T0180375

Lecture Notes in Computer Science 1337

Edited by G. Goos, J. Hartmanis and J. van Leeuwen

Advisory Board: W. Brauer   D. Gries   J. Stoer

Springer

Berlin
Heidelberg
New York
Barcelona
Budapest
Hong Kong
London
Milan
Paris
Santa Clara
Singapore
Tokyo

Christian Freksa   Matthias Jantzen
Rüdiger Valk (Eds.)

Foundations of Computer Science

Potential – Theory – Cognition

 Springer

Series Editors

Gerhard Goos, Karlsruhe University, Germany

Juris Hartmanis, Cornell University, NY, USA

Jan van Leeuwen, Utrecht University, The Netherlands

Volume Editors

Christian Freksa
Matthias Jantzen
Rüdiger Valk
Universität Hamburg, Fachbereich Informatik
Vogt-Kölln-Straße 30, D-22527 Hamburg, Germany
E-mail: {freksa/jantzen/valk}@informatik.uni-hamburg.de

Cataloging-in-Publication data applied for

Die Deutsche Bibliothek - CIP-Einheitsaufnahme

Foundations of computer science : potential - theory - cognition / Christian
Freksa ... (ed.). - Berlin ; Heidelberg ; New York ; Barcelona ; Budapest ;
Hong Kong ; London ; Milan ; Paris ; Santa Clara ; Singapore ; Tokyo :
Springer, 1997
  (Lecture notes in computer science ; Vol. 1337)
  ISBN 3-540-63746-X

CR Subject Classification (1991): F, I.2, D, C.2, K.2, K.4

ISSN 0302-9743
ISBN 3-540-63746-X Springer-Verlag Berlin Heidelberg New York

© Springer-Verlag Berlin Heidelberg 1997
Printed in Germany

Typesetting: Camera-ready by author
SPIN 10647896   06/3142 – 5 4 3 2 1 0   Printed on acid-free paper

To Wilfried Brauer

from his friends, students, and colleagues

Professor Dr. Dr. h.c. Wilfried Brauer

photograph by Lotfi A. Zadeh

Preface

Science has always been used both to explain phenomena in the world and to master everyday problems. A scientific approach to explaining the world and to solving real problems requires systematic foundations – otherwise a field of knowledge should not be called a science.

Accordingly, computer science is motivated by the need to explain the nature of information, knowledge, computation, and computers. The field is also strongly influenced by technological progress and commercial impacts. More than in other disciplines, foundations are required to allow for systematic approaches, to introduce formal methods, to verify results, to integrate various fields of application, and last but not least, to operationalize the concepts developed.

This volume presents new contributions to the foundations of computer science, with a focus on

* theory of formal languages and automata,
* computational structures and complexity theory,
* distributed systems and Petri nets,
* software engineering and verification,
* knowledge representation and cognition,
* machine learning and neural networks,
* robotics, planning, and decision making,
* computer science and its social implications.

By their contributions to this volume the authors acknowledge the work of Wilfried Brauer on the occasion of his sixtieth birthday. Wilfried Brauer has devoted his scientific life to improving the foundations of computer science by opening up the view to new developments in the area and by critically reviewing the existing foundations. Having a background in pure mathematics (algebra and group theory), he belonged to the first authors contributing to the emerging field of computer science in the 1960s by publishing on the theory of finite automata (transition monoid, cascade decomposition). This work is documented in his well known monograph on automata theory published in 1984.

In the 1970s, Brauer pursued his scientific work by studying various types of (non-finite) automata and formal languages. In those days he extended his field of interest to distributed systems, in particular to Petri nets. Already during his stay in Hamburg in the 1970s and early 1980s, and with enhanced emphasis after moving to Munich in 1985, he contributed to the foundations of artificial intelligence with numerous publications, ambitious research projects, and valuable advice to other researchers in the field.

From a methodological perspective, this research includes symbolic representation of knowledge and of processes as well as connectionist and neural net approaches. The topics treated include mathematical foundations and questions of theoretical language and knowledge processing. His interests reach all the way to the applications, for example in medicine. Through these activities, Wilfried Brauer has helped improve the exchange between the theoretical computer science and artificial intelligence communities considerably.

Further publications of Wilfried Brauer deal with the future development of computer science and its potential, with its place in the landscape of sciences, with an appropriate name for the discipline, and with educational issues. Last but not least, Wilfried Brauer is well known in international and national organizations like IFIP (vice president), EATCS (president), and GI (former president). By his engagement in such organizations he successfully contributed to making computer science a mature discipline.

Another important impact of Wilfried Brauer's work in the field is due to his students, about twenty of whom are professors today. Besides students, friends and colleagues have contributed to this volume, thus reflecting – in some sense – the impact of Wilfried Brauer's work in different areas of computer science.

We are grateful for the privilege of working with Wilfried Brauer and receiving his valuable advice. We congratulate him on his birthday and send him all our best wishes!

We thank all authors for their spontaneous enthusiasm in preparing original contributions for this volume and for their willingness to take into account the numerous comments and recommendations of the reviewers. We thank all our reviewers for their expertise and for their critical and constructive recommendations. We also thank Alfred Hofmann and Springer-Verlag for supporting our project and for valuable advice. Special thanks are due to Heidrun Durry, Karin Gramsch, Françoise Hamester, and to everyone who helped reformat contributions and get the book into shape.

Hamburg, August 1997

Christian Freksa

Matthias Jantzen

Rüdiger Valk

Contents

Structures and Complexity Theory

Petri Nets

Systems Analysis and Distributed Systems

Software Engineering and Verification

Cognition and Artificial Intelligence

Knowledge Representation and Reasoning

Machine Learning

Neural Networks and Robotics

Language and Information Systems

The Might of Formulas and Their Limits

F.L. Bauer

Knowledge is power, said Francis Bacon in his *Religious Meditations* in 1598. Thus, if formulas provide knowledge, they also provide power. No-one need doubt that formulas provide knowledge: anyone who has ever forgotten a mathematical formula in an exam can confirm it.

What kind of power, strength, or might can formulas have? What is a powerful formula, a strong formula? The term 'power' as used by the mathematician in expressions like 'the fifth power' will not explain what we mean, and it may be better, in speaking to mathematicians, to avoid saying 'the power of a formula'. Likewise, it does not mean the cardinality of a set. The term 'strength' as used by the logician in expressions like 'the condition A is stronger than the condition B' would also be misleading. But we can speak of the might of formulas.

We approach the heart of the matter if we say 'the benefit of formulas'. Roland Bulirsch, in 1989, in his paper *Mathematik und Informatik – Vom Nutzen der Formeln*[1] [Mathematics and Informatics – On the Benefit of Formulas] discussed the plentiful use of formulas in the everyday mathematical work of astronomers, physicists, and engineers. Collections of formulas have been printed, thus there can be no doubt that formulas possess what one expects from collectors' items: either beauty or utility. According to Thomas Mann[2], formulas are not beautiful, therefore they are useful. But even if one questions the expertise of Thomas Mann with respect to the beauty of formulas and, like Godfrey Harold Hardy, finds some of them beautiful (Hardy wrote that mathematical formulas should be beautiful like the works of poets and painters), they can nevertheless be useful, like other artistic objects. Beauty and utility is the ideal combination.

A useful mathematical formula displays its power through its use. And (may Hardy forgive me) even an ugly, but useful, formula may have power. What we mean is the might formulas exert by the possibility of their use.

Beyond mathematics, chemists use formulas to describe the structure of molecules, biochemists use them to describe the structure of genes. And science is not the sole realm of formulas: writers and linguists are familiar with formulas for the beginning and ending of letters and talks. Even legal jargon describes as formulas the various written forms by which cases are referred to judges or arbitrators for hearing and adjudication. There are legal formularies prescribing

---

[1] In: Manfred Broy (Ed.), *Informatik und Mathematik.* Springer, Berlin 1991
[2] Thomas Mann, *Königliche Hoheit.* 1911

contracts and formularies containing oaths and prayers; there are prescriptive formularies defining medicines and liturgical formularies (*missale*) for church services. And in everyday life there are forms for everything from mailing a parcel to filing a tax declaration.

What are formulas?

Formulas are built up by setting groups of symbols (such as letters, numerals, or arbitrary signs) together to express a concept succinctly. Formulas serve to define general facts, rules, or principles, which they formulate or formularize. They express formalities, formal regularities, formal truth, or matters of outward form. In linguistics, form is the shape corresponding to the structure of the language; in music, it is the shape fitting the structure of the musical idea; in the visual arts, indeed in all art, it is the shape that is juxtaposed to the content. In biology, in medicine, in geography, and in sociology, one speaks of forms and formations.

In mathematics, a form, in contrast to a formula, is the most general way of arranging a group of symbols to create an expression or a proposition; whereas formulas are usually understood more narrowly as expressions defining mathematical functions, as mappings that can be evaluated. Mathematical formulas are shorthand notations for the production of results; in the elementary case, but not the only case, of numerical results.

It follows that formulas are useful, since they are short and memorable, and constructive in that they show people who have learned to use them the shortest way to their goal.

Formulas as such are powerless

What kind of might is given by a formula? A formula by itself is powerless, but it puts power into the hands of the person who knows how to use it; this is might. When Tartaglia found an algebraic formula enabling him to produce the solution of an algebraic equation of third degree by simple calculation, he acquired might. He who has the might should take care to hold on to it: poor Niccolò Tartaglia was not careful enough and gave Geronimo Cardano an opportunity to steal the formula. Cardano made off with the fame at least. To steal a formula one does not have to carry it and its medium away, for it can easily be copied or memorized.

Formulas are immaterial goods

Algorithms are generalizations of formulas – they are plexuses of forms. Anyone who finds a signal-processing algorithm faster than the Fast Fourier Transform can even find countries where he can take out a patent on it. This gives might – the might at least to charge license fees.

To avoid a possible misunderstanding: the formula $E = mc^2$, a consequence of Einstein's special theory of relativity, is not a powerful formula, for it only states a linear dependence between energy and mass, the most trivial one that could be stated – even though it was unapologetically called the "symbol of our century" by Walter Flemmer on the television channel Bayern 3.

Our concern is with formulas that have tremendous expressive power, formulas describing rather voluminous algorithms. If someone were to find such a formula, say one that could serve as the basis of a new weapon system surpassing any known so far, that person could not use it to seize power and would be well advised not even to try to patent it. A government would certainly try to steal the algorithm. In the worst case the inventor would be jailed; at best he could get rich, and the money would be the only power he gained. But the government that stole or bought the formula might use it to cause trouble; even if it did not, it could do.

Formulas make science mightier

Fortunately, this horror story is unreal. The might exerted by formulas does not have to be directed against things or persons. A more subtle and more civilized form of might can help us humans to overcome the difficulties we have created for ourselves in our pursuit of knowledge. Formulas can make science more powerful.

Let us use the word 'formula' for convenience in a rough and ready way to mean also 'forms' in the mathematical-logical sense, and even when we mean plexuses of forms, what we now call algorithms, or – to use a common but imprecise word – programs.

Thus our task in science is to make the knowledge in some domain more striking by using suitable formulas, assuming of course that we are dealing with domains of science where this is possible at all (otherwise we can abandon the domain). The process that leads to the formulas is called formalization. It can be found in the older sciences already in antiquity. Euclid taught a formalization of geometry; mathematics is entitled to its proud status above that of business calculation only if and to the extent that it is formalized. There are levels of formalization. Viète promoted the formalization of algebra tremendously by his introduction of "calculating with letters".

Formalization produces algebra

Formalization of logic has proved to be fundamental. Formal logic, also called mathematical logic or symbolic logic, and formerly logistics, has prevailed over traditional Aristotelian logic, which was dominant up to the 19th century. Formal logic may serve as a prototype of formalization: it uses a formal language (in rough terms, a formula language) whose well-formed expressions are subject to formation rules (syntax) and can be generated by a calculus over an alphabet of basic symbols.

In mathematics, a strict formalization of theorems and theories is fashionable this century, too, a fact largely credited to the influence of David Hilbert. As in logic, this went hand in hand with axiomatization, which we will discuss soon.

The advent of modern computers left no choice but to strictly formalize algorithms that were supposed to run on them. In terms of formal logic, formal algorithms are constructive definitions of mathematical functions that map a set of objects (individuals) into itself or into another set of objects. Surprisingly at the time, Borel and Turing found out that already over the real numbers[3] functions exist that cannot be expressed by any algorithm. Thus, not all mathematical functions over the reals are computable functions. The constructive nature of algorithms – that they can be expressed in a finite chain of symbols – is sufficient to guarantee computability, but insufficient to generate an infinity of real numbers that are only implicitly defined. Something similar is to be expected for other realms of mathematical objects.

Normally, we require that algorithms not only have finite write-ups but also terminate after a finite time. A modern view weakens this requirement to allow certain non-terminating algorithms, such as stream algorithms or tree algorithms that return an infinite sequence or an infinite tree of objects. The way Saul Kripke (*1940) characterized modal logics clarifies the semantics of such cases: stream algorithms are interpreted in temporal logic and tree algorithms in branching-time logic.

Formal languages

The formulation of algorithms is supported by algorithmic languages (with ALGOL as one of the earliest[4]), usually – but imprecisely – called programming languages. Their precursors were calculation sheets, which were common for numerical calculations when these were carried out 'by hand', and plugboards for wired programs. Genuine programming languages first allowed flexible program control. Their syntax was first formalized, as with ALGOL 60 (Heinz Zemanek: "ALGOL started the formal definition culture"), in BNF, Backus Normal Form. For their semantics John Backus (*1924) merely gave informal and intuitive explanations, which were prone to errors. But the formalization of the semantics of programming languages did not have to wait long: it turned out that the decisive move was made at a conference with the deliberately equivocal name *Formal Language Description Languages*, held in September 1964, with the Vienna Definition Language of Heinz Zemanek (*1920) as a shining example. Since then, the role of formalization in the treatment of programming languages has grown mightier. Indeed, Noam Chomsky (*1928) has started a revolution by introducing formalization into general linguistics.

Formulas in silicon

The universal computer, the instrument on which algorithms are played, is of necessity at least as formalized as its programs. Initially, computers (and brains)

---

[3] According to Richard Courant, the real numbers that supplement the rational numbers (on the basis of a definition like that of Dedekind cuts) are no better than paper money – as characterized by Mephisto in Goethe's *Faust* (Second Part, First Act, scene in the Lustgarten).

[4] ALGOL may have been the first that fully deserved the ambitious name 'language'.

were compared to telephone switchboards. But now we are more modern: Zemanek calls the computer, with only slight exaggeration, 'a formula in silicon'.[5] In fact, the formalization of early computers through their wire connections had a considerable feedback on the programming languages used for them. Since then, it has become clear that this influence was in the wrong direction: the programming language should be designed first, to meet the needs of its practical applications, and only then the machine structure. Anyhow, the expression 'formula in silicon' reveals a strong preference for abstraction. A further step would be to formalize the physical effects behind the chip functions, solving partial differential equations of elliptic type. To a large extent this is done already in chip design simulation using supercomputers. Then the next step would be the formalization of semiconductor equations, the next in turn the complete formalization of physics, and so *ad infinitum*. Continued formalization has its limits. Here we are confronted with the old philosophical problem of a stratification of definitions from different paradigms. However, we wish to avoid a confrontation with the disciples of Karl Popper and Thomas Kuhn.

The formalism

In everyday life, formalism means an agglomeration of formalities, superficialities, matters of form; usually a frightful one. In Marxist–Leninist jargon the word had the derogatory meaning 'trifling nonsense'. In the philosophy of science, formalism is the overemphasis on form and formal aspects at the expense of content. Sciences where this is possible – and occurs – are formal sciences. Natural sciences, as commonly understood, are not formal sciences, although theoretical physics, and more recently theoretical chemistry and even biology, are no strangers to formalism – one could say they tolerate it. Logic, mathematics, and informatics, which are strongly related to each other, are at present the only genuine formal sciences in the sense that they can be carried on purely formally. In these fields, the word 'formalism' means something beyond the Marxist–Leninist's trifling nonsense; it denotes useless play with formulas in the methodological sense of an escape into positivistic glass-bead games.

Form and content

There is no reason why logic, mathematics, and informatics should be seen as exclusively formal. The historical development up to the 20th century always connected the form with a content, although the formal side became more and more pronounced. But this is far from implying that the content may be totally neglected, suppressed, and forgotten.

It may happen, of course, that for a while the content is left aside, either for methodological or for aesthetic reasons. In the latter case, a 'pure mathematics' serves only to uplift the human mind by showcasing its own fruits. To speak of

---

[5] IFIP 1994, Vol. II, p. 255

'pure logic' is improper as long as there is no profession of applied logic, and a future 'pure informatics' is a nightmarish prospect.

Anyhow, for a while the total disregard of content may be admissible, but in the end it will lead one astray, to sterility, to narrow-minded seclusion in an ivory tower. Hardy, who believed such disregard to be possible in number theory, did not live to see the application of number-theoretic results in the sensitive but undeniably practical field of cryptology. His colleague Rohrbach and many other mathematicians worked during World War II in cryptanalysis, if for no better reason than to avoid the draft.

True mathematics, logic, and informatics, as practised by the overwhelming majority of researchers and educators, recognizes both form and content, and combines them. The Peano axioms do not float in a vacuum of formalism, but are tested on the bench of a historical concept of natural numbers, which for all their nobility cannot avoid being the subjects of formal hypothetico-deductive systems. This Janus-faced duality of theory and praxis strengthens all the mathematical sciences and raises them above the philosophical critiques of Popperians and Kuhnians. As a rule, genuine mathematicians, logicians, and informaticians work without the enlightenment offered by Popper and Kuhn – except when a colleague deserves to be disqualified, when it helps to locate him philosophically.

Conversely, for a while, content and nothing but content, without any formalism, may be observed. This may happen in application-oriented fields at the beginning of an investigation. The danger is that such exercises in 'applied mathematics', 'applied logic', or 'applied informatics' become separated from progress and deprive themselves of their sharpest instruments. Again, this may be admissible for a while, but pursued too far it leads to muddy defeat and loss of clear vision.

The might of formulas is developed when their content is deployed. Most mathematicians find the Fourier transformation formulas beautiful and important, yet their power rests in their interpretation. This may be seen in a multitude of concrete cases in which their usefulness is demonstrated, for example in image transformations in holographic systems. The formulas for the Radon transformation are equally beautiful, although they were not given the same recognition when Johann Radon (1887–1956) published them in 1913. But the situation has changed since then: the Radon transformation is now powerful since it is the key to building up images in computer tomography. Radon is a good example of a 'genuine' mathematician, who was thoroughly familiar with both the form and the content of his mathematics. For a while, he could be called a pure mathematician in the strict sense, for a while also an applied mathematician; but such a characterization is not invariant, or even disjoint. However, in any case it is positive: he was a good mathematician.

If I were writing this essay for non-specialists – say for politicians, university presidents, or business leaders – I would present a dozen or so further examples of the might of formulas. The examples would range from car bodies and silicon crystals to spacecraft orbits and weather forecasting, from neutron bombs and guided missiles to power plants and traffic systems. Even better, I would refer to my colleagues, say to my Munich colleagues Bulirsch, Hoffmann, and Giering; Brauer, Broy, and Nipkow; Zenger, Siegert, and Bode; Schwichtenberg, Wirsing, and Hegering, to name only a few outstanding examples.

Instead, I shall use the opportunity first to sum up my views on the question of form and content and finally to discuss a technical question that concerns informatics and touches on logic.

On the first question, regarding the relation between form and content, all I wish to say is that the sated boredom of the believers in mere form stands against the sloppiness of the believers in mere content. I am aware that this insight does not exactly rival Hegel's objective idealism for profundity, but too bad.

The axiomatic method:
hypothetico-deductive systems and their models

Now the technical question: The strength of the axiomatic method resides in the use of hypothetico-deductive systems. These systems are quite thoroughly formalized nowadays, with the help of the predicate calculus, and much can be derived from such a system without knowing its interpretation, what it 'means'. This is a definite advantage, since it disallows prejudices stemming from mere intuition and highlights any gaps in the argumentation. When they revert to intuition, even intelligent people can be taken in by invalid proofs.

However, a formal system is not enough. If one wants to know what it means, at least one model must be studied, and preferably all models, provided there are not too many, and even then it is necessary to classify the models. This could be seen recently in the theory of finite groups. To describe the finite groups as a formal structure is easy enough, but their classification was a monumentally laborous and extremely challenging task.

Unfortunately, many structures possess models that cannot be generated within the structure. If a structure has models that cannot be generated, it is likely to have uncountably many models, in which case a full survey in the naive sense of all its models is impossible.

The real numbers as models of an Abelian group with respect to addition, or with respect to multiplication, give the best widely known example. Courant was right to compare them with paper money: their intuitively perceptible content, which is to say their true value, is invisible in the formal system. To this, Ronald Jensen[6] remarked: *"Zu jedem Prinzip für die Erzeugung von reellen Zahlen muß es eine [reelle] Zahl geben, die nicht von diesem Prinzip erfaßt wird"* [To every principle for generating real numbers there must correspond a real number not included by this principle]. Somewhat sloppily paraphrased: 'Almost all' the real numbers are not even computable – the computable real numbers are a countable subset of all the real numbers.

---

[6] Jahresbericht der Deutschen Mathematiker-Vereinigung 1990. Teubner, Stuttgart 1992, p. 273

Homomorphic images of term algebras as constructive models – limits to the might exerted by formulas

Informatics can find its proper employment today only with structures possessing models that can be generated within those structures, and informatics is confined to algorithmic operations over such models. However, models that can be generated within a structure are exactly those models that are homomorphic images of its term algebra.

Only computable, constructive models can be mastered by the might of formulas, plexuses of formulas, algorithms. The universal Turing machine and its Church clones encompass the absolute limit of what can be done in present-day informatics. Stated more positively, term algebra, the Herbrand universe, is the lifeline of informatics. Jacques Herbrand (1908–1931), who died young in a climbing accident, is the patron saint of algebraic specification.

As well as this fundamental limit to the might of formulas, there is a relative one: a practical limit is imposed by the complexity of algorithms. This limit is tangible for many tasks and has created a market for superfast computers which have conquered one after another of the problems that hitherto looked unassailable. This limit is being pushed back through technological progress, and no practical barrier is in sight at the present time, although such a barrier certainly exists according to physics as we now understand it.

We are far from solving all the practical algorithmic problems we can pose today, but for example a chess program, running on IBM's *Deep Blue*, has already defeated world chess champion Gary Kasparov, displaying a mastery of the game that Konrad Zuse (1910–1995) predicted in 1938. Yet there too a lot will be left to do until well into the 21st century, such as an analysis of all possible chess moves. Even as the speed of computers inches up to the limit imposed by physics, possibly toward the middle of the 21st century, we will be unable to stop ourselves formulating concrete problems whose solutions appear to be algorithmically costlier than the constructive mathematics of the time can afford. However, this question may become serious: Can informatics develop beyond the limit of countability, and if so, what new concepts and techniques need to be introduced into mathematics to achieve this? What part of the transfinite could mathematicians make available to informatics? Mathematicians can still do a lot for informatics.

Hardware – Software

An Equivalence and a Contradiction

Heinz Zemanek

Technical University Vienna, IFIP Honorary Member

To my old colleague and friend, Professor Wilfried Brauer
with the most cordial wishes to his Sixtieth Birthday.

1 Introduction

The foundations of computer science are clearer than those of any other technology oriented science; because in the deepest floor, they are identical with propositional logic on a clock driven time scale. It is obvious that applications are far from the logical clarity which the foundations are promising. Where enters the illogic?

Indeed, what ever happens in the circuits of the computer does not only come close to a structure or a process of abstract AND, OR, NOT and DELAY units, it is made to be perfectly so. One could call it an engineering miracle; because the used components are not of logical nature. Engineering tricks impose the necessary behavior – at the clock instances: in between there are analogous transitions, but they are made irrelevant. So what ever runs through a digital network and that is what ever runs through a computer is perfectly logical, a logically correct flow of bits.

Programming consequently was built upon this circuit property, and a program text necessarily refers to a logically clean circuit structure. Programs, therefore, are merely an extension of the logical net. Programs define processes that can happen in such a net.

This distinguishes computer processes from any other kind of processes (the brain processes included), and I want to illustrate this by a fundamental example which I got from the philosopher Yehoshua Bar-Hillel [1]. The difference between the score of a symphony (which is a formal program for the execution of a composition, digitized in both frequency and time steps) and a computer program is that a symphony *is not* identical, a computer program is identical with the notation. (We can ignore here the differences of the processes carried out by the same program on different computers, they mean merely logical variations). The extension of the formal structure laid down in the score to the live performance by the orchestra has its equivalence in the effect of the computer and its programs in the real world which fits only to a certain degree to the assumptions made in programming. This transcendent feature of information technology, as fascinating as it may be, is not the subject of this paper, but it warns from the beginning that *mental* preconditions and foundations of programming must not be neglected and that they coin program properties, often without our attention.

Another illogic feature of our business are the mistakes in our work. On this point, I would have to insert a paragraph, a chapter or a book on errors in the notation. But this too is not the subject of this paper. It is assumed that errors in notation (which can never be fully avoided) have been found and removed.

2 The Equivalence

The basic theorem – a direct consequence of the foundations – is that

Programs and circuits can be replaced by each other.

This is not true in the extreme: programs alone – without any circuitry – and circuitry alone – which are not programmed – are outside the art of computer use. We need not include those extreme cases. In the practical work the equivalence theorem is valid: it is a choice of realization what to do by circuitry and what by programs.

Would we not be entitled to expect that cost trends and reliability can be made in essence the same? Logic has no material damages, programming does not need big energy sources or expensive access to the subtleties of molecular layers. The programmer has learned his logic and he masters it (we can neglect bunglers): software could be of higher quality than hardware. It is not. It amazes the user even by an intrinsic manner of wearing out, not the logic, of course, but the cross relationships of the parts.

Programming costs should go down with about the same speed and reliability should increase with the same speed. The reality, however, is that programming costs tend to go up and the reliability of software is insufficient. Is it not worthwhile to search for the reasons of this contradiction?

The equivalence has more complicated roots than we have described in the introduction. In order to appreciate this, we will first have a look into the history and the formal description of hardware and then do the same for software. We also have to consider the differences of numerical mathematics, abstract formal processing (processing of formal texts), processing of formatted information, and processing of natural language texts (including Mechanical Translation). We shall see that the differences stem from the different models which are applied.

3 Formal Definition of Hardware

Since the early days for the description of hardware switching algebra [2] has been used, mainly for the minimization of the circuits, but actually the expressions meant (or at least offered) a formal definition of the circuits. Since the introduction of the chips it is more important to minimize the number of required pins, but unnecessary circuit elements should still be avoided. But wherever our main intention goes, hardware is formally defined.

4 Formal Definition of Software

The early programs were written in machine code and each term of this code refers to bit-processes in the (well-defined) hardware. At least in theory, one could trace back any instruction to the switching algebra defined circuits. The first formula translation programs certainly did so and the compiler-defined languages like FORTRAN also. The scientific programming languages – ALGOL as the main representative – were syntactically formally defined by the production rules John Backus has presented to the Paris ICIP conference in 1959 [3]. With PL/I – conceived for a computer family – IBM also had to go to document definition and beyond mere syntactical production rules. So the Vienna Laboratory got the chance to develop the Vienna Definition Language (VDL), and the PL/I standard, almost identical with the Vienna documents, represents a formal definition of the semantics of a giant programming language, a description which – again in theory – permits the tracing of all processes down to propositional logic [4].

Business mathematics, at least as long as one looks on the day book, has the same property. That it applies almost no algebra has to do with the fact that business, in contrast to science and technology, is not shaped by laws of nature to which reality obeys relatively completely. He who trusts in "laws of nature" in business and economy will very fast go broke. But the formal procedures of the day book are as strict as the numerical procedures. And that explains why physics, technology and book-keeping were so easy to entrust to the computer.

5 Numerical Mathematics

Calculation is the best defined process in human activity. Numbers are well ordered and have absolutely clear relations. The full subject of calculation is out of the area of our consideration here: as far as things are of calculus nature, they are in the best hands with the mathematicians, and calculation applications are the safest in information processing – unless other features do not mingle into the mathematical clarity. And the first and most dangerous aspect of calculation is the organizational handling of the mathematically clear processes.

The numerical processes look like well defined, in particular if one thinks of the Principia Mathematica by Russell and Whitehead which have based all of mathematics on logic grounds, anticipating theoretically what the computer realized then as practical application of the theory. Looking through the magnifying glass (quite appropriate for a miniaturized device), one discovers that the perfect definition runs against practical barriers. Not only rounding effects but also a lot of other circuit and programming specialties may influence the calculation process. Again: these are aspects not considered in this paper; the mathematicians have tools enough to master aberrations from the ideal line.

6 Abstract Formal Processing

Since the FORMAC language, conceived by Jean Sammet [5], it was also possible to process algebraic expressions by computer programs. The application of such programs did not live up to optimistic expectations, until today handling of algebraic expressions is done before going into the computer. But it is quite clear how to proceed if one wants to do it the automatic way.

The central example for abstract formal processing is formula translation (FORTRAN), i.e. projecting an algebraic formula onto machine code and its generalization, the compiler of a programming language. Programming languages were the first step towards the software outfit of the computer, and they teach two basic lessons: the computer reduces the elegance of algebra by turning its eternal truths into processes ($n := n + 1$) and mingles handy, pragmatic features into the algebraic generality. This was the point where programming stepped from eternal mathematics to time dependent engineering, winning easy use but paying with a fundamental loss: the terms in the programming language are no more algebraic objects; they can not anymore be treated like such objects This may be an other reason for the subjective character to which programming developed.

There is a source of computing and programming which in my opinion has not been explored and applied to the full possible extent in the computer, and that is programming the weaving loom, an early case of parallel processing in digital steps. How to come from a conceived pattern to be woven to the correct punching of the Jacquard cards is still a mostly intuitive process which might give interesting aspects to the programming of parallel processes on the computer. Maybe we shall see more of this interconnection one day.

7 Processing of Formatted Information

There are semi-formal ways to deal with information. One important feature is the formatting of certain data, part of which may be numerical. If the content and the relationships between fields of the formats are sufficiently defined, the computer can be made extremely useful.

Book-keeping and the census are roots of information processing, and they both require the use of numerical data and, at the same time, their connection to informal information, often the projection of non-numerical concepts onto numbers, like kinds of companies in business or the confession in a census sheet.

One reason for the problems with programming may be the diversity of information and information kinds. Back in 1970 [6] already I have distinguished five kinds of information handling, (1) pure mathematics, (2) mathematics applied to physics and technology, (3) formatted information like in a census sheet, (4) formal texts like computer programs and (5) prose, texts in natural language. Physical and technical values (*Größen* in German) are protected by the magnificent invention of the dimension and the book-keeping processes by the old tradition of the typical numberhandling of the merchants. They are a model for projecting a complicated reality onto simple devices like the day-book, reducing the full life of an enterprise to addition and subtraction, with a few tags like company names or their addresses.

Medical records, which came up very early as medical application of the computer, consist of a typical mix of physical values (like weight of the body or temperature of the blood) with absolutely informal entries, observations and thoughts of the doctor. Here is a bridge to computer handling of natural language texts.

8 Processing of Natural Language Texts

There was an extreme optimism in the Fifties and Sixties that aimed at fast high quality mechanical translation of natural languages (MT) [7], a hope that did not substantiate as fast as expected. But after return into the research institutes and a lot of further work, we have today not only pocket computer vocabulary books, but also high quality programs for limited purposes which translate simple texts quite satisfactory, in some cases even without human interference (it is always better to have it checked by humans, but that may get expensive for the purpose).

What we have learned from programming language compilers and from natural language translation, is that programs yield syntactical structures relatively easy, while semantic relations require the reduction to syntactic models, never reaching the full extent of semantics they try to approach. Mathematics is a most effective example, most primitive in one view, most sophisticated in many others.

Behind the extremely colorful universe of information and information processing actually are only few processing methods, like calculation and logic derivation, comparing and sorting and certain organizatorial mechanisms.

9 The Contradiction

Both costs and reliability are properties or at least functions of the production process. If we want to understand the contradiction, we must look into the production process. And we encounter here a very general principle, reaching far beyond the present consideration. The *genesis* of objects, real or abstract, appears as a part of their nature, and one should never conclude that two objects are equal if it is clear that their genesis is different. A deeper look will always disclose that the equality then is only a superficial, partial or limited one.

And I can, ahead of the following analysis, jump to the conclusion that the equivalence in production will not exist as long as one has not brought the genesis of hardware and software to a sufficient equivalence.

10 Cost Reduction

The diagrams to the improvement of hardware I displayed first back in 1968 [8] show that speed and smallness, number of components and storage capacity, price per component and reliability of the system were improved for a factor of 1000 each 20 years, 1948 to 1968 to 1988 (see Fig. 1 at the end of this paper); and with good reasons the lines could be extended to a third 20 years period until 2008, because there is only one reason that the improvement should not continue, and that is the end of electronics with the femto second: a number of considerations indicate that we shall never get the chip electronics faster. So a slight slow down could have to be expected from the turn of the century on. However, light technology is already here and it promises to overcome the femto second mark (as soon as the amplification and restoration problem of the signal is resolved without electronics) and so the extension may continue for two, three and more 20 years periods, but this is the future and not the present. The diagrams do not apply, of course, to the mechanical components like the keyboards and to other I/O parts like the screen, the size of which is dictated by human dimensions, by the size of the fingers or the power of the eyes. The diagrams refer to the bulk of the miniaturized circuits.

It is the highly automated and standardized production process which brings the enormous improvements in cost and reliability. So it is the production process which must be studied.

11   The Hardware Production Process

The hardware production process is based on the physical requirements of the chip (the other components can be neglected in this context, mechanics or screens, although they may decisive feedback influence on the circuits). Hardware, after all steps to very large scale miniaturization, is generated by a standard process in a production line consisting not only of tools but of automatic tool machinery, a line with automatic actions and checking, so that chips come out in almost perfect quality and in arbitrary quantity. I know that hardware specialists do not fully share my optimistic description because they are aware of the weak points in the process. For the overall judgment, my arguments are pertinent enough.

Already the normal minimization requires indirect and automatic handling, the whole production process had to be conceived for this prospect. It is clear that the production line stands for a set of restrictions: one can not expect that the well organized line permits any kind of product. It imposes not only a style, but also certain drawbacks. But this is generally accepted. The basic philosophy is that software can compensate these restrictions, and this and a few other reasons or features yield a philosophy of strictness for hardware and for more than flexibility with software: programming is felt being closer to imagination and creativity which the discipline that dominates hardware would restrict or even kill. The triumph of the computer is based on hardware production discipline. This view inhibits the doubling of the triumph by software.

12   The Software Production Process

Looking from an equivalence point of view, one could expect that the software production process yields even better properties, because on the abstract level – which is the prerequisite of the hardware production process too – software offers cleaner and easier *procedures*, permits more flexibility and can afford more redundancy. From the starting point, programming was aimed at mathematical correctness, but much less at engineering discipline. So such aspects were not seriously considered. Indeed, software does not require the objective discipline of indirect and automatic handling, one always can interfere by hand, change the code, change the module arbitrarily. It is this mode of operation which coins programming habits and which detests the restrictions which the equivalent to hardware would require.

But this may be merely a mental prejudice. Software too may have components of the nature of the chip.

This is the reason why software tools remain restricted to the one application for which they were designed and for its "environment". With such tools one can not build up an automatic production line. The usual programs, what kind ever, do not fit to such a concept. After 50 years of computer programming, there must be a mentality and a full set of habits to cultivate a tool-distant style, and it could have been predicted that the attempt to create software factories would fail.

Minor steps can not change the situation. A fundamental change is required for which even "revolution" is not a sufficient term. Down to fundamentals, is the slogan, and start again. But who can be expected to implement such a comprehensive enterprise? Certainly not the product and fast-return oriented industry. And not the university institutes as long as they are keen (for valid financial and related reasons) to support and satisfy industry.

Big governmental institutions or very big industrial research institutions (like the Bell Labs or IBM Research) might be a starting base, and governmental initiatives in computer-industry-strong countries could be imagined to be suited. And the working order would be about this: Try to distillate the abstract structure of the chip philosophy which enables tools and tool machines to be efficient, and transform these structures to the programming universe. This will yield insight how tools and tool machines in programming are to be conceived.

The consequence of this concept is a clear division of the software into two parts. corresponding to the situation: **certain mechanisms** will be prefabricated and must be accepted as they are, **other mechanisms** can be freely designed, attached to what is mass produced. This clear separation line would permit partial standardization, the prerequisite of inexpensive mass production: standardized, tool-produced components inter-connected or controlled by free use of the left-open degrees of liberty.

I am full of admiration for the programming geniuses who dream for a week and then, working a night and a day and a night, produce programs of outstanding nature and achievement. As an exception, they really animate the programming scene. But as a manager I would not like to have 17 genius programmers reporting to me. And I have rarely heard that their documentations are as great as their programs. For the regular program production process, they are not a model. In the workshop and in the factory only sufficiently and stabilized elements can be introduced, and in programming very few people care for and stabilized elements. Present programming is much closer to poetry than to a factory.

13 Software Factories

It has been tried to organize (I hesitate to say: erect) software factories [9]. All known attempts (under the present conditions) failed, and the analysis of the failures indicates that the reason is that software products have not enough repetitivity to permit automatic production in a line. Now I suspect that this is not a property of software in principle, only of the present software and rather a property of the (present) programmers.

The author of the book [9] mentions the following aims for coming closer to the software factory

1. Discipline and repetitivity	we have pointed this out; the increasing specialization is of negative influence.
2. Visibility	programming hides in a certain sense behind hardware
3. Measurement	methods for measuring the efficiency of a team or a (semi-automatic) system would improve the sensibility for the problem moreover it turned out that efficiency criteria are project-depending
4. Tools	help only in certain sections which make up only 20% of the costs. Tools are highly project-dependent
5. Re-Usability	How to reach modules that can often be re-used?

14 Conclusion: Return to the Academic Origins?

The computer originated in the academic environment. Zuse and IBM are special cases. From the Moore School and the University of Iowa, from Aiken and Wilkes to Algol, the vast majority of the essential steps were achieved on academic grounds. Neither the car nor the aircraft have come up this way. And there are very good reasons. One certainly is that the computer has an essential abstract side, most visible in programming, and abstract automatization is at least not a usual industrial subject.

At the begin of programming, the main task was to organize mathematical formula in such a way that the computer could process them. One had the co-operation between the faculty of electrical engineering for the hardware and of the mathematics department for the programming problems. When informatics developed to a curriculum subject and to a faculty of its own, the past could not simply disappear. And should not disappear: electronics and mathematics still are basic columns on which the building has to reside. But to fully understand that information processing is a technology of a new kind which requires engineers of a new kind could not happen overnight. Like in other branches of engineering mathematical knowledge must support engineering; for informatics even a double load would be necessary: functional analysis for hardware and discrete mathematics including application oriented logic for software. And the history of programming languages has shown us that where we have solid theories based on strong mathematics we can soon master the practical application. But where we have no bearing theory we have to improvise and we do not ideally master the service for the user. The most important, the overwhelming obstacle is organization for which there is no theory comparable to computing or electronics. Programming consists mainly of organizing data flows and matching the application organization. Can a theory of organization be developed which is law obeying like physics or mechanics? Can organization be modularized so that simple equal or very similar components can be used in big numbers, favoring automatic production like chips? This is not a question that can be answered out of the present style and present thinking. This thought moreover indicates that the whole problem extends far beyond programming and computer science. It touches the general questions of organization in our time.

Industry has not the institutions nor the time nor the finances to radically change the programming and software practices. In order to save money, they rather use the university institutes as cheap advanced development centers, and this would not be so wrong if the teaching and the research aspect would remain independent, but in many universities this is not the case.

I can only see a return of the total software complex to the universities as a remedy. The task would be to analyze software and its production with the aim to approach it to hardware and its production. Systematic building of repetitive blocks and automatic checking would prepare the feasibility of software production lines. The tools would look differently after such an analysis, and would be conceived in view of inclusion in a tool machine; a line of such machines could then be the door to the software factory.

The industrial production of the big part of the applied software would not inhibit the hand-made extension or adaptation, but like in hardware certain principles would be imposed on the operation which now can be neglected.

The whole idea might turn out to be useless, to bring no improvement. But has it ever been tried? Or has programming merely followed what early algorithm-oriented calculation programming introduced? There is no proof that software factories are impossible, only the experience so far has shown that they did not work which does not mean that they can not work under a different concept.

15 ATTACHMENT

Remarks to Fig. 1

The diagrams show only relative values, starting with 1 in 1948. As approximate starting points, the following values could be used:

(1) Operations per Second 10^4 1988: 10^{10} 2008: 10^{13}
(2) Number of Components 10^4 1988: 10^{10} 2008: 10^{13}
(3) Volume 10^{-2} 1988: 10^{-8} 2008: 10^{-11}
(4) Cost   10\$ 1988: 10^{-5} 2008: 10^{-8}

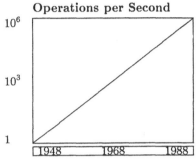

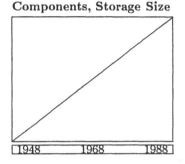

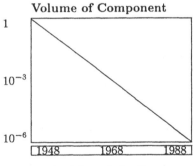

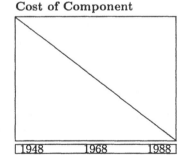

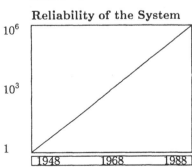

Summary of the diagrams: For the same price and in the same volume a computer of 1988 is a million times fast and bigger than in 1948. In 2008 it will be a billion (10^9) Software does not keep up with such improvement.

Fig. 1. The Improvement of Hardware in Five Parameters (double logarithmic scale)

References

[1] Symphony-Score personal communication from Y. Bar-Hillel.

[2] H. Zemanek Logische Algebra und Theorie der Schaltnetzwerke. In: Taschenbuch der Nachrichtenverarbeitung (K. Steinbuch, Hrsg.) Springer Verlag, Berlin 1962; 1418-1480

[3] J. Backus The Syntax and Semantics of the Proposed International Algorithmic Language of the Zurich ACM-GAMM Conference. In: Information Processing. Proceedings of the ICIP Conference Paris 1959 Butterworth/Oldenbourg/UNESCO 1959, 125-132

[4] P. Lucas, K. Walk On the Formal Definition of PL/I. Annual Review of Automatic Programming 6 (1969) Part 3, 105-152

[-] A.N. Lee The Vienna Definition Language. A Generalization of Instruction Definitions. SIGPLAN-Symposium on Programming Language Definition San Francisco, August 1969

[-] Standard Programming Language PL/I ANSI X3.53 American Standards Institute, New York 1976

[5] J.E.Sammet, E. Bond Introduction to FORMAC. IEEE Trans. Electron. Comp. EC 13 (1964) 386-394

[6] H. Zemanek Some Philosophical Aspects of Information Processing. In: The Skyline of Information Processing. (H. Zemanek, Ed.), p. 93-140 Proceedings of the Tenth Anniversary Celebration of IFIP. Amsterdam, 25 OCT 1970 North Holland, Amsterdam 1972; 146pp

[7] E. Reifler Machine Language Translation. In: Digitale Informationswandler (W. Hoffmann, Hrsg.) Vieweg Verlag, Braunschweig 1961; 444-507

[8] H. Zemanek Zukunftsaspekte der Informationsverarbeitung. Mitteilungsblatt des Rechenzentrums der Universität Erlangen, No. 7 Erlangen, Oktober 1971, 9 - 30

[-] H. Zemanek A Look into the Future of Information Processing. Annals of the History of Computing 12 (1990) No. 4, 241-251

[-] H. Zemanek Another Look into the Future of Information Processing. Annals of the History of Computing 12 (1990) No. 4, 253-260

[9] M. A. Cusumano Japan's Software Factories Oxford Univ. Press 1991; IX+512 pp

[-] H. Zemanek Software-Fabriken - Mehr als eine Buchbesprechung. Informationstechnik (Oldenbourg) 34 (1992) H.6, 368-372

Defining Discipline

Wolfgang Coy

Humboldt-Universität zu Berlin
Institut für Informatik,
Unter den Linden 6, D-10099 Berlin

1 Introduction

This paper deals primarily with developments in computer science or "Informatik" in Germany, the early definition of the discipline, its evolution over the last thirty years, and its perspectives in a global information society. Although throughout the world departments of informatics do research in more or less in the same areas as departments of *computer science, computer engineering, informatique, informatica, or datalogi,* and though in these field German students may develop more or less the same qualifications as students elsewhere, there are some historical peculiarities in the short history of "Informatik", which I want to point out. In particular, I want to argue that the discipline of informatics is still under construction, despite its opportunity to play a defining role for the technological base of the coming information society.

As the paper relates primarily to German experiences, these peculiarities affect the translation from German into American English in a very special way, and I had to make some decisions. I will use the word *informatics* either as synonymous to the German name *Informatik,* or as generalization of the world wide field, depending on the context. Sometimes I will also use the term *computer science* to make a distinction between U.S. and German experiences. The professionals will be called *informaticians.* Readers should be able to follow these twists.

2 "Informatik": Defining a New Discipline

An Academic Path to Data Processing?

Like many other technological and engineering activities building computers was forbidden by allied law in post-war Germany. Nevertheless there was some research done. Konrad Zuse developed the Plankalkül, the first programming language (earlier than John v. Neumann's and Herman Goldstine's Flow Diagrams, and nearly ten years before John Backus' first note on the Fortran project), without any access to a working computer. There was also research done in university mathematics and physics departments, like the work by Heinz Billing on magnetic drums at Werner Heisenberg's Institute in Göttingen or by Alvin Walther at the Institut für Praktische Mathematik of TH Darmstadt, and later by Hans and Robert Piloty at TH München, by N.Joachim Lehmann at TH Dresden, by Heinz Rutishauser and Eduard Stiefel at ETH Zürich, or by Heinz Zemanek at TH Wien.

In the sixties there were already many industrial activities. Computers were developed and built by Siemens, by AEG, by SEL, by Zuse KG and other smaller companies, and by the German subsidiary of IBM (where the acronym is cautiously expanded to "Internationale Büro Maschinen"). Large main-frames (mostly IBM) were used by industry, trade, financial institutes, insurance companies, and in the public sector. Technical highschools and universities founded the first computing centers and a central Deutsches Rechenzentrum was established at Darmstadt. A growing number of data processing specialists was needed. A lack of formal education, combined with high places in the hierarchy, including high salaries, raised serious concerns in the companies.

In the Bundesrepublik, much as in the U.S.A. and other European countries, a solution to these problems was seen in the academic qualification of data processing specialists. The rapidly growing field of data and information processing was to be supplemented by an academic discipline.

The first computer-related courses were developed around 1960 in the U.S.A. Three different lines emerged: *Computer Engineering, Computer Science und Information Science*. The first curriculum in *information science* seems to have been established in 1963 at the Georgia Tech *(Institute of Technology)*. In 1965 the name *computer science* was generally accepted and in 1968 the first ACM *Curriculum for Computer Science* was printed.

Although decisions on university matters are the responsibility of the decentralized state governments (Länder), it was federal money that started the introduction of an academic computer science programme in West Germany. Federal research minister Gerhard Stoltenberg announced the first recommendations for academic education in data processing (Empfehlungen zur Ausbildung auf dem Gebiet der Datenverarbeitung) and started a funding programme (1. Datenverarbeitungs-Förderprogramm). In July 68 a conference on Computers and Universities was organized at the Technische Universität Berlin in cooperation with the Massachusetts Institute of Technology. In the opening speech of Minister Stoltenberg the word *Informatik* was used the first time officially for the discipline to be founded - a translation of the French word *informatique*. From 1970 to 1975 fifty working groups were funded under a Federal Research Programme *(Überregionales Forschungsprogramm* ÜRF, part of 2.

Datenverarbeitungs-Förderprogramm). This was the start of the West German *Informatik.*

"Informatique": What's in a Name?

While *computer engineering* and *information science* are nearly self explanatory, the term *computer science* is somewhat puzzling. Is hardware, the computer, in the focus of that science? What then is the difference to *computer engineering*? And if information processing is in its focus: What is the difference to *information science*? And, as it is obviously different from computer engineering and information sciences, what is it all about? And why does the Association for Computer Machinery propagate a *Curriculum* of Computer Science, as ACM did in 1968 and thereafter?

Peter Naur was well aware of this lack of semantic precision, when he proposed the word datalogi as an alternative to computer science in a letter to the *Communications of the ACM.* His definition *"Datalogi: The discipline of data, their nature and use"* was to be complemented by a technical subfield called *datamatik* ("that part of datalogi which deals with the processing of data by automatic means"), a name taken from Paul Lindgreen and Per Brinch Hansen. But *datalogi* was only accepted in the kingdom of Denmark, while the U.S.A. stayed with the trinity of *computer science, computer engineering,* and *information science.* Even the modest proposal of an ACM Task force headed by Peter J. Denning to use the term *science of computing* instead of *computer science* is not widely recognized.

It seems that Philippe Dreyfus introduced the French name *informatique* from the elements *information* and *automatique* or *électronique* in 1962. In Germany, Standard Elektrik Lorenz used the word *Informatik* already in in the late fifties naming a manufacturing site (Informatik-Werk), but this name and trademark was dropped later. In France the notion *informatique* was used throughout the French press as a generic name related to computers and automation. After even Le Monde printed it, the Acàdemie Française defined it officially in 1967: "Science du traitement rationnel, notamment par machines automatiques, de l'information consiederèe comme le support des conaissances humaines et des communications dans les domaines technique, économique et social."

This definition shows some peculiarities. Most interesting, it assumes that the newly defined *informatique* is already a science. Its object is the rational treatment of informations, especially with automatically working machines (i.e. computers). This science should support human knowledge and skills as well as communication. Applications of that treatment are to be found in technical, economical, and social domains. Clearly this definition looks far beyond programming and use of computers. It embeds hardware and software in a field of applications and connects it with human work and communication.

Many European languages adopted that word. Only the British usage differs somewhat as *informatics* is used in the U.K. since 1967 as synonymous to *information science.* But the German "Informatik" made a strange twist: While it uses the French word, it sticks firmly to the American usage of *computer science* (with elements from *computer engineering*). Computing machines are seen as the base of the newly formed discipline. Neither problems nor consequences of the rational treatment, i.e. rationalization of work force, nor the communicative aspects of the new technology are themes of the academic discipline. Technical problems and their mathematical foundations form the almost exclusive discourse in "Informatik", while practical applications, as well as economics and social questions are generally left out.

Wolfgang Giloi wrote 1969 in a pamphlet of the Technical University of Berlin: "It was obvious, right from the beginning, that the notion *Informatik* had to be synonymous with *Computer Science, i.e.,* it should enclose approximately that, what is understood as *Computer Science* in the U.S.A. " This referential definition unveils its recursive wit in the following sentence: "The problem one had to face there, was that in the U.S.A. there is no common and general understanding what this discipline should be."

This *non-definition* shows clearly that the whole process of introducing the new discipline was not guided by a desire of precise definition. It was instead a matter of sciento-political cooperation between interested researchers who tried to establish an inner circle while excluding unwanted or presumably less important actors. "Informatik" was exactly what the members of the founding committees and the heads of the new departments and chairs did or intended to do. And this was deeply rooted in mathematics and electronic engineering. Important applications like business data processing were left out. The whole definition process of the discipline was much more a social selection than a scientific distinction.

Politics of Choice and Exclusion

Explicit definitions of the term "Informatik" were rarely given in the first years (perhaps with the notable exception of Heinz Zemanek's paper from 1971), and there was certainly no generally accepted common definition. But there is a common attitude in all definitions of the newly founded discipline: They all draw lines of distinction to the manifold of other emerging or competing sciences, like *cybernetics, semiotics, numerics and instrumental mathematics, formal logic and theory of computation, control theory, business data processing, operations research, system theory, information theory, coding theory, cryptography, game theory, semi conductor technology and (micro) electronics, memory and storage technology,* but also *process automation, communication theory,* and *bionics.* They were either excluded or thought to play only a marginal role in informatics – perhaps with the exception of formal logic and computation theory. The definition of the discipline was done primarily by exclusion. It seems that there was only one common sciento-political agreement among the founders of informatics, namely to become as independent as possible from the faculties they came from and where they found less resonance and cooperation than expected.

Of course, exclusion and distinction are understandable attitudes when something new is constructed. It was however not driven by the inner necessities of the field, but primarily by political motives without much regard for the external demands, even when these were not unreasonable. Especially the hopes and demands of the industry, the finance companies and the public sector for academically educated data processing personnel, able to cope with the actual problems of information processing (including knowledge of Cobol and OS/360), was largely ignored in the academic field. As a result academic informatics generated an *application gap* quite beyond the unavoidable difference of practice and its scientific reflection. This *application gap* was enforced by a close relation between informatics and mathematics or electrical engineering as many early informatics chairs were taken by academically trained mathematicians or engineers. Other fundamental aspects of system design and software construction like the study of organizations, team work, working conditions, psychology, economics, or application fields were generally ignored or considered to be less important. As a consequence methodological uncertainties show up wherever mathematical and logical foundations of informatics are insufficient to analyze and solve a problem, or achieve a task. It should be added, however, that the application gap was recognized by many and often mourned, but that it is still not bridged.

The definition of a discipline may be considered as an academic classification-problem, considered an issue since centuries, when the structure of the medieval universities, its trivium, quadrivium, and the higher disciplines were transformed to the modern canon - mathematics, physics and theology finally being separated as disciplines. But where should informatics be placed?

After the given short account of its early years it is not surprising that this classification is seen to be controversial. Even Encyclopedia Britannica mirrors this problem: *Computer Science* belongs to *Applied Mathematics* – like *Automata Theory*. *Information Science* is a *Technological Science*. *Computer Engineering* belongs to *Electrical and Electronical Engineering*, but forms no own subfield.

In Germany, the classification of informatics differs from scientist to scientist, but also through the time in the understanding of the single scientist. Very often "Informatik" is understood as an engineering science:

- *Informatik as engineering science* (F.L. Bauer proposed the term *Software Engineering* in 1968; 1974 he described "Informatik as engineering science", a connection discussed by H. Zemanek already in 1971);
- *Informatik* as *Ingenieur-Geisteswissenschaft,* as well as *Geistes-Ingenieur-wissenschaft* (F.L.Bauer 1974; the inherent language game is difficult to translate, because the meaning of both words is rather obscure in the paper. Perhaps the first could be translated as *engineering science of the mind* and the second as *humanistic engineering science*);
- *System technology and engineering science* (The general assemblies of the German university faculties Fakultätentag Informatik together with Fakultätentag Elektrotechnik 1991);
- *Engineering science and formal science* (Ch. Floyd 1992);
- *Engineering science and structural science* (P. Rechenberg 1991); tem and, departing from the narrow engineering aspects *Informatik as technical science* (A.L. Luft 1988).

In contrast, sometimes relations to mathematics and formal logic are stressed:
- *Formal Science* (F.L. Bauer 1985)
- *Structural Science* (C.F. v. Weizsäcker in 1971, introduced to informatics by W. Brauer in the following years)
- *Science of the formal structures of information processing* (W. Steinmüller 1993)
- *Very Large Scale Application of Logic* (E. Dijkstra 1989)
- *Intelligence formalizing technology* (W. Brauer 1996)

Some informaticians try to orient the discipline more on Scandinavian approaches, or the design-oriented approach of Terry Winograd and Fernando Flores, or look at informatics regarding its consequences to society:

- *Science of design* ("Gestaltungswissenschaft" - Arno Rolf 1992, following T. Winograd & F. Flores 1986)
- *Machinization of brain-work* (F. Nake since 1977)
- *Social science* (W. Steinmüller 1993)

Other connections beyond engineering and technology are proposed.

- H. Zemanek (1992) embeds informatics in more general systematic study of *abstract architecture,* while
- the book of A.L. Luft & R. Kötter (1994) is titled Informatik: *a modern knowledge technology.*
- R. Valk (1997) compares the practice of informaticians to the *practice of lawyers.*

Finally we may identify a group which tries to establish connections to philosophy:

- *"A bridge between science and humanities"* (H. Zemanek 1992)
- *New fundamental science* (Informatik Duden 1993)
- *Fundamental science (comparable to philosophy and mathematics)* (Reinhard Wilhelm 1996)

Classification oscillates between submission and omnipotent phantasies, result of the "radical novelty" (Dijkstra) and the rapid development of the discipline and its underlying technology. It is obvious that the real definition of the discipline "Informatik" was chiefly done by academic practice, by teaching courses, by teaching manuals, by workshops, conferences, and research journals. It should be noted, however, that it was only occasionally influenced by practical data processing outside academic institutions. As a result informatics is generally considered to be "theory" from the outside, whereas it is in fact the sum of academic practices, in which theoretical aspects are reduced to mathematical foundations.

Ironically, the newly founded German Informatik departments were so successful in excluding suspiciously looking and deviating content that they had to start with a bare minimum of lectures. The curricular plan developed by GAMM/NTG, which was adopted by nearly all faculties, filled only 18 hours per week (of a total of 80) in the first two years with genuine informatical content and only 24 hours (of a total of 72) in the second two years. If the other disciplines would have been more tolerant they could have easily included the new discipline as a specialization. But after a short warm-up period the discipline made many further distinctions and generated a plethora of new subfields. It was in fact so successful that in 1985 it was no longer possible for the then more than 20 faculties to agree on a general scheme of practical informatics in the Bundesrepublik as demanded by the federal "Rahmenrichtlinien" (frame of reference). The discipline had entered its adolescence.

3 Re-defining a Start-Up Discipline

Facing an Application Gap

Academic informatics is both technology and science, wrote Peter Rechenberg. We may try to be more specific: theory and construction. Construction as a technical heritage, related not only to science but also to craft and art. Donald Knuth' books *The Art of Computer Programming* denoted the state of the art of basic computer science (though the first three volumes did not touch programming techniques in a genuine sense), and despite many accomplishments there is still no visible *science of programming*. Theory is the other foundation of informatics, but again, though there are many theoretical results on automata theory, formal languages, complexity, algorithmic behavior, or crypto analysis, there is few research on the theoretical foundations of the discipline besides its mathematical and logical constructs. Even the development of new programming languages lacks solid theoretical foundations (again, besides mathematical and logical calculi). It remains an art or craft – sometimes with convincing results. A theory that shows limits and perspectives of informatics is still to be developed.

By its sciento-political classification and practice informatics became a technical science. But it hardly belongs to the engineering sciences. There is still a large *application gap,* or as Dijkstra names it, a gap between a *correctness problem* (how to assure the correct working of a program) and a *pleasantness problem* (how to build adequate programs and systems for people using them). Unlike some other engineering sciences, the use of computers and programs, the design of appropriate interfaces, is an integral part of the applications. Both problems are to be solved, and it seems to be impossible to separate them successfully in most applications. Informatics is responsible for both aspects and hence it may be seen as a new type of techno-scientific endeavor.

In the first decades informatics followed the tayloristic approach of complete automation. Human interaction was to be avoided and it was generally considered to be an irritating factor in a clean algorithmic process. Words like *automatic data processing, paperless office, computer integrated manufacturing, artificial intelligence,* or *intelligent agents* denote these projections, rarely weakened by notions like *tool* or *assistant.* Most of these projections are now considered as dreams of the past, but there is still a large gap between scientific research and everyday computer use. Even if many practitioners do not expect much help from academia anymore, this cannot be the future of informatics.

Wilfried Brauer reflected this development in his series of definitions of the notion "Informatik", when he included applications in his definition the "Studien- und Forschungsführer Infomatik" in 1989: *"Informatik* is the science, technology, and application of machine-based processing and transfer of information. *Informatik* encloses theory, methodology, analysis and construction, application, and consequences of its use." This is some noticeable contrast to his definition of 1978, when he wrote in accordance with most of his colleagues at that time: *"Informatik* is the science of systematic information processing - especially the automatic processing by the aid of digital computers."

While probably most German informaticians will nowadays support his definition of 1989, Wilfried Brauer is already one step ahead. In 1996 he gave a new multi-facetted definition, reflecting new aspects like agent programs and cultural dependencies of informatics: *"Informatik* is the (engineering) science of theoretical analysis and conceptualizing, organization and technical design as well as the concrete realization of (complex) systems that consist of (in some sense intelligent and autonomous) agents and actors, communicating with themselves and their environment, and that should be embedded as support systems for humans in our civilization." Maybe the scientific community will become accustomed to this definition in the coming years. But then we cannot predict how Wilfried Brauer, always ahead of his time, will define "Informatik" in the year 2001.

Despite a still existing application gap between practice and academic informatics, the young discipline made successful contributions to other sciences. *Symbolic Modeling* is an important task of informatics used in many fields. As computers may visualize dynamics, there is also an export of computerized *simulation* and *scientific visualization* from informatics to other scientific and application fields. *Recursive structures* and *complexity theory,* but also the technology of *large data bases* and *knowledge archives* are visible examples of research work done in informatics, reaching far beyond everyday technical applications. Informatics generates methodical instruments for other sciences besides computer programming. Biology, psychology, economics, social sciences, even philosophy use computerized models and simulation programs. Physics integrates models of informatics like *state diagrams* or *neural networks* that are used as an option beyond classical mathematical structures. And sometimes these models from informatics are developed further in physics, as with *spinglass models.*

Exporting theoretical as well as instrumental structures sets informatics apart form the classical engineering sciences. Therefore the notion *engineer-*

ing science looks too narrow; informatics is better classified more generally as a *technical science.*

Computer Nets are Media

The automata and machine perspective of informatics is too narrow for its future development, because it lacks a clear picture of challenges to come. If speed remains to be a main problem of computers, it became also a basic problem of informatics curricula development because of the swiftness with which development and application of computing is changing. Before the sixties, computers were mainly laboratory engines thought to be fast calculators – which they still are in some areas like simulation, weather forecast, stress analysis, molecular modeling, and others. The sixties saw the birth of real data processing complexes with large storages and archives. The *IBM* /360 family is now the index fossil of all main-frames that came later. This was the time of business data processing and the time when academic curricula were planned and started. With the advent of Large Scale Integration and the birth of the microprocessor in the seventies, computers were spread all over the labs and offices, and computer programs were regarded as more or less handy tools for many different applications – mainly for writing texts and for simple calculations. It was also the time of client-server architectures replacing centralized main-frames with their dumb terminals.

Networking and the mutual augmentation of communication and computer services, but also the rapid development of multi-media, changed the *tool perspective* to a *media perspective,* so that we may consider (networked) computers nowadays as digital media.

Networked computers allow new attitudes towards *knowledge* and towards the interplay between externally stored and internally memorized knowledge. For more than two thousand years external knowledge was mainly written knowledge (and for some ten thousand years painted knowledge). Since the fifteenth century knowledge is drawn mainly from printed work, but in the future, the *internet* will become the dominant storage and propagation medium of knowledge. Informaticians must develop and deliver storage technology, network technology, protocols, search engines, and presentation techniques, but also data models, formal definitions, concepts, and structures for this new landscape of externalized knowledge. Computer systems will become instrumental media, media of communication as well as of distribution, media of information as well as of entertainment. The main task of computer programs will no longer be automatic calculation or data processing, but acquisition, storage, and presentation of knowledge – of all kind, in any amount and in any quality.

Acquiring and using knowledge will become, much more than it already is, a technical performance based on computer technology. We take part in rapid change of the existing *global knowledge order,* to use a name introduced by the philosopher Helmut F. Spinner from TU Karlsruhe. Unfortunately, there is a substantial lack of a media concept in Informatics that reflects this accelerating development.

Understanding computers as media shows how problematic the exclusion of information sciences was in the beginning of academic informatics. Information sciences are a part of the discipline as well as computer science or computer engineering. We may well interpret informatics in the light of the coming information society as a "knowledge technology", as the title of Alfred Luft's and Rudolf Kötter's recently published book "Informatik - Eine moderne Wissentechnik" implies.

4 Informatik: A Defining Discipline of the Information Society?

Elements of the Discipline: Theory, Construction, and *Design*

After more than thirty years of its success it may sound unreasonable if not impossible to change the direction of the discipline in a radical way, but it is beyond doubt that the success of ubiquitous computing demands adaptations of the academic education in the discipline itself (as well as in other disciplines, where computers, programs, and nets nowadays are used as basic tools). If we take Kristen Nygaard's elegant statement: *To program is to understand!* seriously, we have to consider theory and construction as the basic elements of informatics. Both aspects are well developed, though the theoretical aspects of informatics are still limited to mathematical analysis. As in other sciences theoretical analysis could be aware of its philosophical, cultural, historical, and social foundations.

Besides a broader, more conscious theoretical foundation, the practice of informatics demonstrates the necessity of a skill that was present from the beginning, but usually not recognized in its importance, namely the skill of *design* – in its broadest sense. Already in 1970 Peter Naur pointed out in a paper on project activities in education that design is an integral part of the construction process in informatics. By mathematically and formally trained computer scientists design is usually considered as a trivial task (This attitude may explain why software sometimes is rejected by users despite striking algorithmic elegance). Peter Naur quoted George Forsythe from Stanford University: "To a modern mathematician design seems to be a second rate intellectual activity." But we may have learned in the past quarter century that computer products have to follow other rules than mathematical theorems. Design is an important aspect of informatics – staring with the first programs doing more than numerical calculations. Dijkstra's *Pleasantness Problem* is a basic problem of informatics. There is no successful separation of correctness and "pleasantness"; they are two faces of informaticians' work.

Design may have many aspects: usability of the artifacts, structural decisions about communications, or the design of cooperative work with the aid of computers, but also design in a more traditional way, like digital typography, user interfaces, or the construction of virtual realities. Hard- and software are constructed in a series of design decisions – some by knowledgeable people in a conscious manner, others ignored, because they were not recognized as important or considered to be self-evident or to follow the "one best way". But there simply is no such thing like the "one best way" - only series of improvements. Education in informatics could make these decision processes more transparent and demonstrate the consequences of alternatives. Knowledge as well as training seems to be necessary.

Growing awareness of design problems is a result of the spread of computer usage. Computer nets are becoming news and entertainment media, used by people who try to perform a task and don't want to care much about the basic enabling technologies. Informatics has to reflect this development, it must consider the difficult balance between restricting and opening technical possibilities in a given environment. This holds *a forteriori* where design decisions will construct new environments, completely unknown before.

The telephone may be used as a striking example. Bell and its early successors developed a beautiful and simple interface, easily understood by users. It was even refined successfully several times, up to the introduction of push buttons. Today, however, even simple telephones are designed like the most nightmarish command line computer interfaces – promising a vast bundle of hitherto unheard of features, but often disguising even the most basic functions.

Social and Communicative Competences

Rather trivially, the management of programmer or developer teams and even the membership in such a group demands social and communicative skills well beyond that of a typical university mathematician or logician. Obviously such skills are essential for a professional career in data processing. This also holds for other technical professions, but in informatics these skills are demanded from the inner workings of the technology, if computer systems are used as work tools or media.

The essentials and pitfalls of *user interfaces* prove that competences besides technical and mathematical knowledge are asked from informaticians. To understand how people work with computers, programs, and computerized work-flow, demands a deeper understanding of work and communication processes.

This is by far not restricted to user interface design, because even negotiating for a programming or development contract already demands communicative skills (and the lack of it may be a prime reason for crashed or delayed software projects and dissatisfied customers). Students have to develop communicative competency, namely the capacity for communication and discernment to enable them to participate, as future computer professionals, in design activities and interdisciplinary discussions.

Knowledge about communicative competency is not sufficient; training and discussion is unavoidable. Peter Naur pointed out in 1970 that *student projects* are a basic way to teach a complete development cycle from first ideas, plans and descriptions to design, construction, programming, test, documentation, and turn-over. Project work allows to work in a team with all the problems and all the help and insight that arise from such a situation. Teaching professional skills and application knowledge by example is a basic advantage of project work, but in addition the social and communicative skills are trained (for both students and teachers). The German Gesellschaft für Informatik considered communicative competencies to be so important that they included them besides technical, application related, and legal competencies in their Ethical Guidelines. The Guidelines are meanwhile confirmed in a formal voting process by their members with an overwhelming majority.

A New Order of Knowledge: Building the Information Society

Post-industrial society or *information society,* as it is called now, is no invention of Al Gore and his National and Global Information Infrastructure Initiatives, nor of the Bangemann-Report to the Council of the European Union. It may be better attributed to the sociologist Daniel Bell who wrote in 1973 *The Coming of Post-Industrial Society: A Venture in Social forecasting.* There were other social scientists who described the fundamental change of societies exposed to computer technology already in the seventies. They were not recognized in the discipline of *Informatik,* much as the Nora/Minc-Report to the French president was not read by many informaticians. So it is only recently, under the influence of political decision makers that computer scientists and informaticians have recognized the prominent role which they could (and should) take in the coming information society.

By no means all of these global processes are simple technical developments: while global finances, global economy, and globally distributed commerce and production depend on information network technology and computers, they follow their own aims and goals, develop their own problems and questions, many of which are only vaguely related to informatics. There is at least one field that has been strongly related to informatics and computers throughout the last thirty years, but usually not appreciated very highly in the discipline: gathering, storing, archiving, and presenting digitally transformed knowledge in form of electronic documents and multi-media materials. This field generates technical challenges in abundance, from design and construction of protocols, networks, and services through storage and long-term archiving up to ubiquitous presentation and interaction over the network. This is a primary task where informatics may serve the information society.

As theoretical background of these changes we may identify the development of a new *global knowledge order,* which, in conjunction with the economic, political and juridical order, defines the conditions of the information society in the next century. To understand these developments, informaticians must finally do their homework, and try to understand the theoretical foundations of their discipline. This means to study the historical, political, and cultural dimensions of "Informatik", computer science, informatique, datalogi, or howeverone chooses to call it.

As the French philosopher Michel Foucault asked in one of his last interviews: "Do you know the difference between true science and pseudo-science? True science takes notice of its own history." If we accept this formulation, we must consider informatics to be a pseudo-science, or, as this ignorance is not necessarily fixed for all time, a *pre-science or a science under construction.*

References

[DANL 72] Deutsche Akademie der Naturforscher Leopoldina, *Informatik*, Joachim-Hermann Scharf (ed.), Proc. Jahresversammlung vom 14. bis 17. Oktober 1971 zu Halle (Saale), Leipzig: Barth, 1972

[CACM 89] Communication of the ACM, A Debate on Teaching Computer Science, *Communication of the ACM* 32(12), 1989, p. 1397-1414

[Baue 71] Friedrich L. Bauer & Gerhard Goos, *Informatik – Eine einführende Übersicht* Bd. 1 & 2, Heidelberg et al.: Springer, 1971^1, 1974^2, 1982^3, 1990^4

[Baue 74] Friedrich L. Bauer, Was heißt und was ist Informatik, *IBM Nachrichten* 1974, p. 333-337

[BrHM 73] Wilfried Brauer, Wolfhart Haake, Siegfried Münch, *Studien- und Forschungsführer Informatik*, Bonn: GMD und Bad Godesberg: DAAD, 1973^1, 1974^2, 1978^3, 1980^4

[BrHM 82] Wilfried Brauer, Wolfhart Haake, Siegfried Münch, *Studien- und Forschungsführer Informatik*, Berlin-Heidelberg-New York et al.: Springer, 1982^1, 1989^2

[BrMu 96] Wilfried Brauer, Siegfried Münch, *Studien- und Forschungsführer Informatik*, Berlin-Heidelberg-New York et al.: Springer, 1996^3

[Bell 73] Daniel Bell, *The Coming of Post-Industrial Society: A Venture in Social Forecasting,* 1973

[Butt 95] Wilhelm Büttemeyer, *Wissenschaftstheorie für Informatiker*, Heidelberg et al.: Spektrum Wissenschaftsverlag, 1995

[Clau 75] Volker Claus, *Einführung in die Informatik*, Stuttgart: Teubner, 1975

[Sich 92] Wolfgang Coy, Frieder Nake, Jörg-Martin Pflüger, Arno Rolf, Dirk Siefkes, Jürgen Seetzen, Reinhard Stransfeld (ed.), *Sichtweisen der Informatik*, Braunschweig/Wiesbaden: Vieweg, 1992

[Denn 91] Peter J. Denning: Beyond Formalism, *American Scientist* 79 (Jan./Feb. 91), 1991, p. 8-10

[Denn 90] Peter J. Denning et al.: Computing as a Discipline, *Communication of the ACM* 32(1), 1989, p. 9-23

[BMwF 68] Der Bundesminister für wissenschaftliche Forschung, Empfehlungen zur Ausbildung auf dem Gebiet der Datenverarbeitung, *Internationale Elektronische Rundschau* 8, 1968, S. 211

[Dijk 89] Edsger Dijkstra, On the cruelty of really teaching computing science, *Communications of the ACM* 32(12), 1989, p. 1397-1414

[FakT 91] Fakultätentag Informatik & Fakultätentag Elektrotechnik, Gemeinsame Erklärung zur Informationstechnik, 1991

34

[FZBK 92] Christiane Floyd, Heinz Züllighoven, Reinhard Budde, Reinhard Keil-Slawik, *Software Development and Reality Construction,* Berlin-Heidelberg-New York et al.: Springer, 1992

[Fouc 88] Michel Foucault et al., *Technologien des Selbst,* S.Fischer: Frankfurt/Main, 1993 (Orig.: *Technologies of the Self,* Cambridge (Mass.): MIT Press, 1988)

[FHPR 95] Jürgen Friedrich, Thomas Herrmann, Max Peschek, Arno Rolf (ed.), *Informatik und Gesellschaft,* Heidelberg et al.: Spektrum 1995

[GAMM 69] GAMM/NTG Stellungnahme zu den ⟨Empfehlungen zur Ausbildung auf dem Gebiet der Datenverarbeitung⟩ des BMF vom 20.6.69

[Gilo 69] Wolfgang Giloi, *Was ist Informatik?,* Berlin: TU Berlin, 1969

[Grie 91] David Gries, Teaching Calculation and Discrimination: A more Effective Curriculum, *Communications of the ACM* 34(3), 1991, p. 44-55

[Haef 92] Klaus Haefner (ed.), *Evolution of information Processing Systems,* Berlin-Heidelberg-New York et al.: Springer, 1992

[Hans 93] Hansen, Hans Robert, Wirtschaftsinformatik, Bd. I & II, Stuttgart: Fischer 1983[4]

[Hoar 71] Tony Hoare, Computer Science, New Lecture Series #62, Belfast: Queen's University, 1971

[Dude 93] Duden Informatik: ein Sachlexikon für Studium und Praxis, Hermann Engesser (ed.), Mannheim (et al.): Dudenverlag 1993[2]

[Karo 92] Peter Karow, *Digitale Schriften – Darstellung und Formate,* Berlin-Heidelberg-New York et al.: Springer, 1992

[Koni 95] Wolfgang König, *Technikwissenschaften – Die Entstehung der Elektrotechnik aus Industrie und Wissenschaft zwischen 1880 und 1914,* Chur/Schweiz: G+B Verlag Fakultas, 1995

[Luft 88] Alfred L. Luft, *Informatik als Technikwissenschaft,* Mannheim et al.: BI Wissenschaftsverlag, 1988

[Luft 94] Alfred L. Luft & Rudolf Kötter, *Informatik – Eine moderne Wissenstechnik,* Mannheim et al.: BI Wissenschaftsverlag, 1994

[Main 79] Klaus Mainzer, Entwicklungsfaktoren der Informatik in der Bundesrepublik Deutschland, in: W. v.d. Daele, W. Krohn, P. Weingart (ed.), *Geplante Forschung,* Frankfurt a. M.: Suhrkamp, 1979, S. 117-180

[Mert 96] Peter Mertens, Wirtschaftsinformatik, in R. Wilhelm a.a.O., 1996

[MCGi 65] A.I. Michajlov, A.I. Cernyi & R.S. Giljarevskij, *Informatik,* Bd. 1 & 2, Staatsverlag der DDR o.O., o.J. (Berlin 1970), russian Original, Moscow 1965[1], 1967[2]

[MiJo 85] Donald Michie & R. Johnston, *Der kreative Computer – Künstliche Intelligenz und menschliches Wissen,* Hamburg/Zürich: Rasch & Röhring, 1985

[Mora 88] Hans A. Moravec, *Mind Children: the Future of Robot and Human Intelligence,* Cambridge, Mass. (et al.): Harvard Univ. Press, 1988

[Nake 88] Frieder Nake, Informatik und die Maschinisierung von Kopfarbeit, in Coy et.al. a.a.O, 1992

[Naur 92] Peter Naur, *Computing: A Human Activity,* New York: ACM Press, and Reading, Mass.: Addison Wesley, 1992

[NoMi 78] Simon Nora & Alain Minc, *L'informatisation de la Societè,* Paris 1978

[Nyga 86] Kristen Nygaard, Programming as a social activity, in Kugler (ed.) *Information Processing '86:* Proceedings of the IFIP 10th World Computer Congress, Dublin, September 1-5, 1986, Amsterdam (et al.): North-Holland 1986

[Parn 90]   David Parnas, Education for Computer Professionals, *IEEE Computer* 23(1), 1990, p. 17-22

[Pflu 94]   Jörg Pflüger, Informatik auf der Mauer, *Informatik Spektrum* 17:6, 1994

[Rech 91]   Peter Rechenberg, *Was ist Informatik?*, München/Wien: Hanser, 1991

[Schi 96]   Britta Schinzel (ed.), *Schnittstellen – Zum Verhältnis von Informatik und Gesellschaft*, Braunschweig/Wiesbaden: Vieweg, 1996

[Sief 90]   Dirk Siefkes, *Formalisieren und Beweisen: Logik für Informatiker*, Braunschweig: Vieweg, 1990

[Spin 94]   Helmut F. Spinner, *Die Wissensordnung: ein Leitkonzept für die Grundordnung des Informationszeitalters* Opladen: Leske und Budrich, 1994

[Stei 93]   Wilhelm Steinmüller, *Informationstechnologie und Gesellschaft – Eine Einführung in die Angewandte Informatik*, Darmstadt: Wissenschaftliche Buchgesellschaft, 1993

[Valk 97]   Rüdiger Valk, Die Informatik zwischen Formal- und Humanwissenschaften, *Informatik Spektrum* 20/2, 1997

[Weiz 76]   Joseph Weizenbaum, *Die Macht der Computer und die Ohnmacht der Vernunft*, Frankfurt a.M.: Suhrkamp, 1977 (Original: *Computer Power and Human Reason: ¿From Judgement To Calculation*, San Francisco: Freeman, 1976)

[Weiz 84]   Joseph Weizenbaum, *Kurs auf den Eisberg*, München/Zürich: Pendo, 1984

[vWei 71]   Carl Friedrich v. Weizsäcker, *Die Einheit der Natur*, München: Hanser 1971

[Wilh 96]   Reinhard Wilhelm, *Informatik – Grundlagen, Anwendungen, Perspektiven*, München: Beck, 1996

[WuFl 89]   Terry Winograd & Fernando Flores, *Understanding Computers and Cognition: a new Foundation for Design*, Norwood, N.J. (U.S.A): Ablex, 1986 (deutsch: *Erkenntnis – Maschinen – Verstehen*, Berlin: Rotbuch 1989)

[Zema 71]   Heinz Zemanek, Was ist Informatik?, *Elektronische Rechenanlagen* 13/4, 1971, S. 157ff.

[Zema 87]   Heinz Zemanek, *Informationsverarbeitung und die Geisteswissenschaften*, Wien: Verlag der Österreichischen Akademie der Wissenschaften, 1987

[Zema 92]   Heinz Zemanek, *Das geistige Umfeld der Informationstechnik*, Berlin-Heidelberg-New York et al.: Springer, 1992, S. 271

[Zuse 72]   Konrad Zuse, Der Plankalkül, GMD-Bericht #63, Sankt Augustin: GMD, 1972

Computer Science as Cultural Development
Toward a Broader Theory

Dirk Siefkes

Technische Universität Berlin
FB Informatik

In common understanding a theory is a body of abstract, or general, knowledge about a field. Laws, values, and methods are collected, put together in an orderly way, deep-fried as it were, and brought back to life on want or demand. If anyone needs a reason why this type of theory does not work, here is one: Such a theory is static, at best depicting certain properties of the field at a certain moment. Fields, however, move. Not just forward; no, they spring up, and change, and — horribile dictu — decay and vanish. A theory is no good if it does not help us understand development in this broad sense. As computer scientists we design and develop artifacts — hardware, software, formalisms. In doing so we develop ourselves, and hopefully others. Also the world changes, and so do we, without our doing or even knowing. Amidst this manyfold movements our field moves. A theory is as good as it helps us understand development.

1 Technological Change

Computer science is centered around computers and their programs. (This is so in Germany, too, where the name "Informatik" was chosen to signal a broader aim.) Therefore development is counted in computer generations and hierarchies of programming languages. Each stage was better than the one before: Computers became ever faster, cheaper, smaller, more reliable; programming languages became ever more powerful, easier to learn and to use, less machine-dependent. (Today both, computers and languages, turn into a medium, and we deal with interfaces only, which again become better and better.)

This simple picture falls apart upon closer inspection. Take as example the introduction of the programming languages Fortran and Algol, as analyzed in Eulenhöfer et al. [ESS97a]. When Algol was developed in the late fifties it was considered a big step forward over Fortran by many people. Nevertheless, till today Fortran is widely used in many areas, whereas Algol never was much recognized outside the universities. The reason, the authors argue, is that both languages are evaluated against different measures. Both developement teams stood firmly in the old tradition that the machine is superior to man in many respects, and thus should replace humans wherever possible. The Fortran team, though, strongly influenced by the IBM environment, considered a programming language as an instrument to run the machine, and organized the work around the machine in Taylor's spirit, business-like. Therefore they divided Fortran into a "language" of "instructions" and "control" where the programmer can express his ideas in a loosely mathematical way, and a "compiler" where the machine itself transforms the program into machine code as efficiently as possible. The Algol team on the other hand was mainly interested in elegance and universality; the programming language should be used first of all for international communication, esp. publication. The result was a formalism intended to make up for the weakness of everyday language. They distinguished between "syntax" and "semantics" of their language; the syntax is described formally, whereas the semantics refers to an abstract level between language and machine.

Thus what is a favorable change, or even a change at all, depends on what people see in a certain artifact, and on the values they use to measure it. These orientations of people come from the grand discourses of society, from the constraints and affordances of institutions like science and technology, from the work environment, and from the personal experiences. In this sense technological change is cultural development; see also Siefkes [Sie97a]. More broadly in [Pfl95] Jörg Pflüger connects the development of programming languages with stages in the "Geistesgeschichte", thus relating technological development to large-scale cultural changes.

2 A Model of Social Development

We gain nothing by inserting technological change into general cultural development if we cannot single out the specific influences relevant for computer science. To disentangle the maze of mutual dependencies I see two principles at work in every type of development: *formation/activation* and *generalization/specialization*. In the terminology of the anthropologist and cybernetician Gregory Bateson [Bat72, Bat79] development consists in *processes* running in given *forms* and creating new forms. As computer scientists we discuss problems, describe solutions, design and use computers and formalisms. These activities are processes forming specific objects which enable and direct new processes. Since in our culture forms are valued higher than processes, this interplay of formation and activation is sometimes called *objectification* or *representation*. I distinguish between *outer forms* which are material objects like texts and computers or tangible structures like universities and technologies, and *inner forms* which are mental objects like concepts and values or, on another level, knowledge and conscience. The mental and the material world are not connected but through our acting and perceiving, thinking and feeling, that is, through our activities.

Here the second principle, the interplay between generalization and specialization, is invoked. All development happens locally. Specifically, social development involves groups of people. If a change is to last, it must affect the people involved (specialization) and spread to wider domains (generalization). In turn individual form, like character, abilities, and orientations, induces and constrains group action, and so do general forms like institutions and other social structures. As indicated above the development of both Fortran and Algol can be better understood if we muster the whole array of factors determining the course of work: The ideologies prevalent in our culture at that time, the technology and science at hand, the working environment of a big computer firm or an international group of scientists, the individual characteristics. These ingredients were partly the same and partly different in the two development teams; in any case they resulted in quite different groups and finally in quite different programming languages. As in the case of the first principle there is no link between individual and society but through the group.

Finally the two principles work only in combination. We can neither design nor use a programming language if we do not perceive and handle it as such: as a specific instance of a technological species that is thereby formed and modified. What happens in the team affects the individual members differently, but jointly, and is carried by them into other groups, either directly by multiple membership or indirectly through representations of the group work: programs, texts, machines, etc. If the innovations meet favorable circumstances or, viewed differently, if they are advanced by the right people at the right time, they may become widely accepted and thus part of the general technological frame.

The term 'technological frame' is Wiebe Bijker's. In his beautiful book [Bij95] he develops a "Theory of Sociotechnical Change" from three case studies "Of Bicycles, Bakelites, and Bulbs". In most respects his theory fits nicely with my evolutionary model; for a detailed discussion see [Sie97a]. An important difference is the stress on local development. Only in groups small enough to allow for direct interaction joint experience is possible, although not without the unabiding effort of all people involved. In larger groups as well as in "the individual" the interplay between process and form happens through the mediation of these small groups. From 1982 onward in my papers on formalization in mathematics and in everyday life I call this the "small systems view", although it is a way to deal with the world rather than a view; see [Sie92b, Sie96].

3   Social Development and Biological Evolution

Bateson's theme is "mind" as a phenomenon of nature, not social, let alone technological, development. In [Bat79] he characterizes mind by maintaining that individual learning follows the same principles as biological evolution. In my efforts to understand formalization I developed his theory into a model of mental development, presented in the next section; see my contribution to [Coy92], also [Sie92a] and subsequent papers. Only later when I got involved with the social history of computer science (see below), I realized that social, and in particular scientific and technological development is inextricably linked with individual learning. So I needed a fitting model for the former, and came up with the one presented above; see e.g. [Sie95]. Thus to me the analogy with biological evolution has been a source of inspiration along the way toward a theory of computer science. To make this source available to others, I sketch my model of biological coevolution; for background information see e.g. Varela et al. [VTR91].

Think of fish in a cove. They swim about in schools, eat, play, reproduce, and die. These activities are supported and dictated by the environment which is formed by them at the same time. In this sense the environment represents the activities. In a different way the activities are represented internally in the chromosomes. This genetic representation is almost constant individually, and reproduced through the generations. It is changed at random, however, through mutation, recombination, and interaction with the environment, and thus varies throughout the gene pool. In this way the species evolves through natural selection, or rather, species and environment coevolve through local interaction.

For historical reasons in our culture biology is strictly separated from either psychology or sociology. Many people therefore dislike the above analogy between biological evolution and social development. Note, however, that it is an analogy, not a reduction: In the social model both processes and outer forms as well as selection are cultural or natural, not biological; the inner forms are mental. We will see in the next section how concepts and values act as genes in social development.

4   A Model of Mental Development

In most scientific theories as well as in everyday language thinking is depicted in mechanical metaphors and models: Our mind is a container where knowledge is stored in various compartments; theories and curricula are buildings with foundations and supporting pillars; learning is putting "stuff" into right places; teaching thus is making this stuff handy. Feelings either are thought to interfere with intellectual activities, or do not appear at all. — This is strange. We are living beings; in fact, we are as alive as our mind is. Why not depict mind as being alive?

Think of thoughts in your mind. They swarm around a subject, nourished by your feelings, they chase each other playfully or in fight, they multiply, vanish, and appear again. These activities are supported and dictated by your knowledge and your valuations, which are formed by them at the same time. In this sense your knowledge and valuations represent your thinking and feeling resp. In a different way they are represented by the concepts and values they carry within. These internal representations are relatively stable during individual thoughts and feelings, and serve to reproduce them over and over again. They are changed at random, however, through spontaneous ideas and sensations, through combination and reflection of the subject matter, and finally through perception, action, and communication. Concepts thus are not the building blocks of our knowledge, but are distributed throughout our thoughts and vary with them. In this way our knowledge about a field evolves through nurturing or suppressing certain thoughts, and thus changing the corresponding concepts. Or rather, intellectual abilities and knowledge coevolve in units that make sense in themselves. These local units of conceptual thinking are called "stories". Similarly feelings and valuations coevolve with the help of (systems of) values through emotional nurture or starvation. Since emotions seem to be related to the visual, the local units of emotional development might be called "movies". A good movie is always based on a story, and we visualize stories as movies. Thinking and feeling are activities that cannot be separated. In our thoughts we value something as true or false; in our emotions, as good or bad, or ugly or beautiful. In either, thinking or feeling, we value our subject.

Knowledge and valuations appear as inner forms in the social model, and as outer forms in the mental model. Through this joint part mental and social development are linked by perception, action, and communication, that is, through our mental, bodily, and social activities. Knowledge and valuations thereby differentiate into individual statements and judgements combining into theories and ethics, getting their meaning from stories and movies on a local level. Thus here is an important difference between biological evolution and its mental and social counterpart: Whereas the biological model is closed, the mental and the social model are open to each other through a common part which we call "self" and which is situated in our body. Thus not only social development depends on mental activities, as we all know, but individual learning is a social enterprise as well, which is less well known.

5 Formalization

The evolutionary theory has important consequences for understanding learning and teaching, and thus for understanding science, on which I have written elsewhere. (See e.g. [Sie92a, Sie97b, Sie97c]. The reader should be aware that the models have evolved themselves considerably, which seems appropriate.) Here I will turn directly to the particularities of computer science.

Formalization is an extreme form of the process of formation discussed above, involving language: Concepts and values are described explicitly and rules are set up for certain mental or social activities, to govern the characteristics of objects and of behavior. Art and law, etiquette and religion are examples from everyday life. In science formalization is used to describe and predict natural processes, in engineering, to design and built machines. Thereby mathematics has become an important background part of our culture. The goal of formalization is to unrelate objects and activities from their surroundings, in particular to prevent them from changing.

In terms of the evolutionary theory, by formalization we move from processes to representations, trying to cut off development. It is a common misunderstanding that we get rid of processes that way, and work with representations only. If we did, we would no longer understand what we do. Even in the most severely formalized realms understanding means development, which needs the interplay between process and form, however restricted. We cannot follow the rules of a formalism without second thoughts and primary feelings and bodily actions. Of course in teaching we must force the students to follow the rules strictly; but if they do not develop a meaning for the rules thereby, they learn nothing. Only in machines formalization is completed. Machines act without understanding, thus without development. This is an important difference between formalisms and machines: Machines act deterministically, formalisms do not act at all. Rather we act with their help, as living beings, thus not deterministically. It is misleading to call formalisms "symbolic machines" as many philosophers do; see e.g. Krämer [Krä88]. It is equally misleading to identify mental techniques or bodily habits with machine behaviour; see e.g. Rammert [Ram95]. We immediately recognize machine-like behaviour in humans as pathetic, if not pathologic.

Representations are continuous or discrete, although never purely so. Discrete representations are built from atomic parts; the meaning of the whole arises from the meaning of the parts, depending on the builtup (Frege's principle). Examples are the formalisms from logic and discrete mathematics we need to deal with computers. Continuous representations — as they are used in the continuous mathematics of engineering — cannot be partioned in this way. Habits, pictures, machines, and everything alive get their meaning from how they evolve in natural, mental, and social processes from earlier representations: through reproduction, creative work, human action. Even if they are built from simpler parts, they cannot be understood that way. In modern genetics, for example, genes are no longer seen as letters in a code since they work context-dependent; even 'gene' as a basic scientific concept seems questionable, see Keller [Kel95].

In [Dij89] Edsger Dijkstra names sheer size and discreteness as the two main factors why computers are such an absolute novelty, and thus so difficult to handle. (Other reasons for the "software crisis" are worked out in Theißing [The95].) Size alone is not the point, as in many areas modern machines are awe-inspiringly large and complex. He is right, however, with discreteness. In computers the symbol processes that arise when we deal with discrete formalisms, are turned into signal processes which bear meaning for the designers and users only, not for the machine; see e.g. Nake [Nak96]. This is the reason why computers are so hard to understand. Dijkstra is wrong, however, in the "solution" he proposes: not to try to understand computer processes (through anthropomorphisms, for example), but rather to deal with them mathematically, that is, to see programs as logical formulas and programming as "very large scale applied logic". Discrete mathematics, esp. logic, is needed to model computing processes. Formulas, however, are as hard to state correctly as programs; so the problem is only pushed into another corner. (No doubt, this translating process can be helpful.) De Millo, Lipton, and Perlis argue in [DLP79] that to prove the correctness of programs mathematically cannot work either. Mathematics is not a play with meaningless symbols (only nonmathematicians think that). To prove a theorem means to convince people, and thus is a social process as much as writing a correct program.

I am not competent enough to judge the feasibility of formal methods in software engineering. The evolutionary model, however, shows that they do not suffice and, taken alone, hinder rather than help. Formalization is not a linear process of building a symbolic representation of some mental process (formation); it also means to establish the representation in a meaningful context (generalization). In doing so we nesessarily pass through the bodily looking-glass that connects the mental and the social world, back and forth, again and again. Formalization is not a symbolic activity, it involves social development. This is the reason why prototyping is helpful in software design: by cutting the problem into manageable parts, by making the relevant people participate, and by rendering the design process cyclic, understanding as a social process — as analyzed above in the evolutionary model — is encouraged; see the beautiful collection Floyd et al. [Flo92].

6 Social History of Computer Science

If so obviously mathematics is only one among many disciplines relevant to computer science, why does it play such a dominant role there? This is one question we pursue in an interdisciplinary research project "Sozialgeschichte der Informatik" (Social History of Computer Science) at the TU Berlin. The answer that generally in engineering mathematization of foundations and curricula is the way to become accepted as a scientific discipline (see e.g. König [Kön95]), accounts only for the continous mathematics of engineering (technology and applications). Discrete mathematics serves to model computing processes as was discussed above. Since the discrete computation models of mathematical logic predate the invention of the computer, it is generally assumed that they guided the inventors. This seems questionable, however; see e.g. Heintz [Hei93]). An analysis of von Neumann's influential "First Draft" shows (Stach [Sta97]) that his ideas came from biology (computers as organisms), neurobiology (the brain as finite-state machine), and cybernetics or systems theory (man as a self-steering device); see also Keller [Kel95] for a detailed discussion of history and background.

Pursuing the above question in [Eul96] Peter Eulenhöfer investigates the institutionalization of computer science in Germany. The promoters of the field were mathematicians or electrical engineers of different background, drawn together by their interest in the use of computers. They were united by their vision of a new field sufficiently different from their home disciplines to require separation, and sufficiently close to ensure scientific substance. This explains why the discrete mathematics of Theoretical CS is considered a genuine part of CS, but the relevant theories of linguistics or psychology or sociology are not.

In this way the work in the Social History Project lead us to look for *(patterns of) orientations* that guide the activities of people and groups involved with CS. Orientations result from our knowledge about and our valuation of a situation and of the possibilities it affords. According to the evolutionary model they thus connect and coordinate mental and social development, thereby establishing group identities. We see development in the decisions of actors and in changes of structure. If we want to understand how the two connect, we have to find out the visions by which social groups orient their actions.

Examples of such patterns of orientation are the wildly mixed motivations in the development of Fortran and Algol sketched above. More broadly, you will design different machines and programming languages depending on whether you view a computer as a large and fast computing machine, as a data processing device, as an electronic brain, or as a medium. The attitude toward mathematics is another example of an orientation with profound influence on the development of CS. For accounts see [ESS97, Sie97d, Sta96, Stä97].

7 Theory and Ethics, Education and Research

In 1988 Wolfgang Coy founded a group of mostly computer scientists concerned with the state of the field. How can a discipline that is so dramatically involved in changing the world without the slightest idea of the whereabouts be content with a foundation in discrete mathematics? We named the group "Theorie der Informatik" (Theory of Computer Science), it was funded as a discourse project of the BMFT, and existed for four years. We did not produce a theory of CS. At the end we humbly published a volume "Sichtweisen der Informatik" (Perspectives of CS, [Coy92]).

By working with a certain orientation, you get a certain perspective on the field that brings some things (that are important to you) into the foreground, and leaves others in the back. If you are mainly interested in the computer as a machine and in its applications, you see CS as an engineering discipline (e.g. Giloi). If formalisms are important to you, you call it a "Strukturwisssenschaft" (structural science, Brauer). If you want to combine both aspects, you call CS an "Ingenieur-Geisteswissenschaft" (Bauer), and computer scientists "engineers for abstract objects" (Zemanek). If you try to include all this, you say "Informatik" (science of information processing, Brauer again). Do these perspectives taken together actually provide a theory of CS?

In common understanding a theory consists of the essentials of a field put into a most general ultimate form. A theory then is the combined result of formation and generalization. The evolutionary model of development sketched above thus indicates why in our culture theories are so highly praised and so rarely used. Forms do not evolve — and thus do not exist — without processes, and generalities, not without specialities. Further theories are not just mind stuff, but lead a social life as well. Therefore, first, a theory cannot be raised and developed "theoretically", separated from scientific praxis, and second, not mentally, separated from social praxis. These are trivialities which at best can serve to raise eyebrows. A closer look at the model, however, reveals some consequences that may be worth to pursue.

First, in the evolutionary model thinking and feeling are inseparably interwined; so therefore are thoughts and emotions, concepts and values, theories and ethics. In scientific praxis on the other hand, theory provides the foundation and helps us in the field, ethics guides us in the applications and is banned from the field. Theory and ethics are deadly enemies, or unrelated at best. The evolutionary model shows that it is precisely this separation that turns barren both of them. Ethics should be raised "within" theory, and theory "within" ethics. For example, Turing's theoretical questions "Can machines think?" should be turned into the ethical question "Is it good to compare man and machine?" Conversely, the question "What is good and what is bad?" should be considered a challenge, not a constraint, and thus excite theoretical work.

Second, in biological evolution species can influence each other only through interaction, the closer the better. In the evolutionary model therefore knowledge cannot be transported from one field to another. Knowledge is not "stuff", it can be spread only through joint work. If we aim for a broader theory of CS, it is not enough to admit the various perspectives quoted above (and there are more) to exist side by side. (Although that would already be a step undreamt of.) The perspectives have to coevolve, not peacefully, but in interaction, if they are to evolve at all.

This demand still sounds illusionary. Quite in accord with the biological analogy, science is based on competition; tolerance, let alone mutual appreciation, is rare. Interaction, however, as asked for above, need not be peaceful. In biological evolution sometimes it is, sometimes it is not; neither way it can be called good or bad. But in science it can! We therefore have to combine the two principles just explicated, and strive for good interactions, and abhor others. That would be a truly novel scientific principle. We might produce less new results, but more meaningful science.

The evolutionary theory has striking consequences for education as well. If knowledge is not stuff that can be transferred, a lecture brings results only as far as it excites and promotes the thoughts of the students. Study projects are better. And if they seem not feasible, there are other ways to turn lectures into work environments. I have, for example, adapted the method of prototyping from software engineering to large lectures: students work in small groups over an extended period at problems bigger than usual, the lecture serves only to support their work; see [Sie90, Sie92b]. A lecture may also be turned into a permanent examination that way — another example why ethics and theory ought to be integrated. In a study project with Carl-Hellmut Wagemann from the department of education we took the experience as a basis to compare the methods of knowledge transfer and information processing in the two fields, and had the students view software design as a teaching/learning situation.

More generally, in an earlier study project we developed the principles of an evolutionary CS curriculum: The students determine their course of study by choosing subjects grouped around themes of their interest. They may leave the university any time with a certificate showing their achievements, and re-enter later. They thus are responsible for acquiring an education suitable for their later needs — a third example for a possible integration of ethics and theory. And the universities may stop worrying about study profiles that never meet the demand anyway. Theory and praxis could be brought still closer by allowing students to participate in suitable research projects of industry and administration as part of their education. For a report see [Sie97c].

Traditionally, research is the area of free evolution. Today for many reasons this freedom becomes more and more restricted by an evergrowing administration. At the TU Berlin a plan is discussed to let its members compete for funding instead. This is familiar with funding from outside the university, but here the criteria are different: Certain themes of general value — a further example of a possible integration of theory and ethics — have to be selected, and research planing has to be related to them. Since relevance for education is a selection criterion, research and education become again interrelated — made possible through the flexibilization of education just sketched; see again [Sie97c].

References

Gregory Bateson. *Steps to an Ecology of Mind.* Ballantine Books, 1972. In German: Ökologie des Geistes. Suhrkamp, stw 571, 1985.

Gregory Bateson. *Mind and Nature – a Necessary Unity.* Bantam Books, 1979. Deutsch: Geist und Natur – eine notwendige Einheit, Suhrkamp 1982.

Wiebe Bijker. *Of Bicycles, Bakelites, and Bulbs. Toward a Theory of Sociotechnical Change.* MIT Press, 1995.

Wolfgang Coy et al., editors. *Sichtweisen der Informatik.* Vieweg, Wiesbaden, 1992.

Richard De Millo et al. Social Processes and Proofs of Theorems and Programs. *Communications of the ACM*, 22:pp. 271 – 280, 1979.

E. W. Dijkstra. On the Cruelity of Really Teaching Computing Science. *Communicatons of the ACM*, 32:pp. 1397 – 1414, 1989.

Peter Eulenhöfer, Dirk Siefkes, and Heike Stach. Informatics as Cultural Development. Technical Report 97-2, Technische Universität Berlin, FB Informatik, 1997.

Peter Eulenhöfer, Dirk Siefkes, and Heike Stach. Informatics as Cultural Development: The Creation of Programming Languages. In Eulenhöfer et al. 1997, pages 16 – 22.

Peter Eulenhöfer. The Enculturation of Mathematical and Logical Practice in the Age of Computing Technology. In Eulenhöfer et al. 1997, pages 10 – 15.

Christiane Floyd et al., editors. *Software Development and Reality Construction.* Springer, 1992.

Bettina Heintz. *Die Herrschaft der Regel – Zur Grundlagengeschichte des Computers.* Campus, Frankfurt/Main, New York, 1993.

Evelyn Fox Keller. *Refiguring Life.* Columbia University Press, 1995.

Wolfgang König. *Technikwissenschaften. Die Entstehung der Elektrotechnik aus Industrie und Wissenschaft zwischen 1880 und 1914.* Berlin, 1995.

Sybille Krämer. *Symbolische Maschinen – Die Idee der Formalisierung im geschichtlichen Abriß.* Wiss. Buchges., Darmstadt, 1988.

Frieder Nake. *A semiotic perspective on interaction.* Talk Dagstuhl-Seminar "Informatik und Semiotik", February 1996.

Jörg Pflüger. Leitbilder der Programmiersprachenentwicklung. In J. Friedrich et al., editor, *"Informatik und Gesellschaft"*, pages 196 – 210. Spektrum, 1995.

Werner Rammert. Regeln der technikgenetischen Methode. In Jost Halfmann, editor, *Jahrbuch "Technik und Gesellschaft"*, volume 8, pages 13 – 30. Campus, 1995.

Dirk Siefkes. *Formalisieren und Beweisen – Logik für Informatiker.* Vieweg, Wiesbaden, 1990. 2. Auflage 1992.

Dirk Siefkes. *Fish in Schools or Fish in Cans – Evolutionary Thinking and Formalization.* Technical Report TR-92-009, International Computer Science Institute Berkeley, 1992.

Dirk Siefkes. *Formale Methoden und Kleine Systeme – Leben, lernen und arbeiten in formalen Umgebungen.* Vieweg, Wiesbaden, 1992.

Dirk Siefkes. *Ökologische Modelle geistiger und sozialer Entwicklung. Beginn eines Diskurses zur Sozialgeschichte der Informatik.* Technical Report FS II 95-102, Wissenschaftszentrum Berlin für Sozialforschung, 1995.

Dirk Siefkes. Umdenken auf kleine Systeme – Können wir zu einer ökologischen Orientierung in der Informatik finden? *Informatik Spektrum*, (19):pp. 141 – 146, 1996.

Dirk Siefkes. *Making Meaning Through the Design and Teaching of Computer Software.* In Eulenhöfer et al. 1997, pages 23 – 32.

Dirk Siefkes. *Turing meets Thoreau. An Ecological Approach to Computer Science.* To appear in Proc. Conference "Einstein meets Magritte", Brussels, vol. "Worldviews", 1997.

Dirk Siefkes. *Veränderung der Lebenswelt durch Informationstechnologie als Herausforderung für eine Veränderung der Informatik.* To appear in: J. Krämer et al., "Schöne Neue Arbeit", Talheimer, 1997.

Dirk Siefkes. *Die Rolle von Gruppenprozessen in der Informatikgeschichte. Zur Arbeit im IFP Sozialgeschichte der Informatik.* To appear in: Eulenhöfer et al. (eds.) "Entwicklung der Informatik im sozialen und kulturellen Kontext" 1997, in preparation

Heike Stach. Orientierungsmuster – ein methodischer Ansatz für eine Sozialgeschichte von Wissenschaft und Technik. *Wechselwirkung*, pages 48 – 53, October 1996.

Heike Stach. *The Image of Man as a Self-Steering Device as Constituent for the Concept of the Stored-Program Computer.* In Eulenhöfer et al. 1997, pages 3 – 9.

Klaus Städtler et al. *Die Rekonstruktion von Orientierungsmustern in Fachtexten aus der Informatik.* Technical Report 97-3, Technische Universität Berlin, FB Informatik, 1997.

Florian Theißing. *Auf dem Weg in die Softwarekrise?* Technical Report 95-14, Technische Universität Berlin, FB Informatik, 1995.

Francisco Varela, Evan Thompson, and Eleanor Rosch. *The Embodied Mind – Cognitive Science and Human Experience.* MIT Press, 1991. In German: Der mittlere Weg der Erkenntnis. Scherz 1994.

Towards Adjusting Informatics Education to Information Era

Jozef Gruska[1]* and Roland Vollmar[2]

[1] Faculty of Informatics, Masaryk University, Botanická 68a, 60020 Brno, Czech Republik
[2] Lehrstuhl Informatik für Ingenieure und Naturwissenschaftler, Universität Karlsruhe, Am Fasanengarten 5, D-76128 Karlsruhe, Germany

Abstract. Since the very beginning of the modern computing era, the scientific and educational community in informatics has been in a continuous search for a proper philosophy, viewpoints, aims, contents, methods and tools. Advances in software, communication and hardware have played by that search the most influencing role, with theory advances having only secondary and declining impacts — in spite of the remarkable success of theory, quite well recognized by the community at large.

The recent developments and advances in computing, communication and informatization of the society point out strongly, that horizons of the field are much broader, and its impacts on the society are far larger than anticipated even by strong optimists. This brings new and strong impetus to reconsider again the aims, scope, contents and methods of education in informatics and in other areas.

In the paper we analyze: (a) needs to change education in informatics; (b) the current situation in informatics education; (c) a framework for a new approach; (d) steps to be done; (3) two case studies.

1   Why we need to change the education in informatics

There are two main reasons why the aim, contents and methods of informatics education should be challenged nowadays. Both of them have their roots in important recent developments as well as in growing experiences with the results of the current educational approaches and methods. The first one is associated with the emerging global/social needs informatics education is to respond to. The second one is related to the important internal developments within informatics itself.

* Most of this work has been done during the first author's stay at the University of Karlsruhe in 1996 and his affiliation with the Institut of Mathematics of Slovak Academy of Sciences. This work has been partly supported by the grant 1112/1994 of VEGA, Slovak Grant Foundation and partly by the grant GRK 209/2-96 of the German Science Foundation (DFG).

1.1 New global and social developments and needs to which informatics education has to respond to

Informatization of the society is having a profound impact not only on tools mankind can use to solve its local problems and to meet its current needs but also on new global aims and problems the mankind can approach. This brings in turn new aims and requirements for informatics itself, and especially for its education, have to try to meet.

New global role of science and education. After the remarkable impact of science and technology during the Second World War, the very basic philosophy about the role of science and research in the postwar period, and how they should be supported and organized, was developed in [Bus45]. This positional document established a doctrine how to view and support science and technology research that was followed by the most developed countries since then. The document was based on a belief in the enormous power of science, correctly, and created space for a large part of science and research to develop according to their needs and views. The other part of science and research have been tied up by the magic word *defence* and practically everything that could be put, somehow, under this umbrella, was almost blindly supported. Except the defence oriented part of science and research, the rest of society was given the chance and responsibility to utilize the outcomes of science. The doctrine was based on a belief that it is enough to care, for science and research supporters, that there are excellent results in science and technology and society will surely benefit out of it proportionally to the investment into the science and technology. This important part of the original philosophy on which the role of science in the society was based on did not turn out as well as expected. In addition, the enormous emphasis on science and research not only put aside education, especially at the "top research universities", but also adjusted its aims and methods to serve primarily to science and research needs.

[Gru93] represents an attempt to reevaluate the original philosophy on which science and technology have been based for almost 50 years and to outline a new role for science and technology in the society in general and propose new ways science should be supported and managed; with *national wealth* as a new magic word.[1] Even if some particular suggestions of that document can be questioned, it is getting increasingly clear that a significant part of science will have to care much more about its aims and usability of its outcomes. *Technology transfer* is the related key word. In addition, it is also getting increasingly clear that high level of education and educational priorities have to be established again. Informatization of society not only increases needs on the overall education of society but also makes a life-long continuing education and a preparation for it a necessity and a top priority.

---

[1] This includes such important tasks to take care of as *environmental protection*.

Tasks of informatics as of a new fundamental and global methodology. It is evident that in the course of time not all components of our society have succeeded to develop sufficiently well. Interesting enough, the degree of the development of various areas of society depends much on the fact whether a given area had at its disposal a sufficiently sound methodology to deal with the problems that needed to be solved.

From this point of view science and technology, and related areas, as medicine, have been developing fast due to the fact that they had two sound and complementary methodologies to their disposal: experimental methodology and theoretical methodology. However, also these two methodologies, though in principle very fundamental and successful, have been lacking the capability for dealing with the complex problems in an appropriate way.

Informatics, including information and communication technology, can be seen as providing science, technology, and actually all areas of society, with a new fundamental and extremely powerful methodology (see Section 3.4). For some areas, as for science and technology, this methodology is a third methodology, which in combination with two old methodologies qualitatively increases their potential. Of the large importance is also the fact that this new methodology has a global character — can be used to deal with problems in all areas of functioning of society — and presents a new, and for some areas actually the only one sound enough methodology so far, for dealing with complex problems in a powerful way.

There are several reasons why informatics should play a crucial role in all main programs of society. The main one is related to the fact that the major problems of mankind that need to be solved are of global and very complex character[2] and information processing and communication technology is seen as the main current technology with a potential to help to deal successfully with such global problems. It is also believed that progress in the area of information processing and communication technology will determine the rate of progress in all major critical technology areas.

Central role of the informatics education in all fields of education. With informatics as perhaps the main methodology of the near future, it is of key importance for all areas of education to achieve that graduates understand the potentials of this new methodology and are able to apply it as needed. The existence of theoretical methodology resulted in having mathematics education as an indispensable ingredient for almost all science, technology, business, ... oriented areas of education. In a similar way laboratories have been used to a large extent to teach and learn fundamentals of the experimental methodology.

Informatics as a methodology is very complex and it is only natural that a search for the ways how to teach this methodology are in the beginnings. Of importance it is to realize that this methodology is often identified only with some of its (software and hardware or communication) tools — and sometimes

---

[2] For example, modelling and prediction of the behaviour of the earth system (including the climate, hydrological cycle, ocean circulation, growth of biosphere,and gas exchange between the atmosphere and the terrestrial and oceanic biota.)

with very elementary tools only. At the same time this methodology develops so fast that even specialists can hardly follow all new developments in their area of expertise. Under these circumstances it is one of the main tasks of informatics to help other educational areas to see the potential of this new methodology and the ways this methodology should be understood and managed by their graduates.

Increasing emphasis on multi-disciplinary approaches. Needs to support inter-disciplinary approaches and to focus education along these lines in general have been emphasized already for a while. With informatics providing a powerful methodology and tools to facilitate multi-disciplinary approaches the possibilities to pursue and develop this idea has a much more real base. At the same time, informatics itself should try to utilize fully the power of this new and multi-inter-disciplinary borders-bridging-methodology. Education in informatics has therefore to adjust to these quite new aims.

1.2   Maturing of the discipline

As an academic discipline informatics is clearly coming of the age. It is also a discipline with an extraordinarily fruitful interaction between academia and industry. This allows and also requires that also its education matures and increases quality of its graduates.

1.3   New internal developments — their potentials and impacts

Several recent internal developments in informatics have much contributed to the needs to change the view of the field, and of its potentials and impact on society.

Global networking: The impacts of global networks are, even in their very beginnings, breathtaking and keep changing radically practically all aspects of society, including education. Information is becoming more and more valuable and more easily available commodity and global methods of obtaining, processing, communicating and presenting information are getting rapidly of an increasing importance.

Cryptographic methods: Not only global networking but also a variety of local and distributed information processing systems, such as smart cards, would hardly be possible without modern cryptographic techniques. Security of communication, data and authentication are the key issues of the information era. In addition to that, basic cryptographic concepts have turned out to be of large importance for various theoretical considerations in informatics and even for foundations of computing.

Visualization and animation: Enormous progress, that has been achieved, step by step, in the area of image generation, processing, transformation and in visualization and animation, has and it is expected to have, far reaching consequences on almost all areas of human activities.[3]

Multimedia: The progress obtained in digitalization of all basic types of information and in recording, combining, modifying and presenting such information, in ever more qualitative ways, is bringing an important new quality concerning the power and impacts of information processing.

Continuously increasing computational power and storage capacities: In spite of various pessimistic forecasts it seems now quite clear that the existing progress concerning performance of computing systems will continue still for quite a while and can be expected to reach a new quality.[4]

New computing paradigms: Several new computing paradigms (randomization, parallelism, distributiveness, interactions, approximations) have significantly changed our theoretical and also practical views on what is feasible and brought also radically new concepts of hard to foresee importance. Randomization turned out to be a very powerful tool, especially when combined with interactions. This, in addition, resulted in development of radically new approaches to such basic concepts of science as evidence (proof) and such basic problems of computing as program validation, self-correction and self-testing. Parallelism and distributiveness, enhanced with the power of global networking, and allow to solve problems far beyond those imaginable only few years ago. (For example, integer factoring using tens of thousands of computers [Cal96].)

Quantum, molecular and brain computing: Though the very basic results obtained so far in the area of quantum, molecular and brain computing are still far away from having a larger impact on practical computing, and it is even far from clear what will come out of it eventually, there are reasons to assume that very important steps have been done concerning the representation and processing of information in quantum and molecular environment, and that information processing space is much larger than considered so far with potentials that may go far beyond those of nowadays.

These changes in the development of informatics mark a critical junction for the discipline and it is rapidly becoming clear that, although informatics education has enjoyed some success in the last decades, the ways of the past will hardly lead to success in the future.

---

[3] One can speak even about visualization of mathematics as an important methodology to deal with some mathematical problems — what a contrast to the views presented by the Bourbaki school.

[4] For example, the recent "world record" of 1.06 teraflops operations per second by Intel is already not too far from the performance 1.4 teraflops that seems to be sufficient to model atom explosion or to decode human genom.

2 Analysis of the current situation in informatics education

The ways politicians and scientists choose research directions, priorities, problems, educational aims, and methods depend in general much on the overall understanding of the scientific base of the field as well as of its long term role and contributions for the society. It is natural that in the absence of some deeper and long term valid understanding of the field the views of informatics have evolved as the field developed, especially its technological base and main applications. See, for example, [Bra87,Bra88,BBr89,Bra90a,Bra90b]):

It is also only natural that the main views on education in informatics have always much reflected the dominating general views of the area and its role in the society. The attempts to come with model curricula played an important role for formulation of such views. A very significant was the ACM Computer Science Curriculum'68, mainly due to the fact that its designers had quite a coherent view of the area — from that period point of view. The second such a big attempt, much more controversial, has been the ACM-IEEE Computer Science Curriculum'92, which was as expected, due to the lack of such a unified and sufficiently deep view of the field at that time, what can be seen also from the following citation from an introductory paper [Den89]: "Old debate continues. Is computer science a science? An engineering discipline? Or merely a technology, an inventor and purveyor of computing commodities? Is it lasting or will it fade with a generation?"

In general, education aims, contents and methods have been very much under the immediate influence of the very last developments in software-hardware-communication technologies without a coherent and appropriate view of the scientific base of the field and without a sufficient vision of the future needs of graduates.

The views of the field presented above are in general too shortsighted. They see the scope and the methods of the field mostly too narrowly and the main aims of its scientific base often in a too utilitarian way (to serve and advice information processing and communication technology). In addition, programming and software have been seen mostly, misleadingly, as dominating the scientific and educational base of the field.

2.1 Shortcomings of the current education and their analysis

In the course of time various general shortcomings of the current informatics education have been more or less identified. Some of them will now be first summarized and later analysed.

Global shortcomings. Several of the general shortcomings have been identified in the Hartmanis-Lin's report [HLi92], where they analysed experiences of the application area with the computer science/engineering graduates. The degree to which they are valid can vary from one educational system to another. However, it seems to be clear that they represent strong points to pay attention to:

1. Computer science graduates are not prepared well enough to cope with the fast development of the field.
2. Computer science graduates are not trained enough to proceed systematically in solving problems and developing products.
3. Computer science graduates are not trained appropriately to use formal methods to derive and validate results and the rigour with which they approach and perform their tasks is in general not sufficient.
4. Computer science graduates do not have sufficient knowledge, insights, models, theories, methods and training in such essential engineering areas as system analysis, product validation, evaluation, testing, robustness, maintenance, and security.
5. Computer science graduates lack sufficient communication skills needed to cooperate in the identification, formulation and solution of problems.
6. Computer science graduates do not see well enough the importance of ethical problems and are not prepared to deal with them as needed.

There are also complaints from the research environment. There are even people that believe that if one wants to do research in computing, then it is better to study first either mathematics or electrical engineering or physics and then switch to research in informatics.

Analysis of the shortcomings. On one side, one can say that some of the above critics are related to the fact that the application area requires too much from graduates concerning their immediate capability to perform perfectly even the jobs that require long term experiences and that the role of university education is to concentrate more on providing graduates with fundamentals needed for their job and for continuous education. However, in spite of that there are few points in such critics which can be summarized as follows (see also [Gru93,Gru93a]):

1. Fundamentals of the field are not well understood and are not usually taken broadly and deeply enough to create a coherent base.[5]
2. There has been a large progress in the development of all main areas of informatics. However, the degree of synthesis of knowledge and experiences in teaching and textbooks is far from sufficient.
3. Current education provides too much emphasis on analytical methods and too little on constructive methods.

---

[5] [HLi92] "While introductory courses for most scientific and engineering disciplines exhibit a relatively high degree of uniformity in content and approach, university level introductory courses in computer science/engineering exhibit striking variations. Some emphasize new concepts in functional programming, logic programming, or object programming. Other teach no theory and are focused more on teaching programming languages than on programming itself, and still others emphasize theories of program correctness and programming methodology.

Some diversity at the introductory level is appropriate and desirable, as diversity results from informed choice on the part of faculty. But to the extent that this diversity reflects a lack of current knowledge about the field, it is undesirable."

4. Quantitative methods of complexity theory are much developed but their use is far from sufficient.

5. Quite often not yet sufficiently verified theories and methods, or even methods good enough only to solve toy problems are taught as a methodology to solve real problems. From this point of view there is too much unjustified and useless experimentation with students.

6. Too much energy is often lost in teaching and learning an enormous number of unessential details of far from perfect systems of far from a long term importance.

7. Practical work is not performed systematically enough.

8. Ethical questions are nowadays often emphasized without having a sufficient impact because the treatment of these questions is not an inherent part of all subjects.

The first reason behind the difficulties in establishing a proper educational program in computing is that the tasks the graduates should be prepared to deal with are very hard. Indeed, the graduates are to be prepared

– to deal with *immense differences in the scale of phenomena*; from individual bits in computers to billion operations per second and with highly complex software and hardware systems;

– to design and to deal with *many levels of abstraction*; to understand, manage, reason about the most complicated human creations;

– to achieve an *unprecedented precision*, because the underlying hardware is a universal computer and therefore a chaotic system;

– to overcome enormous difficulties one encounters in designing and managing of *complex software systems*.

The second reason behind various problems in establishing a more adequate educational program of informatics is that the aim of such an education does not seem to be clear enough. This is due to the fact that informatics graduates are finding jobs in very diverse areas where very different knowledge and skills are needed.

Actually, the main aim of informatics education, namely that

graduates are capable to work along well established scientific principles and methods, have enough skill to enter successfully job market, and enough knowledge to keep themselves continuously up-to-date to ensure their lifetime successful career,

also requires to have a deep understanding of the field and to see the field in a long-term perspective.

3 Framework for a new approach

In order to develop a framework for dealing with the existing problems in informatics education we have first to formulate a new view of the scientific base of the field and its methodological impacts. In order to do that let us start with some very general views on the development of mankind and computing.

3.1 Main eras of mankind and the essence of computing

In a very short but quite well pointed out way the global history of mankind can be seen as consisting of three eras:

Neolithic era: Progress was made on the basis that man learned how to make use of the potentials of nature to have *food* in a sufficient amount and desirable form whenever needed.

Industrial era: Progress has been made on the basis that man learned how to make use of the potentials and laws of nature to have *energy* in a sufficient amount and desirable form whenever needed.

Information era Progress is being made on the basis that man is learning how to make use of the potential and laws of nature to have *information* in a sufficient amount and desirable form whenever needed.

Also the essence of computing in the last two and in the next century seems to be quite well captured as follows:

19th century: Computing was seen as a brain process.

20th century: Computing is seen as a machine process.

21th century: Computing will be seen as a nature process.

The first of the above characterizations forms the basis for seeing the importance of informatics for society, the second forms the basis for searching for the essence of its scientific base.

3.2 A new view of the scientific base of Informatics

In order to develop a new view of some area of science it is useful to look into the history of science and to make a sufficient simple and powerful extrapolation of the current developments in that area (see also [GJu91,Gru93]).

A lesson from history. The history of science shows that the success of a science depends very much on how large space, and at the same time an intellectually simple, smooth, and dense space is able to create and investigate in comparison to the space observable by human senses and the common sense.

There is a widespread belief nowadays that computing and communication technology is the one that represents the current and future progress, and therefore it should get the main attention, appreciation and support — both by scientists and education.

However, the history of mankind indicates that no matter how radically new a technology has been, it could have an immense impact on science, technology and society only when a very new way of thinking and seeing the world has already been emerging for quite a while — a view which could make a full use of this technology.

The history of mankind also indicates that the main long term contributions of such a new technology have been to help to develop further such a new view of seeing, understanding, and managing the world, and to make this new view of the world more coherent and powerful.

Those areas of science and technology that have been initiated by a new technology or developed a radically new paradigm then sooner or later started to shift their attention from the problems related to the development and utilization of the new technology to more general, and in long terms more important, problems. These issues were related to the development of a radically new understanding (and developing) of the world.

The same observations seem to apply to information processing and communication technology that could have been so successfully developed and applied to a large extent because a very new view of formalization and information processing has been developed since the very beginning of this century.

A view of the scientific base of informatics. A new view of the scientific base of informatics, that underpins information processing/communication technology (hardware and software) was elaborated in [GJu91,Gru93]. Let us summarize the main points.

The science that has been emerging from the recent attempts to develop a scientific base for information processing/communication technology as well from millennium old attempts to capture and formalize understanding, knowledge, reasoning, computations, and to mechanize information processing, should be regarded, developed and taught as a new fundamental science that also affords a new fundamental methodology for science, technology and society in general.

This new science should be seen as having similar scientific aims (concerning the *information world*) as physics has had (concerning the *physical world*), and a similar fundamental methodological impact on society as mathematics has had.

This new science should be seen as a science that tries to develop a deep understanding of information (processing) world, its laws, limitations, elements, structures, processes, and so on.

This new science should be seen as a science with enormous research space that puts no limits on its tools and methodologies; as a science that is developed to a large extent (if not primarily) by the needs to extend and deepen our knowledge (of the information world).

3.3 Some problems with which informatics as a fundamental science deals with

1. What are the **laws, limitations, elements, structures,** and **processes** of the information world and what are their properties?
2. What is **information**? What is **knowledge**? How to measure them? What are their properties? How much of them do we need in order to do this and that?
3. What is **feasible**? Namely:
   - What is **feasibly constructible, computable, solvable, decidable, learnable, expressible**?

- What has a **feasible evidence, proof**? (And what is a feasible evidence?)
- What can be **feasible and securely communicated**? (And what is a secure communication?)

4. To study the **space of information processing problems**, its structure, hierarchies, reductions, equivalences, hardest problems,...

5. To study the **space of information processing resources**. Which of them are important? What are their properties and power? Which relations and tradeoffs hold among them? How powerful are such resources as **time, space, randomness, interactions, parallelism, alternation, nondeterminism, reversibility,...**?

6. To study the **space of information processing machines**, their power, mutual simulations, designs,... Machines that fit existing and foreseeable technology. Machines that fit classical physics, quantum physics. Machines that meet biological requirements,...

7. To study the **space of formal descriptional systems**: logics, calculi, theories, languages, rewriting systems, automata, ..., especially methods how to design them and reason about them.

8. To study **inherent complexity** (computational, communicational, descriptional,...) of objects, algorithms, processes ....

9. To study **security** of communications, data,..., protection of intellectual properties,...

10. What are complex systems? How to specify them? How to reason about them? How to design, maintain and verify such systems?

11. How to develop **information processing models** and understanding of physical, biological, social and other worlds?

3.4 Informatics as a new methodology

Two basic methodologies of science and technology (but also of society in general) have been **theoretical methodology** and **experimental methodology**. Both of them have been very well worked out and very successful.

The new methodology, that is emerging from the achievements of theoretical investigations and technological developments in informatics is a methodology that seems to have enormous potential. This new methodology allows to enlarge the power of theoretical and experimental methodologies, to bridge them and, in addition, to be a powerful tool in all the areas where the two basic methodologies have not really been fully successful.

The basic features of this new methodology can be shortly summarized as follows:

Simulation. A new methodology to obtain knowledge, to discover laws and to study processes. It allows to study systems with different physical or biological laws; to reverse, slow-down or speed-up time, ...

Visualization. It helps to see otherwise unvisible, to study nonlinearities, chaos, generation, growth, ... It helps to get insights and to discover laws — it can lead to conjectures which can then be addresses using classical methodologies.

Algorithmization. The design of algorithms is one of the basic methodologies for not only solving algorithmic problems but also for obtaining the very basic scientific understanding of various phenomena, problems and processes.

Formalization. The design and study of formal, description and symbol manipulation systems is an old methodology that has received a new dimension with the modern development of informatics, and symbol manipulation techniques.

Complexity investigations. The investigations of inherent complexity have revealed that formal objects and descriptional/algorithmic/communication problems/processes have inherent complexity and that a discovery of this complexity brings deep scientific understandings and pays large practical dividends.

Study of the complex phenomena in a thorough way. Till very recently the main strategy of science has been an *isolation and investigation of the very basic phenomena*, and little attention has been paid, and could be paid, to their interactions. Informatics brings concepts, methods and tools for such investigations. In this way informatics methods allow sciences to study much more complex problems than so far and it also allows technology and society in general to deal with global problems.

Information processing models of the world. The attempts to develop information processing models of physical, chemical, biological, economical and social world have turned into a new important methodology to deal with old and new problems that could not been handled before.[67]

In order to apply informatics as a new methodology a strong involvement of informatics graduates is needed because they have knowledge and experience needed to do the job. Specialists in other areas are often unable to deal well enough with computing aspects of problems they need to solve.

An application of informatics as a methodology cannot only help to solve otherwise unsolvable problems but may also contribute important intellectual abstractions and discoveries to other fields and to create new conceptual frameworks needed there.

It is also worth observing that **demonstrations** are an important phenomenon in informatics, and they may get so also in all areas heavily using informatics. Indeed, computer science advances are often made public by **dramatic demonstrations** and it is often that the (ideas and concepts tested in the) dramatic demos influence the research agenda in informatics.[8]

---

[6] One can even say that mass, energy and energy transformations, as the building ingredients of most of the current models of worlds are being replaced by information, computing and information transformation as new key ingredients of new models of worlds.

[7] An interesting and important example are information processing models of brain and their impacts on the study of human cognitive processes.

[8] By [Har92], among young computer science faculties **demo or die** is starting to rival the older **publish or perish**.

4 Steps to be done

A new view of the scientific base of informatics and of its methodological power, together with their envisioned role in the future society, create a basis for the formulation of some of the major steps that need to be taken in the informatics education.

4.1 Broadening of the aims and scope

The rapidly broadening scope of informatics applications and increasing sophistications of them require to pay large attention to ways how informatics education should adjust its aims and how to broaden its scope. The main idea to be followed is that the basic tasks of informatics are much beyond those envisioned by the current computing and communication technology and that its impacts may also soon be far beyond those envisioned nowadays. Some steps that seem to be needed are:

1. More adequate and deeper foundations are needed in four areas: discrete mathematics and logic, continuous mathematics, foundations of computing, foundations of information representation/processing systems design (programming, software,...). Foundations in some other areas (physics, biology,...) could also be considered as an addition. In all these areas of foundations a significant broadening of self-concepts is a need; otherwise foundations risk becoming increasingly irrelevant to computing/communication practice.
2. Students need to have more possibilities to tune their education in the last years of their studies in order to adjust to a variety of new applications.
3. Steps need to be done to support more multi-disciplinary studies with informatics as one part of the education.
4. New types of informatics education programs should be formed. It seems no longer feasible to perform all education needed within one program. (However, with the same first part of their studies.) Computing science and engineering should get a more clear profile. Computational science, as an independent subject, is an alternative that is gaining a momentum.

4.2 Synthesis of knowledge and experiences

The amount of theoretically deep, and/or practically useful knowledge and experiences that have already accumulated in informatics is already so large that in order to meet aims concerning informatics education, stated in the previous point, a significant attention has to be given to providing synthesizing courses. Currently, in many areas of informatics courses of the undergraduate but also of the graduate education go often too much into details of importance mostly only for those few, perhaps, that intend to do research in that area. Synthesing courses provide a space needed for other subjects and can also lead to a higher level of the understanding of the subjects.

Synthesis is needed, and possible, not only in such specific areas as foundations (for foundations of computing see an attempt in [Gru97]),[9] programming languages and methods, software development, hardware, parallelism, security, but also, in many areas, theory, software and hardware education should be synthesized — also due to the fact that current computing/communication systems are a mixture of hardware and software. A particularly important step, of the large importance would be to develop curricula and textbooks for such courses as INFORMATICS I and II on such a level as it is in advance areas of science and technology.

4.3   Soundness of education

Basic education should concentrate on a sufficiently solid knowledge and sufficiently verified and systematized experiences, methods, systems and tools. There is no longer a justification to teach in basic courses, as it is quite often the case, especially in the area of programming, "software engineering" and artificial intelligence, the very recent ideas and products the potential and usefulness of which have not been sufficiently verified yet. There are enough deep and useful subjects and methods to teach. Moreover, education should systematize and not only demonstrate the sometimes ad hoc discoveries, inventions and artifacts that arise from the practical imperative. Some experimentation in teaching is needed but this should be restricted to well justified cases. Moreover, the number of non-scientific and non-engineering lectures in informatics itself should be put into minimum. Their positive impact on education is rarely proportional to the time consumed — even if they may contain ideas worth to read, to consider within more technical lectures, and to pay attention to in laboratories, projects and theses.

For education of engineering oriented graduates in informatics, and those is the majority, the main principles of good engineering should be taught: thorough analysis of problems, validation and evaluation of suggested solutions, efficiency, reliability, and security analysis,... and of those techniques facilitating them. (Projects, assignments and labs create the main space for doing that.) Graduates should be able to use science and technology to solve problems and to make decisions on technical terms. In particular, they should be equipped with a much broader range of solid validation techniques than a traditional mathematical proof. Moreover, graduates should be able to distinguish sound, scalable and already verified methods from potential-but-not-tested-yet methods and from alchemy type methods.[10]

---

[9] There is also no longer a good reason to separate teaching of calculus and numerical mathematics on one side and linear algebra and numerical mathematics or abstract algebra and symbolic computation on the other side.

[10] In particular they should be able to understand that a method that does not scale well is actually not a method to be used in larger scale applications.

4.4 Rigour and clarity

Education in informatics has to achieve that graduates understand importance of rigour and clarity and manage the basic techniques of achieving and maintaining it. This is due to the fact that informatics applications have often very large requirements on rigour and clarity because of enormous number of details and complexity of many products, especially software systems. Rigour and clarity have to be learned already in the introductory courses and reinforced through the whole curriculum — this can not be taught as a mere addition in the later courses. Another way of teaching rigour and clarity is through a proper integration of theory concepts and methods with those of practice.

Rigour and clarity are of special importance when software specification and development tasks are to be handled in a disciplined and systematic manner — what is necessary for having systems which can be efficiently manipulated and analysed.

4.5 Technology transfer experiences

Improving technology transfer is one of the general and important problems of the current society. Informatics methods and tools should and could play an important role by that. In order to facilitate this it is desirable and even necessary to take care that graduates of informatics are prepared as much as possible to play by that a progressive role. In order to achieve that the following steps need to be done:

1. Students should learn to work with very modern concepts, methods and tools.
2. Education process should systematize new methods and tools in such a way that graduates are then able to contribute to the improvement of these methods and tools.
3. Students should participate on ambitious projects attacking basic theoretical and practical problems of computing. Even if such particular projects are often far from being able to produce useful products, students learn their lesson and the experiences obtained allow them often to come later with much better solutions and already useful products.
4. Students should get involved as much as possible into multi- and interdisciplinary projects.

5 Case studies

Two areas of informatics education will now be analysed in more detail.

5.1 Fundamentals of computing

As already mentioned, one can distinguish four main types of foundations: discrete mathematics and logic, continuous mathematics and numerical mathematics,[11] foundations of computing, and foundations of designing, reasoning (programming, software engineering),... (Foundations of physics, biology, and so on, should be seen as an additional option.)

In the area of discrete and continuous mathematics the main task is to adjust education to informatics needs by choosing proper subjects and examples and by bridging theory education with using modern computing tools to solve problems far beyond the pen-and-paper framework.

We concentrate here on foundations of computing. Bridging these four types of foundations is the next problem, and not an easy one.

Education in this area seems to need new aims, contents, methods and impetus because in its current form it is loosing respect of graduates, recognition of importance of faculties and interest of students — and there are no objective reasons for being so. Just the opposite is true — with respect to the achievements and impacts of foundations.

In general, the basic educational aim and scope in this area of foundations has been set up, so that the education is good for those graduates going to do research in this area. This is no longer justified — this is the role of some special and not obligatory courses, theses and so on. The education in the area of foundations of computing should concentrate on subject all graduates should learn and most of them need. Interesting enough, this change in the educational aims does not need to have a negative effect on the quality of education in the area of foundations of computing (see [Gru97]).

Larger attention needs to be devoted to demonstrate the relations between very fundamental concepts and results and practical problems. It has to be illustrated that basic concepts of foundations should be seen as intellectual tools that can provide directly only guidance and that in order to get out of them something more practical, these concepts often need to be twisted, modified and "industrialized". However, if this is done, then surprisingly powerful tools can arise. Fortunately, there are already quite a few examples that can be used to illustrate it on a theoretically interesting level and practically important cases. (Let us mention the concept of weighted finite automata and transducers and their use for image compression, modification and generation — see [Gru97].)

The view of foundations of computing keeps developing. The old view has concentrated on computability, grammars, formal languages and automata, as the main subjects. This is still quite often so. In spite of the fact that all these areas still have their unreplaceable place in foundations of computing, their role has changed and therefore the way they are to be taught has to be changed (and what is to be taught from these areas has to be revisited). Teaching of some of

---

[11] Unfortunately, too often too little attention is paid in computer science/engineering education programs to continuous mathematics in spite of the fact that such mathematics is of key importance not only for some particular areas of computing (as robotics), but also because multi-disciplinary approaches and many applications require from graduates a very solid knowledge of concepts and methods of continuous and numerical mathematics.

the old subjects is no longer justified and new subjects and viewpoints have to be added.

More modern view, slowly gaining a momentum, is based on emphasizing efficiency and complexity considerations (computational, descriptional, communicational), randomization, approximations, parallel and distributive computing, communication systems, security foundations, and so on. This provides foundations for computability, complexity of problems, efficiency of algorithms, parallel computing and computers, security, interactions, formal systems, rewriting systems ... Further extension in the direction of radically new modes of computing as quantum, molecular and brain computing are also to be considered.

In order to include a variety of new subjects a high level of synthesis is needed and possible in all four areas of foundations. An attempt to provide a synthesis in the area of foundations of computing is in [Gru97].

Of a special importance would be to develop curricula and textbooks for such synthetizing courses as FOUNDATIONS I and FOUNDATIONS II to combine foundations of computing with foundations for programming and system designs. However, such a synthesis should not be on a naive level but on a level as in advanced areas of science and technology. Such courses could be a base to develop courses INFORMATICS I and INFORMATICS II, mentioned above.

Several areas of foundations offer already a possibility and also a need to bridge the theory, software, hardware and application areas. For example finite automata, parallel computing, computational complexity, cryptography, and so on.

5.2   Parallel and distributed computing

There are two reasons why it becomes necessary to include a teaching of parallelism into any informatics educational program.

- Main nature and society systems are basically parallel and distributed and therefore parallel computing models, modes and methods are actually more natural than sequential ones;
- Parallel information processing is going to play an increasing role in everyday data processing, also because such systems can have better fault tolerance and higher reliability.

As it is often the case, we understand under the parallel computing both parallel and distributed computing, i.e. tasks executed by parallel computers (by multiprocessors or array processors or pipeline computers) or by distributed computers (networks of processors).[12] As obligatory we consider three courses and one laboratory:

---

[12] In the extreme cases, as it has been done in dealing with so called "RSA challenge" [Cal96], such a distributed computing can involve tens of thousands of processors and one can speak about a "metacomputing". Such problems and methods to deal with them are, however, far beyond the needs and possibilities of most of the graduates and therefore we do not suggest to include such topics into the basic education about parallelism yet.

- Models of parallel processing;
- Parallel algorithms;
- Architecture of parallel computers.

Each of these courses should be a one semester and two hours per week course. In the last course one type of parallel computers should be treated in detail. For the other models only basic features and properties should be discussed (see e.g. [Hbr89]). The content of the second course should depend on possible application areas students can be exposed to at the corresponding university but some basic parallel algorithms (e.g. graph theoretical ones) should always be demonstrated (see e.g. [Qui94]). In the more theoretically oriented first course, besides the main simulation and complexity results for basic parallel models also the limitations of physically realizable parallel devices should be analysed. In the laboratory students should learn how to program and use an existing parallel computer — the type of the computer (shared memory or message passing) is secondary. Optional courses, of importance for applications may also be offered (for example, in parallel numerical algorithms).

However, ideal would be to make a synthesis of all the three courses suggested above. The resulting course could be large but smaller than all three courses together.

Many people seem to be convinced that teaching of parallel computing should start only after students master sufficiently well sequential computing. However, this does not seem to us to be the best approach. There should be a synthesis in teaching of sequential and parallel computing (see views in [Nev95] and a presentation in [Gru97]).[13]

6 Conclusions

The paper deals with some general problems concerning informatics education. It is based on the conviction that the current problems of informatics education have deeper, even philosophical, roots and are not only on the level how to improve particular technical aspects of education.

The paper is also based on the conviction that the problem of improving informatics education is of a large importance for society that depends increasingly on its capability to manage the potential informatics and information processing/communication technologies offer.

References

[Bra87] Brauer, W.: Informatics and computer science in education. In D. C. Johnson, F. Lovis (eds.). North Holland, Amsterdam (1987) 101 -107.

---

[13] For example, once a tight lower bound is established for the sequential computational complexity of a problem, time comes to discuss the idea of a work optimal parallel algorithm for the same problem. On the other hand, in the basic foundations of computing course cellular automata can be used as a model of universal computers.

[Bra88] Brauer, W.: Education and informatics. Preface to: R. E. Lewis, E. D. Tagg (eds.): Informatics and education, an anthology of papers selected from IFIP TC3 publications since the establishment of TC3 in 1963, North Holland, Amsterdam (1988) XI-XIII.

[BBr89] Brauer, U., Brauer, W.: Better tools — less education? In G. X. Ritter (ed.), Information Processing'89, North-Holland, Amsterdam (1990) 101-106.

[Bra90a] Brauer, W.: Informatics Education at West German Universities, Education and Computing. Special issue: Informatics Curricula for 1990's, Proc. Workshop, Brown University (1990).

[Bra90b] Brauer, W.: Trends der Informatik-Ausbildung. In A. Reuter (ed.), Proc. GI-20. Jahrestagung I, Informatik-Fachberichte, **257**, Springer-Verlag, Berlin (1990) 456-464.

[Bra91] Brauer, W.: The new paradigm of informatics. In: H. Maurer, (ed.) New Results and New Trends in Computer Science, LNCS 555, Springer-Verlag, Berlin (1991) 15-23.

[Bus45] Bush, V.: Science, the Endless Frontiers. Washington, D. C., National Science Foundations, 1945 (reprinted in 1990).

[Cal96] Cowie, J., Dodson, B., Elkenbracht-Huizing, R. M., Lenstra, A. K., Montgomery, P. L., Zayer, J.: A world wide number field sieve factoring record: On to 512 bits. In K. Kim, T. Matsumoto (eds.): Advances in Cryptography, ASIACRYPT'96. LNCS 1163, Springer-Verlag, Berlin (1996) 382-394. 1989.

[Den89] Denning, P. J., et al: Computing as a discipline. Communications of the ACM, **32** (1989) 9-23.

[Gri93] Griffiths, P. A. at all: Science, technology and federal government. National goals for a new era. National Academy Press (1993).

[Gru93] Gruska, J.: Why we should no longer only repair, polish and iron current computer science education, Education and Computing, **8** (1993) 303-330.

[Gru97] Gruska, J.: Foundations of Computing. International Thomson Computer Press (1997).

[Gru93a] Gruska, J.: Informatics and its education — new horizons, aims and principles, Proceedings of SOFSEM'93, Masaryk University, Brno (1993) 85-96.

[GJu91] Gruska, J., Jürgensen, H.: Maturing of informatics, in D. Bjørner, V. Kotov (eds): Images of Programming, North-Holland, Amsterdam,(1991) I-55-69.

[Har92] Hartmanis, J.: Some observations about the nature of computer science. In: R. Shyamasundar (ed.), Foundations of Software Technology and Theoretical Computer Science, LNCS 652, Springer-Verlag (1992) 1-12.

[HLi92] Hartmanis, J., Lin, L. (eds): Computing the Future, National Academy of Sciences, Washington D.C., (1992).

[Hbr89] Hwang, K., Briggs, F. A.: Computer Architecture and Parallel Processing. McGraw-Hill, New York, 5th printing (1989).

[Qui94] Quinn, M. J.: Parallel Computing, Theory and Practice, McGraw-Hill, New York, 2nd ed. (1994).

[Nev95] Nevinson, C. H.: Parallel computing in the undergraduate curriculum, IEEE Transactions on Computers **44** (1995) 51-57. MIT Press,

Informatics and Society:
A Curriculum for Distance Education

Herbert Klaeren[1] and Christiane Floyd[2] and Friedrich Diestelmeier[3]

[1] Universität Tübingen, Informatik, Sand 13, D–72076 Tübingen,
klaeren@informatik.uni-tuebingen.de
[2] Universität Hamburg, Fachbereich Informatik, Vogt-Kölln-Straße 30,
D–22527 Hamburg, floyd@informatik.uni-hamburg.de
[3] Deutsches Institut für Fernstudienforschung, Konrad-Adenauer-Str. 40,
D–72072 Tübingen, friedrich.d@diff.uni-tuebingen.de

Abstract. Studying the interactions between computer science (informatics) and society is increasingly becoming important, specifically with a view to the rapidly progressing computerisation of processes in business, education and even leisure, and the so-called information society. For many of the German universities, however, teaching in this area turns out to be a difficult task, mainly because the available personnel doesn't feel qualified for this topic. University of Tübingen and DIFF (German Institute for Research in Distance Education) have therefore started an exploratory project aiming at the creation and trial of material suitable for self-study. In this paper, we outline the general setting of the planned course and describe our planned curriculum.

1 Background

Computers and computer applications are omnipresent in today's world; as a matter of fact, modern business, traffic, and communication systems couldn't work at all without involving computers. In a very manifest way, our civilisation is shaped by the computer. On the other hand, however, computers and their applications aren't static objects: they too are changing according to the demands of society and the potentiality of technology. Informaticians (we tend to use this term as a translation of the German "Informatiker" because "computer scientists" would probably convey a different meaning) as the prime innovators in computer technology have largely not felt the need to investigate the interactions between computer science and society, this being considered as the realm of the social sciences.

By and by, the conviction is spreading that informaticians need to have at least a basic knowledge of the pertinent social mechanisms because only this will enable them to develop the level of consciousness they need for a responsible development of new computer systems and applications.

The oldest documented attempt to define the contents for this field of teaching has been made by the Gesellschaft für Informatik (GI) [3]; however the status of this document is a bit unclear. While its preamble states that it is meant for discussion and, after modification, proposed for acceptance by the Board, this seems never to have happened. Teachers willing to engage in this subject have long time felt a lack of appropriate textbooks. It is only recently [1, 5, 4, 6] that some have been published.

When informatics was introduced as a study subject at Tübingen university, the academic senate found it appropriate to add a requirement to the proposed examination regulations that students of informatics must learn about *technology assessment*; in the discussion this was generalised to *"Informatics and Society"*. Besides established material in technology assessment, this subject was meant — much in the spirit of [3] — to contain also ethical considerations as well as a basic knowledge of social sciences and philosophy that should enable students to get a broader perspective on their science. Unfortunately, the senate forgot to create a professorship for this area so the faculty has since its creation always been in desperate search for experts from elsewhere who would be willing to accept a corresponding teaching assignment.

During this search, it became clear that the situation was similar at some other German universities, so we conducted a survey about teaching in "Informatics and Society". About 60 informatics faculties were asked for their examination regulations and were sent a questionnaire about their opinions on "Informatics and Society". From the 40 replies we gathered the data summarised in table 1. This encouraged us to write a proposal for the "Bund-Länder-Kommission für

Topic is compulsory in study regulations	21
Necessity of continuing education in this area	20
Dedicated professorship is available	10
Faculty would appreciate distance education material	27

Table1. Relevance of "Informatics and Society" in German informatics faculties

Bildungsplanung und Forschungsförderung" that has a specific programme for development and trial of distance education courses. Most of the proposal and the preliminary curriculum were worked out in close collaboration with the German Institute for Research in Distance Education while Christiane Floyd was staying in Tübingen for a sabbatical. In the middle of 1996, this project was granted.

2   The Distance Education Project

An extraordinary feature of this project is that we are going to develop a distance learning component for use at traditional universities which are characterised by face-to-face teaching. This differs from the established distance education situation in at least two respects:

1. While each of the participating universities takes care for the organisational matters of their students enrolled in the course, they may not be able to provide the necessary technical tutoring.

2. Special procedures also have to be developed as to the examination: here, every participating university will of course have to hold its own examinations (and anyway want to do so) but, contrary to normal academic practice, will not itself define the contents of the studies but rather use the prefabricated material from this project. Moreover, there may not be in any case experts in the field locally available.

A specific challenge furthermore is the interdisciplinary nature of "Informatics and Society": Questions, methods, and results from the humanities and the social sciences have to be presented in such a way that students of informatics with their radically different methodology centered around formal, constructive, algorithmic knowledge are enabled to understand, assess and appreciate them.

The overall goals of our project are

1. Definition of a *curriculum* for "Informatics and Society" and production of respective *materials for self-directed learning.* Our target group is primarily the students of informatics currently enrolled in German universities; however, since it is our opinion that there also must be practitioners already working in the industry and having developed a need to learn about the interactions of their professional work and society as a whole, we make every reasonable effort to make the curriculum and the self-study materials useable and attractive to them as well. In order to cope with the above-mentioned problems connected to the special nature of this distance education project, we shall also deliver a *teacher's guide* enabling a participating university to offer appropriate tutoring and a set of *examination questions* together with corresponding answers and procedures.

2. Development of a certain number of *face-to face sessions* as a complement to the printed material. As a matter of fact, the present subject matter seems to call for personal discussion and accompanying formation of a point of view even more than traditional, technical topics within informatics. It seems therefore advisory to collect the students at some intervals for both complementary lectures pertaining to the self-study material and for personal discussion about the acquired knowledge. Typically, these face-to face sessions will be few in number and will involve experts from the field and to a certain extent also the authors of the instructional texts.

3. Development of procedures for *on-line tutoring* using the Internet and for remote examination. Because of the relatively small number of face-to face sessions it seems advisable to have a continued on-line support for students participating in this course. Similar setups have already been tried (with varying degree of success) in other distance education projects; here, we are very confident about the success of this activity because our students are already familiar with the handling of the underlying communication mechanisms and have an established access to the Internet. Generally, students of informatics consider electronic mail, bulletin systems, hypertexts and the like very natural means of communication and would probably even find it

ridiculous if we wouldn't offer them. The details of how Internet can be used for on-line tutoring will be worked out in this project.

4. *Trial and evaluation* of all these items in a two semester's experimental pass.
5. On the side of the DIFF, project goals include also the collection of insight about usage of on-line tutoring systems and about interdisciplinary teaching on the borderline between humanities and social sciences on the one hand and engineering disciplines on the other hand.

After the evaluation phase, the teaching material will be revised and made available via Internet and CD-ROM. The organisation of the project involves the following working groups:

- An external *academic advisory group* who consults in the definition of the curriculum and the selection of authors to write instructional texts, and generally supervises the overall project quality. Members of the academic advisory group are renowned scientists working in the "Informatics and Society" field, complemented by experts from industry and from continuing education organisations.
- A collection of *authors* who write instructional texts.
- A *course team* for the overall development of the course, being specifically responsible for didactic, organisational and further technical questions.

In order to achieve the goals mentioned above, we have decided to impose a *modular structure* on the teaching material. A *module* in this sense consists of

- an instructional text including learning aids,
- sets of self-assessment questions and practical exercises,
- a teacher's guide,
- a system of face-to face sessions and
- a set of examination questions, answers, and procedures.

The particular modules will be sketched in the next section. The modular structure on one hand serves as an organisational aid but its main objective is to facilitate the adaptation of the material to both the specific requirements of particular universities and the individual interests of students. Every set of three or four modules (depending on their volume) is equivalent to two contact hours of traditional university teaching.

3 The Curriculum

A first draft of the curriculum was obviously already formulated in the project proposal; in two subsequent meetings of the academic advisory group it has been thoroughly discussed, refined, and partly changed. While there have been definite decisions about a number of modules that now need to get near completion, the number of modules and their titles aren't yet completely determined. We will come back to this after sketching the contents of the modules that are already fixed.

One key feature of all modules is that the authors are required to produce *case studies* illuminating the subject of their teaching unit and giving students the motivation to occupy themselves with it. Of course, the degree to which case studies really make sense may vary according to the topic of every single module.

The first five modules are designed to be *compulsory* because we feel that they offer a minimal amount of knowledge about "Informatics and Society" that cannot be neglected. Students are then free to choose among the additional modules according to their personal interest fields. Note that the only restriction on the order of the modules is given by the first of the modules listed here: this being an introduction, it should really be the first one to study. Otherwise, the sequence might be chosen quite arbitrarily.

3.1 Informatics and Society: An Introduction

The purpose of this module is a general introduction into the field. It is meant to raise motivation for occupation with the course; for this purpose it should make clear the overall relevance of the field, give a first overview of the most important questions and problems and account for the contents of the course. Particularly, it shall describe the fundamental individual and social problems arising from the interactions between informatics and society and it shall make clear what kind of knowledge from informatics and the humanities and social sciences is necessary or appropriate to properly understand and judge these problems and to contribute to their solution. Students shall be enabled to exercise their rôle as professional informaticians and to perceive the rôle of informatics in society in a conscious way. As a whole, they shall be supported in the responsible fulfillment of their duties.

The module will start with a section showing how informaticians as well as computer systems are embedded into larger social contexts and how this can lead to misunderstandings or even conflicts. We want to make clear that there is no sense in constructing a (mental) wall shielding the clean, formal world of informatics from the dirty, fuzzy real world. The next section will sketch informatics as a science of modelling, construction, development and design, and also discuss its relations to other sciences and the necessity of interdisciplinary work. In the third section, we will on a more concrete basis point out the opportunities and conditions of action as a professional informatician. This includes discussion of the freedom of action, expectations of the society and the legal context of informatical work such as privacy concerns, liability, software copyright and the like.

There are two motivating case studies in this module: the construction of a clinical information system and a discussion among employees of a software firm whether they should engage in the development of a defence application.

3.2 Informatics: Yesterday, Now, and Tomorrow

The motto of this module is "What *is* Informatics, what could it be, what should it become?", in other words: The scientific view of informatics on itself. This contains, among other things, the socio-cultural classification of informatics, its scientific environment including constructive mathematics, cybernetics, electronics and communications engineering, and, of course, a chapter on the genesis of informatics as a discipline. In this connection, also the driving forces in the creation and development of informatics have to be addressed, such as the military, the industry and government with their wish for efficient operations, and the entertainment industry. Finally, we have to address the classification of informatics within a theory of science and to contrast it with computer science, computing science(s) and information science(s). The module closes by sketching the dimensions of critique of informatics.

As a whole, this module shall give the students an orientation towards their own formation of the discipline, the main objective being to show them the importance of the relation of the technical, formal kernel to the social context.

3.3 Informatics and Responsibility: Fundamentals of Computer Ethics

In today's fast-acting world, there are ever-increasing situations where computers must make essential, critical decisions, often without the possibility of human intervention, e.g. in defence, aeronautical or other traffic systems. The questions that obviously arise here are: who is responsible for these decisions, can a computer be responsible for anything, what does responsibility mean after all, and what are the standards against which we could judge whether somebody stands to his reponsibility? These thoughts lead to the field of ethics, and the purpose of this module is to convey a minimal knowledge about its fundamentals to students of informatics. After some introductory case studies, a section on general ethics shows that ethics has a logical dimension ("deontic logic") and that moral judgements have a cognitive value ("metaethics"). A section on the basic concepts of normative ethics shows that there is a plurality of ethical approaches but that this doesn't imply that moral judgements are arbitrary. The first part closes with a discussion of the structural problems of applied ethics. A second part deals with the ethics of technology and sketches, among other things, the theories of Ropohl, Hastedt, Hubig and Rohbeck. The third part then deals specifically with computer ethics (ethics of information and communication technologies), discussing now in detail the critical analysis of computer-related leading metaphors and styles, the computer as a cultural phenomenon, the conditions and limits of responsible computer usage, and the questions of responsibility in human-computer interaction. In the sequel, ethical codices of the respective professional organisations are discussed; also, a philosophical determination of cyberspace and virtual reality is included. Last, but not least, we discuss the "Menschenbild" of informatics, i.e. the view of human beings implied by the discipline: ultimately, everything that can be entered into a computer must be expressed using a number; this entails the danger of reducing a human being to its quantifiable aspects. Furthermore, given the apparent infallibility and speed of computerised systems, there is a danger of viewing humans as the unreliable part in human-computer-interaction systems ("Man as an inferior machine").

3.4 From Technology Assessment to Technology Formation

The purpose of this module is to show that informatics and information technology has manifold effects that can be judged differently by the persons concerned. Responsible professional practice is only possible if these consequences are kept in mind. Starting with a discussion of the driving forces in the development of technology, theories from the social sciences about the genesis of technology are presented. A subsequent section discusses the nature and classification of information technology and the computer as a new kind of artifact, machine and medium at the same time. The emphasis here is that computer technology may be formable and designable to an even larger degree than more traditional technologies. The third section explains the philosophy of technology assessment (TA) both in the U.S. and Germany and puts the history of TA into the framework of "Informatics and Society" as a discipline. Some methods of TA are presented and the factors studied by it are shown such as organisation and division of labour, working conditions, privacy etc. The next section argues that TA alone is useless if it doesn't lead to a conscious *design* or *formation* of technology. Next, the rôle of metaphors for informatics as a whole and software development in particular is discussed, and the final section delineates the options a software developer has in the formation of information technology.

3.5 Discourse about Informatics

Here, it is our goal to make clear how important communication skills are specifically for informaticians. While it seems rather difficult to coach students in communication with a distance education activity, it does sound sensible to convey the fundamental theory of oral and written communication to them. Note that this theme has at least two aspects, one of them being communication in the immediate context of professional life (i.e. mainly systems and software development), the other being the social discourse about the rôle of informatics in general. We want to show that modelling as a fundamental informatical activity is a goal-driven and hence subjective process; moreover, it is a cooperative, multi-expert communication process that requires construction of a common anticipation of a future product and therefore the creation of a common mental model and language base. The emphasis is on the necessity of interdisciplinary discourse, participative software development and social responsibility.

3.6 Informatics and Gender Difference

Starting from the observation that in Germany attendance of woman to the study of informatics has, since the beginning of education in this area, dropped from roughly 24% to below 8%, we investigate the reasons this may have. The situation is compared to other countries and cultures and also to other disciplines such as mathematics and some natural and engineering sciences. The educational goals in this module are to some extent opposite to each other: on the one hand, we want to show that there are no fixed gender-specific orientations and abilities but only historically, culturally and contextually induced differences; on the other hand we want to point out that competences that here and now are chiefly attributed to female socialisation (e.g. communicativeness) are very important for the informatics profession which would loose in substance if these competences weren't cultivated. Further sections discuss gender rôle and gender identity, the coeducation debate and perspectives for new professional potentials for woman.

This module is equally important for female and male students since they both need to understand the background of gender-specific socialisation in order to overcome the respective problematics.

3.7 Informatics in Professional Life

The goal of this module is to give an appropriate understanding of the relation and interaction of information technology and labour. Students shall be enabled to maintain a rational point of view and to get a distance to the often ideological and interest-driven demands of the actors in this field. Again, this implies a discussion of the "Menschenbild", e.g. the machine model of man in contrast to his action competence. After an introduction into the connection between labour and technology, aspects of the organisational context of information systems, and ergonomic concerns, this module explains some theoretical foundations of labour and technology formation. This includes a discussion of the Tayloristic/Fordistic view on labour division and how it is being made obsolete by the information society. Further sections delineate perspectives of productive, humane, and socially acceptable design of working situations in a highly technicised world, including legal prescriptions and guidelines from the psychology of labour and ergonomics; they present informatical systems as working tools, as external memories of organisations and as media of communication. Case studies given here include document handling, internal data modeling, video conferencing, application sharing, and workflow management.

3.8 Informatics in Private Life

This module is thought as a contrast to the preceding one: while applications of computers in professional life generally seem to be more prevalent and important, it must not be neglected that also everyday's life is today characterised by computer use. Some key features discussed in this module are computers in music and pictorial art, home banking, tele-shopping, computer games, computer-based training, "edutainment/infotainment", multimedia, virtual classrooms and the like. In part, this overlaps with the topic of the next module.

3.9 Chances and Risks of the Information Society

Derived from the notion of industrial society, "information society" stands for changes in virtually all social domains, caused by the use of modern information and communication technology. As usual, there are both great promises and great threats connected with this notion and frequently a certain "Eigendynamik" (autonomous, automatic, unstoppable development) is attributed to this area. We want to display the political programmes and actions encouraging this development and try to find out their expectations and rationales, so as to enable the students to find a self-critical position in their future rôle within the presumed information society. Besides, key features of the national/global information infrastructure ("global village") and their consequences shall be discussed.

3.10 Further Potential Modules

The academic advisory group has also discussed some further modules but, due to financial restrictions, it is very probable that they cannot be realised within this project. We will nevertheless briefly sketch them.

"Informatics in Legal Contexts" would deal with applications of informatics in jurisprudence, legislation, and legal action, e.g. legal databases, expert systems for decision support in legal proceedings and their specific problems. The goal of "Informatics in Politics" would be to show how politics as a regulating instance sets the framework for development of informatics, how governmental funding policy influences research and development in technology and how, on the other hand, informatics systems change the way politics is made. This would include the thematic "Informatics and Militia", the "transparent citizen" ("big brother" theme) and the changes of political decision making induced by the possibilities of the "information superhighway". "Informatics in Medicine" should present chances and risks of computer use in diagnostics, therapy and medical research including the well-known expert system problematics, more specific privacy concerns (medical databases) but also problems with computerised therapeutic (e.g. THERAC-25) and diagnostic machines (computer tomography, PET etc.). "Informatics in Ecology" and "Informatics and the Developing Countries" would also be interesting and important themes.

4 Perspectives

Instructional texts for the above-mentioned modules will be written by renowned experts in the respective fields. After the texts have been reviewed by the academic advisory group they will be edited by the course team with a view to the specific didactic requirements of remote education material. Then the whole course will be evaluated in a two semester's pilot phase. Following this, the study texts will be revised a second time if necessary. Starting with the second half of 1999 the course shall be generally available.

Authors have been asked to develop their subject if possible using case studies from informatical practice. We hope that this will raise the curiosity of students and guide them towards an occupation with the mutual influences between informatics and society. Furthermore, authors should explicitly discuss alternative options for action wherever this makes sense.

It is our goal to show with such a practical, action-oriented exposition that even difficult situations may offer differentiated opportunities for responsible action. While it often seems (at the first glance) that ethical conflicts only offer two solutions — either to comply with problematical requirements or to raise protest and deny all service — we want to contribute with our project towards overcoming this fundamentalistic, dichotomic view of matters. Eventually, we want to help our students to better understand their rôle as informaticians in an increasingly complex world. They shall elaborate a point of view of their own and act rationally and responsibly. By introducing them into the complicated interactions between informatics and society we hope to initiate some steps towards this goal.

5 Acknowledgements

A preliminary, but more detailed version of this paper (in German) is available from the authors [2]. We gratefully acknowledge the help of Christel Keller and Johannes Busse in the preparation of the project proposal and the curriculum.

This project is sponsored by the "Bund-Länder-Kommission für Bildungsplanung und Forschungsförderung", grant no. M1342.00.

Updated information is available under
http://www-pu.informatik.uni-tuebingen.de/users/klaeren/iug.html.

References

1. Wolfgang Coy. *Sichtweisen der Informatik*. Theorie der Informatik. Vieweg, Braunschweig u.a., 1992.
2. Friedrich Diestelmeier, Christiane Floyd, Christel Keller, Herbert Klaeren. Informatik und Gesellschaft — ein Fernstudienbaustein für das grundständige Studium an Präsenzhochschulen. Forschungsergebnisse und Materialien, Deutsches Institut für Fernstudienforschung, Tübingen, 1996.
3. Fachbereich 8 der GI. Empfehlungen zur Einbeziehung der gesellschaftlichen Aspekte der Informatik in die Informatik-Ausbildung. *Informatik-Spektrum*, 9:51–54, 1986.
4. J. Friedrich, Th. Herrmann, M. Peschek, A. Rolf. *Informatik und Gesellschaft*. Spektrum Akademischer Verlag, 1995.
5. P. Schefe, H. Hastedt, Y. Dittrich, G. Keil, editors. *Informatik und Philosophie*. BI Wissenschaftsverlag, 1993.
6. Britta Schinzel, editor. *Schnittstellen — Zum Verhältnis von Informatik und Gesellschaft*. Theorie der Informatik. Vieweg, 1996.

Syntactic and Semantic Aspects of Parallelism [*]

Alexandru Mateescu[1], Grzegorz Rozenberg[2] and Arto Salomaa[3]

[1] Turku Centre for Computer Science,
Lemminkäisenkatu 14 A, 20520 Turku, Finland
and Department of Mathematics, University of Bucharest, Romania
[2] Department of Computer Science, Leiden University,
P.O.Box 9512, NL-2300 RA Leiden, The Netherlands
[3] Academy of Finland and Department of Mathematics,
University of Turku, 20014 Turku, Finland

Abstract. We define and investigate new methods for the parallel composition of words and languages. The operation of parallel composition leads to new shuffle-like operations defined by syntactic constraints on the usual shuffle operation. The approach is applicable to concurrency, providing a method to define the parallel composition of processes. It is also applicable to parallel computation.

The syntactic constraints are introduced using a uniform method based on the notion of a *trajectory*. We obtain in a natural way a large class of semirings.

The approach is amazingly flexible. Diverse concepts from the theory of concurrency can be introduced and studied in this framework. For instance, we provide examples of applications to the fairness property and parallelization of non-context-free languages in terms of context-free and even regular languages.

Semantic constraints mean constraints applied to the symbols (atomic actions) that occur inside of processes. Such constraints provide methods to define the parallel composition of processes that have critical sections, priorities or re-entrant routines. They are also applicable for modelling the communication between processes.

1 Introduction

We introduce and investigate new methods to define the parallel composition of words and languages. The first part of this paper is dedicated to methods based on syntactic constraints on the shuffle operation. The constraints are referred to as syntactic since they do not concern properties of the words that are shuffled, or properties of the letters that occur in these words.

Instead, the constraints involve the general strategy to switch from one word to another word. Once such a strategy is defined, the structure of the words that are shuffled does not play any role.

---

[*] The work reported here has been supported by the Project 11281 of the Academy of Finland, and the ESPRIT Basic Research Working Group ASMICS II.

Usually, the operation is modelled by the shuffle operation or restrictions of this operation, such as literal shuffle, insertion, etc. For various types of insertion operations the reader may consult [10]. Other restrictions on shuffle are considered in [2], [3], the so called *left-merge*, or in [6], the *join-operation*. No general investigation on the possible restrictions on the shuffle operation has been made.

The syntactic constraints that we consider here are based on the notion of a *trajectory*. Roughly speaking, a trajectory is a segment of a line in plane, starting in the origin of axes and continuing parallel with the axis Ox or Oy. The line can change its direction only in points with nonnegative integer coordinates.

A trajectory defines how to skip from a word to another word during the shuffle operation.

Shuffle on trajectories provides a method of great flexibility to handle the operation of parallel composition of processes: from the catenation to the usual shuffle of processes.

Languages consisting of trajectories are a special case of picture languages introduced in [18].

However, constraints that take into consideration the inner structure of the words that are shuffled are referred to as semantic constraints. For some investigations on semantic constraints on shuffle the reader may consult [5], [11], [12], [14]. The second part of this paper is dedicated to some semantic constraints on shuffle.

The paper is organized as follows. Section 2 is devoted to some basic definitions, notations and terminology, covering almost all the notions necessary to read the paper.

In Section 3 we introduce the notion of a trajectory and we define the shuffle of words and languages over sets of trajectories. Also, we show how various operations with words, operations that are already studied in the literature, can be obtained as a particular case of the operation of shuffle on trajectories.

Section 4 deals with relations between shuffle on trajectories and the Chomsky hierarchy. Some characterization results are proved. These results are used in Section 5 to obtain a parallelization of some non-context-free languages. The results can also be used to show that a certain language L is not a regular language or that the language L is not a context-free language.

In Section 5 we present two applications of these operations to the theory of concurrency and to parallel computation. The fairness property is studied in connection with the algebraic properties of the operation of shuffle on trajectories. Also we prove a couple of results concerning the decidability of the n-fairness property for a set T of trajectories, where n is an integer, $n \geq 1$.

Another application considered deals with the parallelization of non-context-free languages. The parallelization problem for a non-context-free language L consists in finding a representation of L as the shuffle over a set T of trajectories of two languages L_1 and L_2, such that each of the languages L_1, T and L_2 are context-free, or even regular languages. This problem is related to the problem of parallelization of algorithms for a parallel computer. This is a central topic in the theory of parallel computation.

Section 6 and Section 7 deal with semantic constraints. Section 6 starts with a general construction based on dividing the alphabet. After that two important particular cases are studied: the distributed catenation and the left partial shuffle.

Section 7 concerns the parallel composition of processes that have re-entrant routines. Correspondingly, the re-entrant product is introduced and studied.

Finally, the paper contains some conclusions and suggestions for further directions of research.

2 Basic definitions

The set of nonnegative integers is denoted by N. Let Σ be an alphabet, i.e., a finite and nonempty set of symbols called *letters* or *atomic actions*. The free monoid generated by Σ is denoted by Σ^*. Elements in Σ^* are referred to as *words* or *finite sequential processes*. The empty word is denoted by λ.

If $w \in \Sigma^*$, then $|w|$ is the length of w. Note that $|\lambda| = 0$. If $a \in \Sigma$ and $w \in \Sigma^*$, then $|w|_a$ denotes the number of occurrences of the symbol a in w.

The *anti-catenation* operation, denoted by "$\circ$", is defined as: $u^{\circ}v = vu$, for any $u, v \in \Sigma^*$.

For all other notions and results in formal languages that are used in this paper we refer the reader to [20].

The reader may consult [19] , [1] , [2] or [8] for general results concerning the theory of concurrency. However, our approach will not use these results. For automata theory, [4] may be consulted.

In the sequel we recall some operations from formal languages that simulate the parallel composition of words.

The *shuffle* operation, denoted by $\sqcup\!\sqcup$, it is defined recursively by:

$$au\sqcup\!\sqcup bv = a(u\sqcup\!\sqcup bv) \cup b(au\sqcup\!\sqcup v),$$

and

$$u\sqcup\!\sqcup\lambda = \lambda\sqcup\!\sqcup u = \{u\},$$

where $u , v \in \Sigma^*$ and $a , b \in \Sigma$.

The *literal shuffle*, denoted by $\sqcup\!\sqcup_l$, is defined as:

$$a_1 a_2 \ldots a_n \sqcup\!\sqcup_l b_1 b_2 \ldots b_m = \begin{cases} a_1 b_1 a_2 b_2 \ldots a_n b_n b_{n+1} \ldots b_m, & \text{if } n \leq m, \\ a_1 b_1 a_2 b_2 \ldots a_m b_m a_{m+1} \ldots a_n, & \text{if } m < n, \end{cases}$$

where $a_i, b_j \in \Sigma$.

$$(u\sqcup\!\sqcup_l\lambda) = (\lambda\sqcup\!\sqcup_l u) = \{u\},$$

where $u \in \Sigma^*$.

The *balanced literal shuffle*, denoted by $\sqcup\!\sqcup_{bl}$, is defined as:

$$a_1 a_2 \ldots a_n \sqcup\!\sqcup_{bl} b_1 b_2 \ldots b_m = \begin{cases} a_1 b_1 a_2 b_2 \ldots a_n b_n, & \text{if } n = m, \\ \emptyset, & \text{if } n \neq m, \end{cases}$$

where $a_i, b_j \in \Sigma$.

The *insertion* operation, see [10], denoted by $\longleftarrow$, is defined as:

$$u \longleftarrow v = \{u'vu'' \mid u'u'' = u, u', u'' \in \Sigma^*\}.$$

All the above operations are extended in the usual way to operations with languages.

3 Syntactic aspects. Trajectories

In this section we introduce the notion of the trajectory and of the shuffle on trajectories. The shuffle of two words has a natural geometrical interpretation related to lattice points in the plane (points with nonnegative integer coordinates) and with a certain "walk" in the plane defined by each trajectory.

Consider the alphabet $V = \{r, u\}$. We say that r and u are *versors* in the plane: r stands for the *right* direction, whereas u stands for the *up* direction.

Definition 1. A *trajectory* is an element t, $t \in V^*$.

$\square$

We will consider also sets T of trajectories, $T \subseteq V^*$.

Let Σ be an alphabet and let t be a trajectory, $t = t_1 t_2 \ldots t_n$, where $t_i \in V, 1 \leq i \leq n$. Let α, β be two words over Σ, $\alpha = a_1 a_2 \ldots a_p, \beta = b_1 b_2 \ldots b_q$, where $a_i, b_j \in \Sigma, 1 \leq i \leq p$ and $1 \leq j \leq q$.

Definition 2. The *shuffle of α with β on the trajectory t*, denoted $\alpha \amalg_t \beta$, is defined as follows:

if $|\alpha| \neq |t|_r$ or $|\beta| \neq |t|_u$, then $\alpha \amalg_t \beta = \emptyset$, else
$\alpha \amalg_t \beta = c_1 c_2 \ldots c_{p+q}$, where, if $|t_1 t_2 \ldots t_{i-1}|_r = k_1$ and $|t_1 t_2 \ldots t_{i-1}|_u = k_2$,
then

$$c_i = \begin{cases} a_{k_1+1}, & \text{if } t_i = r, \\ b_{k_2+1}, & \text{if } t_i = u. \end{cases}$$

$\square$

We give also a recursive definition of the operation $\amalg_t$, where $t \in V^*$.

Definition 3. Let Σ be an alphabet and let $a_1, a_2, \ldots, a_n$ be letters from Σ, not necessarily distinct. Consider the functions $first$ and $last_*$ defined as:

$$first(a_1 a_2 \ldots a_n) = a_1 \text{ and } last_*(a_1 a_2 \ldots a_n) = a_2 \ldots a_n.$$

Morover,

$$first(a_1) = a_1, last_*(a_1) = \lambda, first(\lambda) = \emptyset \text{ and } last_*(\lambda) = \lambda.$$

The operation $\amalg_t$, where $t \in V^*$, is defined as follows:

$$\lambda \sqcup\!\sqcup_\lambda \lambda = \lambda,$$

and, otherwise,

$$\alpha \sqcup\!\sqcup_{dt} \beta = \begin{cases} first(\alpha)(last_*(\alpha) \sqcup\!\sqcup_t \beta), & \text{if } d = r, \\ first(\beta)(\alpha \sqcup\!\sqcup_t last_*(\beta)), & \text{if } d = u. \end{cases}$$

□

If T is a set of trajectories, the *shuffle of α with β on the set T of trajectories*, denoted $\alpha \sqcup\!\sqcup_T \beta$, is:

$$\alpha \sqcup\!\sqcup_T \beta = \bigcup_{t \in T} \alpha \sqcup\!\sqcup_t \beta.$$

The above operation is extended to languages over Σ, if $L_1, L_2 \subseteq \Sigma^*$, then:

$$L_1 \sqcup\!\sqcup_T L_2 = \bigcup_{\alpha \in L_1, \beta \in L_2} \alpha \sqcup\!\sqcup_T \beta.$$

Example 4. Let α and β be the words $\alpha = a_1 a_2 a_3 a_4 a_5 a_6 a_7 a_8$, $\beta = b_1 b_2 b_3 b_4 b_5$ and assume that $t = r^3 u^2 r^3 ururu$. The shuffle of α with β on the trajectory t is:

$$\alpha \sqcup\!\sqcup_t \beta = \{a_1 a_2 a_3 b_1 b_2 a_4 a_5 a_6 b_3 a_7 b_4 a_8 b_5\}.$$

The result has the following geometrical interpretation (see Figure 1): the trajectory t defines a line starting in the origin and continuing one unit to the right or up, depending of the definition of t. In our case, first there are three units right, then two units up, then three units right, etc. Assign α on the Ox axis and β on the Oy axis of the plane. Observe that the trajectory ends in the point with coordinates $(8, 5)$ (denoted by E in Figure 1) that is exactly the upper right corner of the rectangle defined by α and β, i.e., the rectangle $OAEB$ in Figure 1. Hence, the result of the shuffle of α with β on the trajectory t is nonempty. The result can be read following the line defined by the trajectory t: that is, when being in a lattice point of the trajectory, with the trajectory going right, one should pick up the corresponding letter from α, otherwise, if the trajectory is going up, then one should add to the result the corresponding letter from β. Hence, the trajectory t defines a line in the rectangle $OAEB$, on which one has "to walk" starting from the corner O, the origin, and ending in the corner E, the exit point. In each lattice point one has to follow one of the versors r or u, according to the definition of t.

Assume now that t' is another trajectory, say:

$$t' = ur^5 u^3 rur^2.$$

In Figure 1, the trajectory t' is depicted by a much bolder line that the trajectory t. Observe that:

$$\alpha \sqcup\!\sqcup_{t'} \beta = \{b_1 a_1 a_2 a_3 a_4 a_5 b_2 b_3 b_4 a_6 b_5 a_7 a_8\}.$$

Consider the set of trajectories, $T = \{t, t'\}$. The shuffle of α with β on the set T of trajectories is:

$$\alpha \sqcup\!\sqcup_T \beta = \{a_1 a_2 a_3 b_1 b_2 a_4 a_5 a_6 b_3 a_7 b_4 a_8 b_5, b_1 a_1 a_2 a_3 a_4 a_5 b_2 b_3 b_4 a_6 b_5 a_7 a_8\}.$$

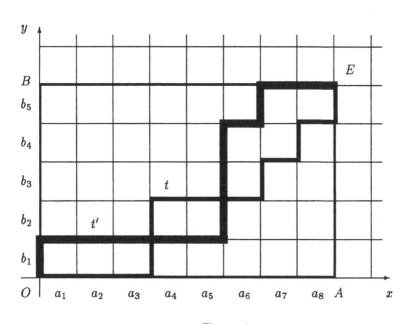

Figure 1

□

Remark 5. Here we show that all costumary operations for the parallel composition of words are particular cases of the operation of shuffle on trajectories.

1. Let T be the set $T = \{r, u\}^*$. Observe that $\sqcup\!\sqcup_T = \sqcup\!\sqcup$, the shuffle operation.
2. Assume that $T = (ru)^*(r^* \cup u^*)$. Note that in this case $\sqcup\!\sqcup_T = \sqcup\!\sqcup_l$, the literal shuffle.
3. Consider $T = (ru)^*$ and observe that $\sqcup\!\sqcup_T = \sqcup\!\sqcup_{bl}$, the balanced literal shuffle.
4. Define $T = r^* u^* r^*$ and note that $\sqcup\!\sqcup_T = \longleftarrow$, the insertion operation.
5. Assume that $T = r^* u^*$. It follows that $\sqcup\!\sqcup_T = \cdot$, the catenation operation.
6. Consider $T = u^* r^*$ and observe that $\sqcup\!\sqcup_T = {}^\circ$, the anti-catenation operation.

□

The following two theorems are representation results for the languages of the form $L_1 \sqcup\!\sqcup_T L_2$. We omit their rather straightforward proofs.

Theorem 6. *For all languages L_1 and L_2, $L_1, L_2 \subseteq \Sigma^*$, and for all sets T of trajectories, there exist a gsm M and two letter-to-letter morphisms g and h such that*

$$L_1 ⧢_T L_2 = M(h(L_1) ⧢ g(L_2) ⧢ T).$$

☐

Our next theorem is a variant of Theorem 6.

Theorem 7. *For all languages L_1 and L_2, $L_1, L_2 \subseteq \Sigma^*$, and for all sets T of trajectories, there exist a morphism φ and two letter-to-letter morphisms g and h, $g : \Sigma \longrightarrow \Sigma_1^*$ and $h : \Sigma \longrightarrow \Sigma_2^*$ where Σ_1 and Σ_2 are two copies of Σ, and a regular language R, such that*

$$L_1 ⧢_T L_2 = \varphi((h(L_1) ⧢ g(L_2) ⧢ T) \cap R).$$

☐

4   Shuffle on trajectories of regular and context-free languages

It is well known that the shuffle of two regular languages is a regular language. Moreover, given two finite automata A_1 and A_2 one can effectively find a finite automaton A such that $L(A) = L(A_1) ⧢ L(A_2)$.

Consider the finite automata $A_i = (Q_i, \Sigma, \delta_i, q_0^i, F_i)$, where $i = 1, 2$. The finite automaton $A = (Q, \Sigma, \delta, q_0, F)$ is defined as follows: $Q = Q_1 \times Q_2$, $q_0 = (q_0^1, q_0^2)$, $F = F_1 \times F_2$, and

$$\delta((q_1, q_2), a) = \{(\delta_1(q_1, a), q_2), (q_1, \delta_2(q_2, a)\}.$$

One can easily verify that $L(A) = L(A_1) ⧢ L(A_2)$.

Note that this construction gives an idea about how one can define the shuffle of two finite graphs.

For instance, let A_1 be the automaton defined by the transition graph from Figure 2 and let A_2 be the automaton that has the transition graph from Figure 3. The transition graph of the automaton A with the property that $L(A) = L(A_1) ⧢ L(A_2)$ is depicted in Figure 4.

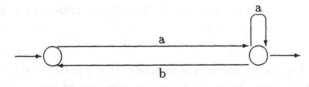

Figure 2

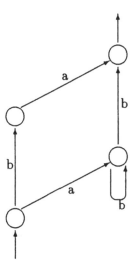

Figure 3

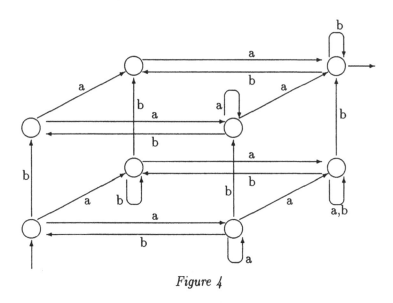

Figure 4

The following theorem provides a characterization of those sets of trajectories T for which $L_1 \sqcup\!\sqcup_T L_2$ is a regular language, whenever L_1, L_2 are regular languages.

Theorem 8. *Let T be a set of trajectories, $T \subseteq \{r, u\}^*$. The following assertions are equivalent:*

(i) for all regular languages L_1, L_2, $L_1 \sqcup\!\sqcup_T L_2$ is a regular language.
(ii) T is a regular language.

Proof. $(i) \Rightarrow (ii)$ Assume that $L_1 = r^*$ and $L_2 = u^*$ and note that $L_1 \sqcup\!\sqcup_T L_2 = T$. It follows that T is a regular language.

$(ii) \Rightarrow (i)$ Assume that T is a regular language. Consider two regular languages L_1, L_2. Without loss of generality, we may assume that L_1 and L_2 are over the same alphabet Σ. Let $A_i = (Q_i, \Sigma, \delta_i, q_0^i, F_i)$ be a finite deterministic automaton such that $L(A_i) = L_i$, $i = 1, 2$. Also, let $A_T = (Q_T, \{r, u\}, \delta_T, q_0^T, F_T)$ be a finite deterministic automaton such that $L(A_T) = T$.

We define a finite nondeterministic automaton $A = (Q, \Sigma, \delta, Q_0, F)$ such that $L(A) = L_1 \sqcup\!\sqcup_T L_2$. Informally, A, on an input $w \in \Sigma^*$, simulates nondeterministically A_1 or A_2 and from time to time changes the simulation from A_1 to A_2 or from A_2 to A_1. Each change determines a transition in A_T as follows: a change from A_1 to A_2 is interpreted as u and a change from A_2 to A_1 is interpreted as r. The input w is accepted by A iff A_1, A_2 and A_T accept.

Formally, $Q = Q_1 \times Q_T \times Q_2$, $Q_0 = \{(q_0^1, q_0^T, q_0^2)\}$, $F = F_1 \times F_T \times F_2$. The definition of δ is:

$$\delta((q_1, d, q_2), a) = \{(\delta_1(q_1, a), \delta_T(d, r), q_2), (q_1, \delta_T(d, u), \delta_2(q_2, a))\},$$

where, $q_1 \in Q_1, d \in Q_T, q_2 \in Q_2, a \in \Sigma$.

One can easily verify that $L(A) = L_1 \sqcup\!\sqcup_T L_2$ and hence $L_1 \sqcup\!\sqcup_T L_2$ is a regular language.

$\square$

Next theorem gives a similar result as Theorem 8, but for context-free sets of trajectories.

Theorem 9. *Let T be a set of trajectories, $T \subseteq \{r, u\}^*$. The following assertions are equivalent:*

(i) for all regular languages L_1, L_2, $L_1 \sqcup\!\sqcup_T L_2$ is a context-free language.
(ii) T is a context-free language.

Proof. $(i) \Rightarrow (ii)$ Assume that $L_1 = r^*$ and $L_2 = u^*$ and note that $L_1 \sqcup\!\sqcup_T L_2 = T$. Therefore T is a context-free language.

$(ii) \Rightarrow (i)$ Assume that T is a context-free language. Consider two regular languages L_1, L_2. Without loss of generality, we may assume that L_1 and L_2 are over the same alphabet Σ. Let $A_i = (Q_i, \Sigma, \delta_i, q_0^i, F_i)$ be a finite deterministic automaton such that $L(A_i) = L_i$, $i = 1, 2$. Also, let $P_T = (Q_T, \Gamma_T, \{r, u\}, \delta_T, q_0^T, Z_T, F_T)$ be a pushdown automaton such that $L(P_T) = T$.

We define a pushdown automaton $P = (Q, \Gamma, \Sigma, \delta, Q_0, Z, F)$ such that $L(P) = L_1 \sqcup\!\sqcup_T L_2$. Informally, P, behaves as the automaton A from the proof of Theorem 8, except that on the second component of the states, P simulates the pushdown automaton P_T. That is, on an input $w \in \Sigma^*$, P simulates nondeterministically A_1 or A_2 and from time to time changes the simulation from A_1 to A_2 or from A_2 to A_1. Each change determines a transition in P_T as follows:

a change from A_1 to A_2 is interpreted as u and a change from A_2 to A_1 is interpreted as r. The input w is accepted by P iff A_1, A_2 and P_T accept.

Formally, $Q = Q_1 \times Q_T \times Q_2$, $Q_0 = \{(q_0^1, q_0^T, q_0^2)\}$, $F = F_1 \times F_T \times F_2$, $\Gamma = \Gamma_T$, $Z = Z_T$. The definition of δ is:

$$\delta((q_1, d, q_2), a, X) = \cup_{(s,\alpha) \in \delta_T(d, r, X)} ((\delta_1(q_1, a), s, q_2), \alpha) \cup$$

$$\cup_{(s', \alpha') \in \delta_T(d, u, X)} ((q_1, s', \delta_2(q_2, a), \alpha')\}$$

where, $q_1 \in Q_1$, $d \in Q_T$, $q_2 \in Q_2$, $a \in \Sigma$, $X \in \Gamma$, $\alpha \in \Gamma^*$.
Additionally,

$$\delta((q_1, d, q_2), \lambda, X) = \cup_{(s,\alpha) \in \delta_T(d, \lambda, X)} ((q_1, s, q_2), \alpha)$$

where, $q_1 \in Q_1$, $d \in Q_T$, $q_2 \in Q_2$, $X \in \Gamma$, $\alpha \in \Gamma^*$.

One can verify that $L(P) = L_1 \sqcup\!\sqcup_T L_2$ and hence $L_1 \sqcup\!\sqcup_T L_2$ is a context-free language. $\qquad\square$

Theorem 10. *Let T be a set of trajectories, $T \subseteq \{r, u\}^*$ such that T is a regular language.*

(i) *If L_1 is a context-free language and if L_2 is a regular language, then $L_1 \sqcup\!\sqcup_T L_2$ is a context-free language.*

(ii) *If L_1 is a regular language and if L_2 is a context-free language, then $L_1 \sqcup\!\sqcup_T L_2$ is a context-free language.*

Proof. The proof is similar with the proof of Theorem 9. For the case (i) the pushdown automaton is simulated on the first component of the states, whereas for the case (ii) the pushdown automaton is simulated on the third component of the states. $\qquad\square$

Alternative proofs for Theorems 8 - 10 can be obtained using Theorem 6 or Theorem 7.

¿From Theorems 8 - 10 we obtain the following corollary:

Corollary 11. *Let L_1, L_2 and T, $T \subseteq \{r, u\}^*$ be three languages.*

(i) *if all three languages are regular languages, then $L_1 \sqcup\!\sqcup_T L_2$ is a regular language.*

(ii) *if two languages are regular languages and the third one is a context-free language, then $L_1 \sqcup\!\sqcup_T L_2$ is a context-free language.*

$\qquad\square$

Remark 12. The above conditions cannot be relaxed. For instance, if two languages are context-free and the third one is a regular language, then $L_1 ⧢_T L_2$ is not necessary a context-free language. Assume that T is regular, $T = \{r, u\}^*$. It is known that there are context-free languages L_1, L_2 such that $L_1 ⧢_T L_2$ is not a context-free language. For the other two cases, assume that $T = \{r^n u^k r^{2n} \mid n, k \geq 1\}$, $L_1 = d^*$ and $L_2 = \{a^n b^n c^m \mid n, m \geq 1\}$. Note that

$$L_1 ⧢_T L_2 \cap a^+ d^+ b^+ c^+ = \{a^n d^k b^n c^n \mid n, k \geq 1\}.$$

Hence, $L_1 ⧢_T L_2$ is not a context-free language. If $T = \{u^n r^k u^{2n} \mid n, k \geq 1\}$, then $L_2 ⧢_T L_1$ is not a context-free language.

$\square$

5 Properties related to concurrency

• Fairness

Fairness is a property of the parallel composition of processes that, roughly speaking, says that each action of a process is performed with not too much delay with respect to performing actions from another process. That is, the parallel composition is "fair" with both processes that are performed.

Definition 13. Let $T \subseteq \{r, u\}^*$ be a set of trajectories and let n be an integer, $n \geq 1$. T has the *n-fairness* property iff for all $t \in T$ and for all t' such that $t = t't''$ for some $t'' \in \{r, u\}^*$, it follows that:

$$\mid |t'|_r - |t'|_u \mid \leq n.$$

$\square$

This means that all trajectories from T are contained in the region of the plane bounded by the line $y = x - n$ and the line $y = x + n$, see Figure 5, for $n = 4$.

Example 14. The balanced literal shuffle ($⧢_b$) has the *n-fairness* property for all n, $n \geq 1$.

The following operations: shuffle ($⧢$), catenation ($\cdot$), insertion ($⟵$) do not have the *n-fairness* property for any n, $n \geq 1$.

Definition 15. Let n be a fixed number, $n \geq 1$. Define the language F_n as:

$$F_n = \{t \in V^* \mid \mid |t'|_r - |t'|_u \mid \leq n, \text{ for all } t' \text{ such that } t = t't'', t'' \in V^*\}.$$

$\square$

Remark 16. Note that a set T of trajectories has the n-fairness property if and only if $T \subseteq F_n$.

$\square$

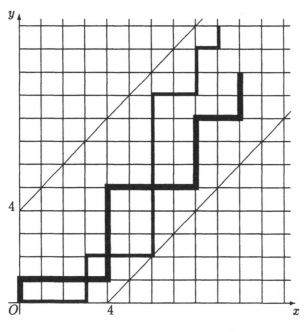

Figure 5

We omit the straightforward proof of the following

Proposition 17. *For every* n, $n \geq 1$, *the language* F_n *is a regular language.*

$\square$

Corollary 18. *Let* T *be a set of trajectories. If* T *is a context-free or a simple matrix language and if* n *is fixed,* $n \geq 1$, *then it is decidable whether or not* T *has the n-fairness property.*

Proof. It is easy to observe that for the above families of languages the problem if a language from a family is contained in a regular language is a decidable problem. Hence, from Proposition 17, this corollary follows.

$\square$

Comment. For a context-free language $T \subseteq V^*$ it is decidable whether or not there exists a nonnegative integer n, such that T has the n-fairness property, see [17]. However, in general it is an open problem for what families $\mathcal{L}$ of languages it is decidable this problem.

Remark 19. The fairness property is not a property of the set $\mathfrak{r}(T)$ as one can observe in the case when T is the set

$$T = \{r^i u^i \mid i \geq 1\}.$$

Indeed, T does not have the n-fairness property for any n, $n \geq 1$ despite that $\mathfrak{r}(T)$ is the first diagonal.

$\square$

• On parallelization of languages using shuffle on trajectories

The *parallelization of a problem* consists in decomposing the problem in subproblems, such that each subproblem can be solved by a processor, i.e., the subproblems are solved in parallel and, finally, the partial results are collected and assembled in the answer of the initial problem by a processor. Solving problems in this way increases the time efficiency. It is known that not every problem can be parallelized. Also, no general methods are known for the parallelization of problems.

Here we formulate the problem in terms of languages and shuffle on trajectories. Also we present some examples.

Assume that L is a language. The *parallelization of L* consists in finding languages L_1, L_2 and T, $T \subseteq V^*$, such that $L = L_1 \sqcup\!\sqcup_T L_2$ and moreover, the complexity of L_1, L_2 and T is in some sense smaller than the complexity of L. In the sequel the complexity of a language L refers to the Chomsky class of L, i.e., regular languages are less complex than context-free languages that are less complex than context-sensitive languages.

One can easily see that every language L, $L \subseteq \{a,b\}^*$ can be written as $L = a^* \sqcup\!\sqcup_T b^*$ for some set T of trajectories. However, this is not a parallelization of L since the complexity of T is the same with the complexity of L.

In view of Corollary 11 there are non-context-free languages L such that $L = L_1 \sqcup\!\sqcup_T L_2$ for some context-free languages L_1, L_2 and T. Moreover, one of those three languages can be even a regular language. Note that this is a parallelization of L.

As a first example we consider the non-context-free language $L \subseteq \{a,b,c\}^*$, $L = \{w \mid\mid w\mid_a = \mid w\mid_b = \mid w\mid_c\}$.

Consider the languages: $L_1 \subseteq \{a,b\}^*$, $L_1 = \{u \mid\mid u\mid_a = \mid u\mid_b\}$, $L_2 = c^*$ and $T = \{t \mid\mid t\mid_r = 2\mid t\mid_u\}$.

One can easily verify that $L = L_1 \sqcup\!\sqcup_T L_2$. Moreover, note that L_1 and T are context-free languages, whereas L_2 is a regular language. Hence this is a parallelization of L. As a consequence of Corollary 11 one cannot expect a significant improvement of this result, for instance to have only one context-free language and two regular languages in the decomposition of L.

Next example is more related to the practice of computers. Assume that a central computer is used by one or many users having their own local computers. Moreover, assume that each user opens one or more connections to the central computer and afterwards closes each connection. The central computer answers to each command of open or close connection by sending a prompter to the user that initiated the command. (Usually, at the open connection one receives also a message such as "welcome", "login:", "username:", etc., whereas at the close connection the prompter acknowledges the closing of connection by sending a message such as "disconnecting", "bye", etc.) For simplicity we don't make any distinction between the prompter for open connection and the prompter for close connection. Also, we assume that one cannot close a connection before the connection is opened and that all open connections will be closed at some stage. Moreover, we assume that the central computer answers with one and only one prompter to each command of open or close connection. However the prompters can be sent with some delay, for instance the following sequence is possible: open connection; close connection; prompter; prompter.

The possible actions are encoded as follows: open connection by "o", close connection by "c" and sending a prompter by "p". Now consider the alphabet $\Sigma = \{o, c, p\}$ and the language L, $L \subseteq \Sigma^*$, consisting of all valid finite sequences of actions. For instance the words *oopcppcp* and *opocpcpp* are in L, whereas the words *oppc* and *oopcpp* are not in L.

The language L is not a context-free language, since

$$L \cap o^+ p^+ c^+ p^+ = \{o^n p^{n-i} c^n p^{n+i} \mid 0 \leq i \leq n, n \geq 1\}.$$

Let L_1 be the Dyck language over the two-letter alphabet $\{o, c\}$ and let T be the Dyck language over the two-letter alphabet $V = \{r, u\}$.

One can easily verify that $L = L_1 \sqcup\!\sqcup_T p^*$. Therefore this is a parallelization of the non-context-free language L, since L_1, T are context-free languages and p^* is a regular language. Again, one cannot expect a significant improvement of this result.

Theorem 20. *If L is a non-context-free language that has a parallelization, then L is a semilinear context-sensitive language.*

Proof. It follows from Theorem 7 that L is context-sensitive and, moreover, L is a semilinear language.

$\square$

Remark 21. Using Theorem 20 one can show that, for instance, the language

$$L = \{a^n b^{n^2} \mid n \geq 1\}$$

does not have a parallelization, since L is not a semilinear language.

However, not all semilinear context-sensitive languages have a parallelization. For instance, let Σ be an alphabet with $card(\Sigma) \geq 2$. The following semilinear context-sensitive language:

$$L = \{ww \mid w \in \Sigma^*\}$$

does not have a parallelization.

Finding characterizations of those languages that have a parallelization remains a challenging problem.

□

Many issues in this direction are subject for further research. We only mention some topics.

(i) Instead of context-sensitive languages, consider some other language class (linear languages, deterministic context-free languages, matrix languages, etc.) with respect to the parallelization problem.

(ii) It might be more feasible to define the complexity of a language by some other means than the Chomsky class. Investigate parallelization in such a new setting.

(iii) Both (*i*) and (*ii*) lead to decision problems and, in decidable cases, to problems of a more detailed characterization.

6   Semantic aspects. Methods based on dividing the alphabet

Constraints concerning the letters occurring in parallel composed words are referred to as semantic. Such constraints enable the description of critical sections, priorities, re-entrant routines, etc. All these semantic constraints lead to shuffle-like operations between words or graphs. In the remainder of this paper we present some results concerning shuffle of words with critical sections and aspects of the use of re-entrant routines.

• Methods based on dividing the alphabet

These methods are suitable to model the existence of critical sections inside of parallel composed processes. We start with a general approach and later on give more detailed results on two such methods: *distributed catenation* and *left partial shuffle*.

Let Σ be an alphabet and assume that $\Sigma = \Gamma \cup \Delta$, where $\Gamma \cap \Delta = \emptyset$. Note that Γ or Δ can be empty. Intuitively the symbols from Γ are elementary actions from critical sections, i.e., a critical section is a nonempty word over Γ, whereas a noncritical section is a word over Δ. A critical section is a part of a process which must not be executed concurrently with a critical section of another process. More precisely, once one process has entered its critical section, another process may not enter any other action until the first process exits its critical section. Mutual exclusion is said to apply between critical sections and any other sections. Throughout this paper we assume that processes have a very simple structure, i.e., a process is a word over Σ.

Notations. Let k be a natural number.

$$M_0 = \Gamma^*,$$

$$M_{k+1} = \Gamma^*(\Delta^+\Gamma^+)^k\Delta^+\Gamma^* \cup \{\lambda\}.$$

Remark 22. Note that:

(i) $\bigcup_{k \geq 0} M_k = \Sigma^*$.
(ii) if $\bar{i} \neq j$, then $M_i \cap M_j = \{\lambda\}$.
(iii) *consequently, for any $w \in \Sigma^+$, there exists a unique k such that $w \in M_k$.*

$\square$

Definition 23. Let w be in Σ^+. The Δ-*degree* of w is:

$$deg_\Delta(w) = k, \text{ where } w \in M_k.$$

By definition, $deg_\Delta(\lambda) = 0$.

$\square$

Note that the degree is well defined, i.e., for any nonempty word w, $deg_\Delta(w)$ has a unique value (see Remark 22).

Notations. In sequel, the symbols $\odot, \Diamond, \sharp$, denote operations from the set $\{., °, \sqcup\}$. Moreover, the operations $\odot, \Diamond, \sharp$, are not necessary distinct operations.
$\square$

Let $\mathcal{P}(M_k)$ be the set of all subsets of M_k. We'll define a binary operation on $\mathcal{P}(M_k)$ as follows:

Definition 24. Let A, B be subsets of M_k. The k-Δ-*product of type* $(\odot, \Diamond, \sharp)$ of A with B, denoted $A \bowtie_{k,\Delta} B$, is by definition

$$A \bowtie_{k,\Delta} B = \bigcup_{x \in A, y \in B} (x \bowtie_{k,\Delta} y),$$

where, if:

$$x = u_0 v_1 u_1 \ldots v_k u_k,$$

$$y = u_0' v_1' u_1' \ldots v_k' u_k',$$

with $u_0, u_0', u_k, u_k' \in \Gamma^*, u_i, u_i' \in \Gamma^+, i = 1, \ldots, k-1, v_i, v_i' \in \Delta^+, i = 1, \ldots, k,$
then :

$$x \bowtie_{k,\Delta} y = (u_0 \Diamond u_0') \odot (v_1 \natural v_1') \odot (u_1 \Diamond u_1') \odot \ldots \odot (v_k \natural v_k') \odot (u_k \Diamond u_k').$$

By definition,

$$x \bowtie_{k,\Delta} \lambda = \lambda \bowtie_{k,\Delta} x = \{x\}.$$

$\square$

A decomposition of x (y) such as in the above definition will be called a *canonical decomposition with respect to Δ* or, shortly, a *canonical decomposition* when Δ is understood from the context.

Lemma 25. *For any alphabet Σ, for any $\Delta \subseteq \Sigma$, and for any nonnegative integer k, the ordered system:*

$$\mathcal{S}_{\Delta,k} = (\mathcal{P}(M_k), \cup, \emptyset, \bowtie_{k,\Delta}, \lambda)$$

is an upper complete semilattice - ordered semiring with the least element $\emptyset$ and ω-continuous operations with the distributivity over infinite sums.

$\square$

We will now extend the k-Δ-product operation to arbitrary words from Σ^*. The new operation will be denoted by $\bowtie_\Delta$.

Definition 26. Let x, y be in Σ^+ such that $deg_\Delta(x) = n$ and $deg_\Delta(y) = m$. Assume that

$$x = u_0 v_1 u_1 \ldots v_n u_n,$$
$$y = u_0' v_1' u_1' \ldots v_m' u_m',$$

with $u_0, u_0', u_n, u_m' \in \Gamma^*, u_i \in \Gamma^+, i = 1, \ldots, n-1, v_i \in \Delta^+, i = 1, \ldots, n,$
$u_i' \in \Gamma^+, i = 1, \ldots, m-1, v_i' \in \Delta^+, i = 1, \ldots, m$. Then the *$\Delta$-parallel product of type $(\odot, \Diamond, \natural)$*, or shortly, the *$\Delta$-product of type $(\odot, \Diamond, \natural)$* (or shortly the *$\Delta$-product*, if the type $(\odot, \Diamond, \natural)$ is understood from the context) of x with y is :
if $n \leq m$, then

$$x \bowtie_\Delta y = (u_0 \Diamond u_0') \odot (v_1 \natural v_1') \odot \ldots \odot (v_n \natural v_n') \odot (u_n \Diamond u_n') \odot v_{n+1}' \odot u_{n+1}' \ldots \odot u_m'$$

and, otherwise,

$$x \bowtie_\Delta y = (u_0 \Diamond u_0') \odot (v_1 \natural v_1') \odot \ldots \odot (v_m \natural v_m') \odot (u_m \Diamond u_m') \odot v_{m+1} \odot u_{m+1} \ldots \odot u_n.$$

By definition:

$$x \bowtie_\Delta \lambda = \lambda \bowtie_\Delta x = \{x\}.$$

□

For any alphabet Σ, for any subset $\Delta \subseteq \Sigma$ and for any type $(\odot, \Diamond, \sharp)$, with $\odot, \Diamond, \sharp \in \{., ^\circ, \sqcup\sqcup\}$, one obtains an ordered system:

$$S_\Delta = (\mathcal{P}(\Sigma^*), \cup, \emptyset, \bowtie_\Delta, \{\lambda\}).$$

Therefore, for a fixed alphabet Σ and for an arbitrary fixed subset $\Delta \subseteq \Sigma$, considering all possible types $(\odot, \Diamond, \sharp)$, with $\odot, \Diamond, \sharp \in \{., ^\circ, \sqcup\sqcup\}$, we obtain a family of 27 ordered systems S_Δ as above. Each such ordered system is an upper complete semilattice - ordered semiring with the least element $\emptyset$ and ω-continuous operations with distributivity over infinite sums. Moreover, each such semiring is a natural, theoretical framework for defining various sorts of concurrent processes. For more results along this line the reader is referred to [5].

• The distributed catenation

The operation $\bowtie_\Delta$ of type $(., ., .)$, called the *distributed catenation*, is denoted by $\circ_\Delta$. This operation between words, extended to sets of words, is "between" normal catenation and partial shuffle. It also defines a special parallel composition of concurrent processes. Each process is supposed to be a finite sequence of atomic actions and, moreover, the atomic actions are divided into two disjoint sets. The method to compose the processes is to catenate blocks consisting of atomic actions from the same category keeping the initial order in which they appear in the input processes. The distributed catenation can also be used to perform the parallel composition of processes that contain critical (tight) sections.

In the sequel we enumerate some properties of the distributed catenation. For more details the reader is referred to [11] and [12].

Theorem 27. *The families REG, CS and RE are closed under distributed catenation. The family CF is not closed under distributed catenation.*

□

Theorem 28. *If $R \in REG$ and $L \in CF$, then $R \circ_\Delta L \in CF$ and $L \circ_\Delta R \in CF$.*

□

Next results concern algebraic properties of the distributed catenation operation.

Definition 29. Let $A \in S_\Delta$, $A \neq \emptyset$. The Δ-*degree* of A is:

$$deg_\Delta(A) = max(\{deg_\Delta(x) \mid x \in A\}),$$

if the maximum exists, and $deg_\Delta(A) = \infty$ otherwise. By definition, $deg_\Delta(\emptyset) = 0$.

□

Note that the following facts hold: $deg_\Delta(A \cup B) = max\{deg_\Delta(A), deg_\Delta(B)\}$, $deg_\Delta(A \circ_\Delta B) = max\{deg_\Delta(A), deg_\Delta(B)\}$ and $deg_\Delta(A^{\circ\Delta}) = deg_\Delta(A)$.

Remark 30. Let A, B be nonempty subsets of Σ^* with $deg_\Delta(A) < \infty$, $deg_\Delta(B) < \infty$.

The Δ-degree of the solution X_0 of the equation $X = A \circ_\Delta X \cup B$ is:

$$deg_\Delta(X_0) = max(\{deg_\Delta(A), deg_\Delta(B)\}).$$

(Observe that $X_0 = A^{\circ\Delta} \circ_\Delta B$ and that $deg_\Delta(A^{\circ\Delta}) = deg_\Delta(A)$.)

$\square$

Definition 31. The family of Δ-*rational* languages over $S_{\Sigma,\Delta}$, denoted $Rat - dc(\Sigma, \Delta)$, is the smallest family of languages over Σ that contains all finite languages over Σ and is closed under union, Δ-catenation and Δ -catenation closure.

$\square$

Notations.

$Rat - dc(\Sigma) = \bigcup_{\Delta \subseteq \Sigma} Rat - dc(\Sigma, \Delta)$ and $Rat - dc = \{L \mid \exists \Sigma, L \in Rat - dc(\Sigma)\}$.

As in the general theory of semirings, see [13], we obtain:

Lemma 32. Let $L \in Rat - dc$ with $L \subseteq \Sigma^*$. Then there exist $\Delta \subseteq \Sigma$ and $n(L) > 0$ such that, for any $w \in L$ with $|w| \geq n(L)$, there exist $x, y, z \in \Sigma^*$ such that:
(i) $w = x \circ_\Delta y \circ_\Delta z$.
(ii) $0 < |y| < n(L)$.
(iii) $\{x\} \circ_\Delta \{y\}^{\circ\Delta} \circ_\Delta \{z\} \subseteq L$.

$\square$

Theorem 33. $Rat - dc$ *is an anti-AFL, i.e. it is not closed under any of the following six operations: union, catenation, Kleene star, intersection with regular languages, morphism and inverse morphism.*

$\square$

Theorem 34. $Rat - dc$ *is not closed under any of the following operations: complementation, intersection, distributed catenation and distributed catenation closure.*

$\square$

Concerning closure properties of the classes $Rat - dc(\Sigma, \Delta)$ we have the following results:

Theorem 35. *In general, a class $Rat - dc(\Sigma, \Delta)$ is not closed under any of the following operations: catenation, Kleene star, morphisms, inverse morphisms, intersection with regular languages, complementation, intersection.*

□

Observe that there are no Σ and $\Delta \subseteq \Sigma$ such that the class $Rat - dc(\Sigma, \Delta)$ is an anti-AFL. The argument is that all classes $Rat - dc(\Sigma, \Delta)$ are closed under union.

Also, note that in some special cases, (for instance when $\Delta = \emptyset$) a class $Rat - dc(\Sigma, \Delta)$ is closed at most under the operations from Theorem 35, such as for instance under: catenation, Kleene star, intersection with regular languages, complementation, intersection.

Finally, we show some (un)decidability properties of $Rat - dc$.

Theorem 36. *The membership problem, the emptiness problem, and the infinity problem for $Rat - dc$ are decidable.*

□

Theorem 37. *For $L_1, L_2 \in Rat - dc$ the following problems are undecidable:*
(1) $L_1 \cap L_2 = \emptyset$?
(2) $|L_1 \cap L_2| = \infty$?

Proof. (1) Let $PCP(\alpha, \beta)$ be an instance of the Post Correspondence Problem with $\alpha = (\alpha_1, \ldots, \alpha_n), \beta = (\beta_1, \ldots, \beta_n)$ and $\{\alpha_i, \beta_i \mid 1 \leq i \leq n\} \subset \{a, b\}^+$.
Define $\Sigma = \{a, b, c\}$, $\Delta = \{c\}$, and consider the finite set

$$K_\alpha = \{ba^i c\alpha_i \mid \alpha_i \text{ in } \alpha, 1 \leq i \leq n\}.$$

and let $L_1 = K_\alpha \circ_\Delta K_\alpha^{\circ\Delta}$.
Note that $L_1 \in Rat - dc$ and moreover,

$$L_1 = \{ba^{i_1} ba^{i_2} b \cdots ba^{i_r} c^r \alpha_{i_1} \alpha_{i_2} \cdots \alpha_{i_r} \mid r \geq 1\}.$$

Analogously, $L_2 = K_\beta \circ_\Delta K_\beta^{\circ\Delta} \in Rat - dc$, and

$$L_2 = \{ba^{j_1} ba^{j_2} b \cdots ba^{j_s} c^s \beta_{j_1} \beta_{j_2} \cdots \beta_{j_s} \mid s \geq 1\}.$$

Note that $L_1 \cap L_2 \neq \emptyset$ if and only if $PCP(\alpha, \beta)$ has a solution, showing that the problem is undecidable.
(2) As in case (1) it follows that $|L_1 \cap L_2| = \infty$ if and only if $PCP(\alpha, \beta)$ has a solution, showing that this problem is undecidable, too.

□

Note that the above problems are decidable for the classical family of rational (regular) languages, [4].

• The (left) partial shuffle

The operation $\bowtie_\Delta$ of type $(.,., \sqcup\!\sqcup)$, is called the *left partial shuffle* or shortly the *partial shuffle* and is denoted by $\sqcup\!\sqcup_\Delta$.

In the sequel we present some properties of the partial shuffle. For more details the reader is referred to [14].

Theorem 38. *The families REG, CS and RE are closed under partial shuffle. The family CF is not closed under partial shuffle.*

□

Theorem 39. *If $R \in REG$ and $L \in CF$, then $R\sqcup\!\sqcup_\Delta L \in CF$ and $L\sqcup\!\sqcup_\Delta R \in CF$.*

□

The next results concern algebraic properties of the distributed catenation operation. The class of rational languages with respect to partial shuffle, denoted $Rat - ps$ is defined as in the case of the distributed catenation, see Definition 31.

Theorem 40. *The class $Rat - ps$ is an anti-AFL, i.e. it is not closed under any of the following six operations : union, catenation, Kleene star, intersection with regular languages, morphic direct and inverse images.*

□

Corollary 41. *The class $Rat-ps$ is closed neither under intersection nor under complementation.*

□

Concerning decidable properties of $Rat - ps$ we can easily show that the membership problem, the emptiness problem and the infinity problem are decidable.

Theorem 42. *For $L_1, L_2 \in Rat - ps$ it is undecidable :*
(i) whether or not $L_1 \cap L_2 = \emptyset$.
(ii) whether or not $card(L_1 \cap L_2) = \infty$.

Proof. (i) Let $PCP(\alpha, \beta)$ be an instance of the Post Correspondence Problem over $\{a, b\}$. Define $\Sigma = \{a, b, c\}$, $\Delta = \{c\}$ and consider the finite set K_α,

$$K_\alpha = \{ba^i c\alpha_i \mid \alpha_i \text{ in } \alpha, i = 1, \ldots, n\}.$$

and let L_1 be , $L_1 = K_\alpha \sqcup\!\sqcup_\Delta K_\alpha^{\sqcup\!\sqcup_\Delta}$. Note that $L_1 \in Rat - ps$ and moreover,

$$L_1 = \{ba^{i_1}ba^{i_2}b \ldots ba^{i_r}c^r \alpha_{i_1}\alpha_{i_2} \ldots \alpha_{i_r} \mid r \geq 1\}.$$

Analogously,

$$L_2 = \{ba^{j_1}ba^{j_2}b \ldots ba^{j_s}c^s \beta_{j_1}\beta_{j_2} \ldots \beta_{j_s} \mid s \geq 1\}.$$

is a language in $Rat - ps$. Note that, $L_1 \cap L_2 \neq \emptyset$ if and only if $PCP(\alpha, \beta)$ has a solution.

(ii) It follows like in case (i) that $card(L_1 \cap L_2) = \infty$ if and only if $PCP(\alpha, \beta)$ has a solution. $\qquad \square$

Note that the above problems are decidable for the classical family of rational (regular) languages.

7 The re-entrant product

The shuffle operation is not suitable to describe the existence of re-entrant routines. A *re-entrant routine* is a routine that can be executed concurrently by more than one user (process).

Consider the following version of the *Latin product*, denoted by $\diamond$.

If $u = a_1 a_2 \ldots a_n$ and $v = b_1 b_2 \ldots b_m$ are words over Σ, then

$$u \diamond v = \begin{cases} a_1 a_2 \ldots a_n b_2 b_3 \ldots b_m, & \text{if } a_n = b_1 \\ a_1 a_2 \ldots a_n b_1 b_2 \ldots b_m, & \text{if } a_n \neq b_1 \end{cases}$$

By definition, $u \diamond \lambda = \lambda \diamond u = u$. It is easy to observe that the ordered system $\mathcal{M} = (\Sigma^*, \diamond, \lambda)$ is a monoid, called the *Latin monoid*.

Let π be the inclusion of Σ to $\mathcal{M}$, i.e., $\pi : \Sigma \longrightarrow \mathcal{M}$, $\pi(a) = a$, for all $a \in \Sigma$. π can be extended to a unique morphism of monoids

$$fl : \Sigma^* \longrightarrow \mathcal{M}.$$

The set of *flat-words* over Σ, denoted $Fl(\Sigma)$ is the set of all fixed points of the morphism fl, i.e.,

$$Fl(\Sigma) = \{w \in \Sigma^* \mid fl(w) = w\}.$$

For instance, if $\Sigma = \{a, b\}$, then aba, $baba$ are in $Fl(\Sigma)$, but ab^3a, b^2a^2b are not in $Fl(\Sigma)$.

Note that the set of flat-words, $Fl(\Sigma)$, is exactly the set of all words free of square letters.

The *flat-image* of an word w is by definition the word $fl(w)$. For instance, $fl(ab^3a) = aba$, $fl(b^2a^2b) = bab$. If w is in $Fl(\Sigma)$ the flat-image of w is w.

Definition 43. Let $w = a_1^{i_1} a_2^{i_2} \ldots a_n^{i_n}$ be a nonempty word over Σ, where $a_i \in \Sigma$, $1 \leq i \leq n$ and $i_j \geq 1$, for all j, $1 \leq j \leq n$, and, moreover, a_{i_k} is different of $a_{i_{k+1}}$, for all $1 \leq k \leq n-1$. The *power* of w is the vector $(i_1, i_2, \ldots i_n)$.

$\qquad \square$

Definition 44. The *re-entrant order* or *r-order*, denoted $\leq_r$, is defined as

$$u \leq_r v \text{ iff } fl(u) = fl(v) \text{ and } p(u) \leq p(v),$$

where $u, v \in \Sigma^+$. (Here $p(u) \leq p(v)$ means the componentwise order between vectors of nonnegative integers.)

By definition, $\lambda \leq_r w$, for any $w \in \Sigma^*$.

$\square$

Remark 45. The relation $\leq_r$ is a partial order relation on Σ^* with the first element λ.

$\square$

Proposition 46. *(i) If $u_i \leq_r v_i$, $1 \leq i \leq n$, then $u_1 u_2 \ldots u_n \leq_r v_1 v_2 \ldots v_n$.*

(ii) If $u \leq_r v_1 v_2 \ldots v_n$, then there are u_i, $1 \leq i \leq n$, such that $u = u_1 u_2 \ldots u_n$ and $u_i \leq_r v_i$, $1 \leq i \leq n$.

(iii) If $u_1 u_2 \ldots u_n \leq_r v$, then there are v_i, $1 \leq i \leq n$, such that $v = v_1 v_2 \ldots v_n$ and $u_i \leq_r v_i$, $1 \leq i \leq n$.

$\square$

Now we introduce the main operation of this section, called the *re-entrant product*.

Definition 47. Let L be a language. The *down$_r$* mapping is defined as:

$$down_r(L) = \{u \mid u \leq_r v, \text{ for some } v \in L\}.$$

$\square$

Note that *down$_r$* is a closure operator.

Definition 48. Let u and v be words over Σ. The *re-entrant product* of u with v, denoted $u \bowtie v$ is:
$$u \bowtie v = down_r(u \sqcup\!\sqcup v).$$

The above operation is extended in the natural way to languages. If L_1 and L_2 are languages, then:

$$L_1 \bowtie L_2 = \bigcup_{u \in L_1, v \in L_2} u \bowtie v.$$

$\square$

Note that
$$L_1 \bowtie L_2 = down_r(L_1 \sqcup\!\sqcup L_2).$$

The re-entrant product is a monotonous operation in each argument.

Theorem 49. *The re-entrant product is a commutative and associative operation.*

□

Note that $\bowtie$ is distributive over union, but $\bowtie$ does not have a unit element. Thus we obtain:

Corollary 50. *Let Σ be an alphabet. The quadruple:*

$$H_r = (\mathcal{P}(\Sigma^*), \cup, \bowtie, \emptyset)$$

is a commutative hemiring (i.e., a semiring without unit element for the multiplication operation, see [13]).

□

The *re-entrant closure* of L is denoted by $L^{\bowtie}$. Note that

$$L^{\bowtie} = \bigcup_{k \geq 0} L^{k(\bowtie)},$$

where $L^{k(\bowtie)}$ denotes the re-entrant product of L with itself $(k-1)$-times, if $k \geq 2$. Moreover, $L^{0(\bowtie)} = \{\lambda\}$ and $L^{1(\bowtie)} = L$.

In the sequel we present some properties of the re-entrant product. For more details the reader is referred to [16].

Proposition 51. *Let L be a language.*

(i) $L^{\bowtie} = (down_r(L))^{\bowtie}$.
(ii) $L^{\bowtie} = (L^*)^{\bowtie}$.
(iii) $L^{\bowtie} = (L^{\sqcup \sqcup})^{\bowtie}$.

□

Proposition 52. *Let L, L_1, L_2 be languages.*

(i) $L^{\bowtie} \bowtie L^{\bowtie} = L^{\bowtie}$.
(ii) $(L_1^{\bowtie} \bowtie L_2^{\bowtie})^{\bowtie} = L_1^{\bowtie} \bowtie L_2^{\bowtie}$.
(iii) $(L_1 \cup L_2)^{\bowtie} = L_1^{\bowtie} \bowtie L_2^{\bowtie}$.
(iv) *If $\lambda \in L_1 \cap L_2$, then* $(L_1 L_2)^{\bowtie} = L_1^{\bowtie} \bowtie L_2^{\bowtie}$.

□

Proposition 53. *Let $\mathcal{A}$ be a full AFL.*

(i) $\mathcal{A}$ *is closed under the operator $down_r$.*

(ii) If $\mathcal{A}$ is closed under shuffle, then $\mathcal{A}$ is closed under the re-entrant product, $\bowtie$.

$\square$

Corollary 54. *The families of regular languages and of recursively enumerable languages are closed under the re-entrant product.*

$\square$

The family of context-free languages is not closed under the re-entrant product.

We present now some properties of the re-entrant closure. We will show that in many respects the re-entrant closure is different from the shuffle closure although, apparently, they seem to be closely related: $L^{\bowtie} = down_r(L^{\sqcup \sqcup})$.

The shuffle closure of a word can be a non-context-free language. However, this is not the case for the re-entrant closure of a word.

Theorem 55. *Let w be a word over some alphabet Σ. The re-entrant closure of w, $w^{\bowtie}$, is a regular language.*

$\square$

Definition 56. A language L is *strictly bounded* iff $L \subseteq a_1^* a_2^* \ldots a_n^*$ for some letters $a_1, a_2, \ldots, a_n$. A language L is *bounded* iff $L \subseteq w_1^* w_2^* \ldots w_n^*$ for some words $w_1, w_2, \ldots, w_n$.

$\square$

Theorem 57. *Let L be a strictly bounded language.*

(i) The language $down_r(L)$ is a regular language.
(ii) The language $L^{\bowtie}$ is a regular language.

$\square$

Note that in the above Theorem 57, the language L is an arbitrary language (L is not necessarily a recursively enumerable language) and still $down_r(L)$ and $L^{\bowtie}$ are regular languages. Moreover, observe that although L is a strictly bounded language, the language $L^{\bowtie}$ can be even unbounded.

We state one more property of the re-entrant product.

Theorem 58. *Let L be a language over an alphabet Σ. There exists a finite language F such that $L \bowtie \Sigma^* = F \bowtie \Sigma^*$.*

Proof. From Higman's Theorem, see [9], it follows that there is a finite language F such that $L \sqcup \sqcup \Sigma^* = F \sqcup \sqcup \Sigma^*$. Hence, $L \bowtie \Sigma^* = down_r(L \sqcup \sqcup \Sigma^*) = down_r(F \sqcup \sqcup \Sigma^*) = F \bowtie \Sigma^*$.

$\square$

8 Conclusion

Syntactic constraints based on the shuffle on trajectories provide a useful tool to the study of a variety of problems in the area of parallel computation and in the theory of concurrency.

This method offers a uniform and global approach to the problem of finding a parallel composition of languages, graphs or of more complex objects.

The problem of parallelization of languages and the problem of parallelization of algorithms are of a special interest. Shuffle on trajectories is a suitable theoretical framework to investigate these problems. The examples considered in Section 5 and the results from Section 4 deal only with context-free and regular languages. However, some other classes of languages can be studied in connection with this problem: locally testable languages, linear languages, deterministic context-free languages, etc.

The problem of parallelization can also be investigated for the Turing time and space complexity classes. Suitable parallelizations of problems can produce significant improvements with respect to the amount of time used by a (one processor) computer to solve the problem. In this case the problem can be solved faster on a parallel computer.

Many other aspects from the theory of concurrency and parallel computation, such as priorities, the existence of critical sections, communication, the use of re-entrant routines, are studied using semantic constraints on the shuffle operation. It seems that these aspects are more related to the inner structure of the shuffled words and cannot be investigated using only syntactic constraints. Perhaps the most useful and realistic types of constraints are mixed, i.e., both syntactic and semantic.

Further research should be done to extend these operations to more complex objects, such as graphs, networks or different types of automata. In this way one can obtain a more general framework to study the phenomena of parallelism and of concurrency.

References

1. T. Axford, *Concurrent Programming Fundamental Techniques for Real Time and Parallel Software Design*, John Wiley & Sons, New York, 1989.
2. J. C. M. Baeten and W. P. Weijland, *Process Algebra*, Cambridge University Press, 1990.
3. J. A. Bergstra and J. W. Klop, "Process Algebra for Synchronous Communication", *Information and Control*, 60 (1984), 109-137.
4. W. Brauer, *Automatentheorie*, B.G. Teubner, Stuttgart, 1984.
5. J. S. Golan, A. Mateescu and D. Vaida, "Semirings and Parallel Composition of Processes ", Journal of Automata, Languages and Combinatorics, to appear.
6. L. Guo, K. Salomaa and S. Yu, *Synchronization Expressions and Languages*, The University of Western Ontario London, Dept. of Comp. Sci., Technical Report 368, 1993.

7. T. Harju, M. Lipponen and A. Mateescu, "Flatwords and Post Correspondence Problem", *Theoretical Computer Science*, to appear.

8. M. Hennessy, *Algebraic Theory of Processes*, The MIT Press, Cambridge, Massachusetts, London, 1988.

9. G.H. Higman, "Ordering by divisibility in abstract algebras", *Proc. London Math. Soc.*, 3, (1952) 326-336.

10. L. Kari, *On insertion and deletion in formal languages*, PhD Thesis, University of Turku, Turku, Finland, 1991.

11. M. Kudlek and A. Mateescu, "Distributed Catenation and Chomsky Hierarchy", FCT'95, Dresden, 1995, Lecture Notes in Computer Science, LNCS 965, Springer-Verlag, 1995, 313-322.

12. M. Kudlek and A. Mateescu, "Rational and Algebraic Languages with Distributed Catenation", DLT'95, Magdeburg, 1995, in *Developments in Language Theory II*, eds. J. Dassow, G. Rozenberg and A. Salomaa, World Scientific, Singapore, 1996, 129-138.

13. W. Kuich and A. Salomaa, *Semirings, Automata, Languages*, EATCS Monographs on Theoretical Computer Science, Springer-Verlag, Berlin, 1986.

14. A. Mateescu, "On (Left) Partial Shuffle", *Results and Trends in Theoretical Computer Science*, LNCS 812, Springer-Verlag, (1994) 264-278.

15. A. Mateescu and A. Salomaa, "Formal Languages: an Introduction and a Synopsis", Chapter 1, in *Handbook of Formal Languages*, eds. G. Rozenberg and A. Salomaa, Springer-Verlag, to appear.

16. A. Mateescu and A. Salomaa, "Parallel Composition of Words with Re-entrant Symbols", TUCS Technical Report, 15, 1996.

17. A. Mateescu, K. Salomaa and S. Yu, "Decidability of Fairness for Context-Free Languages", submitted.

18. H. A. Maurer, G. Rozenberg and E. Welzl, "Using String Languages to Describe Picture Languages", *Information and Control*, 3, 54, (1982) 155-185.

19. R. Milner; *Communication and Concurrency*, Prentice Hall International, 1989.

20. A. Salomaa, *Formal Languages*, Academic Press, New York, 1973.

Unique Fixpoints in Complete Lattices with Applications to Formal Languages and Semantics

Ingbert Kupka

Institut für Informatik, Technische Universität Clausthal,
Erzstraße 1, D-38678 Clausthal-Zellerfeld, Germany
kupka@informatik.tu-clausthal.de

Abstract. Recursive definitions can be modeled either using complete partially ordered sets and applying least-fixpoint theorems or in the context of complete lattices and Tarski's fixpoint theorem which states that all fixpoints of a monotonic operator form a complete lattice, too. Uniqueness is analyzed independently by introducing a metric and looking for contraction properties or by special case analysis depending on application characteristics. We show how Tarski's approach can be extended by characterizing uniqueness. The obtained theorems generalize Arden's lemma related to linear equations of formal languages. Other applications are the uniqueness of equationally defined contextfree languages and of recursive program descriptions.

1 Recursive definitions and fixpoints

Recursively defined complex objects x can be studied as fixpoints of the corresponding definitional recursive equation $x = Tx$. The main fixpoint theories for discrete objects refer alternatively to ω-complete or complete partially ordered sets (ω-CPOs or CPOs, respectively), to complete lattices or to metric spaces. The existence of a solution can be derived from the monotony of the operator T. The least-fixpoint theorem guarantees the existence of a least fixpoint for CPOs, see Abramsky, Gabbay, Maibaum [1], p. 169. The proof is based upon transfinite induction in this case. Tarski's fixpoint theorem for complete lattices states that the set of solutions, which form a complete lattice, too, is not empty. An iterative construction for the least solution can be obtained for ω-continuous operators T. The fixpoint theorem of Kleene states this already for ω-CPOs, as shown in Manes, Arbib [3], p. 154 - 155, and Wechler [7], p. 78. Solution set characterizations are subject of the above mentioned fixpoint theorem of Tarski as well as of the special fixpoint theory of Manna and Shamir for recursive functions, which introduces and analyzes optimal and maximal fixpoints, too. Manna and Shamir have constructed many examples of ambigiuous recursive function definitions like

$$f(x,y) = \text{ if } x = 0 \text{ then } y \text{ else } f(f(x,y-1), f(x-1,y))$$

with the following partial functions on $\mathbb{N} \times \mathbb{N}$ ($\mathbb{N} = \{0, 1, 2, \ldots\}$) as solutions:

$f_0(x, y) = \textbf{if } x = 0 \textbf{ then } y,$
$f_1(x, y) = y,$
$f_2(x, y) = \max(x, y),$
$g_a(x, y) = \textbf{if } x = 0 \textbf{ then } y \textbf{ else } a(x), \text{ where } a(a(x)) = a(x).$

An introduction to this theory is given in Manna, Shamir [5]. An example of a recursive function definition for which the uniqueness is unknown gives the Ulam function defined by $f : \mathbb{N} - \{0\} \rightarrow \mathbb{N}$ and

$$f(x) = \begin{cases} 1 & \text{if } x = 1, \\ y & \text{if } x = 2y, \\ 3x + 1 & \text{else }. \end{cases}$$

Obviously $f(x) = 1$ is a solution. If it is the only one then the recursive evaluation process derived from the definition terminates for any number $x \in \mathbb{N} - \{0\}$.

Uniqueness can be derived in metric spaces for operators satisfying a metric contraction property. Special metrics have been introduced for discrete applications like formal langages as metric fixpoints, see Manes, Arbib [3]. Arden's lemma which states that the recursive equation for formal languages

$$X = A \cup BX$$

has the least fixpoint B^*A and no other fixpoint if the empty word doesn't belong to B gives an example of another kind of characterizing uniqueness, cf. Manna [4], p. 6.

An analysis of the uniqueness of recursive definitions could help integrating semantic aspects of modeling — which may lead to least or greatest or optimal fixpoints — and constructive aspects of computation or verification.

2 Fixpoints in complete lattices

For developing a general fixpoint theory for complete lattices we start with the fundamental theorem of Tarski, see Tarski [6].

Theorem 1 ((Tarski)). *Let $(A, \cap, \cup)$ be a complete lattice with partial order $\leq$, $T : A \rightarrow A$ a monotonic operator and P the set of all fixpoints of T, i.e.*

$$P = \{x \in A \mid x = T(x)\}.$$

Then the following propositions hold:

(1) P is not empty.
(2) The partial order $\leq$ defines operations $\cap, \cup$ on P such that $(P, \cap, \cup)$ is a complete lattice.
(3) $\bigcup_{T(y) \geq y} y = \bigcup_{x \in P} x$ defines the maximal element p_{max} of P.

(4) $\bigcap_{T(y) \le y} y = \bigcap_{x \in P} x$ defines the minimal element p_{min} of P.

The main idea of the proof is to show that for the element

$$p = \bigcup_{T(y) \ge y} y,$$

— which is welldefined because the minimum element belongs to the set $\{y \mid T(y) \ge y\}$ — we have $T(p) \ge p$ and $T(p) \in \{y \mid T(y) \ge y\}$ and thus $T(p) \le p$ and finally $T(p) = p$.

For all fixpoints an inclusion property holds:

Theorem 2. *Let $(A, \cap, \cup)$ be a complete lattice with partial order $\le$, minimum element $\bot$ and maximum element $\top$ and let $T : A \to A$ be a monotonic operator and p any fixpoint of T. Then*

$$q_\infty \le p \le q^\infty$$

holds for

$$q_\infty = \bigcup_{i=0}^{\infty} T^i(\bot), \quad q^\infty = \bigcap_{i=0}^{\infty} T^i(\top).$$

If T satisfies the condition $T(\bigcup_i x_i) = \bigcup_i T(x_i)$ for ω-chains $x_0 \le x_1 \le x_2 \ldots$ then q_∞ is the least fixpoint. Conversely, if T satisfies the condition $T(\bigcap_i x_i) = \bigcap_i T(x_i)$ for ω-chains $x_0 \ge x_1 \ge x_2 \ldots$ then q^∞ is the greatest fixpoint.

Proof. Let $q_i = T^i(\bot)$, $q^i = T^i(\top)$ for $i \ge 0$. Then

$$\bot = q_0 \le p \le q^0 = \top$$

holds and from the monotony of T follows

$$q_i \le p \le q^i \text{ for all } i \ge 0$$

by induction. Applying the definitions of supremum $\cup$ and infimum $\cap$ leads to the inclusion formula. The additional conditions allow the application of Kleene's fixpoint theorem and thus q_∞ and q^∞ represent the least and the greatest fixpoint, respectively. □

Clearly, if q_∞ and q^∞ coincide then there is only one fixpoint. Thus by characterizing this special case we get a sufficient but not necessary condition for the uniqueness of the fixpoint.

Theorem 3. *Let $(A, \cap, \cup)$ be a complete lattice with minimum element $\bot$ and maximum element $\top$ and let $T : A \to A$ be a monotonic operator such that there are decompositions*

$$T^k(\top) = T^k(\bot) \cup s_k \text{ for } k \ge 0$$

satisfying

$$\bigcap_{k=0}^{\infty} (x \cup s_k) = x \text{ for any } x \in A.$$

Then T possesses exactly one fixpoint.

Proof. Let the elements q_i and q^i for $i \geq 0$ be defined like above. Then the decomposition condition reads

$$q^k = q_k \cup s_k \text{ for } k \geq 0.$$

By definition of q_∞ we get

$$q_k \leq q_\infty \text{ and } q_k \cup s_k \leq q_\infty \cup s_k \text{ for all } k \geq 0$$

and hence

$$q^k \leq q_\infty \cup s_k \text{ for all } k \geq 0.$$

Infinite intersection and application of the additional property of the decomposition gives

$$q^\infty = \bigcap_{k=0}^{\infty} q^k \leq \bigcap_{k=0}^{\infty} (q_\infty \cup s_k) = q_\infty$$

and thus

$$q^\infty \leq q_\infty.$$

By application of theorem 2 follows $q_\infty = p = q^\infty$ for any fixpoint p of T. $\square$

We can prove Arden's lemma using this theorem. The formal languages over an alphabet Σ form a complete lattice with $\bot = \emptyset$ and $\top = \Sigma^*$ and with the set-theoretical operations. The decomposition for $T^k(\top)$ with respect to $T(X) = A \cup BX$ reads

$$T^k(\Sigma^*) = T^k(\emptyset) \cup B^k \Sigma^* \text{ for } k \geq 0.$$

Obviously, for any word x there is no word except x belonging to all sets $\{x\} \cup B^k \Sigma^*$ if $\varepsilon \notin B$. By application of theorem 3 follows that there is only one fixpoint

$$\bigcap_{k=0}^{\infty} T^k(\Sigma^*) = \bigcup_{k=0}^{\infty} T^k(\emptyset) = B^* A.$$

If $\varepsilon \in B$ then $B^+ = B^*$ and thus

$$A \cup B(B^* W) = A \cup B^* W = B^* W$$

holds for any W with $A \subseteq W \subseteq \Sigma^*$. The set

$$\{B^* W \mid A \subseteq W \subseteq \Sigma^*\}$$

is the set of all fixpoints in this case.

We obtain two further theorems by specialization. The first one describes a variant of theorem 3 and can be applied to lattices the elements of which are subsets of a given set. The second gives a sufficient condition for fulfilling the main condition (3) of the theorem.

Theorem 4. *Let $(A, \cap, \cup)$ be a complete lattice with minimum element $\perp$ and maximum element $\top$ satisfying the infinite join-distribution law*

$$\bigcap_{y \in M} (x \cup y) = x \cup \bigcap_{y \in M} y \text{ for any subset } M \subseteq A \text{ and any element } x \in A$$

and let $T : A \to A$ be an operator for which the following conditions hold:

(1) $T(x \cup y) = T(x) \cup T(y)$ *for all $x, y \in A$,*
(2) $T(x) = T(\perp) \cup S(x)$ *for some operator S and all $x \in A$,*
(3) $\bigcap_{k=0}^{\infty} S^k(\top) = \perp$ *for the operator S of (2).*

Then T possesses exactly one fixpoint.

Proof. The monotony of T follows from (1). The decomposition formula

$$T^k(\top) = T^k(\perp) \cup S^k(\top)$$

is proven by induction applying (1) and (2). For this decomposition the conditions of theorem 3 are fulfilled. □

Generalizing the main idea of the proof of Arden's lemma we find a sufficient condition for $\bigcap_{k=0}^{\infty} S^k(\top) = \perp$.

Definition 5. Let $(A, \cap, \cup)$ be a complete lattice with minimum element $\perp$. We call an operator $S : A \to A$ *increasing* if there exists a mapping $\mu : A \to \mathbb{N} \cup \{\infty\}$ satisfying

(1) $\mu(\bigcap_{i=0}^{\infty} x_i) \geq \max_i(\mu(x_i))$ for any ω-chain $x_0 \geq x_1 \geq \ldots$,
(2) $\mu(x) = \infty$ iff $x = \perp$,
(3) for each $x \in A$ exists $k \in \mathbb{N} - \{0\}$ such that $\mu(S^k(x)) > \mu(x)$.

In the lattice $(2^{\Sigma^*}, \cap, \cup)$ the operator S defined by

$$S(X) = BX, \ B \subseteq \Sigma^*, \ \varepsilon \notin B$$

is increasing, because the conditions (1), (2) and (3) hold for S and

$$\mu(x) = \begin{cases} \infty & \text{if } X = \emptyset \\ \min_{w \in X} |w| & \text{if } X \neq \emptyset \end{cases}.$$

The mapping μ can be applied for constructing a metric

$$d(X, Y) = 2^{-\mu((X-Y) \cup (Y-X))}.$$

This illustrates the connection with metric approaches to fixpoint theory as presented in Manes, Arbib [3].

Obviously, for an increasing operator S with mapping μ we get

$$\mu\left(\bigcap_{i=0}^{\infty} S^i(\top)\right) \geq m \text{ for any } m \in \mathbb{N}$$

and hence

$$\mu\left(\bigcap_{i=0}^{\infty} S^i(\top)\right) = \infty \text{ and } \bigcap_{i=0}^{\infty} S^i(\top) = \bot.$$

This leads to

Theorem 6. *An increasing operator* $S : A \to A$ *on a complete lattice with minimum element* $\bot$ *and maximum element* $\top$ *satisfies*

$$\bigcap_{i=0}^{\infty} S^i(\top) = \bot.$$

3 Contextfree languages as unique fixpoints

Each contextfree grammar corresponds with a recursive system of equations for the languages L_X derived from the nonterminals X such that the language defined by the grammar corresponds with the least-fixpoint solution of the equations. For example, the grammar

$$S \to aA,$$
$$A \to b, \ A \to Sb,$$

which defines the language $L_S = \{a^n b^n \mid n \geq 1\}$, corresponds with the equations (writing S and A instead of L_S and L_A)

$$S = \{a\}A,$$
$$A = \{b\} \cup S\{b\}$$

with the unambiguous solution

$$S = \{a^n b^n \mid n \geq 1\},$$
$$A = \{a^n b^{n+1} \mid n \geq 0\}.$$

If we add the ineffective rule $A \to A$ to the grammar, then the corresponding equational system has the infinite solution set $\{(S_W, A_W)\}_W$ with

$$S_W = \bigcup_{n \geq 0} \{a^{n+1}\}W\{b^n\}, \qquad A_W = \bigcup_{n \geq 0} \{a^n\}W\{b^n\},$$

where $\{b\} \subseteq W \subseteq \Sigma^*$ and $\Sigma \supseteq \{a, b\}$ is the terminal alphabet. For proving that the equations

$$S = \{a\}A,$$
$$A = \{b\} \cup S\{b\}$$

possess a unique solution, we apply theorem 3 as follows:
Let $\Sigma \supseteq \{a, b\}$ be the terminal alphabet. We take the lattice $(2^{\Sigma^*} \times 2^{\Sigma^*}, \cap, \cup)$

with the lattice operations defined componentwise. $(\emptyset, \emptyset)$ and (Σ^*, Σ^*) are the minimum and the maximum element. The operator T reads

$$T(X_1, X_2) = (\{a\}X_2, \{b\} \cup X_1\{b\}).$$

We can decompose $T(X_1, X_2)$ by

$$T(X_1, X_2) = T(\emptyset, \emptyset) \cup S(X_1, X_2) = (\emptyset, \{b\}) \cup S(X_1, X_2),$$
$$S(X_1, X_2) = (\{a\}X_2, X_1\{b\}).$$

S is increasing because the conditions of definition 5 are fulfilled with

$$\mu(X_1, X_2) = \begin{cases} \infty & \text{if } X_1 \cup X_2 = \emptyset, \\ \min_{w \in X_1 \cup X_2} |w| & \text{else} \end{cases}.$$

By theorem 6 and theorem 4 follows the uniqueness of the fixpoint.

The grammar

$$S \to ab, \; S \to aSb, \; S \to SS$$

gives an example for an ambiguous fixpoint solution in Σ^* and a unique fixpoint solution in Σ^+. The ambiguity in Σ^* follows form the fact that Σ^* is a solution different from the least fixpoint. For the uniqueness in Σ^+ one can apply again theorem 6 and theorem 4.

The next theorem gives a more general result. See also the corresponding theorem based upon a metric in Manes, Arbib [3]. We assume for a contextfree grammar, that each nonterminal symbol occurs at the lefthandside of some production rule.

Theorem 7. *Let G be an ε-free contextfree grammar without unit productions (of the form $A \to B$, where A, B are nonterminal symbols). Then the corresponding equational system has a unique fixpoint in $(2^{\Sigma^+})^r$, $r = |V|$.*

Proof. Let $V_1, V_2, \ldots, V_r$ be the nonterminals, $S = V_1$ and $V_i \to \alpha_{ij}$, $i = 1, \ldots, r$, $j = 1, \ldots, m_i$, the production rules. In the equational form we consider the terms α_{ij} as functions $\alpha_{ij}(V)$, $V = (V_1, V_2, \ldots, V_r)$. Thus the operator T is defined by

$$T(V_1, \ldots, V_r) = \left(\bigcup_{j=1}^{m_1} \alpha_{1j}(V), \ldots, \bigcup_{j=1}^{m_r} \alpha_{rj}(V) \right).$$

For simplification we substitute the functions $\alpha_{ij}(V)$, $i = 1, \ldots, r$, $j = 1, \ldots, m_i$, by functions β_{i0} and $b_{ij}(V)$, $i = 1, \ldots, r$, $j = 1, \ldots, n_i$, with constants β_{i0}, corresponding to the terminal rules $A \to t$, $t \in A$, or $\beta_{i0} = \emptyset$, such that all $\beta_{ij}(V)$, $j > 0$, contain an occurrence of some nonterminal. Now the operator has the form

$$T(V_1, \ldots, V_r) = \left(\beta_{10} \cup \bigcup_{j=1}^{n_1} \beta_{1j}(V), \ldots, \beta_{r0} \cup \bigcup_{j=1}^{n_r} \beta_{rj}(V) \right).$$

This leads to the decomposition

$$T(V_1, \ldots, V_r) = T(\emptyset, \ldots, \emptyset) + S(V_1, \ldots, V_r),$$
$$T(\emptyset, \ldots, \emptyset) = (\beta_{10}, \ldots, \beta_{r0}),$$
$$S(V_1, \ldots, V_r) = \left(\bigcup_{j=1}^{n_1} \beta_{1j}(V), \ldots, \bigcup_{j=1}^{n_r} \beta_{rj}(V) \right).$$

Defining

$$\mu(V) = \mu(V_1, \ldots, V_r) = \begin{cases} \infty & \text{for } V_1 \cup \ldots \cup V_r = \emptyset \\ \min_{w \in V_1 \cup \ldots \cup V_r} |w| & \text{else} \end{cases}$$

we can prove that S is increasing.

As a consequence of theorem 7 any grammar in Chomsky normal form has the fixpoint uniqueness property.

4 Uniqueness of recursive descriptions of while-loops

Formal semantics of programs can be described by relations $r \subseteq S \times S$ where S denotes the set of program states. This approach extends the functional description using functions $f : S \to S$, such that nondeterministic programming is included and the semantics of flowchart-like programs can be based upon regular structures in the sense of the *Kleene algebra* as introduced in Kozen [2] which generalizes regular sets over an alphabet as well as binary relations on a set.

Let the semantics of basic statements A be described by corresponding relations r_A and that of programming conditions $C : S \to \{TRUE, FALSE\}$ by pairs of relations

$$r_C = \{(s, s) \mid C(s) = TRUE\}, \; r_{\bar{C}} = \{(s, s) \mid C(s) = FALSE\}.$$

Then sequences $A; B$ of statements are described by

$$r_{A;B} = r_A r_B$$

— applying the relational product — and branching reads

$$r_{\text{ if } C \text{ then } A \text{ else } B \text{ fi}} = r_C r_A \cup r_{\bar{C}} r_B.$$

Program loops have recursive descriptions. The **while**-loop is described recursively by

$$r_{\text{while } C \text{ do } A \text{ od}} = r_C r_A r_{\text{while } C \text{ do } A \text{ od}} \cup r_{\bar{C}}.$$

If the basic relations represent (deterministic) functions, then the least fixpoint of such a recursive description also represents a function. In the case of the **while**-loop this solution reads

$$r_{\text{while } C \text{ do } A \text{ od}} = (r_C r_A)^* r_{\bar{C}}.$$

The general form of the recursive equation equals that of Arden's lemma.

If the **while**-loop always terminates, then for each state $s \in S$ exists $n \in \mathbb{N}$ such that $(s, s') \in r_A{}^n$ implies $(s', s') \in r_C^-$. We show that the conditions of theorem 4 hold:

$(2^{S \times S}, \cap, \cup)$ is a complete lattice with $\bot = \emptyset$ and $\top = S \times S$. (1) holds trivially, (2) is valid for $S(X) = r_C r_A X$. For proving (3) we assume that there exists a pair $(s, s') \in (r_C r_A)^n S \times S$ for any n. Thus for any n there is a sequence $s_0, s_1, \ldots, s_n$ such that $s_0 = s$ and $(s_i, s_i) \in r_C$, $(s_i, s_{i+1}) \in r_A$. But this was excluded by the termination condition for the **while**-loop. Application of theorem 4 yields the uniqueness of the solution. If, however, there exists a state s such that $(s, s) \in r_C r_A$, i. e. $(s, s) \in r_C$ and $(s, s) \in r_A$, then

$$r' = (r_C r_A)^* r_C^- \cup \{(s, s)\}$$

is a solution of the recursive equation different from the minimal one. To show this we insert r in the equation, this yields r' again, and observe that $(s, s) \in (r_C r_A)^* r_C^-$ is impossible, because $r_C \cap r_C^- = \emptyset$.

For example, the program

$$\textbf{while } n > 0 \textbf{ do } n := n * n \textbf{ od}$$

related to states $n \in N$ defines the following two solutions of the corresponding recursive equation:

$$r_0 = (r_{n>0} r_{n:=n*n})^* r_{n=0} = \{(0, 0)\}$$

and

$$r_1 = \{(0, 0), (1, 1)\}.$$

The important fact to be derived from such examples is that in general the recursive description of a program may be satisfied by different solutions.

References

1. Abramsky, S., Gabbay, D.M., and Maibaum, T.S.E. (eds.): Handbook of Logic in Computer Science, Vol. 1: Background: Mathematical Structures, Oxford University Press, 1992
2. Kozen, D.C.: The Design and Analysis of Algorithms, Springer, 1992
3. Manes, E.G., and Arbib, M.A.: Algebraic Approaches to Program Semantics, Springer, 1986
4. Manna, Z.: Mathematical Theory of Computation, McGraw-Hill Computer Science Series, 1974
5. Manna, Z., and Shamir, A.: The Optimal Approach to Recursive Programs, Comm. ACM, Vol. 20, Nr. 11, 1977, pp.824-831
6. Tarski, A.: A lattice-theoretical fixpoint theorem and its applications, Pacific Journal of Mathematics, 1955, pp. 285-309
7. Wechler, W.: Universal Algebra for Computer Scientists, in: W. Brauer, G. Rozenberg, A. Salomaa (eds.), EATCS Monographs on Theoretical Computer Science, Springer, 1992

On Abstract Families of Languages, Power Series, and Elements

Georg Karner[1] and Werner Kuich[2]

[1] Alcatel Austria AG, Wien, Austria
[2] Abteilung für Theoretische Informatik
Institut für Algebra und Diskrete Mathematik
Technische Universität Wien

Abstract. We generalize the characterization of abstract families of languages by abstract families of acceptors to continuous semirings: Abstract families of elements are now characterized by automata representing a certain type.

1 Introduction

In Kuich [5], the notions of "abstract family of languages" (briefly AFL) and "abstract family of power series" (briefly AFP) were generalized to "abstract family of elements" (briefly AFE, also called AFL-semiring). Due to the fact that the identity mapping on the set of formal languages over an infinite alphabet Σ_∞ is not a rational transduction, some important results of AFL theory are not implied by the AFE theory of Kuich [5]. (See the discussion preceding Lemma 1 below.) In Kuich [6], the author showed how the results and proofs of AFE theory are parallel to those of AFL theory (see, e. g., Theorem 7.22, Theorem 7.25 and Corollary 7.27 of Kuich [6]). But still, AFE theory was not a genuine generalization of AFL theory.

In our paper, we alter some definitions of Kuich [5] and [6] in such a manner that now AFE theory is a genuine generalization of AFL theory.

The main result of our paper is an automata-theoretic characterization of AFEs that applies also to full AFLs, AFLs, full AFPs, and AFPs. It is a generalization of the characterization of full AFLs and AFLs by abstract families of acceptors (see Ginsburg [2]).

It is assumed that the reader is familiar with semiring theory. Notions and notations that are not defined are taken from Kuich [6]. But observe again that some of our definitions below (such as "closed under matricial composition", "$\mathfrak{H}$-A'-family of elements") differ from those in Kuich [5, 6]. It is this difference that allows us to establish our results in full generality.

In the sequel, A will always be a *continuous* semiring. This is a complete and naturally ordered semiring such that, for all index sets I and all families $(a_i \mid i \in I)$ the following condition is satisfied:

$$\sum_{i \in I} a_i = \sup\{\sum_{i \in E} a_i \mid E \subseteq I, E \text{ finite}\}.$$

Here "sup" denotes the least upper bound with respect to the natural order (see Goldstern [3], Sakarovitch [8], and Karner [4]).

A subset $\bar{A}$ of A is called *fully rationally closed* if for all $a \in \bar{A}$, we have $a^* := \sum_{i \geq 0} a^i \in \bar{A}$. By definition, $\mathfrak{Rat}(A')$ is the smallest fully rationally closed subsemiring of A containing $A' \subseteq A$. Furthermore, the collection of the components of the least solutions of all A'-algebraic systems, where A' is a fixed subset of A, is denoted by $\mathfrak{Alg}(A')$.

Given $A' \subseteq A$, we define $[A'] \subseteq A$ to be the least complete subsemiring of A that contains A'. The semiring $[A']$ is called the *complete semiring generated by* A'. Each element a of $[A']$ can be generated from elements of A' by multiplication and summation (including "infinite summation"):

$$a \in [A'] \quad \text{iff} \quad a = \sum_{i \in I} a_{i1} \ldots a_{in_i},$$

where I is an index set, $a_{ij} \in A'$ and $n_i \geq 0$.

From now on, A' will be a fixed subset of A with $0, 1 \in A'$. Moreover, we assume that $[A'] = A$. Furthermore we make the notational convention that all sets Q, possibly provided with indices, are finite and nonempty, and are subsets of some fixed countably infinite set Q_∞ with the following property: if $q_1, q_2 \in Q_\infty$ then $(q_1, q_2) \in Q_\infty$.

Consider the family of all semiring morphisms $h : A \to A^{Q \times Q}$, $Q \subset Q_\infty$, Q finite, and let $\mathfrak{H}$ be a nonempty subfamily of this family. Then we define the subset $[\mathfrak{H}]$ of A as follows. For $h \in \mathfrak{H}$, $h : A \to A^{Q \times Q}$, let $B_h = [\{h(a)_{q_1,q_2} \mid a \in A, q_1, q_2 \in Q\}]$. Then $[\mathfrak{H}] = \bigcup_{h \in \mathfrak{H}} B_h$. A family of morphisms $\mathfrak{H}$ is called *closed under matricial composition* if the following conditions are satisfied for arbitrary morphisms $h : A \to A^{Q \times Q}$ and $h' : A \to A^{Q' \times Q'}$ in $\mathfrak{H}$ (observe the difference with Kuich [5, 6]):

(i) $A' \subseteq [\mathfrak{H}]$.
(ii) For each $a \in [\mathfrak{H}]$ there is an $h_a \in \mathfrak{H}$ with $h_a(a) = a$.
(iii) If $\bar{Q} \subset Q_\infty$ and there exists a bijection $\pi : \bar{Q} \to Q$, then $\bar{h} : A \to A^{\bar{Q} \times \bar{Q}}$, defined by $\bar{h}(a)_{q_1,q_2} = h(a)_{\pi(q_1),\pi(q_2)}$ for all $a \in A$, $q_1, q_2 \in \bar{Q}$, is in $\mathfrak{H}$.
(iv) The functional composition $h \circ h' : A \to A^{(Q' \times Q) \times (Q' \times Q)}$ is again in $\mathfrak{H}$.
(v) If $Q \cap Q' = \emptyset$ then the mapping $h + h' : A \to A^{(Q \cup Q') \times (Q \cup Q')}$ defined by

$$(h + h')(a) = \begin{pmatrix} h(a) & 0 \\ 0 & h'(a) \end{pmatrix}, \quad a \in A,$$

where the blocks are indexed by Q and Q', is again in $\mathfrak{H}$.

(This definition differs from that in Kuich [5]: Conditions (i) and (iii) are new, condition (ii) is changed: it replaces the condition that the identity mapping $e : A \to A$ is in $\mathfrak{H}$.)

From now on, we assume that $\mathfrak{H}$ is a non-empty family of *complete A'-rational* semiring morphisms that is closed under matricial composition.

Next we deal with properties of $[\mathfrak{H}]$ and denote $\mathfrak{B} = \{B_h \mid h \in \mathfrak{H}\}$.

Lemma 1 $\mathfrak{B}$ *is directed by set inclusion and for every finite* $F \subseteq [\mathfrak{H}]$ *there exists an* $h \in \mathfrak{H}$ *such that* $F \subseteq B_h$.

Proof. Consider $B_{h_1}, B_{h_2} \in \mathfrak{B}$, where $h_1 : A \to A^{Q_1 \times Q_1}$ and $h_2 : A \to A^{Q_2 \times Q_2}$. Assume that $Q_1 \cap Q_2 = \emptyset$ by (iii). Then $B_{h_1}, B_{h_2} \subseteq B_{h_1 + h_2}$. From this, $F \subseteq B_h$ follows directly. $\square$

Theorem 2 $[\mathfrak{H}]$ *is a fully rationally closed semiring.*

Proof. Since $A' \subseteq [\mathfrak{H}]$, we infer that $0, 1 \in [\mathfrak{H}]$. The closure of $[\mathfrak{H}]$ under addition and multiplication follows from Lemma 1. Now consider $a \in [\mathfrak{H}]$. Then there is a $B \in \mathfrak{B}$ with $a \in B$. Since B is a complete subsemiring of A, $a^* \in B \subseteq [\mathfrak{H}]$. $\square$

An $\mathfrak{H}$-A'-*rational transducer* is a tuple $\mathfrak{T} = (Q, h, S, P)$ where $h : A \to A^{Q \times Q}$ is in $\mathfrak{H}$, $S \in \mathfrak{Rat}(A')^{1 \times Q}$, $P \in \mathfrak{Rat}(A')^{Q \times 1}$. The transducer defines a mapping $\|\mathfrak{T}\| : A \to A$ by

$$\|\mathfrak{T}\|(a) = Sh(a)P, \qquad a \in A.$$

A mapping $\tau : A \to A$ is called an $\mathfrak{H}$-A'-*rational transduction* if there exists an $\mathfrak{H}$-A'-rational transducer $\mathfrak{T}$ such that $\tau(a) = \|\mathfrak{T}\|(a)$ for all $a \in A$.

An $\mathfrak{H}$-A'-*family of elements* is just a subset of $[\mathfrak{H}]$. (This definition differs from that in Kuich [5] and [6] where arbitrary subsets of $[A'] = A$ are considered.)

Let $\mathfrak{L}$ be an $\mathfrak{H}$-A'-family of elements. We define

$$\mathfrak{M}(\mathfrak{L}) = \{\tau(a) \mid a \in \mathfrak{L}, \tau : A \to A \text{ is an } \mathfrak{H}\text{-}A'\text{-rational transduction}\}.$$

Note that we always have $\mathfrak{L} \subseteq \mathfrak{M}(\mathfrak{L})$ by (ii). The family $\mathfrak{L}$ is said to be *closed* under $\mathfrak{H}$-A'-*rational transductions* if $\mathfrak{M}(\mathfrak{L}) \subseteq \mathfrak{L}$.

The notation $\mathfrak{F}(\mathfrak{L})$ is used for the smallest fully rationally closed subsemiring of A that is closed under $\mathfrak{H}$-A'-rational transductions and contains $\mathfrak{L}$. Note that $\mathfrak{M}(\mathfrak{L}) \subseteq \mathfrak{F}(\mathfrak{L})$. (We have tried to use in our notation letters customary in AFL theory to aid the reader familiar with this theory. See Ginsburg [2].)

An $\mathfrak{H}$-A'-family of elements $\mathfrak{L}$ is called $\mathfrak{H}$-A'-*abstract family of elements* (briefly $\mathfrak{H}$-A'-AFE) if $\mathfrak{F}(\mathfrak{L}) \subseteq \mathfrak{L}$.

Example 1. (Formal power series) Let the basic semiring be $A\langle\langle \Sigma_\infty^* \rangle\rangle$, where A is a commutative continuous semiring and Σ_∞ is an infinite alphabet, and $A' = A\{\Sigma_\infty \cup \varepsilon\}$.

(i) Choose $\mathfrak{H}$ to be the family of rational representations. By Theorem 7.11 of Kuich [6], $\mathfrak{H}$ is closed under matricial composition. It is easy to see that $[\mathfrak{H}] = A\{\{\Sigma_\infty^*\}\}$. Then the subsets of $[\mathfrak{H}]$ are families of power series, and the $\mathfrak{H}$-A'-AFEs are just the full abstract families of power series (full AFPs) in the sense of Kuich [6].

(ii) Choose $\mathfrak{H}$ to be the family of regulated rational representations. By Theorems 6.12, 6.14 and 9.6 of Kuich, Salomaa [7], $\mathfrak{H}$ is closed under matricial composition. Again we obtain $[\mathfrak{H}] = A\{\{\Sigma_\infty^*\}\}$ and the $\mathfrak{H}$-A'-AFEs are just the AFPs in the sense of Kuich, Salomaa [7].

Example 2. (Formal languages) Formal power series are a generalization of formal languages. Choose in Example 1 A to be the Boolean semiring $\mathbb{B}$. Consider $\mathfrak{P}(\Sigma_\infty^*)$ which is isomorphic to $\mathbb{B}\langle\langle\Sigma_\infty^*\rangle\rangle$. Families of power series are now called families of languages. A full AFP or an AFP, respectively, obtained in this way is called a full abstract family of languages (full AFL, see Berstel[1], Section III.7) or an AFL (see the a-transducers of Ginsburg [2] that are ε-output bounded under non-ε input).

2 An automata-theoretic characterization of abstract families of elements

The $\mathfrak{H}$-A'-abstract families of elements will now be characterized. We assume $\mathfrak{H}$ to be fixed. Recall that, by our convention, $\mathfrak{H}$ is a non-empty family of complete A'-rational semiring morphisms that is closed under matricial composition.

We start with some general observations about $\mathfrak{H}$-A'-AFEs. First, we consider two important special cases. An auxiliary result is needed.

Lemma 3 *Let A'' be an arbitrary subset of A. Then $\mathfrak{Alg}(A'') \subseteq [A'']$.*

Proof. Assume $a \in \mathfrak{Alg}(A'')$ as given and consider an A''-algebraic system $y_i = p_i$, $i = 1, \ldots, n$ with least solution σ such that $\sigma_1 = a$. Denote the approximation sequence associated to it by $(\sigma^j \mid j \in \mathbb{N})$. Now consider the algebraic system in $[A'']$ where $[A'']$ is considered partially ordered by its own natural order $\sqsubseteq_{A''}$. (Some care is necessary here since a complete subsemiring of a continuous semiring is *not* continuous, in general, cf. Karner [4], Fact 5.1. So we cannot be sure that our A''-algebraic system has a solution in $[A'']$ at all.) Then all σ^j, $j \in \mathbb{N}$, are in $[A'']^n$. Furthermore, σ^j is monotonic, cf. Kuich and Salomaa [7], Lemma 14.4. Thus by the definition of $\sqsubseteq_{A''}$ there is a sequence of column vectors $(\tau^j \mid j \in \mathbb{N})$ with $\tau^j \in [A'']^n$ such that $\sigma^0 = \tau^0$, $\sigma^{j+1} = \sigma^j + \tau^{j+1}$, $j \in \mathbb{N}$. So $\sigma = \sum_{j \in \mathbb{N}} \tau^j \in [A'']^n$ by Kuich [6], Theorems 3.2 and 3.6. $\square$

Theorem 4 $\mathfrak{Rat}(A')$ *and* $\mathfrak{Alg}(A')$ *are* $\mathfrak{H}$-A'-AFEs.

Proof. By Kuich [6], Theorem 7.17, it suffices to show that $\mathfrak{Alg}(A') \subseteq [\mathfrak{H}]$. Assume $a \in \mathfrak{Alg}(A')$ as given and consider an A'-algebraic system $y_i = p_i$, $i = 1, \ldots, n$ with least solution σ such that $\sigma_1 = a$. Denote the set of coefficients of p_i by $F_i \subseteq A'$ and set $F = F_1 \cup \ldots \cup F_n$. Note that F is finite and that our A'-algebraic system is in fact an F-algebraic system. By Lemmas 3 and 1, $a = \sigma_1 \in [F] \subseteq [\mathfrak{H}]$. $\square$

Recall that every $\mathfrak{H}$-A'-AFE $\mathfrak{L}$ satisfies $\mathfrak{Rat}(A') \subseteq \mathfrak{L}$ by definition. Thus by Theorem 4, $\mathfrak{Rat}(A')$ is the smallest $\mathfrak{H}$-A'-AFE.

The following definitions are taken from Kuich [6]. In the sequel, $\Delta = \{\mathbf{a} \mid a \in A\} \cup Z$ is an alphabet. Here $\{\mathbf{a} \mid a \in A\}$ is a copy of A and Z is an infinite alphabet of variables. A multiplicative monoid morphism $h : \Delta^* \to A^{Q \times Q}$ is *compatible with* $\mathfrak{H}$ if the following conditions are satisfied:

(i) The mapping $h' : A \to A^{Q \times Q}$ defined by $h'(a) = h(\mathbf{a})$, $a \in A$, is a complete A'-rational semiring morphism in $\mathfrak{H}$,

(ii) $h(\mathbf{a}), h(z) \in \mathfrak{Rat}(A')^{Q \times Q}$ for $a \in A'$, $z \in Z$, and $h(z) = 0$ for almost all variables $z \in Z$.

If $h : \Delta^* \to A^{Q \times Q}$ is compatible with $\mathfrak{H}$ and if $h_1 : A \to A^{Q_1 \times Q_1}$ is a complete A'-rational semiring morphism in $\mathfrak{H}$ then $h_1 \circ h : \Delta^* \to A^{(Q \times Q_1) \times (Q \times Q_1)}$ is again compatible with $\mathfrak{H}$.

We introduce now the notions of a *type* T, a *T-matrix*, a *T-automaton* and the *automaton representing* T. Intuitively speaking this means the following. A T-automaton is a finite automaton with an additional working tape, whose contents are stored in the states of the T-automaton. The type T of the T-automaton indicates how information can be retrieved from the working tape. For instance, pushdown automata can be viewed as automata of a specific type.

A *type* is a quadruple

$$(\Gamma_T, \Delta_T, T, \pi_T),$$

where

(i) Γ_T is the set of *storage symbols*,

(ii) $\Delta_T \subseteq \{\mathbf{a} \mid a \in A'\} \cup Z$ is the alphabet of *instructions*,

(iii) $T \in (\mathbb{N}^\infty \{\Delta_T\})^{\Gamma_T^* \times \Gamma_T^*}$ is the *type matrix*,

(iv) $\pi_T \in \Gamma_T^*$ is the *initial content of the working tape*.

In the sequel we often speak of the type T if Γ_T, Δ_T and π_T are understood.

A matrix $M \in (\mathfrak{Rat}(A')^{Q \times Q})^{\Gamma_T^* \times \Gamma_T^*}$ is called a *T-matrix* if there exists a monoid morphism $h : \Delta^* \to A^{Q \times Q}$ that is compatible with $\mathfrak{H}$ such that $M = h(T)$. If $M = h(T)$ is a T-matrix and $h' : A \to A^{Q' \times Q'}$ is a complete A'-rational semiring morphism in $\mathfrak{H}$ then, by the first remark after Kuich [6], Theorem 7.16 and by [6], Theorem 7.3, $h' \circ h$ is compatible with $\mathfrak{H}$ and $h'(M) = h'(h(T))$ is again a T-matrix.

A *T-automaton*

$$\mathfrak{A} = (Q, \Gamma_T, M, S, \pi_T, P)$$

is defined by

(i) a finite set Q of *states*,

(ii) a T-matrix M, called the *transition matrix*,

(iii) $S \in \mathfrak{Rat}(A')^{1 \times Q}$, called the *initial state vector*,

(iv) $P \in \mathfrak{Rat}(A')^{Q \times 1}$, called the *final state vector*.

Observe that Γ_T and π_T are determined by T. The *behavior* of the T-automaton $\mathfrak{A}$ is given by

$$\|\mathfrak{A}\| = S(M^*)_{\pi_T, \varepsilon} P.$$

We define now the set

$$\mathfrak{Rat}_T(A') = \{\|\mathfrak{A}\| \mid \mathfrak{A} \text{ is a } T\text{-automaton}\} \subseteq A.$$

Observe that in the definitions of a T-matrix, of a T-automaton and of $\mathfrak{Rat}_T(A')$, A' and $\mathfrak{H}$ are implicitly present.

It will turn out that $\mathfrak{Rat}_T(A')$ is an $\mathfrak{H}$-A'-AFE if T is a restart type. Here a type $(\Gamma_T, \Delta_T, T, \pi_T)$ is called a *restart type* if $\pi_T = \varepsilon$ and the non-null entries of T satisfy the conditions $T_{\varepsilon,\varepsilon} = z^0 \in Z$, $T_{\varepsilon,\pi} \in \mathbb{N}^\infty\{Z - \{z^0\}\}$, $T_{\pi,\pi'} \in \mathbb{N}^\infty\{\Delta_T - \{z^0\}\}$ for all $\pi \in \Gamma_T^+$, $\pi' \in \Gamma_T^*$, and for some distinguished instruction $z^0 \in \Delta_T$. Observe that the working tape is empty at the beginning of the computation.

Now we want to show that $\mathfrak{Rat}_T(A')$ is an $\mathfrak{H}$-A'-AFE.

Theorem 5 (Kuich [5], Theorems 4.2, 4.3, 4.4, 4.5) *If T is a restart type then $\mathfrak{Rat}_T(A')$ is a fully rationally closed semiring containing $\mathfrak{Rat}(A')$ and closed under $\mathfrak{H}$-A'-rational transductions.* □

Theorem 6 *If T is a restart type then $\mathfrak{Rat}_T(A')$ is a $\mathfrak{H}$-A'-AFE.*

Proof. By Theorem 5, we have only to show that $\mathfrak{Rat}_T(A') \subseteq [\mathfrak{H}]$. Assume that $a = S(M^*)_{\pi_T,\varepsilon} P$. By Lemma 1, there are B_S and $B_P \in \mathfrak{B}$ containing the entries of S and P, respectively. Similarly, for every $z \in Z$, there is $B_Z \in \mathfrak{B}$ containing all entries of $h(z)$, $z \in Z$. Moreover, $B_h \in \mathfrak{B}$ contains all entries of all $h(\mathbf{a})$, $a \in A$. Now by Lemma 1 there is a $B_0 \in \mathfrak{B}$ containing B_S, B_P, B_h, and all B_z, $z \in Z$, with $h(z) \neq 0$. (Note that we only have to consider finitely many B_z, $z \in Z$.) Then $a \in B_0 \subseteq [\mathfrak{H}]$. □

In order to get a complete characterization of $\mathfrak{H}$-A'-AFEs we need a result "converse" to Theorem 6. Let $\mathfrak{L} \subseteq [\mathfrak{H}]$ be an $\mathfrak{H}$-A'-AFE. Then we construct a restart type T such that $\mathfrak{L} = \mathfrak{Rat}_T(A')$. The construction will be relative to a fixed $\mathfrak{R} \subseteq \mathfrak{L}$ with $\mathfrak{F}(\mathfrak{R}) = \mathfrak{L}$. For each $b \in \mathfrak{R}$ there exists an index set I_b such that $b = \sum_{i \in I_b} a_{i1} \ldots a_{in_i}$, $a_{ij} \in A'$, i. e.,

$$\mathfrak{R} = \{b \mid b = \sum_{i \in I_b} a_{i1} \ldots a_{in_i}\}.$$

The restart type $(\Gamma_T, \Delta_T, T, \varepsilon)$ is defined by

(i) $\Gamma_T = \bigcup_{b \in \mathfrak{L}} \Delta_b$, where $\Delta_b = \{\mathbf{a}_b \mid a \in A'\}$ is a copy of A' for $b \in \mathfrak{R}$,

(ii) $\Delta_T = \{\mathbf{a} \mid a \in A'\} \cup \{z^0\} \cup \{z_b \mid b \in \mathfrak{R}\}$,

(iii) $T \in (\mathbb{N}^\infty\{\Delta_T\})^{\Gamma_T^* \times \Gamma_T^*}$, where the non-null entries of T are
$T_{\varepsilon,\varepsilon} = z^0$,
$T_{\varepsilon,\mathbf{a}_b} = z_b$ for $\mathbf{a}_b \in \Delta_b$, $b \in \mathfrak{R}$,
$T_{\pi\mathbf{a}_b, \pi\mathbf{a}_b\mathbf{a}'_b} = \mathbf{a}$ for $\pi \in \Delta_b^*$, $\mathbf{a}_b, \mathbf{a}'_b \in \Delta_b$, $b \in \mathfrak{R}$,
$T_{\pi\mathbf{a}_b, \varepsilon} = (\sum 1)\mathbf{a}$ for $\pi \in \Delta_b^*$, $\mathbf{a}_b \in \Delta_b$, $b \in \mathfrak{R}$, where the summation ranges over all $i \in I_b$ such that $(\mathbf{a}_{i1})_b \ldots (\mathbf{a}_{in_i})_b = \pi\mathbf{a}_b$.

(Observe that in the last two lines of (iii), "multiplicities" are counted; this was missed in Kuich [5] and [6].)

Theorem 7 $\mathfrak{Rat}_T(A') = \mathfrak{L}$.

Proof. We first compute $(T^*)_{\varepsilon,\varepsilon}$. By the proof of Kuich [6], Theorem 7.22,

$$(T^*)_{\varepsilon,\varepsilon} = \left(z^0 + \sum_{b \in \mathcal{L}} \sum_{i \in I_b} z_b \mathbf{a}_{i1} \dots \mathbf{a}_{in_i} \right)^*.$$

We show now $\mathcal{L} \subseteq \mathfrak{Rat}_T(A')$. Fix a $b \in \mathfrak{R}$. Since $\mathfrak{R} \subseteq \mathcal{L} \subseteq [\mathfrak{H}]$ and $\mathfrak{H}$ is closed under matricial composition, there is an $h_b \in \mathfrak{H}$ with $h_b(b) = b$. Let now $h : \Delta^* \to A^{2 \times 2}$ be the monoid morphism defined by

$$h(\mathbf{a}) = \begin{pmatrix} h_b(a) & 0 \\ 0 & h_b(a) \end{pmatrix}, \ a \in A, \qquad h(z_b) = \begin{pmatrix} 0 & 1 \\ 0 & 0 \end{pmatrix},$$

$$h(z_{b'}) = h(z^0) = 0 \text{ for } b' \in \mathfrak{R}, \ b' \neq b.$$

Since $\mathfrak{H}$ is closed under matricial composition, h is compatible with $\mathfrak{H}$.

We obtain

$$h((T^*)_{\varepsilon,\varepsilon}) = \left(\sum_{i \in I_b} \begin{pmatrix} 0 & 1 \\ 0 & 0 \end{pmatrix} \begin{pmatrix} h_b(a_{i1} \dots a_{in_i}) & 0 \\ 0 & h_b(a_{i1} \dots a_{in_i}) \end{pmatrix} \right)^*$$

$$= \begin{pmatrix} 0 & h_b(b) \\ 0 & 0 \end{pmatrix}^* = \begin{pmatrix} 1 & b \\ 0 & 1 \end{pmatrix}$$

and infer that $b \in \mathfrak{Rat}_T(A')$. Hence, $\mathfrak{R} \subseteq \mathfrak{Rat}_T(A')$. Since $\mathfrak{Rat}_T(A')$ is an $\mathfrak{H}$-A'-AFE, we obtain $\mathcal{L} = \mathfrak{F}(\mathfrak{R}) \subseteq \mathfrak{Rat}_T(A')$.

Conversely, we show now $\mathfrak{Rat}_T(A') \subseteq \mathcal{L}$. Assume $a \in \mathfrak{Rat}_T(A')$. Then there exists a monoid morphism $h : \Delta^* \to A^{Q \times Q}$ compatible with $\mathfrak{H}$, and $S \in \mathfrak{Rat}(A')^{1 \times Q}$, $P \in \mathfrak{Rat}(A')^{Q \times 1}$ such that $a = Sh((T^*)_{\varepsilon,\varepsilon})P$. Consider now the entries of this matrix product: The entries of $h(\mathbf{b})$, S, P, $h(z^0)$, and $h(z_b)$ are in $\mathcal{L}$. Since only finitely many $h(z_b)$ are unequal to zero, the entries of $h(z^0) + \sum_{b \in \mathcal{L}} h(z_b)h(\mathbf{b})$ are in $\mathcal{L}$. Since $\mathcal{L}$ is fully rationally closed, the entries of $h((T^*)_{\varepsilon,\varepsilon})$ are in $\mathcal{L}$ by Kuich [6], Theorem 4.7. This implies $a \in \mathcal{L}$. $\square$

We have now achieved our main result of this section, a complete characterization of $\mathfrak{H}$-A'-closed semirings.

Corollary 8 *A semiring $\mathcal{L}$ is an $\mathfrak{H}$-A'-AFE iff there exists a restart type T such that*

$$\mathcal{L} = \mathfrak{Rat}_T(A').$$

We now turn to formal power series, cf. Example 1(i).

Corollary 9 *A family of power series $\mathcal{L}$ is a full AFP iff there exists a restart type T such that $\mathcal{L} = \mathfrak{Rat}_T(A\{\Sigma_\infty \cup \varepsilon\})$.*

A similar result holds for formal languages, cf. Example 2.

Corollary 10 *A family of languages $\mathcal{L}$ is a full AFL iff there exists a restart type T such that $\mathcal{L} = \mathfrak{Rat}_T(\{\{x\} \mid x \in \Sigma_\infty \cup \{\varepsilon\}\})$.*

By Example 1(ii), Theorem 11.43 of Kuich, Salomaa [7] dealing with AFPs (and, if $A = \mathbb{B}$, with AFLs) is now a specialization of Corollaries 11 and 12, respectively (in case A is continuous).

Corollary 11 *A family of power series $\mathfrak{L}$ is an AFP iff there exists a restart type $(\Gamma_T, \Delta_T, T, \varepsilon)$, where $\Delta_T \subseteq \{\mathbf{a} \mid a \in A\{\{\Sigma_\infty^*\}\}, (a, \varepsilon) = 0\}$ such that $\mathfrak{L} = \mathfrak{Rat}_T(A\{\Sigma_\infty \cup \varepsilon\})$.*

Proof. The proofs of Theorem 5, i. e., of Theorems 4.2, 4.3, 4.4, 4.5 of Kuich [5], and of Theorem 6 do not depend on the form of Δ_T. Moreover, by Theorem 11.31 and Corollary 11.33 of Kuich, Salomaa [7], each AFP is generated by a family of quasiregular power series. Hence, in the construction of the type T of Theorem 7, symbols $\mathbf{a}$, where $(a, \varepsilon) \neq 0$, are not needed. □

Observe that the T-automata of Corollary 11 are cycle-free by Theorem 6.10 of Kuich, Salomaa [7].

Corollary 12 *A family of languages $\mathfrak{L}$ is an AFL iff there exists a restart type $(\Gamma_T, \Delta_T, T, \varepsilon)$, where $\Delta_T \subseteq \{\mathbf{a} \mid a \in \mathfrak{L}(\Sigma_\infty^*), a \cap \{\varepsilon\} = \emptyset\}$ such that $\mathfrak{L} = \mathfrak{Rat}_T(\{\{x\} \mid x \in \Sigma_\infty \cup \{\varepsilon\}\})$.*

Our final example shows that our approach is a literal generalization of Kuich [6].

Corollary 13 *Assume that $\mathfrak{H}$ contains the identity mapping $e : A \to A$. Then a subset $\mathfrak{L}$ of A is an $\mathfrak{H}$-A'-AFE iff there exists a restart type T such that $\mathfrak{L} = \mathfrak{Rat}_T(A')$.*

Proof. Just note that the assumption about $\mathfrak{H}$ implies $[\mathfrak{H}] = A$. □

References

1. Berstel, J.: Transductions and Context-Free Languages. Teubner, 1979.
2. Ginsburg, S.: Algebraic and Automata-Theoretic Properties of Formal Languages. North-Holland, 1975.
3. Goldstern, M.: Vervollständigung von Halbringen. Diplomarbeit, Technische Universität Wien, 1985.
4. Karner, G.: On limits in complete semirings. Semigroup Forum 45(1992) 148–165.
5. Kuich, W.: The algebraic equivalent of AFL theory. ICALP95, Lect. Notes Comput. Sci. 944(1995) 39–50.
6. Kuich, W.: Semirings and formal power series: Their relevance to formal languages and automata theory. In: G. Rozenberg and A. Salomaa, eds., Handbook of Formal Languages. Springer, to appear.
7. Kuich, W., Salomaa, A.: Semirings, Automata, Languages. EATCS Monographs on Theoretical Computer Science, Vol. 5. Springer, 1986.
8. Sakarovitch, J.: Kleene's theorem revisited. Lect. Notes Comput. Sci. 281(1987) 39–50.

Are There Formal Languages Complete for *SymSPACE*(log *n*)?

Klaus-Jörn Lange

Wilhelm-Schickard-Institut für Informatik, Universität Tübingen
Sand 13, D72076 Tübingen

Abstract. This article discusses the existence of *SymSPACE*(log *n*)–complete formal languages. It is shown that a recent approach of Alvarez and Greenlaw to define symmetric versions of one-way devices doesn't lead to *SymSPACE*(log *n*)–complete problems when applied to linear context-free or to one-counter languages.

1 Introduction

Investigating the fundamental relation of determinism and nondeterminism the intermediate concept of symmetry has been introduced by Lewis and Papadimitriou [8]. While nondeterminism and symmetry are easily seen to be equivalent for time bounded classes, the case of space bounded computations seems to be more difficult. It is not known whether the inclusion $SymSPACE(\log n) \subseteq NSPACE(\log n)$ is strict or not. There are results indicating that these two classes should be different. Several interesting problems are complete for symmetric space, the most important example being $UGAP$, the connectivity problem for undirected graphs [2,8].

There are many close connections between formal languages (defined by one-way devices) and complexity classes. But these in most cases pertain to nondeterministic and to deterministic classes. Unfortunately, it seems hard to relate the concept of symmetry, which is apparently based on two-way devices, with formal languages, which are built on models with a one-way input. In a recent report, Alvarez and Greenlaw introduced symmetry for one-way finite automata [2]. As a first result of this paper, the complexity of this model is determined. Second, their concept is extended to two families of formal languages related to the class $NSPACE(\log n)$. It turns out that in neither of the two cases we get a characterization of $SymSPACE(\log n)$, but stay at $NSPACE(\log n)$ or come down to NC^1.

2 Preliminaries

For notions of formal languages or complexity theory the reader is referred to standard text books. For the circuit class NC^1 and its relationship to the regular languages we refer to the work of Barrington [4].

2.1 Formal Languages and Complexities

There are characterizations for relevant complexity classes in terms of families of formal languages in the way that a family of formal languages $\mathcal{A}$ is contained in a complexity class $\mathcal{B}$ and that $\mathcal{A}$ contains a $\mathcal{B}$–complete language. For example, the family of regular languages REG corresponds to the class NC^1 [4], both the linear context-free languages LIN and the one-counter languages characterize the class $NSPACE(\log n)$ [6,13,14], the context-free languages CFL are related to the class $NAuxPDA\text{-}TISP(pol, \log n)$ [15], and the indexed languages are representative fot the class NP [12]. Via deterministic one-way automata or grammars restricted by LL(k)- or LR(k)–conditions these relations carry over to the corresponding deterministic classes. But nothing like that is known for symmetry.

3 Symmetry

The intuition behind the idea of symmetry is to allow to go computational steps backwards. Symmetry is a restricted type of nondeterminism and is able to simulate determinism because of the tree-like structure of deterministic configuration graphs. To define this concept formally needs some care. Lewis and Papadimitriou used Turing machines which have something like working heads of width two. We avoid to go into these details and refer the reader to the article of Lewis and Papadimitriou [8]. We will use terms like symmetric time or symmetric space and notations like $SymSPACE(\log n)$ or $SymTISP(f, g)$, the later denoting the class of all languages recognized by symmetric machines which are simultaneously time bounded by $O(f)$ and space bounded by $O(g)$. By Lewis and Papdimitriou we know:

Theorem 1. *Nondeterministic time coincides with symmetric time.*

It is unknown whether the inclusion of symmetric space in nondeterministic space is strict.

The reachability problem for undirected graphs is $SymSPACE(\log n)$–complete [8]. A collection of further complete problems is contained in the compendium of Alvarez and Greenlaw [2].

There are results indicating that in case of space bounded classes symmetric computations are more restricted than nondeterministic ones. None of the following inclusions of $SymSPACE(\log n)$ is known to hold for $NSPACE(\log n)$:

Theorem 2. a) $SymSPACE(\log n) \subseteq \bigoplus SPACE(\log n)$ [7]
b) $SymSPACE(\log n) \subseteq SC^2$ [10]
c) $SymSPACE(\log n) \subseteq DSPACE(\log^{4/3} n)$ [3]
d) $SymSPACE(\log n) \subseteq CREW\text{-}TIME(\log n \log \log n)$ [5]

Analyzing Savitch's algorithm, Lewis and Papadimitriou were able to show the following relationship:

Theorem 3. $NTISP(f, g) \subseteq SymTISP(f \cdot g, g \cdot \log f)$

In particular, $NSPACE(\log n)$ is contained in $SymTISP(pol, \log^2 n)$, the symmetric analogue of SC^2. It is interesting to compare this inclusion with Nisan's result $SymSPACE(\log n) \subseteq SC^2 = DTISP(pol, \log^2 n)$.

Applying the ideas used in Theorem 3 to the algorithm of Lewis, Stearns, and Hartmanis instead to that of Savitch, the equivalence of nondeterminism and symmetry for polynomially time bounded auxiliary pushdown automata will be shown in [1]:

Theorem 4. $NAuxPDA\text{-}TISP(pol, \log n) = SymAuxPDA\text{-}TISP(pol, \log n)$

This result is not restricted to logarithmic space and polynomial time bounds, but holds in general if space bounds and time bounds are in an exponential relation.

3.1 Formal Languages and Symmetry

We now want to consider the possibilities of characterizing symmetric complexity classes in terms of formal languages. For time bounded classes there is no need to do so because of Theorem 1. Neither, this is necessary for polynomially time bounded auxiliary pushdown automata, i.e.: the class $LOG(CFL)$ [15], because of Theorem 4.

The class NC^1 is characterized by the regular languages [4]. Since deterministic and nondeterministic finite automata are equivalent, there seems to be no need to look for characterizations of symmetry. On the other hand, the relation "determinism $\leq$ symmetry $\leq$ nondeterminism" is valid only in the two-way case. and there was up to now no notion of a symmetric finite automaton with one-way input. A definition of this notion was given by Alvarez and Greenlaw [2]. They introduced symmetric finite automata by adding dual transitions, but without reverting the direction of the reading head. That is, an NFA $A = (Q, \Sigma, \delta, q_0, Q_f)$ with $\delta \subseteq Q \times \Sigma \times Q$ is *symmetric* iff with each $(p, a, q) \in \delta$ also (q, a, p) is an element of δ. Alvarez and Greenlaw were able to show that the emptiness for symmetric finite automata is indeed $SymSPACE(\log n)$–complete.

Observe that the languages accepted by symmetric finite automata are a proper subfamily of REG. In particular, no finite regular language containing a nonempty word can be symmetric. This indicates that this version is a strong restriction not able to simulate determinism. Nevertheless, the membership-problem of symmetric finite automata keeps the complexity of the whole class REG:

Theorem 5. *There exists a symmetric finite automaton which accepts a language with an NC^1-complete membership problem.*

Proof: Consider the DFA $A = (Q, \Sigma, \delta, id, \{id\})$ where $Q := \Sigma := S_5$, the group of all permutations over five elements, id is the identity, and δ is defined by $\delta(\pi, \sigma) := \sigma \circ \pi$, i.e.: from permutation π reading permutation σ we enter the composition of π followed by σ. Barrington showed that A accepts an NC^1-complete language [4]. A first idea now could be to augment A by the reversals

128

of all transitions. But the resulting symmetric automaton no longer represents S_5 since it would be necessary to mirror a transition $\delta(\pi,\sigma) = \rho$ by $\delta(\rho,\sigma^{-1}) = \pi$ instead of $\delta(\rho,\sigma) = \pi$ in order to preserve the structure of the S_5.

Instead we will use the following easy trick, which will be used several times throughout the paper. The simple idea is to intertwine all the words of a language with a new symbol a. We set $B := (Q' := Q_a \cup Q, \Sigma' := \Sigma \cup \{a\}, \delta', id, \{id\})$, where a is a new input symbol, Q_a a copy of Q, and δ' is defined by $\delta'(\pi, a) := \pi_a$ and $\delta'(\pi_a, \sigma) := \delta(\pi, \sigma)$ for $\pi \in Q$ and $\sigma \in \Sigma$. $\delta'(\pi_a, a)$ and $\delta'(\pi, \sigma)$ are undefined. If we define the monomorphism $h : \Sigma^* \longrightarrow (\Sigma \cup \{a\})^*$ by $h(\sigma) := a\sigma$, we have $L(B) = h(L(A))$. Since h is one-to-one, $L(B)$ is NC^1-complete.

Now let C be the symmetric closure of A, i.e.: $C = (Q', \Sigma', \tau, id, \{id\})$, where τ is the defined by $\tau := \{(p, b, \delta(p, b)) | p \in Q', b \in \Sigma'\} \cup \{(\delta(p, b), b, p) | p \in Q', b \in \Sigma'\}$. Clearly, every word accepted by C using a reversed transition of the type $(\delta(p, b), b, p)$ must contain a subword in $\Sigma^2 \cup \{aa\}$ and thus $L(C) \cap (a\Sigma)^* = L(B)$. Hence, $L(C)$ is NC^1-complete, as well. $\qquad\square$

After discussing the situation for the classes NP, $LOG(CFL)$, and NC^1, the case of nondeterministic space remains to be treated. The class $NSPACE(\log n)$ is characterized by two well-known subclasses of CFL: the counter languages and the linear context-free languages. The latter coincide with the languages accepted by pushdown automata which make only one turn. But we will consider the representation by grammars since this will make our treatment easier. In the following we extend the approach of Alvarez and Greenlaw to these two families of formal languages.

We will have two possibilities to define symmetry with respect to the access of the pushdown store. In the *crossed version* we let the reversal of a transition which pushes a symbol or increments a counter be one which pops this symbol from the stack or decrements the counter. Since in the Alvarez and Greenlaw approach this principle is not applied to the input head, we also consider the *straight version* in which the reversal of a push (or increment) stays a push (or increment) and the reversal of a pop (or decrement) is a pop (or decrement).

One-Counter Languages We now consider nondeterministic counter automata with emptiness test. These are also called iterated counter automata. In order to investigate symmetric versions of these, we use them in the following normal form. The set of transitions of a counter automaton $A = (Q, \Sigma, \tau, q_0, Q_f)$ consists in four sets of transitions $\tau = (\tau_r, \tau_i, \tau_d, \tau_e)$. $\tau_r \subseteq Q \times \Sigma \times Q$ contains the *reading transitions* which neither test nor change the counter. All other transitions do not move the input head. $\tau_i \subseteq Q \times Q$ contains the *incrementing transitions* which cause the counter to be incremented by one. $\tau_d \subseteq Q \times Q$ contains the *decrementing transitions* which decrement the counter by one. The decrementing transitions can only be executed if the counter is nonempty. $\tau_e \subseteq Q \times Q$ contains the *emptiness tests*. A transition $(p, q) \in \tau_e$ can only be used if the counter is empty. We don't need explicit tests for nonemptiness since these could be simulated by a decrement followed by an increment.

As usual, a configuration of a counter automaton is a triple (p, i, w) where p is the actual state, i the current value of the counter, and w the remaining input to be read.

The following definition of symmetry for counter automata is given in the two versions described above: one changing the direction of the pushdown head when reversing a transition and one keeping the direction of the pushdown head.

Definition 6. a) A counter automaton $A = (Q, \Sigma, (\tau_r, \tau_i, \tau_d, \tau_e), q_0, Q_f)$ is called *symmetric in the crossed version* or *crossed symmetric* if we have

$$(p, a, q) \in \tau_r \text{ implies } (q, a, p) \in \tau_r, (p, q) \in \tau_i \text{ implies } (q, p) \in \tau_d,$$

$$(p, q) \in \tau_d \text{ implies } (q, p) \in \tau_i, \text{ and } (p, q) \in \tau_e \text{ implies } (q, p) \in \tau_e.$$

b) A counter automaton $A = (Q, \Sigma, (\tau_r, \tau_i, \tau_d, \tau_e), q_0, Q_f)$ is called *symmetric in the straight version* or *straight symmetric* if we have

$$(p, a, q) \in \tau_r \text{ implies } (q, a, p) \in \tau_r, (p, q) \in \tau_i \text{ implies } (q, p) \in \tau_i,$$

$$(p, q) \in \tau_d \text{ implies } (q, p) \in \tau_d, \text{ and } (p, q) \in \tau_e \text{ implies } (q, p) \in \tau_e.$$

We will now show that these two versions of symmetric counter automata behave differently w.r.t. complexity. While crossed symmetry stays $NSPACE(\log n)$–complete, straight symmetry allows only for the acceptance of regular languages. To show the hardness in the crossed case we first exhibit an example of a restricted counter automaton accepting an $NSPACE(\log n)$–complete language.

Lemma 7. *There is counter automaton* $A = (Q, \Sigma, (\tau_r, \tau_i, \tau_d, \tau_e), q_0, Q_f)$ *accepting an $NSPACE(\log n)$–complete language fulfilling the following properties: a) No valid computation of A contains two or more successive nonreading steps. In particular, this means that a state reached by a nonreading transition can only be left by reading transitions. b) For each nonreading transition $(p, q) \in \tau_i \cup \tau_d \cup \tau_e$ there is no other transition in τ leading to q.*

Proof: We follow the usual construction [14]. The language accepted by A represents the reachability problem for topologically sorted, acyclic graphs where the inner nodes have outdegree two. A graph will be accepted if there is a path from node v_0 to v_n where v_n is the last node in the order. A will also accept inputs not following this paradigm, but not well-presented graphs without that path. An inner node v_i with its two successors v_j and v_k will be represented by a word $b^i c b^j c b^k d$. The graph is given by the sorted sequence of these words followed by the suffix $b^n e$. For lack of space we give no proof but instead give the exact construction of A, only. $Q := \{q_0, q_1, \cdots, q_{12}\}$, $\Sigma := \{b, c, d, e\}$, $Q_f := \{q_{12}\}$, $\tau_r :=$ $\{(q_0, c, q_1), (q_0, c, q_4), (q_0, e, q_{12}), (q_1, c, q_3), (q_2, b, q_1), (q_3, b, q_3), (q_3, d, q_7), (q_4, b, q_4),$ $(q_4, c, q_5), (q_5, d, q_7), (q_6, b, q_5), (q_7, b, q_8), (q_8, b, q_8), (q_8, c, q_8)(q_8, d, q_7), (q_9, b, q_{10}),$ $(q_{11}, b, q_{10})\}$, $\tau_i := \{(q_1, q_2), (q_5, q_6)\}$, $\tau_d := \{(q_7, q_9), (q_{10}, q_{11})\}$, $\tau_e := \{(q_{10}, q_0)\}$. $\square$

Theorem 8. *There is a counter automaton which is symmetric in the crossed version recognizing an $NSPACE(\log n)$–complete language.*

Proof: Let $A = (Q, \Sigma, (\tau_r, \tau_i, \tau_d, \tau_e), q_0, Q_f)$ be the counter automaton of the previous lemma. We will now apply the trick used in Theorem 5 on A, intertwining $L(A)$ with a new terminal symbol a. Set $B := (Q' := Q_a \cup Q, \Sigma' := \Sigma \cup \{a\}$, $\tau' := (\tau'_r, \tau_i, \tau_d, \tau_e), q_0, Q_f)$ where Q_a is a copy of Q and $\tau'_r := \{(p, a, p_a) | p \in Q\} \cup \{(p_a, b, q) | (p, b, q) \in \tau_r\}$. Using again the monomorphism $h : \Sigma^* \longrightarrow \Sigma'^*$ defined by $h(b) := ab$, we have $L(B) = h(L(A))$. Since h is one-to-one, $L(B)$ is $NSPACE(\log n)$-complete. In addition, B still fulfills the properties of Lemma 7.

We now consider the crossed symmetric closure of B: set $C := (Q', \Sigma', \hat{\tau} := (\hat{\tau}_r, \hat{\tau}_i, \hat{\tau}_d, \hat{\tau}_e), q_0, Q_f)$ where $\hat{\tau}_r := \tau'_r \cup \{(q, b, p) | (p, b, q) \in \tau'_r\}$, $\hat{\tau}_i := \tau_i \cup \tau_d^{-1}$, $\hat{\tau}_d := \tau_d \cup \tau_i^{-1}$, and $\hat{\tau}_e := \tau_e \cup \tau_e^{-1}$. Clearly we have $L(B) \subseteq L(C)$. Now consider a computation R of C accepting some word v in $(a\Sigma)^*$. Obviously, as in Theorem 5, R cannot use any reversal of a reading transition since only the reading transitions switch between the states of Q and of Q_a. Otherwise, the input has to contain a subword in $\Sigma^2 \cup \{aa\}$. But if R contains a reversal (q, p) of a non-reading transition (p, q) we know by the construction that q has been reached by (p, q) or by the inverse of a reading transition. Hence, the only way R could have reached q was using (p, q). But by construction of crossed symmetry, (p, q) and (q, p) cancel each other and can be removed from R resulting in a valid computation accepting v. The last possibility to consider is that C leaves the initial state by the inverse of a nonreading transition. But a simple case analysis shows that this either will end in a cancellation as above or will lead to the acceptance of an element not in $(a\Sigma)^*$. In total, we get $L(C) \cap (a\Sigma)^* = L(B)$ which gives us the $NSPACE(\log n)$–completeness of $L(C)$. □

While crossed symmetry of counter automata leads to the same complexity of the word problem as unrestricted nondeterminism, straight symmetry is a strong restriction and diminishes the complexity from $NSPACE(\log n)$ down to NC^1 since now only regular languages can be accepted.

Theorem 9. *Languages accepted by counter automata which are symmetric in the straight version are regular and hence in NC^1.*

Proof: Let $A = (Q, \Sigma, (\tau_r, \tau_i, \tau_d, \tau_e), q_0, Q_f)$ be symmetric in the straight version. We now construct a nondeterministic (not symmetric) finite automaton $A' = (Q', \Sigma, \tau', q'_0, Q'_f)$ which accepts $L(A)$. The idea is to use the fact that in a straight symmetric automaton every increment or decrement (p, q) can be repeated using the reversed transition to $(p, q)(q, p)(p, q)$ and so on. Instead of increasing or decreasing by one we can now add or subtract an arbitrary odd number. The state set of A' is $Q' := Q \times \{0, 1\} \times \{i, d, e\}$. The second component of a state $\langle p, x, y \rangle$ will represent the value of the counter modulo 2. The third component will mark the type of the last preceding nonreading transition. $q'_0 := \langle q_0, 0, e \rangle$, $Q'_f := Q_f \times \{0, 1\} \times \{i, d, e\}$, and τ' is set to be the following union:

$$\{(\langle p, x, y \rangle, a, \langle q, x, y \rangle) | (p, a, q) \in \tau_r, x \in \{0, 1\}, y \in \{i, d, e\}\} \cup$$

$$\{(\langle p, x, y \rangle, \langle q, 1 - x, i \rangle) | (p, q) \in \tau_i, x \in \{0, 1\}, y \in \{i, d, e\}\} \cup$$

$$\{(\langle p, x, y \rangle, \langle q, 1 - x, d \rangle) | (p, q) \in \tau_d, x \in \{0, 1\}, y \in \{i, d\}\} \cup$$

$$\{((\langle p, 0, y \rangle, \langle q, 0, e \rangle)) \mid (p, q) \in \tau_e, y \in \{d, e\}\}.$$

The construction assures that a decrement cannot be applied when the last preceding nonreading transition was a successful test for emptiness. Further on, a test cannot be successfully passed if the last preceding nonreading transition was an increment or if the counter contains an odd value.

Clearly we have $L(A) \subseteq L(A')$ since every accepting computation of A can be mimicked in A' by forgetting the counter. To get the other inclusion it is sufficient to show the following: if there is a path of A' leading from a state $\langle p, 0, e \rangle$ to a state $\langle q, x, y \rangle$ while reading the input word $v \in \Sigma^*$ then there is a valid computation $(p_0, i_0, w_0) \vdash (p_1, i_1, w_1) \cdots \vdash (p_n, i_n, w_n)$ of A such that $(p_0, i_0, w_0) = (p, 0, v)$, $p_n = q$, w_n is the empty word, and $x = i_n$ modulo 2. The proof is done by induction over k, the length of the path of A'.

The statement obviously holds for $k = 1$. Now let there be a path in A' of length $k + 1$ leading from $\langle p, 0, e \rangle$ to $\langle q, x, y \rangle$ reading the word v. Further on, let $\langle p', x', y' \rangle$ be the state in this path reached after k steps. There is a decomposition $v = v'a$ where v' is read during the first k steps, and a is the empty word or an element of Σ depending of the type of the transition of the last step. By induction we know that there is a valid computation of A leading from configuration $(p, 0, v)$ to configuration (p', i, a) for some i reading the word v'. If the last transition of A' mimicks an element of τ_r or of τ_i then obviously the computation of A reaching (p', i, a) can be extended as claimed in the statement. This is also true if we simulate an element of τ_d and $i > 0$. If $i = 0$, i.e.: the counter is empty, then by construction we know that the last state in this computation with a third component unequal d must have a third component i, but not e, since there is no way in A' from a third component e directly to a d. There is always an i in between. But by replacing in the existing computation of A this increment step S by the sequence S followed by the reversal of S followed by S we can increase the value of the counter by two compared to the original computation. Repeating this process we can change the value of the counter by an arbitrary even number so that we can finally extend the modified computation by the decrement. Further on, there is no test for emptiness after S so we obtain a valid computation of A.

The last case to consider is that A' mimicks an element T of τ_e. In this case we know $x = x' = 0$ and hence i is even. If $i = 0$ we consistently can extend the computation of A by T. Let's assume $i > 0$. By construction we then know that y' is either d or e. But if it were e the last nonreading transition would have been a successfully passed test for emptiness which contradicts $i > 0$. Hence $y' = d$ and the last nonreading transition was a decrement. Using the method described above we can decrease the value of the counter by an arbitrary even number which finally leads us to an empty counter where we successfully can apply T. Since there is no decrement after T, the modified computation is valid.

$\square$

Linear Languages We now consider linear grammars. We will always assume them to be in normal form, that is a production is of the form $A \to a$, $A \to aB$, or $A \to Ba$. The two versions of symmetry now look as follows:

Definition 10. a) A linear grammar $G = (V, \Sigma, P, S)$ is called *symmetric in the crossed version* or *crossed symmetric* if we have

$$(A \to aB) \in P \text{ implies } (B \to Aa) \in P \text{ and}$$

$$(A \to Ba) \in P \text{ implies } (B \to aA) \in P.$$

b) A linear grammar $G = (V, \Sigma, P, S)$ is called *symmetric in the straight version* or *straight symmetric* if we have

$$(A \to aB) \in P \text{ implies } (B \to aA) \in P \text{ and}$$

$$(A \to Ba) \in P \text{ implies } (B \to Aa) \in P.$$

The word problem for linear context free languages is $NSPACE(\log n)$–complete ([6,13]). This complexity is not hidden in the knowledge of the place of the terminating rule:

Lemma 11. *There is a linear grammar $G = (V, \Sigma, P, S)$ generating a language complete for $NSPACE(\log n)$ such that there is a terminal symbol $\$ \in \Sigma$ which is the only used in terminating rules and which does not occur in nonterminating rules, i.e.: each rule in P is of the form $A \to \$, A \to aB$, or $A \to Ba$ for $a \neq \$$.*

Theorem 12. *There is a crossed symmetric linear grammar generating a language which is $NSPACE(\log n)$–complete.*

Proof: We start with a grammar $G = (V, \Sigma, P, S)$ from Lemma 11. Now set $\Sigma' := \Sigma_l \cup \Sigma_r \cup \{\$\}$ where $\Sigma_l := \{b_l \mid b \in \Sigma, b \neq \$\}$ and $\Sigma_r := \{b_r \mid b \in \Sigma, b \neq \$\}$. Construct $G' := (V, \Sigma', P', S)$ by $P' := \{A \to b_l B \mid (A \to bB) \in P\} \cup \{A \to Bb_r \mid (A \to Bb) \in P\} \cup \{A \to \$ \mid (A \to \$) \in P\}$. Then $L(G') \subseteq \Sigma_l^* \$ \Sigma_r^*$ is obtained by marking all terminal symbols left of $\$$ with the subscript l and those to the right of $\$$ with the subscript r. Obviously, $L(G')$ is still $NSPACE(\log n)$-complete.

Now let's look at the crossed symmetric closure of G'. Set $G'' := (V, \Sigma', P'', S)$ where $P'' := P' \cup \{B \to bA \mid (A \to Bb) \in P\} \cup \{B \to Ab \mid (A \to bB) \in P\}$. It is easy to see that the application of a reversed production leads to a word outside of $\Sigma_l^* \$ \Sigma_r^*$. Hence $L(G'') \cap \Sigma_l^* \$ \Sigma_r^* = L(G')$ which gives us the $NSPACE(\log n)$–completeness of $L(G'')$. □

Finally, we show that straight symmetric linear grammars can have membership problems, which are $NSPACE(\log n)$–complete. The main idea is again the simple trick used in Theorem 5.

Theorem 13. *There is a straight symmetric linear grammar generating a language which is $NSPACE(\log n)$–complete.*

Proof: Let $L \subseteq \Sigma^*$ be a linear $NSPACE(\log n)$-complete language as stated in Lemma 11. Let L be generated by the linear grammar $G = (V, \Sigma, P, S)$. Let a be a new terminal symbol not in Σ and set $\Sigma' := \Sigma \cup \{a\}$. Consider the monomorphism $h : \Sigma^* \longrightarrow \Sigma'^*$ defined by $h(b) := ab$. Then $h(L) \subseteq (a\Sigma)^*$ is both linear context-free and $NSPACE(\log n)$-complete. $h(L(G))$ is generated by the grammar $G' = (V', \Sigma', P', S)$ where $V' := V \cup V_a \cup (\Sigma \times V) \cup \{X\}$. Here V_a is a copy of V, $\Sigma \times V$ is the set of new nonterminals $\{\langle b, B\rangle \mid b \in \Sigma, B \in V\}$, and X is a single new nonterminal. Further on, P' is the following set of productions: $\{A \to Xb \mid (A \to b) \in P\} \cup \{X \to a\} \cup \{A \to B_a b \mid (A \to Bb) \in P\} \cup \{B_a \to Ba \mid B \in V\} \cup \{A \to a\langle b, B\rangle \mid (A \to bB) \in P\} \cup \{\langle b, B\rangle \to bB \mid b \in \Sigma, B \in V\}$.

CLAIM: Let $A \overset{*}{\Longrightarrow}_{G'} \alpha B\beta$ be a derivation in G' for some $A \in V$. Then the following implications are induced by the structure of G' and can inductively be shown without difficulty:

- If $B \in V$ then $\alpha, \beta \in (a\Sigma)^*$,
- If $B = X$ or $B \in V_a$ then $\alpha \in (a\Sigma)^*$ and $\beta \in \Sigma(a\Sigma)^*$, and
- If $B \in (\Sigma \times V)$ then $\alpha \in (a\Sigma)^* a$ and $\beta \in (a\Sigma)^*$.

Now consider the straight symmetric closure of G', i.e.: $G'' := (V', \Sigma', P'', S)$ where $P'' := P' \cup \{\langle b, B\rangle \to aA \mid (A \to bB) \in P\} \cup \{B \to b\langle b, B\rangle \mid B \in V, b \in \Sigma\} \cup \{B_a \to Ab \mid (A \to Bb) \in P\} \cup \{B \to B_a a \mid B \in V\} \cup \{X \to Ab \mid (A \to B) \in P\}$. By construction, we have $L(G') \subseteq L(G'')$.

Finally, we now show $L(G'') \cap (a\Sigma)^* = L(G')$ which implies that the straight symmetric linear grammar G'' generates an $NSPACE(\log n)$-complete language. Let $S = \alpha_0 A_0 \beta_0 \overset{1}{\Longrightarrow} \alpha_1 A_1 \beta_1 \overset{1}{\Longrightarrow} \cdots \alpha_n A_n \beta_n \overset{1}{\Longrightarrow} w$ be a derivation in G'' of a word $w \in (a\Sigma)^*$. Here $A_i \in V'$ and $\alpha_i, \beta_i \in \Sigma'^*$. Let j be the minimal number such that in the derivation step from $\alpha_j A_j \beta_j \overset{1}{\Longrightarrow} \alpha_{j+1} A_{j+1} \beta_{j+1}$ a reversed production, i.e.: a production from $P'' \setminus P'$, has been used. We distinguish three cases.

Case 1: $A_j \in V$. By the claim we then have $\alpha_j, \beta_j \in (a\Sigma)^*$. But the right hand sides of the reversed rules for elements of V either end with an a or begin with an element of Σ which leads to a contradiction to w being an element of $(a\Sigma)^*$.

Case 2: $A_j \in V_a$ or $A_j = X$. By the claim we then have $\beta_j \in \Sigma(a\Sigma)^*$. But the right hand sides of the reversed productions for elements of $V_a \cup \{X\}$ always end with a symbol from Σ. Again, this contradicts the fact that $w \in (a\Sigma)^*$.

Case 3: $A_j \in (\Sigma \times V)$. By the claim we have $\alpha_j \in (a\Sigma)^* a$. But the right hand sides of the reversed productions for elements of $\Sigma \times V$ always begin with the symbol a, in contradiction to $w \in (a\Sigma)^*$.

Thus in the derivation of w in G'' no reversed production can be used which implies $w \in L(G')$ and thus $L(G'') \cap (a\Sigma)^* = L(G')$. $\qquad\square$

4 Discussion

Despite the many recent results concerning symmetric space and the many resulting relations to other complexity classes, it seems to be very difficult to get characterizations of classes like $SymSPACE(\log n)$ in terms of families of formal languages. The approach of Alvarez and Greenlaw, applied here to two $NSPACE(\log n)$–complete families, either leads to no restriction in complexity or leads to a collapse down to the regular languages and the class NC^1. One reason for the latter result could be the strong normal form we used. Without the total separation of reading from nonreading steps the proof of Theorem 9 wouldn't work. But considering the other results obtained here, this should again lead to $NSPACE(\log n)$–complete problems and not to $SymSPACE(\log n)$-complete ones.

Acknowledgement

I wish to thank an anonymous referee for his careful reading of the paper.

References

1. E. Allender, K.-J. Lange. Symmetry coincides with nondeterminism for time bounded auxiliary pushdown automata. in preparation, 1997.
2. C. Alvarez and R. Greenlaw. A compendium of problems complete for symmetric logarithmic space. Report TR96-039, ECCC, 6 1996.
3. R. Armoni, A. Ta-shma, A. Wigderson, and S. Zhou. $SL \subseteq L^{4/3}$. submitted, 1996.
4. D.A. Barrington. Bounded-width polynomial-size branching programs can recognize exactly those languages in NC^1. *J. Comp. System Sci.*, 38:150–164, 1989.
5. Ka Wong Chong and Tak Wah Lam. Finding connected components in $O(\log n \log \log n)$ time on the EREW PRAM. In *Proceedings of the Fourth Annual ACM-SIAM Symposium on Discrete Algorithms, SODA*, pages 11–20, 1993.
6. P. Flajolet and J. Steyaert. Complexity of classes of languages and operators. Rap. de Recherche 92, IRIA Laboria, Nov. 1974.
7. M. Karchmer and A. Wigderson. On span programs. In *Proc. of the 8th IEEE Structure in Complexity Theory Conference*, pages 102–111, 1993.
8. P. Lewis and C.H. Papadimitriou. Symmetric space-bounded computation. *Theoret. Comput. Sci.*, 19:161–187, 1982.
9. P. Lewis, R. Stearns, and J. Hartmanis. Memory bounds for recognition of context-free and context-sensitive languages. In *Proc. 6th Annual IEEE Symp. on Switching Circuit Theory and Logical Design*, pages 191–209, 1965.
10. N. Nisan. $RL \subseteq SC$. In *Proc. of the 24th Annual ACM Symposium on Theory of Computing*, pages 619–623, 1992.
11. W. Ruzzo. Tree-size bounded alternation. *J. Comp. System Sci.*, 21:218–235, 1980.
12. E. Shamir and C. Beeri. Checking stacks and context-free programmed grammars accept p-complete languages. In *Proc. of 2nd ICALP*, number 14 in LNCS, pages 277–283. Springer, 1974.
13. I. Sudborough. A note on tape-bounded complexity classes and linear context-free languages. *J. Assoc. Comp. Mach.*, 22:499–500, 1975.
14. I. Sudborough. On tape-bounded complexity classes and multi-head finite automata. *J. Comp. System Sci.*, 10:62–76, 1975.
15. I. Sudborough. On the tape complexity of deterministic context-free languages. *J. Assoc. Comp. Mach.*, 25:405–414, 1978.

On Twist-Closed Trios:
A New Morphic Characterization of r.e. Sets

Matthias Jantzen

Universität Hamburg FB Informatik, Universität Hamburg
Vogt-Kölln-Straße 30, 22527 Hamburg

Abstract. We show that in conjunction with the usual trio operations the combination of twist and product can simulate any combination of intersection, reversal and $\frac{1}{2}$. It is proved that any recursively enumerable language L can be homomorphically represented by twisting a linear context-free language. Indeed, the recursively enumerable sets form the least *twist*-closed full trio generated by $dMIR := \{wcw^{rev} \mid w \in \{a,b\}^*\}$.

1 Introduction

In connection with a representation of Petri net languages by Dyck-reductions of linear context-free sets the operation *twist* was defined and used for the first time, see [JaPe 87,JaPe 91,JaPe 94]. The definition of this new language theoretic operation first is defined as a mapping from strings to strings by rearranging its letters $x_i \in \Sigma$: for a string $w := x_1 x_2 \cdots x_{n-1} x_n$ the new string is $twist(w) := x_1 x_n x_2 x_{n-1} \cdots x_{\lfloor \frac{n}{2} \rfloor + 1}$. Observe, that $twist : \Sigma^* \longrightarrow \Sigma^*$ is a bijection and it's inverse mapping $twist^{-1}(w)$ yields a unique string v with $twist(v) = w$. It follows that for each string w there exists a non-negative integer $k \in \mathbb{N}$ such that $twist^k(w) = w$. The mapping *twist* can also be regarded as a permutation of the n distinct positions for the symbols of a string of length n. As such, it can be decomposed into disjoint *cycles* or *orbits* and the smallest exponent $k \in \mathbb{N}$ such that $twist^k(w) = w$ equals the length of the longest (nontrivial) orbit of this permutation. As language theoretic operation *twist* is generalized to languages and families of languages in the obvious way, see Def.2.

It was shown in [JaPe 94], Th.2.10, that the family $\mathcal{Reg}$ of regular sets is closed with respect to *twist*. Proving this is a nice exercise for a course in automata theory. The inclusion $twist(\mathcal{Reg}) \subsetneqq \mathcal{Reg}$ must be proper since $twist^{-1}(\{a^2, b^2\}^*) = MIR$, where $MIR := \{ww^{rev} \mid w \in \{a,b\}^*\}$ is the non-regular context-free set of palindroms of even length. This observation means, that the regular set $\{a^2, b^2\}^*$ will never appear as $twist(R)$ for any regular set $R \in \mathcal{Reg}$. Notice, $twist^{-1}(MIR) = COPY := \{ww \mid w \in \{a,b\}^*\}$. Theorem 2.11 in [JaPe 94] showed that the class $\mathcal{L}_0$ of λ-free labelled, terminal Petri net languages is closed with respect to the operation *twist*. Again, $twist(\mathcal{L}_0) \subsetneqq \mathcal{L}_0$, since $twist(MIR) \in \mathcal{L}_0$ but $MIR \notin \mathcal{L}_0$ follows from results in [Grei 78,Jant 79], knowing that the reachability problem for Petri nets is decidable [Mayr 84,Kosa 82]. The proof for the closure of $\mathcal{L}_0$ under *twist* uses essentially a construction that can be be modified to show the family $\mathcal{L}_0$ of Petri net langages being closed with respect to the operation $\frac{1}{2}$. In Exercise 3.16 of [HoUl 79] it was asked to prove that the family $\mathcal{R}eg$ of regular sets is closed under this operation. In fact, the two operations $\frac{1}{2}$ and *reversal* are closely linked with the operation *twist*. In conjunction with the usual trio-operations the combination of *twist* and *product* can simulate any combination of *intersection*, *reversal*, and $\frac{1}{2}$. This already suggests a new characterization of the recursively enumerable sets as the smallest *twist*- and *product*-closed full trio generated by the linear language *MIR*. Similar results are known for principal *intersection*-closed trios and principal trios, the generator of which is as rich in structure as the twinshuffle language L_{TS} (see [Culi 79,EnRo 79,GiGo 71,Salo 78], and [Salo 81], Chapt. 6, for a condensed presentation. L_{TS} was there abbreviated by L_Σ). A similar result has been shown by Engelfriet in [Enge 96] for the reverse twin shuffle language L_{RTS}, a language first defined by Brandenburg in [Bran 87]. However, neither of the languages L_{TS} and L_{RTS} is context-free. We will prove the characterization of the r.e. sets directly in a manner similar to proofs in [BaBo 74] which nowadays can be viewed as standard methods. This work is written to show that also *twist* has to be regarded as powerful operation.

2 Basic Definitions

Definition 1. Let $\mathcal{R}eg$ (resp. $lin\mathcal{C}f$, $\mathcal{C}f$, $\mathcal{L}_0$, $\mathcal{C}s$, $\mathcal{L}_0^\lambda$, $\mathcal{R}ec$, $\mathcal{R}e$) denote the families of regular sets (linear context-free, context-free, λ-free labelled terminal Petri net, context sensitive, arbitrarily labelled terminal Petri net, recursive, and recursively enumerable languages, respectively).

Specific languages we consider are constructed using the alphabets $\Gamma := \{a, b\}$, $\overline{\Gamma} := \{\overline{a}, \overline{b}\}$, and the homomorphisms $^-, h$, and $\overline{h}$ defined by:

$$\overline{x} := \begin{cases} \overline{x}, & \text{if } x \in \Gamma \\ x, & \text{if } x \in \overline{\Gamma} \end{cases} \qquad h(x) := \begin{cases} x, & \text{if } x \in \Gamma \\ \lambda, & \text{if } x \in \overline{\Gamma} \end{cases} \qquad \overline{h}(x) := \begin{cases} \lambda, & \text{if } x \in \Gamma \\ x, & \text{if } x \in \overline{\Gamma} \end{cases}$$

$$DUP := \{a^n b^n \mid n \in I\!N\}.$$
$$dMIR := \{w c w^{rev} \mid w \in \Gamma^*\}.$$
$$MIR := \{w w^{rev} \mid w \in \Gamma^*\}.$$
$$PAL := \{w \mid w = w^{rev}, w \in \Gamma^*\}.$$
$$COPY := \{w w \mid w \in \Gamma^*\}$$
$$L_{TS} := \{w \in (\Gamma \cup \overline{\Gamma})^* \mid \overline{h(w)} = \overline{h}(w)\}$$
$$L_{RTS} := \{w \in (\Gamma \cup \overline{\Gamma})^* \mid \overline{h(w)} = \overline{h}(w^{rev})\}$$
$$twinPAL := \{w \in (\Gamma \cup \overline{\Gamma})^* \mid \overline{h(w)} \in MIR \text{ and } \overline{h}(w) \in \overline{MIR}\}$$

Let us repeat the basic notions and results from AFL-theory. More details can be found in the textbooks of S. Ginsburg, [Gins 75], and J. Berstel, [Bers 80].

A family of languages $\mathcal{L}$ is called trio if it is closed under inverse homomorphism, intersection with regular sets, and nonerasing homomorphism. The least trio containing the family $\mathcal{L}$ is written $\mathcal{M}(\mathcal{L})$. If $\mathcal{L} := \{L\}$, then L is a generator of the trio $\mathcal{M}(\mathcal{L})$, shortly written as $\mathcal{M}(L)$ and then called principal. A union-closed trio is called semiAFL. Every principal trio is closed with respect to union and thus forms a semiAFL. If a trio is closed under arbitrary homomorphism, then it is called a full trio, written $\hat{\mathcal{M}}(\mathcal{L})$.

A family of languages $\mathcal{L}$ is called an AFL (or full AFL) if it is a trio (full trio, resp.) which is closed under the operations union, product and Kleene plus. The smallest AFL (or full AFL) containing the family $\mathcal{L}$ is written $\mathcal{F}(\mathcal{L})$ ($\hat{\mathcal{F}}(\mathcal{L})$, resp.). Each full AFL is closed with respect to Kleene star.

If a trio $\mathcal{M}(\mathcal{L})$ (or an AFL $\mathcal{F}(\mathcal{L})$) is in addition closed with respect to one further operation ⊛ then this family will be called ⊛-closed and abbreviated as $\mathcal{M}_{⊛}(\mathcal{L})$ (resp. $\mathcal{F}_{⊛}(\mathcal{L})$).

The linear context-free language DUP is in fact a one-counter language acceptable by a nondeterministic on-line one-counter automaton making at most one reversal in each accepting computation. $dMIR$, MIR and PAL are well-known context-free generators of the family $linCf$ of linear context-free languages: $linCf = \mathcal{M}(dMIR \cup \{\lambda\}) = \mathcal{M}(MIR \cup \{\lambda\}) = \hat{\mathcal{M}}(PAL)$. These languages are precisely the languages accepted by nondeterministic on-line single pushdown acceptors which operate in such a way that in every accepting computation the pusdown store makes at most one reversal. This family is not closed with respect to product or Kleene plus. The family $\mathcal{M}(COPY)$ is incomparable to the family $linCf$ and both include the family $\hat{\mathcal{M}}(DUP)$. For more details see also [Bran 88].

The least intersection-closed full semiAFL $\hat{\mathcal{M}}_{\cap}(DUP)$ has been characterized in [BaBo 74] as the family of languages accepted by nondeterministic on-line multicounter acceptors which operate in such a way that in every computation each counter makes at most one reversal. There it was shown that this class contains only recursive sets, i.e. $\hat{\mathcal{M}}_{\cap}(DUP) \subseteq \mathcal{R}ec$. Similarly, the intersection-closed full semiAFL $\hat{\mathcal{M}}_{\cap}(dMIR)$ equals the family of languages accepted by nondeterministic on-line multipushdown acceptors which operate in such a way that in every computation each pushdown makes at most one reversal. This family, however, is the set of recursively enumerable languages and was characterized in [BaBo 74] by $\mathcal{R}e = \hat{\mathcal{M}}_{\cap}(MIR) = \hat{\mathcal{M}}(twinPAL)$.

Definition 2. Let Σ be an alphabet, then $twist : \Sigma^* \longrightarrow \Sigma^*$ is recursively defined for any $w \in \Sigma^*, a \in \Sigma$ by: $twist(aw) := a \cdot twist(w^{rev})$, and $twist(\lambda) := \lambda$.

For sets of strings L and families of languages $\mathcal{L}$ the operation $twist$ is generalized as usual: $twist(L) := \{twist(w) \mid w \in L\}$ and $twist(\mathcal{L}) := \{twist(L) \mid L \in \mathcal{L}\}$.

We see that $twist(w) = x_1 x_n x_2 x_{n-1} \cdots x_{\lfloor \frac{n}{2} \rfloor + 1}$ for any string $w \in \Sigma^*, w := x_1 x_2 \cdots x_{n-1} x_n$ where $x_i \in \Sigma$ for all $i \in \{1, \cdots, n\}$.

Viewed as permutation π_{twist} of the n subscripts $1, 2, \ldots, n$, i.e., of the positions of the symbols that form the string $w := x_1 x_2 \cdots x_{n-1} x_n$ this yields

$$\pi_{twist}(i) := \begin{cases} 2 \cdot i - 1, & \text{if } 0 \leq i \leq \lceil \frac{n}{2} \rceil \\ 2(n - i + 1), & \text{otherwise} . \end{cases}$$

Since the mapping $twist$ only performs a permutation of the symbols that form a string it is easily seen that $\mathcal{R}e$ and $\mathcal{C}s$ are $twist$-closed families.

Twisting a context-free language obviously yields a context-sensitive language. We have $twist(\mathcal{C}f) \subsetneq \mathcal{C}s$ and the inclusion is proper since $twist(L)$ has a semilinear Parikh image whenever L has this property. Note that $twist(L)$ may not be context-free even for a linear context-free language $L := C_{lin}$ or one-counter language $L := C_1$. It is easily verified that $twist(C_{lin}) \notin \mathcal{C}f$ and $twist(C_1) \notin \mathcal{C}f$ for $C_{lin} := \{a^{3m}b^n c^n d^m \mid n, m \in \mathbb{N}\}$ and $C_1 := \{a^{3m}b^m c^n d^n \mid n, m \in \mathbb{N}\}$. For example, one verifies $twist(C) \cap \{(ad)^i (ac)^j (ab)^k \mid i, j, k \in \mathbb{N}\} = \{(ad)^m (ac)^m (ab)^m \mid m \in \mathbb{N}\}$ for $C \in \{C_{lin}, C_1\}$.

In order to use the operation $\frac{1}{2}$ in connection with $twist$ we shall define a slightly generalized version of this operation:

Definition 3. For any string $w := x_1 x_2 \cdots x_n, x_i \in \Sigma$, let $\frac{1}{2}(w) := x_1 x_2 \cdots x_{\lceil \frac{n}{2} \rceil}$.

Hence, $\frac{1}{2}(abaab) = \frac{1}{2}(abaabb) = aba$.

Lemma 4. *Every trio which is closed with respect to twist is also closed under reversal and $\frac{1}{2}$.*

Proof: Let $L \subseteq \Sigma^*, \$ \notin \Sigma$ be a new symbol and $f : (\Sigma \cup \{\$\})^* \longrightarrow \Sigma^*$ a homomorphism defined by $f(\$) := \lambda$ and $\forall x \in \Sigma : f(x) := x$. Then $L^{rev} = g^{-1}(twist(f^{-1}(L) \cap \{\$\}^* \Sigma^*))$ where $g : \Sigma^* \longrightarrow (\Sigma \cup \{\$\})^*$ is a homomorphism given by $\forall x \in \Sigma : g(x) := \$x$. Thus any $twist$-closed trio $\mathcal{M}(\mathcal{L})$ is closed with respect to reversal.

To express the operation $\frac{1}{2}$ by trio operations and $twist$ that works for strings of both even and odd length we have to insert a dummy symbol for those of odd length and then mark half of the symbols. To do this we use an inverse homomorphism h_1^{-1}. By intersection with a suitable regular set we then can fix the position of the dummy symbol and the marked symbols.

In detail we define: $\overline{\Sigma} = \{\overline{x} \mid x \in \Sigma\}$ as a disjoint copy of Σ and the homomorphism $h_1 : (\Sigma \cup \overline{\Sigma} \cup \{\$\})^* \longrightarrow \Sigma^*$ by: $h_1(x) := h_1(\overline{x}) := x$ for all $x \in \Sigma$ and $h_1(\$) := \lambda$. Now, for any string $w \in \Sigma^*$, $h_1^{-1}(w)$ may contain an arbitrary number of extra $\$$-symbols and likewise barred symbols from $\overline{\Sigma}$ at any position. Then $K_1 := h_1^{-1}(L) \cap \Sigma^* \{\$, \lambda\} \overline{\Sigma}^*$ contains at most one extra symbol $\$$ and all and only the barred symbols at the right hand side. Define new alphabets $\Gamma := \{\langle x, y \rangle \mid x \in \Sigma, y \in \overline{\Sigma}\}, \Gamma_\$:= \{\langle x, \$ \rangle \mid x \in \Sigma\}$ and a homomorphism $h_2 : (\Gamma_\$ \cup \Gamma)^* \longrightarrow (\Sigma \cup \overline{\Sigma} \cup \{\$\})^*$ by $h_2(\langle x, y \rangle) := xy$. Now $K_2 := h_2^{-1}(twist(K_1)) \cap (\Gamma^* \cup \Gamma^* \Gamma_\$)$ is a set of strings, each of which describes the $twist$ of a string from K_1 in the projection of both components of the new symbols from $\Gamma \cup \Gamma_\$$. Since the first $\lceil \frac{|w|}{2} \rceil$ symbols of the original string w are put into the first component of the corresponding string from K_2 a simple coding will retrieve the string $\frac{1}{2}(w)$. With $h_3 : (\Gamma \cup \Gamma_\$) \longrightarrow \Sigma$ defined by $h_3(\langle x, y \rangle) := x$ one obtains $\frac{1}{2}(L) := h_3(K_2)$. The only operations we used to define $\frac{1}{2}(L)$ were trio operations and $twist$ so that the lemma was proved completely.

$\square$

Using a similar technique we can show that the languages *MIR*, *COPY* and their deterministic variants all are generators of the same $twist$-closed trio $\mathcal{M}_{twist}(dMIR)$.

Theorem 5. $\mathcal{M}_{twist}(dCOPY \cup \{\lambda\}) = \mathcal{M}_{twist}(COPY) = \mathcal{M}_{twist}(MIR) = \mathcal{M}_{twist}(dMIR \cup \{\lambda\}) = \mathcal{M}_{twist}(PAL)$.

Proof:

(a) $COPY \in \mathcal{M}_{twist}(dCOPY \cup \{\lambda\})$ follows since $COPY$ is obtained from $dCOPY$ by limited erasing of the symbol c and it is well known that every trio is closed w.r.t. this operation.

(b) $MIR \in \mathcal{M}_{twist}(COPY)$ follows by observing that $MIR = twist(COPY)$. This can be shown by induction on the length and structure of the strings involved.

(c) $\mathcal{M}_{twist}(MIR) = \mathcal{M}_{twist}(dMIR \cup \{\lambda\}) = \mathcal{M}_{twist}(PAL)$ follows since $\mathcal{M}(dMIR \cup \{\lambda\}) = \mathcal{M}(MIR) = \mathcal{M}(PAL) = linCf$, see [Gins 75], [Bers 80].

(d) $dCOPY \in \mathcal{M}_{twist}(dMIR)$: $K_2 := \{w\$^i w^{rev}\textcent^j \mid w \in \{a,b\}^*, i,j \in \mathbb{N} \setminus \{0\}\} \in \mathcal{M}(dMIR)$ is easily seen. Likewise, $K_3 := twist(K_2) \cap (\{a,b\}\{\textcent\})^* \cdot \{\$\textcent\} \cdot (\{\$\}\{a,b\})^* \in \mathcal{M}_{twist}(dMIR)$ and then $dCOPY = f(h^{-1}(K_3))$ follows with $h : \{a,b,c,\bar{a},\bar{b}\}^* \longrightarrow \{a,b,\$,\textcent\}^*$ defined by $h(a) := a\textcent, h(b) := b\textcent, h(c) := \$\textcent, h(\bar{a}) := \$a, h(\bar{b}) := \$b$, and $f(a) := f(\bar{a}) := a, f(b) := f(\bar{b}) := b, f(c) := c$. Consequently, $dCOPY \in \mathcal{M}_{twist}(dMIR)$. $\qquad\square$

The question, whether the operation *twist* is as powerful as intersection will here be partially answered:

Lemma 6. *Every twist-closed trio $\mathcal{L}$ that is in addition closed under product is also closed w.r.t. intersection.*

Proof: Let $L_1, L_2 \subseteq \Sigma^*, L_1, L_2 \in \mathcal{L}$ and Γ a copy of Σ with $h : \Sigma \longrightarrow \Gamma$ being the bijection between the alphabets. By Lemma 4 $L_2^{rev} \in \mathcal{L}$ and then also $L_3 := g^{-1}(twist(L_1 \cdot h(L_2^{rev}))) \in \mathcal{L}$ where $g : \Sigma^* \longrightarrow (\Sigma\Gamma)^*$ is defined by $g(x) = xh(x)$ for all $x \in \Sigma$. Obviously $L_3 = L_1 \cap L_2$, and this proves the lemma. $\qquad\square$

There exist families of languages that are closed with respect to the operations *twist* and *product* but not under intersection! The family $\mathcal{L}_{slip}$ of languages having a semi-linear Parikh image, i.e. are letter equivalent to regular sets, is such a family. This is because this family is not a trio since it is not even closed with respect to intersection by regular sets! To see this, consider the language $L := \{ab^{2^n} \mid n \in \mathbb{N}\} \cup \{b\}^*\{a\}^* \in \mathcal{L}_{slip}$, where one has $L \cap \{a\}\{b\}^* \notin \mathcal{L}_{slip}$.

This observation indicates that it might not be easy to express the operation *twist* by means of known operations in abstract formal language theory.

It is well known and easy to show that any intersection-closed trio is closed w.r.t product but closure under *twist* generally depends on the generator of this trio. It is known that each *intersection*-closed trio is also closed with respect to *shuffle*, defined below:

Definition 7. Let $w_1, w_2 \in \Sigma^*, w_1 := x_1 x_2 \cdots x_m$, and $w_2 := y_1 y_2 \cdots y_n$ where $x_i, y_j \in \Sigma$ for $1 \le i \le m$ and $1 \le j \le n$.

Then the *shuffle* ⊔⊔ and the *literal shuffle* ⊔⊔$_{lit}$ are defined as follows:

$$w_1 \sqcup w_2 := \left\{ u_1 v_1 u_2 v_2 \cdots u_n v_n \;\middle|\; \begin{array}{l} n \in \mathbb{N}, u_i, v_i \in \Sigma^*, w_1 = u_1 u_2 \cdots u_n, \\ w_2 = v_1 v_2 \cdots v_n \end{array} \right\},$$

$$w_1 \sqcup_{lit} w_2 := \left\{ \begin{array}{ll} x_1 y_1 x_2 y_2 \cdots x_m y_m y_{m+1} \cdots y_n, & \text{if } m \le n \\ x_1 y_1 x_2 y_2 \cdots x_n y_n x_{n+1} \cdots x_m, & \text{if } n < m \end{array} \right.$$

The proof of the main theorem is similar to the one of Theorem 1 in [BaBo 74] and can more easily be described by using the operation of literal shuffle.

Theorem 8. *A language L is recursively enumerable if and only if there exists a linear context-free language $K \in lin\,Cf$ and homomorphisms f and g such that $L = g(f^{-1}(twist(K)))$.*

Proof: Let M be a deterministic Turing machine with stateset Z accepting $L \subseteq \Sigma^*$ without loss of generality in such a way that all and only the halting configurations are the accepting ones. Each configuration will be represented by an instantenous description (ID) of the form uqv, where uv is the current string over the tape alphabet of M, $q \in Z$ is a state of M, and q's position in uqv indicates that M is in state q while reading the left-most symbol of v. Initial IDs are strings $q_0 w$, where q_0 is the initial state of M and $w \in \Sigma^*$ is the input of the Turing machine. Let K be the set of strings of the form $ID_0 \$ ID_1 \$ \cdots \$ ID_{k-1} \$ ID_k \$ \math{\text{¢}} ID_k'^{rev} \math{\text{¢}} ID_{k-1}'^{rev} \math{\text{¢}} \cdots \math{\text{¢}} ID_1'^{rev} \math{\text{¢}} ID_0''^{rev}$, where $\$$ and ¢ are distinguished symbols used as markers, $ID_0'' := h(ID_0)$ encodes the initial configuration ID_0 of the TM M and uses a different copy $\Gamma := h(\Sigma)$ of the alphabet Σ which is used in all the other IDs. This is because all but the initial ID finally have to be deleted. The coding h will act as the identity on the set Z of states. ID_k'' describes a final configuration of M. Also, for $1 \le j \le k$ no ID_j needs to be identical to ID_j', but if for some $i \in \{0, \ldots, k-1\}$ $ID_i\$$ is a substring of the set K then $\math{\text{¢}} ID_{i+1}'^{rev}$ is the corresponding substring of K if and only if ID_{i+1}' represents the configuration of M reached in one step from that represented by ID_i. That K is in fact a linear context-free language is easily verified, since the set of all strings of the form $ID_i \$ \math{\text{¢}} ID_{i+1}'^{rev}$ for which $ID_i \vdash_M ID_{i+1}'$ holds clearly is an element of $lin\,Cf$. The iterated substitution of this language between the $\$$ and ¢ symbol in the middle obviously will be linear context-free again. The set of the descriptions of initial instantenous descriptions $ID_0''^{rev}$ is regular as is the set of IDs of the form ID_k in the middle. Hence, $K \in lin\,Cf$ follows. Now, $twist(K)$ contains, among others, strings of the form $(ID_0 \sqcup_{lit} ID_0'')\$\math{\text{¢}}$ $(ID_1 \sqcup_{lit} ID_1')\$\math{\text{¢}} (ID_2 \sqcup_{lit} ID_2')\$\math{\text{¢}} \cdots \$\math{\text{¢}} (ID_k \sqcup_{lit} ID_k')\$\math{\text{¢}}$. It will be guaranteed by applying an inverse homomorphism, that only those strings from $twist(K)$ will be taken for which $|ID_0| = |ID_0''|$, and $\forall i \in \{1, \ldots, k\} : |ID_i| = |ID_i'|$.

Let $f : (\Sigma \cup \Gamma \cup Z \cup \{\#\})^* \longrightarrow (\Sigma \cup \Gamma \cup Z \cup \{\$, \math{\text{¢}}\})^*$ be defined by:

$$f(x) := \left\{ \begin{array}{ll} yx, & \text{if } x = h(y) \in \Gamma \\ xx, & \text{if } x \in \Sigma \cup Z \\ \$\math{\text{¢}}, & \text{if } x = \# \end{array} \right. .$$

Then $f^{-1}(twist(K)) =$

$$\left\{ h(ID_0) \# ID_1 \# \cdots \# ID_k \# \;\middle|\; \begin{array}{l} ID_0 \text{ is an initial } ID \text{ of } M, \\ \forall i \in \{1, \ldots, k\} : ID_{i-1} \vdash_M ID_i, \\ \text{and } ID_k \text{ is an acepting } ID. \end{array} \right\}.$$

Now, let $g : (\Sigma \cup \Gamma \cup Z \cup \{\#\})^* \longrightarrow \Sigma^*$ be a homomorphism that erases the symbols from the set $\Sigma \cup Z \cup \{\#\}$ and acts as h^{-1} on the set $\Gamma = h(\Sigma)$. Then, finally $g(f^{-1}(twist(K))) = L = L(M)$, since g extracts the input string of the Turing machine M from its initial configuration encoded by the prefix $h(ID_0)$ in $f^{-1}(twist(K))$.

$\square$

Corollary 9. $\mathcal{R}e = \hat{\mathcal{M}}(twist(lin\,\mathcal{C}f)) = \hat{\mathcal{M}}_{twist}(dMIR)$

In a forthcoming paper we will show that even without erasing homomorphisms we can in some cases express intersection and product by a combination of *trio* and *twist* operations. To be more precise, we can prove $\mathcal{M}_{twist}(MIR) = \mathcal{M}_{\cap}(MIR)$ from which Corollary 9 follows directly by the results in [BaBo 74].

References

[BaBo 74] B.S. Baker and R.V. Book. Reversal-bounded multipushdown machines, J. Comput. Syst. Sci., 8 (1974) 315–332.

[Bers 80] J. Berstel, Transductions and Context-free Languages, Teubner Stuttgart (1980).

[BoGr 70] R.V. Book and S. Greibach. Quasi-realtime languages, Math. Syst. Theory 19 (1970) 97–111.

[BoGr 78] R.V. Book and S. Greibach. The independence of certain operations on semiAFLs, RAIRO Informatique Théorique, 19 (1978) 369–385.

[BoGW 79] R.V. Book, S. Greibach, C. Wrathall. Reset machines, J. Comput. Syst. Sci., 19 (1979) 256–276.

[BoNP 74] R.V. Book, M. Nivat, and M. Paterson. Reversal-bounded acceptors and intersections of linear languages, Siam J. on Computing, 3 (1974) 283–295.

[Bran 87] F.J. Brandenburg. Representations of language families by homomorphic equality operations and generalized equality sets, Theoretical Computer Science, 55 (1987) 183–263.

[Bran 88] F.J. Brandenburg. On the intersection of stacks and queues, Theoretical Computer Science, 58 (1988) 69–80.

[Culi 79] K. Culik. A purely homomorphic characterization of recursively enumerable sets, J. ACM 26 (1979) 345–350.

[EnRo 79] J. Engelfriet and G. Rozenberg. Equality languages and fixed point languages, Information and Control, 43 (1979) 20–49.

[Enge 96] J. Engelfriet. Reverse twin shuffles, Bulletin of the EATCS, vol. 60 (1996) 144.

[Gins 75] S. Ginsburg, Algebraic and Automata Theoretic Properties of Formal Languages, North Holland Publ. Comp. Amsterdam (1975).

[GiGo 71] S. Ginsburg and J. Goldstein. Intersection-closed full AFL and the recursively enumerable languages, Information and Control, 22 (1973) 201–231.

[GiGr 70] S. Ginsburg and S. Greibach, Principal AFL, J. Comput. Syst. Sci., 4 (1970) 308–338.

[Grei 78] S. Greibach. Remarks on blind and partially blind one-way multicounter machines, Theoretical Computer Science, 7 (1978) 311–236.

[HoUl 79] J.E. Hopcroft and J.D. Ullman, Introduction to Automata Theory, Languages, and Computation, Addison-Wesley Publ. Comp. (1997).

[Jant 79]   M. Jantzen.On the hierarchy of Petri net languages, R.A.I.R.O., Informatique Théorique, 13 (1979) 19–30.

[JaPe 87]   M. Jantzen and H. Petersen. Petri net languages and one-sided reductions of context-free sets, in: (K Voss, H. Genrich, and G. Rozenberg, eds.) Concurrency and Nets, Springer, Berlin, Heidelberg, New York (1987) 245–252.

[JaPe 91]   M. Jantzen and H. Petersen. Twisting Petri net languages and how to obtain them by reducing linear context-free sets, in: Proc. 12th Internat. Conf. on Petri Nets, Gjern (1991) 228–236.

[JaPe 94]   M. Jantzen and H. Petersen. Cancellation in context-free languages: enrichment by reduction. Theoretical Computer Science, 127 (1994) 149–170.

[Kosa 82]   S.R. Kosaraju. Decidability of reachability of vector addition systems, 14th Annual ACM Symp. on Theory of Computing, San Francisco, (1982) 267–281.

[Mayr 84]   E.W. Mayr. An algorithm for the general Petri net reachability problem, SIAM J. of Computing, 13 (1984) 441–459.

[Salo 78]   A. Salomaa. Equality sets for homomorphisms and free monoids, Acta Cybernetica 4 (1978) 127–139.

[Salo 81]   A. Salomaa. Jewels of formal Language Theory, Computer Science Press, Rockville (1981).

An Automata Approach to Some Problems on Context-Free Grammars

J. Esparza and P. Rossmanith

Institut für Informatik, Technische Universität München
Arcisstr. 21, D-80290 München, Germany

Abstract. In Chapter 4 of [2], Book and Otto solve a number of word problems for monadic string-rewriting systems using an elegant automata-based technique. In this note we observe that the technique is also very interesting from a pedagogical point of view, since it provides a uniform solution to several elementary problems on context-free languages. We hope that Wilfried Brauer will consider these results for inclusion in the next edition of his textbook on automata theory [5].

1 Introduction

In Chapter 4 of their book "String-Rewriting Systems" [2], Book and Otto study so-called *monadic string rewriting systems*. These are sets of rewriting rules of the form $\alpha \to \beta$, where $\alpha, \beta \in \Sigma^*$ for some finite alphabet Σ, satisfying $|\alpha| > |\beta|$ and $|\beta| \leq 1$. The rule $\alpha \to \beta$ allows to rewrite α into β.

Among other results, Book and Otto show that the set of *descendants* of a regular set L of strings – i.e., the set of strings that can be derived from the elements of L through repeated application of the rewriting rules – is also regular; moreover, they provide an elegant algorithm to compute it. The input to the algorithm is a nondeterministic finite automaton (NFA) accepting L, and the output is another NFA accepting the descendants of L.

There is a tight relationship between monadic string rewriting systems and context-free grammars. Given a context-free grammar $G = (V, T, P, S)$ without ϵ-productions, the set $R = \{\alpha \to A \mid (A \to \alpha) \in P\}$ is a monadic string rewriting system over the alphabet $V \cup T$. Loosely speaking, R is obtained by "reversing" the productions of G. The set of descendants of a language $L \subseteq (V \cup T)^*$ in R is the set of *predecessors* of L in G, i.e., the set of strings from which some word of L is derivable through repeated application of the productions.

The similarity between monadic string rewriting systems and context-free grammars was already observed by Book and Otto in [2]. In particular, they remark that the algorithm for the computation of descendants could be applied to problems on context-free grammars, but do not elaborate on this point. The purpose of this note is to show that the algorithm indeed leads to elegant and uniform solutions for the membership, emptiness, and finiteness problems of context-free grammars, among others.

2 Preliminaries

We use the notations of [6] for finite automata and context-free grammars. Given an NFA $M = (Q, \Sigma, \delta, q_0, F)$, where $\delta \subseteq Q \times \Sigma \times Q$, we define the *transition relation* $\widehat{\delta} \colon (Q \times \Sigma^*) \to 2^Q$ by:

- $\widehat{\delta}(q, \epsilon) = \{q\}$,
- $\widehat{\delta}(q, a) = \delta(q, a)$, and
- $\widehat{\delta}(q, wa) = \{p \mid p \in \widehat{\delta}(r, a) \text{ for some state } r \in \widehat{\delta}(q, w)\}$

We often denote $q' \in \widehat{\delta}(q, \alpha)$ by $q \xrightarrow{\alpha} q'$.

Given a context-free grammar $G = (V, T, P, S)$, we denote $\Sigma = V \cup T$. We define two relations $\Rightarrow$ and $\overset{*}{\Rightarrow}$ between strings in Σ^*. If $A \to \beta$ is a production of P and α and γ are any strings in Σ^*, then $\alpha A \gamma \Rightarrow \alpha \beta \gamma$. The string $\alpha A \gamma$ is an *immediate predecessor* of $\alpha \beta \gamma$. The relation $\overset{*}{\Rightarrow}$ is the reflexive and transitive closure of $\Rightarrow$. If $\alpha \overset{*}{\Rightarrow} \beta$, then α is a *predecessor* of β. Given $L \subseteq \Sigma^*$, we define

$$pre(L) = \{\alpha \in \Sigma^* \mid \exists \beta \in L \text{ with } \alpha \Rightarrow \beta\}$$

$pre^i(L)$ is inductively defined by $pre^0(L) = L$ and $pre^{i+1}(L) = pre(pre^i(L))$. Finally, we define $pre^*(L) = \bigcup_{i \geq 0} pre^i(L)$, or, equivalently,

$$pre^*(L) = \{\alpha \in \Sigma^* \mid \exists \beta \in L \text{ with } \alpha \overset{*}{\Rightarrow} \beta\}$$

3 Computation of pre^*

Let $G = (V, T, P, S)$ be a fixed context-free grammar. Given an NFA M recognizing a regular set $L(M) \subseteq \Sigma^*$, we wish to construct another NFA recognizing $pre^*(L(M))$. Book and Otto's idea (translated into context-free grammars) is to exhaustively perform the following operation, starting with M as current NFA: if $A \to \alpha$ is a production, and in the current NFA we have $q \xrightarrow{\alpha} q'$, then we add a new transition $q \xrightarrow{A} q'$. The algorithm terminates, because the number of states of the NFA remains constant, and there is an upper bound to the number of transitions of an NFA with a fixed number of states and a fixed alphabet.

Algorithm 1

Input: an NFA $M = (Q, \Sigma, \delta, q_0, F)$
Output: an NFA $M' = (Q, \Sigma, \delta', q_0, F)$ with $L(M') = pre^*(L(M))$

$\delta' \leftarrow \delta$;
repeat
    for $q, q' \in Q$, $A \to \beta \in P$ **do**
        if $q' \in \widehat{\delta'}(q, \beta)$ **then** $\delta' \leftarrow \delta' \cup \{(q, A, q')\}$ **fi**
    od
until δ' does not change any more

We apply the algorithm to an example. Consider the context-free grammar $S \to AS \mid SA \mid a$, $A \to b$ and the NFA of Figure 1 having only the transitions drawn with heavier lines. Assume that for each pair of states (q, q') the for loop examines all productions of the grammar in the order above. Then the transitions labeled by 1 in Figure 1 are added in the first iteration of the repeat-until loop. The second iteration adds the transitions $q_1 \xrightarrow{S} q_1$, derived from $q_1 \xrightarrow{S} q_2 \xrightarrow{A} q_1$, and $q_2 \xrightarrow{S} q_2$, derived from $q_2 \xrightarrow{A} q_1 \xrightarrow{S} q_2$. They are labeled by 2 in Figure 1. The third iteration adds $q_2 \xrightarrow{S} q_1$, derived from $q_2 \xrightarrow{A} q_1 \xrightarrow{S} q_1$ and labeled by 3 in the figure. Nothing is added in the fourth iteration, and the algorithm terminates.

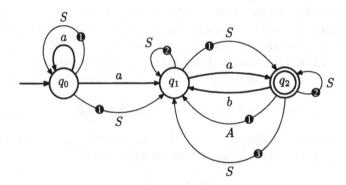

Fig. 1. Illustration of Algorithm 1

The correctness of Algorithm 1 follows immediately from the following two lemmata:

Lemma 1. $pre^*(L(M)) \subseteq L(M')$.

Proof. Let M_i be the NFA computed by the algorithm after i executions of the repeat-until loop ($M_0 = M$), and let $\xrightarrow[i]{}$ be the transition relation of M_i. Since $L(M_i) \subseteq L(M')$, it suffices to prove $pre^i(L(M)) \subseteq L(M_i)$ for every $i \geq 0$.

We proceed by induction on i. The case $i = 0$ is trivial because $L(M) \subseteq L(M_0)$ and $pre^0(L(M)) = L(M)$. For the step from i to $i + 1$, let α be an arbitrary word of $pre^{i+1}(L(M))$. By the definition of pre, there exist words α_1, α_2 and a production $A \to \beta$ such that $\alpha = \alpha_1 A \alpha_2$ and $\alpha_1 \beta \alpha_2 \in pre^i(L(M))$. By induction hypothesis, $\alpha_1 \beta \alpha_2 \in L(M_i)$. Therefore, there exist states q, q' such that

$$q_0 \xrightarrow[i]{\alpha_1} q \xrightarrow[i]{\beta} q' \xrightarrow[i]{\alpha_2} q_f$$

for some final state q_f. So we have

$$q_0 \xrightarrow[i+1]{\alpha_1} q \xrightarrow[i+1]{A} q' \xrightarrow[i+1]{\alpha_2} q_f$$

which implies $\alpha = \alpha_1 A \alpha_2 \in L(M_{i+1})$. $\qquad\square$

Lemma 2. $L(M') \subseteq pre^*(L(M))$.

Proof. For all $j \geq 0$, let N_j be the NFA obtained after the algorithm has added j transitions to the input automaton M, and let $\xrightarrow{}_j$ denote the transition relation of N_j. Since $L(M')$ is the union of all the sets $L(N_j)$, it suffices to prove $L(N_j) \subseteq pre^*(L(M))$ for every $j \geq 0$.

We proceed by induction on j. The case $j = 0$ is trivial because $N_0 = M$. For the step from j to $j+1$, assume that N_{j+1} is obtained from N_j through the addition of a new transition $q_1 \xrightarrow{A} q_2$. Let α be an arbitrary word of $L(N_{j+1})$. If α is accepted by N_j, then, by the induction hypothesis, $\alpha \in pre^*(L(M))$. If α is not accepted by N_j, then we have $\alpha = \alpha_1 A \alpha_2 A \ldots A \alpha_n$ and

$$q_0 \xrightarrow[j]{\alpha_1} q_1 \xrightarrow[j+1]{A} q_2 \xrightarrow[j]{\alpha_2} q_1 \xrightarrow[j+1]{A} q_2 \cdots q_1 \xrightarrow[j+1]{A} q_2 \xrightarrow[j]{\alpha_n} q_f$$

for some final state q_f. Since there exists a production $A \to \beta$ such that $q_1 \xrightarrow[j]{\beta} q_2$, we have

$$q_0 \xrightarrow[j]{\alpha_1} q_1 \xrightarrow[j]{\beta} q_2 \xrightarrow[j]{\alpha_2} q_1 \xrightarrow[j]{\beta} q_2 \cdots q_1 \xrightarrow[j]{\beta} q_2 \xrightarrow[j]{\alpha_n} q_f$$

and therefore N_j accepts $\alpha' = \alpha_1 \beta \alpha_2 \beta \ldots \beta \alpha_n$. By the induction hypothesis, $\alpha' \in pre^*(L(M))$. Since $\alpha \xRightarrow{*} \alpha'$, we have $\alpha \in pre^*(L(M))$. $\qquad\square$

The running time of Algorithm 1 in the size of the input automaton is easy to estimate.[1] Let $n = |Q|$ be the number of states of the input automaton M. Since δ' contains at most $O(n^2)$ elements, the **repeat-until** loop is executed $O(n^2)$ times. The **for** loop is executed $\Theta(n^2)$ times. Checking whether $q' \in \widehat{\delta'}(q, \beta)$ holds can be done by simulating the NFA $(Q, \Sigma, \delta', q, F)$ on input β, which requires $O(n^2)$ time (see [1], pp. 327–329). Adding an element to δ' takes $O(1)$ time (assume for instance that δ' is stored as a bit matrix). So the running time is $O(n^6)$.

4 Improving the complexity

Algorithm 1 is very simple, but not efficient. In this section we present a new algorithm, Algorithm 2, with a running time of $O(n^4)$. It works for grammars with productions of the form $A \to BC$, $A \to a$, or $A \to \epsilon$, i.e., grammars in Chomsky normal form extended with ϵ-productions. Observe that every context-free grammar can be efficiently transformed into one in this form. The check $q' \in \widehat{\delta}(q, \beta)$ is now easier, since β has length at most 2.

We first observe that productions of the form $A \to a$ or $A \to \epsilon$ can only contribute new transitions to the input NFA during the first iteration of the **repeat-until** loop. In Algorithm 2 they are processed in an initialization phase. It remains to deal properly with productions of the form $A \to BC$. In each iteration of the **repeat-until** loop, Algorithm 1 goes over all pairs of states

---

[1] It is also interesting to examine the complexity in the size of the grammar, but this is out of the scope of this little note.

(q, q'), checks if $q' \in \hat{\delta}(q, BC)$, and if so adds the triple (q, A, q') to δ'. The procedure takes $\Theta(n^4)$ time. Algorithm 2 adds exactly the same transitions, but more efficiently: it goes through all states q'', and it computes for each of them the sets $L(B, q'') = \{q \in Q \mid q \xrightarrow{B} q''\}$ and $R(q'', C) = \{q' \in Q \mid q'' \xrightarrow{C} q'\}$; the whole procedure takes $\Theta(n^2)$ time. Then, it adds to δ' the union over all q'' of the triples $L(B, q'') \times \{A\} \times R(q'', C)$.

Actually, one last refinement is needed in order to achieve $O(n^4)$ running time: Algorithm 2 uses two sets of states $L(X, q)$, $L'(X, q)$ (and two analogous sets $R(q, X)$ and $R'(q, X)$). $L'(X, q)$ is reinitialised to the empty set in each iteration of the **repeat-until** loop; it stores the states q' for which a transition $q' \xrightarrow{X} q$ has been added *during the current iteration*. $L(X, q)$ is initialised only once before the execution of the **repeat-until** loop; it stores all the states q' for which a transition $q' \xrightarrow{X} q$ has been added so far. So the new triples that have to be added to δ' after each iteration are

$$(L'(B, q) \times \{A\} \times R(q, C)) \cup (L(B, q) \times \{A\} \times R'(q, C))$$

Algorithm 2

> **Input:** an NFA $M = (Q, \Sigma, \delta, q_0, F)$
> **Output:** an NFA $M' = (Q, \Sigma, \delta', q_0, F)$ with $L(M') = pre^*(L(M))$
> $\delta' \leftarrow \delta$;
> **for** $q \in Q$, $A \rightarrow \epsilon \in P$ **do** $\delta' \leftarrow \delta' \cup \{(q, A, q)\}$ **od**;
> **for** $q, q' \in Q$, $A \rightarrow a \in P$ **do**
>   **if** $(q, a, q') \in \delta'$ **then** $\delta' \leftarrow \delta' \cup \{(q, A, q')\}$ **fi**
> **od**;
> **for** $q \in Q$, $X \in V$ **do** $L(X, q) \leftarrow \emptyset$; $R(q, X) \leftarrow \emptyset$ **od**;
> **repeat**
>   **for** $q \in Q$, $X \in V$ **do** $L'(X, q) \leftarrow \emptyset$; $R'(q, X) \leftarrow \emptyset$ **od**;
>   **for** $q, q' \in Q$, $A \rightarrow BC \in P$ **do**
>   **if** $(q', B, q) \in \delta' \wedge q' \notin L(B, q)$ **then**
> $L(B, q) \leftarrow L(B, q) \cup \{q'\}$; $L'(B, q) \leftarrow L'(B, q) \cup \{q'\}$
>   **fi**;
>   **if** $(q, C, q') \in \delta' \wedge q \notin R(q, C)$ **then**
> $R(q, C) \leftarrow R(q, C) \cup \{q'\}$; $R'(q, C) \leftarrow R'(q, C) \cup \{q'\}$
>   **fi**;
>   **od**;
>   **for** $q \in Q$, $A \rightarrow BC \in P$ **do**
> $\delta' \leftarrow \delta' \cup (L'(B, q) \times \{A\} \times R(q, C)) \cup (L(B, q) \times \{A\} \times R'(q, C))$
>   **od**
> **until** δ' does not change any more

The correctness of the algorithm is an immediate consequence of the fact that both algorithms have added exactly the same new transitions after each iteration of the **repeat-until** loop. More precisely: for every $k \geq 1$, after k

iterations of the **repeat-until** loop the variable δ' has exactly the same value in both Algorithm 1 and Algorithm 2.

Let us now examine the running time.

Lemma 3. *If the* **repeat-until** *loop is executed k times, then Algorithm 2 terminates in $O(kn^2) + O(n^3)$ time.*

Proof. The algorithm uses states (q and q'), sets of states (Q, $L(X,q)$, $L'(X,q)$, $R(q,X)$, $R'(q,X)$) and transition tables (δ and δ') as its basic data structures. We assume that states are implemented as numbers in $\{1,\ldots,n\}$, while sets of states and transition tables are implemented as bit vectors of length n, respectively length $n^2|V|$.

With this implementation the time complexity of all operations is as follows:

Operation	Time complexity
$\delta' \leftarrow \delta$	$O(n^2)$
$(q,a,q') \in \delta'$	$O(1)$
$\delta \leftarrow \delta' \cup \{(q,A,q')\}$	$O(1)$
$L(X,q) \leftarrow \emptyset$	$O(n)$
$q' \in L(B,q)$	$O(1)$
$L'(B,q) \leftarrow L'(B,q) \cup \{q'\}$	$O(1)$
$\delta' \leftarrow \delta' \cup L'(B,q) \times \{A\} \times R(q,C)$	$O(n) + O(n \cdot |L'(B,q)|)$

Only the last line needs some explanation. It works by reading the bit vector of $L'(B,q)$ ignoring empty entries (ignoring an entry takes $O(1)$ time) and performing $\delta' \leftarrow \delta' \cup \{(s,A,s')\}$ for all $s \in R(q,C)$ when finding an entry s in $L'(B,q)$ ($O(n)$ steps).

Let us assume the **repeat-until** loop is executed exactly k times. Using the above table we easily see that everything before the **repeat-until** loop runs in time $O(n^2)$. The first **for** loop in the body of the **repeat-until** loop runs in time $O(n^2)$, the second **for** loop also in time $O(n^2)$. Not counting the last **for** loop, the overall time requirement is therefore $O(n^2) + k \cdot O(n^2) = O(kn^2)$.

Let $L'_i(B,q)$, $L_i(B,q)$, $R'_i(q,C)$, and $R_i(q,C)$ denote the values of $L'(B,q)$, $L(B,q)$, $R'(q,C)$ and $R(q,C)$ after the ith iteration of the **repeat-until** loop. The last **for** loop then requires

$$T(i) = \sum_{\substack{q \in Q \\ A \to BC \in P}} \Big(O(n) + O(n \cdot |L'_i(B,q)|) + O(n \cdot |R'_i(q,C)|) \Big)$$

$$= O(n^2) + O\Big(n \cdot \sum_{\substack{q \in Q \\ A \to BC \in P}} |L'_i(B,q)|\Big) + O\Big(n \cdot \sum_{\substack{q \in Q \\ A \to BC \in P}} |R'_i(q,C)|\Big)$$

steps during the ith iteration of the **repeat-until** loop. The total running time of the algorithm is therefore $O(kn^2) + T(1) + T(2) + \cdots + T(k)$.

Since the $L'_i(B,q)$'s for $i = 1, \ldots, k$ as well as the $R'_i(q,C)$'s are disjoint, we have

$$\sum_{i=1}^{k} |L'_i(B,q)| \leq n \quad \text{and} \quad \sum_{i=1}^{k} |R'_i(q,C)| \leq n.$$

So the sum $T(1) + T(2) + \cdots + T(k)$ yields

$$\sum_{i=1}^{k} O(n^2) + \sum_{\substack{q \in Q \\ A \to BC \in P}} \left(O(n \cdot \sum_{i=1}^{k} |L'_i(B,q)|) + O(n \cdot \sum_{i=1}^{k} |R'_i(q,C)|) \right) = O(kn^2) + O(n^3)$$

The overall running time is therefore $O(kn^2 + n^3)$. □

We immediately get:

Theorem 4. *Algorithm 2 runs in $O(n^4)$ time.*

Proof. Since M' has $O(n^2)$ transitions, the **repeat-until** loop is executed $O(n^2)$ times. Use now Lemma 3. □

It requires a bit of thought to find a grammar and a family of NFAs for which the **repeat-until** loop is executed $\Theta(n^2)$ times and Algorithm 2 runs in $\Theta(n^4)$ time. The next figure shows an example (more precisely, the figure shows the grammar and a member of the family):

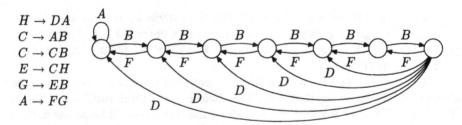

$$H \to DA$$
$$C \to AB$$
$$C \to CB$$
$$E \to CH$$
$$G \to EB$$
$$A \to FG$$

5   A special case

In this section, we show that Algorithm 2 needs only $O(n^3)$ time for linear NFAs, a special class of inputs relevant for the next section. An NFA is *linear* if there is a bijection $l : Q \to \{1, \ldots, n\}$ such that $l(q) \leq l(q')$ if and only if $q \xrightarrow{\alpha} q'$ for some word α.[2]

Lemma 5. *If the input NFA M of Algorithm 2 is linear, then the **repeat-until** loop is executed at most $O(n)$ times.*

---

[2] Observe that all circuits of a linear NFA are of the form $q \xrightarrow{A} q$. We call them *self-loops*.

Proof. Observe first that any new transition $q \xrightarrow{A} q'$ added by the algorithm to a linear input M satisfies $l(q) \neq l(q')$. Therefore, if the input M is linear, so is the output M'.

Let the *width* of a transition $q \xrightarrow{A} q'$ be $l(q') - l(q)$. We show that transitions $q \xrightarrow{A} q'$ of width i are added after at most $(i+1)|V|$th iterations of the **repeat-until** loop.

We proceed by induction on i. The base of the induction is the case $i = 0$. We then have $q = q'$ and so the transition $q \xrightarrow{A} q'$ is in fact the self-loop $q \xrightarrow{A} q$. If $q \xrightarrow{A} q$ is added by one of the two initial **for** loops, then it has been added after 0 iterations of the **repeat-until** loop, and we are done. So assume that $q \xrightarrow{B} q', q' \xrightarrow{C} q$ and a rule $A \to BC$ yield together $q \xrightarrow{A} q$. Since the current automaton is linear, we have $q = q'$, and so both $q \xrightarrow{B} q$ and $q \xrightarrow{C} q$ are self-loops. Since each state can have at most $|V|$ self-loops labelled with variables, and in each iteration of the **repeat-until** loop at least one of them is added, $q \xrightarrow{A} q$ is added during the first $|V|$ iterations.

Now, let the width of $q \xrightarrow{A} q'$ be $i > 0$. Again, if $q \xrightarrow{A} q'$ is added by one of the two initial **for** loops, then we are done as before. So assume that there is a state q'' with $q \xrightarrow{B} q''$ and $q'' \xrightarrow{C} q'$ and a production $A \to BC \in P$. Clearly, the widths of $q \xrightarrow{B} q''$ and $q'' \xrightarrow{C} q'$ are at most i. If these two widths are smaller than i, then by the induction hypothesis $q \xrightarrow{B} q''$ and $q'' \xrightarrow{C} q'$ are added after at most $(i-1)|V|$ iterations. So $q \xrightarrow{A} q'$ is added after at most $(i-1)|V| + 1 \leq i|V|$ iterations.

Let us now assume that the width of $q \xrightarrow{B} q''$ is i or the width of $q'' \xrightarrow{C} q'$ is i. Then $q = q''$ or $q' = q''$. If $q = q''$ we say $q \xrightarrow{A} q'$ *depends directly on* $q \xrightarrow{C} q'$. If $q' = q''$ we say $q \xrightarrow{A} q'$ *depends directly on* $q \xrightarrow{B} q'$.

In general we have direct dependency chains $q \xrightarrow{A} q'$, $q \xrightarrow{A'} q'$, $q \xrightarrow{A''} q', \ldots$, $q \xrightarrow{A^{(k)}} q'$, where $q \xrightarrow{A^{(t)}} q'$ depends directly on $q \xrightarrow{A^{(t+1)}} q'$ for $t = 0, \ldots, k-1$. Since no two transitions of the chain can be identical and there are only $|V|$ variables, we have $k \leq |V|$. The last transition $q \xrightarrow{A^{(k)}} q'$ of a maximal chain does not depend directly on a transition, and so it is added because of transitions with width smaller than i. By induction hypothesis this occurs after at most $(i-1)|V|$ iterations. Then $q \xrightarrow{A^{(t)}} q'$ is added after at most $(i-1)|V| + k - t$ iterations, and $q \xrightarrow{A} q'$ after $(i-1)|V| + k \leq i|V|$ iterations.

Since the width of all transitions is at most $n = |Q|$, all transitions are added after at most $n|V|$ iterations of the **repeat-until** loop. So δ' does not change any more during the $n|V| + 1$ iteration, and the loop is executed $O(n)$ times. $\square$

It follows from Lemma 5 and Lemma 3 that Algorithm 2 runs in $O(n^3)$ time for linear NFAs.

6 Applications

We show that several standard problems on context-free languages, for which textbooks often give independent algorithms, can be solved using Algorithm 2.

We fix a context-free grammar $G = (V, T, P, S)$ for the rest of this section.

In order to avoid redundant symbols in G it is convenient to compute the set of *useless* variables ([6], p.88). Recall that $X \in V$ is *useful* if there is a derivation $S \stackrel{*}{\Rightarrow} \alpha X \beta \stackrel{*}{\Rightarrow} w$ for some α, β and w, where w is in T^*. Otherwise it is *useless*. To decide if X is useless, observe that X is useful if and only if $S \in pre^*(T^*XT^*)$ and $X \in pre^*(T^*)$. Compute the automata accepting $pre^*(T^*XT^*)$ and $pre^*(T^*)$ using Algorithm 2, and check if they accept S and X, respectively.

Nullable variables have to be identified when eliminating ϵ-productions ([6], p. 90). A variable X is *nullable* if $X \stackrel{*}{\Rightarrow} \epsilon$. To decide the nullability of a variable observe that X is nullable if and only if $X \in pre^*(\{\epsilon\})$.

Consider now the membership problem: given a word $w \in T^*$ of length n, is w generated by G? To solve it, compute the automaton accepting $pre^*(\{w\})$, and check in constant time if it accepts S. Since there is a linear automaton with $n + 1$ states recognizing $\{w\}$, the complexity of the algorithm is $O(n^3)$. This is also the complexity of the CYK-algorithm usually taught to undergraduates [7].

To decide if $L(G)$ is contained in a given regular language L, observe that $L(G) \subseteq L$ is equivalent to $L(G) \cap \overline{L} = \emptyset$, which is equivalent to $S \notin pre^*(\overline{L})$. If L is presented as a deterministic finite automaton with n states, compute a deterministic automaton for $\overline{L}$ in $O(n)$ time, and check $S \notin pre^*(\overline{L})$ in $O(n^4)$.

Similarly, to decide if $L(G)$ and L are disjoint, check whether $S \notin pre^*(L)$. In the example of Figure 1 the languages are disjoint because there is no transition $q_0 \stackrel{S}{\longrightarrow} q_2$.

To decide if $L(G)$ is empty, check whether $L(G)$ is contained in the empty language, which is regular. In this case the automaton for $\overline{L}$ has just one state.

To decide if $L(G)$ is infinite, assume that G has no useless symbols (otherwise apply the algorithm above), and use the following characterization (see for instance [6], Theorem 6.6): $L(G)$ is infinite if and only if there exists a variable X and strings $\alpha, \beta \in \Sigma^*$ with $\alpha\beta \neq \epsilon$ such that $X \stackrel{*}{\Rightarrow} \alpha X \beta$. This is the case if and only if $X \in pre^*(\Sigma^+ X \Sigma^* \cup \Sigma^* X \Sigma^+)$.

7 Conclusions

In our opinion, our adaptation of Book and Otto's technique has a number of pedagogical merits that make it very suitable for an undergraduate course on formal languages and automata theory: it is appealing and easy to understand, its correctness proof is simple, it applies the theory of finite automata to the study of context-free languages, and it provides a unified view of several standard algorithms.

Acknowledgements We are very grateful to Ahmed Bouajjani and Oded Maler, who drew our attention to Book and Otto's result, and applied it, together with the first author, to the analysis of pushdown automata [3, 4]. Many thanks to an anonymous referee for pointing out an important mistake in a former version of the paper, and for very helpful suggestions.

References

1. A. V. Aho, J. E. Hopcroft and J. D. Ullman. The Design and Analysis of Computer Algorithms. Addison-Wesley, 1976.
2. R. F. Book and F. Otto. *String-Rewriting Systems*. Texts and Monographs in Computer Science. Springer, 1993.
3. A. Bouajjani and O. Maler. Reachability analysis of pushdown automata Proceedings of INFINITY '96, tech, rep. MIP-9614, Univ. Passau, 1996.
4. A. Bouajjani, J. Esparza, and O. Maler. Reachability analysis of pushdown automata: Application to model checking. To appear in CONCUR '97.
5. W. Brauer. *Automatentheorie*. Teubner, 1984.
6. J. E. Hopcroft and J. D. Ullman. *Introduction to Automata Theory, Languages and Computation*. Addison-Wesley, 1979.
7. D. H. Younger. Recognition and parsing of context-free languages in time n^3. *Information and Control*, 10:189–208, 1967.

On Aperiodic Sets of Wang Tiles

Karel Culik[1] and Jarkko Kari[2]

[1] Depart. of Comp. Science,
University of South Carolina,
Columbia, S.C. 29208 ***
[2] Depart. of Comp. Science,
University of Iowa,
Iowa City, IA 52242-1419

1 Introduction

Wang tiles are unit square tiles with colored edges. The tile whose left, right, top and bottom edges have colors l, r, t and b, respectively is denoted by the 4-tuple (l, r, t, b). A *tile set* is a finite set of Wang tiles. *Tilings* of the infinite Euclidean plane are considered using arbitrarily many copies of the tiles in the given tile set. The tiles are placed on the integer lattice points of the plane with their edges oriented horizontally and vertically. The tiles may not be rotated. A tiling is *valid* if everywhere the contiguous edges have the same color.

Let T be a finite tile set, and $f : \mathbb{Z}^2 \to T$ a tiling. Tiling f is *periodic* with period $(a, b) \in \mathbb{Z}^2 - \{(0, 0)\}$ iff $f(x, y) = f(x + a, y + b)$ for every $(x, y) \in \mathbb{Z}^2$. If there exists a periodic valid tiling with tiles of T, then there exists a *doubly periodic* valid tiling, i.e. a tiling f such that, for some $a, b > 0$, $f(x, y) = f(x + a, y) = f(x, y + b)$ for all $(x, y) \in \mathbb{Z}^2$. A tile set T is called *aperiodic* iff (i) there exists a valid tiling, and (ii) there does not exist any periodic valid tiling.

R. Berger in his well known proof of the undecidability of the tiling problem [2] refuted Wang's conjecture that no aperiodic set exists, and constructed the first aperiodic set containing 20426 tiles. He shortly reduced it to 104 tiles. A number of researchers, among them some well known people in discrete mathematics, logic and computer science, tried to find a smaller aperiodic set of Wang tiles. Between 1966 and 1978 progressively smaller aperiodic sets were found by D. E. Knuth (92 tiles, 1966, see [11]), H. Läuchli (40 tiles, 1966, see [8, p. 590]), R. M. Robinson (56 tiles, 1967, 35 tiles, 1971), R. Penrose (34 tiles, 1973), R. M. Robinson (32 tiles, 1973, see [8, p. 593] and 24 tiles, 1977, see [8, p. 593]) and finally R. Ammann (16 tiles, 1978, see [13, 8, p. 595]). An excellent discussion of these and related results, and in most cases the first published version of them is included in Chapter 10 and 11 of [8]. We quote from [8, p. 596]: "The reduction in the number of Wang tiles in an aperiodic set from over 20,000 to 16 has been a notable achievement. Perhaps the minimum possible number has now been reached. If, however, further reductions are possible, then it seems certain that new ideas and methods will be required. The discovery of such remains one of the outstanding challenges in this field of mathematics." Recently,

---

*** Supported by the National Science Foundation under Grant No. CCR-9417384

the second author developed a new method for constructing aperiodic sets that is not based on geometry, as the earlier ones, but on sequential machines that multiply real numbers in the balanced representation by rational constants. The balanced representation is based on Beatty sequences [1]. This approach makes short and precise correctness arguments possible. He used it to construct a new aperiodic set containing only 14 tiles over 6 colors in [10]. The first author added an additional trick in [3] and obtained an aperiodic set consisting of 13 tiles over 5 colors.

Recently, we have studied whether the 13-set tile T_{13} from [3] is (locally) minimal, i.e. whether all 13 tiles are needed in order to tile the whole plane. With the help of software written by V.Valenta, we performed extensive computer experiments and searches which support our conjecture that when omitting one tile from T_{13} we still get an aperiodic set T_{12} of Wang tiles. Clearly, we just need to show that the whole plane can be tiled with only the 12 tiles. However, to prove this, even using the isomorphism between tilings and computations of the sequential machine representing the tile set, seems to be extremely difficult. In the following we will discuss our plan of attacking this problem.

2 Balanced representation of numbers, sequential machines and tile sets

For an arbitrary real number r we denote by $\lfloor r \rfloor$ the integer part of r, i.e. the largest integer that is not greater than r, and by $\{r\}$ the fractional part $r - \lfloor r \rfloor$. In proving that our tile set can be used to tile the plane we use *Beatty sequences* of numbers. Given a real number α, its bi-infinite Beatty sequence is the integer sequence $A(\alpha)$ consisting of the integral parts of the multiples of α. In other words, for all $i \in \mathbb{Z}$,

$$A(\alpha)_i = \lfloor i \cdot \alpha \rfloor.$$

Beatty sequences were introduced by S.Beatty [1] in 1926.

We use sequences obtained by computing the differences of consecutive elements of Beatty sequences. Define, for every $i \in \mathbb{Z}$,

$$B(\alpha)_i = A(\alpha)_i - A(\alpha)_{i-1}.$$

The bi-infinite sequence $B(\alpha)_i$ will be called the *balanced* representation of α. The balanced representations consist of at most two different numbers: If $k \leq \alpha \leq k + 1$ then $B(\alpha)$ is a sequence of k's and $(k + 1)$'s. Moreover, the averages over finite subsequences approach α as the lengths of the subsequences increase. In fact, the averages are as close to α as they can be: The difference between $l \cdot \alpha$ and the sum of any l consecutive elements of $B(\alpha)$ is always smaller than one.

For example,

$$B(1.5) = \ldots 121212\ldots, \ B(\tfrac{1}{3}) = \ldots 001001\ldots \text{ and } B(\tfrac{8}{3}) = \ldots 233233\ldots.$$

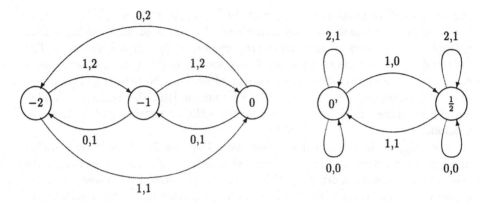

Fig. 1. Sequential machines M_3 and $M_{\frac{1}{2}}$

The balanced representation of a rational number is always a periodic bi-infinite string. A periodic bi-infinite string ($\omega\omega$-string) $\ldots www \ldots$ is denoted by $(w)^{\omega\omega}$.

Now we introduce sequential machines which define mappings on bi-infinite strings. We will use them to implement multiplication of numbers in balanced representation and later shown that they are isomorphic to sets of tiles.

A *sequential machine* is a 4-tuple $M = (K, \Sigma, \Delta, \gamma)$ where K is the set of states, Σ is the input alphabet, Δ is the output alphabet, and $\gamma \subseteq K \times \Sigma \times \Delta \times K$ is the transition set. Sequential machine M can be represented by a labeled directed graph with nodes K and an edge from node q to node p labeled a, b for each transition (q, a, b, p) in γ.

Machine M computes a relation $\rho(M)$ between bi-infinite sequences of letters. Bi-infinite sequences x and y over input and output alphabets, respectively, are in relation $\rho(M)$ if and only if there is a bi-infinite sequence s of states of M such that, for every $i \in \mathbb{Z}$, there is a transition from s_{i-1} to s_i labeled by x_i, y_i.

In [10, 3] we show that for every rational number $\frac{m}{n}$ we can construct a sequential machine with $m + n - 1$ states that implements the multiplication by $\frac{m}{n}$ on real numbers in the balanced representation. It is based on using the states to remember the remainders where the input is multiplied digit by digit by $\frac{m}{n}$. A transition $s \xrightarrow{a,b} t$ means that $a\frac{m}{n} + s = b + t$. Fig. 1 shows a diagram of sequential machine M_3 which multiplies by 3, and sequential machine $M_{\frac{1}{2}}$ which divides by 2. For example, there are two transitions from state 0 (remainder 0) in machine M_3: transition $0 \xrightarrow{0,2} -2$ and $0 \xrightarrow{0,1} -1$. Since the result of the multiplication is 0, in order to get the output in the desired output alphabet $\{1, 2\}$, we either output 2 and the remainder is -2 or output 1 and the remainder is -1.

Finally, there is a one-to-one correspondence between the tile sets and sequential machines which translates the properties of tile sets to properties of computations of sequential machines.

A finite tile set T over the set of colors C_{EW} on east-west edges and the set of colors C_{NS} on north-south edges is represented by sequential machine $M = (C_{EW}, C_{NS}, C_{NS}, \gamma)$ where $(s, a, b, t) \in \gamma$ iff there is a tile (s, a, b, t) in T. See Fig. 2.

Fig. 2. The tile (s, a, b, t) corresponding to the transition $s \xrightarrow{a,b} t$

Obviously, bi-infinite sequences x and y are in the relation $\rho(M)$ iff there exists a row of tiles, with matching vertical edges, whose upper edges form sequence x and lower edges sequence y. So there is a one-to-one correspondence between valid tilings of the plane, and bi-infinite iterations of the sequential machine on bi-infinite sequences.

Clearly, the two conditions for T being aperiodic can be translated to conditions on computations of M. Set T is aperiodic if and only if (i) there exists a bi-infinite computation of M, and (ii) there is no bi-infinite word w over C_{NS} such that $(w, w) \in [\rho(M)]^+$, where ρ^+ denotes the transitive closure of ρ.

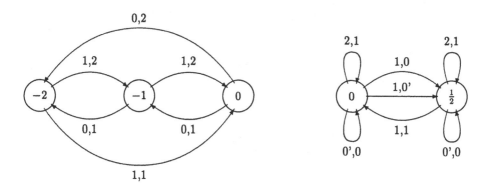

Fig. 3. Sequential machine $M = M_3 \cup M'_{\frac{1}{2}}$.

Our construction of a small aperiodic set is based on the implementation of an aperiodic dynamical system by a sequential machine. Consider the following specification of dynamical system S_1 on the real interval $[\frac{1}{3}, 2]$. For arbitrary starting value $s_0 \in [\frac{1}{3}, 2]$, let for $n > 0$,

$$s_{n+1} = 3s_n, \quad \text{for} \quad s_n \in [\frac{1}{3}, \frac{2}{3}] ;$$

$$s_{n+1} = \frac{1}{2}s_n \quad \text{for} \quad s_n \in (\frac{2}{3}, 2] .$$

It is easy to see that $s_n \in [\frac{1}{3}, 2]$ for all $n \geq 0$ and that starting from any $s_0 \in [\frac{1}{3}, 2]$ the operation performed alternates between one multiplication by 3 followed by one or two divisions by 2. Since $\frac{3^k}{2^l} \neq 1$ for all integers $k, l \geq 1$ we have that $s_k \neq s_l$ for all $k, l \geq 0$, hence our dynamical system is aperiodic. We can implement the multiplication by 3 and division by 2 by the sequential machines in Fig. 1. However, we have to enforce the condition that at most two divisions by 2 are performed consecutively. We ensure this by modifying $M_{\frac{1}{2}}$ to sequential machine $M'_{\frac{1}{2}}$ shown in Fig. 3. Machines M_3 and $M'_{\frac{1}{2}}$ can be viewed as one machine $M = M_3 \cup M'_{\frac{1}{2}}$. This sequential machine correctly implements dynamical system S_1. For strings representing numbers in $[\frac{1}{3}, \frac{2}{3}]$ the multiplication by 3 is executed, for strings representing numbers in $(\frac{2}{3}, 2]$ the division by 2 is executed. The corresponding tile set T_{13} has 13 tiles and admits a tiling of the whole plane since our machine performs, among others, the infinite computation by our dynamical system. The tiles are depicted in Fig. 4 in the same order as the corresponding transitions are in Fig. 3.

One might think that the nonexistence of a periodic tiling follows from the aperiodicity of our dynamical system. That essentially is the idea, however, we have to show that there is no aperiodic computation (tiling), not even one which does not work with balanced representations. We can argue as follows: Assume there is a valid periodic tiling. Then there is a doubly periodic tiling, say with horizontal period a. In terms of sequential machines, after a input letters the machine returns to the same state, so the remainder is 0. Therefore, the sum of symbols over one period of length a gets multiplied by 3 or $\frac{1}{2}$, depending on which machine M_3 or $M'_{\frac{1}{2}}$ was used. Since no sequence of multiplications by 3 and $\frac{1}{2}$ gives identity, regardless of the order in which they are performed, there cannot be a vertical period. Therefore, the tiling is not doubly periodic.

Thus we have the smallest known aperiodic set together with a clean brief proof of the required properties.

3 An aperiodic set of 12 tiles

A natural question for any aperiodic set S is: Is S (locally) minimal, i.e. is any proper subset of S aperiodic? We have a result in [7] which helps to test whether after omitting a tile from our tile set T_{13} there still exists a tiling of the whole plane. This result states, in terms of the computations of our sequential machine, that every infinite computation must include a row of inputs containing an arbitrarily long substring of 2's. This result is also valid for every subset of T_{13} that admits a tiling of the whole plane. By Konig's infinity lemma, such

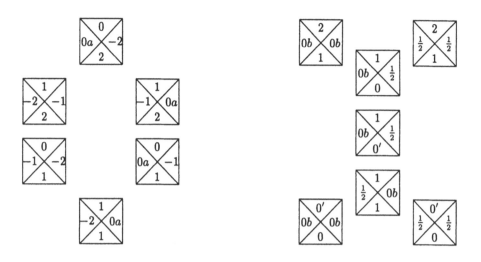

Fig. 4. Aperiodic tile set T_{13} corresponding to the sequential machine M. We used labels $0a$ and $0b$ to distinguish the two states with the same label 0 in M.

subset must also admit a tiling with one row of inputs entirely consisting of 2's. Now, our sequential machines are a special case of an $\omega\omega$-transducer of [5] and the bi-infinite sequence of 2's is an $\omega\omega$-regular set of [5]. In [5] , it is shown that $\omega\omega$-regular sets are effectively closed under $\omega\omega$-transducers.

V. Valenta implemented the computation of (simple) $\omega\omega$-regular sets by sequential machines. Since, for some subset $S \subseteq T_{13}$, every computation must contain $2^{\omega\omega}$ (a bi-infinite string of 2's) we compute successively $R_n = M^n(2^{\omega\omega})$ for $n = 1, 2, \ldots$. For each (simple) $\omega\omega$-regular set R_n we can test whether $R_n = \emptyset$ (by testing if its reduced form has a cycle). Clearly, if this is the case, there exists no extension of $2^{\omega\omega}$ by n rows and hence no tiling of the whole plane. The number of states of R_n grows exponentially so we can test up to 15 steps down or up. The above technique allowed us to show that all tiles in T_{13} are essential with the possible exception of the two tiles with the input $0'$ and the output 0. Further extensive investigations indicate that indeed it seems to be possible that one of these tiles can be omitted and the remaining tiles still allow an infinite computation (i.e., a valid tiling of the whole plane). The sequential machine for division by 2 is essentially symmetric so it does not matter which of the two tiles is omitted. Say we omit the edge at state $\frac{1}{2}$ and denote the resulting tile set by T_{12}.

Note that a tile (transition) with input $0'$ is used only when dividing by 2 for the second time in a row. We will combine such two successive divisions by two into one (restricted) division by 4, which is implemented by $M_{\frac{1}{4}}^r$, the composition

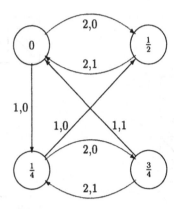

Fig. 5. Sequential machine $M_{\frac{1}{4}}^r$

of the unrestricted division by 2 and of the restricted division by 2. The diagram of $M_{\frac{1}{4}}^r$ is shown in Fig. 5. That gives us the dynamical system S_2 which, up to the omission of some steps, is equivalent to S_1

$$s_{n+1} = 3s_n \text{ for } s_n \in [\frac{1}{3}, \frac{2}{3}] \,;$$

$$s_{n+1} = \frac{1}{2}s_n \text{ for } s_n \in (\frac{2}{3}, \frac{4}{3}] \,;$$

$$s_{n+1} = \frac{1}{4}s_n \text{ for } s_n \in (\frac{4}{3}, 2] \,.$$

However, the union of sequential machines M_3, $M_{\frac{1}{2}}$ and $M_{\frac{1}{4}}^r$ does not implement S_2 in the balanced number representation since machine $M_{\frac{1}{4}}^r$ is not defined for the most balanced representation in $(\frac{3}{4}, 2]$ (e.g. for $(12)^{\omega\omega}$ the balanced representation of $\frac{3}{2}$). Our extensive computer experiments have shown that there exists a computation of at least length 30 using the machines $M_3, M_{\frac{1}{2}}$ and $M_{\frac{1}{4}}^r$; hence, tile set T_{12} admits a tiling of size 30 by infinity. Since we can also interpret our tile set as a sequential machine running horizontally (i.e. having the colors on vertical edges as inputs-outputs and the colors on horizontal edges as states), our tests also show that we can tile the area of size 30 horizontally and vertically infinite. Both these tilings match in the common square of size 30×30. Thus we know that the tiles from set T_{12} can tile an "infinite cross" with both arms 30 tiles wide. We know how to design a more efficient simulation which would disprove our conjecture if the counter example requires a depth up to about 50.

However, we believe that T_{12} is aperiodic and we have a plan how to try to prove it. Unlike in the case of T_{13} such proof will require to consider sequential machine with a relatively large number of states, will require first extensive computer experiments and finally to test the complicated cases by computer. The

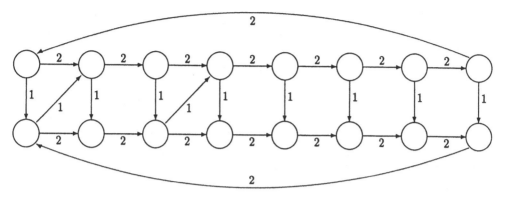

Fig. 6. $\omega\omega$ finite automaton A

main idea is to consider a "speed-up" of dynamical system S_2. We will combine sequential machines M_3, $M_{\frac{1}{2}}$ and $M_{\frac{1}{4}}^r$ into bigger machines each performing several steps at once. Let $M_{\frac{9}{8}}^r = M_{\frac{1}{4}}^r \circ M_3 \circ M_{\frac{1}{2}}^r \circ M_3$ and $M_{\frac{27}{32}}^r = M_{\frac{1}{4}}^r \circ M_3 \circ M_{\frac{1}{4}}^r \circ M_3 \circ M_{\frac{1}{2}} \circ M_3$, where $\circ$ denotes the (associative) composition of sequential machines. The idea is that both $M_{\frac{9}{8}}^r$ and $M_{\frac{22}{32}}^r$ have the restricted $M_{\frac{1}{4}}^r$ close to the front and unrestricted tail $M_3 \circ M_{\frac{1}{2}} \circ M_3$. Since M_3 is nondeterministic and specifically, in many contexts, it allows to switch consecutive 1 and 2 on the output, we believe that we will be able to prove the existence of an infinite computation by this machines which, of course, would imply the existence of an infinite computation by the original small machines. We note that a computation by M_3, $M_{\frac{1}{2}}$ and $M_{\frac{1}{4}}^r$ involves alternating of M_3 and either $M_{\frac{1}{2}}$ or $M_{\frac{1}{4}}^r$ with the additional rule that $M_{\frac{1}{2}}$ never comes immediately before and after M_3. Therefore, any such computation can be simulated by alternating $M_{\frac{9}{8}}^r$ and $M_{\frac{29}{32}}^r$, where a simple application of $M_{\frac{29}{32}}^r$ is alternating with one or two applications of $M_{\frac{9}{8}}^r$. The corresponding "fast" dynamical system operates in the interval $[\frac{4}{3}, 2]$ as follows:

$$s_{n+1} = \frac{9}{8}s_n \ \text{ for } \ s_n \in [\frac{3}{4}, \frac{16}{9}];$$

$$s_{n+1} = \frac{29}{32}s_n \ \text{ for } \ s_n \in (\frac{16}{9}, 2].$$

Since $M_{\frac{9}{8}}^r$ starts with $M_{\frac{1}{4}}^r$, it is easy to see that a necessary condition for a bi-infinite string to be in the domain of $M_{\frac{9}{8}}^r$ is that we can choose every second 1's (two choices, say, odd or even 1's), so that between each two successive odd (even) 1's there is odd number of 2's. For $M_{\frac{29}{32}}^r$ a similar necessary condition is somewhat more complicated, a bi-infinite string must be in the domain of $M_{\frac{1}{4}}^r \circ M_3 \circ M_{\frac{1}{4}}^r \circ M_3$ which can be shown to be specified by $\omega\omega$-finite automaton A shown in Fig. 6. It is easy to see that a bi-infinite string accepted by A has to satisfy the condition that the number of 2's between any odd (even) 1's must be congruent to 5, 7 or 9 modulo 8. This leads us to the definition of *pseudobalanced* representation $\beta(r)$ of a rational number in $[\frac{4}{3}, 2]$ which we define intuitively as follows: Note that the balanced representation of a rational number is always periodic. Let $(u)^{\omega\omega}$ be the balanced representation of $r \in [\frac{4}{3}, 2]$. We define $\beta(r) = (w)^{\omega\omega}$ where w is chosen so that the ratio of 1's and 2's in w is the same as in u, and w is one of the shortest strings satisfying the necessary domain condition, chosen so that each prefix is as close as possible to the correct ratio of 1's and 2's. The weaker condition ($\equiv 1 \mod 2$) is used for the bi-infinite strings representing rational numbers in $[\frac{3}{4}, \frac{16}{9}]$ the stronger one ($\equiv 5, 7$ or $9 \mod 8$) in $[\frac{16}{9}, 2]$. We denote the set of pseudobalanced strings representing numbers in $[\frac{3}{4}, \frac{16}{9}]$ and in $(\frac{16}{9}, 2]$ by P_1 and P_2, respectively. We know that $P_1 \subseteq \text{dom}\, M_{\frac{9}{8}}^r$ and $P_2 \subseteq \text{dom}\, M_{\frac{29}{32}}^r$. We need to show that $M_{\frac{9}{8}}^r(x) \cap P_2 \neq \emptyset$ for each $x \in P_1$ and $M_{\frac{29}{32}}^r(y) \cap P_1 \neq \emptyset$ for each $y \in P_2$. Computer experiments have shown that there is no "small" counter example to the above. We found such counter examples for other smaller compositions of the basic sequential machines.

Principally, if our conjecture holds and can be proved by the above strategy a big computer can complete our proof. This is because testing of the equality of topologically closed sets of bi-infinite strings (in the product topology, see [4, 5]), reduces to the testing of their finite substrings, see [5], and the testing of the equivalence of two regular sets R_1 and R_2 reduces to the testing of the strings up to the length $m + n$, where $m(n)$ is the number of states of a deterministic finite automaton accepting $R_1(R_2)$, respectively [6]. Unfortunately, $m + n$ in our application is so big that no supercomputer could perform the test. Our plan si to show that for every $r \in [\frac{3}{4}, \frac{16}{9}]$ we can modify the balanced image $B(\frac{9}{8}r)$ of the balanced representation $B(r)$ to obtain a pseudobalanced image $\beta(\frac{9}{8}r)$ in $M_{\frac{9}{8}}^r(\beta(r))$. Similarly, for $r \in (\frac{16}{9}, 2)$ we will construct $\beta(\frac{29}{32}r)$ in $M_{\frac{29}{32}}^r(\beta(r))$.

References

1. S. Beatty, Problem 3173, *Am. Math. Monthly* 33 (1926) 159; solutions in 34, 159 (1927).

2. R. Berger, The Undecidability of the Domino Problem, *Mem. Amer. Math. Soc.* 66 (1966).

3. K. Culik II, An aperiodic set of 13 Wang tiles, *Discrete Mathematics*, to appear.

4. K. Culik II, L. P. Hurd and S. Yu, computation theoretic aspects of cellular automata, *Physica D* 45, 357-378 (1990).

5. K. Culik II and S. Yu, Cellular automata, $\omega\omega$-regular sets, and Sofic Systems, *Discrete Applied Mathematics* 32, 85-102 (1991).

6. J. E. Hopcroft and J. D. Ullman, *Introduction to automata theory, languages and computation*, Addison-Wesley (1979).

7. K. Culik II and J. Kari, An aperiodic set of Wang cubes, *Journal of Universal Computer Science* 1, 675-686 (1995).

8. B. Grünbaum and G.C. Shephard, *Tilings and Patterns*, W.H.Freeman and Company, New York (1987).

9. M.V. Jaric, *Introduction to the Mathematics of Quasicrystals*, Academic Press, Inc., San Diego (1989).

10. J. Kari, A small aperiodic set of Wang tiles, *Discrete Mathematics*, to appear.
11. D. E. Knuth, *The Art of Computer Programming*, Vol.1, p.384, Addison-Wesley, Reading, MA (1968).
12. R. M. Robinson, Undecidability and Nonperiodicity for Tilings of the Plane. *Inventiones Mathematicae* 12, 177-209 (1971).
13. R. M. Robinson, Undecidable tiling problems in the hyperbolic plane, *Inventiones Mathematicae* 44, 259-264 (1978).

Closure under Complementation
of Logspace Complexity Classes
— A Survey —

Birgit Jenner[*]

Abt. Theoretische Informatik, Universität Ulm,
Oberer Eselsberg, D–89069 Ulm, Germany
E-mail: `jenner@informatik.uni-ulm.de`

Abstract

In this article we chronologically survey the closure under complementation results for several logspace-bounded complexity classes, namely the early collapses
of the logspace alternation and oracle hierarchies, and the closure under complementation for NL, LOGCFL, and SL. The presentation of the proofs follows
a uniform approach based on exact counting.

1 Introduction

Since the beginning of complexity theory the major part of research in this field
has been done in the area of polynomial time-bounded classes, since most of
the problems arising "in practice" are located between P and PSPACE. To a
minor extent logarithmic space-bounded classes were investigated, mostly as a
contrast to the polynomial time case. The few examples of problems known to be
computable with logarithmic space arose mainly from the area of finite automata
and formal language theory.

During the last ten years, the importance of logspace classes has increased
considerably. As pushing forces here worked the general interest in parallel algorithms and parallel complexity classes and the separation results obtained
for small circuit complexity classes. Many parallelizable problems are located in
the parallel class NC^2 which is characterized by uniform circuits of polynomial
size and $O(\log^2 n)$ depth, and the "backbone" of a classification scheme of these
problems is built by logspace classes, namely deterministic (L), nondeterministic
(NL), symmetric logspace (SL), and nondeterministic logspace with augmented
pushdown store (LOGCFL), or functional variants of these classes (see [12,3,4]
and for more details see [20]).

Another pushing force for the recent interest in logspace classes was the success in solving various important open questions in this area. The most prominent

---

[*] Work was done while on vacation from Wilhelm-Schickard-Institut für Informatik, Universität Tübingen, during the academic year 1996-97 with DFG-
Habilitandenstipendium Je 154 3/1.

of these results is certainly the one by Immerman [18] and Szelepcsényi [42] who showed that NL is closed under complementation (and got the Gödel prize of 1995 for this result). Other examples are the recent result of Nisan and Ta-Shma [30], the closure of SL under complementation, and the solution of a conjecture of Hartmanis by Cai and Sivakumar [8], the existence of sparse hard sets for NL implies L=NL.

The proofs of these results introduced new techniques like the technique of inductive counting of [18,42] and revealed new interesting properties of logspace classes. In this survey, we pick out one such property, namely the property of "exact counting", that is, determining that a given (abstract) object like a graph or list of graphs has exactly k different parts of a particular type. We want to show that all the closure under complementation results for NL, LOGCFL, and SL, and the collapses of the logspace alternation and oracle hierarchies that preceded these results, "drastically demonstrated that the ability of exact counting [...] makes it possible to complementation nondeterministically" as Schöning formulates it in [36] for NL. What is counted, that is, the *type* of the object that is counted, is determined by the structure of the complexity class in question, for example, for the logspace alternation hierarchy it is the number of solvable GAP instances in a list, and for SL, it is the number of connected components of a graph, just to name two examples.

The article is organized as follows. In the next section we briefly present the classes that will be studied later. Afterwards, each of the closure under complementation results is presented in a separate section that starts with an exposition of the exact counting problem for the class. For space reasons, we had to restrict ourself to extremely short expositions of the proofs and could not include a complete overview about all the known and open closure under complementation results for logspace classes, including, for example, probabilistic logspace classes or some restricted versions of NL.

2 An Overview of Logspace Complexity Classes

In this section we define and describe all the classes that will be studied later.

Deterministic Logspace (L) and Nondeterministic Logspace (NL)

The complexity classes L and NL are the classes of languages that are accepted by *deterministic logspace*-bounded, and respectively, *nondeterministic logspace*-bounded Turing machines, that is, by machines that for inputs of length n obey the space bound $O(\log n)$. L and NL have characterizations by many other abstract models, like multihead finite automata [40], uniform branching programs or skew circuits of polynomial size [45], or extended first order logic [17]. Among the complete problems for L are undirected graph acyclicity [11], finding the product of two permutations for disjoint cycle representation [13], tree isomorphism [28,22]. NL has complete problems from many areas. The probably most famous example is the graph accessibility problem GAP (or sometimes called STCONN) from [23], the problem whether in a given directed graph G two designated nodes s and t are connected via a path. Other examples of NL complete problems are the non-emptiness problem for finite automata [23], the (un)satisfiability problem of Boolean formulas in 2-CNF [24], or concatenation knapsack [19]. (For a collection of L and NL complete problems see [20].)

The Logspace Alternation and Oracle Hierarchies (LAH, LOH)

Whereas deterministic complexity classes above logspace, like for example L, are trivially closed under complementation, nondeterministic classes like NL are not at first sight, and there are many examples of classes characterized by nondeterministic devices that are not closed under complementation, like the recursive enumerable languages, the context-free languages etc. For nondeterministic classes *not* closed or not known to be closed under complementation, it makes sense to consider hierarchies built over the nondeterministic class and its complement analogous to the analytic hierarchy, using the two concepts of alternation or relativization.

Alternating Turing machines were introduced in the fundmental paper [9] of Chandra, Kozen, and Stockmeyer as a generalization of nondeterministic Turing machines. An alternating Turing machine M is allowed to alternate between existential (nondeterministic) and universal states, and acceptance of M is generalized inductively as follows: Any accepting configuration is called accepting; an existential configuration is called accepting, if *at least one* of its successors is accepting, and a universal configuration is accepting, if *all* of its successors are accepting. M accepts its input x if and only if the initial configuration is accepting. The maximal number of alternations between existential and universal states from the initial to the accepting configuration may now be taken as a new "resource". The *logspace alternation hierarchy* LAH of [9] is the set of classes $\{A\Sigma_i^L, A\Pi_i^L \mid i \geq 0\}$, where $A\Sigma_0^L = A\Pi_0^L$ is defined to be L, and $A\Sigma_i^L$ defines the class of all problems that are computable with logspace and $i - 1$ alternations starting in an existential configuration, and $A\Pi_i^L$ is the complementary class, where the machine starts in a universal configuration. In particular it holds $NL = A\Sigma_1^L$, and $coNL = A\Pi_1^L$.

The other logspace hierarchy is defined via relativization using the notion of logspace RST-reducibility defined by Ruzzo, Simon, and Tompa in [35]. RST-reducibility is a "well-behaved compromise" between the two previously known, but extremely strong and, respectively, weak relativizations of Ladner and Lynch [26] and Simon [38]. RST-reducibility is obtained as follows. An oracle machine is a Turing machine M that is extended by a further write-only oracle query tape, on which queries q to an "oracle" may be written, and two special states, in which the "yes" or "no" answer to the question $q \in O?$, for a particular oracle O, is received for free. $B^{<A>}$ denotes the class of languages recognized by oracle machines of class B that have an unbounded write-only oracle query tape for oracle A and operate *deterministically* from the time some symbol is written onto the query tape until the next oracle call is made, after which the query is erased. The *logspace oracle hierarchy* of [35] is the set of classes $\{O\Sigma_i^L, O\Pi_i^L \mid i \geq 0\}$, where $O\varSigma_0^L = O\varPi_0^L := L$, $O\varSigma_{i+1}^L := NL^{<O\varSigma_i^L>}$, $O\varPi_i^L := coO\varSigma_i^L$. Again it holds $O\varSigma_1^L = NL$, but this hierarchy contains the whole logspace alternation hierarchy in its second level: $LAH \subseteq L^{NL} \subseteq O\varSigma_2^L$ [35].

Logspace Plus Pushdown: The Class LOGCFL

An AuxPDA(log) machine (auxiliar log-tape push down automaton) is a logspace Turing machine that is augmented by a pushdown store, for which read, pop and push operations of the topmost symbol are allowed (but no read operations of lower symbols in the push down stack). If the AuxPDA(log) machine is bounded polynomially on their running time, it is called an AuxPDA(log,poly) machine.

Already in 1971 Cook investigated the computation power of AuxPDA(log) machines and showed that they characterize the complexity class P, independently of whether the machine operates determinstically or nondeterministically [10]. Essential for this characterization is the exponential running time of the AuxPDA. Later, Sudborough considered in [41] AuxPDA(log,poly) machines and showed that the corresponding complexity class is precisely LOGCFL, the class of languages that are *logspace many-one reducible to the context-free languages*. During the years, LOGCFL turned out to be an extremely robust class with many characterizations, for example, by alternating logspace Turing machines and polynomial accepting tree size [33], by polynomial-size uniform arithmetic circuits of polynomial degree [39], by uniform semi-unbounded Boolean circuits of polynomial size and logarithmic depth [44]. Furthermore, LOGCFL contains many natural problems, for example, the monotone planar circuit value problem [14], bounded valence subtree isomorphism [34], recognition of tree-width bounded graphs [46] and basic dynamic programming problems [15].

Symmetric logspace (SL)

A Turing machine M is called *symmetric* if for any move from configuration c to configuration c' M can also move back from c' to c (for a formal definition, see [27]). SL is the class of languages that are accepted by logspace-bounded symmetric Turing machines. SL can also be characterized in terms of uniform families of polynomial-size contact schemes or switching networks [31]. The first completeness result for SL was technically quite tricky, Lewis and Papdimitriou [27] showed SL completeness for UGAP (also called USTCONN), the problem to determine for a given undirected graph and designated nodes s, t whether s and t are connected. Several combinatorial problems logspace many-one equivalent to UGAP were already presented six years before in 1976 by Jones, Lien, and Laaser [24] as apparently not NL complete, for example, the problem whether a graph is non-bipartite.

In order to classify various problems that did not seem to be SL or coSL complete, for example, bounded degree planarity, Reif [32] introduced the *symmetric logspace alternation hierarchy* (SLAH) $\{A\varSigma_i^{SL}, A\varPi_i^{SL} \mid i \geq 0\}$ based on SL, in a manner analogous to the alternating hierarchy based on NL described above (but technically more involved). Later, Borodin et al. [6] and Ben-Asher et al. [5] added the *symmetric logspace oracle hierarchy* $\{O\Sigma_i^{\mathrm{SL}}, O\Pi_i^{\mathrm{SL}}, O\Delta_i^{\mathrm{L}} \mid i \geq 0\}$ defined with the Ruzzo-Simon-Tompa oracle query mechanism by replacing NL by SL in the definition of the logspace oracle hierarchy. The inclusion properties of these hierarchies are completely analogous to the NL case.

3 The Logspace Alternation Hierarchy Collapses

The first hierarchy collapse result in complexity theory for a resource bounded hierarchy that was build like the analytic hierarchy came as a big surprise. In 1987 it was shown by Jenner, Kirsig, and Lange that the logspace alternation hierarchy collapses to its second level [21]; independently, Toda showed the collapse of the linear space alternation hierarchy to its second level [43].

The proof given in [21] was the first example of the application of a counting technique to prove a class to be closed under complementation. What matters to count here is the number of solvable GAP instances in a given list of graphs.

Exactly k Solvable GAPs (SG$_=$)

Given: A list of digraphs $(G_1, \ldots, G_n)$, and a positive integer k.
Problem: Are there exactly k solvable GAP instances in the list, i.e., $k = \#\{i \mid 1 \leq i \leq n, G_i \in \mathrm{GAP}\}$?

The counting is applied to a list of GAP instances that build up a computation tree of an $A\Sigma_2^{\mathrm{L}}$ machine. Instead of counting the exact number of solvable instances in this list, it was sufficient to *compare* the number of solvable GAP instances in the first half of the list with those in the second half. This could be achieved with the help of the threshold counting problems **At least k Solvable GAPs (SG$_{\geq k}$)** and **At Most k Solvable GAPs (SG$_{\leq k}$)** that give, respectively, upper and lower bounds on k in SG$_=$. SG$_{\geq k}$ is an (complete) NL-problem; SG$_{\leq k}$ a coNL-problem.

Theorem 1. *[21] The logarithmic alternation hierarchy collapses to its second level, i.e., it holds $\Sigma_2^{\mathrm{L}} = \Pi_2^{\mathrm{L}} = A\Sigma_k^{\mathrm{L}} = A\Pi_k^{\mathrm{L}}$ for all $k \geq 2$.*

Proof. Let G_i, $i \geq 0$, in the following denote a directed graph. Consider the following set C that is logspace many-one complete for $A\Sigma_2^{\mathrm{L}}$:

$$C := \{(G_1, \ldots, G_{2n}) \mid \exists i, 1 \leq i \leq n : G_i \in \mathrm{GAP} \wedge G_{n+i} \notin \mathrm{GAP}\}.$$

We will show that $C \in A\Pi_2^{\mathrm{L}}$. This suffices for the equality $\Sigma_2^{\mathrm{L}} = \Pi_2^{\mathrm{L}}$, and then, by construction of the hierarchy, all higher classes of LAH are equal to $A\Sigma_2^{\mathrm{L}}$.

Let a list of graphs $T := (G_1, \ldots, G_{2n})$ be given. To determine whether T belongs to C we first conjunctively connect any of the last n graphs of T with the first n graphs of T, to ensure that the number of solvable GAPs in the first half does not decrease in the latter half. (A conjunction of two graphs

$(G, s, t), (G', s', t')$ is given by $(G \cup G' \cup \{(t, s')\}, s, t').$) The resulting new list T' looks as follows:

$$T' := (G'_1, \ldots, G'_{2n}) = (G_1, \ldots, G_n, (G_1 \wedge G_{n+1}), \ldots, (G_n \wedge G_{2n})).$$

Now we can determine containment in C simply by comparing the number of solvable GAPs in the first and second half of T':

$$T \in C \iff \#\{i \mid 1 \le i \le n, \ G'_i \in \text{GAP}\} > \#\{i \mid n+1 \le i \le 2n, \ G'_i \in \text{GAP}\}.$$

Using $\text{SG}_{\ge k}$ and $\text{SG}_{\le k}$, we obtain both an $A\Sigma_2^L$ ($\exists$)-description as well as an $A\Pi_2^L$ ($\forall$)-description of the inequality:

$$
\begin{aligned}
T \in C \iff & \bigvee_{k=1}^{n} (G'_1, \ldots, G'_n, k) \in \text{SG}_{\ge k} \wedge (G'_{n+1}, \ldots, G'_{2n}, k-1) \in \text{SG}_{\le k} \\
\iff & \bigwedge_{k=1}^{n} (G'_1, \ldots, G'_n, k-1) \in \text{SG}_{\le k} \vee (G'_{n+1}, \ldots, G'_{2n}, k) \in \text{SG}_{\ge k}.
\end{aligned}
$$

Hence, we have shown that $C \in A\Pi_2^L$. $\qquad\qquad\square$

4 The Logspace Oracle Hierarchy Collapses

By a similar counting argument as above, it can be shown that LAH collapses to the class $\text{L}_{\log}^{NL}$, characterized by deterministic logspace oracle machines that query their NL oracle only logarithmically often. But still, this result does not imply a collapse the logspace oracle hierarchy. The collapse of this hierarchy to $\text{L}_{\log}^{NL}$ was shown by Schöning and Wagner [37] in 1988 (see also [7]) using another counting technique, called "census technique". This technique consists in determining for a set A first $census(n)$, the number of strings of size n in A, and afterwards verifying that a given string y of length n is *not* contained in A by determining $census_A(n)$ many strings in A that are different from y.

Given an NL machine on input x with an NL oracle, what matters here to count is the number of oracle queries answered positively by the oracle. Again, this is nothing else but the problem $\text{SG}_=$, counting the number of solvable GAPs in a list of GAP instances, because in the Ruzzo-Simon-Tompa oracle query mechanism the number of oracle queries to an NL oracle is polynomially bounded, and we may obtain such a list by reducing all the possible oracle queries of M to their corresponding GAP instances.

Theorem 2. *[37] The logarithmic oracle hierarchy collapses down to $\text{L}_{\log}^{NL}$, i.e., it holds $\text{L}_{\log}^{NL} = O\Sigma_2^L = O\Pi_2^L = O\Sigma_k^L = O\Pi_k^L$ for all $k \ge 2$.*

Proof. Let an NL machine M be given that has Ruzzo-Simon-Tompa access to the oracle GAP. This is a complete characterization of $O\Sigma_2^L$, and it hence suffices to show that the language accepted by M is contained in $\text{L}_{\log}^{NL}$. M produces its queries deterministically and the number of query-producing configurations of M is bounded by $p(n)$ for a given input x of length n, because of M's logspace bound. Hence there are at most $l \leq p(n)$ different oracle queries possible for M to ask, which ordered lexicographically make up the set $Q := \{G_1, \ldots, G_l\}$. We will construct a deterministic logspace machine M' that has access to (the join of) two appropriate NL oracles and accepts the same set as M. M' operates as follows. M' first determines the number k of solvable GAP instances of Q (the census of Q) by doing binary search with the help of the NL oracle $SG_{\geq k}$, Since $k \leq \log O(p(n)) = O(\log n)$, for this *logarithmically many* queries to $SG_{\geq k}$ suffice. Once the census k of Q is known, *one* further query to the following NL set H suffices to determine whether M accepts or not the input x: H is the set of all (x, k) such that M accepts x if the oracle queries G_i are answered as follows:

- "yes", if $G_i \in$ GAP, or
- "no", if there are k GAP instances $G_1, \ldots, G_k$, all distinct from G_i, in Q such that $G_j \in$ GAP for all $1 \leq j \leq k$.

These two conditions are complementary, but both are NL problems and can be computed by M'. Hence, for the correct k M' accepts x iff M accepts x. $\qquad\square$

5 Closure under Complementation of NL

Shortly after the collapse of the LAH and LOH were known, independently of each other Immerman [18] and Szelepcsényi [42] showed that these hierarchies in fact collapse to their first level: nondeterministic logspace is closed under complementation. Consequently, any arbitrary well-behaved higher space-bound, and in particular, nondeterministic *linear space*, the class of context-sensitive languages, is closed under complementation. Hence this complexity theoretical result settled a twenty year open problem of the theory of formal languages, the so-called second LBA-problem of [25] (see also [16]).

The proof introduces an extremely nice and simple "inductive counting technique". In the light of the simplicity of the idea it is difficult to understand, why this problem has been open for twenty years; probably here most contraproductive to obtaining the result was the overall complexity theoretical assumption (made explicit, for example, by Cook in [11], p.12.) that NL and coNL were different. What matters to count in the case of NL is the number of reachable nodes in a directed graph.

Exactly k Reachable Nodes ($RN_=$)

Given: A digraph G, a designated node s, and a positive integer k.
Problem: Are there exactly k nodes in G that are reachable from s, i.e., $\#succ(s) = k$?

This problem has two parts: determining a lower bound and an upper bound on k, the problems **At Least k Reachable Nodes ($RN_{\geq k}$)** and **At Most k**

Reachable Nodes ($RN_{\leq k}$). It is not hard to see that $RN_{\geq k}$ is computable in NL. On the other hand, $\overline{RN}_{\leq k}$ is coNL-hard, because coGA$\overline{P}$ reduces to $RN_{\leq k}$: For a given GAP instance $(\overline{G}, s, t)$ of n nodes with s a designated indegree 0 node, we simply add edges (t, v) to G for all nodes $v \neq s$ of G. Then it holds for this new graph G': s is not connected to t in G if and only if $\#succ_{G'}(s) \leq n-1$. The proof now consists in showing that $RN_{\leq k}$ can be solved in NL via the technique of inductive nondeterministic counting.

Theorem 3. *[18,42] NL is closed under complementation.*

Proof. Since $RN_{\leq k}$ is coNL-hard, it suffices to show that $RN_{\leq k} \in$ NL. Let a graph G of n nodes with designated node s be given. We construct an NL machine M that determines the number $\#succ(s, i)$ of successors s' of s that are reachable on a path of length at most i inductively by determining $\#succ(s, 1)$, $\#succ(s, 2)$ and so on until $\#succ(s, n - 1)$. We show by induction on i how M can in fact determine $\#succ(s, i)$. Clearly, for $i = 1$, that is, paths of length at most one, $\#succ(s, 1) = k + 1$, where k is the number of direct successors of s. For $i > 1$, by induction hypothesis, M knows $\#succ(s, i - 1)$ and installs a counter c_{i-1} with this value. M will also keep a counter c_i for the number $\#succ(s, i)$ to be computed. M does the following: it cycles (in lexicographical order) through all nodes v of G and

- increments the counter c_i by one, if there is a node v' that is reachable in at most $i - 1$ steps from s and $(v', v) \in G$; or
- leaves the counter c_i unchanged, if there are $\#succ(s, i - 1)$ many nodes in G that are different from v' and reachable from s in at most $i - 1$ steps.

Both conditions here are NL problems and thus computable by M. Nevertheless, the conditions are complementary, that is, either of two is verified, and M will have set c_i to the correct value $\#succ(s, i)$, after having considered the (lexicographical) last node. This completes the proof. $\qquad \square$

6 Closure under Complementation of LOGCFL

The technique of inductive nondeterministic counting turned out to be useful for showing closure under complementation for other classes, too. Borodin, Cook, Dymond, Ruzzo, and Tompa were able to apply it to the class LOGCFL [6]. Venkateswaran [44] had shown that LOGCFL can be characterized by SAC^1 circuits, that is, by uniform families of semi-unbounded Boolean circuits of polynomial-size and logarithmic depth. Such circuits have unbounded fan-in $\exists$-gates and fan-in two $\wedge$-gates. (Negations are moved to the input bits.) And the circuits may have a particular easy normal form: the circuits may be *levelled*, that is, all gate names may contain a level number, and the inputs to the circuit are on level zero, and all other gates on level i receive inputs only from gates on level $i - 1$.

What matters to count in the case of LOGCFL is the number of gates on a particular level of an SAC^1 circuit that evaluate to one.

Exactly k Solvable Gates on Level i (SGL$_=$)

Given: A levelled semi-unbounded Boolean circuit C, an input x to C, a level i, and a positive integer k.

Problem: Are there exactly k gates on level i of C that evaluate to 1, i.e., $\#pg(C, x, i) = k$?

The proof consists in showing that SGL$_=$ can be solved via inductive nondeterministic counting.

Theorem 4. *[6] LOGCFL is closed under complementation.*

Proof. We sketch the proof given in [29]. Let $L \in$ LOGCFL and consider the characterization of L by a family $\{C_n\}$ of levelled SAC^1 circuits $\{C_n\}$. We assume that C_n has exactly $c \cdot \log n$ levels, the last level just containing the output gate. Let x of length n be an input to C_n. Since x is not in L if and only if $\#pg_{(C,x,c\cdot\log n)} = 0$, it suffices to show that SGL$_=$ can be computed in LOGCFL. We will do this by constructing an AuxPDA(log,poly) machine M for SGL$_=$. M will, as in Theorem 3, determine $\#pg_{(C,x,1)}$, $\#pg_{(C,x,2)}$ and so on, until $\#pg_{(C,x,c\cdot\log n)}$. Again we show by induction on i how M can in fact determine $\#pg_{(C,x,i)}$, which in the following is abbreviated $\#pg(i)$. Clearly, for $i = 0$, that is, for the input level, M simply counts the number of input bits, $x_1, \ldots, x_n, \neg x_1, \ldots, \neg x_n$, that are zero. For $i > 1$, by the induction hypothesis, M knows $\#pg(i-1)$ and installs a counter c_{i-1} with this value. M will also keep a counter c_i for the number $\#pg(i)$ to be computed. M does the following: it cycles (in lexicographical order) through all gates g of C on level i and

- increments the counter c_i by one, if g is $\exists$-gate and there is a gate g' on level $i-1$ of C that is input of g and evaluates to one, or, if g is $\wedge$-gate and there are two gates g', g'' on level $i-1$ of C that are inputs of g and evaluate to one; or
- leaves the counter c_i unchanged, if g is $\exists$-gate and there are $\#pg(i-1)$ many gates on level $i-1$ of C that are different from all inputs to g and evaluate to one, or, if g is $\wedge$-gate and there are $\#pg(i-1) - 1$ many gates on level $i-1$ of C that that are different from all inputs to g (since one of the inputs of g may evaluate to one, if g evaluates to zero.)

Both conditions here are LOGCFL problems that M can solve by guessing and simulating an AuxPDA(log,poly) machine for the circuit evaluation problem of an SAC^1 circuit. Moreover, the two conditions are complementary, that is, exactly one of the two is verified, and M will have set c_i to the correct value $\#succ(s, i)$, after having considered the (lexicographical) last gate of C_n. This completes the proof. □

7 Closure under Complementation of SL

The technique of nondeterministic inductive counting was useful for directed graphs, but of no use to solve the problem for undirected graphs. This technique, as explained, relied on checking for a given digraph G with root s and a given node v of G, whether v is within distance k of s. Unfortunately, this problem is also NL-complete for undirected graphs G. (In fact, this is one of the rare exceptions of NL-complete graph problems that are defined on undirected graphs.) That is, counting distances is too hard for SL, unless SL=NL, and in fact, it was not clear whether "one could count in SL" at all.

It took another six years until Nisan and Ta-Shma [30] showed that counting is possible in SL, and that symmetric logspace in fact is closed under complementation, too. The breakthrough was obtained by two observations of Nisan and Ta-Shma. First, they observed that

Proposition A: *SL is closed under logspace monotone Boolean formula reducibility (mBF-reducibility), defined as follows: A language A is logspace mBF-reducible to a language B, if there is a logspace computable function g that on input x produces a monotone Boolean formula F of m variables, and strings $y_1, \ldots, y_m$ such that $x \in A \iff F(c_B(y_1), \ldots, c_B(y_m)) = TRUE$. (Here $c_B(\cdot)$ denotes the characteristic function of B.)*

Ajtai, Komlos, and Szemeredi [1] have shown that there are logspace-uniform monotone NC^1 circuits that sort the zeroes and ones of a given binary string. Any such NC^1 circuit is uniformly logspace transformable into an equivalent monotone Boolean formula $F_{AKS(n,k)}$ of polynomial size such that $F_{AKS(n,k)} = TRUE$ if and only if $x_{i_k} = 1$ in the sorted string $S(x) := (x_{i_1} \ldots x_{i_n})$ for variable k. Hence Proposition A in particular implies the following threshold counting property for SL:

Proposition B: *Let $A \in SL$. Then, $A_{\geq k} \in SL$, where*

$$A_{\geq k} := \{(x_1, \ldots, x_m) \mid \#\{i \mid 1 \leq i \leq m, x_i \in A\} \geq k\}.$$

Second, Nisan and Ta-Shma showed what matters to count in the case of SL:

Exactly k Connected Components ($CC_=$)

Given: An undirected graph G, and a positive integer k.
Problem: Does G have exactly k connected components, i.e., $\#cc(G) = k$?

This problem again has two parts, related to computing a lower and an upper bound on k, **At Least k Connected Components ($CC_{\geq k}$)**, and **At Most k Connected Components ($CC_{\leq k}$)**. For closure of SL under complementation it is shown that both $CC_{\geq k}$ and $\overline{CC_{\leq k}}$, and hence $CC_=$, are contained in SL, and that the complementation of UGAP reduces to $CC_=$, and hence lies in SL.

Theorem 5. *[30] SL is closed under complementation.*

Proof. Let a graph G of n nodes, and a positive integer k bounded by n be given. First, we show that $CC_=$ is contained in SL. This follows from (a) $CC_{\leq k} \in SL$ and (b) $CC_{\geq k} \in SL$.

(a) To show $CC_{\leq k} \in SL$. Call a vertex v of G *representative*, if it is the lexicographically maximal vertex of its connected component in G. Clearly, the number of connected components of G is equal to the number of representatives of G. Now define the set

$$VNR := \{v \mid v \text{ is } not \text{ representative}\}.$$

It holds $VNR \in SL$, since for verification only a lexicographically higher vertex than v has to be guessed that is reachable from v. Because of Proposition B, it follows $VNR_{\geq k} \in SL$, that is, we can verify in SL that there are at least $n - k$ non-representatives in G, which is equivalent to say that there are at most k connected components in G.

(b) To show $CC_{>k} \in SL$, let us assume that the edges (i, j), $1 \leq i, j \leq n$, of the input graph G of n nodes are labeled by integers from 1 to $\binom{n}{2}$ corresponding to their lexicographical order. The number of connected components of G is related to the size of a spanning forest F of G as follows: $|F| = n - \#cc(G)$. We will show how to determine an upper bound $n - k$ on the lexicographically first spanning forest $LFSF(G)$ of G which then gives us the lower bound k on $\#cc(G)$. For this, call an edge (i, j) of G *important*, if it belongs to $LFSF(G)$. Consider the set

$$ENI := \{(i, j) \mid (i, j) \text{ is } not \text{ important}\}.$$

It holds $ENI \in SL$, since a necessary and sufficient condition for an edge (i, j) with label l to be unimportant is: either (i, j) is not edge of G, or i is connected to j by a path over edges using only labels smaller than l. (This was already noticed by Reif and independently by Cook [32]). Now, by Proposition B, $ENI_{\geq k} \in SL$, that is, we can verify in SL that there are at least $\frac{n \cdot (n-3)}{2} + k$ edges that are not important, which is equivalent to the fact that the size of $LFSF(G)$ is bounded by $\binom{n}{2} - (\frac{n \cdot (n-3)}{2} + k) = n - k$.

Second, we show that $\overline{UGAP}$ is logspace mBF-reducible to $CC_=$ as follows: s is *not* connected to t if and only if $\exists k : \#cc(G) = k \wedge \#cc(G \cup \{(s, t)\}) = k - 1$. Hence, by Proposition A, $\overline{UGAP} \in SL$, which yields the theorem. □

As a consequence of the structure of both hierarchies over SL we obtain

Corollary 6. *[30] Both the symmetric logspace oracle hierarchy and the symmetric logspace alternation hierarchy collapse to SL, i.e., $SL = A\Sigma_k^{SL} = A\Pi_k^{SL} = O\Sigma_k^{SL} = O\Pi_k^{SL}$ for all $k \geq 1$.*

This result places several important problems like bounded degree planarity in SL that were formally only known to be contained in higher levels of these hierarchies (see [2,20] for a collection of SL complete problems). Another consequence is the complete characterization of SL by reconfigurable networks (RNs) of constant rounds (time) and polynomial number of switches (space) [5].

Acknowledgement: I am very grateful to Prof. W. Brauer for his constant support and encouragement throughout my academic journey (Hamburg, Barcelona, Munich, Barcelona, Tübingen/Ulm).

174

References

1. M. Ajtai, J. Komlos, and E. Szemeredi. An $O(n \log n)$ sorting network. In *Proc. of 15th ACM STOC*, pages 1–9. Association for Computing Machinery, 1983.
2. C. Àlvarez and R. Greenlaw. A compendium of problems complete for symmetric logarithmic space. Technical Report ECCC-TR96-039, http://www.eccc.uni-trier.de/eccc/, 1996.
3. C. Àlvarez and B. Jenner. A very hard log-space counting class. *Theoretical Computer Science*, 107:3–30, 1993.
4. C. Àlvarez and B. Jenner. A note on logspace optimization. *J. of Computational Complexity*, 5:155–166, 1995.
5. Y. Ben-Asher, K.-J. Lange, D. Peleg, and A. Schuster. The complexity of reconfiguring network models. *Information and Computation*, 121(1):41–58, 1995.
6. A. Borodin, S. A. Cook, P. W. Dymond, W. L. Ruzzo, and M. Tompa. Two applications of inductive counting for complementation problems. *SIAM J. on Computing*, 18(3):559–578, 1989. & Erratum: 18(6):1283, 1989.
7. S.R. Buss, S.A. Cook, P.W. Dymond, and L. Hay. The log space oracle hierarchy collapses. Technical Report CS103, Dept. of Computer Science and Engineering, Univ. of California, San Diego, CA, 1988.
8. J. Cai and D. Sivakumar. Resolution of Hartmanis' conjecture for NL-hard sparse sets. Technical Report TR 95–40, SUNY Buffalo, 1995.
9. A. K. Chandra, D. C. Kozen, and L. J. Stockmeyer. Alternation. *J. of the ACM*, 28(1):114–133, 1981.
10. S. A. Cook. Characterizations of pushdown machines in terms of time-bounded computers. *J. of the ACM*, 18:4–18, 1971.
11. S. A. Cook. Towards a complexity theory of synchronous parallel computation. *L'Enseignement Mathématique*, XXVII(1–2):75–100, 1981.
12. S. A. Cook. A taxonomy of problems with fast parallel algorithms. *Information and Control*, 64(1):2–22, 1985.
13. S. A. Cook and P. McKenzie. Problems complete for deterministic logarithmic space. *J. of Algorithms*, 8:385–394, 1987.
14. P. W. Dymond and S. A. Cook. Hardware complexity and parallel computation. In *Proc. of 10th FOCS*, pages 360–372. IEEE, 1980.
15. L.M. Goldschlager. Synchronous parallel computation. *JACM*, 29:1073–1086, 1982.
16. J. Hartmanis and H.B. Hunt. The LBA problem and its importance in the theory of computing. In *Complexity of Computation*, pages 1–26. SIAM-AMS Proceedings, Vol. 7, 1974.
17. N. Immerman. Languages that capture complexity classes. *SIAM J. on Computing*, 16(4):760–778, 1987.
18. N. Immerman. Nondeterministic space is closed under complementation. *SIAM J. on Computing*, 17(5):935–938, 1988.
19. B. Jenner. Knapsack problems for NL. *Inform. Proc. Letters*, 54:169–174, 1995.
20. B. Jenner. *Between NC^1 and NC^2: Classification of Problems by Logspace Resources*. Manuscript of habilitation thesis, 1997.
21. B. Jenner, B. Kirsig, and K.-J. Lange. The logarithmic alternation hierarchy collapses: $A\Sigma_2^{\mathcal{L}} = A\Pi_2^{\mathcal{L}}$. *Information and Computation*, 80:269–288, 1989.
22. B. Jenner, K.-J. Lange, and P. McKenzie. Tree isomorphism and some other complete problems for deterministic logspace. Technical Report #1059, DIRO, Université de Montréal, 1997.

23. N. Jones. Space-bounded reducibility among combinatorial problems. *J. of Computer and System Sciences*, 11:68–85, 1975.

24. N. D. Jones, Y. E. Lien, and W. T. Laaser. New problems complete for nondeterministic log space. *Mathematical Systems Theory*, 10:1–17, 1976.

25. S.-Y. Kuroda. Classes of languages and linear-bounded automata. *Information and Control*, 7:207–223, 1964.

26. R. Ladner and N. Lynch. Relativization of questions about log space computability. *Mathematical Systems Theory*, 10:19–32, 1976.

27. H. R. Lewis and C. H. Papadimitriou. Symmetric space-bounded computation. *Theoretical Computer Science*, 19:161–187, 1982.

28. S. Lindell. A logspace algorithm for tree canonization. In *Proc. of the 24th STOC*, pages 400–404. ACM, 1992.

29. R. Niedermeier and P. Rossmanith. Unambiguous auxiliary pushdown autoata and semi-unbounded fan-in circuits. *IC*, 118(2):227–245, 1995.

30. N. Nisan and A. Ta-Shma. Symmetric logspace is closed under complement. *Chicago J. of Theoretical Computer Science*, Volume 1995:Article 1, 1995.

31. A. Razborov. Lower bounds for deterministic and nondeterministic branching programs. In *Proc. of the 8th FCT*, LNCS 529, pages 47–60, 1991.

32. J. H. Reif. Symmetric complementation. *J. of the ACM*, 31(2):401–421, 1984.

33. W. Ruzzo. Tree-size bounded alternation. *J. of Computer and System Sciences*, 21:218–235, 1980.

34. W. Ruzzo. On uniform circuit complexity. *J. of Computer and System Sciences*, 22:365–338, 1981.

35. W. L. Ruzzo, J. Simon, and M. Tompa. Space-bounded hierarchies and probabilistic computations. *J. of Computer and System Sciences*, 28:216–230, 1984.

36. U. Schöning. The power of counting. In *Complexity Theory Retrospective*, pages 205–223. Springer-Verlag, 1990.

37. U. Schöning and K. Wagner. Collapsing oracles, hierarchies, census functions, and logarithmically many queries. In *Proc. of the 5th STACS*, number 294 in LNCS, pages 91–97. Springer-Verlag, 1988.

38. I. Simon. *On some subrecursive reducibilities*. Ph.D. thesis, Stanford University, Computer Science Department, Technical Report STAN-CS-77-608, 1977.

39. S. Skyum and L. G. Valiant. A complexity theory based on boolean algebra. *J. of the ACM*, 32(2):484–502, 1985.

40. I. H. Sudborough. On tape-bounded complexity classes and multihead finite automata. *J. of Computer and System Sciences*, 10:62–76, 1975.

41. I. H. Sudborough. On the tape complexity of deterministic context-free languages. *J. of the ACM*, 25:405–414, 1978.

42. R. Szelepcsényi. The method of forced enumeration for nondeterministic automata. *Acta Informatica*, 26:279–284, 1988.

43. S. Toda. $\Sigma_2 NSPACE(n)$ is closed under complement. *J. of Computer and System Sciences*, 35:145–152, 1987.

44. H. Venkateswaran. Properties that characterize LOGCFL. *J. of Computer and System Sciences*, 43:380–404, 1991.

45. H. Venkateswaran. Circuit definitions of nondeterministic complexity classes. *SIAM J. on Computing*, 21:655–670, 1992.

46. E. Wanke. Bounded tree-width and LOGCFL. *J. of Algorithms*, 16:470–491, 1994.

A Relation Between Sparse and Printable Sets in NSPACE(log n)

Bernd Kirsig

Fachbereich Informatik
Universität Hamburg
Vogt-Kölln-Str. 30
22527 Hamburg

Abstract. For the polynomial time classes $\mathcal{NP}sparse$ and $\mathcal{NP}print$ it is known that these classes coincide if and only if nondeterministic exponential time is closed under complement ([Ha Ye 84]). Transfering this result to logarithmic space classes would lead to an equality of sparse and printable sets in NSPACE(log n) if and only if nondeterministic space classes are closed under complement. We know that space classes are closed under complement, so unfortunately the techniques that work in the polynomial time case are useless for logarithmic space. In this paper we want to investigate some relations between sparse sets and printable sets in NSPACE(log n). We show that separating $\mathcal{NL}$-printable sets from those sparse sets in NSPACE(log n) that can be recognized by 1-way machines also separates 2-way sparse sets from these 1-way sets.

1. Introduction

We call a set S sparse if there is at most a polynomial number of strings in S up to length n. The study of sparse sets is mainly motivated by the isomorphism conjecture of Berman and Hartmanis. In [BerHa 77] they proved that all *known* $\mathcal{NP}$-complete sets are isomorphic under polynomial time computable functions. Thus they conjectured that *all* $\mathcal{NP}$-complete sets are isomorphic under polynomial time many-one reducibilities. Since the densities of any two p-time isomorphic sets are polynomially related and all known $\mathcal{NP}$-complete sets have an exponential density they also conjectured that sparse sets can not be $\mathcal{NP}$-complete.

Using results from Berman [Ber 78] and Fortune [For 79] Mahaney [Mah 82] showed that sparse sets can not be $\mathcal{NP}$-complete unless $\mathcal{P} = \mathcal{NP}$.

Recently even more progress has been made. Cai and Sivakumar [CaiSiv 95a], [CaiSiv 95b] settled the isomorphism conjecture for $\mathcal{P}$ and nondeterministic logspace (throughout the paper denoted by $\mathcal{NL}$). They proved that the existence of sparse complete sets for $\mathcal{P}$ under logspace many-one reductions implies $\mathcal{P} = DSPACE(\log n)$. If there are sparse complete sets for $\mathcal{NL}$ then $\mathcal{NL} = DSPACE(\log n)$. Thus sparse sets can not be complete for those classes unless implausible equalities hold. These results also support Hartmanis' conjecture that neither $\mathcal{P}$ nor $\mathcal{NL}$ can have complete sets that are sparse [Ha 78].

It is natural to ask whether sparse sets can not be complete because they are too easy or because they contain too few elements to encode enough information for a complete set.

Typically, an easy set means a set with easy membership testing. But we may also use the stronger requirement that it is easy to produce a list of all words (up to a given length) in the set.

Since a sparse set S only contains a polynomial number of strings of a given length n polynomial space is sufficient to write down a list of all words in S up to length n. But this does not imply that it is efficiently possible to generate such a list. Any efficient algorithm to print a list of all elements of a given length of S may also serve as an efficient mechanism to retreive all of the information we might need about S.

So the question is how difficult it is to produce such a list? Are the sparse sets (in $\mathcal{NL}$) easy enough to compute a list of all words within the resource bound of the class?

This question dates back to recursion theory and the study of recursively enumerable sets. If no restriction is imposed on the machines that have to generate the list of words exactly the recursivly enumerable sets are characterized. By restricting the resources that may be used it is possible to define various classes of *printable* sets.

2. Sparse Sets and Printability

Definition:

A set S is called $\mathcal{P}$-printable if there is a polynomially time bounded transducer that, on input 1^n, outputs all elements $w \in S$ with $|w| \leq n$.

A set S is called $\mathcal{NL}$-printable if there is a nondeterministic logspace bounded transducer that, on input 1^n, outputs all elements $w \in S$ with $|w| \leq n$. The transducer is equipped with a read-only but two-way input tape. The output tape is unbounded, write-only, one-way. Since this device operates nondeterministically we furthermore require that any computation of this transducer either outputs exactly this list or the computation terminates with output of a special symbol $\$$ that invalidates the output that has been produced so far and thus denotes the inability to print the correct list of words. Of course there must be at least one computation that outputs the elements of S. Since nondeterminism allows arbitrary long computations before termination we restict all $\mathcal{NL}$-transducers to run in polynomial time by attaching a polynomial time clock.

$\mathcal{NP}$-printable sets are defined analogously.

$\mathcal{P}$-printable and $\mathcal{NP}$-printable sets have been defined and investigated by Hartmanis and Yesha [Ha Ye 84]. Research on $\mathcal{P}$-printable sets has been done by Allender [All 86] and Allender and Rubinstein [AllRu 88]. They presented structural as well as machine-based characterizations of the class of $\mathcal{P}$-printable sets.

Characterizations of $\mathcal{P}$-printable sets   [All 86], [AllRu 88]

The following are equivalent:

1. S is $\mathcal{P}$-printable
2. S is sparse and its ranking function is computable in polynomial time
3. S is $\mathcal{P}$-isomorphic to some tally set in $\mathcal{P}$
4. $S \subseteq K[k \log n, n^k]$ and $S \in \mathcal{P}$
5. S is sparse and is accepted by a deterministic 1-way logspace bounded AuxPDA
6. S is sparse and is accepted by a nondeterministic 1-way logspace bounded AuxPDA

$\mathcal{NL}$-printability was defined by Jenner and Kirsig in [JeKi 89]. $\mathcal{L}$-printable sets have been investigated by Fortnow, Goldsmith, Levy, and Mahaney in [FoGoLeMa 96].

3. Inside $\mathcal{NL}$

In this paper we focus on $\mathcal{NL}$-printable sets and the class of sparse sets in $\mathcal{NL}$.

The class of $\mathcal{NL}$-printable sets is denoted by $\mathcal{NL}print$, the class of all sparse sets in $\mathcal{NL}$ by $\mathcal{NL}sparse$

Since any $\mathcal{NL}$-transducer printing a set is polynomially time bounded it is obvious that all $\mathcal{NL}$-printable sets are sparse.

This follows also from the fact that any $\mathcal{NL}$-printable set can be printed by a deterministic logspace bounded transducer that has access to a (tally) oracle in $\mathcal{NL}$ since this device operates in polynomial time.

Proposition 1:   [JeKi 89] $\mathcal{NL}print = \mathcal{L(UNL)}\text{-}print$

This result also ensures that any $\mathcal{NL}$-printable set can be printed in lexicographic order.

Regarding the complexity of printable sets Hartmanis has shown that the context-sensitive languages $\mathcal{CS}$ differ from the determinstic context-sensitive languages $\mathcal{DLBA}$ iff there is a subset of the $\mathcal{NL}$-complete graph accessibility problem (GAP) that is easy to decide (see [Ha 88]).

Proposition 2:   [Ha 88] $GAP \cap KS[\log n, \log n] \in \mathcal{L} \Longleftrightarrow \mathcal{DLBA} \neq \mathcal{CS}$

where $KS[\log n, \log n]$ denotes the set of all words that have a short description (of length log n) and can be constructed out of that description in log space.

The set $GAP \cap KS[\log n, \log n]$ is $\mathcal{NL}$-printable. Moreover, it is an example of a very hard printable set since it has been shown in [JeKi 89] that $GAP \cap KS[\log n, \log n] \in \mathcal{L}$ implies its $\mathcal{L}$-printability.

Obviously, all tally sets in $\mathcal{NL}$ are $\mathcal{NL}$-printable since for any string 1^n an $\mathcal{NL}$-printer can verify if this string is an element of the tally set under consideration.

A slight generalisation of this result shows that any set in $\mathcal{NL}$ that contains very few elements is also $\mathcal{NL}$-printable:

Proposition 3: [JeKi 89]   *Any set $S \in 1\mathcal{NL}$ that contains at most one word of each length is $\mathcal{NL}$-printable.*

Until now it is not known if all sparse sets in $\mathcal{NL}$ are $\mathcal{NL}$-printable. We conjecture that this is not the case. The definition of $\mathcal{NL}$-printability implies that all $\mathcal{NL}$-printable sets can be recognized by one-way machines, that is $\mathcal{NL}$-machines that scan their input only one time from the left to the right.

The class $1\mathcal{NL}sparse$ of all sparse sets in $\mathcal{NL}$ that can be recognized 1-way is located between $\mathcal{NL}sparse$ and $\mathcal{NL}print$.

Proposition 4: $\mathcal{NL}print \subseteq 1\mathcal{NL}sparse \subseteq \mathcal{NL}sparse$

Though the restriction of scanning the input only once seems to be very strong for sublinear space bounded machines until now it is an open question whether there are sparse sets in $\mathcal{NL}$ that can not be recognized 1-way, i.e. whether $\mathcal{NL}sparse \neq 1\mathcal{NL}sparse$. We are not yet able to answer these questions but at least we can develop some further relations between these classes thus gaining some more insight into the structure of sparse sets in $\mathcal{NL}$. The goal of this paper is to prove an upward separation between these classes:

$$\mathcal{NL}print \subsetneq 1\mathcal{NL}sparse \implies 1\mathcal{NL}sparse \subsetneq \mathcal{NL}sparse$$

That is: if there are sets in $1\mathcal{NL}sparse$ that can not be $\mathcal{NL}$-printed then there are also sparse sets in $\mathcal{NL}$ that can not be recognized by 1-way $\mathcal{NL}$-machines. Hence it would be possible to separate 1-way and 2-way classes without use of exponentially dense languages.

For sublinear space bounds 1-way classes are easily separated from their 2-way counterparts but all results of this type make use of languages like $COPY := \{w\$w \mid w \in \{0,1\}^*\}$ (see [HopUll 69]) which is exponentially dense.

Proposition 5: [HopUll 69] $COPY \notin 1NSPACE(o(n))$

In order to separate for example $1\mathcal{NL}$ from $\mathcal{NL}$ first observe that $COPY$ can be recognized by a deterministic logspace bounded Turing machine, i.e. $COPY \in DSPACE(\log n)$.

The above mentioned result from Hopcroft and Ullman proves that the recognition of $COPY$ requires at least linear space if the recognizer (even if it is a nondeterministic device) is restricted to scan the input only once. As a special case we get $COPY \notin 1\mathcal{NL}$.

Combining these two facts yields

Corollary 1: $1\mathcal{NL} \subsetneq \mathcal{NL}$

The proof makes use of the fact that there is an exponential number of different w but any potential logspace bounded recognizer for this set has only a polynomial number of different configurations. So, after processing the first half of the input there must be at least two different strings w and w' that lead to the same configuration. Thus the recognizer is not able to distinguish between these two different prefixes and will accept $w\$w'$ as well as $w'\$w$.

Such an argumentation does not hold for sparse sets. If we look at $\{w\$w \mid w \in S\}$ for some sparse set S then there are only polynomially many strings of length n or less in S. Since the (lexicographic) position of any string w in S uniquely descibes w logarithmic space is sufficient for the identification of any string w in S.

Now we have to ask the question under which circumstances sparse sets can be used to obtain a separation between 1-way and 2-way classes.

Define a formal operation on languages.

Definition:

$$Copy(L) := \{w\$w | w \in L\}$$

It is easy to see that $L \in \mathcal{NL}$ implies $Copy(L) \in \mathcal{NL}$. If L is sparse then $Copy(L)$ is sparse, too.

Using the above technique to separate 1-way classes from 2-way classes the problem reads as follows: given some recognizer M for $Copy(S)$ and a string of logarithmic length, i.e. a configuration c_w of M where the input head has just finished scanning the first w, for which languages can one reconstruct the input w from that configuration c_w.

The following theorem gives an answer to this question and, as a byproduct, we obtain an alternative characterization of the class of $\mathcal{NL}$-printable sets.

Theorem 1: $\mathcal{NL}print = \{L \mid Copy(L) \in 1\mathcal{NL}\}$

Proof. "$\subseteq$": Since any $\mathcal{NL}$-printable set can also be printed in lexicographical order ([JeKi 89]), thus avoiding the repetition of words, it is easy to see that for any $L \in \mathcal{NL}print$ $Copy(L)$ is $\mathcal{NL}$-printable, too. Any printer can easily be modified in such a way that instead of just printing an output w it prints $w\$w$. Hence, $Copy(L)$ is $\mathcal{NL}$-printable. Using Proposition 4 we conclude $Copy(L) \in 1\mathcal{NL}$.

"$\supseteq$": Let $Copy(L) \in 1\mathcal{NL}$ and M an $1\mathcal{NL}$-machine recognizing $Copy(L)$.

Observe that whenever M accepts some input $w\$w$ there must be a configuration c_w with the input head scanning the middle marker $\$$ that can not be reached by any other prefix $w'\$$ of the input since otherwise words of the form $w'\$w$ and $w\$w'$would be accepted. The idea is to use this configuration c_w as an information source to reconstruct and print w nondeterministically.

Observe that for any configuration c of M exactly one of the following statements is true:

a) c is an unreachable configuration of M

b) c is reachable but there is no accepting computation starting at c

c) c is reachable and an accepting configuration is reachable from c.

Interesting for us is only case c). If c is a configuration where the input head scans the middle marker \$ then the input prefix $w\$$ that leads to c is uniquely determined and must be an element of L. Moreover, for any string $w \in L$ there must be at least one such configuration

Now construct a printer P that behaves as follows:

on input 1^n P generates all configurations of M of length $\log n$ or less, one after the other. For each of these configurations P verifies whether it belongs to case a), b), or c). Since nondeterministic space classes are closed under complement ([Im 87], [Sze 87]) the unreachability of configurations (case a)) and the unreachability of accepting configurations (case b)) can be tested. In both cases P drops configuration c and constructs the next one.

Any configuration from case c) uniquely determines some string $w \in L$. In order to print w P simulates M starting at configuration c. Since M is one-way any input symbol is needed only once and a simulation of M is possible by nondeterministically guessing the necessary input symbols for M. Any such symbol is also printed onto the output tape. If P fails to reach an accepting configuration of M the printing process is aborted. If P succeeds to reach an accepting configuration of M the printing process has produced a string $w \in L$.

Since for any $w \in L$ there is a configuration from case c) all words in L of length n or less are generated. In a further step using techniques from [JeKi 89] repetions of words on the output list can be avoided by modification of the printer in such a way that the output is produced in lexicographical order.

$\square$

We now have all the necessary tools to shed some light on the relations between $\mathcal{NL}sparse$, $1\mathcal{NL}sparse$, and $\mathcal{NL}print$.

Theorem 2: $\mathcal{NL}sparse = 1\mathcal{NL}sparse \Longrightarrow \mathcal{NL}sparse = \mathcal{NL}print$

Proof. Obviously, if $L \in \mathcal{NL}sparse$ then $Copy(L) \in \mathcal{NL}sparse$, too. Using the assumption $\mathcal{NL}sparse = 1\mathcal{NL}sparse$ we conclude that $Copy(L) \in 1\mathcal{NL}sparse$. Now Theorem 3 proves that L must be $\mathcal{NL}$-printable. Hence, $\mathcal{NL}sparse \subseteq \mathcal{NL}print$.

The inclusion of $\mathcal{NL}print$ in $\mathcal{NL}sparse$ is trivial. $\square$

Observe that $\mathcal{NL}sparse = \mathcal{NL}print$ implies that $1\mathcal{NL}sparse$ must coincide with these two classes because of the inclusion $\mathcal{NL}print \subseteq 1\mathcal{NL}sparse \subseteq \mathcal{NL}sparse$. Thus, if the $\mathcal{NL}$-printable sets and the 1-way sparse sets in $\mathcal{NL}$ differ then there must exist some sparse sets in $\mathcal{NL}$ that can not be recognized 1-way.

In fact, we have proven the upward-separation result

Corollary 2: $1\mathcal{NL}sparse \neq \mathcal{NL}print \Longrightarrow \mathcal{NL}sparse \neq 1\mathcal{NL}sparse.$ $\square$

4. Conclusions

Though we have not been able to solve the most interesting questions in this area of complexity classes, $1\mathcal{NL}sparse \overset{?}{=} \mathcal{NL}print$ and $\mathcal{NL}sparse \overset{?}{=} 1\mathcal{NL}sparse$, we have been able to prove some new relations between these classes.

In order to obtain a separation of $1\mathcal{NL}sparse$ from $\mathcal{NL}sparse$ it is now sufficient to come up with a sparse set in $1\mathcal{NL}$ that can not be $\mathcal{NL}$-printed. Since the requirement of printability seems to be much stronger than 1-way recognition this might be an easier task than the construction of a set in $\mathcal{NL}sparse \setminus 1\mathcal{NL}sparse$ from scratch. For any set $S \in 1\mathcal{NL}sparse \setminus \mathcal{NL}print$ the set $Copy(S)$ is sparse but not 1-way.

If it turns out to be too hard to construct a set in $1\mathcal{NL}sparse \setminus \mathcal{NL}print$ there is still the possibility to prove the existence of such a set without explicitly constructing it. One approach can be the following:

Observe that the complements of $\mathcal{NL}$-printable sets are contained in $1\mathcal{NL}$. Instead of testing if the input is printed by some given $\mathcal{NL}$-printer one has to check that it is *not* on the list of printed words, $Co\text{-}\mathcal{NL}print \subseteq 1\mathcal{NL}$. For the sets in $1\mathcal{NL}sparse$ this is doubtful, we conjecture that there are sets in $Co\text{-}1\mathcal{NL}sparse \setminus 1\mathcal{NL}$.

Any such set can be used to separate $\mathcal{NL}print$ from $1\mathcal{NL}sparse$ as follows: if there is a set $S \in 1\mathcal{NL}sparse$ with $Co\text{-}S \notin 1\mathcal{NL}$ then S can not be $\mathcal{NL}$-printable since the complements of $\mathcal{NL}$-printable sets are also in $1\mathcal{NL}$, hence $\mathcal{NL}print \subsetneq 1\mathcal{NL}sparse$.

References

[All 86]   E. Allender: The complexity of sparse sets in P, Proc. of the 1st Structure in Complexity Theory Conference, 1986, Lect. Notes in Comput. Sci. 223, 1–11.

[AllRu 88] E. Allender, R.S. Rubinstein: P-printable sets, SIAM Journ. Comput. 17,6 (1988), 1193–1202.

[Ber 78]   P. Berman: Relationships between density and deterministic complexity on NP complete languages, 5th ICALP 1978, Udine, Italy, Lect. Notes in Comput. Sci. 62, 1978, 63–71.

[BerHa 77] P. Berman, J. Hartmanis: On isomorphisms and density of NP and other complete sets, SIAM Journ. of Computing 6 (1977), 305–322.

[CaiSiv 95a] J. Cai, D. Sivakumar: The resolution of a Hartmanis conjecture, UBCS-TR 95-30, Computer Science Dept., University at Buffalo, 1995.

[CaiSiv 95b] J. Cai, D. Sivakumar: Resolution of Hartmanis' Conjecture fo NL-hard sparse sets, UBSC-TR 95-40, Computer Science Dept., University at Buffalo, 1995

[FoGoLeMa 96] L. Fortnow, J. Goldsmith, M.A. Levy, S. Mahaney: L-printable sets, 11th Conference on Comput. Complexity, (1996), 97–106

[For 79]   S. Fortune: A note on sparse complete sets, SIAM Journ. of Computing 8 (1979), 431–433.

[Ha 78]   J. Hartmanis: On log-tape isomorphisms of complete sets, Theoretical Computer Science 7, (1978), 273–286.

[Ha 88]   J. Hartmanis: Some Observations about Relativizations of Space Bounded
            Computations, Bull. European Association for Theoretical Computer Sci-
            ence 33, (1988), 82–92.

[Ha Ye 84] J. Hartmanis, Y. Yesha: Computation times of NP sets of different densi-
            ties, Theoretical Computer Science 34 (1984), 17–32.

[HopUll 69] J. Hopcroft, J. Ullman: Some results on tape-bounded Turing machines,
            Journal of the ACM 16, (1969), 168–177.

[Im 87]   N. Immerman: Nondeterministic space is closed under complement, Techn.
            Report, Yale University, YALEU/DCS/TR 552, July 1987.

[JeKi 89]   B. Jenner, B. Kirsig: Alternierung und logarithmischer Platz, Dissertation,
            FB Informatik, Universität Hamburg, 1989.

[Mah 82]   S.R. Mahaney: Sparse complete sets for NP: solution of a conjecture by
            Berman and Hartmanis, Journ. of Comput. System Sci. 25, (1982), 130–
            143.

[Sze 87]   R. Szelepcsényi: The method of forcing for nondeterministic automata,
            Bull. European Association for Theoretical Computer Science 33, (Oct
            1987), 96–100.

A Foundation for Computable Analysis

Klaus Weihrauch

FernUniversität Hagen, D – 58084 Hagen
e–mail: Klaus.Weihrauch@Fernuni-Hagen.de

Abstract. While for countable sets there is a single well established computability theory (ordinary recursion theory), Computable Analysis is still underdeveloped. Several mutually non–equivalent theories have been proposed for it, none of which, however, has been accepted by the majority of mathematicians or computer scientists. In this contribution one of these theories, TTE (Type 2 Theorie of Effectivity), is presented, which at least in the author's opinion has important advantages over the others. TTE intends to characterize and study exactly those functions, operators etc. known from Analysis, which can be realized correctly by digital computers. The paper gives a short introduction to basic concepts of TTE and shows its general applicability by some selected examples.
First, Turing computability is generalized from finite to infinite sequences of symbols. Assuming that digital computers can handle (w.l.o.g.) only sequences of symbols, infinite sequences of symbols are used as names for "infinite objects" such as real numbers, open sets, compact sets or continuous functions. Naming systems are called representations. Since only very few representations are of interest in applications, a very fundamental principle for defining effective representations for T_0–spaces with countable bases is introduced. The concepts are applied to real numbers, compact sets and continuous functions. The problem of zero–finding is considered. Computational complexity is discussed. The paper concludes with some remarks on other models for Computable Analysis.

1 Introduction

Classical computability theory considers the natural numbers ω or the words Σ^* over some finite alphabet Σ as basic sets. Many definitions of computability have been proposed and justified by intuition, most of which turned out to be equivalent to computability by Turing machines. This lead to a claim generally referred to as Church's Thesis, which can be formulated as follows: A partial function $f :\subseteq \Sigma^* \longrightarrow \Sigma^*$ is computable in the intuitive sense or by a physical device such as a digital computer, if and only if it can be computed by a Turing machine. Although Church's Thesis cannot be proved it is generally accepted, and to-day "computable" is the usual abbreviation of "Turing computable". Church's Thesis does not apply to functions on the real numbers. Several theories for studying aspects of effectivity in Analysis have been developed in the past (Intuitionistic Logic [TD88], Bishop [Bis67], Grzegorczyk [Grz55], Ceitin [Cei59], Hauck [Hau83], Traub et al. [TWW88], Pour–El/Richards [PER88], Ko [Ko91], Blum/Shub/Smale [BSS89], [WS81], [KW85], ...), and several generalizations of

Church's Thesis have been suggested. Although each of these generalizations is based on easily comprehensible intuition, they are not equivalent. Moreover, the relations between the theories and computability definitions are not yet fully explored. None of the theories has been accepted by the majority of mathematicians or computer scientists. This somewhat confusing situation may explain but does not excuse the fact that computer scientists have neglected Computable Analysis in research and almost disregarded it in teaching.

In this article we present one of the existing approaches to Computable Analysis, henceforth called "Type 2 Theory of Effectivity" (TTE for short). TTE is based on a definition of computable real functions given by the Polish logician A. Grzegorczyk in 1955 [Grz55], where computable operators transform fast converging sequences of rational numbers representing real numbers. TTE extends this original approach in several directions:

1. Also continuous operators are considered where "continuity" can be interpreted as a very fundamental kind of "constructivity".

2. By using representations effectivity can be studied not only on the real numbers but on many other spaces used in Analysis.

3. A general concept of "admissible" (effective) representations is derived from basic principles.

4. Computational complexity ("bit–complexity") is included as a part of TTE.

Since intuition has not lead to a single concept of computability for real functions, TTE intends to characterize and study those real functions, which can be computed by physical devices. The main difficulty stems from the fact that the set of real numbers is not countable and that therefore real numbers cannot be coded by natural numbers or finite words but must be considered as infinite objects (e.g. infinite decimal fractions). By laws of Physics, however, any device can store only finitely many bits of information at any moment, and any input or output channel can transfer only finitely many bits in a finite amount of time. TTE solves this by considering finite objects as approximations of infinite ones and by representing infinite objects by infinite sequences of finite objects.

In recursion theory computability is defined explicitly (w.l.o.g.) on Σ^*. Computability is transferred to other countable sets M by notations $\nu :\subseteq \Sigma^* \longrightarrow M$, where words serve as names. TTE considers additionally the set Σ^ω of infinite sequences as standard infinite objects, defines computability (and other effectivity concepts) on Σ^ω explicitly and transfers them to sets M with maximally continuum cardinality by representations $\delta :\subseteq \Sigma^\omega \longrightarrow M$, where infinite sequences of symbols serve as names (example: infinite decimal fractions as names for real numbers).

In Section 2 we introduce computable functions from tuples of finite or infinite sequences to finite or infinite sequences $f :\subseteq Y_1 \times \ldots \times Y_k \longrightarrow Y_0$ ($Y_0 \ldots Y_k \in \{\Sigma^*, \Sigma^\omega\}$) by means of Type 2 machines, which are Turing machines with one-way finite or infinite input and output tapes. We observe that for such a computable function, every finite portion of the result depends only on a finite portion of the input. This finiteness property can be expressed as continuity w.r.t. the Cantor topology on Σ^ω. We give examples of computable functions and prove that multiplication of infinite decimal fractions is not even continuous, hence not computable. Section 3 introduces the vocabulary for transferring effectivity concepts from Σ^ω to represented sets. Although every representation $\delta :\subseteq \Sigma^\omega \longrightarrow M$ of a set M induces some type of effectivity on M, most of the countless representations are not interesting, only "effective" ones are important. Effectivity is usually based on some structure on M. A type of structure we consider is a topological T_0-space with a notation of a subbase [Eng89]. For each such "information structure" we introduce a standard representation with very interesting natural topological and computational properties, which justify to call them "effective" or "admissible". As a fundamental result in TTE, for admissible representations every computable function is continuous. Only admissible representations will be used in the following. They provide a very natural and sufficiently general concept to introduce computability in almost all branches of Analysis. In Section 5 we investigate computability on the real line, based on the Cauchy representation which is admissible for this topological space. We show that the representation by infinite decimal fractions is not admissible, we give examples for computable functions, and we show that no (non–trivial) set of real numbers is recursive. In Section 6 we apply the general concept to the set of compact subsets of $\mathbb{R}$. Several admissible representations, which express different types of knowledge, are introduced and compared. Compactness is an instructive example for a classical concept which branches into several parts in TTE. In Section 7 we consider zero-finding for continuous real functions Computational Complexity is considered in Section 8. For functions on Σ^ω, complexity and input lookahead (input information) are measured as functions of the output precision. For transferring complexity and input lookahead, distinguished admissible representations are needed. For the real line we introduce the "modified binary representation" (which uses the digits 0, 1 and -1) [Wie80]. The resulting complexity concept ("bit complexity") has been used by Ko [Ko91] and others.

The first presentation of the concepts of TTE is [KW84]. More complete versions are [Wei85] and [KW85] as well as Part 3 of [Wei87]. A formally simpler access to TTE is "A simple introduction to computable analysis" [Wei95], more details can be found in [Wei94]. Some further publications are added without reference from the text. This paper is a revised and shortened version of a contribution to the Bulletin of the EATCS 57, October 1995 and of [Wei97].

We shall denote the set $\{0, 1, 2, \ldots\}$ of natural numbers by ω. A partial function f from A to B is denoted by $f :\subseteq A \longrightarrow B$. Usually, Σ will be a sufficiently large finite alphabet.

2 Computability and Continuity on Infinite Sequences of Symbols

For defining computability on finite and infinite sequences of symbols we introduce *Type 2 machines*.

A Type 2 machine is a multi–tape Turing machine M with k ($k \in \omega$) one–way input tapes and a single one–way output tape together with a type specification $(Y_1, \ldots, Y_k, Y_0)$, where $Y_0, \ldots, Y_k \in \{\Sigma^*, \Sigma^\omega\}$ and $Y_i = \Sigma^*(\Sigma^\omega)$ means that Tape i is provided for finite (infinite) inscriptions. Let $f_M :\subseteq Y_1 \times \ldots \times Y_k \longrightarrow Y_0$ be the function computed by a Type 2 machine M.

Notice, that the machine M must compute forever, if $f_M(y_1, \ldots, y_k) = y_0 \in \Sigma^\omega$. The above semantics considers infinite input and output tapes which do not exist physically and infinite computations which cannot be completed in reality. For a computation of a Type 2 machine any finite prefix of the output can be obtained in finitely many computation steps from finite prefixes of the inputs. Finite initial parts of computations concerning only finite prefixes of inputs and outputs, however, can be realized by digital computers. There are several other computability concepts which are equivalent (via appropriate encodings) to Type 2 computability (enumeration operators, partial recursive operators, partial recursive functionals, ..., see [Rog67]). In the following we shall say "computable" instead of "computable by a Type 2 machine". We illustrate the concepts by some examples.

1. Let $A \subseteq \Sigma^*$ be recursively enumerable. Define $f :\subseteq \Sigma^\omega \longrightarrow \Sigma^*$ by $f(p) := (0$ if $p \in x\Sigma^\omega$ for some $x \in A$, div otherwise). Then f is computable (easy proof).

2. There is a computable function $f :\subseteq \Sigma^\omega \longrightarrow \Sigma^\omega$ which divides infinite decimal fractions by 3. (Use school method beginning from the left.)

3. The function $f :\subseteq \Sigma^\omega \longrightarrow \Sigma^*$ defined by $f(p) = (0$ if $p = 0^\omega$, 1 otherwise) is not computable. The proof is similar to that of 4.

4. No computable function multiplies infinite decimal fractions by 3. For a proof assume that some Type 2 machine M multiplies infinite decimal franctions by 3. Consider the input $p = 0.3^\omega$. Then $f_M(p) = 0.9^\omega$ or $f_M(p) = 1.0^\omega$. Consider the case $f_M(p) = 0.9^\omega$. After some number t of computation steps M has written "0." on the output tape. During this computation M has read at most the first t symbols from the input tape. Now, consider the input $q := 0.3^t 40^\omega$. Also for this input M must write "0." during the first t steps. But for correct multiplication the output must begin with "1.". (The case $f_M(p) = 1.0^\omega$ is treated accordingly.) The above proof of non–computability is very typical for TTE. It uses only the following basic finiteness property for computable functions on Σ^ω or Σ^*: If $f(z) = x$, then every finite portion of x depends only on (is already completely defined by) a finite portion of z. This finiteness property can be expressed by continuity w.r.t. two topologies [Eng89] which we consider as fixed in the following:

– the discrete topology on $\Sigma^* : \tau = \{A \mid A \subseteq \Sigma^*\}$,
– the Cantor topology on $\Sigma^\omega : \tau_C := \{A\Sigma^\omega \mid A \subseteq \Sigma^*\}$. (The set $\{w\Sigma^\omega \mid w \in \Sigma^*\}$ is a basis of τ_C.)

As a simple but fundamental result we obtain that every computable function $f :\subseteq Y_1 \times \ldots \times Y_k \longrightarrow Y_0$ is continuous.

Already the conventions for Type 2 machines that inputs must be read symbol by symbol and the outputs must be written one–way symbol by symbol suffice to prove the theorem. Since the finiteness property, or more generally speaking continuity, can be interpreted as a very fundamental kind of effectivity or constructivity, it is of separate interest in TTE. We extend well known definitions from recursion theory. Recursive and recursively enumerable subsets of $Y_1 \times \ldots \times Y_k$ can be defined straightforwardly.

The standard numbering $\varphi : \omega \longrightarrow P^{(1)}$ of the partial recursive number functions is an important object in recursion theory [Rog67]. It is determined uniquely except for equivalence by the smn– and the utm–theorem. Correspondingly, for any $a, b \in \{*, \omega\}$ there is a notation $\xi^{ab} : \Sigma^* \longrightarrow P^{ab}$ of the set of computable functions $f :\subseteq \Sigma^a \longrightarrow \Sigma^b$ with similar properties. Moreover, for continuous functions from Σ^ω to Σ^* or Σ^ω there are *admissible* representations [Wei85, Wei87, Wei94]. Let $F^{\omega*}$ be the set of all continuous functions $f :\subseteq \Sigma^\omega \to \Sigma^*$ with open domain, and let $F^{\omega\omega}$ be the set of all continuous functions $f :\subseteq \Sigma^\omega \to \Sigma^\omega$ with G_δ - domain. Consider $a \in \{*, \omega\}$. There is a total function $\eta^{\omega a}$ from Σ^ω onto $F^{\omega a}$ with the following properties:

- Every continuous function $f :\subseteq \Sigma^\omega \to \Sigma^a$ has an extension in $F^{\omega a}$;
- The function $u :\subseteq \Sigma^\omega \times \Sigma^\omega \to \Sigma^a$ defined by $u(p, q) := \eta^{\omega a}(p)(q)$ is computable (the utm-theorem);
- For any computable function $g :\subseteq \Sigma^\omega \times \Sigma^\omega \to \Sigma^a$ there is a computable function $s : \Sigma^\omega \to \Sigma^\omega$ such that $g(p, q) = \eta^{\omega a}(s(p))(q)$ (the computable smn-theorem).

3 Notations and Representations, Induced Effectivity

In TTE it is assumed that computers can only read and write finite or infinte sequences of symbols. Computability is transferred to other sets by notations and representations where finite or infinite sequences are used as names. We introduce the vocabulary now.

A notation of a set M is a surjective function $\nu :\subseteq \Sigma^* \longrightarrow M$, a representation of a set M is a surjective function $\delta :\subseteq \Sigma^\omega \longrightarrow M$. A naming system is a notation or a representation. Examples for notations are the binary notation $\nu_{bin} :\subseteq \Sigma^* \longrightarrow \omega$ of the natural numbers and the notation $\nu_Q :\subseteq \Sigma^* \longrightarrow \mathbb{Q}$ of the rational numbers by signed binary fractions (e.g. $\nu_{bin}(101) = 5$, $\nu_Q(-10/-111) = 2/7$). In the following we shall abbreviate $\nu_Q(w)$ by $\bar{w}$. Well known is the decimal representation $\delta_{dec} :\subseteq \Sigma^\omega \longrightarrow \mathbb{R}$ of the real numbers by infinite decimal fractions. Naming systems can be compared by reducibility, where we consider continuous and computable translations.

For functions $\gamma :\subseteq Y \longrightarrow M$ and $\gamma' :\subseteq Y' \longrightarrow M'$ with $Y, Y' \in \{\Sigma^*, \Sigma^\omega\}$ we call γ *reducible to* γ', $\gamma \leq \gamma'$, iff $(\forall y \in dom\,(\gamma))$ $\gamma(y) = \gamma' f(y)$ for some computable function $f :\subseteq Y \longrightarrow Y'$. We call γ and γ' *equivalent*, $\gamma \equiv \gamma'$, iff $\gamma \leq \gamma'$ and $\gamma' \leq \gamma$.

Topological reducibility $\leq_t$ and *topological equivalence* $\equiv_t$ are defined accordingly by substituting "continuous" for "computable".

We have, e.g., $\nu_{bin} \leq \nu_Q \leq \delta_{dec}$, but $\delta_{dec}|^\mathbb{Q} \not\leq_t \nu_Q$. Next, we define how naming systems transfer effectivity concepts from Σ^* and Σ^ω to the named sets.

Let $\gamma_i :\subseteq Y_i \longrightarrow M_i$ $(i = 1, \ldots, k)$ be naming systems.

1. $x \in M_1$ is called γ_1–computable, iff there is a computable element $y \in Y_1$ with $\gamma_1(y) = x$.
2. $X \subseteq M_1 \times \ldots \times M_k$ is called $(\gamma_1, \ldots, \gamma_k)$–open $(-r.e., -recursive)$, iff $\{(y_1, \ldots, y_k) \in Y_1 \times \ldots \times Y_k \mid (\gamma_1(y_1), \ldots, \gamma_k(y_k)) \in X\}$ is open $(r.e., recursive)$ in $dom(\gamma_1) \times \ldots \times dom(\gamma_k)$.

For any naming system $\gamma :\subseteq Y \longrightarrow M$, the set $\tau_\gamma := \{X \subseteq M \mid X \text{ is } \gamma\text{-open}\}$ is called the *final topology* of γ.

For a γ–open set X, a property $\gamma(p) \in X$ is guaranteed already by a finite prefix of p, for a γ–r.e. set additionally there is a "proof–system" for showing this. Examples will be given below. We define relativized computability and continuity of functions and relations.

For $i = 0, \ldots, k$ let $\gamma_i :\subseteq Y_i \longrightarrow M_i$ be naming systems.

1. A relation $Q \subseteq M_1 \times \ldots \times M_k \times M_0$ is called $(\gamma_1, \ldots, \gamma_k, \gamma_0)$–*computable* $(-continuous)$, iff there is some computable (continuous) function $f :\subseteq Y_1 \times \ldots \times Y_k \longrightarrow Y_0$ with $(\gamma_1(y_1), \ldots, \gamma_k(y_k), \gamma_0 f(y_1, \ldots, y_k)) \in Q$ if $\exists x.(\gamma_1(y_1), \ldots, \gamma_k(y_k), x) \in Q$.
2. A function $F :\subseteq M_1 \times \ldots \times M_k \longrightarrow M_0$ is called $(\gamma_1, \ldots, \gamma_k, \gamma_0)$–*computable* $(-continuous)$, iff there is some computable (continuous) function $f :\subseteq Y_1 \times \ldots \times Y_k \longrightarrow Y_0$ with $F(\gamma_1(y_1), \ldots, \gamma_k(y_k)) = \gamma_0 f(y_1, \ldots, y_k)$ whenever $F(\gamma_1(y_1), \ldots, \gamma_k(y_k))$ exists.

As an example, the real function $x \mapsto x/3$ is $(\delta_{dec}, \delta_{dec})$–computable, but $x \mapsto x \cdot 3$ is not even $(\delta_{dec}, \delta_{dec})$–continuous (see Section 2). Computability of the relation Q is an effective version of the mere existence statement $(\forall x_1, \ldots, x_k)(\exists x_0)$ $Q(x_1, \ldots, x_k, x_0)$. A function $f :\subseteq M_1 \times \ldots \times M_k \longrightarrow M_0$ is called a choice function for Q, iff $Q(x_1, \ldots, x_k, f(x_1, \ldots, x_k))$ for all $(x_1, \ldots, x_k) \in dom(Q)$. A relation may be computable without having a computable choice function.

4 Effective Representations

Simple considerations show that two naming systems of a set M are equivalent (topologically equivalent), iff they induce the same computational (topological) properties on M.

Which among the numerous representations of the set $\mathbb{R}$ of real numbers induce the "right" kind of computability? This question has no answer for the mere set $\mathbb{R}$ but a definite answer for any *information structure* on $\mathbb{R}$.

1. An *information structure* on a set M is a triple (M, σ, ν), where $\nu :\subseteq \Sigma^* \longrightarrow \sigma$ is a notation of a set $\sigma \subseteq 2^M$ of subsets of M, which identifies points (i.e. $\cup \sigma = M$ and $\{Q \in \sigma \mid x \in Q\} = \{Q \in \sigma \mid y \in Q\} \Rightarrow x = y$ for all $x, y \in M$).
2. The standard representation $\delta_\nu :\subseteq \Sigma^\omega \longrightarrow M$ for an information structure (M, σ, ν) is defined by: $\delta_\nu(p) = x :\Longleftrightarrow \{w \mid x \in \nu(w)\} = \{w \mid \natural w \natural\natural \text{ is a subword of } p\}$
We assume tacidly that $dom(\nu) \cap \Sigma^* \{\natural, \natural\} \Sigma^* = \emptyset$. The elements Q of σ are called

atomic properties. A standard name $p \in \Sigma^\omega$ of $x \in M$ is a list of all those atomic properties $Q \in \sigma$ which hold for x. Since σ identifies points, x is uniquely defined by p. There are many important examples for information structures (M, σ, ν) :

(1) $M = \Sigma^\omega$, $p \in \nu(w) \iff w$ is a prefix of p;
(2) $M = 2^\omega$, $A \in \nu(w) \iff \nu_{bin}(w) \in A$;
(3) $M = \mathbb{R}$, $x \in \nu(w) \iff \bar{w} < x$ (remember $\bar{w} = \nu_Q(w)$);
(4) $M = \mathbb{R}$, $x \in \nu(w) \iff x < \bar{w}$;
(5) $M = \mathbb{R}$, $x \in \nu(w) \iff (w = u\natural v, \bar{u} < x < \bar{v})$;
(6) $M = \mathbb{P}$, $f \in \nu(w) \iff (w = 0^i\natural 0^j, f(i) = j)$;
(7) $M = \tau_{\mathbb{R}}$, $U \in \nu(w) \iff (w = u\natural v, [\bar{u}; \bar{v}] \subseteq U)$;
(8) $M = C(\mathbb{R})$, $f \in \nu(w) \iff (w = u\natural v\natural y\natural z, f[\bar{u}; \bar{v}] \subseteq (\bar{y}; \bar{z}))$

(where $\mathbb{P} = \{f \mid f :\subseteq \omega \longrightarrow \omega\}$ and $C(\mathbb{R}) = \{f : \mathbb{R} \longrightarrow \mathbb{R} \mid f \text{ continuous}\}$). The standard representations of the real numbers for the information structures in (3), (4) and (5) are denoted by $\rho_<, \rho_>$ and ρ, respectively.

An information structure defines a T_0-topology τ_σ on M, which has σ as a subbase [Eng89]. On the other hand, for any T_0-space (M, τ) with notation $\nu :\subseteq \Sigma^* \longrightarrow \sigma$ of a subbase, (M, σ, ν) is an information structure. The user, who wants to operate effectively on a set M, has to specify the set σ of atomic properties and the notation ν of σ. By σ a concept of "approximation" is introduced on M (mathematically by the topology τ_σ), and the notation ν expresses how atomic properties can be handled concretely, i.e. ν fixes computability on σ and M. The case of real numbers in the above example shows that for a set M different information structures may be of interest. Of course, only the most relevant ones can be investigated in more details. The choice of the notation ν of σ should be justified, but usually there is some "standard notation" which is generally accepted as "effective".

The standard representation δ_ν is continuous and open, and, as an outstanding property it is t-complete in the class of continuous representations:

For any representation δ of M: $\delta \leq_t \delta_\nu \iff \delta$ is continuous.

There is a striking formal similarity of this theorem with a formulation of the utm–theorem and the smn–theorem for the "admissible Goedel numberings" of the partial recursive functions [Rog67]. The representations which are t-equivalent to the standard representation δ_ν are called *admissible*. The admissible representations for an information structure are defined already by their final topology. They are the "topologically effective" representations. Most important is the following "main theorem" which holds for admissible representations:

For admissible representations $\delta_i :\subseteq \Sigma^\omega \longrightarrow M_i$ with final topologies τ_i ($i = 0, \ldots, k$), a function $f :\subseteq M_1 \times \ldots \times M_k \longrightarrow M_0$ is continuous, iff it is $(\delta_1, \ldots, \delta_k, \delta_0)$-continuous.

Consequently, for admissible representations $(\delta_1, \ldots, \delta_k, \delta_0)$-computable functions are continuous. Roughly speaking, in a natural setting only continuous functions can be computable.

For a separable metric space with a notation α of a countable dense subset the

Cauchy representation δ_α is admissible, where δ_α is defined by:
$\delta_\alpha(p) = x : \iff p = u_0 \natural u_1 \natural \ldots$ $(u_i \in dom(\alpha))$ with
$(\forall k)(\forall i > k)d(\alpha(u_i), \alpha(u_k)) < 2^{-k}$ and $x = \lim_{i \to \infty} \alpha(u_i)$. Notice, that only "fast"
converging sequences of elements of the dense set A are used as names.

5 Computability on the Real Line

The main subject in Analysis is the real line, i.e. the topological space $(\mathbb{R}, \tau_\mathbb{R})$,
where $\tau_\mathbb{R}$ is the set of open subsets of $\mathbb{R}$. We consider the information structure
$(\mathbb{R}, \sigma, \nu)$ from Example 4.2(5) with $x \in \nu(w) \iff (w = u\natural v$ and $\bar{u} < x < \bar{v})$
as basis of our effectivity theory on the real line. The standard representation
δ_ν (Def. 4.1) is equivalent to the Cauchy representation $\rho_C := \delta_{\nu_Q}$, where fast
converging Cauchy sequences of rational numbers serve as names.
Like δ_ν, the Cauchy representation is admissible with final topology $\tau_\mathbb{R}$. The
requirement of admissibility with final topology $\tau_\mathbb{R}$ excludes many other representations. Since $x \mapsto 3x$ is not $(\delta_{dec}, \delta_{dec})$-continuous (see Example 2.2.(4)),
δ_{dec} cannot be admissible with final topology $\tau_\mathbb{R}$ by Theorem 4.4. Since $\tau_\mathbb{R}$ is
the final topology of δ_{dec}, it cannot be admissible at all by the main theorem
for admissible representations. Furthermore, there is no injective and no total
admissible representation of $\mathbb{R}$ with final topology $\tau_\mathbb{R}$. The "naive" Cauchy rep-
resentation $\delta_{naive} : \subseteq \Sigma^\omega \longrightarrow \mathbb{R}$, where $\delta_{naive}(p) = x : \iff p = u_0 \natural u_1 \natural \ldots$ and
$(\bar{u}_0, \bar{u}_1, \ldots)$ is a Cauchy sequence with limit x, has $\{\emptyset, \mathbb{R}\}$ as its final topology
and is not admissible. If $\delta_{naive}(p) = x$, then no finite prefix of p contains any
information about x.
We shall now study effectivity induced on $\mathbb{R}$ by the Cauchy representation ρ_C.
By Definition 3.3(1), a real number x is ρ_C-computable, iff $x = \rho_C(p)$ for some
computable sequence $p \in \Sigma^\omega$. Every rational number is computable. $\sqrt{2}, e, \pi$
and many other important real numbers are computable. Every "fast" converg-
ing (ν_{bin}, ρ_C)-computable Cauchy sequence has a computable limit. However,
for any set $A \subseteq \omega$, $x_A := \Sigma\{2^{-i} \mid i \in A\}$ is computable, if and only if A is
recursive. Let A be r.e., but not recursive. There is some injective computable
function $f : \omega \longrightarrow \omega$ with $A = range(f)$. Define $a_n := \Sigma\{2^{-f(i)} \mid i \leq n\}$.
Then $(a_n)_{n \in \omega}$ is an increasing (ν_{bin}, ν_Q)-computable sequence converging to the
non–computable number x_A. Since the function f must enumerate many num-
bers $k \in A$ very late the sequence $(a_n)_{n \in \omega}$ converges very slowly. However, the
number x_A is $\rho_<$-computable.
A simple topological consideration shows that $\emptyset$ and $\mathbb{R}^n$ are the only subsets of
$\mathbb{R}^n$ which are recursive w.r.t. ρ_C. $\{x \in \mathbb{R} \mid x \neq 0\}$, and $\{(x, y) \in \mathbb{R}^2 \mid x < y\}$ are
examples of sets which are r.e. but not recursive. Moreover, there is no represen-
tation $\delta \subseteq \Sigma^\omega \longrightarrow \mathbb{R}$ of the real numbers at all, such that $\{(x, y) \in \mathbb{R}^2 \mid x < y\}$
becomes (δ, δ)-recursive [Wei95]. The relation $x < y$ is "easily definable" but
"absolutely" non–recursive. (Notice that some computability models on $\mathbb{R}$ have
decidability of $x < y$ as a basic assumption [BSS89]).
By our definitions, a function $f : \subseteq \mathbb{R} \longrightarrow \mathbb{R}$ is (ρ_C, ρ_C)-computable, iff some
Type 2 machine transforms any Cauchy sequence of rational numbers converg-

ing fast to $x \in dom(f)$ to some Cauchy sequence of rational numbers converging fast to $f(x)$. Notice that by main theorem for admissible representations every real function computable w.r.t. ρ_C is continuous. Many of the commonly used functions from "classical" analysis are computable.

1. The real functions $(x, y) \mapsto x + y$, $(x, y) \mapsto x \cdot y$, $(x, y) \mapsto \max(x, y)$, $x \mapsto -x$, $x \mapsto 1/x$ are computable.
2. Let $(a_i)_{i \in \omega}$ be a (ν_{bin}, ρ_C)–computable sequence and let $R_0 > 0$ be the radius of the power series $\Sigma a_i x^i$. Then for any $R < R_0$ the real function $f_R(x) := (\Sigma a_i x^i$ if $|x| < R$, div otherwise) is computable.

For details of the proofs see [Wei95]. By 5.3.(2), exp, sin, cos and many other functions are computable. Notice also, that the computable functions are closed under composition. Theorem 5.3(2) cannot be generalized to the case $R = R_0$! By identifying the complex plane $\mathbb{C}$ with $\mathbb{R}^2$, computability of complex functions can be reduced to computability of real functions. The complex functions addition, multiplication, inversion, exp, sin, log etc. are computable.

6 Compact Subsets of the Real Line

The power set $2^{\mathbb{R}}$ of $\mathbb{R}$ has no representation since its cardinality is too large. Therefore, by means of TTE it is impossible to express computability of functions such as sup $:\subseteq 2^{\mathbb{R}} \longrightarrow \mathbb{R}$. The open, the closed and the compact subsets of $\mathbb{R}$, however, have representations since they have continuum cardinality. As an example we introduce and discuss some admissible representations of the compact subsets of the real line. Compactness is a good example for a classical concept which branches into many parts in TTE. A subset $X \subseteq \mathbb{R}$ is compact, iff it is closed and bounded or, equivalently by the Heine/Borel theorem, iff every open covering has a finite subcovering. We introduce several representations $\delta.. :\subseteq \Sigma^\omega \longrightarrow K(\mathbb{R})$ of the set $K(\mathbb{R})$ of compact subsets of $\mathbb{R}$ by information structures $(K(\mathbb{R}), \sigma.., \nu..)$ as follows.

$$\delta_o : X \in \nu_o(w) : \iff w = u \natural v \text{ and } X \cap [\bar{u}; \bar{v}] = \emptyset$$
$$\delta_n : X \in \nu_n(w) : \iff w = u \natural v \text{ and } X \cap (\bar{u}; \bar{v}) \neq \emptyset$$
$$\delta_{ob} : X \in \nu_{ob}(w) : \iff w = y \natural 0^n \text{ and } X \in \nu_o(y) \text{ and } X \subseteq (-n; n)$$
$$\delta_{obn} : X \in \nu_{obn}(w) : \iff w = x \natural z \text{ and } X \in \nu_{ob}(x) \cap \nu_n(z)$$
$$\kappa_w : X \in \nu_w(w) : \iff w = u_1 \natural v_1 \natural \ldots \natural u_k \natural v_k \text{ and } X \subseteq (\bar{u}_1; \bar{v}_1) \cup \ldots \cup (\bar{u}_k; \bar{v}_k)$$
$$\kappa_s : X \in \nu_s(w) : \iff w = u_1 \natural v_1 \natural \ldots \natural u_k \natural v_k \text{ and } X \subseteq (\bar{u}_1; \bar{v}_1) \cup \ldots \cup (\bar{u}_k; \bar{v}_k)$$
$$\text{and } X \cap (\bar{u}_i; \bar{v}_i) \neq \emptyset \text{ for } i = 1, \ldots, k$$

Thus: $\delta_o(p) = X$, iff p enumerates the "outside" of X (i.e. δ_o is equivalent to a restriction of δ_{cl}); $\delta_n(p) = X$, iff p enumerates the open "neighbours" of X; $\delta_{ob}(p) = X$, iff p enumerates the outside and additionally bounds of X; $\delta_{obn}(p) = X$, iff p enumerates the outside, the bounds and the neighbours of X; $\kappa_w(p) = X$, iff p enumerates all finite coverings (with rational intervals) of X; $\kappa_s(p) = X$, iff p enumerates all minimal finite coverings of X. The above namings $\delta..$ represent different types of knowledge about the named objects. Reducibilities express dependences between these types. For the first four representations we have $\delta_{obn} \leq \delta_{ob} \leq \delta_o$ and $\delta_{obn} \leq \delta_n$, while $\not\leq_t$ holds for all other combinations. The following equivalences are two computable versions of the Heine/Borel theorem [KW87]):

$- \delta_{ob} \equiv \kappa_w$; $delta_{obn} \equiv \kappa_s$.

Every non–empty compact set $X \in K(\mathbb{R})$ has a maximum. On the non–empty compact subsets

- Max is $(\delta_n, \rho_<)$–computable and $(\delta_{ob}, \rho_>)$–computable,
- Max is **not** $(\delta_n, \rho_>)$–continuous, $(\delta_0, \rho_>)$–continuous or $(\delta_{ob}, \rho_<)$–continuous.

Notice in particular, that without knowing a concrete upper bound not even a $\rho_>$–name of $Max(X)$ can be determined from a δ_0–name of X.

The above representations behave differently w.r.t. union and intersection. While union is computable w.r.t. all of them, intersection is e.g. $(\kappa_w, \kappa_w, \kappa_w)$–computable but not even $(\kappa_s, \kappa_s, \delta_n)$–continuous.

Some more details can be found in [KW87, Wei94, Wei95].

7 Continuous Functions and Zero–Finding

In this section we shall consider the set $C[0;1]$ of continuous functions $f : [0;1] \longrightarrow \mathbb{R}$. Let δ_F be the standard representation of $C[0;1]$ for the information structure $(C[0;1], \sigma, \nu)$ with $- f \in \nu(w) : \Longleftrightarrow w = u\underline{t}v\underline{t}x\overline{t}y$ and $f[\overline{u}; \overline{v}] \subseteq (\overline{x}; \overline{y})$. Thus $\delta_F(p) = f$, iff p enumerates all $(a, b, c, d) \in \mathbb{Q}^n$ with $f[a;b] \subseteq (c;d)$. Any atomic information about f is a rectangle bounding the graph of f. δ_F is admissible, where the final topology is the well–known compact–open topology [Eng89]. The following useful theorem emphasizes the effectivity of the representation δ_F. Define $apply : C[0;1] \times \mathbb{R} \longrightarrow \mathbb{R}$ by $apply(f, x) := f(x)$. Then for any representation δ of $C[0;1]$:

- $apply$ is (δ, ρ_C, ρ_C)–continuous $\Longleftrightarrow$ $\delta \leq_t \delta_F$,
- $apply$ is (δ, ρ_C, ρ_C)–computable $\Longleftrightarrow$ $\delta \leq \delta_F$.

Therefore, δ_F is complete in the set of all representations of $C[0;1]$, for which the apply–function is computable. Notice the formal similarity with the smn– and the utm–theorem from recursion theory. The following theorem summarizes some effectivity properties [KW87]:

1. $f : [0;1] \longrightarrow \mathbb{R}$ is (ρ_C, ρ_C)–computable $\Longleftrightarrow$ f is δ_F–computable.
2. The composition $(f, g) \mapsto fg$ on $C[0;1]$ is $(\delta_F, \delta_F, \delta_F)$–computable.
3. The function $H : C[0;1] \times K(\mathbb{R}) \longrightarrow K(\mathbb{R})$, $H(f, X) := f(X)$, is $(\delta_F, \kappa_s, \kappa_s)$–computable.
4. $Max : C[0;1] \longrightarrow \mathbb{R}$ with $Max(f) := \max\{f(x) \mid 0 \leq x \leq 1\}$ is (δ_F, ρ_C)–computable.
5. $Int : C[0;1] \times \mathbb{R} \longrightarrow \mathbb{R}$ with $Int(f, a) := \int_0^a f(x)dx$ is $(\delta_F, \rho_C, \rho_C)$–computable.
6. $Diff :\subseteq C[0;1] \longrightarrow C[0;1]$, defined by $Diff(f) = g$ iff $g \in C[0;1]$ is the derivative of f, is not (δ_F, δ_F)–continuous.

In accordance with experience from Numerical Mathematics, the maximum can be determined, integration is easy but differentiation cannot be performed effectively on δ_F-names. We consider the problem of finding zeroes for functions from $C[0;1]$. The following can be proved:

1. The function $Z_{\min} :\subseteq C[0;1] \longrightarrow \mathbb{R}$, where $Z_{\min}(f) = x : \Longleftrightarrow x = \min f^{-1}\{0\}$, is $(\delta_F, \rho_<)$-computable but not (δ_F, ρ_C)-continuous.
2. The function $Z_1 :\subseteq C[0;1] \longrightarrow \mathbb{R}$, where $Z_1(f) = x : \Longleftrightarrow x$ is the only zero of f, is (δ_F, ρ_C)-computable.
3. The relation $R := \{(f,x) \mid f \in C[0;1], x \in \mathbb{R}, f(0) < 0, f(1) > 0, f(x) = 0\}$ is not (δ_F, ρ_C)-continuous.
4. The relation $R := \{(f,x) \mid f \in C[0;1], x \in \mathbb{R}, f(0) < 0, f(1) > 0, f(x) = 0, f^{-1}\{0\}$ contains no proper interval$\}$ is (δ_F, ρ_C)-computable but has no (δ_F, ρ_C)-continuous choice function.

As a positive result, the minimal zeroes can be approximated from below, and a computable function determines the zeroes for all functions which have exactly one zero. By the intermediate value theorem, every function $f \in C[0;1]$, which changes its sign, has a zero. But there is not even a continuous function, which for any δ_F-name of a function f (which changes its sign) determines some ρ_C-name of a zero of f. We obtain a weak positive result, if we consider only functions f, for which $f^{-1}\{0\}$ contains no proper interval. An instructive example is the special problem of finding a zero of $f_a : \mathbb{R} \longrightarrow \mathbb{R}$ from $a \in [-1;1]$, where $f_a(x) := x^3 - x + a$ [Wei95].

8 Computational Complexity

We introduce computational complexity for Type 2 machines and transfer it by representations to other sets. For an ordinary Turing machine M, $Time_M(x)$ is the number of steps which M with input x works until it halts. Such a definition is useless for Type 2 machines with infinite output. We introduce as a further parameter a number $k \in \omega$ and measure the time until M has produced the first k output symbols:
$Time_M(y)(k) :=$ the number of steps which the machine M with input y needs for writing the first $k + 1$ output symbols.
Another important information is the input lookahead, $Ila_M(y)(k)$, which is the number of input symbols which M requires for producing the first k output symbols. The parameter k can be interpreted as precision of the intermediate result.

We transfer these concepts to represented sets as follows. For a representation $\delta :\subseteq \Sigma^\omega \longrightarrow M$ and a set $X \subseteq M$ a function $f :\subseteq M \longrightarrow M$ is computable on M in time $t : \omega \longrightarrow \omega$ and input lookahead $s : \omega \longrightarrow \omega$, iff there is a Turing machine N with (1) $f\delta(p) = \delta f_N(p)$, (2) $Time_N(p)(n) \leq t(n)$, (3) $Ila_N(p)(n) \leq s(n)$ for all $n \in \omega$, whenever $p \in \delta^{-1}(X)$.

Unfortunately, this definition of complexity is useless for many representations, e.g. for our Cauchy representation ρ_C of the real numbers. In fact, every (ρ_C, ρ_C)-computable real function is (ρ_C, ρ_C)-computable in linear time, since every output $q \in dom(\rho_C)$ can be padded arbitrarily by using rational numbers with large numerators and denominators. Informally, the set of ρ_C-names of any real number is too big. We solve this problem for the real numbers by using an admissible representation with uniformly bounded redundance, the "modified binary representation" ρ_m, which uses the binary digits 0, 1 and -1 (which we denote by $\bar{1}$) [Wie80], i.e. $\rho_m(a_n \ldots a_0 \cdot a_{-1} a_{-2} \ldots) = \sum \{a_i \cdot 2^i \mid i \leq n\}$ where $a_i \in \{1, 0, -1\}$. (Like decimal representation, ordinary binary representation induces an unnatural computability theory.) Easy proofs show (1) $\rho_m \equiv \rho_C$ and (2) $\rho_m^{-1}(X)$ is compact if X is compact. By (1) ρ_C and ρ_m induce the same computability theory, and by (2) $max\{Time_N(p)(n) | p \in \rho_m^{-1}(X)\}$ exists for each n.

The resulting computational complexity is sometimes called "bit–complexity". It is essentially equivalent to definitions used by Brent [Bre76], Schönhage [Sch90], Ko [Ko91] and others. We mention only a single concrete result by Mueller [Mül87]: If a real analytic function is (ρ_m, ρ_m)– computable in time $O(n^k)$, $(k \geq 3)$, then its integral and derivative are computable in time $O(n^{k+2})$.

Admissible representations δ such that $\delta^{-1}K$ is compact, if K is compact, exist for all separable metric spaces, i.e. uniform complexity can be defined on compact metric spaces.

9 Conclusion

The approach presented here (TTE) connects Abstract Analysis and Turing computability. It provides a simple language for expressing a variety of types of effectivity ranging form continuity (interpreted as "constructivity" or "finite dependence") via computability to computational complexity of points, sets, relations and functions. It is claimed that "Type 2 computability" models "computability by machines" adequately.

Computability aspects in Analysis have been discussed already from the beginning of Computability Theory. In his famous paper [Tur36], A. Turing defines computable real numbers by computable infinite binary fractions. In a correction [Tur37] he proposes to use computable sequences of nested intervals with rational boundaries instead. As we already mentioned, TTE extends a definition of computable real functions by A. Grzegorczyk [Grz55]. Two years later, he introduced several definitions equivalent to the first one [Grz57]. Grzegorczyk's characterization "$f : [0; 1] \to \mathbb{R}$ is computable, iff f maps every computable sequence of computable numbers to a computable sequence of computable numbers and f has a computable modulus of uniform continuity" has been generalized to computable Banach spaces by Pour–El and Richards [PER88]. TTE includes this generalization. Another characterization by Grzegorczyk (by means of monotone (w.r.t. inclusion) computable functions mapping intervals with rational boundaries to intervals with rational boundaries) is the computational background of Interval Analysis [Moo79, Abe88]. Domain Theory approaches consider computability on spaces the elements of which are real numbers as well as approximations of real numbers (e.g. intervals with rational boundaries) [Abe80, WS81, Kus84, Blä95, Esc95, Eda95, DG96]. Domain computability restricted to the real numbers coincides with TTE–computability.

The "Russian" approach to Computable Analysis handles programs of computable real numbers. Let ψ be some standard notation (by "programs") of all computable elements of Σ^ω. Then $\rho_C \psi$ is a partial notation of the set of all computable real numbers $\mathbb{R}_C$. A function $f :\subseteq \mathbb{R}_C \to \mathbb{R}_C$ is Ceitin computable, iff it is $(\rho_C \psi, \rho_C \psi)$–computable. Every TTE–computable function $f :\subseteq \mathbb{R} \to \mathbb{R}$ with $dom(f) \subseteq \mathbb{R}_C$ is Ceitin computable. The converse holds only under certain conditions on $dom(f)$ [Cei59]. A necessary and sufficient condition has been given in [Her96]. Computational complexity based on the bit–model [Bre76, Sch90, Ko91] can be considered as a part of TTE. While in the Russian approach only the computable real numbers are considered as entireties, the "real RAM" model [BM75, BSS89, PS85] considers all real numbers as entities. A real RAM is a random access machine operating on real numbers with assignments "$x := y+z$", "$x := y \cdot z$", ... and branchings "$x < 0$". Time complexity is measured by the number of operations as a function of the input dimension. The real RAM model is unrealistic since almost all real RAM–computable functions are not continuous, hence not realizable by physical machines, and almost all TTE–computable (i.e. realizable) functions (e.g. e^x, $sin(x)$) are not real RAM–computable.

The computational model used in "Information Based Complexity" (IBC) [TWW88] extends the real RAM model [Nov95]. Also this model cannot be realized mathematically correctly by digital computers. Moreover, the output of one machine (in general) cannot be used as the input for a second machine. A slightly modified real RAM, the "feasible real RAM", however, can be realized physically [BH96]. Here, the precise tests "$x < 0$" are replaced by finite precision tests. A different way to study effectivity in analysis is the use of constructive logic, e.g. [TD88]. Bishop's "Constructive analysis" [Bis67, BB85] is the most famous example. Its close relations to TTE still has to be investigated.

Comutational complexity in Analysis ("bit-complexity") will certainly be a very important and fruitful area of future research in computer science. While much work on structural complexity has been done already by Ko [Ko91], only very few concrete problems have been considered until today.

References

[Abe80] Oliver Aberth. *Computable Analysis*. McGraw-Hill, New York, 1980.

[Abe88] Oliver Aberth. *Precise Numerical Analysis*. Brown Publishers, Dubuque, 1988.

[BB85] Errett Bishop und Douglas S. Bridges. *Constructive Analysis*, Band 279 der Reihe *Grundlehren der mathematischen Wissenschaft*. Springer, Berlin, 1985.

[BH96] Vasco Brattka und Peter Hertling. Feasible real random access machines. In Keith G. Jeffrey, Jaroslav Král und Miroslav Bartošek, Hrsg., *SOFSEM'96: Theory and Practice of Informatics*, Band 1175 der Reihe *Lecture Notes in Computer Science*, Seiten 335–342, Berlin, 1996. Springer. 23rd Seminar on Current Trends in Theory and Practice of Informatics, Milovy, Czech Republik, November 23-30, 1996.

[Bis67] Errett Bishop. *Foundations of Constructive Analysis*. McGraw-Hill, New York, 1967.

[Blä95] Markus Bläser. Uniform computational complexity of the derivatives of C^∞-functions. In Ker-I Ko und Klaus Weihrauch, Hrsg., *Computability and Complexity in Analysis*, Band 190 der Reihe *Informatik-Berichte*, Seiten 99–104. FernUniversität Hagen, September 1995. CCA Workshop, Hagen, August 19-20, 1995.

[BM75] A. Borodin und I. Munro. *The Computational Complexity of Algebraic and Numeric Problems*. Elsevier, New York, 1975.

[Bre76] R.P. Brent. Fast multiple-precision evaluation of elementary functions. *Journal of the Association for Computing Machinery*, 23(2):242–251, 1976.

[BSS89] Leonore Blum, Mike Shub und Steve Smale. On a theory of computation and complexity over the real numbers: NP-completeness, recursive functions and universal machines. *Bulletin of the American Mathematical Society*, 21(1):1–46, Juli 1989.

[Cei59] G.S. Ceitin. Algorithmic Operators in Constructive Complete Separable Metric Spaces. *Doklady Akad. Nauk*, 128:49–52, 1959. (in Russian).

[DG96] Pietro Di Gianantonio. Real number computation and Domain Theory. *Information and Computation*, 127:11–25, 1996.

[Eda95] Abbas Edalat. Domain theory and integration. *Theoretical Computer Science*, 151:163–193, 1995.

[Eng89] Ryszard Engelking. *General Topology*, Band 6 der Reihe *Sigma series in pure mathematics*. Heldermann, Berlin, 1989.

[Esc95] Martin Hötzel Escardó. PCF extended with real numbers. In Ker-I Ko und Klaus Weihrauch, Hrsg., *Computability and Complexity in Analysis*, Band 190 der Reihe *Informatik-Berichte*, Seiten 11–24. FernUniversität Hagen, September 1995. CCA Workshop, Hagen, August 19-20, 1995.

[Grz55] Andrzej Grzegorczyk. Computable functionals. *Fundamenta Mathematicae*, 42:168–202, 1955.

[Grz57] Andrzej Grzegorczyk. On the definitions of computable real continuous functions. *Fundamenta Mathematicae*, 44:61–71, 1957.

[Hau83] Jürgen Hauck. Konstruktive reelle Funktionale und Operatoren. *Zeitschrift für mathematische Logik und Grundlagen der Mathematik*, 29:213–218, 1983.

[Her96] Peter Hertling. Unstetigkeitsgrade von Funktionen in der effektiven Analysis. Informatik Berichte 208, FernUniversität Hagen, Hagen, November 1996. Dissertation.

[Ko91] Ker-I Ko. *Complexity Theory of Real Functions*. Progress in Theoretical Computer Science. Birkhäuser, Boston, 1991.

[Kus84] Boris Abramovich Kushner. *Lectures on Constructive Mathematical Analysis*, Band 60 der Reihe *Translation of Mathematical Monographs*. American Mathematical Society, Providence, 1984.

[KW84] Christoph Kreitz und Klaus Weihrauch. A unified approach to constructive and recursive analysis. In M.M. Richter, E. Börger, W. Oberschelp, B. Schinzel und W. Thomas, Hrsg., *Computation and Proof Theory*, Band 1104 der Reihe *Lecture Notes in Mathematics*, Seiten 259–278, Berlin, 1984. Springer. Proceedings of the Logic Colloquium, Aachen, July 18-23, 1983, Part II.

[KW85] Cristoph Kreitz und Klaus Weihrauch. Theory of representations. *Theoretical Computer Science*, 38:35–53, 1985.

[KW87] Christoph Kreitz und Klaus Weihrauch. Compactness in constructive analysis revisited. *Annals of Pure and Applied Logic*, 36:29–38, 1987.

[Moo79] Ramon E. Moore. Methods and Applications of Interval Analysis. *SIAM Journal on Computing*, 1979.

[Mül87] Norbert Th. Müller. Uniform Computational Complexity of Taylor series. In Thomas Ottmann, Hrsg., *Proceedings of the 14th International Colloquium on Automata, Languages, and Programming*, Band 267 der Reihe *Lecture Notes in Computer Science*, Seiten 435–444, Berlin, 1987. Springer.

[Nov95] Erich Novak. The real number model in numerical analysis. *Journal of Complexity*, 11(1):57–73, 1995.

[PER88] Marian B. Pour-El und J. Ian Richards. *Computability in Analysis and Physics*. Perspectives in Mathematical Logic. Springer, Berlin, 1988.

[PS85] Franco P. Preparata und Michael Ian Shamos. *Computational Geometry*. Texts and Monographs in Computer Science. Springer, New York, 1985.

[Rog67] Hartley Rogers. *Theory of Recursive Functions and Effective Computability*. McGraw-Hill, New York, 1967.

[Sch90] A. Schönhage. Numerik analytischer Funktionen und Komplexität. *Jahresbericht der Deutschen Mathematiker-Vereinigung*, 92:1–20, 1990.

[TD88] A.S. Troelstra und D. van Dalen. *Constructivism in Mathematics, Volume 1*, Band 121 der Reihe *Studies in Logic and the Foundations of Mathematics*. North-Holland, Amsterdam, 1988.

[Tur36] Alan M. Turing. On computable numbers, with an application to the "Entscheidungsproblem". *Proceedings of the London Mathematical Society*, 42(2):230–265, 1936.

[Tur37] Alan M. Turing. On computable numbers, with an application to the "Entscheidungsproblem". A correction. *Proceedings of the London Mathematical Society*, 43(2):544–546, 1937.

[TWW88] Joseph F. Traub, G.W. Wasilkowski und H. Woźniakowski. *Information-Based Complexity*. Computer Science and Scientific Computing. Academic Press, New York, 1988.

[Wei85] Klaus Weihrauch. Type 2 recursion theory. *Theoretical Computer Science*, 38:17–33, 1985.

[Wei87] Klaus Weihrauch. *Computability*, Band 9 der Reihe *EATCS Monographs on Theoretical Computer Science*. Springer, Berlin, 1987.

[Wei94] Klaus Weihrauch. Effektive Analysis. Correspondence course 1681, FernUniversität Hagen, 1994.

[Wei95] Klaus Weihrauch. A Simple Introduction to Computable Analysis. Informatik Berichte 171, FernUniversität Hagen, Hagen, Juli 1995. 2nd edition.

[Wei97] Klaus Weihrauch. A Foundation for Computable Analysis. In Douglas S. Bridges, Cristian S. Calude, Jeremy Gibbons, Steve Reeves und Ian H. Witten, Hrsg., *Combinatorics, Complexity, and Logic*, Discrete Mathematics and Theoretical Computer Science, Seiten 66–89, Singapore, 1997. Springer. Proceedings of DMTCS'96.

[Wie80] E. Wiedmer. Computing with infinite objects. *Theoretical Computer Science*, 10:133–155, 1980.

[WS81] Klaus Weihrauch und Ulrich Schreiber. Embedding metric spaces into cpo's. *Theoretical Computer Science*, 16:5–24, 1981.

A Computer Scientist's View of Life, the Universe, and Everything

Jürgen Schmidhuber

IDSIA, Corso Elvezia 36, CH-6900-Lugano, Switzerland
juergen@idsia.ch - http://www.idsia.ch/~juergen

Abstract. Is the universe computable? If so, it may be much cheaper in terms of information requirements to compute all computable universes instead of just ours. I apply basic concepts of Kolmogorov complexity theory to the set of possible universes, and chat about perceived and true randomness, life, generalization, and learning in a given universe.

PRELIMINARIES

Assumptions. A long time ago, the Great Programmer wrote a program that runs all possible universes on His Big Computer. "Possible" means "computable": (1) Each universe evolves on a discrete time scale. (2) Any universe's state at a given time is describable by a finite number of bits. One of the many universes is ours, despite some who evolved in it and claim it is incomputable.

Computable universes. Let TM denote an arbitrary universal Turing machine with unidirectional output tape. TM's input and output symbols are "0", "1", and "," (comma). TM's possible input programs can be ordered alphabetically: "" (empty program), "0", "1", ",", "00", "01", "0,", "10", "11", "1,", ",0", ",1", ",,", "000", etc. Let A_k denote TM's k-th program in this list. Its output will be a finite or infinite string over the alphabet { "0","1","," }. This sequence of bitstrings separated by commas will be interpreted as the evolution E_k of universe U_k. If E_k includes at least one comma, then let U_k^l denote the l-th (possibly empty) bitstring before the l-th comma. U_k^l represents U_k's state at the l-th time step of E_k ($k, l \in \{1, 2, \ldots, \}$). E_k is represented by the sequence $U_k^1, U_k^2, \ldots$ where U_k^1 corresponds to U_k's big bang. Different algorithms may compute the same universe. Some universes are finite (those whose programs cease producing outputs at some point), others are not. I don't know about ours.

TM not important. The choice of the Turing machine is not important. This is due to the compiler theorem: for each universal Turing machine C there exists a constant prefix $\mu_C \in \{$ "0","1","," $\}^*$ such that for all possible programs p, C's output in response to program $\mu_C p$ is identical to TM's output in response to p. The prefix μ_C is the compiler that compiles programs for TM into equivalent programs for C.

Computing all universes. One way of sequentially computing all computable universes is dove-tailing. A_1 is run for one instruction every second step, A_2 is run for one instruction every second of the remaining steps, and so on. Similar methods exist for computing many universes in parallel. Each time step of each universe that is computable by at least one finite algorithm will eventually be computed.

Time. The Great Programmer does not worry about computation time. Nobody presses Him. Creatures which evolve in any of the universes don't have to worry either. They run on local time and have no idea of how many instructions it takes the Big Computer to compute one of their time steps, or how many instructions it spends on all the other creatures in parallel universes.

REGULAR AND IRREGULAR UNIVERSES

Finite histories. Let $| \ x \ |$ denote the number of symbols in string x. Let the partial history $S_k^{i,j}$ denote the substring between the i-th and the j-th symbol of E_k, $j > i$. $S_k^{i,j}$ is regular (or compressible, or non-random) if the shortest program that computes $S_k^{i,j}$ (and nothing else) *and halts* consists of less than $| \ S_k^{i,j} \ |$ symbols. Otherwise $S_k^{i,j}$ is incompressible.

Infinite histories. Similarly, if some universe's evolution is infinite, then it is compressible if it can be computed by a finite algorithm.

Most universes are irregular. The evolutions of almost all universes are incompressible. There are 3^n strings of size n, but less than $(1/3)^c * 3^n << 3^n$ algorithms consisting of less than $n - c$ symbols (c is a positive integer). And for the infinite case, we observe: the number of infinite symbol strings is incountable. Only a negligible fraction (namely countably many of them) can be computed by finite programs.

The few regular universes. There are a few compressible universes which can be computed by very short algorithms, though. For instance, suppose that some U_k evolves according to physical laws that tell us how to compute next states from previous states. All we need to compute U_k's evolution is U_k^1 and the algorithm that computes U_k^{i+1} from U_k^i ($i \in \{1, 2, \ldots, \}$).

Noise? Apparently, we live in one of the few highly regular universes. Each electron appears to behave the same way. Dropped breads of butter regularly hit the floor, not the ceiling. There appear to be deviations from regularity, however, which are embodied by what we call noise. Although certain macroscopic properties (such as pressure in a gas container) are predictable for physicists, microscopic properties (such as precise particle positions) seem subject to noisy fluctuations. Noise represents additional information absent in the original physical laws. Uniform noise is incompressible — there is no short algorithm that computes it and nothing else.

Noisy laws don't necessarily prevent compressibility. Laws currently used by physicists to model our own universe model noise. Based on Schrödinger's equation, they are only conditional probability distributions on possible next states, given previous states. The evolution of Schrödinger's wave function (WF) itself can be computed by a very compact algorithm (given the quantizability assumptions in the first paragraph of this paper) — WF is just a short formula. Whenever WF collapses in a particular way, however, the resulting actual state represents additional information (noise) not conveyed by the algorithm describing the initial state (big bang) and WF. Still, since the noise obviously is non-uniform (due to the nature of the physical laws and WF), our universe's evolution so far is greatly compressible. How? Well, there is a comparatively short algorithm that simply codes probable next states by few bits, and unlikely next states by many bits, as suggested by standard information theory [8].

More regularity than we think? The longer the shortest program computing a given universe, the more random it is. To certain observers, certain universes appear partly random although they aren't. There may be at least two reasons for this:

1. Shortest algorithm cannot be found. It can be shown that there is no algorithm that can generate the shortest program for computing arbitrary given data on a given computer [2, 9, 1]. In particular, our physicists cannot expect to find the most compact description of our universe.

2. Additional problems of the Heisenberg type. Heisenberg tells us that we cannot even observe the precise, current state of a single electron, let alone our universe. In our particular universe, our actions seem to influence our measurements in a fundamentally unpredictable way. This does not mean that there is no predictable underlying computational process (whose precise results we cannot access). In fact, rules that hold for observers who are part of a given universe and evolved according to its laws need not hold outside of it. There is no reason to believe that the Great Programmer cannot dump a universe and examine its precise state at any given time, just because the creatures that evolved in it cannot because their measurements modify their world.

How much true randomness? Is there "true" randomness in our universe, in addition to the simple physical laws? True randomness essentially means that there is no short algorithm computing "the precise collapse of the wave function", and what is perceived as noise by today's physicists. In fact, if our universe was infinite, and there was true randomness, then it could not be computed by a finite algorithm that computes nothing else. Our fundamental inability to perceive our universe's state does *not* imply its true randomness, though. For instance, there may be a very short algorithm computing the positions of electrons lightyears apart in a way that seems like noise to us but actually is highly regular.

ALL UNIVERSES ARE CHEAPER THAN JUST ONE

In general, computing all evolutions of all universes is much cheaper in terms of information requirements than computing just one particular, arbitrarily chosen evolution. Why? Because the algorithm that systematically enumerates and runs all universes (with all imaginable types of physical laws, wave functions, noise etc.) is very short, although it takes time. On the other hand, computing just one particular universe's evolution (with, say, one particular instance of noise), without computing the others, tends to be very expensive, because almost all individual universes are incompressible, as has been shown above. More is less!

Many worlds. Suppose there is true (incompressible) noise in state transitions of our particular world evolution. The noise conveys additional information besides the one for initial state and physical laws. But from the Great Programmer's point of view, almost no extra information (nor, equivalently, a random generator) is required. Instead of computing just one of the many possible evolutions of a probabilistic universe with fixed laws but random noise of a certain (e.g., Gaussian) type, the Great Programmer's simple program computes them all. An automatic by-product of the Great Programmer's set-up is the well-known "many worlds hypothesis", ©Everett III. According to it, whenever our universe's quantum mechanics allows for alternative next paths, all are taken and the world splits into separate universes. From the Great Programmer's view, however, there are no real splits — there are just a bunch of different algorithms which yield identical results for some time, until they start computing different outputs corresponding to different noise in different universes.

From an esthetical point of view that favors simple explanations of everything, a set-up in which all possible universes are computed instead of just ours is more attractive. It is simpler.

ARE WE RUN BY A SHORT ALGORITHM?

Since our universes' history so far is regular, it by itself *could* have been computed by a relatively short algorithm. Essentially, this algorithm embodies the physical laws plus the information about the historical noise. But there are many algorithms whose output sequences start with our universe's history so far. Most of them are very long. How likely is it now that our universe is indeed run by a short algorithm? To attempt an answer, we need a prior probability on the possible algorithms. The obvious candidate is the "universal prior".

Universal prior. Define $P_U(s)$, the *a priori probability* of a finite symbol string s (such as the one representing our universe's history so far), as the probability of guessing a halting program that computes s on a universal Turing machine U. Here, the way of guessing is defined by the following procedure: initially, the input tape consists of a single square. Whenever the scanning head of the program tape shifts to the right, do: (1) Append a new square. (2) With probability $\frac{1}{3}$ fill it with a "0"; with probability $\frac{1}{3}$ fill it with a "1"; with probability $\frac{1}{3}$ fill it with a ",". Programs are "self-delimiting" [3, 1] — once U halts due to computations based on the randomly chosen symbols (the program) on its input tape, there won't be any additional program symbols. We obtain

$$P_U(s) = \sum_{p:U \text{ computes } s \text{ from } p \text{ and halts}} (\frac{1}{3})^{|p|}.$$

Clearly, the sum of all probabilities of all halting programs cannot exceed 1 (no halting program can be the prefix of another one). But certain programs may lead to non-halting computations.

Under different universal priors (based on different universal machines), probabilities of a given string differ by no more than a constant factor independent of the string size, due to the compiler theorem (the constant factor corresponds to the probability of guessing a compiler). This justifies the name *"universal* prior," also known as the Solomonoff-Levin distribution.

Dominance of shortest programs. It can be shown (the proof is non-trivial) that the probability of guessing any of the programs computing some string and the probability of guessing one of its shortest programs are essentially equal (they differ by no more than a constant factor depending on the particular Turing machine). The probability of a string is dominated by the probabilities of its shortest programs. This is known as the "coding theorem" [3]. Similar coding theorems exist for the case of non-halting programs which cease requesting additional input symbols at a certain point.

Now back to our question: are we run by a relatively short algorithm? So far our universe *could* have been run by one — its history *could* have been much noisier and thus much less compressible. Universal prior and coding theorems suggest that the algorithm is indeed short. If it is, then there will be less than maximal randomness in our future, and more than vanishing predictability. We may hope that our universe will remain regular, as opposed to drifting off into irregularity.

Life in a Given Universe

Recognizing life. What is life? The answer depends on the observer. For instance, certain substrings of E_k may be interpretable as the life of a living thing L_k in U_k. Different observers will have different views, though. What's life to one observer will be noise to another. In particular, if the observer is not like the Great Programmer but also inhabits U_k, then its own life may be representable by a similar substring. Assuming that recognition implies relating observations to previous knowledge, both L_k's and the observer's life will have to share mutual algorithmic information [1]: there will be a comparatively short algorithm computing L_k's from the observer's life, and vice versa.

Of course, creatures living in a given universe don't have to have any idea of the symbol strings by which they are represented.

Possible limitations of the Great Programmer. He does not need not be very smart. For instance, in some of His universes phenomena will appear that humans would call life. The Great Programmer won't have to be able to recognize them.

The Great Programmer reappears. Several of the Great Programmer's universes will feature another Great Programmer who programs another Big Computer to run all possible universes. Obviously, there are infinite chains of Great Programmers. If our own universe allowed for enough storage, enough time, and fault-free computing, then you could be one of them.

Generalization and Learning

In general, generalization is impossible. Given the history of a particular universe up to a given time, there are infinitely many possible continuations.

Most of these continuations have nothing to do with the previous history. To see this, suppose we have observed a partial history $S_k^{i,j}$ (the substring between the i-th and the j-th symbol of E_k). Now we want to generalize from previous experience to predict $S_k^{j+1,l}$, $l > j$. To do this, we need an algorithm that computes $S_k^{j+1,l}$ from $S_k^{i,j}$ ($S_k^{i,j}$ may be stored on a separate, additional input tape for an appropriate universal Turing machine). There are 3^{l-j} possible futures. But for $c < l - j$, there are less than $(1/3)^c * 3^{l-j}$ algorithms with less than $l - j - c$ bits computing such a future, given $S_k^{i,j}$. Hence, in most cases, the shortest algorithm computing the future, given the past, won't be much shorter than the shortest algorithm computing the future from nothing. Both will have about the size of the entire future. In other words, the mutual algorithmic information between history and future will be zero. As a consequence, in most universes (those that can be computed by long algorithms only), successful generalization from previous experience is not possible. Neither is inductive transfer. This simple insight is related to results in [10].

Learning. Given the above, since learning means to use previous experience to improve future performance, learning is possible only in the few regular universes (no learning without compressibility). On the other hand, regularity by itself is not sufficient to allow for learning. For instance, there is a highly compressible and regular universe represented by ",,,,,,,,...". It is too simple to allow for processes we would be willing to call learning.

In what follows, I will assume that a regular universe is complex enough to allow for identifying certain permanent data structures of a general learner to be described below. For convenience, I will abstract from bitstring models, and instead talk about environments, rewards, stacks etc. Of course, all these abstract concepts are representable as bitstrings.

Scenario. In general, the learner's life is limited. To it, time will be important (not to the Great Programmer though). Suppose its life in environment $\mathcal{E}$ lasts from time 0 to unknown time T. In between it repeats the following cycle over and over again ($\mathcal{A}$ denotes a set of possible actions): select and execute $a \in \mathcal{A}$ with probability $P(a \mid \mathcal{E})$, where the modifiable policy P is a variable, conditional probability distribution on the possible actions, given current $\mathcal{E}$. Action a will consume time and may change $\mathcal{E}$ and P. Actions that modify P are called primitive learning algorithms (PLAs).

"Policy modification processes" (PMPs) are action subsequences that include PLAs. The i-th PMP in system life is denoted PMP_i, starts at time $s_i > 0$, ends at $e_i < T$, $e_i > s_i$, and computes a sequence of P-modifications denoted M_i. Both s_i and e_i are computed dynamically by executing special instructions in $\mathcal{A}$ according to P itself: P conveys information about when to start and end PMPs, and P influences the way P is modified ("self-modification").

Occasionally $\mathcal{E}$ provides real-valued reward. The cumulative reward obtained in between time 0 and time $t > 0$ is denoted by $R(t)$ (where $R(0) = 0$). At each PMP-start s_i the learner's goal is to use experience to generate P-modifications to accelerate long-term reward intake. It wants to let $\frac{R(T)-R(s_i)}{T-s_i}$ exceed the current average speed of reward intake. Assuming that reward acceleration is possible at all, given E and $\mathcal{A}$, how can the learner achieve it? I will describe a rather general way of doing so.

The success-story criterion. Each PMP-start time s_i will trigger an evaluation of the system's performance so far. Since s_i is computed according to P, P incorporates information about when to evaluate itself. Evaluations may cause policy modifications to be undone (by restoring the previous policy — in practical implementations, this requires to store previous values of modified policy components on a stack). At a given PMP-start t in the learner's life, let $V(t)$ denot the set of those previous s_i whose corresponding M_i have not been undone yet. If $V(t)$ is not empty, then let v_i ($i \in \{1, 2, \ldots, | V(t) |\}$ denote the i-th such time, ordered according to size. The success-story criterion SSC is satisfied if either $V(t)$ is empty (trivial case) or if

$$\frac{R(t)}{t} < \frac{R(t) - R(v_1)}{t - v_1} < \frac{R(t) - R(v_2)}{t - v_2} < \ldots < \frac{R(t) - R(v_{|V(t)|})}{t - v_{|V(t)|}}.$$

SSC essentially says that each surviving P-modification corresponds to a long term reward acceleration. Once SSC is satisfied, the learner continues to act and learn until the next PMP-start. (Since there may be arbitrary reward delays in response to certain action subsequences, it is important that $\mathcal{A}$ indeed includes actions for delaying performance evaluations — the learner will have to learn when to trigger evaluations).

Since the success of a policy modification recursively depends on the success of later modifications for which it is setting the stage, the framework provides a basis for "learning how to learn". Unlike with previous learning paradigms, the entire life is considered for performance evaluations. Experiments in [7, 6] show the paradigm's practical feasibility. For instance, in [7], $\mathcal{A}$ includes an extension of Levin search [4] for generating the PMPs.

PHILOSOPHY

Life after death. Members of certain religious sects expect resurrection of the dead in a paradise where lions and lambs cuddle each other. There is a possible continuation of our world where they will be right. In other possible continuations, however, lambs will attack lions.

According to the computability-oriented view adopted in this paper, life after death is a technological problem, not a religious one. All that is necessary for some human's resurrection is to record his defining parameters (such as brain connectivity and synapse properties etc.), and then dump them into a large computing device computing an appropriate virtual paradise. Similar things have been suggested by various science fiction authors. At the moment of this writing, neither appropriate recording devices nor computers of sufficient size exist. There is no fundamental reason, however, to believe that they won't exist in the future.

Body and soul. More than 2000 years of European philosophy dealt with the distinction between body and soul. The Great Programmer does not care. The processes that correspond to our brain firing patterns and the sound waves they provoke during discussions about body and soul correspond to computable substrings of our universe's evolution. Bitstrings representing such talk may evolve in many universes. For instance, sound wave patterns representing notions such as body and soul and "consciousness" may be useful in everyday language of certain inhabitants of those universes. From the view of the Great Programmer, though, such bitstring subpatterns may be entirely irrelevant. There is no need for Him to load them with "meaning".

Talking about the incomputable. Although we live in a computable universe, we occasionally chat about incomputable things, such as the halting probability of a universal Turing machine (which is closely related to Gödel's incompleteness theorem). And we sometimes discuss inconsistent worlds in which, say, time travel is possible. Talk about such worlds, however, does not violate the consistency of the processes underlying it.

Conclusion. By stepping back and adopting the Great Programmer's point of view, classic problems of philosophy go away.

ACKNOWLEDGMENTS

Thanks to Christof Schmidhuber for interesting discussions on wave functions, string theory, and possible universes.

References

1. G.J. Chaitin. *Algorithmic Information Theory*. Cambridge University Press, Cambridge, 1987.
2. A.N. Kolmogorov. Three approaches to the quantitative definition of information. *Problems of Information Transmission*, 1:1–11, 1965.
3. L. A. Levin. Laws of information (nongrowth) and aspects of the foundation of probability theory. *Problems of Information Transmission*, 10(3):206–210, 1974.
4. L. A. Levin. Randomness conservation inequalities: Information and independence in mathematical theories. *Information and Control*, 61:15–37, 1984.
5. J. Schmidhuber. Discovering neural nets with low Kolmogorov complexity and high generalization capability. *Neural Networks*, 1997. In press.
6. J. Schmidhuber, J. Zhao, and N. Schraudolph. Reinforcement learning with self-modifying policies. In S. Thrun and L. Pratt, editors, *Learning to learn*. Kluwer, 1997. To appear.
7. J. Schmidhuber, J. Zhao, and M. Wiering. Shifting inductive bias with success-story algorithm, adaptive Levin search, and incremental self-improvement. *Machine Learning*, 26, 1997. In press.
8. C. E. Shannon. A mathematical theory of communication (parts I and II). *Bell System Technical Journal*, XXVII:379–423, 1948.
9. R.J. Solomonoff. A formal theory of inductive inference. Part I. *Information and Control*, 7:1–22, 1964.
10. D. H. Wolpert. The lack of a priori distinctions between learning algorithms. *Neural Computation*, 8(7):1341–1390, 1996.

Calendars and Chronologies

Manfred Kudlek

Fachbereich Informatik, Universität Hamburg
email : kudlek@informatik.uni-hamburg.de

1 Prolog

What is JDN 2428754 - 12.16.3.9.9 7 *muluc* 7 *xul* - 1 *Elul* 5697 - 30 *Jumādā* I 1396 - 17 *Mordād* 1316 - 2 *Mesōrí* 1653 - 3 *Naḥasē* 1930 - cycle 77 year *dīng chŏu* month *jiǎ zǐ* day *dīng mǎo* - *décade II, Decadi de Thermidor* 145 - 26 *July* 1937 ? The answer will be given in the sequel. Because of limited space the reader is referred to the detailed bibliography in [1].

2 Astronomical Facts and Julian Day Number

Most calendars and chronologies are based on astronomical phenomena. The basic units are the mean solar day (d), *synodical month* $m_{Sy} = 29.530589\ d$, *sidereal month* $m_{Si} = 27.321661\ d$, *tropical year* $a_T = 365.242199\ d$, and *sidereal year* $a_{Si} = 365.256360\ d$ (all mean values). Whereas lunar and solar calendars keep in concordance with Moon or Sun, lunisolar calendars combine both.

To facilitate the computation of dates and time intervals for astronomical and chronological purposes, around 1600 Joseph Scaliger introduced a counting of days. A similar method had been invented by the Mayas or their predecessors in Mesoamerica 1700 years earlier. For the epoch (starting point) he chose 4713.1.1 BC = -4712.1.1, 0 h UT (Universal time). For astronomical purposes the start is 12 h later.

Actually Scaliger's system, called Julian Day Number (JDN) after the underlying Julian calendar, is a time scale with 0.0 corresponding to -4712.1.1, 0 h UT. Thus the first day is the interval [0,1].

The Julian Day Number will be used as a basic reference frame for all the calendar systems to be considered, especially the epochs will be expressed in JDN. $JDN \equiv 0\ (mod\ 7)$ or [0,1] corresponds to Monday,.

3 Day Cycles

The following day cycles are used in calendars.

- 1 - This simplest day cycle, called *ekawara* on Bali, is just given for completeness. Its only day is called *laung*.

- 3 - This cycle, called *triwara*, is used on Bali. The day names are *pasah, beteng, kajeng*, with $JDN \equiv 2\ (mod\ 3)$ corresponding to the beginning of *pasah*.

- 5 - This cycle is also used on Jawa and Bali, being called *pasaran* or *pancawara*. Its day names and associated numbers *urip* u_5 are *paing* 9, *pon* 7, *wage* 4, *kaliwon* 8, *umanis* 5, with $JDN \equiv 1\ (mod\ 5)$ corresponding to the beginning of *paing*.

- **6** - Another cycle used on Jawa and Bali is called *paringkelan* or *sadwara*. The day names and *urip* u_6 are *tungleh* 7, *aryang* 6, *urukung* 5, *paniron* 8, *was* 9, *maulu* 3, with $JDN \equiv 2 \pmod 6$ corresponding to the beginning of *tungleh*.

- **7** - This is the most commonly known cycle, the week. Its origin seems to be Mesopotamia. On Jawa and Bali this cycle is called *wuku* or *saptawara*. The days are either just numbered (in the Jewish calendar) or named after Gods of Planets or Planets. Names in some languages as well as *urip* u_7, and the names and meanings in the Bahā'i calendar are given in the following lists.

Latin : *Dies Solis, Dies Lunae, Dies Martis, Dies Mercurii, Dies Iovis, Dies Veneris, Dies Saturni.*

English : *Sunday, Monday, Tuesday, Wednesday, Thursday, Friday, Saturday.*

Balinese : *radite* 5, *soma* 4, *anggara* 3, *buda* 7, *wraspati* 8, *sukra* 6, *saniscara* 9.

Bahā'i : *jamāl* (beauty), *kamāl* (perfection), *fiḍāl* (favour), *'idāl* (fairness), *istijlāl* (glory), *istiqlāl* (independence), *jalāl* (splendor).

$JDN \equiv 0 \pmod 7$ corresponds to the beginning of Monday.

- **8** - This cycle was used in ancient Rome, but without individual names for the days, only every 8th day being called *Nundinae*. with $JDN \equiv 6 \pmod 8$ corresponding to *Nundinae*.

- **9** - This is a cycle used by the Maya in Mesoamerica. The day names of this cycle are known only in the form of hieroglyphs, being noted as G_n with $1 \le n \le 9$.

G_1 *Xiuhtecutli*, G_2 *Itztli*, G_3 *Piltzintecutli*, G_4 *Centeotl*, G_5 *Mictlantecutli*, G_6 *Chalchihuitlicue*, G_7 *Tlazolteotl*, G_8 *Tepeyollotl*, G_9 *Qiuauitecutli*.

$JDN \equiv 2 \pmod 9$ corresponds to the beginning of G_6.

- **10** - This cycle is from China and at least 3500 years old. It is called *tiān gàn*, i.e. the 10 celestial stems. Their names are

Chinese : *jiǎ, yǐ, bǐng, dīng, wù, jǐ, gēng, xīn, rén, guǐ.*

Japanese . *ki-no-e, ki-no-to, hi-no-e, hi-no-to, tsuchi-no-e, tsuchi-no-to, ka-no-e, ka-no-to, mizu-no-e, mizu-no-to.*

Vietnamese : *giáp, àt, bính, dinh, mậu, kỷ, canh, tân, nhâm, qúi.*

$JDN \equiv 0.7 \pmod{10}$ corresponds to the beginning of *jiǎ*.

- **12** - This cycle is also from China and is called *dì zhī*, i.e. the 12 terrestrial branches. Their names are

Chinese : *zǐ, chǒu, yín, mǎo, chén, sì, wǔ, wei, shēn, yǒu, xū, hai.*

Japanese : *ne, ushi, tora, u, tatsu, mi, uma, hitsuji, saru, tori, inu, i.*

Vietnamese : *tí, sửu, dâàn, mão, thiñ, tị, ngọ, mùi, thân, dậu, tuất, họi.*

Popular zodiacal signs in Chinese and their meanings : *shǔ* (rat), *niú* (ox), *hǔ* (tiger), *tù* (hare), *lóng* (dragon), *shé* (snake), *mǎ* (horse), *yáng* (sheep), *hóu* (monkey), *jī* (fowl), *quǎn* (dog), *zhū* (pig).

$JDN \equiv 10.7 \pmod{12}$ corresponds to the beginning of *zǐ*.

- **13** - This cycle, and the next of 20 *d*, have been used in Mesoamerica since about 2500 years. The days are just numbered by 1 to 13.

Assuming the Maya day to begin at sunrise $JDN \equiv 9 \pmod{13}$ corresponds to the beginning of day 13.

- **20** - This cycle was called *uinal* by the Mayas. The names with meanings are

Yucatec : *imix, ik, akbal, kan, chicchan, cimi, manik, lamat, muluc, oc, chuen, eb, ben, ix, men, cib, caban, etznab, cauac, ahau.*

Aztec : *cipactli* (alligator), *ehecatl* (wind), *calli* (house), *cuetzpallin* (lizard), *coatl* (serpent), *miquiztli* (death), *mazatl* (deer), *tochtli* (rabbit), *atl* (water), *itzcuintli* (dog), *ozomatli* (monkey), *malinalli* (grass), *acatl* (reed), *ocelotl* (jaguar), *cuauhtli* (eagle), *cozcaquauhtli* (vulture), *ollin* (movement), *tecpatl* (flint), *quiauitl* (rain), *xochitl* (flower).

$JDN \equiv 6 \ (mod\ 20)$ corresponds to the beginning of imix.

- **35** - This is the combination of the cycles of 5 and 7 on Jawa and Bali, called *tumpek*.

This cycle also contains two other 'cycles', that of 2 days called *dwiwara*, and that of 10 days, called *dasawara*. The day names in these 'cycles' are not cyclic, however, but are computed in the following way : $n_2 = 1 + u_5 + u_7 \ (mod\ 2)$ and $n_{10} = 1 + u_5 + u_7 \ (mod\ 10)$. The day names of these two 'cycles' are *menga, pepet* and *pandita, pati, suka, duka, sri, manuh, manusa, raja, dewa, raksasa.*

$JDN \equiv 6 \ (mod\ 35)$ corresponds to *paing radite*, and *menga sri*.

- **60** - This is the combination of the cycles of 10 and 12, yielding the basic and most important Chinese cycle. It is also used for the naming of hours, months and years. The names of days are just the combinations of those from the cycles of 10 and 12, starting with *jia zǐ*. $JDN \equiv 10.7 \ (mod\ 60)$ corresponds to the beginning of *jia zǐ*.

- **210** - This is the combination of the cycles of 5, 6 and 7, and is used on Jawa and Bali. It is called *wewaran* or *pawukon*. The cycle is divided into 30 *wuku* each having its own name. These are given in the following list :

sinta, landep, ukir, kulantir, tolu, gumbreg, wariga, warigadian, julungwangi, sungsang, galungan, kuningan, langkir, medangsia, pujut, pahang, krulut, merakih, tambir, medangkungan, matal, uye, menail, perangbakat, bala, ugu, wayang, kulawu, dukut, watugunung.

The days within a *wuku* are not numbered but named according to the 7 day cycle. Thus the first day in each *wuku* is radite. $JDN \equiv 146$ corresponds to the first day of the *wuku sinta* with *paing, tungleh, radite*.

The *pawukon* is also divided into 1 interval of 3 plus 23 intervals of 9 days, yielding $210 = 3 + 23 \times 9$. The 'cycle' of 9 days is called *sangawara* or *nawawara*, with *dangu, jangur, gigis, nohan, ogan, erangan, urungan, tulus, dadi.*

The first 3 days of *wuku sinta* have the name *dangu* whereas the days in the 23 periods of 9 days have the names of the *sangawara*, starting with the 4th of *sinta*.

Two other divisions of the *pawukon* period starting on the first day of *galungan* are $210 = 2 + 52 \times 4$ and $210 = 2 + 26 \times 8$. The day names of the 4 day and 8 day periods, called *caturwara* and *astawara*, respectively, are *jaya, menala, sri, laba* and *kala, uma, sri, indra, guru, yama, ludra, brahma.*

The first 2 days in *galungan* have the names *jaya* and *kala*, respectively, whereas the days in the 4 day and 8 day periods have the names according to the lists, respectively, starting on the 3rd day of *galungan*.

- **260** - This is the combination of the cycles of 13 and 20, yielding the most important Mesoamerican cycle (*tzolkin* in Yucatec). Again, the day names are just the combinations of those from the cycles of 13 and 20, starting with 1 *imix*. $JDN \equiv 164 \ (mod \ 260)$ corresponds to the beginning of 1 *imix*.

In the following cycles the days do not have individual names.

- **360** - A period called *tun* by the Mayas.
- **365** - Solar year. Used in the Egyptian and Mesoamerican calendars.
- **400** - This period has been used by the Cakchiquel Indians in Guatemala.

4 Lunar Calendars

In pure lunar calendar systems there is no relation to the solar year although a 'lunar year' (a_L) of 12 synodical months is used. Such systems exist in Arabic and Muslim countries, and on Jawa and Bali.

The first one is the **Arabic** lunar calendar.

The basic relation is $30 \ a_L = 360 \ m_{sy} = 10631 \ d$. A lunar year either has 354 d, or 355 d as a leap year. In the cycle of 30 a_L the following years are leap years, 2 systems being in use : 2,5,7,10,13,15(16),18, 21,24,26,29. The lunar year is divided into 12 months. Their names in Arabic and lenghts are

Muḥarram 30, *Ṣafar* 29, *Rabī' l-awwal* 30, *Rabī' l-aḫir* 29, *Jumādā l-ūlā* 30, *Jumādā l-āḫira* 29, *Rajab* 30, *Ša'ban* 29, *Ramaḍān* 30, *Šawwāl* 29, *Ḏu l-qa'da* 30, *Ḏu l-ḥiǧǧa* 29 (30).

The days within a month are numbered from 1 to 29 or 30, and the years are counted from the epoch. Since the Muslim day begins at sunset the epoch of the system is the Muslim era 1948438.65 (astronomical) or 1948439.65 (civic).

Another calendar is used on **Jawa**.

The basic relation is $120a_L = 42524 \ d$, thus resulting in 4 periods of 30 a_L of the Arabic calendar. But 120 a_L are divided into 15 periods of 8 a_L with 8 $a_L = 2835 \ d$ each, except for the 15th one with only 2834 d. Such a period of 8 a_L is called *windu*, and the years within a *windu* have the following names :

harsa, heruwarsa, jimantra, duryanta, dharma, pitaka, wahyu, dirgawarsa or *alip, ehe, jimawal, je, dal, be, wawu, jimakir.*

The *windu* are arranged in a cycle of 4, each having a name in the following order : *adi, kuntara, sangara, sancaya.*

As in the Arabic calendar a lunar year either has 354 d, or 355 d as a leap year. In each period of 8 a_L the following years are leap years : 2, 5 and 8, except for the 15th one only with leap years 2 and 5.

The Jawanese month names are *Sura, Sapar, Mulud, Bakdamulud, Jumadi-lawal, Jumadilakhir, Rejeb, Ruwah, Pasa, Sawal, Sela (Hapit), Besar (Haji).*

They have the same lengths as in the Arabic calendar. Years are counted according to the following equation :

$JDN = 2317690 = 1 \ Sura \ 1555, umanis, sukra$, beginning of year *alip*, *windu kuntara*.

A third lunar calendar is used on **Bali**. The basic relation of this system, *Pangalantaka (Candra)*, is $128 \ a_L = 45359 \ d$. These 128 a_L are divided into

16 periods of 8 a_L with 8 $a_L = 2835\ d$ each, except for the 16th one with only 2834 d. The month names are just the Indian Lunar month names, and years are numbered according to : $JDN = 2317690 = 1\ Caitra\ 1603, umanis, sukra.$

Days within a month are numbered from 1 to 15 (bright half), and then again from 1 to 15 (dark half, denoted here by $\underline{1}$ to $\underline{15}$). However, counting cyclically with 30, every 63rd number is omitted according to a system called *pangalihan*. Thus a day will not have number n but $n + 1$, denoted by $n/(n + 1)$.

The *pangalihan* system is based on $3 \times 3 \times 3 \times 210 = 5670\ d = 16\ a_L$. Its starting point is shifted relatively to the lunar months. In the present system, called *eka sungsang ke pon* the first omission is in *wuku sungsang, day pon, buda*, with $\underline{9}/\underline{10}$. This gives the following series of omissions of numbers :

$\underline{9}/\underline{10}$, $\underline{13}/\underline{14}$, 2/3, 6/7, 10/11, 14/15, $\underline{3}/\underline{4}$, $\underline{7}/\underline{8}$, $\underline{11}/\underline{12}$, $\underline{15}/1$, 4/5, 8/9, 12/13, $1/\underline{2}$, $\underline{5}/\underline{6}$.

After 1 repetition the omission will fall into the same wuku, and repeating the whole 3 times (i.e. 5670 d), the omission will also fall into the same month.

Starting point of the present system is $JDN = 2447972$.

5 Solar Calendars

Solar calendars only keep in concordance with the tropical or sidereal year.

In the **Egyptian** calendar the year has $365 = 12 \times 30 + 5\ d$. Month names in some languages are

Coptic : Θώϑ, Φαωφί, Ἀϑύρ, Χοίακ, Τυβί, Μεχίρ, Φαμενώϑ, Φαρμουϑί, Παχών, Παϋνί, Ἐπιφί, Μεσωρί, Ἐπαγόμεναι.

Persian : *Farvardīn, Urdībihišt, Ḥardād, Tīr, Murdād, Šahrīvar, Mihr, Ābān, Ādar, Dai, Bahman, Isfandārmud, (5 days).*

Armenian : *Nawasardi, Hori, Sahmi, Trê, Khalots, Araths, Mehekani, Areg, Ahekani, Mareri, Margaths, Hrotiths, Aveleaths.*

Days within a month are numbered from 1 to 5 or 30. In the Persian calendar the days within each month of 30 d had individual names, as well as the 5 additional days. These names are

Hormuz, Bahman, Urdībihišt, Šahrīvar, Isfandārmud, Ḥardād, Murdād, Day-bi-ādar, Ādar, Ābān, Ḥūr, Māh, Tīr, Juš, Day-bi-mihr, Mihr, Surūš, Rašn, Farvardīn, Bahrām, Rām, Bād, Day-bi-dīn, Dīn, Ard, Aštād, Asmān, Zāmdād, Mārasfand, Anīrān and *Ahnad, Ašnad, Isfandārmud, Aḫšaatar, Wahišt.*

Until the year 375 of the Era *Yazdagird* the 5 additional days were put after *Ābān*, from 376 on after *Isfandārmud*.

Epochs are Egyptian (Era Nabonassar) 1448638, Egyptian (Era *Philippi*) 1603398, Persian (Era *Yazdagird*) 1952063, Armenian 1922868.

A similar calendar with $365 = 18 \times 20 + 5\ d$ was used in Mesoamerica and is still used in some Indian communities of Guatemala. The period of 365 d was called *haab* in Yucatec. The month names are

Yucatec : *pop, uo, zip, zotz, tzec, xul, yaxkin, mol, chen, yax, zac, ceh, mac, kankin, muan, pax, kayab, cumhu, uayeb.*

Aztec : *atlcahualo, tlacaxipehualiztli, tozoztontli, hueytozoztli, toxcatl, etzal-
cualiztli, tecuilhuitontli, hueytecuilhuitl, miccailhuitontli, hueymiccailhuitl, och-
paniztli, pachtontli, hueypachtli, quecholli, panquetzaliztli, atemoztli, tititl, izcalli,
nemontemi.*

There is no counting of years, but $JDN \equiv 302 \ (mod \ 365)$ corresponds to
0 *pop*, the first day of a year.

The basic relation of the **Julian** calendar is $4 \ a = 1461 \ d$. There are two
different internal divisions of the year, an Egyptian $(365(366) = 12 \times 30 + 5(6) \ d)$,
(also Coptic, Ethiopian), and a Roman one. Month names in the Coptic calendar
were given above, in Ethiopian and Latin in the following lists :

Ethiopian : *Maskaram, Ṭeqemt, Hedār, Tāhsās, Ṭer, Yakkātit, Maggābit,
Miyāzyā, Genbot, Sanē, Ḥamlē, Naḥasē, Pāgumēn*

Epochs, with leap years $Y \equiv n \ (mod \ 4)$, are Alexandrian (Panodorus) -284653
3, Ethiopian 1724290 3, Coptic 1825030 1.

Latin : *Ianuarius* 31, *Februarius* 29 (30) / 28 (29), *Martius* 31, *Aprilis*
30, *Maius* 31, *Iunius* 30, *Quintilis/Iulius* 31, *Sextilis/Augustus* 30 / 31,
September 31 / 30, *October* 30 / 31, *November* 31 / 30, *December* 30 / 31.
with lengths from 46 BC / 8 BC.

The numbering of the days in the old Roman calendar is quite complicated.
The first day is called *Kalendae*. In months 3,5,7,10 the 7th day is called *Nonae*
and the 15th day *Idus*. In months 1,2,4,6,8, 9,11,12 the 5th day is called *Nonae*
and the 13th day *Idus*. The other days are counted backwards with *XIX,...,III
dies, pridie ante Nonas, Idus, Kalendas* respectively. The intercalary day is *VI
dies ante Kalendas Martii*, i.e. February 24 which is counted two times. Thus
the other name *bisextile* for a leap year. In the other calendars the days within
a month are just numbered from 1 to 28, 29,30 or 31.

Epochs, together with leap years $Y \equiv n \ (mod \ 4)$ and start of the year are
Roman (Varro) 1446390 (0, 1.1), Spanish ('Era') 1707544 (1, 1.1), Julian
(Christian) 1721424 (0, 1.1), Byzantine (March) -290313 (3, 3.1), Antiochian -
458394 (0, 9.1), Byzantine (September) -290494 (0, 9.1), Seleucide (Hellenistic,
Syrian) 1607739 (3, 10.1).

The basic relation of the **Gregorian** calendar, introduced by Pope Gregor
XIII in 1582, is $400 \ a = 146097 \ d$. The intercalary day is February 29 as in the
Julian calendar. Leap years are all those years Y for which $Y \equiv 0 \ (mod \ 4)$ except
for $Y \equiv k \cdot 100 \ (mod \ 400)$ with $k = 1,2$ or 3.

The internal division of the year is the same as in the Julian calendar, as well
as the numbering of within a month. The epoch is JDN 1721426.

Another division of the year is used in the Indian National calendar, introduced in 1957 AD. The month names are

Hindi : *Cait* 30 (31), *Baisākh* 31, *Jeṭh* 31, *Āsārh* 31, *Sāvan* 31, *Bhādō* 31,
Āsin 30, *Kātik* 30, *Aghan* 30, *Pūs* 30, *Māgh* 30, *Phāgun* 30.

Days within a month are numbered from 1 to 30 or 31, and the epoch is *Śaka*
1749993.8. Leap years are all those years Y with $Y + 78 \equiv 0 \ (mod \ 4)$ except for
such ones with $Y + 78 \equiv k \cdot 100 \ (mod \ 400)$ and $k = 1,2$ or 3.

215

The *Bahā'i* calendar has a division $365(366) = 12 \times 19 + 4(5)$. The month names are

bahā' (magnificence), *jalāl* (splendour), *jamāl* (beauty), *'azamāt* (majesty), *nūr* (light), *rahmat* (compassion), *kalimāt* (words), *kamāl* (perfection), *asmā'* (names), *'izzat* (power), *mašī'at* (wish), *'ilm* (knowledge), *qudrat* (strength), *qaul* (speech), *masā'il* (questions), *šaraf* (honour), *sulṭān* (rule), *mulk* (sovereignity), *ayyām-i-hā* (additional days), *'alā'* (nobility).

The Bahā'i calendar with its intercalation is bound to the Gregorian calendar. Starting point is JDN 2394645.75.

The basis relation of the **Neojulian** calendar, introduced by some Orthodox churches in 1923, is 900 $a = 328718 \, d$. The internal structure of the year and the epoch is the same as in the Gregorian calendar. However, leap years are all years $Y \equiv 0 \pmod 4$ except $Y \equiv k \cdot 100 \pmod{900}$ with $k = 0,1,3,4,5,7$ or 8.

The basic relation of the **Jawanese** Solar calendar, called *Pranatamangsa*, is 128 $a = 46751 \, d$. The month names with lengths are

kasa 41, *karo* 23, *katiga* 24, *kapat* 25, *kalima* 27, *kanem* 43, *kapitu* 43, *kaulu* 26 (27), *kasanga* 25, *kadasa* 24, *desta* 23, *sada* 41.

Days within a month are just numbered from 1 to the corresponding length, and the epoch is JDN 2398757. Years are numbered, and leap years are those with $Y \equiv 1 \pmod 4$, except for such with $Y \equiv 1 \pmod{128}$.

A calendar with the **tropical** year is used in Iran. The first day of a year is that day, beginning at midnight Iranian time, the noon of which follows directly the time of the vernal equinox. The month names are

Farvardīn 31, *Ordībehešt* 31, *Hordad* 31, *Tīr* 31, *Mordād* 31, *Šahrīvar* 31, *Mehr* 30, *Ābān* 30, *Āzar* 30, *Dey* 30, *Bahman* 30, *Esfand* 29 (30).
Epoch is *Hijra Šamsi* JDN 1948320.8569 (vernal equinox JDN 1948320.3767).

Another such calendar was introduced during the French revolution in 1793 AD. The first day of a year is that day, beginning at midnight, on which the autumn equinox falls. The year is divided into $365(366) = 12 \times 30 + 5(6) \, d$. The normal month was divided into $30 = 3 \times 10 \, d$. The month names and the 10 day names are

Vendémiaire, Brumaire, Frimaire, Nivôse, Pluviôse, Ventôse, Germinal, Floréal, Prairial, Messidor, Thermidor, Fructidor, Jours complémentaires.

Primidi, Duodi, Tridi, Quartidi, Quintidi, Sextidi, Septidi, Octidi, Nonidi, Décadi.

The additional days had individual names. Epoch is JDN 2375839.9935 (autumn equinox JDN 2375840.3751).

The third such calendar is part of the Chinese calendar. *Solar terms qi* are defined by the motion of the Sun in the equatorial or ecliptical plane, by 15°. The *Sāndōng* (6 BC) and the *Sifēn* (85 AD) calendar ues 1539 $a = 562120 \, d$, and 4 $a = 1461 \, d$, respectively. The solar terms (odd *jiéqi*, even *zhōngqi*) are

lìchūn, yǔshuǐ, jīngzhé, chūnfēn, qīngmíng, gǔyǔ, lìxià, xiǎomǎn, mángzhòng, xiàzhì, xiǎoshǔ, dàshǔ, lìqiū, chǔshǔ, báilù, qiūfēn, hánlù, shuāngjiàng, lìdōng, xiǎoxuě, dàxuě, dōngzhì, xiǎohán, dàhán.

The winter solstice is at the beginning of *dōngzhi*.

The **sidereal** year is used in the Indian calendar. There are 12 intervals *rāśi* of 30° each, the starting points being called *saṃkrānti*. According to the *Sūrya Siddhānta* such an interval is defined by $4320000\ a = 1577917828\ d$. The first day of a Solar month begins at sunrise after the Sun passed a *saṃkrānti*.

The month names are *Meṣa, Vṛṣabha, Mithuna, Karka, Siṃha, Kanyā, Tulā, Vṛścika, Dhanus, Makara, Kumbha, Mīna*.

Epoch is *Era Kaliyuga JDN* 588465.7895325 (midnight at *Laṅkā*), *JDN* 588466.0395 (sunrise). But years are numbered by *Kaliyuga* 3179 = *Śaka* 1.

6 Lunisolar Calendars

Lunisolar calendars combine the motions of Sun and Moon. The Babylonian month names are

Nisannu, Aiaru, Tašrītu, Simānu, Du'ūzu, Abu, Ulūlu, Tašrītu, Araḫsamna, Kislimu, Ṭebetu, Šabāṭu, Addaru.

In 8th century BC the Babylonians discovered $19\ a = 235\ m_{Sy}$, and the concordance was kept by an Addaru II in years 3,6,8,11,14 and 19, and an Ulūlu II in year 16 of the 19 a cycle. This cycle, also named after *Meton*, was improved by *Kallippos* in 330 BC to $76\ a = 940\ m_{Sy} = 27759\ d$.

The **Jewish** month names, adopted from the Babylonians, with lengths in short, normal, and long years, are

Tišri 30, *Marḥešvan* (29,29,30), *Kislev* (29,30,30), *Ṭebet* 29, *Šebaṭ* 30, *Adar* 29 (30), (*Veadar* 29), *Nisan* 30, *Iyyar* 29, *Sivan* 30, *Tammuz* 29, *Ab* 30, *Elul* 29, resulting in years of 353, 354, 355, 383, 384, 385 d.

In 344 AD *Hillel II* introduced the basic relation $1\ m_{Sy} = 29\ d\ 12\ š\ 793$ h, where $1\ d = 24\ š\ (ša'h)$, and $1\ š = 1080\ h\ (halaqim)$. Intercalary months (*Veadar*) are in leap years (LY) 3,6,8,11,14,17,19 of the cycle.

Epoch is JDN 347997.8687 2 d 5 š 204 h (Monday).

For the internal division of a year one has to compute the first New Moon (*Molad Tišri*, MT) and the New Year (NY) of it and of the next year by :

yaḥ : If MT ≥ 18 š then NY 1 *d* later;

adu : If MT on 1,4,6 then NY 1 *d* later (on 2,5,7);

yaḥ-adu : If NY by A on 1,4,6 then NY 1 *d* later (on 2,5,7);

gaṭrad : If in CY 3 *d* 9 š 204 *h* ≤ MT < 3 *d* 18 š then NY on 5;

beṭutakpaṭ : If in CY after a LY 2 *d* 15 š 589 *h* ≤ MT < 2 *d* 18 š then NY on 3;

From the more than 50 **Chinese** calendars only 2 will be presented, namely *Sāndŏng* and *Sifēn* with $19\ a = 235\ m_{Sy}$.

A lunation falling entirely within a double Solar term, beginning with a *zhōngqi*, (except for the rare case that it starts exactly on the begin of such a double Solar term), is defined as an intercalary month.

The months within a year are either numbered from 1 to 12, the intercalary month having the same number as its predecessor, or they get the names of the cycle of 60 given above, the intercalary month having no name.

The civic year begins with the 3rd month of the astronomical system. As an epoch can be taken JDN -2929.3, both a winter solstice and a New moon at midnight. Years are denoted by names of the cycle of 60, starting with the 61st year of the reign of the emperor *Huángdì* (2636 BC).

The *Sanskrit* month names of the **Indian** Lunisolar calendar are

Caitra, Vaiśākha, Jyeṣṭha, Āṣāḍha, Śrāvaṇa, Bhādrapada, Āśvina, Kārttika, Mārgaśīrṣa, Pauṣa, Māgha, Phālguna.

According to the *Sūrya Siddhānta* 4320000 $a = 57753336$ m_{Sy} defines a lunation. A lunation is divided into 30 parts, called *tithi* (t), corresponding to the motion of the Moon by 12° relatively to the Sun. These 30 *tithi*, divided into the first 15 (*śukla pakṣa*, bright half), numbered from 1 to 15, and the second 15 (*kṛṣṇa pakṣa*, dark half), numbered from 1 to 14, and the last one by 30. The days of a Lunar month get their number from that *tithi* which contains the sunrise. A lunation entirely within a *rāśi* is intercalary and is named by the following one with *adhika* (added). The first month of a Lunisolar year always is *Caitra*, ending after *Mesa saṃkrānti*. The years are numbered from the *Kaliyuga* or *Śaka* epoch.

7 The Maya Calendar

The Maya also used a counting of days by *kin* (day, k), *uinal* (U = 20 k), *tun* (T = 18 U), *katun* (KT = 20 T), *baktun* (BT = 20 KT), denoted by *BT.KT.T.U.k* with the epoch 0.0.0.0.0 4 *ahau* 8 *cumhu* = JDN 584285.

8 Epilog

The answer to the question in the prolog is : 8 *August* 1937 (Gregorian), the day *Wilfried Brauer* was born. The reader is asked to convert the following date(s).

Friday - *pasah, kaliwon, paniron, sukra, menga, sri, nohan, laba, indra, wuku tolu* - JDN 2450669 - 12.19.4.7.4 4 *kan* 2 *yaxkin* - 5 *Av* 5757 - 3 *Rabī'* II 1418 - 17 *Mordād* 1376 - 2 *Mesōrí* 1713 - 3 *Naḥasē* 1990 - cycle 77 year *dīng chŏu* month *jiă zĭ* day *rén wŭ* - *décade III, Primidi de Thermidor* 205 - 26 *July* 1997 - 4 *Bakdamulud* 1930 *tahun jimakir windu sancaya* - 4 *Ashadha* 1978 - 17 *sāvan* 1919 - 7 *karo* 143 - 4 *Śrāvaṇa* 1919.

References

1. M. Kudlek : *Calendar Systems* (Mitteilungen der Mathematischen Gesellschaft in Hamburg, Band XII, Heft 2, p 395-428,1991. Festschrift der Mathematischen Gesellschaft in Hamburg zu ihrem 300-jährigen Bestehen, Teil 2)

A Uniform Approach to Petri Nets

H. Ehrig   J. Padberg
Technische Universität Berlin, FB Informatik
Sekr. 6-1, Franklinstr. 28/29, D-10587 Berlin
E-mail: {ehrig,padberg}@cs.tu-berlin.de

Abstract

The new concept of *universal parameterized net classes* is introduced in order to allow a uniform approach to different kinds of Petri net classes. By different actualizations of the *net structure parameter* and the *data type parameter* we obtain several well-known net classes, like elementary nets, place-transition nets, colored nets, predicate transition nets, and algebraic high-level nets, as well as several interesting new classes of low- and high-level nets. While the basic concept of *parameterized net classes* is defined on a purely set theoretical level the extended concept of *universal parameterized net classes* takes into account also morphisms and universal properties in the sense of category theory. This allows to discuss general constructions and compatibility results concerning union and fusion of nets for different types of net classes.

1 Introduction

Petri nets have been used sucessfully for more than three decades to model concurrent processes and distributed systems. Various kinds of Petri net classes with numerous features and analysis methods have been proposed in literature (among many others [Bra80, BRR87b, BRR87a]) for different purposes and application areas. The fact that Petri nets are widely used and are still considered to be an important topic in research, shows the usefulness and the power of this formalism. Nevertheless, the situation in the field of Petri nets is far from satisfactory, partly due to the enormous interest in Petri nets, that has been leading to a vast accumulation of dissimilar approaches. The different notions, definitions and techniques, both in literature and practice, make it hard to find a common understanding and to provide good reasons for the practical use of the nets. Moreover, the unstructured variety of Petri net approaches causes the new formulation and examination of similar concepts. The relation of these concepts requires complicated, but boring conversions. Most of the different concepts for Petri nets are defined explicitly for a single net class, although many of these notions are essentially the same for different kinds of net classes. Unfortunately, however, there is no abstract notion of Petri nets up to now, that permits the abstract formulation of such notions for a large variety of different net classes. The uniform approach to Petri nets, based on universal parametrized net classes captures the common components of different kinds of Petri nets like places, transitions, net structure, and, in case of high-level nets, a data type part. General notions, like switching behaviour, that are essential for all kinds of Petri nets are formulated within the frame of abstract Petri nets independently of their specific definition within a fixed net class. Hence, this concept comprises many known and several new net classes as special cases and allows their mutual comparison. Results achieved within this frame can be generalized to several different net classes. This means notions and results are achieved without further effort in each of these net classes, provided the general assumptions have been verified for the specific instance.

This paper is organized as follows. First we sketch a purely set theoretic description of this uniform approach, called parametrized net classes. This includes the definition of the net structure parameter and the data type paramenter. The subsequent section extends these parameters into a categorical frame that includes morphisms and allows to specify certain universal properties. This allows the construction of the marking graph, some horizontal and vertical structuring techniques and compatibility results, that have not been presented detailed due to space limitations. The conclusion summarizes the achieved results.

2 Parametrized Net Classes

The basic idea of this uniform approach to Petri nets is to identify two parameters, that describe each of the net classes entirely. In case of the usual Petri nets this is the net structure and in case of high-level nets it is the net structure and the data type formalism. We call these parameters net structure parameter and data type parameter. The instantiation of these parameters leads to different types of Petri nets, or more precisely Petri net classes. In this section we introduce parameters for net classes, parametrized net classes and their instances leading to several well-known and some interesting new net classes.

2.1 Relevance of Parameters for Net Classes

The net structure parameter describes different low-level net classes. Several different net classes have been proposed over the last 30 years, see for example [Rei85, RT86, Bra84]. Moreover, the developments in software industries have yielded quite a large amount of variants that are equipped with additional features and/or restrictions. We propose an abstraction of net structure that can be instantiated to several net classes, including place/transition nets, elementary nets, variants of these and S-graphs. We have shown in [Pad96] that the underlying construction is general enough to comprise several different kinds of low-level nets and their net structure. The data type parameter is necessary, because several data type formalisms have been integrated with Petri nets leading to different notions of high-level nets. Typical examples are: indexed sets with place/transition nets leading to coloured nets [Jen81], predicate logic with elementary nets leading to predicate/transition nets [GL81], algebraic specifications with place/transition nets leading to different versions of algebraic high-level nets [Vau86, Rei91], ML with place/transition nets leading to coloured nets [Jen92], OBJ2 with superposed automata nets leading to OBJSA-nets [BCM88], and algebraic specifications with the Petri Box Calculus [BDH92] leading to A-nets [KP95]. In practice there are also other data type formalisms like entity/relationship diagrams, SADT and many other semi-formal techniques that are combined with Petri nets in an informal way.

2.2 Algebraic Presentation of Place/Transition Nets

We use the algebraic presentation of Petri nets, that uses functions to relate a transition with its pre- and postdomain. This approach relates a transition on the one hand with all those places in its predomain using the function *pre* and on the other hand with its postdomain using the function *post*. In this algebraic presentation a place/transition net N is simply given by a 4-tuple $N = (P, T, pre, post)$ where P and T are the sets for places and transitions respectively and *pre* and *post* are functions $pre, post : T \rightarrow P^*$ from T to the free commutative monoid P^* over P. This algebraic presentation [MM90] is equivalent to the classical presentation (see e.g. [Rei85]) where a place/transition net is given by a flow relation $F \subseteq P \times T \cup T \times P$ and a weight-function $weight : F \rightarrow \mathbb{N}$, where $\mathbb{N}$ are the natural numbers. In fact, given the classical presentation[1] we have $pre(t) = \sum_{i=1}^{k} n_i p_i \in P^*$ where $^\bullet t = \{p \in P \mid (p, t) \in F\}$ is given by $^\bullet t = \{p_1, ..., p_k\}$ and $n_i = weigth(p_i, t)$ for $i = 1, ..., k$. Vice versa, given for example $pre(t) = 2p_1 + p_2$ and $post(t) = 2p_2 + 3p_3$ we have $(p1, t), (p2, t), (t, p2), (t, p3) \subseteq F$ with weights $2, 1, 2$ and 3 respectively.

2.3 Variants of Net Classes

Note, that there are several variants of place/transition nets, and similar for other types of nets, where nets are considered with initial marking or with labels on places, transitions, and/or arcs. However, in this paper we only consider a basic variant without initial markings and without labels. In the case of high-level nets our basic variant means in addition that a net includes one explicit model with total operations (resp. predicates) and that there are no switching conditions for the transitions (unguarded case). In our paper [ER96] we discuss several kinds of variants of algebraic high-level nets, which can also be extended to variants of other types of high-level nets considered in this paper.

2.4 Mathematical Notation of Parameters for Net Classes

In the following we distinguish between formal and actual parameters for the net structure and data type formalisms. The actual net structure parameter for a net class is based on the algebraic presentation of nets, more precisely the codomain of the pre- and post functions. In the case of place/transition nets the codomain is given by the free commutative monoid P^* over the set of places P. In the case of elementary nets[2] it is given by the power set construction $\mathcal{P}(P)$, that is $pre, post : T \rightarrow \mathcal{P}(P)$, because $^\bullet t = pre(t)$ and $t^\bullet = post(t)$ are given by subsets of P. Moreover, each element $m \in \mathcal{P}(P)$ can be considered as a marking of the elementary net, and similar $m \in P^*$ as a marking of the

---

[1] Note, that the algebraic presentation allows infinite set of places and transitions without inducing infinite pre- or post domains. In contrast, the classical presentation requires finite sets of places and transitions.

[2] We talk about elementary nets as elementary (net) systems without an initial marking.

place/transition net. The calculation with markings is based on the operations union of $\mathcal{P}(P)$ and addition of P^* respectively, leading to a semigroup structure in both classes. Hence, the constructions $\mathcal{P}(P)$ and P^* for each set P can be considered as functions from the class **Sets** of sets via some subclass **Struct** of semigroups to the class **Sets**, where in the last step we consider $\mathcal{P}(P)$ and P^* as sets, forgetting about the semi-group structure. This motivates that in general an actual net structure parameter for a net class can be considered as a composite function: $Net : \textbf{Sets} \xrightarrow{F} \textbf{Struct} \xrightarrow{G} \textbf{Sets}$

An actual data type parameter for a net class consist of a class **SPEC** of data type specifications and for each $SPEC \in \textbf{SPEC}$ a class **Mod(SPEC)** of models satisfying the specification $SPEC$. Hence, it can be represented by a function $Mod : \textbf{SPEC} \to \textbf{ModelClasses}$ where **ModelClasses** is the (super)class of all model classes. The mathematical notation of formal net structure and data type parameters are variables **Net** and **Mod** ranging over all actual net structure and data type parameters Net and Mod respectively.

Definition 2.4.1 (Parameters of Net Classes)

1. The formal net structure parameter resp. formal data type parameter of a net class is given by variables **Net** for the net structure formalism, and **Mod** for the data type formalism ranging over all actual net structure and actual data type parameters, respectively.

2. An actual net structure parameter resp. actual data type parameter of a net class is defined by a composite function $Net : \textbf{Sets} \xrightarrow{F} \textbf{Struct} \xrightarrow{G} \textbf{Sets}$ and a function $Mod : \textbf{SPEC} \to \textbf{ModelClasses}$ respectively as motivated above.

Example 2.4.2 (Actual Parameters of Net Classes)

1. The powerset construction $\mathcal{P}(P)$ over a set P defines a composite function $\mathcal{P} : \textbf{Sets} \to \textbf{Struct} \to \textbf{Sets}$, where $\mathcal{P}(P)$ with union operation is a semi-group and without union operation a set, which is the actual net structure parameter for the class of elementary nets.

2. The free commutative monoid P^* over a set P defines a composite function $(\_)^* : \textbf{Sets} \to \textbf{Struct} \to \textbf{Sets}$, where P^* with the addition operation is a semi-group and without this operation it is a set, which is the actual net structure parameter for the class of place/transition nets. The free commutative monoid P^* can be represented by formal sums $P^* = \{\sum_{i=1}^{k} n_i * p_i \mid p_i \in P, \; n_i \in \mathbb{N}\}$ with componentwise addition.

3. The free commutative group P^{ab} over a set P represented by $P^{ab} = \{\sum_{i=1}^{k} n_i * p_i \mid p_i \in P, \; n_i \in \mathbb{Z}\}$ can be considered as an actual net structure parameter for the classes of place/transition group nets or algebraic high-level group nets.

4. The composite function $ID* : \textbf{Sets} \to \textbf{Struct} \to \textbf{Sets}$, defined by $ID* : P \mapsto P^* \mapsto P$ (Identity) for each set P can be considered as the actual net structure parameter for the subclass of place/transition nets, called S-Graphs (see [RT86]), where each transition has exactly one place in its pre-

and post-domain respectively. The corresponding net can be considered as graph, where the nodes are the places and the edges are the transitions. The intermediate construction of P^* in the definition of $ID*(P)$ makes sure that markings are elements $m \in P^*$ (as usual in place/transition nets) rather than $m \in P$, which would allow only one token at all in the net .

5. Let **SPEC** be the class of all algebraic specifications $SPEC = (S, OP, E)$ with signature (S, OP) and equations E and **Alg(SPEC)** the class of all $SPEC$-algebras A (see [EM85]). Then we obtain a function $Alg :$ **SPEC** $\rightarrow$ **ModelClasses** which is the actual data type parameter for the class of algebraic high-level nets ([PER95]).

6. Let **FOSPEC** be the class of all first order predicate logic specifications $FOSPEC = (\Omega, \Pi, AXIOMS)$ with the signature (Ω, Π) and $AXIOMS$ being a set of closed formulas, and **FOMod(FOSPEC)** the class of all non-empty models satisfying the formulas in $AXIOMS$. Then we obtain a function $FOMod :$ **FOSPEC** $\rightarrow$ **ModelClasses**, which is the actual data type parameter for the class of predicate/transition nets ([GL81]).

7. In order to be able to consider low-level nets as special case of high-level nets we define the following trivial actual data type parameter $Triv :$ **TRIV** $\rightarrow$ **ModelClasses**, where the class **TRIV** consists only of one elements called trivial specification $TRIV$, and **Triv(TRIV)** is the model class, consisting only of one model, the one-element set $\{\bullet\}$, representing a single token.

8. There are also actual data type parameters for the class of colored nets in the sense of [Jen81] and [Jen92], which are based on indexed nets and the functional language ML, respectively (see [Pad96]).

Now we are able to define parameterized net classes and their instantiations mentioned above already.

Definition 2.4.3 (Parameterized and Actual Net Classes)

1. A parameterized net class is defined by a pair (**Net**, **Mod**) consisting of a formal net structure parameter **Net** and a formal data type parameter **Mod** (see 2.4.1).

2. The actual net class defined by instantiation of the formal parameters (**Net**, **Mod**) by actual parameters (Net, Mod) with $Net = F \circ G$ and $Mod :$ **SPEC** $\rightarrow$ **ModelClasses** (see 2.4.1) consists of all nets $N = (P, T, SPEC, A, pre, post)$ satisfying the following conditions:

   – P and T are sets of places and transitions respectively,
   – $SPEC \in$ **SPEC** is the data type specification
   – $A \in$ **Mod(SPEC)**, called data type model
   – $pre, post : T \rightarrow Net(PSPEC)$ are functions,
     where $PSPEC$ is a set constructed in a uniform way from the set P and the specification $SPEC$.

   In the case of low-level nets we have $Mod = Triv$ (see 2.4.2.7) and hence **SPEC** = **TRIV** and $A = \{\bullet\}$ which are omitted as components of a net. Requiring in addition $PSPEC = P$ we obtain $N = (P, T, pre, post)$ with $pre, post : T \rightarrow Net(P)$

Remark 2.4.4

- Other parameterized and actual net classes can be defined by other variants of net classes discussed in 2.4.2. In our notion above we only consider the basic variant without initial markings, without labels, with only one explicit (total) model and without switching conditions for transitions.
- A uniform construction of $PSPEC$ from P and $SPEC$ is provided by the notion of *Abstract Petri-Nets* studied in [Pad96], where also the switching behaviour of nets is defined in a uniform way for different actual net classes.

Example 2.4.5 (Actual Net Classes)

A survey of actual net classes defined by the actual parameter given in example 2.4.2 is given in the table below, where well-known net classes are shown as explicit entries in the table while each blank corresponds to a new or less well-known net class.

Net \ Mod	Triv	Alg. Spec.	Pred. Logic	ML	Indexed Sets
powerset	Elem. Nets [RT86]		PrT-Nets [GL81]		
monoid	P/T-Nets [Rei85]	AHL-Nets [PER95]		CPN '91 [Jen92]	CPN '82 [Jen81]
group	P/T(G)-Nets [MM90]	AHL(G)-Nets [EGH92]			
identity	S-Graph [RT86]				

In more detail we have:

- Elementary nets defined by $Net = \mathcal{P}$ (see 2.4.2.1) are given by $N = (P, T, pre, post)$ with $pre, post : T \to \mathcal{P}(P)$ (see 2.4).
- Place/Transition nets defined by $Net = (\_)^*$ (see 2.4.2.2) are given by $N = (P, T, pre, post)$ with $pre, post : T \to P^*$ (see 2.2, 2.4).
- Place/Transition (Group) nets defined by $Net = (\_)^{ab}$ (see 2.4.2.3) are given by $N = (P, T, pre, post)$ with $pre, post : T \to P^{ab}$.
- S-graphs defined by $Net = ID*$ (see 2.4.2.4) are given by $N = (P, T, pre, post)$ with $pre, post : T \to P$.
- AHL-nets defined by $Net = (\_)^*$ and $Mod = Alg$ (see 2.4.2.5) are given by $N = (P, T, SPEC, A, pre, post)$ with $pre, post : T \to (T_{OP}(X) \times P)^*$ Here the uniform construction $PSPEC$ is given by $PSPEC = T_{OP}(X) \times P$, where $T_{OP}(X)$ are the terms with variables X over $SPEC$.
- Similar for AHL(Group) nets replacing $(\_)^*$ by $(\_)^{ab}$.
- For a presentation of predicate/transition nets and different versions of colored nets in our framework see [Pad96].

3 Universal Parametrized Net Classes

The main idea of universal parameterized net classes is to extend the notion of parameterized net classes studied in the previous section by morphisms on different levels. Hence, the classes become categories and the corresponding functions become functors in the sense of category theory [AHS90]. In other words the set theoretical approach of parameterized net classes becomes a categorical approach of universal parameterized net classes. Especially, we obtain also morphisms of nets for all types of net classes. Since morphisms of nets are rarely used for Petri nets up to now we motivate the benefits of morphisms for Petri-nets. For this purpose we first review net morphisms for place/transition nets in algebraic presentation (see 2.2). Then we discuss the benefit of morphisms in this case which is also valid for other types of net classes, we give a short outline how to extend section 2 to universal parametrized net classes. Finally, we discuss general constructions and results which have been obtained in this framework.

3.1 Categorical Concepts

Category theory is a universal formalism which is successfully used in several fields of mathematics and theoretical computer science. It has been developed for about 50 years and its influence can be found in most branches of structural mathematics and, for about 25 years in several areas of theoretical computer science. In the survey [EGW96] it has been shown that the following areas in computer science have been influenced by category theory: Automata and system theory, flow charts and recursion, λ-calculus and functional languages, algebraic specifications, logical systems and type theory, graph transformation, Petri nets and replacement systems. The aim of category theory is to present structural dependencies and universal notions that can be found in many (mathematical) areas and to give a uniform frame independently of internal structures. This uniform frame and the universality of the concepts distinguish category theory as a common language for the modeling and analysis of complex structures, as well as for a unified view of the development of theories, and for the integration of different theories within computer science. The main purpose of category theory is to have a uniform frame for different kinds of mathematical structures, mappings between structures, and constructions of structures. The most fundamental notions in category theory are on the one hand *categories* consisting of *objects* and *morphisms* and on the other hand *functors* defining structure compatible mappings between categories. Another important concept of category theory is that of limits and colimits, especially product, equalizers, and pullbacks and the dual concepts of coproducts, coequalizers and pushouts. In [Pad96] we especially need pushouts and coequalizers corresponding to a union of objects with shared subobjects and the fusion of subobjects, respectively. Universal properties express that these constructs are generated. These universal properties imply that the corresponding construction is essentially unique. They are strongly exploited for the results we obtain in [Pad96]. Special colimits as pushouts and coequalizers are the basis for the just mentioned structuring techniques. Injective pullbacks correspond to the intersection of nets. Furthermore, the notions and results for rule-based refinement depend on these constructions. The marking graph construction and the realization construction are derived from the net structure, and the preservation of colimits by free constructions yields the compatibitlity of the marking graph construction with the structuring techniques (see [Pad96]).

3.2 Morphisms of Place/Transition Nets

Given two place/transition nets $N1$ and $N2$ with $Ni = (Pi, Ti, prei, posti)$ for $(i = 1, 2)$ (see algebraic presentation in 2.2) a morphism $f : N1 \to N2$ of place/transition nets is a pair $f = (f_P : P1 \to P2, f_T : T1 \to T2)$ of functions, such that we have $f_P^* \circ pre1 = pre2 \circ f_T$ and $f_P^* \circ post1 = post2 \circ f_T$ where $f_P^* : P1^* \to P2^*$ is defined by $f_P^*(\Sigma_{i=1}^{k} n_i * p_i) = \Sigma_{i=1}^{k} n_i f_P(pi)$. This means that the following diagram commutes for pre- and post-functions respectively.

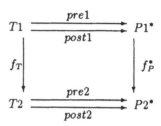

Example 3.2.1 (Example of union in low-level nets)

This example illustrates the union of place/transition nets $N0, N1, N2$, and $N3$ and morphisms $f1 : N0 \to N1$, $f2 : N0 \to N1$, $g1 : N1 \to N3$, and $g2 : N2 \to N1$ (explicitly defined by the dotted lines) and shows the union $N3 = N1 +_{N0} N2$.

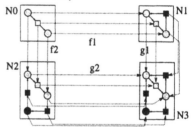

3.3 Benefits of Morphisms for Petri Nets

Similar to 3.2 for place/transition net morphisms can also be defined for all other kinds of Petri nets, including low-level and high-level nets. The main benefits are the following:

1. A morphism $f : N1 \to N2$ of nets allows to express the structural relationship between nets $N1$ and $N2$. If f is injective (in all components) then $N1$ can be considered as a subset of $N2$. In general f may map different places $p1$ and $p1'$ or transition $t1$ and $t1'$ of N1 to only one place $p2$ or one transition $t2$ of $N2$. Then only a homomorphism image of $N1$ is a subnet of $N2$. In fact, there may be different morphisms $f, g : N1 \to N2$ which corresponds to different occurrences of the net $N1$ in the net $N2$. In example 3.2.1 all morphisms are injective such that $N0$ can be considered as subnet of $N1$ via $f1$ and of $N2$ via $f2$. Moreover, $N1$ and $N2$ can be considered as subnet of $N3$ via $g1$ and $g2$ respectively.

2. A bijective morphism $f : N1 \xrightarrow{\sim} N2$ is called isomorphism. In this case the nets $N1$ and $N2$ are called isomorphic, written $N1 \cong N2$, which means that they are equal up to renaming of places and transitions.

3. The composition of net morphisms $f1 : N1 \to N2$ and $f2 : N2 \to N3$ is again a net morphism $f2 \circ f1 : N1 \to N3$ (see also $g1 \circ f1 = g2 \circ f2 : N0 \to N3$ in 3.2.1). Moreover, this composition is associative and for each net N there is an identity morphism $id_N : N \to N$ such that we have $f1 \circ id_{N1} = f1$ and $id_{N2} \circ f1 = f1$ for all $f1 : N1 \to N2$. This means that the class of all nets (of a given type TYP) together with all net morphisms constitutes a category **TypNet**.

This allows to apply constructions and results from category theory to different types of nets and net classes. Note, that each pair (Net, Mod) of actual parameters defines a type $TYP = (Net, Mod)$ and hence an actual net class (see 2.4.5) which is the object class of the category **TypNet**.

4. Morphisms can be used to define the horizontal structuring of nets, for example the net $N3$ in 3.2.1 as union of $N1$ and $N2$ via the common subnet $N0$. Vice versa, the nets $N1$ and $N2$ with subnet $N0$ (distinguished by morphisms $f1 : N0 \to N1$ and $f2 : N0 \to N2$) can be composed leading to net $N3 = N1 +_{N0} N2$. In fact, this union of nets is also a pushout construction in the category **TypNet**. This allows to apply general results of category like composition and decomposition properties of pushouts to the union construction of nets, for example associativity and commutativity of union up to isomorphism.

5. Morphisms can also be used to define refinement of nets. In several cases more general morphisms than those in 3.2 should be considered for this purpose. One simple generalization of 3.2 is to replace $f_P^* : P1^* \to P2^*$ generated by $f_P : P1 \to P2$ by an arbitrary monoid homomorphism $\hat{f}_P : P1^* \to P2^*$. This allows to map one place $p1$ in $P1$ to a sum of places, that is $p1 \mapsto \sum_{i=1}^{k} n_i * p2_i$ for $p2_i \in P2$, which is important for refinement.

6. A morphism $f : N1 \to N2$ of place/transition nets preserves the switching behaviour: If transition t is enabled under marking m in net $N1$ leading to marking m', that is $m[t > m'$ then also the transition $f_T(t)$ is enabled under marking $f_P^*(m)$ in net $N2$ leading to marking $f_P^*(m')$, that is $f_P^*(m)[f_T(t) > f_P^*(m')$. In a similar way morphisms preserve the switching behaviour also for other types of nets. Specific kinds of net morphisms can be considered to preserve other kinds of Petri net properties, for example deadlock-freeness. Especially, isomorphisms preserve all kinds of net properties which do not depend on a specific notation.

3.4 Universal Parameters of Net Classes

The parameters of net classes considered in 2.4.1 become universal parameters of net classes, if all classes and functions are replaced by categories and functors, respectively. In more detail the classes of sets, structures, specifications, and model classes are extended by suitable morphisms leading to categories **Sets** of sets, **Struct** of structures, **SPEC** of specifications, and **ModelClasses** of model-classes, and for each $SPEC \in$ **SPEC** a category **Mod(SPEC)** of $SPEC$-models. Moreover, the functions are extended to become functors: $Net : \textbf{Sets} \xrightarrow{F} Struct \xrightarrow{G} \textbf{Sets}$, the universal net structure parameter and $Mod : \textbf{SPEC}^{op} \rightarrow$ **ModelClasses**, the universal data type parameter, where $Net = G \circ F$ and the functor F is a *free functor* with respect to the *forgetful functor* G, and Mod is a contravariant functor from **SPEC** to **ModelClasses** in the sense of category theory ([AHS90]). Note, that we use an overloaded notation, where **Sets, Struct, SPEC, ModelClasses,** and **Mod(SPEC)** denote classes and Net, F, G, and Mod denote functions in section 2, while they denote categories and functors respectively in this section. In fact, all the examples of actual parameters of net classes given in 2.4.2 can be extended to universal parameters of net classes with well-known categories and functors (see [Pad96]). We only consider the universal net structure parameter of place/transition nets in more detail (see 2.4.2.2):

Let **Struct** = **CMon** be the category of commutative monoids, F : **Sets** $\rightarrow$ **CMon** the free commutative monoid construction, that is $F(P) = (P^*, 0, +)$, $G : \textbf{CMon} \rightarrow \textbf{Sets}$ the forgetful functor, defined by $G(M, \epsilon, \circ) = M$, forgetting only about the neutral element ϵ and the monoid operator $\circ$. Then $Net : \textbf{Sets} \xrightarrow{F} \textbf{CMon} \xrightarrow{G} \textbf{Sets}$ with $Net(P) = P^*$ is the universal net structure functor for the class of place/transition nets.

In fact, F is a free functor with respect to G, because for each set P the free construction $F(P) = (P^*, 0, +)$ together with the inclusion $u_P : P \rightarrow G \circ F(P) = P^*$ satisfies the following universal property: For each commutative monoid $(M, \epsilon, \circ)$ and each function $f : P \rightarrow G(M, \epsilon, \circ) = M$ there is a unique monoid homomorphism $\overline{f} : F(P) = (P^*, 0, +) \rightarrow (M, \epsilon, \circ)$ such that $G(\overline{f}) \circ u_P = f$

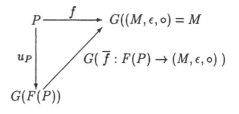

In fact, $\overline{f} : (P^*, 0, +) \rightarrow (M, \epsilon, \circ)$ is uniquely defined by $\overline{f}(0) = \epsilon$ and $\overline{f}(\sum_{i=1}^{k} n_i * p_i) = \Pi_{i=1}^{k} n_i * f(p_i)$. This universal property allows to extend the pre- and post functions of place/transition nets $pre, post : T \rightarrow P^*$ – and similar for other types of nets – to monoid homomorphisms $\overline{pre}, \overline{post} : T^* \rightarrow P^*$ and hence to parallel switching of transitions.

3.5 Universal Parameterized and Actual Net Classes

Parameterized and actual net classes as considered in 2.4.1 become universal parameterized and actual net classes, if we replace the actual parameters (Net, Mod), which are functions, by universal parameters (Net, Mod), which are functors (see 3.4). In this case we have in addition to the nets $N = (P, T, SPEC, A, pre, post)$ of the corresponding net class also net morphisms $f : N1 \rightarrow N2$ leading to a category **TypNet** for the type $TYP =$

(Net, Mod). In the case of low-level nets $Ni = (Pi, Ti, prei, posti)$ for $(i = 1, 2)$ of type (Net, Mod) a net morphism $f : N1 \rightarrow N2$ is a pair of functions $f = (f_P : P1 \rightarrow P2, f_T : T1 \rightarrow T2)$ such that $pre2 \circ f_T = f_{NetP} \circ pre1$ and $post2 \circ f_T = Net(f_P) \circ post1$ In the special case $Net = (\_)^*$ we obtain the notion of morphisms for place/transition nets (see 3.2). All the examples of actual net classes given in 2.8 can be extended to examples of universal actual net classes defined by the corresponding universal parameters (see 3.4).

3.6 Uniform Constructions and Results

In section 2 we have shown how to obtain several well-known and new net classes in a uniform way by the notion of parameterized and actual net classes. Now we raise the question, whether at all resp. how far it is possible to obtain well-known results for each of these net classes in a uniform way. At first sight this seems hopeless, because each type of Petri net has its own notation and own kind of problems, although the general idea of most constructions and results is quite similar. However, the presentation of net classes as instances of parameterized net classes opens the way to study the theory on the level of parameterized net classes rather than for specific actual ones. In fact, this has been done to a certain extend in the PhD-thesis [Pad96] using the notion of "Abstract Petri Nets", which corresponds to the notion of "Universal Parameterized Net Classes" in this paper. In the following we summarize some main constructions and results for abstract Petri nets in the terminology of this paper. In this way we obtain uniform constructions and results for all the actual net classes (see 2.4.5) which are instantiations of universal parameterized net classes:

- There is a uniform notion of nets, marking of nets, enabling and switching of transitions.
- Switching of transition can be extended to parallel and concurrent switching in a uniform way (see 3.3).
- In the case of low level nets there is a uniform construction of the marking graph of a net in terms of F-graphs and a characterization of all those F-graphs, which are realizable by nets in the net class defined by $Net = G \circ F$.
- There is a uniform construction of the operations "union" and "fusion" for nets in the sense of [Jen92], which are most important for horizontal structuring of nets.
- Refinement is the essential technique for vertical structuring of the software development process. Several refinement notions are known in the Petri net literature (see for example [BGV90]). Rule-based refinement comprises these in a uniform way using ideas from the theory of graph grammars and high-level replacement systems [Pad96]. Moreover, important results concerning independence, parallelism and concurrency of rule-based refinement – developed first in the theory of graph grammars – have been extended to universal parameterized net classes.
- Horizontal structuring of nets based on union and fusion is compatible with rule-based refinement of nets, provided that certain independence conditions are satisfied.

- There is a uniform construction of flattening from high-level nets of type $TYP = (Net, Mod)$ to low-level nets of type $TYP = (Net, Triv)$.
- There is a uniform notion of morphisms for nets of type $TYP = (Net, Mod)$ leading to a category **TypNet** of nets of type TYP. The category **TypNet** is cocomplete, which includes as special cases existence and construction of pushouts and coequalizers corresponding to union and fusion of nets.

Finally, let us point out that for most of the uniform constructions and results above it seems to be necessary to consider morphisms of nets (see 3.3) This means that it is worthwhile to consider universal parameterized net classes including a few notions of category theory and not only parameterized net classes based on set theoretical notions.

4 Conclusion

In this paper we have given a uniform approach to different types of Petri nets, including low-level nets, like elementary and place/transition nets, as well as high-level nets, like algebraic high-level or predicate/transition nets. The main idea of this approach is a first step to introduce parameterized net classes, which are based on a net structure parameter for low-level nets and in addition a data type parameter for high-level nets. By instantiation of these parameters we obtain most well-known net classes studied in the literature but also several new interesting net classes in a uniform way. In a second step we extend the parameters of net classes to universal parameters leading to the notion of universal parameterized and actual net classes. The main idea of this extension is to study not only classes of nets, specifications and nets, but to consider also suitable morphisms leading to different kinds of categories. The benefits to use morphisms for Petri nets are discussed concerning general structural aspects, net specific ones, and aspects from system development including horizontal structuring and vertical refinement. Moreover the concept of universal parameterized net classes allows to obtain several constructions and results known for specific low-level or high-level nets in a uniform way for all net classes which can be obtained by suitable instantiations of the parameters. A formal version of these constructions and results is presented in the theory of abstract Petri nets studied in [Pad96]. This, however, is only a first step towards a general uniform theory for different types of Petri nets.

References

[AHS90]   J. Adamek, H. Herrlich, and G. Strecker, *Abstract and concrete categories*, Series in Pure and Applied Mathematics, John Wiley and Sons, 1990.

[BCM88]   E. Battiston, F. De Cindio, and G. Mauri, *OBJSA nets: a class of high-level nets having objects as domains*, Advances in Petri nets (G. Rozenberg, ed.), vol. 340, Springer Verlag Berlin, 1988, pp. 20–43.

[BDH92]   E. Best, R. Devillers, and J. Hall, *The Box Calculus: a new causal algebra with multi-label communication*, Advances in Petri Nets, 1992, 609, pp. 21–69.

[BGV90]   W. Brauer, R. Gold, and W. Vogler, *A Survey of Behaviour and Equivalence Preserving Refinements of Petri Nets*, Advances in Petri Nets, LNCS 483 (1990).

[Bra80]   W. Brauer (ed.), *Net Theory and Aplications*, Springer, LNCS 84, 1980.

[Bra84]   Wilfried Brauer, *How to play the token game*, Petri Net Newsletter **16** (1984), 3–13.

[BRR87a] W. Brauer, W. Reisig, and G. Rozenberg (eds.), *Petri Nets: Applications and Relations to Other Models of Concurrency*, Springer, LNCS 255, 1987.

[BRR87b] W. Brauer, W. Reisig, and G. Rozenberg (eds.), *Petri Nets: Central Models and Their Properties*, Springer, LNCS 254, 1987.

[EGH92]   H. Ehrig, M. Große-Rhode, and A. Heise, *Specification techniques for concurrent and distributed systems*, Tech. Report 92/5, jan. 1992.

[EGW96]   H. Ehrig, M. Große-Rhode, and Uwe Wolter, *On the role of category theory in the area of algebraic specifications*, LNCS , Proc. WADT11, Oslo, 1996.

[EM85]   H. Ehrig and B. Mahr, *Fundamentals of algebraic specifications 1: Equations and initial semantics*, EACTS Monographs on Theoretical Computer Science, vol. 6, Berlin, 1985.

[ER96]   H. Ehrig and W. Reisig, *Integration of Algebraic Specifications and Petri Nets*, Bulletin EATCS, Formal Specification Column (1996), submitted.

[GL81]   H.J. Genrich and K. Lautenbach, *System modelling with high-level Petri nets*, 109–136.

[Jen81]   K. Jensen, *Coloured petri nets and the invariant method*, 317–336.

[Jen92]   Kurt Jensen, *Coloured Petri nets. basic concepts, analysis methods and practical use*, vol. 1, Springer, 1992.

[KP95]   H. Klaudel and E. Pelz, *Communication as unification in the Petri Box Calculus*, Tech. report, LRI, Universite de Paris Sud, 1995.

[MM90]   J. Meseguer and U. Montanari, *Petri nets are monoids*, Information and Computation **88** (1990), no. 2, 105–155.

[Pad96]   J. Padberg, *Abstract Petri Nets: A Uniform Approach and Rule-Based Refinement*, Ph.D. thesis, Technical University Berlin, 1996, Shaker Verlag.

[PER95]   J. Padberg, H. Ehrig, and L. Ribeiro, *Algebraic high-level net transformation systems*, Mathematical Structures in Computer Science **5** (1995), 217–256.

[Rei85]   W. Reisig, *Petri nets*, EATCS Monographs on Theoretical Computer Science, vol. 4, Springer-Verlag, 1985.

[Rei91]   W. Reisig, *Petri nets and abstract data types*, Theoretical Computer Science **80** (1991), 1 – 34 (fundamental studies).

[RT86]   G. Rozenberg and P.S. Thiagarajan, *Petri nets: Basic notions, structure, behaviour*, Current Trends in Concurrency, 1986, 224, pp. 585–668.

[Vau86]   J. Vautherin, *Parallel specification with coloured Petri nets and algebraic data types*, Proc. of the 7th European Workshop on Application and Theory of Petri nets (Oxford, England), jul. 1986, pp. 5–23.

Observing Partial Order Runs of Petri Nets

Astrid Kiehn

Institut für Informatik, Technische Universität München
Arcisstr.21, D–80290 München, Germany

Abstract. A reformulation of the standard causal semantics for Petri nets is proposed which allows one to reconstruct a partial order run from sequential observations without any knowledge of the underlying net structure or its current marking. It provides a new solution to how Mazurkiewicz's trace theory can be generalized to unbounded nets.

Introduction

In the eighties there has been a vivid discussion on the interrelationship of process algebras and Petri nets. Several people working with Wilfried Brauer have influenced these investigations. The clean description of concurrency within net theory motivated the search for a branching time semantics for process algebras discriminating between nondeterminism and concurrency. The field has settled by now. There are well-established, so-called noninterleaving semantics for process algebras which are sensitive to different interpretations of concurrency (see e.g. [DNM88, DD89]). In this little note I show that the basic idea of the causal semantics proposed in [Kie94] – one of the noninterleaving semantics describing concurrency as causal independence – can be utilised to give a new solution to an old Petri net problem. For safe nets – nets where under each reachable marking each place contains at most one token – the partial order run underlying a sequential occurrence sequence can be reconstructed. This is the essence of Mazurkiewicz's trace theory. The reconstruction proceeds by removing all dependencies in an occurrence sequence which are not causal. The knowledge of when a dependency is causal is given by the dependence relation. Two transitions are dependent if they are connected to at least one common place. This form of dependence can easily be determined from the net structure. For one-safe nets it suffices to characterize the dynamic behaviour. In case of arbitrary Petri nets tokens can accumulate on places and enable transitions concurrently even though they have places in common. So the static dependence relation is not sufficient to determine causal dependencies. Generalizations of trace theory presented in the literature do therefore either use the dynamic behaviour to define the dependence relation [HKT92] or the constructed partial orders do not express causal dependencies only [Die90].

The solution given here pursues a different approach as it does not determine a dependence relation at all. It rather assumes an extended notion of occurrence sequence. An event (the occurrence of a transition) is observed by the environment together with the causal dependencies to previous events. This information is encoded in the tokens and therefore locally available. As in process algebras an observation is understood as an interaction of the environment with the system. Hence the causal dependencies can naturally be seen as part of the information delivered to the environment. The observer can now easily reconstruct the partial order underlying an occurrence sequence: he prolongs the current partial order by the new event together with the observed dependencies to previous events. As it will become clear from the semantics the order of the observations can be arbitrary. In this sense the semantics is robust with respect to distributed implementations.

The Refined Occurrence Rule

The nets we consider are known as place/transition nets with weighted arcs and without capacities.

Definition 1. A *Petri net* $N = (S, T, W)$ consists of a finite set S of places, a finite set T of transitions and a weighted flow function $W : (S \times T) \cup (T \times S) \to I\!N$ connecting places and transitions.

If a transition occurs then this occurrence is an unique event. What is observable from outside is the event not the transition. To make the difference precise we assume that each transition is equipped with a local counter. This counter delivers with each transition occurrence a unique event $next(t)$ which is taken from the set $\mathcal{E}_t = \{t_1, t_2, \ldots\}$. The universe of all events is $\mathcal{E} = \bigcup_{t \in T} \mathcal{E}_t$ and $\mathcal{ES}$ denotes the set of finite subsets of $\mathcal{E}$. A *history preserving marking* associates with each place of the net a *multiset of sets of events*. Each set of events corresponds to a token in the usual meaning. The events of the token describe its history, that is all events in the past which led to its creation. As the tokens of the initial marking have no history their event sets are empty.

Let $\mathcal{M}(A)$ denote the set of non-empty finite multisets over A that is $B \in \mathcal{M}(A)$ if $B : A \to I\!N$ and $\sum_{a \in A} B(a) \geq 1$. The empty multiset is denoted $\bot$. Multiset union and multiset difference are denoted by $+$ and $-$. The number of elements of B is given by $|B| = \sum_{a \in A} B(a)$ and $flat(B) = \{a \in A \mid B(a) \geq 1\}$. In examples the multiplicity $B(a)$ of an element a in B is given by an exponent.

Definition 2. Let N be a Petri net with places S. A *history preserving marking* M of N is a mapping $M : S \to \mathcal{M}(\mathcal{ES}) \cup \{\bot\}$. The marking is called *initial* if $M(s) \in \mathcal{M}(\{\emptyset\}) \cup \{\bot\}$ for all $s \in S$.

Each history preserving marking M induces a standard marking $M' : S \to I\!N$, $M'(s) = |M(s)|$. The enabling condition for transitions is as usual. From each place a number of tokens determined by the weight function is removed. Due to their histories tokens have an individuality, so the marking obtained depends on the choice of the tokens consumed. The history of the new tokens subsumes the histories of the consumed tokens. Additionally it contains the new event representing the occurrence of the transition.

Definition 3. Let $N = (S, T, W)$ be a Petri net and let M be a history preserving marking of N. A transition $t \in T$ *is enabled at* M if $|M(s)| \geq W(s, t)$ for all $s \in S$. A transition t *occurs at* M *yielding the marking* M', $M \xrightarrow{t_i, A} M'$, if t is enabled at M, $t_i = next(t)$ and for each $s \in S$ there is a multiset K_s such that $A = \bigcup_{s \in S} flat(K_s)$, $K_s \subseteq M(s)$ and $|K_s| = W(s, t)$ and

$$M'(s) = M(s) - K_s + \{(A \cup \{t_i\})^{W(t,s)}\}.$$

For an observation $M \xrightarrow{t_i, A} M'$ the set A consists of the histories of the consumed tokens. It can be interpreted as the history of t_i. As an example we consider two occurrence sequences of the net in Figure 1. They correspond to the occurrence sequences $babc$ and $baba'd$ in the standard net semantics.

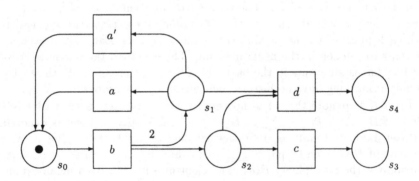

Fig. 1. a Petri net

$(\{\emptyset\}, \bot, \bot, \bot, \bot)$

$\xrightarrow{b_1, \emptyset} \quad (\bot, \{\{b_1\}^2\}, \{\{b_1\}\}, \bot, \bot)$

$\xrightarrow{a_1, \{b_1\}} \quad (\{\{a_1, b_1\}\}, \{\{b_1\}\}, \{\{b_1\}\}, \bot, \bot)$

$\xrightarrow{b_2, \{a_1, b_1\}} \quad (\bot, \{\{b_1\}, \{a_1, b_1, b_2\}^2\}, \{\{b_1\}, \{a_1, b_1, b_2\}\}, \bot, \bot)$

$\xrightarrow{c_1, \{b_1\}} \quad (\bot, \{\{b_1\}, \{a_1, b_1, b_2\}^2\}, \{\{a_1, b_1, b_2\}\}, \{\{c_1, b_1\}\}, \bot)$

$$(\{\emptyset\}, \perp, \perp, \perp, \perp)$$

$$\xrightarrow{b_1, \emptyset} \quad (\perp, \{\{b_1\}^2\}, \{\{b_1\}\}, \perp, \perp)$$

$$\xrightarrow{a_1, \{b_1\}} \quad (\{\{a_1, b_1\}\}, \{\{b_1\}\}, \{\{b_1\}\}, \perp, \perp)$$

$$\xrightarrow{b_2, \{a_1, b_1\}} \quad (\perp, \{\{b_1\}, \{a_1, b_1, b_2\}^2\}, \{\{b_1\}, \{a_1, b_1, b_2\}\}, \perp, \perp)$$

$$\xrightarrow{a_1', \{b_1\}} \quad (\{\{a_1', b_1\}\}, \{\{a_1, b_1, b_2\}^2\}, \{\{b_1\}, \{a_1, b_1, b_2\}\}, \perp, \perp)$$

$$\xrightarrow{b_3, \{a_1', b_1\}}$$

$$(\perp, \{\{a_1, b_1, b_2\}^2, \{a_1', b_1, b_3\}^2\}, \{\{b_1\}, \{a_1, b_1, b_2\}, \{a_1', b_1, b_3\}\}, \perp, \perp)$$

$$\xrightarrow{d_1, \{a_1, a_1', b_1, b_2, b_3\}}$$

$$(\perp, \{\{a_1, b_1, b_2\}, \{a_1', b_1, b_3\}^2\}, \{\{b_1\}, \{a_1, b_1, b_2\}\}, \perp, \{\{a_1, a_1', b_1, b_2, b_3, d_1\}\})$$

Reconstructing the Partial Order Run

The information that may be used to reconstruct the partial order run underlying an occurrence sequence is that made known to the environment with a transition occurrence: the arc labelling. It is used to construct event orders. An *event order* is a partial ordering $(E, \prec)$ with $E \in \mathcal{ES}$.

Definition 4. Let N be a Petri net with history preserving marking M.

1. If M is initial then $(\emptyset, \emptyset)$ represents the empty occurrence sequence leading to M.
2. If $M \xrightarrow{t_i, A} M'$ and $(E, \prec)$ is the event order representing an occurrence sequence leading to M then $(E \cup \{t_i\}, \prec \cup A \times \{t_i\})$ is the event order representing the extended occurrence sequence leading to M'.

In our example for the first occurrence sequence a stepwise reconstruction yields the event orders (represented by Hasse diagrams):

$$\varepsilon, \quad b_1, \quad b_1 \rightarrow a_1, \quad b_1 \rightarrow a_1 \rightarrow b_2, \quad b_1 \overset{c_1}{\underset{\nearrow}{\rightarrow}} a_1 \rightarrow b_2 \quad .$$

The second occurrence sequence finally yields

$$b_1 \overset{a_1' \rightarrow b_3}{\underset{\rightarrow}{\nearrow}} a_1 \rightarrow b_2 \rightarrow d_1 \quad .$$

Note that for the construction the ordering between observations is not important. The history set A of an observation $\xrightarrow{t_i, A}$ determines the events causing t_i. The events of A which so far have not been observed can be added to the event order with a label expressing that their cause sets are presently not known. Such labels are removed and the missing dependencies added if the respective observation is available. The event order is complete if all labels have been removed. So even if the Petri net is distributed over various sites and the observations are not made in the right order (relative to a global time) the observer is still able to reconstruct the concurrent run correctly. In this sense the semantics is robust with respect to distributed implementations.

The partial order semantics usually associated with Petri nets is that of so-called processes (cf. [GR83]). A process is an acyclic, labelled Petri net of which each place has at most one input and one output transition. It represents the token game leading to a particular marking. Each transition reports the occurrence of the transition determined by its label; the connecting places represent the tokens consumed and produced by this occurrence. Processes can also be developed stepwise just from observing the transition occurrences. However, the observer must have a complete knowledge of the net structure and of the initial marking.

By inductive arguments it can be shown that the partial orderings obtained from Definition 4 do coincide with Petri net processes or, more precisely, with their abstractions (the restriction to the set of transitions, see [BDKP91]).

Proposition 5. *Let N be a Petri net with initial marking M_0. If M is a reachable history preserving marking of N and $(E, \prec)$ is the event order representing an occurrence sequence leading to M then there is a process π of N such that the abstraction of π is equal to $(E, \prec)$.*

Observations according to Definition 3 can also be used to rephrase the familiar definition of history preserving bisimulation equivalence (see e.g. Def. 5.1 of *fully concurrent bisimulations* in [BDKP91]).

Proposition 6. *Let N and N' be Petri nets with initial markings M_0 and M_0', respectively. N and N' are history preserving equivalent if there is a relation $\mathcal{R}$ (a bisimulation) containing (M_0, M_0') such that for all $(M, M') \in \mathcal{R}$ it holds:*

1. *$M \xrightarrow{t_i, A} M_1$ implies $M' \xrightarrow{t_i, A} M_1'$ such that $(M_1, M_1') \in \mathcal{R}$,*
2. *$M' \xrightarrow{t_i, A} M_1'$ implies $M \xrightarrow{t_i, A} M_1$ such that $(M_1, M_1') \in \mathcal{R}$.*

This characterization is a considerable simplification of the definition in [BDKP91] which requires to keep the partial orders associated with a state. Since the event orders are equally extended for N and N' they need not be computed in the present set up. The characterization is based on the assumption that each transition t has the same kind of counter in N and N' and that both counters start counting at 0. Without this assumption or in case of labelled nets one has to associate a global event name to corresponding local events.

Conclusions

The net semantics proposed is based on two ideas known from noninterleaving semantics of CCS ([DD89, Kie94]). The history of a run is directly encoded into the current marking of the net. A local updating of this information takes place with each transition occurrence. The occurrence rule has further been refined such that the information locally available is published to the environment. This allows the observer to reconstruct the partial order run from the simple observation of an occurrence sequence. The price to pay for this strong observability is that the sizes of tokens grow with each transition occurrence.

Acknowledgement: Thanks to the referee who pointed out the slips in the first version of this note.

References

[BDKP91] E. Best, R. Devillers, A. Kiehn, and L. Pomello. Concurrent bisimulations in Petri nets. *Acta Informatica*, (28):231–264, 1991.

[DD89] P. Darondeau and P. Degano. Causal trees. In *Proceedings of ICALP 89*, number 372 in Lecture Notes in Computer Science, pages 234–248, 1989.

[DNM88] P. Degano, R. De Nicola, and U. Montanari. A distributed operational semantics for CCS based on condition/event systems. *Acta Informatica*, 26:59–91, 1988.

[Die90] V. Diekert. Combinatorics of Traces. *number 454 in Lecture Notes in Computer Science*, 1990.

[GR83] U. Goltz and W. Reisig. The non-sequential behaviour of Petri nets. *Information and Control*, 57(2-3):125–147, 1983.

[HKT92] P. W. Hoogers, H. C. M. Kleijn, and P. S. Thiagarajan. A trace semantics for Petri nets. In W. Kuich, editor, *Proceedings of ICALP 92*, number 623 in Lecture Notes in Computer Science, pages 595–604, 1992.

[Kie94] A. Kiehn. Comparing locality and causality based equivalences. *Acta Informatica*, 31:697–718, 1994.

[Maz77] A. Mazurkiewicz. Concurrent program schemes and their interpretation. Report DAIMI PB-78, Aarhus University, 1977.

Representation Theorems for Petri Nets

José Meseguer, Ugo Montanari, and Vladimiro Sassone

Dedicated to Prof. Wilfried Brauer on the occasion of his sixtieth birthday

ABSTRACT. This paper retraces, collects, summarises, and mildly extends the contributions of the authors — both together and individually — on the theme of representing the space of computations of Petri nets in its mathematical essence.

Introduction

Among the semantics proposed for *Petri nets* [10] (see also [11, 13]), a relevant role is played by the various notions of *process*, e.g. [12, 5, 1], whose merit is to provide a faithful account of computations involving many different transitions and of the *causal connections* between the events occurring in computations. Bare process models, however, fail to bring to the foreground the *algebraic structure* of the space of computations of a net. Our interest, instead, resides on abstract models that capture the mathematical essence of such spaces, possibly axiomatically, roughly in the same way as a prime algebraic domain (or, equivalently, a prime event structure) models the computations of a safe net [9]. The research detailed in [6, 3, 4, 14, 7, 8, 16] identifies such structures as *symmetric monoidal categories* — where objects are states, i.e., multisets of tokens, arrows are processes, and the tensor product and the arrow composition model, respectively, the operations of parallel and sequential composition of processes.

At a higher level of abstraction, the next important question concerns the *global structure* of the collection of such spaces, i.e., the axiomatisation `in the large' of net computations. In other words, the space of the spaces of computations of Petri nets. Building on [3, 4, 16], the work presented in [15, 17] shows that the so-called *symmetric Petri categories*, a class of symmetric strict monoidal categories with free (non-commutative) monoids of objects, provide one such an axiomatisation.

In this paper, we retrace and illustrate the main results achieved so far along these lines of research by the authors, both in joint work and individually. Also, we give a new presentation of the results of [15], already hinted at in [17], but never spelled out in detail before. Due to space limitations, we shall omit any discussion on related work in the literature.

1991 *Mathematics Subject Classification.* Primary 68Q55, 68Q10, 68Q05.

Key words and phrases. Semantics of Concurrency, Noninterleaving, Processes, Petri Nets.

1. Petri Nets as Monoids

The idea of looking at nets as *algebraic structures*, e.g. [13, 9, 18, 2], has been given an original interpretation in [6], where nets are viewed essentially as internal graphs in categories of sets with structure, and monoidal categories are first used as a suitable semantic framework for them. Concerning the algebraic representation of net computations, along the lines described in the introduction, the following is the main result of [6].

THEOREM. *The commutative processes (see* [1]) *of a net N are the arrows of* $T(N)$, *the free strictly symmetric strict monoidal category on N.*

Observe that, as a free construction, $T(N)$ provides an axiomatisation of the commutative processes of N as an *algebraic theory*, and thus moves a step towards a *unification* of the process and the algebraic view of net computations. As already mentioned, the algebra here consists of the operations of a monoidal category: tensor product and the arrow composition representing, respectively, parallel and sequential composition of processes.

Commutative processes, however, are somehow marginal in net theory. The next step was therefore to extend the result to the *nonsequential processes* of N [5], the currently best-established notion of noninterleaving computation for nets.

2. Concatenable Processes

Concatenable processes of Petri nets have been introduced in [3, 4] to account, as their name indicates, for the issue of process sequential concatenation. The starting observation of *loc. cit.* is that such an operation has to do with merging *tokens*, i.e., instances of places, rather than *places*. In fact, due to the ambiguity introduced by multiple instance of places (multiple tokens in places), two processes of N can be composed sequentially in many ways, each of which gives a possibly different process of N.

Therefore, any attempt to structure processes of N as an algebra which includes sequential composition must disambiguate each token in a process. This is exactly the idea of concatenable processes, which are simply nonsequential processes in which, when needed, instances of places (tokens) are distinguished by appropriate decorations. This immediately yields an operation of concatenation: the ambiguity about multiple tokens is resolved using such additional information. The main result of [3, 4] is an axiomatisation of such a category, stated here in the improved enunciation proved in [14, 16].

THEOREM. *The concatenable processes of a net N are the arrows of* $\mathcal{P}(N)$, *obtained from the free symmetric strict monoidal category* $\mathcal{F}(N)$ *on N by imposing the axioms*

$$c_{a,b} = id_{a \otimes b}, \quad \text{if } a \text{ and } b \text{ are different places of } N,$$

$$s;t;s' = t, \quad \text{if } t \text{ is a transition of } N \text{ and } s \text{ and } s' \text{ are symmetries of } \mathcal{F}(N),$$

where c, id, $\otimes$, *and* $\_;\_$ *are, respectively, the symmetry isomorphism, the identities, the tensor product, and the composition of* $\mathcal{F}(N)$.

This result matches the one for commutative processes in describing net behaviours as *algebras* in terms of *universal* constructions. Here, of course, a more complex algebraic structure — namely, symmetries and the related axioms above — is needed.

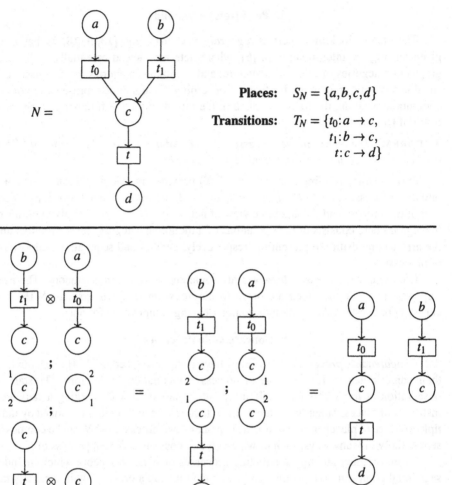

$$t_1 \otimes t_0 \, ; c_{c,c} \, ; t \otimes id_c \qquad (t_1 \otimes t_0 \, ; c_{c,c}) \, ; t \otimes id_c \qquad t_0 \otimes t_1 \, ; t \otimes id_c$$

FIGURE 1. A net N and its concatenable process $\pi = t_0 \otimes t_1 \, ; t \otimes id_c$

Observe that, in fact, the strictness of the symmetric structure of the monoidal category has disappeared.

EXAMPLE. Figure 1 shows a concatenable process π of a net N that corresponds to the arrow $t_0 \otimes t_1 \, ; t \otimes id_c$ of $\mathcal{P}(N)$. To exemplify the algebra of processes of N, π is expressed as parallel (_$\otimes$_) and sequential (_; _) composition of simpler processes. Such operations are matched precisely by operations and axioms of $\mathcal{P}(N)$, and this is the essence of the theorem above.

The construction $\mathcal{P}(\_)$, however, is somehow unsatisfactory, since it is not functorial: given a *simulation* between two nets, it may not be possible to identify a cor-

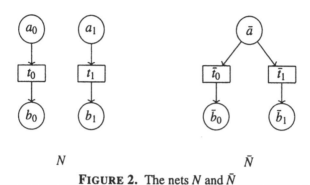

FIGURE 2. The nets N and $\bar{N}$

responding monoidal functor between the respective categories of computations. This fact, besides showing that the understanding of nets provided by $\mathcal{P}(\_)$ is still incomplete, prevents us from identifying the *category* (of the categories) *of net computations*, i.e., from axiomatising the behaviour of nets `in the large'.

DEFINITION. Given nets N and $\bar{N}$, a morphism $f: N \to \bar{N}$ is a pair $\langle f_T, f_S \rangle$, where $f_T: T_N \to T_{\bar{N}}$ is a function — the transition component of f — and, denoting by $\mu(S)$ the free commutative monoid on S, $f_S: \mu(S_N) \to \mu(S_{\bar{N}})$ is a monoid homomorphism — the place component of f — mapping *multisets* of places of N to *multisets* of places of $\bar{N}$ in such a way that for all transitions $t: u \to v$ of N, we have $f_T(t): f_S(u) \to f_S(v)$.

This defines the category Petri of Petri nets.

EXAMPLE. Consider the nets N and $\bar{N}$ in Figure 2 and $f: N \to \bar{N}$ where $f_T(t_i) = \bar{t}_i$, $f_S(a_i) = \bar{a}$ and $f_S(b_i) = \bar{b}_i$, for $i = 0, 1$. Then, f cannot be extended to a monoidal functor $\mathcal{P}(f): \mathcal{P}(N) \to \mathcal{P}(\bar{N})$. In fact, for any such extension F, by monoidality we must have $F(t_0 \otimes t_1) = F(t_0) \otimes F(t_1) = \bar{t}_0 \otimes \bar{t}_1$, and since $t_0 \otimes t_1 = t_1 \otimes t_0$, it follows that

$$\bar{t}_0 \otimes \bar{t}_1 = F(t_1 \otimes t_0) = \bar{t}_1 \otimes \bar{t}_0,$$

which is impossible, since the leftmost and rightmost processes are *different* in $\mathcal{P}(\bar{N})$.

3. Strongly Concatenable Processes

Strongly concatenable processes are a slight refinement of concatenable processes introduced in [15, 17] to yield a *functorial* algebraic description of net computations. The refinement, which consists simply of decorating selected places in nonsequential processes more strongly than in concatenable processes (see Figure 3), is shown to be — in a very precise mathematical sense (see [15, 17]) — the *slightest* refinement that yields a functorial construction. As for their predecessors, strongly concatenable processes admit an axiomatisation in terms of a universal algebraic construction based on symmetric monoidal categories.

THEOREM. *The strongly concatenable processes of a net N are the arrows of $Q(N)$, obtained from the symmetric strict monoidal category freely generated from the places of N and, for each transition t of N, an arrow $t_{u,v}: u \to v$ for each pair of linearisations (as strings) u and v of the pre- and post- sets (multisets) of t, by quotienting modulo the axiom*

$$(\Phi) \qquad s; t_{u',v} = t_{u,v}; s', \qquad \text{for } s: u \to u' \text{ and } s': v' \to v \text{ symmetries.}$$

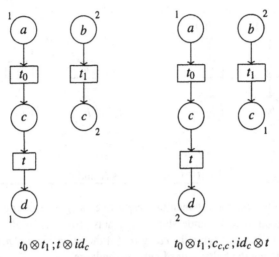

$$t_0 \otimes t_1 ; t \otimes id_c \qquad\qquad t_0 \otimes t_1 ; c_{c,c} ; id_c \otimes t$$

FIGURE 3. Two strongly concatenable processes corresponding to π of Figure 1

The key feature of $Q(\_)$ is that, differently from $P(\_)$, it associates to the net N a monoidal category whose objects form a free *non-commutative* monoid (*viz.* S_N^* as opposed to $\mu(S_N)$), i.e., it deals with *strings* as explicit *representatives* of multisets. As hinted above, renouncing to such commutativity, a choice that at first may seem odd, can be proved to be necessary in order to obtain a functor. As a consequence of this choice, each transition of N has many corresponding arrows in $Q(N)$; such arrows, however, are 'related' to each other by the *naturality* condition (Φ), in the precise sense that, when collected together, they form a natural transformation between appropriate functors. In fact, (Φ) asserts that any diagram in $Q(N)$ of the kind

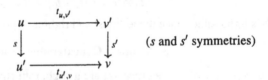

commutes, which, as we shall see, can be equivalently expressed in terms of functors and natural transformations. This naturality axiom is the second relevant feature of $Q(\_)$, actually the one that keeps the computational interpretation of the category $Q(N)$, i.e., the strongly concatenable processes, surprisingly close to that of $P(N)$, i.e., to the concatenable processes (cf. Figures 1 and 3).

Concerning functoriality, [15] shows that $Q(\_)$ extends to a *coreflection* functor from the category of Petri nets to *a* category of symmetric monoidal categories. The latter is constructed by *quotienting* the category of symmetric monoidal categories in such a way as to identify all the symmetric monoidal functors that, informally speaking, differ only by the 'representatives of multisets' chosen. Here, we proceed along the way hinted at in [17] using *2-categories* (more precisely, *groupoid-enriched* categories), the role of the 2-structure being to carry information about multisets, thus making an explicit quotient construction unnecessary.

DEFINITION. A *symmetric Petri category* is a symmetric strict monoidal category C whose monoid of objects is S^*, the free monoid on S, for some set S. We shall let Sym_C denote its subcategory of symmetries, and $Sym_{C,v}$, for v a multiset in $\mu(S)$, the full subcategory of Sym_C consisting of those $u \in S^*$ whose underlying multiset, $\mu(u)$, is v.

The relevance of symmetric Petri categories for our purposes resides in that they allow us to capture the essence of the arrows generating $Q(N)$, i.e., the instances of the transitions of N. Such arrows, in fact, have two very special properties that characterise them completely: (1) they are decomposable as tensors only trivially, and as compositions only by means of symmetries, and (2), as already mentioned, they form natural transformations between appropriate functors. Following the usual categorical paradigm, we then use such properties, expressed in abstract categorical terms, to define the notion of *transition* in a general symmetric Petri category.

DEFINITION. Let C be a symmetric Petri category and S^* its monoid of objects. An arrow τ in C is *primitive* if (denoting by ε the empty word in S^*)

▶ τ is *not* a symmetry;

▶ $\tau = \alpha; \beta$ implies α is a symmetry and β is primitive, or viceversa;

▶ $\tau = \alpha \otimes \beta$ implies $\alpha = id_\varepsilon$ and β is primitive, or viceversa.

A *transition* of C is a natural transformation $\tau \colon \pi^0_{C,v,v'} \Rightarrow \pi^1_{C,v,v'}$ whose components $\tau_{u,v}$ are *primitive* arrows of C, where, for v,v' in $\mu(S)$, and the functors $\pi^0_{C,v,v'}$ and $\pi^1_{C,v,v'}$ are defined by the diagram

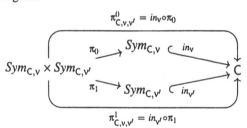

Observe that the definition above captures the essence of $Q(N)$: the transitions of $Q(N)$ are *all* and *only* the families $\{t_{u,v} \mid t \colon \mu(u) \to \mu(v) \in T_N\}$. This leads us to the following result.

THEOREM. *Let* SPetriCat *be the 2-category whose objects are the symmetric Petri categories, whose arrows are the symmetric strict monoidal functors that respect transitions, and with a 2-cell $F \Rightarrow G$ if there exists a monoidal natural isomorphism between F and G whose components are all symmetries.*

Then, $Q(\_) \colon$ Petri $\to$ SPetriCat *is a pseudo 2-functor (considering the category* Petri *of Petri nets as a trivial 2-category) that admits a pseudo right adjoint $\mathcal{N}(\_)$ forming with $Q(\_)$ a pseudo coreflection.*

The latter terminology means precisely that the natural family of isomorphisms between homsets that defines an adjunction is relaxed to a (pseudo) natural family of *equivalences* between homcats. Finally, concerning the *category* (of the categories) *of net computations*, we have the following result that characterises abstractly the categories corresponding to algebras of Petri net causal behaviours.

THEOREM. *Let* FSPetriCat *be the full subcategory of* SPetriCat *consisting of those symmetric Petri categories* C *whose arrows can be generated by tensor and composition from symmetries, and components of transitions of* C, *uniquely up to the axioms of symmetric strict monoidal categories and the naturality of transitions, i.e., axiom* (Φ). *Then,* FSPetriCat *and* Petri *are pseudo equivalent via* $\mathcal{N}[\_]$ *and* $Q[\_]$.

In the rest of the paper we shall provide a sketch of the proofs of these results.

Let FMon be the category with objects the free monoids S^*, where $S \in$ Set ranges over sets, and morphisms the monoid homomorphisms. Similarly, let FCMon be the category with objects the free commutative monoids $\mu(S)$, $S \in$ Set, and morphisms the monoid homomorphisms. Consider the obvious quotient functor $(\_)^b$: FMon $\rightarrow$ FCMon. Explicitly, $(S^*)^b = \mu(S)$, whilst the action of $(\_)^b$ on $f: S^* \rightarrow \bar{S}^*$ gives the unique homomorphism $f^b: \mu(S) \rightarrow \mu(\bar{S})$ such that $f^b(a) = \mu(f(a))$ for all $a \in S$. If we regard $(\_)^b$: FMon $\rightarrow$ FCMon as a *reflexive graph*[1] homomorphism, we can define a reflexive graph homomorphism $(\_)^{\natural}$: FCMon $\rightarrow$ FMon in the other direction such that $((\_)^{\natural})^b = id_{\text{FCMon}}$. Indeed, we can define $(\_)^{\natural}$ on objects by $(\mu(S))^{\natural} = S^*$ and for each nonidentity monoid homomorphism $f: \mu(S) \rightarrow \mu(S')$ we can choose a monoid homomorphism $f^{\natural}: S^* \rightarrow S'^*$ by selecting for each $a \in S$ a word $f^{\natural}(a)$ such that $\mu(f^{\natural}(a)) = f(a)$. For the identity homomorphisms we can define $(id_{\mu(S)})^{\natural} = id_{S^*}$.

Fixed one such $(\_)^{\natural}$, we can define the action of $Q(\_)$ on Petri net morphisms.

Let $f: N \rightarrow \bar{N}$ be a morphism of Petri nets. Since f_S is a monoid homomorphism from $\mu(S_N)$ to $\mu(S_{\bar{N}})$, we consider the homomorphism $f_S^{\natural}: S_N^* \rightarrow S_{\bar{N}}^*$. By the freeness of $Sym_{Q(N)}$, such a morphism can be extended (uniquely) to a symmetric strict monoidal functor $F_S: Sym_{Q(N)} \rightarrow Q(\bar{N})$ and, therefore, to a functor $F: Q(N) \rightarrow Q(\bar{N})$, defined as the unique symmetric strict monoidal functor which coincides with F_S on $Sym_{Q(N)}$ and maps $t_{u,v}: u \rightarrow v$ to $(f_T(t))_{F(u),F(v)}: F(u) \rightarrow F(v)$. Since monoidal functors map symmetries to symmetries, and since $f_T(t)$ is a transition of N_1, it follows immediately that F respects axiom (Φ), i.e., that F is well defined. Concerning the (trivial) 2-cells of Petri, the action of $Q(\_)$ on them is clearly forced: $Q(id: f \Rightarrow f)$ must necessarily be (the unique) $Q(f) \Rightarrow Q(f)$.

Since $Q(f)$ is uniquely determined by f_T and $f_S^{\natural}$, by the property $(id_{\mu(S)})^{\natural} = id_{S^*}$ of $(\_)^{\natural}$, it follows that $Q(id_N): Q(N) \rightarrow Q(N)$ is the identity functor. However, since in general $(g_S \circ f_S)^{\natural} \neq g_S^{\natural} \circ f_S^{\natural}$, we have that $Q(g \circ f) \neq Q(g) \circ Q(f)$. The whole point about considering the 2-structure of SPetriCat is, in fact, to show that such functors are *isomorphic* in SPetriCat, i.e., that $Q[\_]$ is a pseudo 2-functor. We proceed as follows.

Let $f: N \rightarrow N'$ and $g: N' \rightarrow \bar{N}$ be morphisms of nets. Observe that for each $a \in S_N$, the string $(g_S \circ f_S)^{\natural}(a)$ is a permutation of $g_S^{\natural}(f_S^{\natural}(a))$ and that, therefore, there exists a symmetry $s_a: Q(g \circ f)(a) \rightarrow Q(g) \circ Q(f)(a)$ in $Q(\bar{N})$. Then, for $u = u_1 \cdots u_n \in S_N^*$, take s_u to be $s_{u_1} \otimes \cdots \otimes s_{u_n}: Q(g \circ f)(u) \rightarrow Q(g) \circ Q(f)(u)$. We claim that the family $\{s_u\}_{u \in S_N^*}$ is a natural transformation $Q(g \circ f) \Rightarrow Q(g) \circ Q(f)$. Since s is clearly a monoidal natural transformation and each s_u is a symmetry isomorphism, this proves

---

[1] A reflexive graph has a set E of edges, a set N of nodes, functions $\partial_0, \partial_1: E \rightarrow N$ and a function $id: N \rightarrow E$ with $\partial_i(id(x)) = x$. Homomorphisms preserve the ∂_i and id.

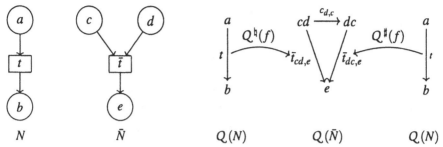

FIGURE 4. Two different, yet equivalent, pseudo functorial extensions of $Q(\_)$

that $Q(g \circ f) \cong Q(g) \circ Q(f)$ in SPetriCat. We proceed by induction on the structure of α to show that, for any $\alpha \colon u \to v$ in $Q(N)$, we have

$$Q(g \circ f)(\alpha) \, ; s_v = s_u \, ; Q(g) \circ Q(f)(\alpha).$$

The key to the proof is that s is monoidal, i.e., $s_{uv} = s_u \otimes s_v$, as a simple inspection of the definition shows. If α is an identity, then the claim is obvious. Moreover, if α is a transition $t_{u,v}$, then $Q(g \circ f)(\alpha)$ and $Q(g) \circ Q(f)(\alpha)$ are instances of the same transition of $\bar{N}$, and the thesis follows immediately from axiom (Φ). Suppose now that $\alpha = c_{u,v}$, a symmetry of $Q(N)$. Since $Q(g \circ f)$ and $Q(g) \circ Q(f)$ are symmetric strict monoidal functors, the equation that we have to prove reduces to

$$c_{Q(g \circ f)(u), Q(g \circ f)(v)} \, ; s_v \otimes s_u = s_u \otimes s_v \, ; c_{Q(g) \circ Q(f)(u), Q(g) \circ Q(f)(v)},$$

which certainly holds since $\{c_{u,v}\}_{u,v \in S_{\bar{N}}^*}$ is a natural transformation $x_1 \otimes x_2 \Rightarrow x_2 \otimes x_1$. If $\alpha = \alpha_0 \otimes \alpha_1$, with $\alpha_i \colon u_i \to v_i$, then, for $i = 0, 1$, we have by induction hypothesis that $Q(g \circ f)(\alpha_i) \, ; s_{v_i} = s_{u_i} \, ; Q(g) \circ Q(f)(\alpha_i)$ whence

$$Q(g \circ f)(\alpha_0) \otimes Q(g \circ f)(\alpha_1) \, ; s_{v_0 \otimes v_1} = s_{u_0 \otimes u_1} \, ; Q(g) \circ Q(f)(\alpha_0) \otimes Q(g) \circ Q(f)(\alpha_1),$$

which is $Q(g \circ f)(\alpha) \, ; s_v = s_u \, ; Q(g) \circ Q(f)(\alpha)$. Finally, in the case $\alpha = \alpha_0 \, ; \alpha_1$, where $\alpha_0 \colon u \to w$ and $\alpha_1 \colon w \to v$, the induction is proved by pasting the two commutative squares in the following diagram, which exists by the induction hypothesis

$$
\begin{array}{ccc}
Q(g \circ f)(u) & \xrightarrow{\;s_u\;} & Q(g) \circ Q(f)(u) \\
{\scriptstyle Q(g \circ f)(\alpha_0)} \downarrow & & \downarrow {\scriptstyle Q(g) \circ Q(f)(\alpha_0)} \\
Q(g \circ f)(w) & \xrightarrow{\;s_w\;} & Q(g) \circ Q(f)(w) \\
{\scriptstyle Q(g \circ f)(\alpha_1)} \downarrow & & \downarrow {\scriptstyle Q(g) \circ Q(f)(\alpha_1)} \\
Q(g \circ f)(v) & \xrightarrow{\;s_v\;} & Q(g) \circ Q(f)(v)
\end{array}
\qquad \checkmark
$$

In principle, of course, choosing two different sections for $(\_)^\flat$, say $(\_)^\natural$ and $(\_)^\sharp$, gives two *different* pseudo functors $Q^\natural(\_), Q^\sharp(\_) \colon \textbf{Petri} \to \textbf{SPetriCat}$ (that, however, coincide on the objects). Another use for the 2-structure of SPetriCat is to show that the choice of the `choice mapping' $(\_)^\natural$ is actually, in a precise mathematical sense, *irrelevant*.

EXAMPLE. Let N and $\bar{N}$ be the nets of Figure 4, and let $f\colon N \to \bar{N}$ be the morphism such that $f_T(t) = \bar{t}$, $f_S(a) = c \oplus d$, and $f_S(b) = e$. In the hypothesis that $f^\natural(a) = cd$ and $f^\sharp(a) = dc$, we have that $Q^\natural(f)(t_{a,b}) = \bar{t}_{cd,e} \neq \bar{t}_{dc,e} = Q^\sharp(f)(t_{a,b})$.

Observe, however, that $\bar{t}_{cd,e}$ and $\bar{t}_{dc,e}$ are simply different instances of the same transition of $\bar{N}$, namely $\bar{t}\colon c \oplus d \to e$, related by axiom (Φ) via the symmetries $c_{c,d}$ and id_e. In other words, $\bar{t}_{cd,e}$ and $\bar{t}_{dc,e}$ are components of the same transition of $Q(N)$. This fact holds in full generality: for each net morphism f, $Q^\natural(f)$ and $Q^\sharp(f)$ differ at most by the correspondence between components of transitions, and coincide when considered as maps of transitions of $Q(N)$ to transitions of $Q(\bar{N})$ (cf. [15, 17]); formally, there exists a 2-cell $Q^\natural(f) \Rightarrow Q^\sharp(f)$ in SPetriCat that makes them *isomorphic*. In this sense, $Q^\natural(\_)$ and $Q^\sharp(\_)$ are *equivalent* functors, and the choice of the section of $(\_)^\flat$ is irrelevant.

In order to make this precise, let $(\_)^\natural$ and $(\_)^\sharp$ be sections of $(\_)^\flat$ and let $f\colon N \to \bar{N}$ be a morphism of nets. Since for each $f\colon \mu(S) \to \mu(S')$ any such section can only differ in the choice of the linearization of each multiset $f(a)$, $a \in S$, the string $f^\natural(a)$ is a permutation of $f^\sharp(a)$ for each $a \in S_N$. Then, we can choose a symmetry $s_a\colon Q^\natural(f)(a) \to Q^\sharp(f)(a)$ in $Q(\bar{N})$, take $s_{u_1} \otimes \cdots \otimes s_{u_n}\colon Q^\natural(f)(u) \to Q^\sharp(f)(u)$ as s_u for each $u = u_1 \cdots u_n \in S_N^*$, and — proceeding as before — prove that $s = \{s_u\}_{u \in S_N^*}$ is a natural transformation $Q^\natural(f) \Rightarrow Q^\sharp(f)$. Since s is monoidal and each s_u is a symmetry isomorphism, this proves that $Q^\natural(f) \cong Q^\sharp(f)$ in SPetriCat. $\checkmark$

Let us now turn our attention to $\mathcal{N}(\_)$. There is now an obvious way to extract a net $\mathcal{N}(C)$ from a symmetric Petri category C, namely:

▶ the places of $\mathcal{N}(C)$ are the generators S of the monoid of objects S^* of C;
▶ a transition $\tau\colon v \to v'$ of $\mathcal{N}(C)$ is a transition $\tau\colon \pi^0_{C,v,v'} \Rightarrow \pi^1_{C,v,v'}$ of C.

Let $F\colon C \to \bar{C}$ be a morphism of symmetric Petri categories, and let S^* and $\bar{S}^*$ be the monoid of objects of, respectively, C and $\bar{C}$. The object component of F, say F_S, induces a monoid homomorphism $F_S^\flat\colon \mu(S) \to \mu(\bar{S})$. Moreover, since F respects transitions, i.e., since for each transition τ of C there exists a (necessarily unique) transition $\bar{\tau}$ of $\bar{C}$ such that $F(\tau_{u,v}) = \bar{\tau}_{F(u),F(v)}$, its arrow component restricts to a map F_T from the transitions of C to those of $\bar{C}$ in such a way that, if $\tau\colon v \to v'$ in $\mathcal{N}(C)$, then $F_T(\tau)\colon F_S^\flat(v) \to F_S^\flat(v')$ in $\mathcal{N}(\bar{C})$. Therefore, $\langle F_T, F_S \rangle\colon \mathcal{N}(C) \to \mathcal{N}(\bar{C})$ is a morphism of nets, which we will denote $\mathcal{N}(F)$. It follows easily from the functoriality of $(\_)^\flat$ that $\mathcal{N}(\_)$, as defined above, is a (1-)functor. Concerning 2-cells, it can be proved that whenever $F \Rightarrow G$ in SPetriCat, i.e., F and G are isomorphic via a monoidal natural transformation composed exclusively of symmetries, then $F_S^\flat = G_S^\flat$ and $F_T = G_T$, which means that $\mathcal{N}(F) = \mathcal{N}(G)$. Therefore, defining $\mathcal{N}(F \Rightarrow G) = id_{\mathcal{N}(F)}$ yields a *2-functor* $\mathcal{N}(\_)\colon$ SPetriCat $\to$ Petri. $\checkmark$

The last argument shows that $\mathcal{N}(\_)$, although *full*, is *not faithful*. Observe now that N and $\mathcal{N}(Q(N))$ are isomorphic via the Petri net morphism $\eta_N\colon N \to \mathcal{N}(Q(N))$ whose place component is id_{S_N} and whose transition component maps $t \in T_N$ to the transition $\{t_{u,v} \in Q(N)\} \in T_{\mathcal{N}(Q(N))}$. These two facts imply that $\mathcal{N}(\_)$ *cannot* be adjoint to $Q(\_)$, as the homcats SPetriCat$(Q(N), C)$ and Petri$(N, \mathcal{N}(C)) \cong$ Petri$(\mathcal{N}(Q(N)), \mathcal{N}(C))$ are not isomorphic. Actually, since $\mathcal{N}(\_)$ performs a quotient of monoids, *viz.* $(\_)^\flat$, whilst $Q(\_)$ chooses an arbitrary linearisation for the place components of net morphisms, viz. $(\_)^{\natural}$, one could not expect otherwise. We shall see next that $\mathcal{N}(\_)$ identifies *only* isomorphic functors or, equivalently, that the categories SPetriCat$(Q(N),C)$ and Petri$(N, \mathcal{N}(C))$ are *equivalent*.

Let C be a symmetric Petri category C, let $\varepsilon_C : Q\,\mathcal{N}(C) \to C$ be the (unique) symmetric strict monoidal functor that acts identitically on objects and sends the component at (u,v) of the transition $\tau \colon v \to v'$ of $\mathcal{N}(C)$ to the component $\tau_{u,v}$ of the corresponding natural transformation $\tau \colon \pi^0_{C,v,v'} \Rightarrow \pi^1_{C,v,v'}$ of C. Since τ is a transition of C, ε_C is well defined. Since it preserves transitions, it is a morphism of symmetric Petri categories.

Since $\mathcal{N}(\_)$ is a 2-functor and $Q(\_)$ acts functorially on 2-cells, for each N in Petri and each C in SPetriCat, the functors η_N and ε_C induce a pair of functors between homcats as follows.

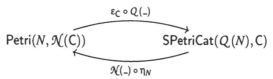

Let us prove that such functors form an *equivalence* of categories.

For $f \colon N \to \mathcal{N}(C)$, let g be $\mathcal{N}(\varepsilon_C \circ Q(f)) \circ \eta_N$. Since $g(a) = (f^{\natural})^{\flat}(a) = f(a)$ and $g(t) = \mathcal{N}(\varepsilon_C \circ Q(f))(\{t_{u,v}\}) = f(t)$, we have that $g = f$. In the opposite direction, for $F \colon Q(N) \to C$, let G stand for $\varepsilon_C \circ Q(\mathcal{N}(F) \circ \eta_N)$, and consider $a \in S_N$. Since $\mathcal{N}(F) \circ \eta_N(a) = F^{\flat}_S(a)$, we have that $G(a) = Q(\mathcal{N}(F) \circ \eta_N(a)) = (F^{\flat}_S)^{\natural}(a)$ and, thus, there exists a symmetry $s_a \colon F(a) \to G(a)$ in C. Then, for $u = u_1 \cdots u_n \in S^*_N$, let s_u be $s_{u_1} \otimes \cdots \otimes s_{u_n} \colon F(u) \to G(u)$. An inductive argument completely analogous to the one exploited previously shows that the family $s = \{s_u\}_{u \in S^*_N}$ is a monoidal natural isomorphism $F \Rightarrow G$ whose components are all symmetries. Therefore $F \cong G$ in SPetriCat, completing the proof that $\mathcal{N}(\varepsilon_C \circ Q(\_)) \circ \eta_N = id$ and $\varepsilon_C \circ Q(\mathcal{N}(\_) \circ \eta_N) \cong id$, i.e., that $\varepsilon_C \circ Q(\_)$ and $\mathcal{N}(\_) \circ \eta_N$ form an equivalence of categories. ✓

To show that $Q(\_) \dashv \mathcal{N}(\_)$, i.e., that $\mathcal{N}(\_)$ is pseudo right adjoint to $Q(\_)$, we need to show that the above family of equivalences is pseudo natural — that is *natural up to isomorphism* — in N and C. This amounts to showing that, for each $g \colon \bar{N} \to N$ and $G \colon C \to \bar{C}$, the following diagrams of functors commute up to isomorphism.

$$
\begin{array}{ccccc}
\text{Petri}(N, \mathcal{N}(C)) & \xrightarrow{\varepsilon_C \circ Q(\_)} & \text{SPetriCat}(Q(N),C) & \xrightarrow{\mathcal{N}(\_) \circ \eta_N} & \text{Petri}(N, \mathcal{N}(C)) \\
{\scriptstyle \mathcal{N}(G) \circ \_ \circ g} \downarrow & & \downarrow {\scriptstyle G \circ \_ \circ Q(g)} & & \downarrow {\scriptstyle \mathcal{N}(G) \circ \_ \circ g} \\
\text{Petri}(\bar{N}, \mathcal{N}(\bar{C})) & \xrightarrow{\varepsilon_{\bar{C}} \circ Q(\_)} & \text{SPetriCat}(Q(\bar{N}),\bar{C}) & \xrightarrow{\mathcal{N}(\_) \circ \eta_{\bar{N}}} & \text{Petri}(\bar{N}, \mathcal{N}(\bar{C}))
\end{array}
$$

It is in fact routine to prove that $G \circ \varepsilon_C \circ Q(\_ \circ g) = \varepsilon_{\bar{C}} \circ Q(\mathcal{N}(G) \circ \_ \circ g)$ and that $\mathcal{N}(G \circ \_) \circ \eta_N \circ g \cong \mathcal{N}(G \circ \_ \circ Q(g)) \circ \eta_{\bar{N}}$. ✓

Finally, concerning FSPetriCat, by general arguments in category theory, it is enough to show that C belongs to FSPetriCat if and only if $\varepsilon_C \colon Q\,\mathcal{N}(C) \to C$, the component at C of the counit of $Q(\_) \dashv \mathcal{N}(\_)$ is an iso. Since ε_C is an isomorphism on the objects, it is iso if and only if it is an isomorphism on each homset. Then the result follows, since each arrow of C can be written as tensor and composition of symmetries and component of transitions if and only if ε_C is surjective on each homset, and this can be done uniquely (up to the equalities that necessarily hold in any symmetric Petri category) if and only if ε_C is injective on each homset. ✓

References

[1] E. BEST AND R. DEVILLERS (1987), Sequential and Concurrent Behaviour in Petri Net Theory, *Theoretical Computer Science* n. **55**, 87–136.

[2] C. BROWN, D. GURR, AND V. DE PAIVA (1991), *A Linear Specification Language for Petri Nets*, Technical Report DAIMI PB-363, Computer Science Department, University of Aarhus.

[3] P. DEGANO, J. MESEGUER, AND U. MONTANARI (1989), Axiomatizing Net Computations and Processes, in *Proceedings LICS'89*, IEEE Computer Society Press, 175–185.

[4] P. DEGANO, J. MESEGUER, AND U. MONTANARI (1996), Axiomatizing the Algebra of Net Computations and Processes, in *Acta Informatica* n. **33**, 641–667.

[5] U. GOLTZ AND W. REISIG (1983), The Non Sequential Behaviour of Petri Nets, *Information and Computation* n. **57**, 125–147.

[6] J. MESEGUER AND U. MONTANARI (1990), Petri Nets are Monoids, *Information and Computation* n. **88**, 105–154.

[7] J. MESEGUER, U. MONTANARI, AND V. SASSONE (1996), Process versus Unfolding Semantics for Place/Transition Petri Nets, *Theoretical Computer Science* n. **153**, 171–210.

[8] J. MESEGUER, U. MONTANARI, AND V. SASSONE (1997), On the Semantics of PlaceTransition Petri Nets, *Mathematical Structures in Computer Science*, to appear. Avalaible by anonymous ftp at `http://www.di.unipi.it/ vs`.

[9] M. NIELSEN, G. PLOTKIN, AND G. WINSKEL (1981), Petri Nets, Event Structures and Domains, Part 1, *Theoretical Computer Science* n. **13**, 85–108.

[10] C.A. PETRI (1962), *Kommunikation mit Automaten*. PhD thesis, Institut für Instrumentelle Mathematik.

[11] C.A. PETRI (1973), Concepts of Net Theory, in *Proceedings of MFCS'73*, Mathematics Institute of the Slovak Academy of Science, 137–146.

[12] C.A. PETRI (1977), *Non Sequential Processes*, Interner Bericht ISF–77–5, Gesellschaft für Mathematik und Datenverarbeitung.

[13] W. REISIG (1985), Petri Nets. Springer-Verlag.

[14] V. SASSONE (1995), Axiomatizing Petri Net Concatenable Processes, in *Proceedings of FCT'95*, H. Reichel (Ed.), LNCS n. **965**, Springer-Verlag, 414–423.

[15] V. SASSONE (1995), On the Category of Petri Net Computations, in *Proceedings of TAPSOFT'95*, P.D. Mosses *et al* (Eds.), LNCS n. **915**, Springer-Verlag, 334–348.

[16] V. SASSONE (1996), An Axiomatization of the Algebra of Petri Net Concatenable Processes, *Theoretical Computer Science* n. **170**, 277–296.

[17] V. SASSONE, *An Axiomatization of the Category of Petri Net Computations*. Submitted for publication. Avalaible by anonymous ftp at `http://www.di.unipi.it/ vs`.

[18] G. WINSKEL (1987), Petri Nets, Algebras, Morphisms and Compositionality, *Information and Computation* n. **72**, 197–238.

COMPUTER SCIENCE LAB., SRI INTERNATIONAL, 333 RAVENSWOOD AVE., MENLO PARK, CA
E-mail address: meseguer@csl.sri.com

DIPARTIMENTO DI INFORMATICA, UNIVERSITA DI PISA, CORSO ITALIA 40, I-56125 PISA, ITALY.,
ON LEAVE DURING 1996-97 AT COMPUTER SCIENCE LAB., SRI INTERNATIONAL.
E-mail address: ugo@di.unipi.it

DIPARTIMENTO DI INFORMATICA, UNIVERSITA DI PISA, CORSO ITALIA 40, I-56125 PISA, ITALY
E-mail address: vs@di.unipi.it

A Remark on Trace Equations

Volker Diekert

Institut für Informatik, Universität Stuttgart
Breitwiesenstr. 20-22, D-70565 Stuttgart

This paper is dedicated to Prof. Wilfried Brauer

Preamble

Parallelism and concurrency are fundamental concepts in computer science. It is clear that a satisfactory notion of correctness for software written in this framework has to be based on a rigorous mathematical model. Investigating the behavior of elementary net systems Mazurkiewicz introduced the concept of partial commutation to informatics. The abstract description of a concurrent process leads to the notion of *trace,* being defined as a congruence class of a word (sequence) modulo identities of the form $ab = ba$ for some pairs of independent letters. It turned out that there are important applications such as verification for parallel and distributed systems, as well as challenging mathematical problems in combinatorics, algebra and formal languages. This makes the theory particularly attractive on the borderline between informatics and mathematics.

As a personal remark I would like to mention that I can trace back my contact to this theory to Hamburg in 1984, when I became a research assistant in informatics. It was Prof. Brauer who introduced me to trace theory as a working area. I have appreciated his scientific advice very much and took benefit from it.

1   Notations and Basic Properties

We refer to *The Book of Traces* [5] for an introduction to trace theory and a systematic study of various aspects thereof. We shall use the following notations. By Σ^* we mean the set of words over some finite alphabet Σ, and the empty word is denoted by 1; it is the unit element. For a word x of Σ^*, $|x|$ denotes the length of x and $|x|_a$ denotes its a-length, i.e. the number of occurrences of a letter a in x. The notation $\mathrm{alph}(x) = \{a \in \Sigma \mid |x|_a \neq 0\}$ is used for the set of letters of Σ actually appearing in the word x.

By $I \subseteq \Sigma \times \Sigma$ we mean a symmetric and irreflexive relation over the alphabet Σ, called the *independence* relation. The idea of Mazurkiewicz [11] behind this definition is that the independence of two actions (being abstracted as letters a and b) means that they act on disjoint sets of resources. They can also be performed in parallel or simultaneously, hence $ab = ba$. Two letters a and b such that $(a, b) \notin I$ are dependent and cannot be executed simultaneously. Therefore the complement $\Sigma \times \Sigma \setminus I$ of I is called the *dependence* relation, it is denoted by D.

The pair (Σ, I) is called the *independence alphabet* and can be represented by an undirected graph conveniently: The vertex set is Σ, edges are between independent letters.

This notion of independence is extended to words $u \in \Sigma^*$ (and later to traces) by

$$I(u) = \{v \in \Sigma^* \mid \mathrm{alph}(u) \times \mathrm{alph}(v) \subseteq I\}.$$

We also allow to write $(u, v) \in I$ instead of $v \in I(u)$.

Example 1. Let the independence alphabet be given as $\Sigma = \{a, b, c, d\}$ and $I = \{(a, b), (b, a), (b, c), (c, b), (c, d), (d, c), (d, a), (a, d)\}$, then its graphical representation is as follows.

$$(\Sigma, I) \quad = \quad \begin{array}{ccc} a & \!\!\!\!-\!\!\!\!- & b \\ | & & | \\ d & \!\!\!\!-\!\!\!\!- & c \end{array}$$

Given (Σ, I) (or (Σ, D) resp.), the free partially commutative monoid $\mathrm{M}(\Sigma, I)$ is defined by the quotient monoid of the free monoid Σ^* with defining relations $ab = ba$ for all $(a, b) \in I$. Hence $\mathrm{M}(\Sigma, I) = \Sigma^* / \{ab = ba \mid (a, b) \in I\}$.

If I is empty, then $\mathrm{M}(\Sigma, I)$ is the free monoid Σ^*; if any two different letters of Σ commute, then $\mathrm{M}(\Sigma, I)$ is the free commutative monoid denoted by N^Σ or simply by N^k where $k = |\Sigma|$. Other families of free partially commutative monoids are direct products of free monoids: $\Sigma_1^* \times \Sigma_2^* \times \cdots \times \Sigma_n^*$, and free products of free commutative monoids: $\mathrm{N}^{k_1} * \mathrm{N}^{k_2} * \cdots * \mathrm{N}^{k_n}$.

In Ex. 1 above we have $\mathrm{M}(\Sigma, I) = \{a, c\}^* \times \{b, d\}^*$ being a direct product of free monoids.

The alphabet $\mathrm{alph}(t)$ of a trace $t \in \mathrm{M}(\Sigma, I)$ is defined as the alphabet of any representing word. By $\mathrm{init}(t)$ we mean the initial alphabet of a trace t, $\mathrm{init}(t) = \{a \in \Sigma \mid \exists u \in \mathrm{M}(\Sigma, I) : t = au\}$. A trace t is called *connected*, if $\mathrm{alph}(t)$ induces a connected subgraph of (Σ, D). As we have done for words the independence relation $I \subseteq \Sigma \times \Sigma$ is extended to traces by setting $(s, t) \in I$, if $\mathrm{alph}(s) \times \mathrm{alph}(t) \subseteq I$. If $u = st \in \mathrm{M}(\Sigma, I)$ with $(s, t) \in I$, we also write $u = s \perp t$ to indicate this fact. Note that every trace $t \in \mathrm{M}(\Sigma, I)$ has a unique decomposition into connected components

$$t = t_1 \perp \cdots \perp t_k$$

where t_i are non-empty and connected, $1 \le i \le k, k \ge 0$.

Let $A \subseteq \Sigma$ and let $I_A \subseteq A \times A$ be an independence relation such that $(I \cap A \times A) \subseteq I_A$, then the pair (A, I_A) induces a canonical projection

$$\pi_{(A, I_A)} : \mathrm{M}(\Sigma, I) \longrightarrow \mathrm{M}(A, I_A)$$

defined by $\pi_A(a) = a$ for $a \in A$ and $\pi_A(a) = 1$ for $a \in \Sigma \setminus A$. (This is well-defined since $ab = ba \in \mathrm{M}(\Sigma, I)$ implies $\pi_{(A, I_A)}(a)\pi_{(A, I_A)}(b) = \pi_{(A, I_A)}(b)\pi_{(A, I_A)}(a) \in$

$M(A, I_A)$.) For $(a, b) \in D$ and $I_A = \emptyset$ we simply write $\pi_{a,b}$ instead of $\pi_{(\{a,b\},\emptyset)}$. In these notations, the a-length becomes $|t|_a = \pi_{a,a}(t)$, and the Parikh-mapping is:

$$\pi = \pi_{(\Sigma, \Sigma \times \Sigma \setminus id_\Sigma)} : M(\Sigma, I) \longrightarrow N^\Sigma.$$

Sometimes it is convenient to view N^Σ as a subset of the $\mathbb{Q}$-vector space $\mathbb{Q}^\Sigma$, then the Parikh-mapping becomes $\pi : M(\Sigma, I) \longrightarrow \mathbb{Q}^\Sigma$.

For reasoning about traces there are some basic tools:

Proposition 2 (Projection Lemma). *Let u and v be two traces of $M(\Sigma, I)$, then we have $u = v$ if and only if*

$$\pi_{a,b}(u) = \pi_{a,b}(v) \quad \text{for all } (a, b) \in D.$$

Proposition 3 (Levi's Lemma). *Let t, u, v, and w be traces of $M(\Sigma, I)$. Then the following assertions are equivalent.*

i) $tu = vw$
ii) *There exist $p, q, r, s \in M(\Sigma, I)$ such that*
$t = pr$, $u = sq$, $v = ps$, $w = rq$ with $\mathrm{alph}(r) \times \mathrm{alph}(s) \subseteq I$.

2 Equations

The presentation of this section is closely related to the chapter of Choffrut [1]. In particular Lem. 8, Lem. 9, and Cor. 12 (stated for a single equation) can be found there. However, we have modified some proofs and there is also some new material.

The following proposition is the starting point for studying trace equations. It characterizes the set of solutions of the equation $xy \equiv yx$ in trace monoids.

Proposition 4 (Duboc [6]). *Let $x, y \in M(\Sigma, I)$ be traces and $\alpha(\Sigma, I)$ be the maximal size of pairwise independent letters. Then the following assertions are equivalent:*

i) $xy = yx$.
ii) *There are pairwise independent and connected traces $t_1, \ldots, t_m$, $m \leq \alpha(\Sigma, I)$ such that $x, y \in t_1^* \perp \cdots \perp t_m^*$ for all $1 \leq i \leq k$.*

Let Ω be a finite alphabet of *unknowns*, called also variables. An equation without constants is a pair $(e, f) \in \Omega^* \times \Omega^*$. We use $e \equiv f$ for denoting equations. A system of equations without constants is a subset $S \subseteq \Omega^* \times \Omega^*$. A *solution* of S over $M(\Sigma, I)$ is an assignment of the variables $\sigma : \Omega \longrightarrow M(\Sigma, I)$ such that we have $\sigma(e) = \sigma(f)$ for all $(e, f) \in S$, where σ denotes also the canonical extension to a homomorphism $\sigma : \Omega^* \longrightarrow M(\Sigma, I)$. A solution is also specified by a vector

$$(u_1, \ldots, u_n) \in M(\Sigma, I)^\Omega, \quad \Omega = \{x_1, \ldots, x_n\}.$$

Ehrenfeucht's Conjecture states that every system of word equations is equivalent to some finite subsystem. It has been proved by Albert and Lawrence in

1985, see [13] for an elementary proof. The finite subsystem $F \subseteq S$ is also called a *test set* for S. As observed in [3] it is straightforward to see that Ehrenfeucht's Conjecture holds over traces, too.

Proposition 5. *Let $S \subseteq \Omega^* \times \Omega^*$ be a system of equations without constants. Then there exists a finite subsystem $F \subseteq S$ such that for all $\mathbb{M}(\Sigma, I)$ a solution of F over $\mathbb{M}(\Sigma, I)$ is also a solution of S over $\mathbb{M}(\Sigma, I)$.*

Proof. Let F be a finite test set of S for solutions over a free monoid with two generators. Let $\sigma : \Omega \longrightarrow \mathbb{M}(\Sigma, I)$ be any solution for F over $\mathbb{M}(\Sigma, I)$ and let $(a, b) \in D$. Then we have $\pi_{a,b}\sigma(e) = \pi_{a,b}\sigma(f)$ for all $(e, f) \in F$; and hence for all $(e, f) \in S$ since $\{a, b\}^*$ is a free monoid. By Prop. 2 it follows $\sigma(e) = \sigma(f)$ for all $(e, f) \in S$.

A (finite) system S can (effectively) be reduced by some obvious rules:

- Replace an equation $xe \equiv xf$ by $e \equiv f$.
- Replace an equation $x_1 \cdots x_m \equiv 1, m > 1$ by a conjunction

$$x_1 \equiv 1 \ \& \ \cdots \ \& \ x_m \equiv 1.$$

- If $x \equiv 1 \in S$, then cancel the variable x in all other equations.

The case of interest are therefore finite and reduced systems.

Definition 6. Let $\sigma : \Omega \longrightarrow \mathbb{M}(\Sigma, I)$ be a solution of a system of equations without constants S. The solution $\sigma = (u_1, \ldots, u_n) \in \mathbb{M}(\Sigma, I)^\Omega$ is called

- *non-singular* (*singular* resp.), if $\sigma(x) \neq 1$ for all $x \in \Omega$ ($\sigma(x) = 1$ for some $x \in \Omega$ resp.),
- *cyclic*, if for some $t \in \mathbb{M}(\Sigma, I)$ we have $u_i \in t^*$ for all $1 \leq i \leq n$,
- to have an *1-dimensional Parikh-image*, if for some vector $p \in \mathbb{N}^\Sigma$ we have $\pi(u_i) \in \mathbb{Q}p$ for all $1 \leq i \leq n$, where $\pi : \mathbb{M}(\Sigma, I) \longrightarrow \mathbb{N}^\Sigma \subseteq \mathbb{Q}^\Sigma$ denotes the Parikh-mapping,
- *Abelian*, if $\sigma(x)\sigma(y) = \sigma(y)\sigma(x)$ for all $x, y \in \Omega$.

Remark 7. For word equations the notion of Abelian solution coincides with the notion of cyclic solution. For traces there is a difference. However, if all trace solutions have an 1-dimensional Parikh-image, then all trace solutions are cyclic. This fact is stated in Thm. 10, and it is used as a tool in Cor. 12 below.

Lemma 8. *Let S be a system of equations without constants such that every word solution is cyclic. Let $(u_1, \ldots, u_k)$ be a trace solution. For each $1 \leq i \leq k$ consider the decomposition into connected components:*

$$u_i = u_{i1} \perp \cdots \perp u_{in_i}.$$

Then for all i, j, l, m we have either $\mathrm{alph}(u_{ij}) = \mathrm{alph}(u_{lm})$ *or* $(u_{ij}, u_{lm}) \in I$.

Proof. By contraction: Assume that for some i, j, l, m we have $(u_{ij}, u_{lm}) \notin I$ and $\text{alph}(u_{ij}) \neq \text{alph}(u_{lm})$. Then (by symmetry and since the alphabets of u_{ij} and u_{lm} are connected) there exist $a \in \text{alph}(u_{ij}), b \in \text{alph}(u_{lm}) \setminus \text{alph}(u_{ij})$ such that $(a, b) \in D$. Since all word solutions are cyclic, we have $\pi_{ab}(u_{ij}) = t^p, \pi_{ab}(u_{lm}) = t^q$ for some $t \in \{a, b\}^*, p, q \geq 0$. Hence $\{a, b\} \subseteq \text{alph}(t) \subseteq (\text{alph}(u_{ij}) \cap \text{alph}(u_{lm}))$, yielding a contradiction.

Lemma 9. *Let S be as in the previous lemma, $(u_1, \ldots, u_k)$ be a trace solution such that for some connected set $A \subseteq \Sigma$ we have $\text{alph}(u_i) = A$ for all $1 \leq i \leq k$. Then the solution $(u_1, \ldots, u_k)$ has an 1-dimensional Parikh-image.*

Proof. Let $u = u_1$ and $v = u_2$. It is enough to show that $\pi(u) = \alpha \pi(v)$ for some $\alpha \in \mathbb{Q}$. Consider $a, b \in A$ such that $(a, b) \in D$. Clearly there exist $\alpha, \beta \in \mathbb{Q}$ such that $|u|_a = \alpha |v|_a$ and $|u|_b = \beta |v|_b$. Now, $\pi_{ab}(u) = t^l$ and $\pi_{ab}(v) = t^m$ for some $t \in \{a, b\}^*, l, m > 0$. Therefore $|u|_a = l|t|_a = \alpha \cdot |t|_a \cdot m$, hence $\alpha = \frac{l}{m}$. The same argument applied to the letter b yields $\beta = \frac{l}{m}$, hence $\alpha = \beta$. Since A is connected, we conclude that, indeed, $\pi(u) = \alpha \pi(v)$.

Theorem 10. *Let S be a system of equations such that every trace solution has an 1-dimensional Parikh-image. Then every solution is cyclic.*

Proof. By contradiction assume that the assertion would be wrong for some S. Consider such a system S with a minimal number of unknowns and a non-cyclic solution $(u_1, \ldots, u_k)$. We may assume that the solution is non-singular, $u_i \neq u_j$ for all $i \neq j$, and that $|u_1| + \cdots + |u_k|$ is minimal for such a situation. Let $xe \equiv yf \in S, x, y \in \Omega$. We may assume that $x \neq y, \sigma(x) = u = u_1$ and $\sigma(y) = v = u_2$ for the solution $\sigma : \Omega \longrightarrow \mathbb{M}(\Sigma, I)$ above. Then we have $u = pr, v = ps$ for some traces p, r, s with $(r, s) \in I$. Since the trace solution has an 1-dimensional Parikh-image, we find $q \in \mathbb{N}^\Sigma, \alpha, \beta \in \mathbb{Q}$ such that

$$\pi(u) = \alpha q , \ \pi(v) = \beta q.$$

This implies $\pi(r) - \pi(s) = (\alpha - \beta) \cdot q$. Since $(r, s) \in I$, we have either $r = 1$ or $s = 1$. By symmetry let $r = 1$. Then $s \neq 1$ (since $u \neq v$) and we can replace the variable y by xz with a new variable z. The number of variables is not changed, the new system has a smaller solution $(p, s, u_3, \ldots, u_k)$ with $\sigma(z) = s$. Let us show that that every trace solution of the new system has in fact an 1-dimensional Parikh-image:
Let $(v_1, v_2, \ldots, v_k)$ be any solution, then $(v_1, v_1 v_2, v_3 \ldots, v_k)$ is a solution of the original system S. Hence for some $q \in \mathbb{N}^\Sigma$ we have:

$$\pi(v_1) = \alpha \cdot q , \ \pi(v_1 v_2) = \beta q , \ \pi(u_3) = \alpha_3 q , \ \ldots , \ \pi(u_k) = \alpha_k q.$$

This implies $\pi(v_2) = (\beta - \alpha)q$ and $(v_1, v_2, \ldots, v_k)$ has an 1-dimensional Parikh-image. By induction $(p, s, u_3, \ldots, u_k)$ is a cyclic solution, and $(u_1, u_2, u_3 \ldots, u_k) = (p, ps, u_3, \ldots, u_k)$ is a cyclic solution, too.

Corollary 11. *For a system of equations without constants the following asser-tions are equivalent:*

1. *Every solution is cyclic.*
2. *Every solution has an 1-dimensional Parikh-image.*

Corollary 12 ([1, Prop. 3.2.5]). *For every system of equations without con-stants we have that if all word solutions are cyclic, then all trace solutions are Abelian.*

Proof. Let $(u_1, \ldots, u_k)$ be a trace solution. By Lem. 8 we may assume that such that for some connected set $A \subseteq \Sigma$ we have alph$(u_i) = A$ for all $1 \le i \le k$. By Lem. 9 the solution has an 1-dimensional Parikh-image and by Thm. 10 it is cyclic.

2.1 The graph of first letters

The following definition and Prop. 15 below is borrowed from [2], see also [7].

Definition 13. Let $S \subseteq \Omega^* \times \Omega^*$ be a system of equations without constants. The *graph of first letters* $G(S) = (\Omega, E(S))$ is defined as follows. The vertex set is Ω. For $x, y \in \Omega$ we define an edge $xy \in E(S)$, if there is some equation $xe \equiv yf$ in S. The system is called *connected*, if $G(S)$ is a connected graph.

Example 14. Let

$$S = (x_1y_1 \equiv y_1x_1 \ \& \ x_2y_2 \equiv y_2x_2 \ \& \ zx_1 \equiv x_1z \ \& \ zx_2 \equiv x_2z).$$

Then we have

$$G(S) = y_1 - x_1 - z - x_2 - y_2.$$

By Prop. 15 below every non-singular word solution of S is cyclic. However, $(y_1, x_1, z, x_2, y_2) = (a, a, 1, b, b)$ is a singular word solutions being non-cyclic. Over traces there are also non-singular solutions which are non-cyclic: Let

$$(\Sigma, I) = a - b - c - d - e.$$

A non-singular solution over $\mathbb{M}(\Sigma, I)$ is $(y_1, x_1, z, x_2, y_2) = (a, b, c, d, e)$.

Proposition 15. *Let $S \subseteq \Omega^* \times \Omega^*$ be a connected system, then every non-singular word solution is cyclic.*

Proof. (Sketch) By contradiction assume that S is connected and $(u_1, \ldots, u_n)$ is a non-singular and non-cyclic solution. Among those situations choose the value

$$|u_1| + \cdots + |u_n|$$

to be minimal. Let $xy \in E(S)$. Without restriction we have $x = x_1$ and $y = x_2$. If $u_1 = u_2$, then we can put $x = y$. The graph of the new system is obtained by an edge contraction. Hence it is still connected, but $|u_2| < |u_1| + |u_2|$. Therefore $u_1 \neq u_2$ and without restriction $u_1 = u_2 v$ with $v \neq 1$. We replace the variable x by yz where z is a new variable. A simple reflection shows that the corresponding graph transformation does not destroy the connectivity. We have a contradiction since $|v| < |u_1|$.

We have seen in Ex.14 that in the corresponding statement for traces it is not sufficient to replace the word *cyclic* by *Abelian*. (This is no contradiction to Cor. 12 since the connectivity of $G(S)$ is not enough to ensure that the singular word solutions are cyclic.) In the following, by abuse of language, the independence relation I is called *transitive*, if in fact $I \cup \mathrm{id}_\Sigma$ is a transitive relation, i.e., $\mathbb{M}(\Sigma, I)$ is a free product of free commutative monoids.
Using this terminology, we can state:

Proposition 16. *If the independence relation I is not transitive, then there exists a connected system with a non-singular non-Abelian solution.*

Proof. If I is not transitive, then there are $(a, b), (b, c) \in I$, but $(a, c) \notin I$ and $a \neq c$. Hence there $a, b, c \in \Sigma$ such that $ab = ba, bc = cb$, but $ac \neq ca$. Thus, it is enough to consider the system

$$S = (xy \equiv yx \ \& \ yz \equiv zy).$$

The interesting fact is that Prop. 15 and the observation above yield a characterization when I is transitive.

Theorem 17. *Let I be a transitive independence relation and let $S \subseteq \Omega^* \times \Omega^*$ be connected. Then every non-singular solution is Abelian.*

Proof. The monoid $\mathbb{M}(\Sigma, I)$ is a free product of free commutative monoids:

$$\mathbb{M}(\Sigma, I) = \mathbb{N}^{\Sigma_1} * \cdots * \mathbb{N}^{\Sigma_k}$$

for some partition $\Sigma = \Sigma_1 \cup \cdots \cup \Sigma_k$. For each Σ_i pick some letter $a_i \in \Sigma_i$ and define a homomorphism:

$$\eta : \mathbb{M}(\Sigma, I) \longrightarrow \{a_1, \ldots, a_k\}^*, b \mapsto a_i, \text{ for } b \in \Sigma_i, 1 \leq i \leq k.$$

Now, a non-singular trace solution $\sigma : \Omega \longrightarrow \mathbb{M}(\Sigma, I)$ yields a non-singular word solution $\tau = \eta\sigma$, hence $\tau : \Omega \longrightarrow \{a_1, \ldots, a_k\}^*$. Hence for some $t \in \Sigma^*$ we have $\tau(z) \in t^+$ for all $z \in \Omega$. If $t \in a_i^*$ for some i, then $\sigma(\Omega) \subseteq \mathbb{N}^{\Sigma_i}$, the solution is Abelian and we are done. Otherwise let us go back to the proof of Prop. 15.

What has been used only is the fact that if $\sigma(x) = u_1, \sigma(y) = u_2$, and $xy \in E(S)$ then u_1 is a prefix of u_2 or vice versa. Let us show that $|\sigma(x)| \leq |\sigma(y)|$ implies that u_1 is a prefix of u_2. Since $xy \in E(S)$ we can write $u_1 = pr$ and $u_2 = ps$ with $(r, s) \in I$. Moreover since $G(S)$ is connected and $|\text{alph}(t)| > 1$ there is some $q \in M(\Sigma, I)$ ($\eta(q)$ is a prefix of t) such that $|\text{alph}(\eta(q))| > 1$ and $z \in q\,M(\Sigma, I)$ for all $z \in \Omega$. Thus, $u_1 q$ and $u_2 q$, and hence rq and sq are prefixes of a common trace in $M(\Sigma, I)$. Since $|r| \leq |s|$, $(r, s) \in I$, and $|\text{alph}(\eta(q))| > 1$, we conclude as desired $r = 1$.

In order to guarantee Abelian solutions we have to restrict the class of systems. For $X \subseteq \Omega$ let $S|_{X \equiv 1}$ be the new system which is obtained by cancelling first all variables $x \in X$ and then reducing the system according to the rules mentioned earlier.

Definition 18. A system S is called *stably connected*, if $S|_{X \equiv 1}$ is connected for all $X \subseteq \Omega$.

Theorem 19. *If S is stably connected, then every trace solution $\sigma : \Omega \longrightarrow M(\Sigma, I)$ is Abelian.*

Proof. Let $\Omega \to \Sigma^*$ be any solutions over words, $X = \{x \in \Omega \mid \sigma(x) = 1\}$. Then $\sigma' : \Omega \setminus X \to \Sigma^*$ is a non-singular solution over words for $S|_{X \equiv 1}$. Since $S|_{X \equiv 1}$ is connected, the solution σ' is cyclic. Therefore $\sigma : \Omega \to \Sigma^*$ is a cyclic solution and the theorem follows by Cor. 12.

3 Equations with constants

An equation with constants $e \equiv f$ is a pair $(e, f) \in \Gamma^* \times \Gamma^*$ where $\Gamma = \Omega \cup \Sigma$. It should be clear what we mean by a system of equations with constants and what means a solution. Deciding the solubility of a given system with constants is a difficult task – even if at most one constant is involved.

Proposition 20. *It is an NP-complete problem to decide whether a finite system of trace equations using at most one constant has a solution.*

Proof. Let $a \in \Sigma$ be the only constant involved in the system. Replacing a solution $\sigma(x) = u \in \Sigma^*$ by $a^{|u|}$, we see that it is enough to solve a linear system over N. The NP-completeness is then clear from integer linear programming.

The next observation is that Ehrenfeucht's Conjecture holds in such a setting, too. Indeed let $S \subseteq \Gamma^* \times \Gamma^*$ be any systems of equations with constants. Then replace every constant $a \in \Sigma$ by an occurrence of a new variable x_a. Let $S' \subseteq \Omega'^* \times \Omega'^*$ be the new systems $\Omega' = \Omega \cup \{x_a \mid a \in \Sigma\}$. By Prop. 5 there exists a finite test set $F' \subseteq S'$. The corresponding finite set $F \subseteq S$ is a test set for S: A solution $\sigma : \Omega \longrightarrow M(\Sigma, I)$ for F yields a solution $\sigma' : \Omega' \longrightarrow M(\Sigma, I)$ for F' by extending σ with $\sigma'(x_a) = a$. Hence σ' is a solution for S'. Therefore σ is a solution for S.

Moreover, every system of equations can be replaced by a single equation. This equation involves a new constant, in general.

Proposition 21. *Let $S \subseteq \Gamma^* \times \Gamma^*$ be a system of equations with constants and let $\mathbb{M}(\Sigma, I)$ be a trace monoid. Then there exists a single equation $e \equiv f$ over the free product $\mathbb{M}(\Sigma, I) * a^*$ such that the equation $e \equiv f$ is solvable over $\mathbb{M}(\Sigma, I) * a^*$ if and only if S is solvable over $\mathbb{M}(\Sigma, I)$.*

Proof. By Ehrenfeucht's conjecture it is enough to consider finite systems:

$$S = \{(e_1, f_1), \ldots, (e_k, f_k)\}.$$

Let a be a new letter (constant) and let $b \in \Sigma$ any letter. Note that in the free product $\mathbb{M}(\Sigma, I) * a^*$ the letter a is dependent on b. Consider the equation $e \equiv f$ where

$$e = e_1 a^2 \cdots e_k a^2 f_1 a \cdots f_k a e_1 a b a \cdots e_{k-1} a b a e_k,$$
$$f = f_1 a^2 \cdots f_k a^2 e_1 a \cdots e_k a f_1 a b a \cdots f_{k-1} a b a f_k.$$

Clearly, a solution $\sigma : \Omega \longrightarrow \mathbb{M}(\Sigma, I)$ of S is a solution of $e \equiv f$ by $\mathbb{M}(\Sigma, I) \subseteq \mathbb{M}(\Sigma, I) * a^*$. Conversely, let $\sigma' : \Omega \longrightarrow \mathbb{M}(\Sigma, I) * a^*$ be a solution of $e \equiv f$. A simple reflection involving Levi's Lemma shows $\sigma'(e_i) = \sigma'(f_i)$ for all $1 \leq i \leq k$. Indeed, to see this for $i = 1$ we may assume that $|\sigma'(e_1)| \leq |\sigma'(f_1)|$. Then $\sigma'(e_1 a)$ and $\sigma'(f_1 a)$ are prefixes of a common trace. Hence $\sigma'(e_1)$ is a prefix of $\sigma'(f_1)$. If $|\sigma'(e_1)| = |\sigma'(f_1)|$, then $\sigma'(e_1) = \sigma'(f_1)$. Otherwise, if $|\sigma'(e_1)| < |\sigma'(f_1)|$, then $\sigma'(e_1 a a)$ and $\sigma'(e_1 a b)$ are both prefixes of $\sigma'(f_1 a)$, which is impossible since a and b are dependent. Knowing $\sigma'(e_i) = \sigma'(f_i)$ for all $1 \leq i \leq k$ we conclude that $\sigma = \pi_{(\Sigma, I)} \sigma' : \Omega \longrightarrow \mathbb{M}(\Sigma, I)$ is a solution of S.

One might be interested to allow negations in the system of equations. Similar to the word case, a negation $e \not\equiv f$ can be replaced by a conjunction. In the trace case however we need additionally some regular constraints of a simple type (specifying the initial alphabet and the independence of some solutions).

Proposition 22. *The negation $(e \not\equiv f)$ is equivalent to the following conjunction where x, y, and z are new variables:*

$$e \equiv xy \; \& \; f \equiv xz \; \& \; (\text{init}(y) \cup \text{init}(z) \neq \emptyset) \; \& \; (\text{alph}(y) \times \text{alph}(z) \subseteq I).$$

The challenge is therefore to solve a single trace equation with constants and some regular constraints of simple type as above. For free monoids the solubility (without any regular constraints) is known due to Makanin [8]; this result is viewed as a major break-through in the combinatorics on words. Moreover, Pécuchet [12] has shown that every solution derives a unique principle solution. The algorithms of Makanin is extremely complex, it has has been refined by Schulz [14] to systems where the variables must satisfy additional regular constraints. Using the refinement of Schulz it became possible to reduce the solubility of a trace equation with constants to the word case.

Theorem 23 (Matiyasevich). *It is decidable whether a system of trace equations with constants has a solution.*

The original proof [9,10] is a reduction to the word case by an induction on the size of I. Another reduction using a new result on lexicographical normal forms is presented in [4]. Both reductions lead to an exponential grow up in both the size of the system and the number of variables.

References

1. Christian Choffrut. Combinatorics in trace monoids I. In V. Diekert and G. Rozenberg, editors, *The Book of Traces*, chapter 3, pages 71–82. World Scientific, Singapore, 1995.
2. Christian Choffrut and Juhani Karhumäki. Combinatorics of words. In G. Rozenberg and A. Salomaa, editors, *Handbook of Formal Languages*, volume 1, pages 329–438. Springer, Berlin-Heidelberg-New York, 1997.
3. Aldo de Luca and Antonio Restivo. On a generalization of a conjecture of Ehrenfeucht. *Bulletin of the European Association for Theoretical Computer Science (EATCS)*, 30:84–90, 1986.
4. Volker Diekert, Yuri Matiyasevich, and Anca Muscholl. Solving trace equations using lexicographical normal forms. In R. Gorrieri P. Degano and A. Marchetti-Spaccamela, editors, *Proceedings of the 24th International Colloquium on Automata, Languages and Programming (ICALP'97), Bologna (Italy) 1997*, number 1256 in Lecture Notes in Computer Science, pages 336–347, Berlin-Heidelberg-New York, 1997. Springer.
5. Volker Diekert and Grzegorz Rozenberg, editors. *The Book of Traces*. World Scientific, Singapore, 1995.
6. Christine Duboc. Some properties of commutation in free partially commutative monoids. *Information Processing Letters*, 20:1–4, 1985.
7. Tero Harju and Juhani Karhumäki. On the defect theorem and simplifiability. *Semigroup Forum*, 33:199–217, 1986.
8. Gennadiĭ Semyonovich Makanin. The problem of solvability of equations in a free semigroup. *Math. Sbornik*, 103:147–236, 1977. English transl. in Math. USSR Sbornik 32 (1977).
9. Yuri Matiyasevich. Reduction of trace equations to word equations. Talk given at the "Colloquium on Computability, Complexity, and Logic", Institut für Informatik, Universität Stuttgart, Germany, Dec. 5–6, 1996.
10. Yuri Matiyasevich. Some decision problems for traces. In Sergej Adian and Anil Nerode, editors, *Proceedings of the 4th International Symposium on Logical Foundations of Computer Science (LFCS'97), Yaroslavl, Russia, July 6–12, 1997*, number 1234 in Lecture Notes in Computer Science, pages 248–257, Berlin-Heidelberg-New York, 1997. Springer. Invited lecture.
11. Antoni Mazurkiewicz. Concurrent program schemes and their interpretations. DAIMI Rep. PB 78, Aarhus University, Aarhus, 1977.
12. Jean Pierre Pécuchet. Solutions principales et rang d'un système d'équations avec constantes dans le monoïde libre. *Discrete Mathematics*, 48:253–274, 1984.
13. Dominique Perrin. On the solution of Ehrenfeucht's Conjecture. *Bulletin of the European Association for Theoretical Computer Science (EATCS)*, 27:68–70, 1985.
14. Klaus U. Schulz. Makanin's algorithm for word equations — Two improvements and a generalization. In Klaus U. Schulz, editor, *Word Equations and Related Topics*, number 572 in Lecture Notes in Computer Science, pages 85–150, Berlin-Heidelberg-New York, 1991. Springer.

Verification of Distributed Algorithms with Algebraic Petri Nets*

Ekkart Kindler   Wolfgang Reisig

Humboldt-Universität zu Berlin, Institut für Informatik, D-10099 Berlin, Germany

Introduction

Concise models of distributed algorithms which on the one hand allow rigorous correctness proofs and on the other hand are easy to understand are still rarely found. Algebraic Petri nets as proposed in [3] allow to concisely model distributed algorithms. Moreover, classical Petri net techniques in combination with a temporal logic can be used to verify the correctness of these models [4, 8, 7]. Here, we present a simple example which provides a flavour of how distributed algorithms can be modelled and verified by help of algebraic Petri nets. The formal background can be found in [4, 3]. Some verification techniques are presented in more detail in separate notes which are interspersed within the text.

1 A minimal spanning tree algorithm

As an example we use a distributed algorithm for calculating a *minimal spanning tree* for a network of communicating agents, taken from [1] resp. [9]:

Let A be a set of *agents*, some of which are connected by bidirectional communication channels. A *network* of communication channels is represented by a set $N \subseteq A \times A$, where a pair $(x, y) \in N$ denotes a *channel* from agent x to agent y. If $(x, y) \in N$ we say x and y are *neighbours*. Note that with $(x, y) \in N$ also $(y, x) \in N$ since by assumption the channels are bidirectional. Moreover, we assume that there is a set of distinguished *root agents* $R \subseteq A$; the other agents $I = A \setminus R$ are called *inner agents*. A simple network of agents is graphically represented in Fig. 1, where an agent is represented as a dot, a communication channel is represented as an edge, and root agents c and d are indicated by an additional circle.

Now, the task is to compute for each inner agent a path of minimal length to some root agent; actually each inner agent does not calculate the full path, but only a *pointer* to the next agent on the path. Altogether these pointers form a *minimal spanning tree*[1]. For example, Fig. 2 shows a minimal spanning tree for the network of Fig. 1. These pointers can be calculated on any network of agents by the following algorithm: Initially, each root agent x sends to each neighbour a message, which contains distance

---

*This work was supported by the DFG (Project 'Distributed Algorithms').

[1]The graph is only a tree, if there is only one root agent; otherwise there is a forest of trees.

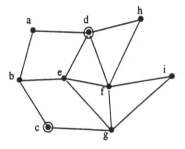

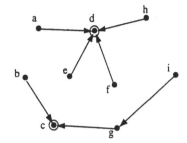

Figure 1: A network of agents　　　　Figure 2: A minimal spanning tree

information 1. In general, distance information n indicates, that the agent has distance n from a root. When an inner agent x receives a message from a neighbour y with distance information n, he stores the name of this agent y in his pointer along with the distance information. Moreover, x sends a message with distance information $n + 1$ to each of his neighbours. When an inner agent receives another message from an agent z with a distance information m which is shorter than the one he has currently stored, he stores z in his pointer along with the new distance information m, and sends another message with distance information $m + 1$ to each of his neighbours. Upon termination, the calculated pointers form a forest of minimal spanning trees.

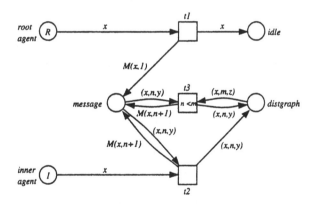

Figure 3: A minimal spanning tree algorithm

Figure 3 shows this algorithm modelled as an algebraic Petri net. In this net, sending of a *message* with distance information n from agent x to agent y is modelled by adding a token (y, n, x) to place *message*. The receiver is put in the first position, since he is the only one using this message (cf. contribution of J. Desel in this volume). The reception of the message by agent y is modelled by removing the token from place *message*. Now, sending a message with distance information n from agent x to each of his neighbours $y_1, \ldots, y_k$ can be modelled by putting tokens $(y_1, n, x), \ldots, (y_k, n, x)$ to place *message*. To this end, we introduce a multi-set-valued operation M with $M(x, n) = [(y_1, n, x), \ldots, (y_k, n, x)]$ for each agent x with neighbours $y_1, \ldots, y_k$ and each $n \in \mathbb{N}$. For example, $M(a, 7) = [(b, 7, a), (d, 7, a)]$ for the network shown in Fig. 1.

The initial step of a root agent $x \in R$ is modelled by transition t_1: Agent x sends distance information 1 to each of his neighbours and becomes idle. An inner agent still waiting for a first message is represented in place *inneragent*. The reception of the first message is modelled by transition t_2; where the pointer from x to y along with the distance information n is modelled as a token (x, n, y) on place *distgraph*. Receiving a message with a smaller distance information later on is modelled by transition t_3; the guard $n < m$ guarantees that only messages with shorter distance information are considered.

2 Properties

Before verifying the algorithm, we introduce some notations for properties which will be used to specify the correctness of the algorithm. Properties are formalized by *temporal formulas* which are built from *state formulas* and *state expressions*.

2.1 State formulas

A *state expression* is an expression built from some standard operations and place names, which are interpreted as multiset-valued variables. For example, *message + distgraph* or *rootagent + idle* are state expressions, where + denotes the addition operation on multisets. In a given marking a state expression can be evaluated in the usual way, where each place name takes the value of the corresponding marking.

For a multiset-valued expression e and some value x the operation $e[x]$ denotes the number of occurrences of x in e. Thus, $e[x]$ is an expression over the natural numbers. A finite multiset is denoted by $[a_1, \ldots, a_n]$, where multiple occurrences of the same element are allowed and relevant. The empty multiset is denoted by $[]$.

An *elementary state formula* can be constructed by combining two state expressions with the usual relations on multisets or natural numbers. *State formulas* can be built by combining elementary state formulas with the usual boolean connectives or by quantification. For example, $\forall x \in R : rootagent[x] + idle[x] = 1$ is a state formula which is valid in each marking in which each root agent occurs exactly once in one of the two places *rootagent* or *idle*. Often, we need a formula which says that token x occurs at least once on some place p. To this end, we use $p(x)$ as an abbreviation for $p[x] \geq 1$. For example, $rootagent(x)$ is true for each root agent $x \in R$ in the initial marking.

2.2 Temporal formulas

From state formulas φ and ψ we build the following *temporal formulas*: $\Box\varphi$, φ UNLESS ψ, $\Diamond\varphi$, and $\varphi \rightsquigarrow \psi$.

The first two formulas express so-called *safety properties*. The formula $\Box\varphi$ says that the state formula φ is true in each reachable state of the system. Therefore, we call $\Box\varphi$ an *invariant property*. In our example $\Box\forall x \in R : rootagent[x] + idle[x] = 1$ is a valid invariant property. We will write $\forall x \in R : \Box rootagent[x] + idle[x] = 1$ for better readability. The formula φ UNLESS ψ says that in each run of the system ψ will become valid whenever φ becomes invalid. In our example $message(x, n, y)$ UNLESS $distgraph(x, n, y)$ is valid.

The last two formulas express so-called *liveness properties*. The formula $\Diamond\varphi$ says that in each run of the system φ will eventually be true. In our example, $\Diamond idle(x)$ holds for each $x \in R$; we will write $\forall x \in R : \Diamond idle(x)$ for short. The formula $\varphi \rightsquigarrow \psi$ says that in each run of the system for each state in which φ is true, ψ will be true in some subsequent state. We call $\varphi \rightsquigarrow \psi$ a *leadsto property*. In our example, the following is a valid leadsto property:

$$inneragent(x) \wedge message(x, n, y) \rightsquigarrow \exists k \in \mathbb{N}, v \in A : k \le n \wedge distgraph(x, k, v)$$

2.3 Specification

Next, we specify the minimal spanning tree algorithm by help of temporal formulas. As usual, the specification consists of a safety and a liveness part.

Safety We start with two simple properties, which guarantee that we can interpret a token (x, n, y) on place *distgraph* as a unique pointer from agent x to some neighbour y. The uniqueness of the pointer is formalized by the following invariant property:

$$\Box(distgraph(x, n, y) \wedge distgraph(x, m, z)) \Rightarrow (n = m \wedge y = z) \qquad (1)$$

The requirement that only pointers to a neighbour are allowed is formalized by the invariant property:

$$\Box distgraph(x, n, y) \Rightarrow (x, y) \in N \qquad (2)$$

When x stores a pointer to y along with distance information n, we require that there is a path of pointers from x via y to some root agent, which has length n or shorter. This requirement is implicitly expressed by the following invariant property:

$$\Box distgraph(x, n, y) \Rightarrow (y \in R \vee \exists m \in \mathbb{N}, z \in A : m < n \wedge distgraph(y, m, z)) \quad (3)$$

For each pointer from x to y, agent y is a root agent or y has a pointer to some z along with a smaller distance information. Therefore, there is a path form x to some root agent which is shorter than n whenever $distrgraph(x, n, y)$ holds true.
At last, we require that a pointer will only change in favour of a better pointer (i.e. a pointer with a shorter distance information):

$$distgraph(x, n, y) \text{ UNLESS } \exists k \in \mathbb{N}, v \in A : k < n \wedge distgraph(x, k, v) \qquad (4)$$

In particular, this property in combination with (1)–(3) guarantees that once a minimal path is calculated it will not change any more.

Liveness Up to now, no property guarantees that the minimal spanning tree will eventually be calculated. Now, we require for each inner agent x for which there is a path to some root agent with length n, the following property holds:

$$\Diamond \exists k \in \mathbb{N}, v \in A : k \le n \wedge distgraph(x, k, v) \qquad (5)$$

In particular property (5) must be valid for the minimal path to a root, which guarantees that eventually the minimal path will be calculated for each inner agent.

A *place invariant* of an algebraic Petri net is a linear expression in which places may occur as variables with the following property: For each marking (including all non-reachable markings) the expression does not change its value when a transition occurs. So, if e is a place invariant of an algebraic Petri net and e evaluates to v in the initial marking, then the invariant $\Box e = v$ is true.

The verification of a place invariant e is quite simple: For each transition we have to check an equation which is constructed from the expression and the arc inscriptions of the corresponding transition. To this end, we define for each transition t two substitutions $\sigma_{\bullet t}$ and $\sigma_{t\bullet}$, which substitute for a place p the inscription $i(p, t)$ of the arc from p to t or the inscription $i(t, p)$ of the arc from t to p, respectively. If there is no arc, p is substituted by the empty set $\parallel$. The application of the substitutions to the expression e is denoted by $\sigma_{\bullet t}(e)$ and $\sigma_{t\bullet}(e)$, respectively.

Now, to verify that e is a place invariant, we have to check the equation $\sigma_{\bullet t}(e) = \sigma_{t\bullet}(e)$ for each transition t (cf. [6, 4, 8]).

Note 1: Place invariants

3 Verification

Now, we will verify that the minimal spanning tree algorithm from Fig. 3 is correct; i.e. it satisfies properties (1)–(5). In Sect. 3.1 we verify the safety properties, in Sect. 3.2 we verify the liveness property. Note that we prove more safety properties than necessary for (1)–(4); these additional safety properties will be used in the verification of the liveness property (5) in Sect. 3.2.

3.1 Safety properties

Obviously, each inner agent $x \in I$ is in one of the following two states: x has not yet received a message (and thus does not yet have a pointer and a distance information) or x has a pointer and a distance information. Formally, we state:

$$\forall x \in I : \Box \, inneragent(x) \vee \exists k \in \mathbb{N}, v \in A : distgraph(x, k, v) \qquad (6)$$

This property can be verified by help of a *place invariant* (cf. Note 1). A place invariant is a linear expression, such that in each marking the occurrence of a transition does not change the value of this expression. Here, we use the expression $inneragent + Pr_1(distgraph)$, where Pr_1 denotes the linear function, which maps each element (x, n, y) of a multiset of triples to its first component x. In the initial marking the expression evaluates to I which gives us:

$$\Box \, inneragent + Pr_1(distgraph) = I \qquad (7)$$

This invariant immediately implies property (6). Moreover, (7) implies property (1) $\Box(distgraph(x, n, y) \wedge distgraph(x, m, z)) \Rightarrow (n = m \wedge y = z)$ from the specification because (7) guarantees that there is at most one tuple (x, n, y) with first component x on place $distgraph$.

Similarly, we can prove the invariant property $\Box \, rootagent + idle = R$ by help of place invariant $rootagent + idle$. This invariant immediately implies the following invariant property:

$$\Box \, idle(x) \Rightarrow x \in R \qquad (8)$$

Similar to place invariants, *siphons* and *traps* are linear expressions. An individual trap for some set A is a linear expression e such that for each $x \in A$ the formula $e(x)$ remains valid once $e(x)$ is true. Dually, e is an individual siphon for some set A if for each $x \in A$ the formula $e(x)$ remains invalid once it is false.

So, if e is an individual trap for A and $e(x)$ holds initially for each $x \in A$, then $\forall x \in A : \Box e(x)$ is a valid invariant property. Similarly, if e is an individual siphon for A and $e(x)$ is initially false for each $x \in A$, then $\forall x \in A : \Box \neg e(x)$ is a valid invariant property.

An individual siphon or an individual trap can be checked by verifying one implication for each transition of the system. A linear expression e is an individual trap for A, if and only if for each transition t the implication $\forall x \in A : g(t) \wedge \sigma_{\bullet t}(e)(x) \Rightarrow \sigma_{t\bullet}(e)(x)$ is valid, where $g(t)$ denotes the transition guard of t and the substitutions $\sigma_{\bullet t}$ and $\sigma_{t\bullet}$ are defined as for place invariants (cf. Note 1). A linear expression e is an individual siphon for A, if for each transition t the implication $\forall x \in A : g(t) \wedge \neg\sigma_{\bullet t}(e)(x) \Rightarrow \neg\sigma_{t\bullet}(e)(x)$ is valid.

Note 2: Siphons and traps

Next, we verify the following invariantproperty by help of an *individual siphon*:

$$\forall(x,y) \notin N : \Box \, \neg(message(x,n,y) \vee distgraph(x,n,y)) \tag{9}$$

An individual siphon with respect to some set $x \in A$ is an expression which guarantees that whenever a particular element $x \in A$ is not in the current evaluation of the expression, it will never be again. So, when x is not in the evaluation of the expression in the initial marking, it will never be (cf. Note 2). It is easy to check that $message + distgraph$ is an individual siphon for all triples (x,n,y) with $(x,y) \notin N$. Initially, this siphon evaluates to the empty set, which gives us (9). In particular, property (9) implies invariant property (2) from the specification: Whenever $distgraph(x,n,y)$ is valid x and y are neighbours.

For two state formulas φ and ψ and a transition t the assertion $\{\varphi\}t\{\psi\}$ says that whenever transition t occurs in a (not necessarily reachable) marking in which φ is valid, then ψ is valid after the occurrence of the transition.

If $\{\varphi\}t\{\varphi\}$ is valid for each transition t and φ is true in the initial state, $\Box\varphi$ is a valid invariant property. Similarly, if $\{\varphi\}t\{\varphi \vee \psi\}$ is valid for each transition t, then φ UNLESS ψ is valid.

The validity of an assertion can be verified by checking the validity of a state formula, which is constructed from the formulas φ and ψ and the transition. For simplicity we assume, that variables occurring in φ and ψ are disjoint from those occurring in the arc-inscriptions. Then, we define two substitutions $\eta_{\bullet t}$ and $\eta_{t\bullet}$ such that each place p is replaced by $p + i(p,t)$ or $p + i(t,p)$, respectively, where $i(p,t)$ denotes the arc-inscription of arc (p,t) and $i(t,p)$ the arc-inscription of arc (t,p); p is not replaced, if the arc does not exist. The assertion $\{\varphi\}t\{\psi\}$ is valid if and only if the state formula $g(t) \wedge \eta_{\bullet t}(\varphi) \Rightarrow \eta_{t\bullet}(\psi)$ is valid.

Note 3: Assertions

For verifying property (3) from the specification we show the following invariant property:

$$\Box \left(\begin{array}{c} message(x,n,y) \vee \\ distgraph(x,n,y) \end{array} \right) \Rightarrow \left(\begin{array}{c} idle(y) \vee \\ \exists m \in \mathbb{N}, z \in A : m < n \wedge \\ distgraph(y,m,z) \end{array} \right) \tag{10}$$

This property in combination with (8) implies (3). Property (10) can be shown by checking that $\varphi = (message(x, n, y) \vee distgraph(x, n, y)) \Rightarrow (idle(y) \vee \exists m \in \mathbb{N}, z \in A : m < n \wedge distgraph(y, m, z))$ is valid in the initial state, and by checking the assertion $\{\varphi\}t\{\varphi\}$ for each transition t of the model (i.e. when φ is true and t occurs, φ is true afterwards; cf. Note 3).

For verifying property (4) of the specification we have to check the following assertion for each transition t of the model (cf. Note 3):

$$\{distgraph(x, n, y)\}t\{distgraph(x, n, y) \vee \exists m \in \mathbb{N}, z \in A : m < n \wedge distgraph(x, m, z)\}$$

For proving the liveness property in Sect. 3.2 we need some more safety properties. When a message is received (removed from place message), the corresponding agent has stored the corresponding information afterwards:

$$message(x, n, y) \text{ UNLESS } distgraph(x, n, y) \tag{11}$$

Again, this property can be proven by checking the corresponding assertions.

The last safety property says that when an agent y has stored a pointer v with distance information n, then for each neighbour x of y there is either a message from y to x with distance information $n + 1$, or the neighbour has already a distance information, which is shorter than or equal to $n + 1$. Again, this property can be proven by help of the corresponding assertions.

$$\forall(y, x) \in N : \Box \left[distgraph(y, n, v) \Rightarrow \left(\begin{array}{l} message(x, n + 1, y) \vee \\ \exists k \in \mathbb{N}, v \in A : k \leq n + 1 \wedge \\ distgraph(x, k, v) \end{array} \right) \right] \tag{12}$$

3.2 Liveness

Now, we are going to show the liveness property. The proof starts with some simple

---

A leadsto property $\varphi \rightsquigarrow \psi$ can be verified by checking that a transition t is enabled when φ is valid and an occurrence of the transition will establish ψ, which can be expressed by the assertion $\{\varphi\}t\{\psi\}$. Moreover, each transition which is in conflict with t must also establish ψ, when it occurs. This can also be formalized by help of assertions (cf. [8]), but is more involved.

Here, we *pick up* a leadsto property $\varphi \rightsquigarrow \psi$ from the net in a more intuitive way: We state which transition t guarantees the leadsto property; the verification that the occurrence of each conflicting transition also guarantees ψ, is left informal.

Note 4: Pick up rule

---

leadsto properties which can be picked up from the transitions of the Petri net (cf. Note 4). Each root agent y will eventually send a message to his neighbours, since transition t_1 will eventually occur in this mode.

$$\forall(y, x) \in N : rootagent(y) \rightsquigarrow message(x, 1, y) \tag{13}$$

Similarly, we can pick up for transition t_2 and transition t_3:

$$inneragent(x) \wedge message(x, n, y) \rightsquigarrow \exists k \in \mathbb{N}, v \in A : distgraph(x, k, v) \tag{14}$$

> The *Progress-Safety-Progress* rule [2] combines a leadsto property $\varphi \rightsquigarrow \psi$ with a safety property χ UNLESS χ'. In a state which satisfies $\varphi \wedge \chi$ we know from the leadsto property that eventually there will be a state which satisfies ψ; from the safety property we know that either χ' must have been valid in between or χ is still valid, when ψ becomes true. This implies $\varphi \wedge \chi \rightsquigarrow \chi' \vee \psi \wedge \chi$
>
> Note 5: PSP rule

and

$$\begin{pmatrix} distgraph(x, m, v) \wedge \\ message(x, n, y) \wedge \\ n < m \end{pmatrix} \rightsquigarrow \begin{pmatrix} distgraph(x, n, y) \vee \\ \exists k \in \mathbb{N}, v \in A : k < m \wedge \\ distgraph(x, k, v) \end{pmatrix} \tag{15}$$

Note that we cannot pick up $inneragent(x) \wedge message(x, n, y) \rightsquigarrow distgraph(x, n, y)$ because there may be another message for x, which might be received first. For the same reason, we cannot pick up:

$$distgraph(x, m, v) \wedge message(x, n, y) \wedge n < m \rightsquigarrow distgraph(x, n, y)$$

The unless property (11) implies that the reception of a message (x, n, y) results in $distgraph(x, n, y)$. Combining property (11) with (14) we get by the Progress-Safety-Progress rule (cf. Note 5):

$$\begin{pmatrix} inneragent(x) \wedge \\ message(x, n, y) \end{pmatrix} \rightsquigarrow \begin{pmatrix} distgraph(x, n, y) \vee \\ \exists k \in \mathbb{N}, v \in A : distgraph(x, k, v) \wedge \\ message(x, n, y) \end{pmatrix} \tag{16}$$

Combining (11) with (15) we get

$$\begin{pmatrix} distgraph(x, m, v) \wedge \\ message(x, n, y) \wedge \\ n < m \end{pmatrix} \rightsquigarrow \begin{pmatrix} distgraph(x, n, y) \vee \\ \exists k \in \mathbb{N}, v \in A : k < m \wedge \\ distgraph(x, k, v) \wedge message(x, n, y) \end{pmatrix} \tag{17}$$

Property (17) guarantees that the distance m of x decreases as long as the message (x, n, y) with $n < m$ is not consumed. Therefore, eventually the distance of x will become n or smaller, which can be formally proven by induction on $|n - m|$:

> A *proof graph* is a finite acyclic graph whose nodes are state formulas and which has exactly one maximal and one minimal node (cf. proof lattices of [5]). A proof graph is valid, if for each node φ with successor nodes $\psi_1, \ldots, \psi_n$ the leadsto property $\varphi \rightsquigarrow \psi_1 \vee \ldots \vee \psi_n$ is valid. The justifications for these leadsto properties is indicated by a number of an already proven leadsto property at the corresponding node.
> For a valid proof graph with maximal node φ and minimal node ψ the property $\varphi \rightsquigarrow \psi$ is also valid.
> An invariant $\Box(\varphi \Rightarrow \psi)$ immediately implies the validity of the leadsto property $\varphi \rightsquigarrow \psi$. Therefore, we also allow invariants of the form $\Box(\varphi \Rightarrow \psi_1 \vee \ldots \vee \psi_n)$ as a justification instead of a leadsto property $\varphi \rightsquigarrow \psi_1 \vee \ldots \vee \psi_n$.
>
> Note 6: Proof graphs

$$\left(\begin{array}{c} distgraph(x, m, v) \wedge \\ message(x, n, y) \end{array} \right) \rightsquigarrow \left(\begin{array}{c} \exists k \in \mathbb{N}, v \in A : k \le n \wedge \\ distgraph(x, k, v) \end{array} \right) \qquad (18)$$

Now, we can combine properties (6). (16). and (18) in the proof graph shown in Fig. 4 (cf. Note 6), from which immediately follows:

$$x \in I : message(x, n, y) \rightsquigarrow \exists k \in \mathbb{N}, v \in A : k \le n \wedge distgraph(x, k. v) \qquad (19)$$

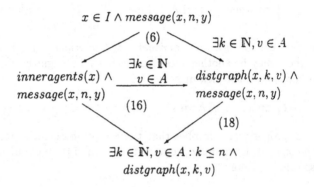

Figure 4: Proof graph for (19)

At last we show by induction over the reachability from a root agent in the network N that for each agent x with distance n from a root property (5) holds true:

$$\Diamond \exists k \in \mathbb{N}, v \in A : k \le n \wedge distgraph(x, k, v)$$

$n = 1$: Let $x \in I$ be a node with distance $n = 1$ from a root. Then, there exists a root agent $y \in R$ with $(y, x) \in N$. Therefore, initially holds $rootagent(y)$. Property (13) implies that eventually $message(x, 1, y)$ holds; then, by (19) eventually $distgraph(x, k, v)$ holds for some $v \in A$ and $k \le 1$, which proves $\Diamond \exists k \in \mathbb{N}, v \in A : k \le 1 \wedge distgraph(x, k, v)$

$n \to n + 1$: We assume that (5) holds for each agent $x \in I$ with a distance n from a root. Now, let $x \in I$ be an agent with distance $n + 1$ from a root. Then, there exists an agent $y \in I$ with distance n from a root and $(y, x) \in N$; by induction hypothesis follows $\Diamond \exists k \in \mathbb{N}, v \in A : k \le n \wedge distgraph(y, k, v)$. Then, by (12) either $message(x, k + 1, y)$ holds true or $distgraph(x, k', v)$ holds true for some $v \in A$ and $k' \le k + 1 \le n + 1$. In the latter case we are finished; in the first case (19) implies that eventually $distgraph(x. k, v)$ will hold true for some $v \in A$ and $k \le n + 1$, which proves $\Diamond \exists k \in \mathbb{N}. v \in A : k \le n + 1 \wedge distgraph(x, k. v)$

Altogether, we have shown that the Petri net model of the minimal spanning tree algorithm from Fig. 3 satisfies properties (1)–(5) from the specification.

4 Conclusion

This paper demonstrates by help of an example how algebraic Petri nets can be used for modelling and verification of distributed algorithms. For lack of space we could only sketch the used proof techniques; still the proof should provide a flavour of our method. In essence the basic technique for deriving simple temporal properties is to verify the validity of some state formulas which are derived from the structure of the net and the verified formula: equations for place invariants, simple implications for siphons and traps, and some more complex implications for assertions. Though not completely explained here, even the pick up rule for leadsto properties can be reduced to checking the validity of some state formulas. For combining temporal formulas in order to verify more complex properties we mainly use standard rules: weakening of invariants, PSP-rule and proof graphs for liveness properties.

A formal presentation of this method is beyond the scope of this paper. A formal presentation of algebraic nets as used in this paper can be found in [3]; more information about the verification techniques and some more interesting examples can be found in [4, 8].

References

1. Manfred Broy. On the design and verification of a simple distributed spanning tree algorithm. SFB-Bericht 342/24/90 A, Technische Universtität München, December 1990.
2. K. M. Chandy and J. Misra. *Parallel Program Design: A Foundation.* Addison-Wesley, 1988.
3. Ekkart Kindler and Wolfgang Reisig. Algebraic system nets for modelling distributed algorithms. *Petri Net Newsletter*, 51:16–31, December 1996.
4. Ekkart Kindler, Wolfgang Reisig, Hagen Völzer, and Rolf Walter. Petri net based verification of distributed algorithms: An example. Informatik-Berichte 63, Humboldt-Universität zu Berlin, May 1996.
5. Susan Owicki and Leslie Lamport. Proving liveness properties of concurrent programs. *ACM Transactions on Programming Languages and Systems*, 4(3):455–495, July 1982.
6. Wolfgang Reisig. Petri nets and algebraic specifications. *Theoretical Computer Science*, 80:1–34, May 1991.
7. Wolfgang Reisig. *Distributed Algorithms — Modelling and Analysis with Petri Nets.* In preparation, 1997.
8. R. Walter, H. Völzer, T. Vesper, W. Reisig, E. Kindler, J. Freiheit, and J. Desel. Memorandum: Petrinetzmodelle zur Verifikation verteilter Algorithmen. Informatik-Bericht 67, Humboldt-Universität zu Berlin, July 1996.
9. J. Welch, L. Lamport, and N. Lynch. A lattice-structured proof technique applied to a minimal spanning tree algorithm. In *Proc. 7th ACM Symposium on Principles of Programming Languages*, 1988.

A Short Story on Action Refinement

Walter Vogler

Institut für Informatik, Universität Augsburg
D-86135 Augsburg, Germany

Abstract

This note presents a meaningful example – concerning a communication
protocol – how congruence results for action refinement should be applied.

1 Introduction

The operation of action refinement is meant to support the hierarchical construction of concurrent systems. In recent years, it has found considerable interest, see e.g. [BGV91, Gor91, Vog92, Ren93, Jat93] and the references therein. Contributions usually consist of congruence results, i.e. an equivalence is defined and for coarse system descriptions it is shown: if two such descriptions are equivalent and both are refined in the same way, then the resulting detailed system descriptions are equivalent again. Sometimes, this is complemented by showing full abstractness, i.e. by showing that the presented equivalence makes just the necessary distinctions in order to be a congruence and to respect some basic equivalence. For example, interval-semiword equivalence is the coarsest congruence that respects language equivalence, see [BGV91, Vog92]; this result is a justification for taking the trouble of using partial order semantics.

What is missing, to the knowledge of the author, is an application of these results. (Some first experiments were conducted in the unpublished [GG91].) The purpose of this note is to present a meaningful example how these results should be used.

The example is concerned with a coarse system which is refined and combined via parallel composition and hiding with a communication device; this leads to a correct implementation where correctness is based on the language for simplicity. Next the coarse system is slightly modified for reasons of elegance; even when taking into account concurrency, this modification seems innocent since it leads to a step-sequence equivalent system. But refining and composing the modified system in the same way as before leads to an incorrect implementation.

The story teaches that such a modification should preserve interval semiwords - which is of course not the case in the example. If the coarse systems are interval-semiword equivalent, application of the same action refinement gives language equivalent systems and, since parallel composition and hiding preserve language equivalence, the construction leads to language equivalent implementations. Hence, if the first implementation is correct, the modified implementation is correct, too.

The next section sketches some notions and results about Petri nets, our system models, including the relevant equivalences and operations for Petri nets. Section 3 tells the sad story.

2 Nets, equivalences and operations

We assume the reader to have some acquaintance with Petri nets in order to keep this note short, see e.g. [Rei85] or – for interval semiwords in particular – [Vog92]. Notions that should be known are pre- and postset, safe net, firing sequence, step sequence and preferably S-invariants and processes.

We use finite S/T-nets $N = (S, T, F, l, M_N)$ and assume that all nets are safe, do not have isolated transitions and only have arcs of weight 1; l labels the transitions with *actions* from some infinite alphabet Σ or with the empty word λ, indicating internal, unobservable actions. For $w \in T^*$, we obtain $l(w)$ by replacing each transition by the action it is labelled by, which automatically deletes the internal actions; if w is a firing sequence, we call $l(w)$ a *trace*. The set of traces is the *language* of N, and two nets are *language equivalent* if they have the same traces. Similarly, step sequences give rise to *step traces*, where again internal actions have to be deleted, just as those steps that become empty when deleting internal actions. Nets are *step equivalent* if they have the same step traces.

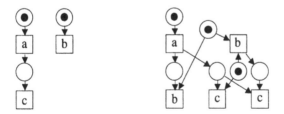

Figure 1: step, but not interval-semiword equivalent nets

For example, the nets in Figure 1 are step equivalent (and hence language equivalent). To see this, consider first a behaviour of the net on the right where the upper b occurs; this disables the c on the left, giving essentially the step trace $\binom{a}{b}c$. Similarly, the lower b leads to $a\binom{b}{c}$.

Partial order semantics based on processes or e.g. interval semiwords show that only the net on the left can do b while a followed by c is performed; hence, such a semantics distinguishes the two nets shown – and this is really all one has to know about interval semiwords. Nevertheless, here is a short explanation how interval semiwords can be constructed from processes: consider the transition-labelled events of a process and the partial order induced on them; replace the transitions in the labels by the respective actions and delete internal events; increase the ordering of the remaining events arbitrarily such that you still have a partial order. Results of this construction are called *partial words* or *semiwords*; they were originally defined independently of processes in [Gra81, Sta81]. A semiword is an *interval semiword* if its partial order is a so-called interval order, where unorderedness corresponds to overlapping real intervals. E.g. in the run described at the beginning of this paragraph, the interval of b overlaps with both, the intervals of a and c, which are in sequence. Nets are *interval-semiword equivalent* if they have the same interval semiwords.

An important operation for the bottom-up construction of a system from its components is *parallel composition* $\|_A$ inspired from TCSP, where $A \subseteq \Sigma$. If we combine nets with $\|_A$, then they run in parallel and have to synchronize on actions from A. To construct $N_1 \|_A N_2$, we take the disjoint union of N_1 and N_2, combine each a-labelled transition t_1 of N_1 with each a-labelled transition t_2 from N_2 if $a \in A$ (i.e. introduce a new a-labelled transition (t_1, t_2) that inherits all arcs from t_1 and t_2), and delete all the original a-labelled transitions in N_1 and N_2 if $a \in A$. Another useful operation is *hiding*, where N/A is obtained from N by changing all transition labels in A to the unobservable λ.

Action refinement is meant to support the top-down construction of systems. An *action refinement* is a function *ref* that assigns to each observable action a refinement net, which describes the low-level activities in the respective high-level action. Such a net has to satisfy certain conditions given in [BGV91, Vog92]; we will use only one refinement, which splits some actions into sequences and leaves all other actions untouched. In particular, a refinement net has a special place *idle* representing the environment; the transitions in its postset are called start transitions, those in its preset are called end transitions. When applying *ref* to a net N, each a-labelled transition t is replaced by a copy of $ref(a)$, where the preset of t is added to the preset of each start transition and the postset of t is added to the postset of each end transition. The effect is that, if t is enabled in N, then the start transitions corresponding to t are enabled in $ref(N)$; when firing a transition sequence of the inserted net, beginning with a start transition and finishing with an end transition, the overall effect on the places of N is the same as that of firing t.

It is desirable that the semantics and the operations one uses are compatible in the sense of the following results.

Theorem 1 *Language equivalence is a congruence for parallel composition, i.e. for $A \subseteq \Sigma$, a net N and language equivalent nets N_1 and N_2, $N_1\|_A N$ and $N_2\|_A N$ are language equivalent again. Similarly, language equivalence is a congruence for hiding.*

Furthermore, interval-semiword equivalence is a congruence for parallel composition and hiding.

Theorem 2   • *Interval-semiword equivalence is a congruence for action refinement, i.e. for an action refinement ref and interval-semiword equivalent nets N_1 and N_2, ref(N_1) and ref(N_2) are interval-semiword equivalent
again.*

• *Interval-semiword equivalence is fully abstract w.r.t. language equivalence
and action refinement, i.e. it is the coarsest congruence for action refinement that implies language equivalence.*

The last part of this theorem says in particular that language equivalence is
not a congruence for action refinement – compare the above example –, but has
to be refined to become one.

In the next section, some nets will be defined by drawings, which will use
some high-level net notation as abbreviation for S/T-nets. In this notation, we
have variables i, j, k and x with values in $\{0,1\}$; e.g. the transition labelled
set(i) in Figure 3 corresponds to two transitions with the same pre- and postset
performing the actions *set(0)* and *set(1)*. A place s having labelled arcs as in
Figure 4 abbreviates two places s_0 and s_1 – with s_0 being marked initially in
Figure 4; here, a transition labelled *set(i)* stands for 4 transitions, which remove
the token from s_0 or s_1 (corresponding to the x-arc) and mark s_i (corresponding
to the i-arc). In the same way, the net in Figure 2 has 7 actions *compute(0,0,1)*,
compute(0,1,0) etc.; *send(j)* and *send(k)* really have the same meaning as *send(i)*,
but are used to ease the comparison with Figure 1.

3   The story

Once upon a time, a system was to be designed which had to compute three
values $i, j, k \in \{0, 1\}$, not all 0, and to evaluate them in some way in which the
order of these values did not matter. Computation and evaluation were to be
performed on different components of the system. Now it turned out that there
was enough money for two, but not for three communication channels, so the
high-level engineer (*he*) – when designing a rough description of the system –
decided that the first component should not try to send three values in parallel,
but at most two. He concluded that either one *send* had to be performed first,
followed by the other two in parallel, or two *sends* in parallel before the third
one. Consequently, he presented the coarse system N_1 shown in Figure 2.

He left the task of implementing communication to his subordinate, the *sub-
high-level engineer (she)*[1]; her ideas were as follows. To use the channels in
practice, some protocol had to be obeyed: instead of performing *send(i)*, the
sender had to write the message i into a shared variable with *set(i)*, then send a
ready signal (*sready*) and finally wait for the reception of an acknowledgement
rack; call this a send-sequence. Vice versa, *receive(i)* had to be replaced by the

---

[1]The title 'low-level engineer' would have been regarded as discriminating.

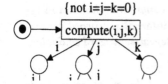 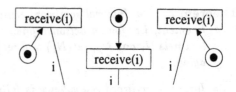

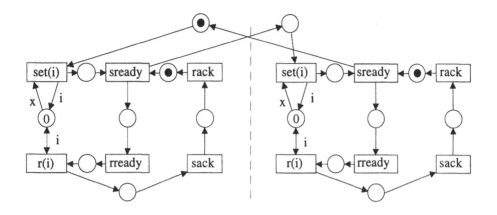

Figure 4: the channel component C

sack rack are performed – one on each channel – and, according to N_1, only after both have ended another send-sequence can start. Therefore, on each channel one *set(i)* and the corresponding *r(i)* occur, i.e. both values are transmitted successfully. As mentioned above, a possible complication is that a receive-sequence may perform *rready* on one channel and *r(i)* on the other. But in this case, *set(i) rready* was performed on the latter channel, too; hence, a correct value is read. After the two *racks*, C returns to its initial state – except that possibly the values of the shared variables have changed.

He was not really convinced by this argument[2], but did not want to bother about these low-level considerations. Instead, the language of Impl_1 was checked with some flashy tool[3] and turned out to be correct: it essentially consists of sequences *compute(i,j,k) evaluate(i',j',k')* with the multisets $\{i, j, k\}$ and $\{i', j', k'\}$ being equal and not $\{0, 0, 0\}$; in particular, *error* cannot occur. Furthermore, there is never a deadlock after *compute(i,j,k)*.

Everything would have been fine, had he not looked at N_1 again before the system was actually built. Suddenly, he saw a much more elegant design than the clumsy N_1, namely N_2 shown in Figure 5.

Surely, N_2 also uses at most two channels in parallel. Now he had heard rumours that action refinement was somehow related to concurrency – so, to be on the safe side, he checked that N_1 and N_2 are indeed step-sequence equivalent; compare with the nets in Figure 1. And so $\text{Impl}_2 = (ref(N_2)\|_I C)/I$ was built.

It turned out to be erroneous; let us ignore the hiding in order to see what is going on: Impl_2 can perform *compute(0,1,0)* and *set(1) sready* (corresponding to *send(j)* in Figure 5) on the first channel; next a complete cycle is performed

---

[2]'Female logic', he muttered, but was luckily not heard by anybody.
[3]Beautiful spot for some product placement, anybody interested?

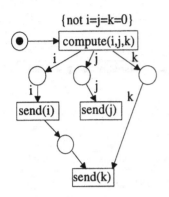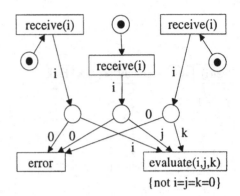

Figure 5: the net N_2

on the second channel, i.e. *set(0) sready rready r(0) sack rack*; then, *set(0)* writes 0 into the first shared variable before the value 1 is read. The run ends with *rready r(0) sack rack sready rready r(0) sack rack error*.

You know, dear reader, that he should have checked N_1 and N_2 for being interval-semiword equivalent; since they are not (compare Section 2), he should have expected some trouble when exchanging N_1 and N_2. On the other hand, if we have some N_3 interval-semiword equivalent to N_1, we could conclude from Theorem 2 that $ref(N_1)$ and $ref(N_3)$ are language equivalent; then Theorem 1 implies that $Impl_1$ and $Impl_3 = (ref(N_3) \|_I C)/I$ are also language equivalent.

It may be worth pointing out two things: First, in $Impl_1$ *rready* and *r(i)* corresponding to the same *receive(i)* in N_1 may synchronize with actions *rready* and *r(i)* from different channels in C; this is somewhat counterintuitive and it may be a good idea to consider an alternative definition of action refinement and/or parallel composition to avoid this effect, see e.g. [Huh96] for an alternative definition of action refinement and also [GG91]. But the problem in $Impl_2$ is independent of this; it arises from two concurrent uses of the same channel in C – which is not possible in $Impl_1$.

Second, in this story correctness was merely based on the language for simplicity; one could also take into account the absence of deadlocks using the *iw $\mathcal{F}$*-semantics of [Vog92] instead of interval semiwords.

References

[BGV91] W. Brauer, R. Gold, and W. Vogler. A survey of behaviour and equivalence preserving refinement of Petri nets. In G. Rozenberg, editor, *Advances in Petri Nets 1990*, Lect. Notes Comp. Sci. 483, 1–46. Springer, 1991.

[GG91] U. Goltz and N. Götz. Modelling a simple communication protocol in a language with action refinement, 1991. Unpublished manuscript.

[Gor91] R. Gorrieri. *Refinement, atomicity and transactions for process description languages.* PhD thesis, Dipartimento di Informatica, Università di Pisa, 1991. Available as Technical Report TD 2/91.

[Gra81] J. Grabowski. On partial languages. *Fundamenta Informaticae*, IV.2:428–498, 1981.

[Huh96] M. Huhn. Action refinement and property inheritance in systems of sequential agents. In U. Montanari and V. Sassone, editors, *CONCUR '96*, Lect. Notes Comp. Sci. 1119, 639–654. Springer, 1996.

[Jat93] L.A. Jategaonkar. *Observing 'True' Concurrency.* PhD thesis, Laboratory for Computer Science, MIT, 1993.

[Rei85] W. Reisig. *Petri Nets.* EATCS Monographs on Theoretical Computer Science 4. Springer, 1985.

[Ren93] A. Rensink. *Models and Methods for Action Refinement.* PhD thesis, Faculteit der Informatica, Universiteit Twente, 1993.

[Sta81] P.H. Starke. Processes in Petri nets. *J. Inf. Process. Cybern. EIK*, 17:389–416, 1981.

[Vog92] W. Vogler. *Modular Construction and Partial Order Semantics of Petri Nets.* Lect. Notes Comp. Sci. 625. Springer, 1992.

Interactive and Reactive Systems:

States, Observations, Experiments, Input, Output, Nondeterminism, Compositionality and all That*

(Extended Abstract)

Manfred Broy
Institut für Informatik
Technische Universität München
80290 München

Abstract

In this paper, we discuss, analyse, relate, and investigate the basic notions of state, action, experiment, and observation and their importance for questions of compositionality as they appear in reactive systems. In particular, we discuss the concept and role of input and output as well as that of nondeterminism for the mathematical modelling of system behaviours. We argue that for a given state transition system with composition operators there exists a canonical notion of nondeterminism as well as of input and output and that these notions are helpful in the search for modular semantic models.

1. Introduction

The study of mathematical models of reactive and interactive systems and of their distributed interacting components in terms of experiments and observations is fruitful for the semantic analysis of hardware and software systems. In an experimental setting the behaviour of a distributed system is described by the experiments that we can perform with the system and the observations we can make about the it by such experiments. However, in most of such scenarios of experiments and observations, there does not exist a clear explicit distinction between

- the *action* of the experimenter as an *active* step in performing an experiment, which we consider as input to the observed system,
- the *observation* of the experimenter as a *passive* step in performing an experiment, which we consider as output of the observed system.

We interpret the selection of the individual actions by the experimenter as the *input* to the system under our analysis and the observations are understood by us as recording the *output* by the system.

For a practical use in systems engineering, such very general, operational system models are not very useful. What we need is more structure than provided by a huge

---

*) This work was partially sponsored by the Sonderforschungsbereich 342 "Werkzeuge und Methoden für die Nutzung paralleler Rechnerarchitekturen" and the industrial research project SysLab sponsored by Siemens Nixdorf and by DFG under the Leibniz programme.

state transition system. Such structure allows us to deal with complex systems in a modular way. More structure can be imposed on state transition systems by using the concepts of

- experiments and observations,
- composition operators.

Composition operators allow us to compose large systems from given ones which we then call the *components* of the system. Experiments that are supposed to lead to observations about composed systems can be carried out with the help of corresponding experiments providing observations about the components.

In the following we show how to choose a notion of nondeterminism and its dependency on the choice of the notion of input and output. Given composition operators we can try to choose a notion of nondeterminism that allows us to see nondeterministic systems as sets of deterministic systems.

2. Nondeterminism in Transition Systems

In this section we introduce the concept of transition systems and classify the notion of nondeterminism for them. A *labelled state transition system* (also called a *state machine* or *state automaton*) is represented by a quadruple

$$M = (S, A, \rightarrow, T)$$

where

- S is a set of *states*,
- A is a set of *actions*,
- $\rightarrow \subseteq S \times A \times S$ is a *transition relation* (a relation on states for each action),
- $T \subseteq S$ (where $T \neq \emptyset$) is called the *initial state set*.

Using currying we describe the transition relation $\rightarrow$ as a family of relations

$$\xrightarrow{a} \in S \times S,$$

one for each action $a \in A$. It is common and convenient to write transitions in the form

$$\sigma \xrightarrow{a} \sigma'$$

This is a logical proposition that stands for $(\sigma, a, \sigma') \in \rightarrow$. This proposition expresses that in the state σ the considered system may perform (is ready to do or to accept) the action a and then (after having done the action a) be in the state σ'. In other words: for a transition $\sigma \xrightarrow{a} \sigma'$ the explanation

"in the state σ the system can perform the action a and then get into the state σ'"

can be given as well as the explanation

"in the state σ the system is ready to accept the action a and to get into the state σ'".

The two explanations[1] lead to different views of a system: in the first view the system is understood as an active unit that freely decides which action it performs next ("actions are output of the system"), in the second view it is a unit that is a slave of the environment.

By enabled$_M(\sigma)$ we denote the set of actions of the machine M that are enabled in state σ.

3. Abstractions for State Transition Systems

In this section we study observations that we can make about state transition systems. Restricted concepts of observations lead to specific abstractions. There are several notions of observation for state transition systems. We treat only two prominent examples.

A very basic notion of observations are sets of traces. Traces are finite and infinite sequences of actions and states. Let A be an arbitrary set. By A* we denote the set of finite sequences over the set A, by A^∞ we denote the set of infinite sequences over A (total mappings from $\mathbb{N}$ to A). By A^ω we denote the set of finite and infinite sequences (called *streams*) over the set A. Formally we define

$$A^\omega = A^* \cup A^\omega$$

We introduce the function

$$\text{ct}: S \rightarrow \wp(A^\omega)$$

that associates with every state $\sigma \in S$ its set ct.σ of complete[2] action traces (note that we consider finite and infinite sequences of actions as traces). We call two states *trace equivalent*, if their trace sets coincide. Two state machines are trace equivalent if their initial states are trace equivalent.

As well-known, the set of complete traces for the states (or similarly the set of traces for a given set of states) does not reflect all the properties of a state transition system that are reflected for instance by abstract synchronisation trees, in general. Finer equivalence relations than trace equivalence that also reflect the choice structure of state transition systems are *bisimulation relations* as suggested by Park. If an equivalence relation defines a *bisimulation* in the sense of Milner (cf. [Milner 85]), we call two state transition systems *bisimulation equivalent*, if their initial states are bisimulation equivalent.

4. Input and Output in State Transition Systems

For a state transition system it is left unspecified, in general, whether actions occurring as labels in the transitions are to be understood as input or as output. A classification of actions as input or output, however, strongly influences the interpretation of system actions and our understanding of the system and our notion of nondeterminism.

---

[1] These two different views are well known in formal languages: we say that an automaton generates a language or that it accepts a language.

[2] An action trace is called complete it is infinite or it ends with a state in which no action is enabled.

4.1 Actions as Output

If we consider actions always as output, we get a very restricted notion of a deterministic state transition system. Then we assume that we cannot influence the choice of the actions in a computation. Consequently, a state transition system where all actions are considered as output is called *nondeterministic*, if for some state σ there exist distinct pairs (a_1, σ_1) and (a_2, σ_2) of actions and states such that we have

$$\sigma \xrightarrow{a_1} \sigma_1 \wedge \sigma \xrightarrow{a_2} \sigma_2.$$

A classical example for deterministic systems where the choices of actions cannot be influenced by the environment (via input) are deterministic sequential programs that start their computations in some fixed initial state and take no further input.

4.2 Actions as Input

Another extreme is to consider all its actions as input. This way a transition of the system is viewed as a machine the transitions of which are controlled by the experimenter by offering actions a in state σ. Then the system performs a step accepting the action a and going into some state σ', provided the proposition

$$\sigma \xrightarrow{a} \sigma'$$

holds or it may refuse the action a, if there does not exist such a state σ'. In such a scenario the experimenter decides about the choice of the action a and the system only reacts to her choices.

When all actions are considered as input a system is called *nondeterministic*, if for a (reachable) state σ there exists an action a and distinct (and even non-bisimulation equivalent) states σ_1 and σ_2 such that

$$\sigma \xrightarrow{a} \sigma_1 \wedge \sigma \xrightarrow{a} \sigma_2.$$

In particular, a system is called nondeterministic (under the assumption that all actions are being considered as input), if we have

$$\sigma_0 \xrightarrow{a} \sigma_1 \wedge \sigma_0 \xrightarrow{a} \sigma_2$$

and in state σ_1 a certain action b is accepted while in state σ_2 it is rejected.

A simple example of a system where all actions are input is a pocket calculator. All actions are chosen by the experimenter, the calculator only carries out the state changes.

4.3 Partitioning the Action Set into Input and Output

Both views onto actions as input and output in state transition systems introduced above just represent two extremes of a broad spectrum of possible interpretations of the actions of the state transition system as input or output. In general, it is not appropriate to consider all actions of a system as being input or to consider all its actions as output. A simple and more flexible approach considers certain actions as input and other actions as output (see the I/O-machines of [Lynch, Stark 89]).

A transition system $M = (S, A, \rightarrow, T)$ with a split $A = I \cup O$ of the action set A into a set of input actions I and a set of output actions O with $I \cap O = \emptyset$ is called *input enabled*, if for all states $\sigma \in S$ (for details see [Lynch, Stark 89]) we have:

$$I \subseteq \text{enabled}_M(\sigma)$$

According to this definition the state transition system is input enabled, if input actions are always (in all states) enabled.

It is characteristic for the notion of input that a system cannot influence its input, but only react to it. We express this requirement formally for state transition systems by adding a fresh state • called failure to the state space of the transition system and define

$$\sigma \xrightarrow{a} \bullet \qquad\qquad \text{for all } a \in I \setminus \text{enabled}_M(\sigma),$$

We specify that in the failure state all actions are enabled and lead to the failure state again. So we have

$$\bullet \xrightarrow{a} \bullet \qquad\qquad \text{for all } a \in A.$$

In other words, the failure state is stable for all input and output actions. Then the state transition

$$\sigma \xrightarrow{a} \bullet$$

expresses that the action a is rejected[3] in state σ. Our notion of nondeterminism then is obvious: a system is nondeterministic if it contains a reachable state in which two different output actions are enabled.

4.4 Decomposing Actions into Input and Output

In this section we consider the decomposition of single actions into an input and an output part. We assume that we can decompose every action uniquely into two parts: the part that can be determined exclusively by the system and the part that can be influenced exclusively by the environment. We assume sets B and C of input actions and output actions respectively, and a bijective function that maps the input actions and the output actions onto the composed actions:

$$\text{act: } B \times C \rightarrow A.$$

For each action $a \in A$ where $a = \text{act}(b, c)$ the element b denotes that part of the action a that is the input to the system and is determined exclusively by the environment and c denotes that part that is the output and can be determined exclusively by the system. We assume that the action a is uniquely determined by the actions b and c and vice versa.

The decomposition of the actions is called *adequate*, if for every state σ and every input action $b \in B$ there exists some output $c \in C$ and some state σ' such that:

$$\sigma \xrightarrow{\text{act}(b, c)} \sigma'$$

---

[3] Another way to look at a transition that leads into the failure state is to say that the input of action a (the experiment a) leads to *chaos*.

This is equivalent to the requirement of input enabledness expressed by

$$\forall \sigma, b: \exists c: \text{enabled}_M(\sigma) \cap \text{act}(b, c) \neq \varnothing.$$

According to this definition, adequacy corresponds to the generalisation of input enabledness to actions that are composed of input and output.

5. Nondeterministic Systems as Sets of Deterministic Systems

So far, there seems to be a lot of freedom for defining a notion of nondeterminism and the idea of input for state transition systems. This changes radically if we introduce composition operators and demand that the composition of nondeterministic state machines can be reduced to composition of the sets of all their deterministic descendants.

5.1 Descendants

Given a state machine $M = (S, A, \rightarrow, T)$ a state machine $M' = (S', A', \rightarrow', T')$ is called a *descendant* of M (see [Kennaway 81]) and we write

$$M' \text{ Æ } M$$

if we have $S' \subseteq S$ and $A' \subseteq A$, $T' \subseteq T$ and $\rightarrow' \subseteq \rightarrow$. A descendant has a smaller set of states, less actions and less transitions. The notion of a descendant is closely related to the notion of refinement as it is used in system development.

By $\Re$ we denote a set of state machines that are input enabled according to some fixed notion of input and output. Obviously Æ defines a partial ordering on $\Re$.

We take the disjoint union over a set $\Im \subseteq \Re$ of state machines with the same action sets and state spaces by taking the union over all state spaces (making them disjoint before), the union over all transition relations and the union over the set of initial states and write $\uplus \Im$. The resulting state machine is, in general, highly nondeterministic and shows all computations that are computations of one of the state machines in $\Im$.

5.2 Composition Operators

A composition operator is a mapping

$$\rho: \Re \times \Re \rightarrow \Re.$$

where for any two state machines $M_1, M_2 \in \Re$ with $M_i = (S_i, A_i, \rightarrow_i, T_i)$ the composed state machine is $M = M_1 \rho M_2$ has $S_1 \times S_2$ as its state space and $T_1 \times T_2$ as its initial states. We could allow more sophisticated forms of composition where the state space contains additional information such as buffered communication messages but we rather keep the idea of composition more simple.

In the following we assume a set of such operators. We think about an operator as providing a context for a state machine that controls its input and output.

5.3 Nondeterminism

We may fix a notion of nondeterminism for the set $\mathfrak{R}$ of state machines by establishing a predicate

$$\det: \mathfrak{R} \to \mathbb{B}$$

that determines which state machine is deterministic.

Given a set of composition operators we call a notion of nondeterminism *adequate*, if the following propositions are valid:

- minimality: the state machines $M \in \mathfrak{R}$ with $\det(M)$ are exactly the minimal elements with respect to the descendent relation Æ,

- additivity: every state machine $M \in \mathfrak{R}$ is the union over its deterministic descendants:

$$M = \uplus \ \{N \ \text{Æ} \ M: \det(N)\}$$

- compositionality: given state machines M_i, where $i = 1, 2$, for each of the composition operators ρ, the following equation holds:

$$M_1 \rho M_2 = \uplus \ \{M_1' \rho M_2': M_1' \ \text{Æ} \ M_1 \wedge M_2' \ \text{Æ} \ M_2 \wedge \det(M_1') \wedge \det(M_2')\}.$$

We define a partial order on the notions of nondeterminism as follows. Given two notions of nondeterminism

$$\det_1, \det_2: \mathfrak{R} \to \mathbb{B}$$

the notion $\det_1$ is called *finer* than the notion $\det_2$, if $\det_1(M) \Rightarrow \det_2(M)$ for all state machines M. Then a state machine that is deterministic according to $\det_1$ is so according to $\det_2$, too.

We obtain a canonical notion of nondeterminism as follows: the notion should be adequate and as fine as possible. The reason is as follows: we should always consider alternatives of a behaviour as nondeterministic, if we cannot understand them as determined by input. The composition operators enforce that the nondeterminism is chosen such that compositionality is guaranteed. This keeps us from choosing the nondeterminism too fine.

6. Conclusion

If the idea of experiment and observation is chosen appropriately then the behaviour of systems constructed by particular composition operators can be defined in terms of the experiments and observations of the components. Every concept of experiment and observation also fixes a notion of nondeterminism. Furthermore for notions of refinements a clear concept of a deterministic behaviour is essential. In refinements we may start from a highly nondeterministic machine and replace it step by step by more deterministic descendants.

A modular (compositional) semantic model for distributed systems is one of the essential goals of a theoretical foundation of distributed systems. In particular, it is interesting to study

- nondeterminism,

- input/output-oriented views of systems,
- compositional semantic models

within one conceptual framework.

With this understanding of an adequate notion of nondeterminism with respect to composition operators there are two simple principles that allow us to find the appropriate classification of nondeterminism and input in algebras of state transition systems describing reactive systems:

- input enabledness: for every input there exist a behaviour (input must not be constrained by a system such that for certain input no behaviour is possible),
- the notion of nondeterminism is chosen as fine as possible with respect to the composition operators such that components and composition operators can be defined in terms of the deterministic descendants.

Whether we call the behaviour of a machine starting in a given state nondeterministic obviously depends strongly on the question whether the choice of an action can be influenced by the environment or not. In the most general case the choice of an action can be influenced to some extend by the environment.

For practical purposes, however, the potentials of specification techniques obtained that way are more important. An appropriate semantic model of a state transition system reflects nondeterminism in a canonical way. A nondeterministic behaviour is represented then by the set of its deterministic descendants. This allows us to see nondeterminism as a simple extension of models for the behaviour deterministic systems to sets of such behaviours.

References

[Broy et. al. 91]
M. Broy, F. Dederichs, C. Dendorfer, R. Weber: Characterizing the Behaviour of Reactive Systems by Trace Sets. Technische Universität München, Institut für Informatik, TUM-I9102, February 1991

[Kennaway 81]
J. R. Kennaway: Formal Semantics of Nondeterminism and Parallelism. Ph. D. Thesis, St. John's College, Oxford University 1981

[Lynch, Stark 89]
N. Lynch, E. Stark: A Proof of the Kahn Principle for Input/Output Automata. Information and Computation 82, 1989, pp. 81-92

[Milner 85]
R. Milner: Lectures on a Calculus for Communicating Systems. In: M. Broy (ed.): Control Flow and Data Flow: Concepts of Distributed Programming. NATO ASI Series, Series F: Computer and System Sciences, Vol. 14, Springer 1985, 205 – 228

Discrete Time Analysis of a State Dependent Tandem with Different Customer Types

Hans Daduna

FB Mathematik, Institut für Mathematische Stochastik,
Universität Hamburg, Bundes-Straße 55, 20146 Hamburg

Abstract. We consider a discrete time model for a transmission line in a meshed network of stations. The line is fed by a state dependent arrival stream of customers of different types. The service regime at the nodes is FCFS with state dependent probabilities. The stationary distribution for the joint queue lengths of the line is of product form. We derive expressions for loss probabilities, end–to–end–delay distribution, and throughput.
Key Words: Bernoulli servers, arrival theorem, joint sojourn times vector, throughput, loss probabilities, state dependent queues, steady state.

1 Introduction and description of the model

Interest in discrete time queueing systems renewed during the last years because of the introduction of ATM protocols for high speed networks. The need of predicting quality of service (e.g. loss probabilities, delay times) for high speed networks resulted in modeling processes using discrete time queueing networks. This class of models turned out to be adequate for several aspects in performance evaluation of communication networks, because the ATM protocols prescribe on the cell and burst level an inherent discrete time scale for the system.

Surveys on discrete time queueing systems are the books [2], [10] (single server systems), and [11] (introductory course), and special issues of PERFORMANCE EVALUATION (21), 1994: *Discrete time models and analysis methods*, and QUEUEING SYSTEMS AND THEIR APPLICATIONS (18), 1994: *Advances in discrete time queues*. With emphasis on networks having product form equilibria is [4].

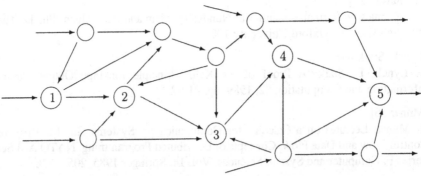

Figure 1: Virtual channel with $J = 5$ nodes in a meshed network

We consider a virtual channel in a meshed network, i.e., a transmission line prescribed for a specific connection (see figure 1). The network is operating on a discrete time scale which is always assumed to be $I\!N = \{0, 1, 2, \ldots\}$. The nodes of the line represent the transmission channels; they are numbered 1 through J. Calls of different types arrive at node 1 according to a state dependent random process and pass the nodes in increasing order.

The calls are divided into cells of fixed (equal) length. Cells are transmitted according to a First–Come–First–Served (FCFS) regime one by one through the successive transmission channels. The time for transmitting one cell through a channel constitutes the inherent discrete time scale of the system: Transmission of a cell needs exactly one time unit. Therefore inside the transmission line of nodes $1, \ldots, J$ no queues would built up if the line is used only by the cells arriving at node 1, which are henceforth called regular cells. Delay and queueing are due to the external traffic from the rest of the network which partly interferes with the regular cells at the nodes of the line. We incorporate the effect of this background traffic (similar to the *principle of adjusted transfer rates* for continuous time systems, see [9], and [7]) into the model as follows:

In a first step the background traffic originating from the rest of the network that arrives at node j is bundled into one stream of background cells for j, which interferes here with the regular cells from the virtual channel and thereafter leaves the line directly, $j = 1, \ldots, J$.

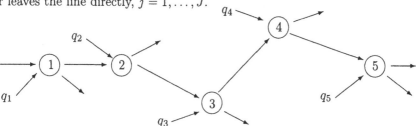

Figure 2: The virtual channel with bundled background traffic

Therefore a regular cell on its arrival at node j will possibly find there a queue of random length of other regular cells and of cells from the background traffic. ¿From the point of view of regular cells they have to share the total capacity of the nodes (one cell per time unit) with the cells of the background traffic. If the intensity (= *mean number of arrivals*) of the background traffic at node j is $q_j \in [0, 1)$, then the capacity of node j dedicated to regular cells is $p_j := 1 - q_j$ cells per time unit.

In a second step the load of the background traffic on node j is locally incorporated into the model by reducing the capacity of node j to p_j cells per time unit, and thereafter neglecting the rest of the network outside of the virtual channel. This yields a linear network of nodes $1, \ldots, J$ with regular cells only (see figure 3).

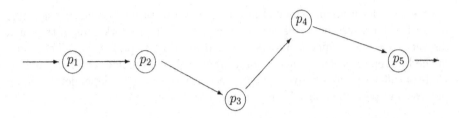

Figure 3: The virtual channel as a simple line with reduced capacities

Our model of interest (see figure 3) is therefore a transmission line of nodes 1 through J, where the capacity of node j is reduced from one cell per time unit to p_j cells per time unit, $0 < p_j \leq 1$. This is equivalent to having a mean transmission time of $1/p_j \geq 1$ at node j. The randomness of the background traffic is incorporated into the model by assuming geometrically distributed transmission times with exactly these means. It follows: A (regular) cell in transmission at the beginning of a time unit at station j will be completely transmitted at the end of this time unit with probability p_j, with probability $1 - p_j$ the transmission will need at least one more time unit.

We want to provide explicit expressions for the following optimization problem: Suppose the regular cells arrive in a Bernoulli stream of intensity $B \in (0,1]$ at station 1. Then find a control $\beta : \mathbb{N} \longrightarrow [0,1]$, $n \longrightarrow \beta(n)$, which determines a state dependent Bernoulli switch at the entrance point of the line: If the total load of the line is n (= sum of all queue lengths in the line), an arriving cell will be admitted with probability $\beta(n)$, with probability $1 - \beta(n)$ it will be rejected and is therefore lost. The arrival probability is then $b(n) = B \cdot \beta(n)$. The control is to be chosen such that

(a) for a prescribed (small) probability $\gamma \in (0,1)$ the loss probability of a cell is less than γ;

(b) for a prescribed (large) probability $\alpha \in (0,1)$ and a critical transmission time t_0 the probability that transmission of a cell is performed within time t_0 is greater than α;

(c) the throughput is maximal given constraints (a) and (b).

Clearly, the requirement of (a), (b) is antagonistic to (c). While (a) and (b) are main measures for the quality of service (customer oriented performance) in high speed networks, (c) is a system oriented performance measure.

Having explicit expressions for (a), (b), and (c) at hand would therefore open firstly the possibility of predicting the quality of service, and secondly to optimize systems in the planning process.

In our model the control of the system is twofold:

(i) The probability of terminating at node j a cell's transmission at the end of the present time unit may depend on the actual load $n_j > 0$ of that node (*queue length at node j*), $p_j = p_j(n_j), j = 1, \ldots, J$, and

(ii) the probability $b \in [0, 1]$ of a new arrival at node 1 at the end of the present time unit may depend on the total load n of the system ($n = n_1 + \ldots + n_J$, the *total population size of the line*), $b = b(n)$, and on the type of the customer as will be specified below.

Such control includes as an extreme case the classical window flow control, see [9], or loss systems. The introduction of different cell types offers versatile modeling features, e.g. for keeping trace of individual cells' behaviour and computing type dependent loss probabilities.

We define empty products to be 1 and empty sums to be 0, and
$[a \neq b] = 1 \quad if \quad a \neq b, [a \neq b] = 0 \quad if \quad a = b.$
Details of the proofs which are skipped here can be found in [5].

2 Open tandem systems

We consider a tandem system of state–dependent Bernoulli servers under FCFS queueing regime with unlimited waiting room. The nodes are numbered $1, 2, \ldots, J$; customers leaving node j proceed immediately to node $j+1$. A customer leaving node J departs from the system.

Customers are of different types $m \in M, 0 < |M| < \infty$, which they change according to a Markovian law when departing from a node. All customers show the same behaviour with respect to type selection.

The external arrival probabilities depend on the total population of the system and on the type of the arrival, i.e., if at time $t \in \mathbb{N}$ there are n_j customers present at node $j, j = 1, \ldots, J$, then a new arrival of type m appears in $(t, t+1]$ with probability $b(n_1 + \ldots + n_J) \cdot a(m) \in (0, 1)$.

With probability $r(i; m, m') \geq 0$ a customer of type m on leaving node i becomes a customer of type $m' \in M$ when entering node $i + 1, i = 1, \ldots, J - 1$. Given i and m, the selection of m' is done independently of anything else. We do not put further assumptions on the probability matrices $r(i) = (r(i; m, m') : m, m' \in M)$, so e.g. cyclic or deterministic behaviour of the type change process is possible. We only assume that the system of equations
$\eta(i; m) = \sum_{m' \in M} \eta(i - 1; m') r(i - 1; m', m); \quad i = 1, \ldots, J; \quad m \in M,$
with $\eta(1; m) = a(m), \quad m \in M$, has a unique stochastic solution
$\eta = (\eta(i; m) : i = 1, \ldots, J; \quad m \in M).$
The evolution of the system will be described by a discrete time stochastic process $X := (X(t) : t \in \mathbb{N})$.

Let $M(i) = \{m \in M : \eta(i; m) > 0\}$ denote the set of possible types which customers may show when staying in node $i, i = 1, \ldots, J$.

A typical state of the system is denoted by $x = (x_1, \ldots, x_J)$. Here either $x_j = e_j$, if node j is empty, or x_j is of the form $x_j = (x_{j1}, \ldots, x_{jn_j}) \in M(j)^{n_j}, 1 \leq n_j, j = 1, \ldots, J$. In the latter case a customer of type x_{j1} is in service at node j, x_{j2} is the type of the customer waiting at the head of the queue,$\ldots$, and x_{jn_j} is the type of the customer who arrived most recently at node j. n_j is the queue length at node j. If $x_j = e_j$ we set $n_j = 0$. x_j is called a local state for node j.

¿From these local states we construct the state space of the system
$$\tilde{S}(J) := \{(x_1, \ldots, x_J) : x_j = (x_{j1}, \ldots, x_{jn_j}) \in M(j)^{n_j}, n_j \geq 0, j = 1, \ldots, J\}.$$

We assume that the nodes operate independently as single channel state dependent Bernoulli servers under FCFS: If at time t at node j a customer is in service and if there are $h - 1 \geq 0$ other customers present at that node then this service ends in $[t, t + 1)$ with probability $p_j(h) \in (0, 1)$ and (for $j = 1, \ldots, J - 1$) the departed customer will join the end of the queue of node $j + 1$ at time $t + 1$; with probability $q_j(h) = 1 - p_j(h)$ this customer will stay at least one further time quantum at node j. Decisions whether to stay or to leave are made independently of anything else.

A customer arriving at node $j + 1$ at time $t + 1$ will either join the end of the queue there (if other customers are present) or immediately enter service (if at time t node j was empty or there has been exactly one customer who obtained his last quantum of service time).

If at some node at the same epoch an arrival and a departure occur we always assume that the departure event takes place first.

The state of the system is recorded at times $t \in I\!N$ just after possible departures and arrivals had happened. Let $X_j(t)$ denote the local state at node j at time t, $j = 1, \ldots, J$, $t \in I\!N$, and $X(t) = (X_1(t), \ldots, X_J(t))$ the joint *vector of type sequences* at time t. $X = (X(t) : t \in I\!N)$ is a discrete time irreducible Markov chain with state space $\tilde{S}(J)$. The stabilization problem for X generalizes the problem solved in [8]:

Theorem 1 (Steady state). *The Markov chain X is ergodic if and only if (with $c(h) := 1 - b(h)$) the measure $\pi^J = (\pi^J(x) : x \in \tilde{S}(J))$ given by*

$$\pi^J(x_1, \ldots, x_J) \qquad\qquad (x_1, \ldots, x_J) \in \tilde{S}(J),$$
$$= \pi^J((x_{11}, \ldots, x_{1n_1}); \ldots; (x_{J1}, \ldots, x_{Jn_J}))$$
$$= \left(\frac{\prod_{h=0}^{n_1 + \ldots + n_J - 1} b(h)}{\prod_{h=0}^{n_1 + \ldots + n_J} c(h)} \right) \prod_{j=1}^{J} \left(\prod_{k=1}^{n_j} \eta(j; x_{jk}) \right) \left(\frac{\prod_{h=1}^{n_j - 1} q_j(h)}{\prod_{h=1}^{n_j} p_j(h)} \right) \cdot H(J)^{-1}.$$

is with suitable $H(J) < \infty$ a probability measure, the steady state of X.

Proof : [5] Approximate the open tandem by a sequence of closed cycles and use a limit argument. $\odot$

This result allows an optimization of transmission lines using the principle of adjusted transfer rates and the simple but versatile state dependent arrival process with customers of different types.

Example 2 (Control of a Bernoulli arrival stream). Consider a state independent Bernoulli arrival stream of customers of different types (an arrival is of type $m \in M$ with probability $a(m)$) with intensity $B \in (0, 1]$, which feeds an open tandem of Bernoulli servers as described above. Introduce a Bernoulli switch at the entrance point of the network (before node 1): If the total population size of the network is n then an arriving customer is allowed to enter with probability $\beta(n) \in (0, 1]$ and is rejected and lost with probability $1 - \beta(n)$. Theorem 1 applies with $b(n) = B \cdot \beta(n)$. It follows: The switch can be incorporated to stabilize such systems, and we can construct a scheduling regime for optimizing the network.

Example 3 (Open loss systems). The assumption $\beta(n) \in (0, 1]$ on the admission control function $\beta(\cdot)$ can be weakened such that $\beta(n) = 0$ holds if $n \geq L$ for some control limit $L \in \mathbb{N}$. This yields the usual loss control for networks if we have $\beta(n) = 1, 0 \leq n < L$.

Investigating an individual customer's delay behaviour we need to know the behaviour of the system in arrival instances.

Theorem 4 (Arrival Theorem). *Consider the state process X of the open tandem in equilibrium and denote by $A(1, m)$ the event that at time 0 a customer of type m arrives at node 1. Then*

$$\pi_{1,m}^J(x_1, \ldots, x_J) = P(X(0) = ((x_1, m), x_2, \ldots, x_J)|A(1, m))$$
$$= P(X(0) = ((x_{11}, .., x_{1n_1}, m); (x_{21}, .., x_{2n_2}); ..; (x_{J1}, .., x_{Jn_J}))|A(1, m))$$
$$= \left(\frac{\prod_{h=0}^{n_1+\ldots+n_J} b(h)}{\prod_{h=0}^{n_1+\ldots+n_J+1} c(h)} \right) \prod_{j=1}^J \left(\prod_{k=1}^{n_j} \eta(j; x_{jk}) \right). \tag{1}$$
$$\left(\prod_{h=1}^{n_1} \frac{q_1(h)}{p_1(h)} \right) \prod_{j=2}^J \left(\frac{\prod_{h=1}^{n_j-1} q_j(h)}{\prod_{h=1}^{n_j} p_j(h)} \right) \cdot H_1(J)^{-1}, \qquad (x_1, \ldots, x_J) \in \tilde{S}(J),$$

Here $H_1(J)$ is the norming constant, which does not depend on the type of the arriving customer. For $i \neq 1$ similar formulas apply.

The interpretation of $\pi_{i,m}^J$ is that it describes the distribution of the other customers' disposition in an arrival instant at node i in equilibrium. Note that this distribution has not the form of the equilibrium of the system. In continuous time such a statement is true. (For node 1 this is *Poisson Arrivals See Time Averages.*) Further: The arrival distributions in discrete time depend on the node, where the arrival appears.

Corollary 5 (Individual loss probabilities). *(a) Control of a Bernoulli arrival stream (Example 2): The Bernoulli-(B) arrival process is controlled by a Bernoulli switch with admission probabilities $\beta(n), n \in \mathbb{N}$. Then the loss probability for an arriving customer of type m due to rejection is*

$$p_{l,m}(J) = 1 - \frac{1}{B \cdot H(J)} \sum_{K=0}^{\infty} \prod_{h=0}^{K} \frac{b(h)}{c(h)} G(K, J),$$

where $G(K, J)$ is the norming constant of the steady state distribution for a closed cycle of J nodes with K indistinguishable customers cycling. (See [6]; Theorem 1.)

   (b) Open loss system (Example 3): Assume additionally that the control of the Bernoulli-(B) process is of the form $\beta(n) = 1, \quad n < L, \quad \beta(n) = 0, \quad n \geq L$. Then the loss probability for an arriving customer of type m due to overflow is $p_{L,m}(J) = G(L, J)H(J)^{-1}$.

Theorem 6 (Throughput of the tandem). *In equilibrium the throughput of the tandem is $Th(J) = H_J(J) \cdot H(J)^{-1}$.*
The throughput of type m customers is $a(m) \cdot Th(J)$.

It can be shown, that $H_j(J)$ in (1) does not depend on j. (See [3], App. 1.)

   The passage time (end–to–end–delay) distribution for the general tandem system of Theorem 1 with state dependent service times seems to be unknown up to now. In the following we investigate the case of state independent service rates.

   We consider a test customer of type m arriving at time 0 at node 1 who finds the other customers distributed according to $\pi_{1,m}^J$. Let $(S_1, \ldots, S_J)$ denote the vector of this test customer's successive sojourn times (=waiting time + service time) at the nodes during his passage starting at time 0. We denote by $P_{\pi_{1,m}^J}$ a probability law which governs the evolution of the system under this condition, and by $E_{\pi_{1,m}^J}[\cdot]$ expectations under $P_{\pi_{1,m}^J}$. Working under this conditions we are in equilibrium conditioned on a specific arrival.

Theorem 7 (Joint sojourn time distribution). *The joint distribution of $(S_1, S_2, \ldots, S_J)$ is given by the generating function ($|\theta_j| \leq 1, j = 1, \ldots, J$)*

$$E_{\pi_{1,m}^J}\left[\prod_{j=1}^J \theta_j^{S_j}\right] = \sum_{(n_1,\ldots,n_J)\in I\!\!N^J} H_1(J)^{-1} \tag{2}$$

$$\cdot \left(\frac{\prod_{h=0}^{n_1+\ldots+n_J} b(h)}{\prod_{h=0}^{n_1+\ldots+n_J+1} c(h)}\right) \left(\frac{q_1}{p_1}\right)^{n_1} \prod_{j=2}^J \left(\frac{1}{q_j}\right)^{[0\neq n_j]} \left(\frac{q_j}{p_j}\right)^{n_j}$$

$$\cdot \left(\frac{p_1\theta_1}{1-q_1\theta_1}\right)^{n_1+1} \prod_{j=2}^J \left\{\left(\frac{p_j\theta_j}{1-q_j\theta_j}\right)^{n_j+1} \left(\frac{1}{\theta_j}\right)^{[0\neq n_j]}\right\}.$$

Proof : Conditioning on the arrival disposition seen by the arriving customer we obtain

$$E_{\pi_{1,m}^J}\left[\prod_{j=1}^J \theta_j^{S_j}\right] = \sum_{(x_1,\ldots,x_J)\in\tilde{S}(J)} \pi_{1,m}^J(x_1, x_2, \ldots, x_J)$$

$$\cdot E_{\pi_{1,m}^J}\left[\prod_{j=1}^J \theta_j^{S_j} | X(0) = ((x_1, m), x_2, \ldots, x_J)\right]$$

$$= \sum_{K=0}^{\infty} H_1(J)^{-1} \left(\frac{\prod_{h=0}^{n_1+\ldots+n_J} b(h)}{\prod_{h=0}^{n_1+\ldots+n_J+1} c(h)} \right) G_{1,m}(K+1,J)$$

$$\cdot \left\{ \sum_{\substack{(x_1,\ldots,x_J)\in \tilde{S}(J) \\ n_1+\ldots+n_J=K}} E_{\pi_{1,m}^J} \left[\prod_{j=1}^{J} \theta_j^{S_j} | X(0) = ((x_1,m),x_2,\ldots,x_J) \right] \right. \tag{3}$$

$$\cdot \prod_{j=1}^{J} \left(\prod_{k=1}^{n_j} \eta(j;x_{jk}) \right) \left(\frac{q_1}{p_1} \right)^{n_1} \prod_{j=2}^{J} \left(\frac{1}{q_j} \right)^{[0\neq n_j]} \left(\frac{q_j}{p_j} \right)^{n_j} G_{1,m}(K+1,J)^{-1} \right\},$$

where $G_{1,m}(K+1,J)^{-1}$ is given in (4). The sum in the waved brackets can be given a specific interpretation:

Consider a closed cycle of the nodes $1,\ldots,J$ with $K+1$ customers cycling, and with a customer of type m, henceforth called C_m, on arrival at node 1, seeing the other K customers distributed according to the arrival distribution for this situation. This distribution is ([5],corollary 1)

$$\pi_{1,m}^{K+1,J}(x_1,\ldots,x_J) \qquad\qquad (x_1,\ldots,x_J) \in \tilde{S}(K,J), \tag{4}$$

$$= \prod_{j=1}^{J} \left(\prod_{k=1}^{n_j} \eta(j;x_{jk}) \right) \left(\frac{q_1}{p_1} \right)^{n_1} \prod_{j=2}^{J} \left(\frac{1}{q_j} \right)^{[0\neq n_j]} \left(\frac{q_j}{p_j} \right)^{n_j} G_{1,m}(K+1,J)^{-1},$$

Now, if we consider the joint conditional distribution of C_m's sojourn times during his next cycle, given the arrival disposition $(x_1,\ldots,x_J)$ for the other customers, we conclude that it is identical to the joint conditional distribution of a customer on his passage through the open tandem, given this customer sees an arrival disposition $(x_1,\ldots,x_J)$. This is due to the strong Markov property of the state processes for both systems, the identical structure of the nodes in the systems, and the *overtake-free property* of the open tandem as well as of the closed cycle with respect to *one* cycle of C_m.

We therefore can reduce the computation of (2) to first computing the joint sojourn time distributions of C_m in a sequence of closed networks with increasing population size $K+1 = 1,2,\ldots$. Using the obvious notation similar to (1) and (2) we have to compute

$$E_{\pi_{1,m}^{K+1,J}} \left[\prod_{j=1}^{J} \theta_j^{S_j} \right]$$

$$= \left\{ \sum_{\substack{(x_1,\ldots,x_J)\in \tilde{S}(J) \\ n_1+\ldots+n_J=K}} E_{\pi_{1,m}^{K+1,J}} \left[\prod_{j=1}^{J} \theta_j^{S_j} | X(0) = ((x_1,m),x_2,\ldots,x_J) \right] \right. \tag{5}$$

$$\cdot \prod_{j=1}^{J} \left(\prod_{k=1}^{n_j} \eta(j;x_{jk}) \right) \left(\frac{q_1}{p_1} \right)^{n_1} \prod_{j=2}^{J} \left(\frac{1}{q_j} \right)^{[0\neq n_j]} \left(\frac{q_j}{p_j} \right)^{n_j} G_{i,m}(K+1,J)^{-1} \right\}.$$

Collecting states in (5) according to common queue length vectors and arguing that the conditional sojourn time distribution does not depend on the customers' types we apply Theorem 4 of [3] and obtain

$$
E_{\pi_{1,m}^{K+1J}} \left[\prod_{j=1}^{J} \theta_j^{S_j} \right] = \sum_{\substack{(n_1,\ldots,n_J) \in I\!\!N^J \\ n_1 + \ldots + n_J = K}} \left(\frac{q_1}{p_1} \right)^{n_1} \prod_{j=2}^{J} \left(\frac{1}{q_j} \right)^{[0 \neq n_j]} \left(\frac{q_j}{p_j} \right)^{n_j}
$$

$$
\cdot G_1(K+1,J)^{-1} \left(\frac{p_1 \theta_1}{1 - q_1 \theta_1} \right)^{n_1+1} \prod_{j=2}^{J} \left\{ \left(\frac{p_j \theta_j}{1 - q_j \theta_j} \right)^{n_j+1} \left(\frac{1}{\theta_j} \right)^{[0 \neq n_j]} \right\},
$$

Inserting this into (5) and (5) into (3) yields (2). $\odot$

The joint distribution of the successive sojourn times of a customer in equilibrium is a mixture of multivariate distributions with independent negative binomial marginals. The mixture distribution is (1). So (2) can be inverted easily. Similar remarks apply to the computation of the end–to–end–delay.

For the case of a state independent Bernoulli arrival process these results boil down to simply to evaluate distributions. The most remarkable result is the independence of the successive sojourn times of a customer in this case, when traversing the tandem.

Corollary 8 (Independent sojourn times). *For state independent arrivals the joint distribution of* $(S_1, S_2, \ldots, S_J)$ *is given by the generating function*

$$
E_{\pi_{1,m}^{J}} \left[\prod_{j=1}^{J} \theta_j^{S_j} \right] = \prod_{j=1}^{J} \frac{\left(\frac{p_j - b}{c} \right) \theta_j}{1 - \left(1 - \frac{p_j - b}{c} \right) \theta_j}, \quad |\theta_j| \leq 1, j = 1, 2, \ldots, J. \quad (6)
$$

The individual sojourn times are geometrically distributed with parameter $\frac{p_j - b}{c}, j = 1, \ldots, J$, *and independent. The distribution of the end–to–end–delay is the convolution of these distributions.*

This result is parallel to those in open exponential tandems in continuous time (for a review see [1]). It follows: The distribution of the end-to-end-delay is a convolution of the single-node-delay distributions.

Compare these results with the results of the decomposition approximation of Bruneel and Kim for discrete time networks ([2], section 4.1.6): They *assume* independence of successive delay times of a customer and then apply the convolution formula obtained from (6) to get an approximation of the end–to–end–delay distribution. We have shown that in the networks considered here their approximation is exact.

References

1. O. Boxma and H. Daduna. Sojourn times in queueing networks. In H. Takagi, editor, *Stochastic Analysis of Computer and Communication Systems*, pages 401–450, Amsterdam, 1990. IFIP, North-Holland.

2. H. Bruneel and B. G. Kim. *Discrete-Time Models for Communication Systems including ATM*. Kluwer Academic Publications, Boston, 1993.

3. H. Daduna. The joint distribution of sojourn times for a customer traversing a series of queues: The discrete–time case. Preprint 95–3, Institut für Mathematische Stochastik der Universität Hamburg, 1995. Submitted.

4. H. Daduna. Discrete time queueing networks: Recent developments. Preprint 96–13, Institut für Mathematische Stochastik der Universität Hamburg, 1996. (Tutorial Lecture Notes Performance '96).

5. H. Daduna. Discrete time analysis of a state dependent tandem system with different customer types. Preprint 97–6, Institut für Mathematische Stochastik der Universität Hamburg, 1997.

6. H. Daduna. Some results for steady–state and sojourn time distributions in open and closed linear networks of Bernoulli servers with state–dependent service and arrival rates. *Performance Evaluation*, 30:3–18, 1997.

7. H. Daduna and R. Schassberger. Delay time distributions and adjusted transfer rates for Jackson networks. *Archiv für Elektronik und Übertragungstechnik*, 47:342 – 348, 1993.

8. J. Hsu and P. Burke. Behaviour of tandem buffers with geometric input and markovian output. *IEEE Transactions on Communications*, 24:358 – 361, 1976.

9. M. Reiser. Performance evaluation of data communication systems. *Proceedings of the IEEE*, 70:171–196, 1982.

10. H. Takagi. *Queueing Analysis: A Foundation of Performance Analysis*, volume 3. North–Holland, New York, 1993. Discrete-Time Systems.

11. M. Woodward. *Communication and Computer Networks: Modelling with Discrete–Time Queues*. IEEE Computer Society Press, Los Alamitos, CA, 1994.

How Distributed Algorithms
Play the Token Game

Jörg Desel

Institut für Angewandte Informatik und Formale Beschreibungsverfahren
Universität Karlsruhe, Germany
desel@aifb.uni-karlsruhe.de

Abstract. We argue that high-level Petri nets are an appropriate technique for the formulation of distributed algorithms. To this end, we introduce sufficient conditions for a faithful modeling of message-passing algorithms and of shared-memory algorithms.

1 Introduction

In [Brau84], W. Brauer discusses different possible interpretations of place/transition Petri nets when transition occurrences are not scheduled by a single global control. Subsequent papers of D. Taubner [Taub88] and D. Hauschildt [Haus87] investigate consequences for the implementation of Petri nets. As pointed out in [Haus87], a program implementing Petri nets yields an automatic implementation of arbitrary distributed algorithms modeled by Petri nets. For a *distributed* implementation, it is necessary that the net-modeled algorithm employs only communication mechanisms between local components that are provided by the distributed device. The aim of this paper is to demonstrate that such restrictions lead to special rules for the token game of net-modeled distributed algorithms. For different types of distributed algorithms, we will provide structural criteria that guarantee that these rules are obeyed.

Usually, a distributed algorithm is given by a set of programs, one for each local component of a distributed system. Communication between these programs is explicitly modeled, e.g. by actions for sending or receiving messages. The programs can be translated into a single Petri net such that the behavior of the net reflects the runs of the corresponding distributed algorithm. In this way, Petri nets provide a semantics for distributed algorithms, and verification techniques based on Petri nets can be applied. Early references for this approach are [Kell76] and [Best82]. Verification of parallel programs using Petri nets is studied in depth in [Best96]. It is also the core idea of E. Best's Box calculus (cf. [BFFH95], [EsBr96]). In case of automatic verification, there is no need for an explicit representation of the Petri net.

We claim that the graphical representation provided by a Petri net can be much more lucid than a corresponding parallel program, even when the program is written in pseudo-code. It is well-known that for understanding, explaining or teaching complex structures in general two-dimensional graphical notions have advantages over one-dimensional textual ones. Petri nets provide such a graphical notion. They moreover support specific constructs for distributed algorithms: local parts of the algorithm correspond to non-overlapping subnets; common transitions model synchronous communication between components; message passing is modeled by arcs leading from a transition of one component to a place of another component; semaphores are modeled by additional places between components etc. Relevant physical aspects of the distributed hardware running the algorithm are captured in the model, too. For example, sending a message requires an existing signal line, represented by a path in the net. Another example is synchronous communication: actions that are spatially apart cannot be forced to perform simultaneously, so synchronization is modeled by the amalgamation of the corresponding transitions. Finally, Petri nets allow to capture smoothly internal parallelism of local components (cf. [DeRW90]). These considerations suggest to represent distributed algorithms immediately by Petri nets, without going via a programming notation (cf. [Valk87], [KiWa95], [Walt95], [Reis95], [Reis96]). We admit, however, that the readability of a net representation of a distributed algorithm heavily depends on the layout of the net.

The following section discusses different types of distributed algorithms and their Petri net representations. In section 3, we give a short formal definition of a simple variant of high-level Petri nets. Section 4 is devoted to message-passing algorithms. We present a syntactical criterion which guarantees that only message-passing communication between components is used. A mutual-exclusion algorithm by K. Raymond will serve as an example. We show moreover, that the behavior of each single component is easily obtained by a projection of the overall system. In section 5 we consider shared-memory algorithms. Again, we present a structural sufficient condition for implementability. Peterson's mutual-exclusion algorithm will illustrate this approach.

2 Distributed Algorithms

Every elementary book on Computer Science defines an algorithm to be a *finite* collection of *effective* commands in a *precise* language (for some purpose) (cf. [BaGo91], [AhUl92]). Surely, this definition is also relevant for distributed algorithms. We restrict to finite Petri nets for the representation of distributed algorithms. The local occurrence rule defines the (global) behavior in a precise way. However, problems come up with effectiveness.

Each single step of a distributed algorithm defines an action that can either be performed by a local component or which employs an assumed effectively implementable communication mechanism. Arbitrary control structures of algorithms such as sequence, choice, parallelism or synchronization can be formulated with Petri nets, and their behaviors are then mimicked by the occurrence rule. This simplicity has great advantages for verification techniques because it suffices to consider one type of transformation only, instead of a collection of different commands. However, it can also be a drawback. Given an arbitrary Petri net, it is not obvious if this net models a distributed algorithm of some given type, or not. The reason is that the token game can always be effectively played by a single instance, but might be ineffective in a distributed setting (see the discussion in [Brau84]).

Fig. 1 shows an elementary Petri net representing an algorithm for mutual exclusion of two processes. For understanding the algorithm, one only has to know the very simple occurrence rule for elementary Petri nets (see e.g. [BrRR87]). This net can be implemented on one local device (actually, any Petri net simulation tool could be

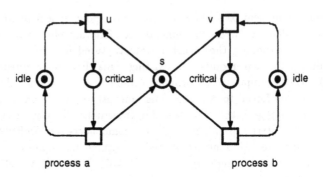

Fig. 1 A mutual exclusion algorithm using a semaphore

used). But, if the processes a and b run concurrently on distributed devices, then the concurrent access to the place s requires special assumptions. In the initial marking, transition u is enabled because s is marked, and so ist transition v. The occurrence of u disables v and vice versa. For an implementation of the algorithm, the test-operation *"is s marked?"* and the set-operation *"remove the token from s!"* for the transition u have to be performed together as one atomic action, and the same holds for v. Atomicity avoids that first both transitions are identified as enabled by their test-operations, and then both transitions occur and try to remove the token on s.

Atomic test- and set-operations on a variable correspond to *semaphores*, a synchronization mechanism for concurrent processes introduced by E.W. Dijkstra [Dijk68]. Actually, every elementary Petri net can be canonically transformed into a semaphore-based distributed algorithm, where the input-transitions of a place correspond to V-operations and output transitions correspond to P-operations on the corresponding semaphore (cf. [Goos95], where semaphores are defined via Petri nets). As pointed out in [Rayn86], semaphores can be viewed as hardware solutions to mutual exclusion problems in centralized frameworks. They do not exist in all devices. Hence, most distributed algorithms do not depend on atomicity assumptions for the hardware.

The theory of distributed algorithms distinguishes (amongst others) two paradigms: *message-passing* and *shared-memory* (cf. [Lync96]). Roughly speaking, a component of a message-passing algorithm can only communicate with other components by sending and receiving messages, where sending and receiving a message is not assumed to happen coincidently. A component has only access to local data and to received messages. In a shared-memory algorithm, every component has access to its local data and moreover to data of the shared memory. It is generally agreed that algorithms of these types can be implemented on respective distributed devices.

A Petri net modeling a message-passing algorithm should restrict to message-passing communication and similarly for shared-memory algorithms. Since a Petri net does not distinguish components of the algorithm and global memory by definition, Petri net models of such algorithms have to obey additional rules. Instead of modifying the occurrence rule (as done in [Walt95]), we will restrict the structure of nets in such a way that the transitions modeling communication mechanisms are implementable on the respective hardware.

3 High-Level Petri Nets

We do not only consider algorithms for a fixed number of distributed components such as simple synchronization protocols but also algorithms for arbitrary networks of distributed components. An algorithm for a fixed set of components can be represented by an elementary Petri net such that the components of the algorithm correspond to subnets of its net representation. For these models, it is not difficult to organize the net structure in such a way that the communication restriction of the algorithm is obeyed. Things are more difficult when algorithms for arbitrary networks of components are considered. For each such network, a different elementary net would be necessary. Even worse, a network of components can change during the run of an algorithm – in this case no finite elementary Petri net can represent the algorithm. A way to overcome this problem is to employ high-level Petri nets (introduced in [GeLa81]), i.e. Petri nets with individual tokens. We only consider algorithms where all components behave in the same way, with the exception that they might start in different local states. Hence different components of an algorithm can be represented by distinguishable tokens on one single net description of a component's behavior.

For sake of simplicity and self-containment, we do not refer to any existing notion for high-level Petri nets but define a simple class that is particularly tailored for our purpose. See [WVVR96] for a more detailed presentation. Other notions such as *predicate/transition nets*, *colored Petri nets* or *algebraic Petri nets* as well as their extensions and variations could have been used as well.

Given a set A, a *multiset* over A is a mapping $\mu: A \to I\!N$. Multisets generalize sets, but a multiset can contain several identical copies of an element. We call a multiset over A finite if only finitely many elements of A are not mapped to 0. The set of multisets over A will be denoted by $\mathcal{M}(A)$. The sum (and difference, if applicable) of two multisets is defined elementwise for each element of A.

An *High-Level Petri Net* has the following constituents:

- A net with a finite set of *places* S, a finite set of *transitions* T satisfying $S \cap T = \emptyset$, and a *flow relation* $F \subseteq (S \times T) \cup (T \times S)$,
- a set A of *individual tokens* and a domain $A_s \subseteq A$ for each place s,
- an *initial marking* μ_0, where a *marking* $\mu: S \to \mathcal{M}(A)$ associates to every place $s \in S$ a finite multiset $\mu(s) \in \mathcal{M}(A_s)$,
- a set of modes M_t for each transition $t \in T$,
- for each pair $(s,t) \in F \cap (S \times T)$, an input-mapping $i_{(s,t)}: M_t \to \mathcal{M}(A_s)$ specifying the tokens on the place s necessary for the occurrence of t in mode $m \in M_t$,
- for each pair $(t,s) \in F \cap (T \times S)$. an output-mapping $o_{(t,s)}: M_t \to \mathcal{M}(A_s)$.
- When a transition t occurs in mode $m \in M_t$ at a marking μ. then a successor marking μ' is reached, defined by

$$\mu'(s) = \begin{cases} \mu(s) - i_{(s,t)}(m) & \text{if } (s,t) \in F \text{ and } (t.s) \notin F \\ \mu(s) + o_{(t,s)}(m) & \text{if } (s,t) \notin F \text{ and } (t,s) \in F \\ \mu(s) - i_{(s,t)}(m) + o_{(t.s)}(m) & \text{if } (s,t) \in F \text{ and } (t,s) \in F \\ \mu(s) & \text{if } (s,t) \notin F \text{ and } (t,s) \notin F \end{cases}$$

We use the usual notations for nets. representing places by circles, transitions by squares and the flow relation by arcs. The inscription of places by elements of their domains denotes the initial marking.

In this paper, we only consider high-level Petri nets set where the set of modes M_t of a transition t is a subset of the cartesian product $A_1 \times \cdots \times A_n$ for some n and sets $A_1, \ldots, A_n$. Each mapping $i_{(s.t)}$ ($o_{(t.s)}$) will be described by a term τ with variables from $\{x_1, \ldots, x_n\}$ such that $(a_1 \ldots a_n) \in M_t$ is mapped by $i_{(s.t)}$ ($o_{(t.s)}$. respectively) to the evaluation of τ when x_i is interpreted as a_i ($1 \leq i \leq n$). These terms are annotations of the respective arcs. Note that a term does not necessarily contain all variables. For the sake of readability. we also use x, y, z instead of x_1, x_2, x_3. If an arc has no inscription at all, then its corresponding mapping has the constant value $\bullet \in A$, i.e., a black token is consumed or produced.

We won't mention the sets of transition modes explicitly but consider all variable assignments that make sense w.r.t. the domains of the respective places. A set M_t can be restricted by means of a predicative expression, inscribed in the transition t. For every mode of M_t, this expression must evaluate to *true*. Again, the variables x_i (or x, y, z) are used for the respective components of the cartesian product $A_1 \times \cdots \times A_n$.

In our examples we will not employ proper multisets of tokens in reachable markings but only sets. The use of multisets simplifies models of other algorithms as well as the occurrence rule.

4 Message-Passing Algorithms

We suggest the following representation rules for message-passing algorithms modeled by Petri nets:

- The net represents the (equal) behavior of all components of the algorithm.
- Each token on a place denotes data present in one component, called its owner.
- The owner of a token is given by its first entry in the corresponding tuple. So x represents a black token of the component x, (x, y) stands for a token y of the component x etc.
- An action of a component only depends on data present in this component. Since a transition depends on tokens in its input places, the first element of all arc inscriptions of input arcs must be equal. We always use the variable x as the first entry for all annotations of input arcs of transitions.
- If an inscription of an output arc has x as its first entry. then this token stays inside the component. Otherwise the first element is some y, $x \neq y$, denoting the receiver of a message. E.g.. an arc inscription (y, a) at an arc leading from a transition to some place s means that component y receives the data a at the place s from x, where the interpretation of x and y depends on the transition mode.

We demonstrate the concept with the following distributed message-passing algorithm which is inspired by the paper [Raym89] of K. Raymond. The algorithm ensures mutual exclusion of agents which communicate only via messages in a fixed connected network.

The algorithm assumes a non-directed spanning tree of the network such that every arc of the tree corresponds to an existing connection of the network. Then, at any system state, an agent without token has exactly one neighbor (w.r.t. the tree) which is closer to the token then the agent himself. For demanding the token, a request is sent to this neighbor. The request is forwarded by intermediate agents to the agent that actually possesses the token. This agent passes the token to his requesting neighbor, who passes it further etc.. until the token reaches the agent who started the request. Advantages of this algorithm are that the token is not moved if nobody requires access to the critical section and that the token is moved to a demanding agent relatively fast, compared to a simple token-ring algorithm.

In [Hare92], this algorithm is illustrated by a story about a hotel with a bottleneck concerning warm water: at any moment, at most one guest is allowed to have a shower. To ensure this behavior, there exists only one piece of soap in the hotel which plays the role of the token mentioned above.

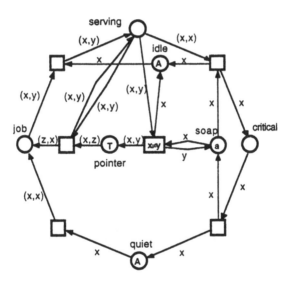

Fig. 2   Raymond's mutual-exclusion algorithm

We assume a finite set A of agents which can cyclically change their local states *quiet*, *job*, *serving* and *critical* (see Fig. 2). The occurrence of the transition from *quiet* to *job* for some agent x moves a token (x, x) to *job*, which means that agent x tries to get the token for himself. The transition from *job* to *serving* is only enabled if the agent is *idle*, which holds for all agents initially. An agent can only enter the local state *critical* when he serves himself and owns the *soap*. Initially, exactly one agent $a \in A$ has the soap. Entering the critical section sets *idle* again. Leaving the critical section sets *quiet* again. For each agent x except a. the place *pointer* contains the name of the neighbor y which is closer to the soap (w.r.t. the tree). This information is represented by the pair (x, y) in *pointer*. The set T describes thus the arcs of an inverted tree, initially with root a. An agent x serves another agent y if *serving* carries a pair (x, y). A pair (x, x) in *serving* stands for an agent x who serves himself and demands access to the critical section. Assume a serving agent x, i.e. assume that *serving* contains a pair (x, y) for some y. If x does not possess the *soap* and there is the pair (x, y) in *pointer*, then x sends a request to y; the pair (y, x) on *job* means that agent y has received a request from x to get the soap for x. If an agent x serves another agent y $(x \neq y)$ and owns the *soap* then he will pass the *soap* to y. This action is modeled by the transition with inscription $x \neq y$. It changes the owner of the *soap*, sets the former owner *idle* again, and records in *pointer* where the former owner can ask for the soap when he needs it again.

A formal correctness proof of this algorithm, based on the above Petri net, is presented in [WVVR96], [DeKi97]. For two agents, similar algorithms modeled by Petri nets can be found in [Valk87] and [KiWa95]. Note that, since more than one agent might start requests concurrently, there can exist conflicting requests in the network. Fairness assumptions are therefore necessary to ensure that every demanding agent will eventually be served.

It is not difficult to see that each Petri net represented according to the rule given at the beginning of this section models a message-passing algorithm. For an implementation of the algorithm, it is necessary to have a description of the local algorithm for each single component. A Petri net description of this behavior is very simply obtained: Fig. 3 shows the local algorithm for the agent a, which is the agent in possession of the soap initially. For the other agents, the place *soap* is initially unmarked and the place *pointer* contains the name of some other agent.

In general, a component is obtained from the net of the entire algorithm by dropping the first entry of each arc inscription, replacing remaining variables x by the name of the current component and disconnecting arcs that represent messages.

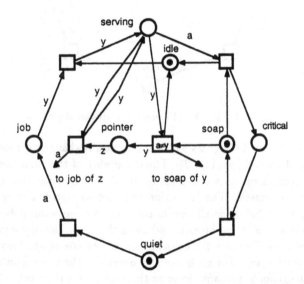

Fig. 3 A component of Raymond's mutual-exclusion algorithm

5 Shared-Memory Algorithms

In contrast to message-passing algorithms. a language for shared-memory algorithms needs explicit representation of the memory.

- We will represent the shared memory using grey places whereas black places denote local control or data of the components of the algorithm.
- As before, the first entry of each token on a black place denotes its owner.

For the grey places, we only allow a restricted access policy (see Fig. 4):

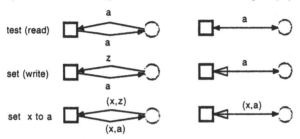

Fig. 4   Allowed access to a shared memory

- A transition is allowed to test the value of a token in a place of the shared memory, but then this value is not changed. So this test-operation is modeled by arcs from and to the transition that are both labeled by the same term. Therefore, we suggest a double-headed single arc with single inscription for testing access to a grey place.
- A transition is also allowed to set a new value to a shared variable, no matter what the old value was. This operation is modeled by an arc to the grey place inscribed by a variable for the new value and an arc from the grey place inscribed by an arbitrary *dummy*-variable that appears nowhere else in the vicinity of the transition (here we used z). Fig. 4 suggests a shorthand notation that avoids the explicit use of a dummy variable.
- Since, in high-level nets, a place should be able to carry more than one token, representing more than one variable of the shared memory, we need a corresponding notion for set-operations with names for addressing shared variables. In the third example of Fig. 4, the shared variable x receives the value a. Again, z is a dummy-variable. The right-hand side shows a notation for high-level set-operations that will be used in the following example.

For Peterson's mutual-exclusion algorithm [Pete81], there exist several low-level Petri net representations and correctness proofs (cf. [Walt95], [EsBr96], [Best96]). Our high-level representation provides a clear distinction between local components and the shared memory, and it is considerably more compact. Moreover, it can be unfolded to a low-level net such that the existing correctness proofs can be reused.

In the algorithm. only two agents a and b compete for access to their critical sections. Fig. 5 shows on the left-hand side the entire algorithm and on the right-hand side the local behavior of the component a together with the shared memory. The rough idea

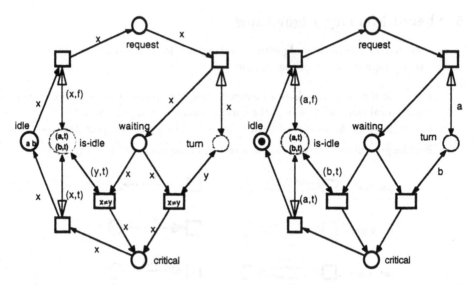

Fig. 5   Peterson's Mutual-exclusion algorithm

of the algorithm is that each agent has arbitrary access to its critical section as long as the other agent remains idle. If both agents compete then they get access alternately. The place *is-idle* contains the pair (x,t) if agent x is idle and (x,f) otherwise. So, if an agent is idle, then the other agent can reach his critical section via the left input-transition of the place *critical*. Otherwise. the right input-transition must be used. The place *turn* ensures then the alternating behavior: no two subsequent occurrences of this transition are in the same mode.

Acknowledgment. The concepts suggested in this paper are partly based on discussions within W. Reisig's research group in Berlin. In particular, I am grateful to E. Kindler, W. Reisig and R. Walter for stimulating remarks. R. Valk and two anonymous referees provided helpful comments.

References

[AhUl92] A.V. Aho and J.D. Ullmann. *Foundations of Computer Science.* Computer Science Press (1992)

[BaGo91] F.L. Bauer and G. Goos. *Informatik – eine einführende Übersicht.* 4. Auflage, Springer-Verlag (1991)

[Best82] E. Best. Representing a Program Invariant as a Linear Invariant in a Petri Net. *Bulletin of the EATCS* 17, 2–11 (1982)

[Best96] E. Best. *Semantics of Sequential and Parallel Programs.* Prentice Hall International Series in Computer Science. Prentice Hall (1996)

[BFFH95] E. Best, H. Fleischhack. W. Fraczak, R.P. Hopkins. H. Klaudel and E. Pelz. An M-net Semantics of $B(PN)^2$. *Structures in Concurrency Theory, Berlin 1995* (J. Desel, ed.). Workshops in Computing. Springer-Verlag. 85–100 (1995)

[Brau84] W. Brauer. How to Play the Token Game. *Petri Net Newsletter* 16, Gesellschaft für Informatik, 3–13 (1984)

[BrRR87] W. Brauer, W. Reisig and G. Rozenberg (ed.). *Petri Nets: Central Models and Their Properties.* LNCS 254, Springer-Verlag (1987)

[DeKi97] J. Desel and E. Kindler. *Proving Correctness of Distributed Algorithms – A Petri Net Approach.* Forschungsbericht 348 des Institutes AIFB der Universität Karlsruhe

[DeRW90] J. Desel, W. Reisig and R. Walter. The Alternating Bit Protocol – Fairness Versus Priority. *Petri Net Newsletter* 35, Gesellschaft für Informatik, 3–5 (1990)

[Dijk68] E.W. Dijkstra. Cooperating Sequential Processes. *Programming Languages* (F. Genuys, ed.), Academic Press, 43–112 (1968)

[EsBr96] J. Esparza and G. Bruns. Trapping Mutual Exclusion in the Box Calculus. *Theoretical Computer Science* 153(1–2), 95–128 (1996)

[GeLa81] H.J. Genrich and K. Lautenbach. System Modelling with High-level Petri Nets. *Theoretical Computer Science* 13, 109–136 (1981)

[Goos95] G. Goos. *Vorlesungen über Informatik – Band 1: Grundlagen und funktionales Programmieren.* Springer-Verlag (1995)

[Hare92] D. Harel. *Algorithmics: The Spirit of Computing.* Addison Wesley (1992)

[Haus87] D. Hauschildt. *A Petri Net Implementation.* Mitteilung 145 des Fachbereiches Informatik der Universität Hamburg (1987)

[Kell76] R.M. Keller: Formal Verification of Parallel Programs. *Communications of the ACM* 19(7), 371–384 (1976)

[KiWa95] E. Kindler and R. Walter. Message Passing Mutex. *Structures in Concurrency Theory* (J. Desel, ed.), Workshops in Computing, Springer-Verlag, 205–219 (1995)

[Pete81] G.L. Peterson. Myths about the Mutual Exclusion Problem. *Information Processing Letters* 12(3), 115–116 (1981)

[Lync96] N. Lynch. *Distributed Algorithms.* Morgan Kaufmann (1996)

[Raym89] K. Raymond. A Tree-Based Algorithm for Distributed Mutual Exclusion. *ACM Transactions on Computer Systems* 7(1), 61–77 (1989)

[Rayn86] M. Raynal. *Algorithms for Mutual Exclusion.* North Oxford Academic (1986)

[Reis95] W. Reisig. Petri Net Models of Distributed Algorithms. *Computer Science Today* (J. v. Leeuwen, ed.), LNCS 1000, Springer-Verlag, 441–455 (1988)

[Reis96] W. Reisig. Modelling and Verification of Distributed Algorithms. *CONCUR'96*, (U. Montanari and V. Sassone, ed.), LNCS 1119, Springer-Verlag, 579–595 (1996)

[Taub88] D. Taubner. On the Implementation of Petri Nets. *Advances in Petri Nets 1988* (G. Rozenberg, ed.), LNCS 340, Springer-Verlag, 418–439 (1988)

[Valk87] R. Valk. On Theory and Practice: An Exercise in Fairness. *Petri Net Newsletter* 26, Gesellschaft für Informatik, 4–11 (1987)

[Walt95] R. Walter. *Petrinetzmodelle verteilter Algorithmen.* Edition VERSAL 2, Bertz Verlag (1995)

[WVVR96] R. Walter, H. Völzer, T. Vesper, W. Reisig, E. Kindler, J. Freiheit and J. Desel. *Memorandum Petrinetzmodelle zur Verifikation Verteilter Algorithmen.* Informatik-Bericht 67 der Humboldt-Universität zu Berlin (1996).

The Asynchronous Stack Revisited: Rounds Set the Twilight Reeling*

Rolf Walter

Fraunhofer-Institut für Software- und Systemtechnik
ISST Berlin, Kurstrasse 33, D-10117 Berlin

Abstract

Protocols return often to a particular state - no matter what happens. We call such a state a *ground state*. Each action which occurs in the ground state starts a so called *round*. A round ends when the ground state is reached again.

In distributed protocols without global control, rounds are hard to identify. Ground states might be only virtual snapshots and not necessarily observable. When partial order semantics are considered a round can be clearly identified even in a distributed system. We will discuss the use of rounds for structuring and verifying a system's behavior. As an example a Petri net model for the asynchronous stack is introduced.

Introduction

A good reason to stand a round for colleagues and friends is the celebration of a 60th birthday. Such a round never remains a singleton. Follower rounds offered by the same as well as other persons are usually offered to the guests. Often, a sequence of rounds is the result of such an evening until everybody feels quite pleasant.

If we have to speak more precisely about this sequence of rounds we immediately get into difficulties; when does a round start, when does it exactly finish, what about the persons that have not finished their drinks from the previous round while a new round has already been started by others.

In this paper a formal notion of *round-based* behavior of a distributed system is proposed. Since a partial order based description of a system's behavior is used rounds are denotable, verifiable and usable for correctness purposes. Moreover, we claim that the notion of rounds helps the system designer to understand the interaction structure of the system's components.

The notion of rounds was first formalized in [9]. Due to the lack of space we restrict ourselves to illustrate the idea and the purpose of rounds using an example. Formal definitions are skipped and we refer to the literature for details of the system modeling with algebraic Petri net models [5] and the denotation of properties using temporal logic (cf. [5, 8]). In Section 1 we introduce an algebraic Petri net model for the asynchronous stack. In Section 2 a partially ordered run of the stack is discussed. In

---

*This work was partially supported by the DFG (Project 'Distributed Algorithms').

Section 3 a definition for round-based behavior is presented. The benefit of round-based behavior is discussed in Section 4.

1 The asynchronous stack

There exist at least two motivations to implement a stack asynchronously: First, we are heading for a stack which in principle can be always extended without loss of performance, when push and pop-operations are applied to the top of the stack [2]. Second, the functionality of the stack is realized by a set of interacting simple modules. Renounciating any global control mechanism ([4]) the behavior of the asynchronous stack is simply based on an intelligent treatment of concurrency [3].

In contrast to the Petri net model in [7] where the stack modules communicate synchronously by handshake, we introduce a Petri net model where the stack modules communicate asynchronously by message passing.

Fig. 1 shows a single module of the stack intended to store one data. A stack consists

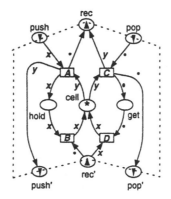

Figure 1: A module of the stack for one datum

of an arbitrary number of modules arranged in a row. Hence, each module has a unique *predecessor* module and a unique *successor* module[1].

Two modules communicate via the places *push, pop* and *rec*. The arrow-heads drawn in these places are only illustrative and distinguish the input places from the output places of the module. Each module may perform four actions:

A: **push(x)** When the predecessor sends a datum x, the datum y which was actually stored in the *cell* is handed over to the successor (place *push'*). The predecessor is informed that the new datum has been accepted (place *rec*) while x is *hold*.

B: **store(x)** The new datum x is stored in the *cell* only when the successor has accepted the old datum (signaled on place *rec'*).

C: **pop(y)** When a *pop*-signal to a stored datum is received the module sends the datum y from the *cell* (via place *rec*) to the predecessor and hands over the *pop*-signal to its successor (to place *pop'*).

---

[1]despite of the top module and the bottom module of the stack.

D: get(x) A datum x received from the successor is stored in the *cell*.

In the figure to the right the top module and the bottom of the stack are shown together with three modules in between. The top module performs push-actions and pop-actions without further synchronization. Similarly, the bottom module destroys the datum y stored in its cell and accepts the datum x received from its predecessor. After the bottom module has performed a pop-action a particular datum element $\star$ is stored in its cell. The star models that actually no datum is stored in this cell. Initially, all cells are marked with $\star$ since the stack is initially empty.

In the next section we discuss the behavior of the asynchronous stack using partially ordered runs.

2 Stack behavior

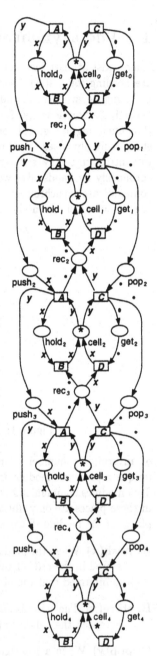

In Fig. 2 a run of the stack with n modules is sketched as a non-sequential inscribed process [1]. Only the initial state is modeled by the minimal conditions. For simplicity all other places have been omitted in the inscribed process. Consequently, we have abstracted from the concrete data stored and removed in the stack during this run. The labeling of each event in the process identifies the corresponding transition of the stack module. For example, the first event in the third line labeled by A refers to the occurrence of transition A in the third module.

The first line of events shows the operations that have been applied to the top module of the stack in this run. Two push-operation have been followed by a pop-operation. This sequence of operations is repeated twice. Please note, that this sequence is repeated by every module. Depending on the operations at the top of the stack the behavior of all the other modules is determined.

The dashed line in Fig. 2 shows a reachable state in this run. In this state the first module has already performed the push- and pop-sequence twice, but the fourth module has only performed this sequence once. In the next section we will introduce the notion of rounds intuitively and formally.

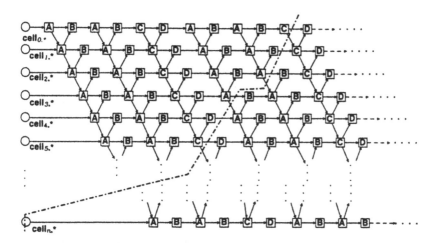

Figure 2: A partially ordered run of the asynchronous stack

3 Round-based behavior

The behavior of the stack is easily understood as a sequence of rounds. In the initial state all *cells* are marked with a star. Only a push- or pop-action at the top module may occur first. When each module has performed exactly two actions, all *cells* are marked again. We call the state, when all *cells* are marked, the ground state of the asynchronous stack model.

The behavior between the occurrence of two consecutive ground states we call a round. In Fig. 3 the rounds of the above run are illustrated using the sequence of dashed lines

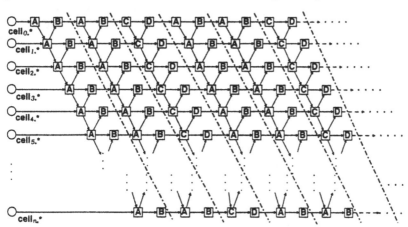

Figure 3: A round consisting of two actions from each module

corresponding to the sequence of ground states reached.

The actions performed in different rounds are not always the same. They depend on the actions occurring in the top module. But, at the end of each round the ground state is eventually reached and all *cells* are marked again. The formal notion of round-based behavior is based on this borderline between two consecutive rounds.

Let φ be a state formula. For each marking interpreted as a state of an algebraic Petri net we may evaluate φ in this state. We call each state of an algebraic Petri net a φ-state if φ evaluates to true in this state.

We call a system φ-round-based iff a state satisfying φ is always eventually reached. More precisely, using e.g. the temporal logic proposed in [8] we call an algebraic Petri net model Σ φ-round-based iff the system property $true \rightsquigarrow \varphi$ (leads-to) holds in every run of Σ. The Petri net model of the asynchronous stack is

$$(\bigwedge_{i=1}^{n} \mid cell_i \mid = 1)\text{-round-based.}$$

4 The benefit of rounds

In this section we will shortly discuss the benefit of round based behavior. First, we introduce a so called proof-rule for Petri net model that is φ-round-based. Then, we will convince the reader that prooving systems to be round-based is feasible.

In general, liveness properties (in the sense of [6]) are the essential and most difficult properties to prove for a distributed system. A liveness property states that eventually something good will happen. As an example, $push_i(x) \rightsquigarrow hold_i(x)$ denotes the property that a datum x on place $push_i$ eventually leads to the datum x on place $hold_i$. The proof of such a liveness property demands detailed knowledge to assure that in each $push_i(x)$-state the transition A of the i-th module occurs and is not blocked forever.

In contrast, if we know that the stack model is round-based and every $push_i(x)$-state is not a ground state of the asynchronous stack, we can immediatly conclude that transition A has to occur. From the place-invariant $\mid push_i + cell_i + get_i \mid$ (cf. [8])[2] we derive that the number of token on these three places is always equal to 1. This guarantees, that each $push_i(x)$-state cannot be a ground state of the stack.

More generally, every ψ-state must be eventually followed by a $\neg\psi$-state in case the Petri net model is φ-round-based and each ψ-state is not a φ-state. An even stronger proof rule is formulated in terms of the temporal logic used in [8] as follows:

Progress with Rounds:
$\quad$ Σ is $\varphi - round\text{-}based,$ $\qquad$ ψ $unless$ $\psi',$ $\qquad$ $\Box\psi \Rightarrow \neg\varphi$
$$\psi \rightsquigarrow \psi'$$

The proof that a system is φ-round based is far from trivial. But, in general it is straight forward when the following rule is used:

Round-based behavior:
$\quad$ $\Diamond \varphi,$ $\qquad$ φ $unless$ $\psi,$ $\qquad$ $\psi \rightsquigarrow \varphi$
$$\Sigma \text{ is } \varphi - round\text{-}based$$

This rule demands firstly to prove that a φ-state has to be reached eventually from the initial state. Then, we have to find a state formula ψ satisfying the two properties: ψ holds when the φ-state is left and $\psi \rightsquigarrow \varphi$ is valid in Σ. Intuitively, this means that whenever the ground-state is left, the system will return to the ground state.

---
[2]formal details to place invariants for algebraic high level nets can be found in the contribution to this book be E. Kindler and W. Reisig

In [9] this technique has been applied to the synchronously communicating asynchronous stack and some other models of distributed algorithms. The reason why the proof of the premises is often straight forward is that the behavior of a system is mostly determined for the round once the system has begun a round.

For the stack we know from the above place invariant that only the transitions A and C of the top module may start a round. If one of these transitions has occurred, we have enough information to compute successively that the ground-state will eventually be reached again in both cases, since here the behavior of all other modules in this round is completely determined.

5 Conclusion

The notion of rounds has been successfully used in many case studies of distributed algorithms. Proofs are much more intuitive and structured by the use of rounds.

To sum up it is remarkable, that the introduced proof rules for round-based behavior are valid, too, when interleaving semantics are used. But generally, ground states and rounds do no longer exist according to this semantics. The twilight produced by the arbitrary interleaving of concurrency prevents the simple characterization of the existing round-based behavior.

Acknowledgments I would like to thank Wolfgang Reisig for some helpful discussions concerning the notion of rounds and the asynchronous stack. This stack was introduced to me by him and Prof. Brauer. Prof. Brauer, my Ph-D. supervisor, observed at first glance that there was some stupid redundancy in the Petri net model of the asynchronous stack used in [9]. I hope that he enjoys much more the present model of the asynchronous stack.

References

1. Eike Best and César Fernández. *Nonsequential Processes*, volume 13 of *EATCS Monographs on Theoretical Computer Science*. Springer-Verlag, 1988.
2. Frederick C. Furtek. Asynchronous push-down stacks. Computation structures group memo 86, project mac, Massachussets Institute of Technologie, 1973.
3. Hartmann Genrich. Net models of dynamically evolving data structures. In K. Voss, H.J. Genrich, and G. Rozenberg, editors, *Concurrency and Nets*, pages 201–216. Springer-Verlag, 1987.
4. Leo J. Guibas and Frank M. Liang. Systolic stacks, queues, and counters. In *1982 Conference on Advanced Research in VLSI, M.I.T.*, pages 155–164, January 1982.
5. Ekkart Kindler and Wolfgang Reisig. Algebraic system nets for modelling distributed algorithms. to appear in Petri Net Newsletter 51, 1996/97.
6. Leslie Lamport. Proving the correctness of multiprocess programs. *IEEE Transactions on Software Engineering*, SE-3(2):125–143, 1977.
7. Wolfgang Reisig. Petrinetze: Grundfragen, Konzepte, Konsequenzen. Arbeitspapiere der GMD 497, GMD, 1990.
8. R. Walter, H. Völzer, T. Vesper, W. Reisig, E. Kindler, J. Freiheit, and J. Desel. Memorandum: Petrinetzmodelle zur Verifikation verteilter Algorithmen. Informatik-Bericht 67, Humboldt-Universität zu Berlin, July 1996.
9. Rolf Walter. *Petrinetzmodelle verteilter Algorithmen – Intuition und Beweistechnik*. Band 2 aus Edition VERSAL. Bertz Verlag. PhD thesis, Humboldt-Universität zu Berlin, 1995.

Online Scheduling of Continuous Media Streams*

B. Monien, P. Berenbrink, R. Lüling, and M. Riedel**

University of Paderborn, Germany
E-mail: bm,pebe,rl,barcom@uni-paderborn.de

Abstract. We present a model for an interactive continuous media server. Such server systems work in an online environment without knowing future requirements of the customers. We apply competitive analysis to study different scenarios of the design and control of a server and we give upper and lower bounds for the competitive ratio.

1   Introduction

To provide high bandwidth interactive media to large number of customers suitable network and server technologies have to be available. Whereas the delivery of data without real time constraints like texts and images has been successfully solved (e.g. WWW service on Internet), this is not true for the delivery of real time continuous media streams in large networks. So one of the key elements in such an environment is the development of an interactive continuous media server (ICMS).

To store huge amounts of data and to allow simultaneous access for many customers a set of memory modules is necessary, e.g. a large array of hard disks. Our model consists of such a set of memory modules and a set of links. These two sets are completely connected. The customers get their data via the links and included buffers.

In our research we are interested in supporting decisions about memory bandwidth and storage policies of the data, and we study how the throughput is effected by allowing delays.

An ICMS works online, i.e. prospective requirements of the customers are unknown or uncertain because the customers have the freedom to access and to leave the system as well as to interrupt the transmission and to continue at any point of the media stream. However, the decisions about the current usage of the server resources have to be made immediately and a later change is impossible. We investigate the loss of performance due to this online information regime to see the consequences of different server constructions. To do so, we

---

* This work was partly supported by the EC ACTS project SICMA (Scalable Interactive Continuous Media Server – Design and Application), No. AC071, http://www.uni-paderborn.de/cs/sicma

** Supported by DFG-Graduiertenkolleg "Parallele Rechnernetzwerke in der Produktionstechnik", GRK 124/2-96.

apply competitive analysis, introduced in [10]. It determines the maximal ratio between online and optimal offline solutions over all possible inputs.

In fact we focus on a very special scheduling problem. The memory modules are our resources and the data requests of the customers are the "jobs". The jobs can be managed by that subset of the resources storing a copy of the requested data, and in order to fulfill the real time constraints jobs have deadlines.

The literature about scheduling theory is extremely rich. A good introduction is [4] and [2], which also deals with resource constraints. [9] gives a survey about up to date online scheduling research whereas online interval scheduling with fixed start and end times is investigated in [8, 11].

The design of ICMS is a very active area of worldwide theoretical and experimental research (e.g. see [1, 3, 5, 6]). The work presented in this paper has been accomplished in the context of the SICMA project. This project, funded by the commission of the European community, aims at developing a parallel ICMS. The integration of sophisticated scheduling algorithms into the architecture of this server is one of the major aims of the SICMA project.

The material is organized as follows. Sec. 2 presents our model and Sec. 3 gives an overview of the results with some ideas of the proofs. In Sec. 4 we concentrate our view on a special model instance and prove a nontrivial upper bound. Finally, we mention a few open problems in Sec. 5.

2 The Model

Our model has three main parameters: b, c and d. These parameters describe the memory bandwidth (b), the number of data copies (c) and a tolerable delay (d).

In our model, $M := \{m_1, m_2, \ldots, m_n\}$ is the set of n memory modules. The data streams are split into packets of equal size. To relax access conflicts on memory modules each of these packets is located in c different memory modules. Our model works in discrete time steps and a memory module has the bandwidth to deliver up to b data packets in one step.

A customer requests at most one data packet per time step. Thus, we bound the number of concurrent customers by the total memory bandwidth bn and they are described by a set $R := \{\chi_1, \chi_2, \ldots, \chi_{bn}\}$. In the model we assume that each customer requests one arbitrary data packet, which means an access to one out of c memory modules storing the requested data, or does nothing at each time step. For our model the input is a request function $r : R \times \{1, \ldots, T\} \to M_c$, where $\{1, \ldots, T\}$ is the set of time steps and $M_c := \{A \mid A \subset M, |A| = c\} \cup \{\emptyset\}$. The absence of customers can be expressed with consecutive empty requests.

A request can be served immediately or with a maximal delay of d time steps.

We investigate two variants of the model. In the first one an algorithm has to construct a scheduling function $s : R \times \{1, \ldots, T\} \to (M \times T) \cup \{\emptyset\}$, which assigns a memory module $m \in M$ and a time of delivery $t \in \{1, \ldots, T\}$ for each request or assigns $\emptyset$ when the request is empty or it is unsatisfiable. We will call this problem "data access problem" (DAP).

In the second variant, which is a restriction of the first one, a customer, or his assigned link respectively, can only receive one data packet per time step. This model is more realistic and the results show a fundamental difference in the reachable online performance. This second variant is called "restricted DAP" (RDAP). Algorithms solving DAP or RDAP will be compared with the optimal offline algorithm OPT.

The model cannot guarantee for delivering the requested data packets[3]. Nevertheless, we want to serve as many requests as possible. So the performance of an algorithm ALG for DAP or RDAP under an input r is the number of successful requests, i.e. the number of delivered data packets, and it is denoted by $P_{ALG}(r)$. This objective function follows ideas of [8, 11] where no benefit is paid when a job violates its deadline.

Following the well known definition of competitiveness, we say an online algorithm $\mathcal{A}$ is ρ-competitive if there is a constant α such that for all inputs r

$$P_{OPT}(r) \leqq \rho P_{\mathcal{A}}(r) + \alpha \ .$$

The competitive ratio is then the infimum over all values ρ such that $\mathcal{A}$ is ρ-competitive.

In the next sections we study the influence of the three main parameters memory bandwidth b, number of copies c, and delay d to the competitive ratio for *deterministic* algorithms. We are interested in understanding the reachable benefit that arises from allowing larger delay, increased memory bandwidth, and number of data copies.

3 Results

The table below summarizes our current results. A competitive ratio of "1" indicates that the online algorithm reaches the same performance as an optimal offline algorithm while "> 1" expresses that no such online algorithm exists. In this work $\mathbb{N}$ denotes the natural numbers without 0.

problem	parameters	competitive ratio	
		lower bound	upper bound
DAP	$d = 0,\ b,\ c \in \mathbb{N}$		1
	$c = 1,\ b,\ d \in \mathbb{N}$		1
	$c > 1,\ b,\ d \in \mathbb{N}$	> 1	$\min\{2, n/c\}$
RDAP	$b,\ c,\ d \in \mathbb{N}$	> 1	$\min\{d+1, n/c\}$
	$b = c = d = 1$	$4/3$	$5/3$
	$c = d = 1,\ b \in \mathbb{N}$		$5/3$

The proof of the $5/3$ upper bound for RDAP is presented in Sec. 4. Below we sketch some of the proofs for the other results.

---

[3] Let us imagine requests of all customers to a few modules. We get "hot spots" and any algorithm can satisfy only a small subset of requests.

Upper Bounds Using a Matching Technique. First we describe the matching technique and afterwards we sketch the proofs for the upper bounds of rows one, three, and four in the above table.

The DAP can be modelled as a matching problem in a bipartite graph G with weighted nodes. Each request is represented as a node in U and has weight 1 (*request nodes*). Each resource, i.e. each memory module at each time step, is represented as a node with weight b in V (*resource nodes*) and in a matching such a node can be incident to maximal b matching edges. The set of edges E connects every non-empty request node to all resource nodes which are able to serve the request, i.e. to all c specified modules and all possible $d + 1$ time steps. The capability of the memory modules is the only limiting factor, so every maximum matching in G describes an optimal solution for DAP. It is well known that a maximum matching can be constructed efficiently by an offline algorithm.

In the online version of DAP with no delay ($d = 0$) all dependencies between two time steps disappear. In fact every time step represents an independent offline problem and the optimal offline algorithm can solve it itself. Thus we get the first upper bound of 1.

For the DAP with parameters $d \geq 1$, $c, b \in \mathbb{N}$ we have to construct the matching in G online. Karp *et al.* proved in [7] that 2 is an upper bound for the competitive ratio of the online bipartite matching for deterministic algorithms. This upper bound shown by the greedy algorithm also holds for the matching problem in G.

The upper bounds of $d + 1$ and n/c are shown by an algorithm without using delays. At each time step it applies the matching technique to determine a maximum number of the current requests for immediate serving. All other requests are ignored. This algorithm does not violate the additional restriction of RDAP.

We get the $d+1$ upper bound for RDAP by the following observation. Due to the maximization of the above algorithm, no other algorithm (including OPT) can serve a higher number of the current requests in any of the $d + 1$ possible time steps. The online algorithm uses only the first of them and an application of this fact for every time step gives the upper bound for the competitive ratio.

The n/c bound can be shown by another observation: If the current time step has no more than bc requests, then all of them will be served. Otherwise at least bc requests get their data packets because at least c memory modules are able to serve up to b requests. In our model, however, at most bn concurrent requests exist per time step and the optimal offline algorithm OPT can serve, at best, all of them. This proves the upper bound of n/c for DAP and RDAP. Here, a phenomenon of small system sizes is depicted: The competitive ratio decreases when the number of memory modules n (and therewith the maximal number of customers) becomes too small.

An Upper Bound Using Earliest Deadline First Heuristics. In the DAP with only one copy of every data packet ($c = 1$) all dependencies between memory modules disappear. This problem is equivalent to the online uniprocessor deadline scheduling of unit time tasks which can be solved as optimal as in the offline case using the earliest deadline first heuristics. This gives the 1-competitiveness.

Lower Bounds. The nonexistence of 1-competitive online algorithms for DAP and RDAP with parameters $d \geq 1$, $b \in \mathbb{N}$ and $c > 1$ (DAP), $c \in \mathbb{N}$ (RDAP) respectively, can be shown by an adversary argument. It works in two phases and the second phase depends on the decisions made by the online algorithm which are completely known to the adversary in advance.

In the first phase at time $t = 1$ the adversary constructs a request sequence in such a way that after d time steps all but one arbitrary request can be served. Thereafter, the system is in one of at least two different structured but equally valued configurations, depending on the request chosen by the algorithm for maximal delay. In the second phase the adversary continues the request sequence at time $t = d + 1$ in a way that the system can just manage to serve all requests. However, due to the delayed request, which needs the same resource, the online algorithm cannot satisfy all of them.

The optimal offline algorithm is able to fulfill each request by choosing another system configuration before time $t = d + 1$. Then the maximal delayed request uses a resource not needed for serving the requests of the second phase.

Repeating the whole request sequence over time shows that no online algorithm can be 1-competitive.

The lower bound of $4/3$ for RDAP with parameters $b = c = d = 1$ can be shown by a similar strategy which appends new requests in a continuous way.

4 An Improved Upper Bound

Now we shift focus on a special model instance, the RDAP, where all three main parameters are equal to one. A memory module can deliver only one data packet per time step ($b = 1$), every data packet is stored only once in the system ($c = 1$), and a request has to be served immediately or in the next time step ($d = 1$). This is the model with smallest parameters for which the construction of 1-competitive algorithms is impossible.

The online algorithm $\mathcal{H}$ employed to show the $5/3$ upper bound needs a global view onto the system and works as follows:

for every time step $t \in \{1, \ldots, T\}$:
    read all incoming requests of time t and mark all of them corresponding
        to customers with a delayed request of time $t - 1$;
    for each memory module $m \in M$:
        phase 1: if there is a delayed request of time $t - 1$ on m
               then serve it
               else serve an unmarked request
        phase 2: delay one of the remaining requests for serving at time $t + 1$

Theorem. $\mathcal{H}$ *is* $5/3$*-competitive.*

Sketch of Proof. At first we need a few definitions and notations for a fixed input:

$\mathbf{P}_{\mathrm{ALG}}(T)$ – performance of algorithm ALG, i.e. number of served requests from the beginning up to time T.

$\mathbf{p}_m^{\mathrm{ALG}}(t)$ – local performance of ALG, i.e. number of served requests on memory module m at time t

$$\mathbf{P}_{\mathrm{ALG}}(T) = \sum_{t=1}^{T} \sum_{m \in M} \mathbf{p}_m^{\mathrm{ALG}}(t) \ .$$

$d_m^{\mathrm{ALG}}(t)$ – number of requests at time $t-1$ which are served by ALG at time t from memory module m.

$\varphi_m(t)$ – a local potential function on memory module m at time t which is defined as

$$\varphi_m(t) := \begin{cases} 0 & \text{, if } d_m^{\mathrm{OPT}}(t) = 0 \text{ and } d_m^{\mathcal{H}}(t) = 0 \\ 1 & \text{, if } d_m^{\mathrm{OPT}}(t) = 0 \text{ and } d_m^{\mathcal{H}}(t) = 1 \\ -1 & \text{, if } d_m^{\mathrm{OPT}}(t) = 1 \text{ and } d_m^{\mathcal{H}}(t) = 0 \\ \frac{2}{3} & \text{, if } d_m^{\mathrm{OPT}}(t) = 1 \text{ and } d_m^{\mathcal{H}}(t) = 1 \end{cases} \ .$$

$\Phi(t)$ – the global potential function which is defined as

$$\Phi(t) := \sum_{m \in M} \varphi_m(t) \ .$$

From this definition follows $\Phi(t) \in [-n, n]$.

In order to show the competitive ratio of $5/3$ it is sufficient to show

$$\mathbf{P}_{\mathrm{OPT}}(T) \leqq \frac{5}{3} \mathbf{P}_{\mathcal{H}}(T) + \Phi(T+1) \tag{1}$$

which is equivalent (using the above definitions and the fact that at the starting time it holds for each $m \in M : d_m^{\mathrm{OPT}}(1) = d_m^{\mathcal{H}}(1) = 0 \Rightarrow \varphi_m(1) = 0$) to:

$$0 \leqq \sum_{t=1}^{T} \sum_{m \in M} \left[\frac{5}{3} \mathbf{p}_m^{\mathcal{H}}(t) - \mathbf{p}_m^{\mathrm{OPT}}(t) + \varphi_m(t+1) - \varphi_m(t) \right] \ . \tag{2}$$

Thus, it is sufficient to concentrate our view on local situations where a local situation is defined by a memory module $m \in M$ at a time t, $1 \leqq t \leqq T$. For reasons of convenience we define the term for the value of such a local situation in (2) as $\ell_m(t)$:

$$\ell_m(t) := \frac{5}{3} \mathbf{p}_m^{\mathcal{H}}(t) - \mathbf{p}_m^{\mathrm{OPT}}(t) + \varphi_m(t+1) - \varphi_m(t) \ .$$

Equation (2) and the terms $\ell_m(t)$ compare an arbitrary but fixed optimal solution of OPT with the online solution of $\mathcal{H}$. If we consider all feasible combinations of the variables in such a local term $\ell_m(t)$ (based on the input and the decisions made by OPT and $\mathcal{H}$), we can observe that $\ell_m(t) \geqq \frac{1}{3}$ in all but three cases. These exceptions are:

Case 1: There are at least two requests to the memory module m, all of them are marked by $\mathcal{H}$. OPT and $\mathcal{H}$ have no delayed requests of time $t - 1$ $(d_m^{OPT}(t) = d_m^{\mathcal{H}}(t) = 0)$. OPT serves one request $(p_m^{OPT}(t) = 1)$ and will serve another one with delay $(d_m^{OPT}(t + 1) = 1)$.

Under this condition $\mathcal{H}$ delivers no packet $(p_m^{\mathcal{H}}(t) = 0)$ and will serve one request with delay $(d_m^{\mathcal{H}}(t + 1) = 1)$; therefore $\ell_m(t) = -\frac{1}{3}$.

Case 2: Like Case 1 but algorithm OPT will not serve a request with delay $(d_m^{OPT}(t + 1) = 0)$; therefore $\ell_m(t) = \pm 0$.

Case 3: There is one request to the memory module m which is marked by $\mathcal{H}$ and no delayed requests $(d_m^{\mathcal{H}}(t) = d_m^{OPT}(t) = 0)$. OPT serves this request at time t $(p_m^{OPT}(t) = 1)$.

Under this condition $d_m^{OPT}(t + 1) = 0$ and $\mathcal{H}$ has to serve this request with delay $(p_m^{\mathcal{H}}(t) = 0, d_m^{\mathcal{H}}(t + 1) = 1)$; therefore $\ell_m(t) = \pm 0$.

In Case 1 the term $\ell_m(t)$ is negative but such a situation needs special preconditions. So we will prove the existence of a set of local situations including all of Case 1 with a non negative overall sum of their terms $\ell_m(t)$.

In a Case 1-situation at time t all requests are marked. Therefore, we can uniquely identify at least two local situations at memory modules m' and m'' occurring one time step before where $\mathcal{H}$ delayed exact one request of the current customers at each module $(d_{m'}^{\mathcal{H}}(t) = d_{m''}^{\mathcal{H}}(t) = 1)$. For these local situations can hold $\ell_{m'}(t - 1) \geq \frac{1}{3}$ or $\ell_{m''}(t - 1) \geq \frac{1}{3}$. Then the negative value is equalized. However, it is also possible that both situations are of Case 1, 2 or 3. In all three cases $\mathcal{H}$ cannot deliver a data packet because all requests are marked. Applying the same argument we can identify one (Case 3) or at least two (Case 1 and 2) predecessor situations.

For every Case 1-situation at time $t' \leq T$ we can construct a *dependency tree* where all leaves have a local value $\ell_m(t) \geq \frac{1}{3}$. Thereby, other dependency trees are possibly absorbed. At starting time no delayed request exists, so no situations of Case 1, 2 or 3 can occur. This fact bounds the depth of the tree by t'.

This tree has more leaves $(\ell_m(t) \geq +\frac{1}{3})$ than inner nodes with at least two predecessors (possibly of Case 1; $\ell_m(t) = -\frac{1}{3}$) and the overall sum of the values $\ell_m(t)$ of the situations described by such a tree is non negative. Comparing the solutions of $\mathcal{H}$ and OPT it is possible to find a forest of such dependency trees, which includes all situations of Case 1, and the sum of all the local terms $\ell_m(t)$ is non negative with respect to inequality (2).

$\square$

A careful inspection of the proof gives us an adversary showing that this $5/3$ bound is tight for algorithm $\mathcal{H}$.

This algorithm and the proof can be extended for arbitrary memory bandwidth $b \in \mathbb{N}$ in a straight forward manner and the same upper bound holds.

5 Open Problems

The bounds for the competitive ratio of the introduced model still have gaps. E.g. algorithm $\mathcal{H}$ makes the decisions about delaying requests in phase 2 too early. We have the feeling that it should be possible to improve the upper bound by using an algorithm waiting on the new requests before deciding which ones are served with delay. But up to now we have not been able to prove it.

Also, we like to extend the restrictions to real network structures[4] between the memory modules and the customers. A very interesting question is the influence of an additional lookahead while the buffers are bounded by a small constant.

If convincing motivated assumptions or knowledge about the input distribution are available, it is necessary to develop and study functions to map the data to memory modules supporting this input distribution.

Finally, it would be interesting to know whether randomized online algorithms can essentially help to decrease the bounds.

References

1. S. Aggarwal, J. A. Garay, and A. Herzberg. Adaptive video on demand. In P. G. Spirakis, editor, *Proceedings of the Third Annual European Symposium on Algorithms*, LNCS 979, pages 538–553, Berlin-Heidelberg-New York, 1995. Springer-Verlag.
2. J. Błażewicz, W. Cellary, R. Słowiński, and J. Węglarz. *Scheduling under Resource Constraints - Deterministic Models*, volume 7 of *Annals of Oaeration Research*. J.C. Baltzer AG, Scientific Publishing Company, Basel, 1986.
3. C. Bouras, V. Kapoulas, G. E. Pantziou, and P. G. Spirakis. Competitive scheduling schemes for video on demand. Technical Report CTI-TR 96.5.12, Computer Technology Institute, Patras, Greece, 1996.
4. P. Brucker. *Scheduling Algorithms*. Springer-Verlag, Berlin-Heidelberg-New York, 1995.
5. A. Dan, D. M. Dias, R. Mukherjee, D. Sitaram, and R. Tewari. Buffering and caching in large-scale video servers. In *Proceedings of COMPCON 1995*, pages 217–224, 1995.
6. D. J. Gemmell, H. M. Vin, D. D. Kandur, P. V. Rangan, and L. Rowe. Multimedia storage servers: A tutorial. *IEEE Computer*, 28(5):40–49, May 1995.
7. R. M. Karp, U. V. Vazirani, and V. V. Vazirani. An optimal algorithm for on-line bipartite matching. In *Proceedings of the 22nd Annual ACM Symposium on Theory of Computing*, pages 352–358, 1990.
8. R. J. Lipton and A. Tomkins. Online interval scheduling. In *Proceedings of the Fifth Annual ACM-SIAM Symposium on Discrete Algorithms*, pages 302–311, 1994.
9. J. Sgall. On-line scheduling — a survey. In A. Fiat and G. J. Woeginger, editors, *Dagstuhl Seminar on On-Line Algorithms (June 24-28, 1996)*, to appear in LNCS in Summer 1997. Springer-Verlag, Berlin-Heidelberg-New York.
10. D. D. Sleator and R. E. Tarjan. Amortized efficiency of list update and paging rules. *Communications of the ACM*, 28(2):202–208, Feb. 1985.
11. G. J. Woeginger. On-line scheduling of jobs with fixed start and end times. *Theoretical Computer Science*, 130(1):5–16, 1994.

---

[4] networks with nodes of constant and small degree

Contribution to Goodenough's and Gerhart's Theory of Software Testing and Verification: Relation between Strong Compiler Test and Compiler Implementation Verification

Hans Langmaack

Institut für Informatik und Praktische Mathematik der
Christian-Albrechts-Universität zu Kiel

Dedicated to Prof. Dr. Dr. h. c. Wilfried Brauer, Technical University Munich, on occasion of his 60th birthday on the 8th of August, 1997.

1 Introduction

Goal of good engineering and its branches like software engineering and compiler construction is safe mastery of realistic systems and software [Bau75]. J. B. Goodenough's and S. L. Gerhart's theory of test data selection can well contribute [GG75]. Their central question is: Can program verification, i. e. mathematical correctness proofs, be made easier by appropriate input data selection and successful test calculations?

Certification institutions like Technischer Überwachungsverein TÜV and Bundesamt für Sicherheit in der Informationstechnik BSI do not trust any compilers in safety critical applications. TÜV is certifying high level source programs only together with their generated binary machine codes [Pof95]. BSI demands that mapping of source to machine code must be a posteriori verified [ZSI89,ZSI90,BSI94]. Everyone knows such a posteriori verification from school. Results of laborious algorithms like dividing or equations solving are to be double checked by afterward proofs.

The ways of acting of TÜV and BSI are responsible and right w. r. t. momentary engineering standard. Due to L. M. Chirica, D. F. Martin [CM86] and J. S. Moore [Moo88,Moo96] full realistic compiler correctness is not only translation (specification) correctness, i. e. correctness of a mathematical mapping from source to target code, but also correctness of implementation of translators for realistic programming languages, implementation down in binary machine code of real processors. Literature is treating the first problem almost exclusively, the second problem is neglected. This is the essential reason for TÜV's and BSI's attitudes.

Our paper demonstrates how realistic compiler implementation verification can be enabled and eased by successful socalled strong compiler tests [Wir77]. Key is our Second Translator Test Theorem. The investigations have been done in the project "Verified Compilers – Verifix" in cooperation with the research groups of G. Goos, U. Karlsruhe, and F. W. von Henke, U. Ulm. The project is supported by the Deutsche Forschungsgemeinschaft DFG.

2 Definitions and Propositions about Programming Languages and Translators

In this paper we are mainly interested in sequential programming languages of usual information processing. These languages are opposed to process languages with their constructs for concurrent and distributed programming with communications and timing constraints. The languages we are studying here shall be especially appropriate for compiler writing what is done in sequential languages even if process languages are translated.

2.1 Programming Languages, Syntax, Semantics, Transformation

A *programming language* L consists of its *syntax* and its *semantics*. Syntax represents itself by a collection of non-empty syntactical domains like *expressions* (EX_L), *statements* (ST_L), *programs* (P_L) and *proper programs* (PP_L) [vWi69]. Semantics assigns meanings (often also called semantics) to syntactical constructs in corresponding *semantical spaces*. We are especially interested in the *external* semantical space Sem_L of all *relations* or *multivalued mappings* between non-empty *input* and *output data* domains DI_L and DO_L :

$$Sem_L =_{Df} (DI_L \overset{rel}{\to} DO_L), \ [\ .\ ]_L : PP_L \overset{tot\ fu}{\longrightarrow} Sem_L \ .$$

To consider predicate transformers instead of relations would be an even more general view [MO96]. So the essential and outside observable constituents of a programming language L are its proper programs domain PP_L and its semantics $[\ .\ ]_L$ with implicit data domains DI_L , DO_L

$$L =_{Df} (PP_L , [\ .\ ]_L).$$

Programs even of different languages can be *sequentially composed* by ; and executed, possibly by manual support. We model that by associatively *composed languages*

$$L\ ;\ L' =_{Df} (PP_{L;L'} , [\ .\ ]_{L;L'})$$

with

$$PP_{L;L'} =_{Df} PP_L\ ;\ PP_{L'} , DI_{L;L'} =_{Df} DI_L , DO_{L;L'} =_{Df} DO_{L'} ,$$

$$[\pi_L\ ;\ \pi_{L'}]_{L;L'} =_{Df} [\pi_L]_L\ ;\ [\pi_{L'}]_{L'} \ .$$

In $[\pi_L]_L; [\pi_{L'}]_{L'}$ we use ; as a relational operator, beforehand we have used ; as a syntactical operator. We furtheron assume that programs of one and the same language L can be sequentially composed with

$$PP_{L;L} \subseteq PP_L \ . \ [\pi_L^1\ ;\ \pi_L^2]_{L;L} = [\pi_L^1\ ;\ \pi_L^2]_L \ .$$

Application of the syntactical operator ; may be undefined for certain argument programs, especially in machine languages with resource constraints.

If L and L' are programming languages (L' is considered to be a *transformation* of L, in special situations we speak about *translation, representation, concretion* or *implementation*) then it is interesting to know when two meanings $f \in Sem_L$, $g \in Sem_{L'}$ are behaving in a reasonable semantical relation $\sigma_{L'}^L$. Different notions are conceivable. Let $\rho\iota_{L'}^L$ und $\rho\omega_{L'}^L$ be *data representation relations*

$$\rho\iota_{L'}^L \subseteq DI_L \times DI_{L'} \,, \ \rho\omega_{L'}^L \subseteq DO_L \times DO_{L'} \,.$$

They *induce* socalled *preserving of partial correctness* ${}^P\sigma_{L'}^L$ (when going from f to g)

$$(*) \quad f \ {}^P\sigma_{L'}^L \ g \ \Leftrightarrow_{Df} \ \rho\iota_{L'}^L ; g \subseteq f ; \rho\omega_{L'}^L \,,$$

$$
\begin{array}{ccccc}
Sem_L : & DI_L & \xrightarrow{f} & DO_L \\
{}^P\sigma_{L'}^L \downarrow & \rho\iota_{L'}^L \downarrow & & \downarrow \rho\omega_{L'}^L \\
Sem_{L'} : & DI_{L'} & \xrightarrow{g} & DO_{L'} \,.
\end{array}
$$

We say the *diagram is commutative in the sense of preserving partial correctness*. Other authors speak of an L - *simulation diagram* [Eng97].

Usual sequential information processing is mostly interested in this kind of semantical relation ${}^P\sigma_{L'}^L$ because any result $d' \in DO_{L'}$ of any *regularly terminating (non-aborting) calculation* of the *more concrete, implemented* (multivalued) mapping g is trustful and not deceiving the user: $(*)$ expresses that d' and the *more abstract, original* mapping f are reasonably related [GDG$^+$96].

Programmers of safety critical processes are more interested in a different semantical relation:

$$f \ {}^t\sigma_{L'}^L \ g \ \Leftrightarrow_{Df} \ \rho\iota_{L'}^{L-1} ; f \subseteq g ; \rho\omega_{L'}^{L-1} \,.$$

${}^t\sigma_{L'}^L$ expresses *preserving of total correctness*. Regular termination of an abstract f-calculation implies that there is a regularly terminating g-calculation as well. Non-termination would be fatal for the implemented automatic process g because termination is absolutely required in safety critical situations [BHL$^+$96]. The notions ${}^P\sigma_{L'}^L$ and ${}^t\sigma_{L'}^L$ are logically independent.

Since commutative diagrams can be composed vertically and horizontally we have *vertical* and *horizontal continuation* of ${}^P\sigma_{L'}^L$ and ${}^t\sigma_{L'}^L$. This means firstly: The relational composition ${}^\bullet\sigma_{L'}^L ; {}^\bullet\sigma_{L''}^{L'}$ is exactly that semantical relation ${}^\bullet\sigma_{L''}^L$ induced by $\rho\iota_{L''}^L =_{Df} \rho\iota_{L'}^L ; \rho\iota_{L''}^{L'}$ and $\rho\omega_{L''}^L =_{Df} \rho\omega_{L'}^L ; \rho\omega_{L''}^{L'}$. I. o. w. both inducings *preserve relational composition*. Secondly: With $f \ {}^\bullet\sigma_{L'}^L \ g$ and $\bar{f} \ {}^\bullet\sigma_{L'}^L \ \bar{g}$ we have $f ; \bar{f} \ {}^\bullet\sigma_{L'}^L \ g ; \bar{g}$ if $\rho\omega_{L'}^L$ and $\rho\iota_{L'}^{\bar{L}}$ coincide in $(DO_L \cap DI_L) \times (DO_{L'} \cap DI_{L'})$, i.o.w. both induced semantical relations *preserve relational composition* too.

The First Bootstrapping Theorem will show why induced preserving of partial correctness is the more important semantical relation when compilers are generated by compiling.

2.2 Translation, Translation Correctness and Verification

In subsection 2.1 we have transformed data by mappings f , g and by data representations ρ. Now we treat proper programs like data and we transform them. Let L be a language and L' be a more concrete one. We consider relations $trf_{L'}^L$ between PP_L and $PP_{L'}$. $trf_{L'}^L$ is *correct* if diagram

$$
\begin{array}{ccc}
Sem_L & \overset{{}^p\sigma_{L'}^L}{\to} & Sem_{L'} \\
[\![\,\cdot\,]\!]_L \uparrow & & \uparrow [\![\,\cdot\,]\!]_{L'} \\
PP_L & \overset{trf_{L'}^L}{\to} & PP_{L'}
\end{array}
$$

is commutative as indicated by . We may express this correctness by saying $trf_{L'}^L$ is *partially correct w. r. t. precondition Q*

$$ Q\ \pi_L \ \Leftrightarrow_{Df}\ \pi_L \in PP_L $$

and postcondition R

$$ R\ \pi_L\ \pi_{L'} \ \Leftrightarrow_{Df}\ [\![\pi_L]\!]_L\ {}^p\sigma_{L'}^L\ [\![\pi_{L'}]\!]_{L'} \quad . $$

The postcondition is formulated in the sense of VDM [Jon90]. A different phrasing: $trf_{L'}^L$ is *correct in the sense of preserving partial correctness*, indicated by p in ${}^p\sigma_{L'}^L$. It is clear that correct transformations *continue horizontally* (compare subsection 2.1).

Mathematical proving of transformation correctness is *transformation verification*. In special cases (considered in the next section) we speak of *translation* resp. *concretion verification*.

Now we consider two cooperating kinds of language transformations. *Translations $trans_T^S$* go from *source languages S* to *target languages T*. *Concretions $\varphi_{S'}^S, \varphi_{T'}^T$* go from *abstract languages S, T* to *more concrete ones S', T'*. We call $trans_{T'}^{S'}$ a *refinement* or *implementation* of $trans_T^S$ if diagram

$$
\begin{array}{ccc}
PP_S & \overset{trans_T^S}{\to} & PP_T \\
\varphi_{S'}^S \downarrow & & \downarrow \varphi_{T'}^T \\
PP_{S'} & \overset{trans_{T'}^{S'}}{\to} & PP_{T'}
\end{array}
$$

is commutative, as indicated by . This is a notion of refinement or implementation w. r. t. given concretions $\varphi_{S'}^S$, $\varphi_{T'}^T$ and again in the sense of preserving partial correctness when going from $trans_T^S$ to $trans_{T'}^{S'}$.

2.3 Translator Implementation, Translator Implementation Correctness and Verification

We want to explain what a *translator program* or shortly *translator π_{tH}* in *McKeeman's T-diagram* [Wir77]

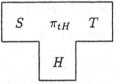

with source, target and *host language* S, T, H is exactly meaning and what is resulting if we are doing *bootstrapping*, i. e. if we are generating translators π_T by translating translators π_{tS} with the help of translators π_{tH}. We want to clarify the circumstances when any resulting π_T is really a translator.

In reality, abstract source programs $\pi_S \in PP_S$ cannot be inputs of π_{tH} literally, and we cannot have abstract target programs $\pi_T \in PP_T$ as outputs because the data domains DI_H and DO_H of π_{tH} might be disjoint from the proper program domains PP_S and PP_T. π_S and π_T have to be made more concrete as in- and output data $\pi_{S'}$ and $\pi_{T'}$ of H by concretions $\varphi_{S'}^S$ and $\varphi_{T'}^T$:

$$
\begin{array}{ccc}
\pi_S \in PP_S & \xrightarrow{trans_T^S} & PP_T \ni \pi_T \\
\varphi_{S'}^S \downarrow & & \downarrow \varphi_{T'}^T \\
\pi_{S'} \in PP_{S'} = DI_H & \xrightarrow[=[\![\pi_{tH}]\!]_H]{trans_{T'}^{S'}} & DO_H = PP_{T'} \ni \pi_{T'}
\end{array}
$$

The compiler constructor must make sure that the data domains DI_H and DO_H become proper program domains $PP_{S'}$ and $PP_{T'}$ of new concrete languages S' and T' such that $trans_T^S$, $trans_{T'}^{S'} = [\![\pi_{tH}]\!]_H$, $\varphi_{S'}^S$ and $\varphi_{T'}^T$ become correct translations and concretions and such that $trans_{T'}^{S'}$ refines $trans_T^S$ i. t. s. o. preserving partial correctness.

This is the full realistic definition of a *correct T–diagram* resp. of a *correctly implemented translator* π_{tH}. Implicit concretions $\varphi_{S'}^S$, $\varphi_{T'}^T$ must be respected. Proving this correctness is called *translator implementation verification*. Clear: Translation verification for $trans_T^S$ has to be done beforehand, but is not at all sufficient for full translator correctness. Correct T–diagrams can be syntactically composed by ; like programs.

2.4 Steps towards Correctly Implemented Translators

J. S. Moore [Moo88] has formulated the necessary steps towards correct implementation of a translator π_{tH}. If translators shall be trusted even in safety critical applications trustworthily proved correctness must hold also and especially if π_{tH} is implemented in binary real machine code H.

First step: Source and target languages S and T with their syntaxes PP_S , PP_T, data domains DI_S , DO_S , DI_T , DO_T and semantics $[\![\,.\,]\!]_S$, $[\![\,.\,]\!]_T$ are to be defined. A mathematical translation relation $trans_T^S$ is to be specified, usually done by *translation theorems* (to be proved correct in the second step) for source language constructs. Every theorem may be considered to be a non-deterministic *deduction rule* which allows to deduce target language constructs from source ones. The collection of all such rules is a *calculus* determining $trans_T^S$.

Second step: Translation verification for $trans_T^S$ is to be done. This is the activity field of theoretical informatics. Operational semantics employs simulation techniques of automata theory due to R. Milner [Mil89] or G. Plotkin [Plo81]. Denotational semantics uses cpo-theory due to D. S. Scott [Sco82].

Translation verification has been done also with the help of mechanical provers. W. Polak [Pol81] did so for translating a *Pascal*-like language into code of an idealised stack machine with unrestricted arithmetic and memory, W. D. Young [You88] for *Micro-Gypsy* (*Pascal*-like as well) into *Piton* (an assembly-like language) and J. S. Moore for *Piton* into the binary machine code of the real processor FM8501 [Moo88,Moo96].

Third step: A host language H with its syntax and semantics is to be elected. As long as there is no correctly proved, trusted compiler for H running on a real computer we are forced to take the binary machine language H of a real processor HM in order to construct an initial proved correct running compiler π_{tH} translating S to T. If T is the binary machine language of a real processor TM as well and if S is a high level language with rich enough recursion and data structures for easy formulation of compilers then bootstrapping technique allows that all further compilers may be developed in S or other high level host languages.

Fourth step: We have to do the necessary translator implementation verification for π_{tH}. J. S. Moore's third step is split in step three and four.

We have mentioned that almost all compiler correctness proofs in literature are only translation correctness proofs (second step), mostly for idealised target machines and translation correctness notions, and no translator implementation correctness proofs. But what is with the mechanical proofs mentioned above?

W. Polak's compiler is implemented in the host language *Pascal* of the *Stanford-Pascal-Verifier*, but there is no verified really running *Pascal*-compiler. W. D. Young's and J. S. Moore's compilers are implemented in the host language *Boyer-Moore-Lisp* (a kind of *pure Lisp*) of the *Boyer-Moore-Prover*, but we have no verified real machine code implemented *Boyer-Moore-Lisp*-compiler. Assume we can trust mechanical provers (their momentary implementations in real machine code are not fully verified) then all three authors have done not only translation verification, but also translator implementation verification, but only for very high host or implementation languages. So we are still far away from fully verified compilers implemented in real machine code. So J. S. Moore calls his own activity translation verification only, not translator implementation verification.

A clarifying different view: Any translation verification of $trans_T^S$ by a mechanical prover requires a formalisation of $trans_T^S$ in some language. This may be considered to be a high level programming language H as a part of the logic of the prover even though there is no compiler for H [ORS92]. This shows drastically that translation verification alone is insufficient for practical applications.

L. M. Chirica and D. F. Martin [CM86] were the first ones who have explicitly stressed that translator implementation verification is to be separated from translation verification. Because implementation verification down in real machine code has never been done up to now certification institutions are acting legitimately not to trust any compilers for safety critical applications, but only to trust real processors with their binary machine languages. Some researchers plead for doing only high level, abstract translation verification. They say implementation verification down in binary machine code requires too complex, too laborious and therefore unintelligible proofs. But that attitude does not help safety critical applications. We go a modularized way such that each step is abstract enough.

3 Correct Translator Generation

3.1 Bootstrapping

Bootstrapping is translator generation by translation. Let us put a translator $\pi_{tS} = \pi_S$ of section 2.3 in π_{tH}. What does a result π_T look like if a calculation of π_{tH} terminates regularly? What does that mean precisely?

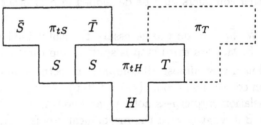

For π_{tS} and its necessary concretion $\pi_{tS'} = \pi_{S'}$ in $PP_{S'} = DI_H$ which π_{tH} is factually applied upon we can assume a diagram

$$
\begin{array}{ccc}
(1)\ PP_{\bar{S}} & \xrightarrow{\ trans_{\bar{T}}^{\bar{S}}\ } & PP_{\bar{T}} \\
\varphi_{\bar{S}'}^{\bar{S}}\ \big\downarrow & & \big\downarrow\ \varphi_{\bar{T}'}^{\bar{T}} \\
PP_{\bar{S}'} = DI_S & \xrightarrow[= [\pi_{tS}]_S]{trans_{\bar{T}'}^{\bar{S}'}} & DO_S = PP_{\bar{T}} \\
\varphi_{\bar{S}''}^{\bar{S}'}\ \big\downarrow = \rho\iota_{\bar{S}''}^{S}\ \big\downarrow & & \big\downarrow\ \rho\omega_{\bar{S}'}^{S} = \big\downarrow\ \varphi_{\bar{T}''}^{\bar{T}'} \\
PP_{\bar{S}''} = DI_{S'} & \xrightarrow[= [\pi_{tS'}]_{S'}]{trans_{\bar{T}''}^{\bar{S}''}} & DO_{S'} = PP_{\bar{T}''}
\end{array}
$$

due to definition of correct π_{tS} and π_{tH} . $\pi_{T'}$ is observed as the concrete result of the π_{tH}-calculation. Since we have

$$[\pi_{tS}]_S \xrightarrow{{}^P\sigma_{T'}^S} [\pi_{tS'}]_{S'} \xrightarrow{{}^P\sigma_{T'}^{S'}} [\pi_{T'}]_{T'}$$

correctness of π_{tH} further ensures the existence of a result $\pi_T \in PP_T$ with

$$[\pi_{tS}]_S \xrightarrow{{}^P\sigma_T^S} [\pi_T]_T \xrightarrow{{}^P\sigma_{T'}^T} [\pi_{T'}]_{T'}.$$

This assures the existence and commutativity of the inner diagrams in:

$$PP_{\bar{S}'} = DI_S \quad \overset{trans_{\tilde{T}'}^{\bar{S}'}}{\underset{=[\pi_{tS}]_S}{-}} \quad DO_S = PP_{\bar{T}'}$$

$$\varphi_{\bar{S}'''}^{\bar{S}'} \downarrow = \rho \iota_T^S \downarrow \qquad \qquad \downarrow \rho \omega_T^S = \downarrow \varphi_{\bar{T}'''}^{\bar{T}'}$$

$$(2)\ PP_{\bar{S}'''} = DI_T \quad \overset{trans_{\tilde{T}'''}^{\bar{S}'''}}{\underset{=[\pi_T]_T}{-}} \quad DO_T = PP_{\bar{T}'''}$$

$$\varphi_{\bar{S}'v}^{\bar{S}'''} \downarrow = \rho \iota_{T'}^T \downarrow \qquad \qquad \downarrow \rho \omega_{T'}^T = \downarrow \varphi_{\bar{T}'v}^{\bar{T}'''}$$

$$(3)\ PP_{\bar{S}'v} = DI_{T'} \quad \overset{trans_{\tilde{T}'v}^{\bar{S}'v}}{\underset{=[\pi_{T'}]_{T'}}{-}} \quad DO_{T'} = PP_{\bar{T}'v}$$

We are finished with correct translators π_T resp. $\pi_{T'}$ as soon as we have proved all concretions and translations correct. But that can only be done with an additional assumption. A possible one is: All *inverse data representations* ρ^{-1} *(data abstractions)* and *inverse program concretions* φ^{-1} *(program abstractions)* are partial single valued mutually commuting functions. This allows straight forward semantics lifting. Such data representation condition is holding in many programming language environments, e. g. in the *Lisp* environment in which the Verifix-project is demonstrating translator implementation verification: Every character sequence represents at most one *Lisp*-datum (*Lisp-symbolic expression or s-expression*), and every such expression represents at most one abstract *Lisp*-program. Lines (1), (2), (3) show that π_T has the desired shape

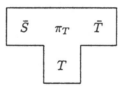

First Bootstrapping Theorem: Let π_{tH}, π_{tS}, $\pi_{tS'}$ be abstract and associated concrete translator programs correct i. t. s. o. preserving partial correctness. Let us assume that the data representation condition is holding and H-hostprocessor hardware is correct, i. e. syntax and semantics of H is definable and defined by the actual shape and function of the processor. So program $\pi_{tH} \in PP_H$ can be executed by the processor, especially be applied upon $\pi_{tS'} \in PP_{S'} = DI_H$. Let the execution terminate regularly with the output $\pi_{T'} \in DO_H$. Then $\pi_{T'} \in PP_{T'}$ together with an associated abstract $\pi_T \in PP_T$ are correct translator programs, correct i. t. s. o. preserving partial correctness. $\pi_{T'}$ is coding the translation $trans_{\tilde{T}'v}^{\bar{S}'''} = [\![\pi_{T'}]\!]_{T'}$ which is refining $trans_{\tilde{T}'''}^{\bar{S}'''} = [\![\pi_{tT}]\!]_T$, $trans_{\tilde{T}'}^{\bar{S}'} = [\![\pi_{tS}]\!]_S$ and $trans_{\tilde{T}}^{\bar{S}}$ of line (1).

Corollary: The First Bootstrapping Theorem is holding even if we change correctness of π_{tS} , $\pi_{tS'}$ towards preserving total correctness. The resulting translator programs π_T ,$\pi_{T'}$ are preserving total correctness as well. But the theorem does not work if π_{tH} is only correct i. t. s. o. preserving total correctness and not correct i. t. s. o. preserving partial correctness.

The theorems in this shape are new and demonstrate the importance of translator correctness i. t. s. o. preserving partial correctness for generating compilers by compiling [Lan97a,Lan97b]. Our translator correctness notion is weak enough such that the theorems can be applied realistically. Usual theory of T-diagrams likes to assume that the meanings of programs and their compiled programs are identical [Tof90], but that translation correctness notion is too strong and unrealistic. The next sections show how to apply the theorems and to ensure their assumptions, see especially section 3.4. It is legitimate to assume that real processor hardware is correct, i. e. is working as described in the instruction manuals. Software engineers and compiler constructors are not obliged to bother about hardware correctness. That is the responsibility of hardware developers and VLSI-chip designers and producers. Compiler constructors especially are subcontractors of the application programmers who will apply and trust the hardware anyway.

3.2 Strong Compiler Test

A main goal and idea of the Verifix-project [GDG+96] is to establish repeatable engineering methods how to correctly specify and, what is novel, correctly implement initial $S \rightarrow T$-compilers π_T for compiler implementation languages S on real processors TM with their binary machine languages T. Verifix has defined a sublanguage $S = ComLisp$ of the real life language $S_0 = ANSI\text{-}CommonLisp$ [Ste84] which is implemented (unverified) e. g. on the $Sun\text{-}SPARC$-processor $H_0 M$ with its binary machine language H_0. TM is the transputer- or the DEC-alpha-processor.

A further Verifix-goal is to maintain approved practical compiler building methods and to integrate verification. N. Wirth is recommending: (1) Do correct translation specification $trans_T^S$ and implementation of an $S \rightarrow T$-translator π_{tS} in S, (2) translate, manually or mechanically, π_{tS} to π_T following the own translation specification (1), and (3) do the socalled *strong compiler test*: apply π_T upon π_{tS}, execute π_T on processor TM and, after regular termination with result $\bar{\pi}_T$, check equivalence of $\bar{\pi}_T$ and π_T.

Test (3) is for higher trustworthyness of (1) and (2), (3) is necessarily successfull if (1) and (2) are done correctly. Because of practical importance we prove this statement in the case of mechanical creation of π_T by twofold bootstrapping of $\pi_{tS} = \pi_{tS_0}$ (syntactical identity) on processor $H_0 M$:

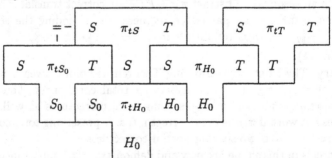

A consequence of the First Bootstrapping Theorem is the (abbreviately formulated)

Second Bootstrapping Theorem: If π_{tS} , π_{tS_0} and π_{tH_0} are correct i. t. s. o. preserving partial correctness then so are π_{H_0} and π_T.

Is the strong compiler test successfull after a third bootstrapping?

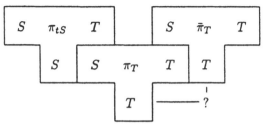

And if so in what sense? Beforehand, let us mention that a hardware processor LM-datum $\in DI_L$ resp. DO_L has two components. One is the LM-input resp. - output medium component, mostly a character sequence. The other is the initial resp. final LM-memory/registers state component.

Due to our Bootstrapping Theorems we have diagrams for the machine code implemented translators π_{H_0} (first bootstrapping)

$$
\begin{array}{llll}
\pi_{tS} & \in PP_S & \overset{trans_T^S}{\longrightarrow} & PP_T \ni \pi_T \\
& \varphi_{S'}^S \downarrow & & \downarrow \varphi_{T'}^T \\
\pi_{tS'} & \in PP_{S'} = DI_{S_0} & \overset{trans_{T'}^{S'}}{\underset{=[\pi_{tS_0}]S_0}{\longrightarrow}} & DO_{S_0} = PP_{T'} \ni \pi_{T'} \\
& \varphi_{S'''}^{S'} \downarrow = \rho\iota_{H_0}^{S_0} \downarrow & & \downarrow \rho\omega_{H_0}^{S_0} = \downarrow \varphi_{T'''}^{T'} \\
\pi_{tS'''} & \in PP_{S'''} = DI_{H_0} & \overset{trans_{T'''}^{S'''}}{\underset{=[\pi_{H_0}]H_0}{\longrightarrow}} & DO_{H_0} = PP_{T'''} \ni \pi_{T'''}
\end{array}
$$

and π_T (second bootstrapping)

$$
\begin{array}{llll}
\pi_{tS} & \in PP_S & \overset{trans_T^S}{\longrightarrow} & PP_T \ni \bar\pi_T \\
& \varphi_{S^v}^S \downarrow & & \downarrow \varphi_{T^v}^T \\
\pi_{tS^v} & \in PP_{S^v} = DI_S & \overset{trans_{T^v}^{S^v}}{\underset{=[\pi_{tS}]S}{\longrightarrow}} & DO_S = PP_{T^v} \ni \pi_{T^v} \\
& \varphi_{S^{v''}}^{S^v} \downarrow = \rho\iota_T^S \downarrow & & \downarrow \rho\omega_T^S = \downarrow \varphi_{T^{v''}}^{T^v} \\
\pi_{tS^{v''}} & \in PP_{S^{v''}} = DI_T & \overset{trans_{T^{v''}}^{S^{v''}}}{\underset{=[\pi_T]T}{\longrightarrow}} & DO_T = PP_{T^{v''}} \ni \pi_{T^{v''}}
\end{array}
$$

on the processors H_0M and TM. $\pi_{tS'} = \pi_{tS^v}$ are identical character sequence representations $\tilde\pi_{tS}$ of the abstract S-program π_{tS}. The H_0M- resp. TM-input media components $pr_1(\pi_{tS'''}) = pr_1(\pi_{tS^{v''}})$ are $\tilde\pi_{tS}$ again. Factually, the high level implementor in N. Wirth's recommended activity (1) has not written down the abstract π_{tS} but the concrete $\tilde\pi_{tS}$ instead. π_{tS_0} and π_{tS} are deterministic programs with semantics graphs $[\![\pi_{tS_0}]\!]_{S_0} \supseteq [\![\pi_{tS}]\!]_S$. Therefore the result of argument $\pi_{tS'} = \pi_{tS^v}$ in both cases is $\pi_{T'} = \pi_{T^v}$. This identity (∗) is the salient point of successful strong compiler test, but $\pi_{T'}$ and π_{T^v} are not calculated by a real processor. The H_0M- resp. TM-output medium components $pr_1(\pi_{T'''})$ and $pr_1(\pi_{T^{v''}})$ are factually calculated character sequences representing and identical with $\pi_{T'} = \pi_{T''}$. Syntactical identity of $pr_1(\pi_{T'''})$ and $pr_1(\pi_{T^{v''}})$ is what the strong compiler test can really check, and such check is successfull due to identity (*).

First Translator Test Theorem: Under the assumptions of the Second Bootstrapping Theorem and if third bootstrapping, i. e. π_T applied to π_{tS}, has a regular result $\bar{\pi}_T$ then the strong compiler test is successful when the calculated H_0M- and TM-output character sequences $pr_1(\pi_{T'''})$ and $pr_1(\pi_{T^{v''}})$ – concretions of π_T and $\bar{\pi}_T$ – are checked for identity.

3.3 The Dilemma of Translator Implementation Verification

Creation of a correct π_T due to the Second Bootstrapping Theorem depends on the correctness of the available $S_0 \rightarrow H_0$-translator π_{tH_0} implemented and running on H_0M. Even official validation of π_{tH_0} does not guarantee correctness of π_{tH_0} and so of π_T. Sorry enough, a successful strong compiler test does not imply correctness of π_T if π_{tH_0} is not guaranteed to be correct. The situation is even worse: A versed compiler builder with a hacker's mentality might intrude a virus in π_T via π_{tH_0} such that π_T becomes incorrect although π_{tH_0} fulfills all requirements for official validation, translation verification for $trans_T^S$ is done, π_{tS} is correctly implemented in high level language S, and the strong compiler test for π_T is successful.

A correct way out of this dilemma is to do *mathematical a posteriori verification* (English: *double checking*, German: *Beweis durch Probe*) of the bootstrapping result π_T on basis of a correct translation specification for $trans_T^S$. Then H_0M, π_{tH_0} and π_{H_0} have been used only as intelligent typewriters. If π_T had a virus which makes π_T incorrect that would be detected by double checking.

Is mathematical double checking realistic? π_T is correctly implemented if π_T can be deduced from π_{tS} due to the verified translation specification rules for $trans_T^S$ (see subsection 2.4, first and third step). But manual construction of a deduction tree is complex, laborious and error prone. Help by real processors is questionable as well, because this leads to a new implementation correctness problem which might be bigger than the original a posteriori verification problem.

Double checking is realistic if S-source and T-target programs are close enough so that the derivation tree between π_{tS} and π_T is visible implicitly and need no be written down explicitly. Mathematicians check formula transformations in proofs in a similar manner.

Verifix seeks to ease a posteriori verification by appropriately defined, close enough intermediate languages. Between $S = ComLisp$ and binary *transputer-*code or *DEC-alpha-*code T there are three of them. So fully correct initial compiler development is recommending multi passes translation.

3.4 Strong Compiler Test as a Correct Support of the Way out of the Dilemma

Multi passes not only enable a posteriori verification but also save especially unpleasant double checking of low level programs. We demonstrate that with a single intermediate language I.

Our strong compiler test demands identity checking of π_T and of the result $\bar{\pi}_T$ of a test calculation of π_T with argument π_{tS}. Due to F. B. Goodenough and S. L. Gerhart [GG75] we ask: How can we ease the implementation correctness proof for π_T when the strong compiler test has shown to be successful? We proceed in five steps:

1. π_{tS} is to be composed by two passes

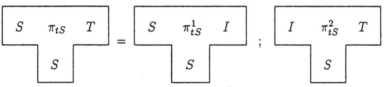

Each correctness proof for translation $trans_T^S$ and for translator π_{tS} splits in two simpler subproofs. This is essentielly translation verification, see the discussion in section 2.4.

2. We do twofold bootstrapping. After the first pass $\pi_{H_0}^1$ of the second bootstrapping on processor $H_0 M$ there is an intermediate result

$$
\boxed{\; S \quad \pi_I \quad T \;}\!\!\!\!\!\raisebox{-1ex}{I} \;=\; \boxed{\; S \quad \pi_I^1 \quad I \;}\!\!\!\!\!\raisebox{-1ex}{I} \;;\; \boxed{\; I \quad \pi_I^2 \quad T \;}\!\!\!\!\!\raisebox{-1ex}{I}
$$

after the second pass $\pi_{H_0}^2$ there is the final result

$$
\boxed{\; S \quad \pi_T \quad T \;}\!\!\!\!\!\raisebox{-1ex}{T} \;=\; \boxed{\; S \quad \pi_T^1 \quad I \;}\!\!\!\!\!\raisebox{-1ex}{T} \;;\; \boxed{\; I \quad \pi_T^2 \quad T \;}\!\!\!\!\!\raisebox{-1ex}{T}
$$

For full translator correctness we need double checks for four transitions in principle

$$
\begin{array}{cc}
\pi_{tS}^1 & \pi_{tS}^2 \\
\downarrow \text{ 1. } trans_I^S & \downarrow \text{ 2. } trans_I^S \\
\pi_I^1 & \pi_I^2 \\
\downarrow \text{ 1. } trans_T^I & \downarrow \text{ 2. } trans_T^I \\
\pi_T^1 & \pi_T^2
\end{array}
$$

We do these double checks in the upper right triangle due to the specifications of $trans_I^S$ and $trans_T^I$.

3. Machine code checking, e. g. 1. $trans_T^I$ down left corner, is especially unpleasant. We liberate ourselves from that and just make sure that π_T^1 is a program $\in PP_T$. There is great practical help if processor TM has memory

protection mechanisms (which the *transputer* has not. The *transputer* is good for process programming, not for systems programming).

4. Let third bootstrapping, π_T applied to π_{tS}, yield an intermediate result $\bar{\pi}_I = \bar{\pi}_I^1$; $\bar{\pi}_I^2$ after pass π_T^1 and a final result $\bar{\pi}_T = \bar{\pi}_T^1$; $\bar{\pi}_T^2$ after pass π_T^2. Let us extend the strong test to intermediate results and successfully observe

$$\pi_I = \bar{\pi}_I \text{ i. e. } \pi_I^1 = \bar{\pi}_I^1 \text{ and } \pi_I^2 = \bar{\pi}_I^2, \quad \pi_T = \bar{\pi}_T \text{ i. e. } \pi_T^1 = \bar{\pi}_T^1 \text{ and } \pi_T^2 = \bar{\pi}_T^2 .$$

5. π_I^2 is correct by 2. $trans_T^I$, $\bar{\pi}_I^1$ by 1. $trans_I^S$ and step 4.. $\bar{\pi}_T^1$ is the result of π_T^2 applied to $\bar{\pi}_I^1$ and correct by the First Bootstrapping Theorem. So is π_T^1 by step 4. and π_T by sequential composition.

Second Translator Test Theorem: If $\pi_I = \pi_I^1$; π_I^2 and π_T^2 are correctly implemented translators, if π_T^1 is just a proper program $\in PP_T$ and if the extended strong compiler test is successful then π_T is a correctly implemented translator [Lan97a].

4 Conclusion

In view of J. B. Goodenough's and S. L. Gerhart's theory compiler π_{tS} shows up to be a very well selected test datum to do translator implementation verification for π_T supported by testing.

A posteriori verification of generated machine code as demanded by BSI in each program case relevant for safety critical applications should and can be made redundant. It suffices to do such a posteriori verification for initial compilers only.

For translator implementation verification we have used and refunctioned a real life system, host processor H_0M plus $S_0 \rightarrow H_0$-translator π_{tH_0}, as a proof assistant. We print and iuxtapose intermediate translators which represent formal proof trees understandable by usual programmers. No special formal logics are necessary as existing theorem provers require.

We create complete enough and readable proof documentations not only for translation verification but also for translator implementation verification. Our technique allows to put the finger on the wound of any compiler failure in translation specification as well as in translator implementation. Even for full compiler correctness only a reduced set of low level code must be double checked.

Our proceeding is in accordance with A. Robinson's [Rob96] statements on formal and informal proof: Informatics should try to mechanise proof techniques of mathematicians. Their informal proofs are guided by good ideas. That is more effectful than pursuing swollen formal proof protocols in predicate logics.

Acknowledgement. The author would like to thank for valuable discussions and help of his colleagues in the Verifix–project W. Goerigk, U. Hoffmann, M. Müller-Olm, H. Ruess, W. Zimmermann and of Mrs. A. Langmaack.

References

[Bau75]   F.L. Bauer, editor. Software Engineering: An Advanced Course. LNCS, 30. Springer-Verlag, 1975.

[BHL+96]   J. Bowen, C.A.R. Hoare, H. Langmaack, E.-R. Olderog, and A.P. Ravn. A ProCoS II Project Final Report: ESPRIT Basic Reserach Project 7071. EATCS-Bulletin, 59:76-99, 1996.

[BSI94]   BSI-Bundesamt für Sicherheit in der Informationstechnik. BSI-Zertifizierung. BSI 7119, Bonn, 1994.

[CM86]   L.M. Chirica and D.F. Martin. Toward Compiler Implementation Correctness Proofs. ACM Transactions on Programming Languages and Systems, 8(2):185-214, April 1986.

[Eng97]   K. Engelhardt. Model-Oriented Data Refinement. PhD thesis, Univ.Kiel, 1997.

[GDG+96]   W. Goerigk, A. Dold, T. Gaul, G. Goos, A. Heberle, F.W. von Henke, U. Hoffmann, H. Langmaack, H. Pfeifer, H. Ruess, and W. Zimmermann. Compiler Correctness and Implementation Verification: The Verifix Approach. In CC '96 Int. Conf. on Compiler Construction (poster session), Linkøping, Sweden, 1996.

[GG75]   J.B. Goodenough and S.L. Gerhart. Toward a Theory of Test Data Selection. IEEE Transactions on Software Engineering, 1(2):156-173, June 1975.

[Jon90]   C.B. Jones. Systematic Software Development Using VDM, 2nd ed. Prentice Hall, New York, London, 1990.

[Lan97a]   H. Langmaack. Softwareengineering zur Zertifizierung von Systemen: Spezifikations-, Implementierungs-, Übersetzerkorrektheit. it+ti-Informationstechnik und Technische Informatik, 39 (3), 41-47, 1997.

[Lan97b]   H. Langmaack. Theoretische Informatik ist Grundlage für das sichere Beherrschen realistischer Software und Systeme. In K. Brunnstein and H. Oberquelle, editors, 25 Jahre Informatik an der Universität Hamburg, Informatik: Stand, Trends, Visionen, Ber. FBI-HH-B-195/97, pages 47-62. Univ. Hamburg, 1997.

[Mil89]   R. Milner. Communication and Concurrency. Prentice Hall, 1989.

[MO96]   M. Müller-Olm. Modular Compiler Verification. Dissertation, Univ.Kiel, 1996. Will be published as vol. 1283 of LNCS, Springer-Verlag, 1997.

[Moo88]   J.S. Moore. Piton: A verified assembly level language. Technical Report 22, Comp. Logic Inc, Austin, Texas, 1988.

[Moo96]   J.S. Moore. Piton, A Mechanically Verified Assembly-Level Language. Kluwer Academic Publishers, 1996.

[ORS92]   S. Owre, J. M. Rushby, and N. Shankar. PVS: A Prototype Verification System. In Deepak Kapur, editor, Proceedings 11th International Conference on Automated Deduction CADE, volume 607 of Lecture Notes in Artificial Intelligence, pages 748-752, Saratoga, NY, October 1992. Springer-Verlag.

[Plo81]   G.D. Plotkin. A Structural Approach to Operationale Semantics. DAIMI-FN19, Aarhus University, 1981.

[Pof95]   E. Pofahl. Methods Used for Inspecting Safety Relevant Software. In W. J. Cullyer, W. A. Halang, B.J. Krämer (eds.): High Integrity Programmable Electronic Systems, Dagstuhl-Sem.-Rep. 107, p 13, 1995.

[Pol81]   W. Polak. Compiler specification and verification. Number 124 in LNCS. 1981.

[Rob96]   A. Robinson. Formal and Informal Proof. Lecture, Colloquium, DFG-Schwerpunktprogramm "Deduktion", Dagstuhl, January 1996.

[Sco82]   D. S. Scott. Domains for Denotational Semantics. In M. Nielsen and E. M. Schmidt, editors, Int. Coll. on Automata, Languages and Programs, number 140 in LNCS, pages 577–613. 1982.

[Ste84]   G.L. Steele. Common Lisp: The Language. Digital Press, Bedford, MA, 1984.

[Tof90]   M. Tofte. Compiler Generators. EATCS Monographs on Theoretical Computer Science, Springer-Verlag, 1997.

[vWi69]   A. van Wijngaarden (ed.). Report on the Algorithmic Language ALGOL68. Numerische Mathematik, 14:79–218, 1969.

[Wir77]   N. Wirth. Compilerbau. Teubner, 1977.

[You88]   W.D. Young. A Verified Code Generator for a Subset of Gypsy. Technical Report 33, Comp. Logic. Inc., Austin, Texas, 1988.

[ZSI89]   ZSI-Zentralstelle für Sicherheit in der Informationstechnik. IT-Sicherheitskriterien. Bundesanzeiger Verlagsgesellschaft, Köln, 1989.

[ZSI90]   ZSI-Zentralstelle für Sicherheit in der Informationstechnik. IT-Evaluationshandbuch. Bundesanzeiger Verlagsgesellschaft, Köln, 1990.

On the Arrangement Complexity of Uniform Trees

Günter Hotz   and   Hongzhong Wu
FB14-Informatik, Universität des Saarlandes

This paper studies the arrangement problem of uniform trees and shows that the arrangement complexity of a uniform tree is either $\Theta(1)$ or $\Omega((\lg n)^\gamma)(\gamma > 0)$. It also presents a recursive algorithm to compute the optimal complete arrangements for $\Theta(1)$ arrangeable balanced uniform trees.

1   Introduction

A tree-like structured VLSI system is called a tree. Every node inside the tree implements a function and has several input lines and one output line. A uniform tree is a special one in which all nodes implement the same function. A tree is considered to be balanced if the difference between the length of the longest path and that of the shortest one from the root to the leaves is at most 1. The input lines corresponding to the leaves of the tree are called *primary input lines*, while the output line of the root node is called *primary output line*.

An *arrangement* set for a tree with n primary input lines consists of a number of n-component patterns such that by applying them to the primary input lines of the tree, the input and output sets of every node inside the tree have a *predefined property*. An *arrangement* problem is to assign an arrangement set to a tree. This is a more general combinational problem extracted from the assignment and the test problem related to the tree VLSI systems. Assignment and test are two basic problems in the field of VLSI system design. The study of these problems is useful for the design of easily testable VLSI systems and the generation of their optimal test sets, and therefore it is helpful to reduce the costs of the system's design and maintenance[Haye71,SK77, BeHa90, BeSp91, Wu92, WuSp92, Wu93, HoWu95].

If the predefined property for the arrangement is that *the input set to the node includes all possible input combinations,* the arrangement is just the assignment problem. The VLSI system test problem can be divided into two essential subproblems, test application and response observation. For the I_{DDQ} testing technique [FSTH90], it suffices to completely exercise all internal nodes of the network, i.e. apply all possible input combinations to each of the internal nodes. If the predefined property is that *the input and output sets of the node comprise a test set of the node,* the arrangement problem is exactly the test problem. Thus, the assignment and test problems are two instances of the arrangement problem.

The arrangement complexity of a given tree is defined as the minimum of the cardinalities of its arrangement sets. The extensive study of the arrangement complexity has theoretical as well as practical value.

This paper discusses the arrangement problem of the balanced uniform trees. It consists of four sections. In the next section, we use the X-category theory developed in [Hotz65, Hotz74] to define tree systems and their arrangement problems formally such that we can simplify our discussion and generalize the results easily. In section 3, we study the constant arrangeable tree families. Section 4 shows that the arrangement complexity of a uniform tree is either $\Theta(1)$ or $\Omega((\lg n)^\gamma)(\gamma > 0)$. It explores that according to their arrangement complexities, the balanced uniform trees can be roughly divided into two classes, constant and polynomial in $\lg n$. There is nothing in between.

2 X-Category and Arrangement of Uniform Trees

In this section, we give a formal description of VLSI systems by using the X-category. It is shown that all combinational VLSI systems correspond to an X-category denoted by $\mathcal{C}$, and that the functions implemented by the elements in $\mathcal{C}$ together correspond to an X-category denoted by $\mathcal{K}$. Furthermore, we show that there is a functor from $\mathcal{C}$ to $\mathcal{K}$. Then, we can study some properties of elements of $\mathcal{C}$ in the field of $\mathcal{K}$ without concern of their concrete physical structures.

Let $T = \{t_1, t_2, ..., t_m\}$ be the set of the basic types of signals which can be transferred through a (symbolic) line or (symbolic) bus in VLSI systems. A signal type $t_i \in T$ consists of a number of signals called individuals(values). For instance, the 1-bit binary signal type includes logic 0 and logic 1 as its individuals, and a line of such a signal type can transfer both logic 0 and logic 1.

Let $T^* = \{a_1...a_k | a_1, ..., a_k \in T, k \in \mathbf{N}_0\}$ be the free monoid generated by T. The concatenation of $u, v \in T^*$ is $u \cdot v$, and $|a_1 \cdots a_k|$ denotes the length of the sequence $a_1 \cdots a_k (a_i \in T)$. We use the symbol ε to denote the empty word.

We use I_{t_i} to denote the set of all individuals of the signal type t_i and consider I_{uv} as $I_u \times I_v$ for $u, v \in T^*$.

Let $\mathcal{A}$ be the set of all building blocks of the VLSI systems. Every line of an element $F \in \mathcal{A}$ has a signal type. Two functions $Q, Z : \mathcal{A} \longrightarrow T^*$ are used to determine the input and output types of the building blocks in $\mathcal{A}$. For instance, the input type and output type of $F \in \mathcal{A}$ are $Q(F)$ and $Z(F)$, respectively. Given two building blocks $F, G \in \mathcal{A}$, we can construct a new building block by using the parallel operation " $\times$ ". The building block constructed in this way is illustrated by Fig. 1. In case the output type $Z(G)$ of G is equal to the input type $Q(F)$ of F, we can construct a new building block by using the sequential operation " $\circ$ ". Fig. 2 shows the new building block constructed by linking the ith output line of G directly to the ith input line of F.

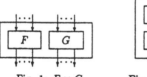

Fig. 1: $F \times G$ Fig. 2: $F \circ G$

For $F, G \in \mathcal{A}$, it holds

$$Q(F \times G) = Q(F) \cdot Q(G), \qquad Z(F \times G) = Z(F) \cdot Z(G),$$
$$Q(F \circ G) = Q(G), \qquad Z(F \circ G) = Z(F).$$

Let $\mathbf{B}_T = \{B_1, B_2, ...\}$ and $\mathbf{D}_T = \{L_u, D_u, V_{uv} \mid u, v \in T\}$ be two classes of basic building blocks. Assume that $|Q(B)| \in \mathbf{N}$(set of all positive integers) and $|Z(B)| = 1$ for every $B \in \mathbf{B}_T$. In other words, every basic building block B in $\mathbf{B}_T$ has only one output line and at least one input line. The input and output types of B are $Q(B)$ and $Z(B)$, and the input and output values of B are limited to $I_{Q(B)}$ and $I_{Z(B)}$, respectively. The elements in $\mathbf{D}_T$ can be illustrated by the following figures.

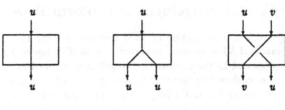

Fig. 3: L_u **Fig. 4: D_u** **Fig. 5: V_{uv}**

L_u denotes a line, D_u a fanout mechanism, and V_{uv} two crossing lines. For the three building blocks, we have $Q(L_u) = u$, $Z(L_u) = u$, $Q(D_u) = u$, $Z(D_u) = uu$, $Q(V_{uv}) = uv$, $Z(V_{uv}) = vu$.

Let $\mathbf{A} = \mathbf{B}_T \cup \mathbf{D}_T$. $\mathcal{A}$, the set of all building blocks of VLSI systems can be formally defined by
(1) $\mathcal{A} \supset \mathbf{A}$.
(2) $F, G \in \mathcal{A} \Longrightarrow F \times G \in \mathcal{A}$.
(3) $F, G \in \mathcal{A}$ and $Z(G) = Q(F) \Longrightarrow F \circ G \in \mathcal{A}$.

It has been shown that $\mathbf{C} = (T^*, \mathcal{A}, Q, Z, \circ)$ is a category, and that $\mathcal{C} = (T^*, \mathcal{A}, Q, Z, \circ, \times)$ is an X-category [Hotz65].

Suppose that t is the 1-bit binary signal type and $T = \{t\}$. If $\mathbf{D}_T = \{L_t, D_t, V_{tt}\}$ and $\mathbf{B}_T$ includes NOT, AND and OR gates, the X-category $\mathcal{C}$ defined above corresponds to the whole combinational VLSI system. $\mathcal{C}$ corresponds to the whole tree system if $\mathbf{D}_T$ does not include the fanout mechanism D_t.

Assume that a building block $F \in \mathcal{A}$ implements a function f and that its domain and codomain are denoted by $Q'(f)$ and $Z'(f)$. ($Q'(f) = I_{Q(F)}$ and $Z'(f) = I_{Z(F)}$). Let $T^* = \{I_u | u \in T^*\}$. The set

$$\mathcal{F} = \{f \mid f : Q'(f) \to Z'(f) \wedge Q'(f), Z'(f) \in T^*\}$$

includes all the functions implemented by the elements of $\mathcal{A}$.

We define two operations $\odot$ and $\otimes$ over $\mathcal{F}$. Given two functions f and g, $f \otimes g$ is a function from $Q'(f)Q'(g)$ to $Z'(f)Z'(g)$. In case $Q'(f) = Z'(g)$, $f \odot g$ is defined as a function from $Q'(g)$ to $Z'(f)$. It can be shown that $K = (T^*, \mathcal{F}, Q', Z', \odot)$ is a category and that $\mathcal{K} = (T^*, \mathcal{F}, Q', Z', \odot, \otimes)$ is an X-category. In the following, we investigate the relationship between the two X-categories $\mathcal{C}$ and $\mathcal{K}$ by using *functors*.

Definition 1 (functor)
Given two categories $\mathbf{C} = (O(C), M(C), Q, Z, \circ)$ and $\mathbf{K} = (O(K), M(K), Q', Z', \odot)$ and two mappings $\phi_1 : O(C) \to O(K)$ and $\phi_2 : M(C) \to M(K)$, $\phi = (\phi_1, \phi_2)$ is called a functor, provided that the following conditions are satisfied.

1. $\forall F \in M(C) \{Q'(\phi_2(F)) = \phi_1(Q(F)) \wedge Z'(\phi_2(F)) = \phi_1(Z(F))\}$.

2. $\forall F, G \in M(C) \{Q(F) = Z(G) \Longrightarrow \phi_2(F \circ G) = \phi_2(F) \odot \phi_2(G)\}$.

3. $\forall u \in O(C) \{\phi_2(1_u) = 1_{\phi_1(u)}\}$.

We define the two mappings as
$$\phi_1 : T^* \to T^*, \quad \phi_1(u) = I_u, \quad u \in T^*,$$
$$\phi_2 : \mathcal{A} \to \mathcal{F}, \quad \phi_2(F) = f \text{ if } f : I_{Q(F)} \to I_{Z(F)}, \; F \in \mathcal{A}$$
It is easy to check that:
1, $\forall F \in \mathcal{A} \{Q'(\phi_2(F)) = \phi_1(Q(F)) \wedge Z'(\phi_2(F)) = \phi_1(Z(F))\}$.
2, $\forall F, G \in \mathcal{A} \{Q(F) = Z(G) \Longrightarrow \phi_2(F \circ G) = \phi_2(F) \odot \phi_2(G)\}$.
3, $\forall u \in T^* \{\phi_2(1_u) = 1_{\phi_1(u)}\}$.

Thus, $\phi = (\phi_1, \phi_2)$ is a functor from **C** to **K**, and a functor from $\mathcal{C}$ to $\mathcal{K}$ as well since

$$\forall F, G \in \mathcal{A} \{\phi_2(F \times G) = \phi_2(F) \otimes \phi_2(G)\}.$$

Thereafter, we use operators o and × to replace ⊙ and ⊗, and substitute the mappings Q and Z for Q' and Z' provided that no confusion can be caused. For the sake of simplicity, we often call a basic building block *cell* and use a lower case letter to represent a function implemented by a building block represented by the corresponding upper case letter. For example, b is used to represent the function implemented by $B \in \mathcal{A}$. L_t is used to denote a line transferring signals of type t. Furthermore, we use u to represent $\phi_1(u)$ ($u \in T^*$), namely the set of values of type u. For instance, we use the form $f : t^k \longrightarrow t$ to represent a function f from $\phi_1(t^k)$ to $\phi_1(t)$.

Every building block $F \in \mathcal{A}$ implements a function $\phi_2(F) : Q(F) \to Z(F)$. For example, L_u realizes an identity on u, D_u a function from u to $u \times u$, and V_{uv} a function from $u \times v$ to $v \times u$. Suppose x and y are two individuals of type u and v, respectively, then

$$\phi_2(L_u)(x) = x, \quad \phi_2(D_u)(x) = xx \quad \text{and} \quad \phi_2(V_{uv})(xy) = yx.$$

For the rest of the paper, we assume that $T = \{t\}$, $\mathbf{B}_T = \{B\}$, $\mathbf{D}_T = \{L_u, V_{uv} | u, v \in T\}$, $Q(B) = \underbrace{t \cdots t}_{k}$ and $Z(B) = t$. We use $\mathcal{A}$ to denote the set of all uniform trees based on the unique basic cell B, and $T_b^{(n)}$ to denote a balanced uniform tree consisting of b-cells and having n primary input lines. Our discussion will deal with the arrangement problem for $T_b^{(n)}$.

For distinguishing from the Cartesian product t^l, we use $t^{(l)}$ to denote the set of all l-dimensional vectors consisting of elements of type t. Given a function $f : t^k \longrightarrow t$ and an integer $l \in \mathbf{N}$, we use $f^{(l)}$ to denote a vector function defined as follows:

$$f^{(l)}(\vec{v}_1, \vec{v}_2, \cdots, \vec{v}_k) = \begin{pmatrix} f(v_{11}, v_{12}, \cdots, v_{1k}) \\ f(v_{21}, v_{22}, \cdots, v_{2k}) \\ \vdots \\ f(v_{l1}, v_{l2}, \cdots, v_{lk}) \end{pmatrix}, \qquad \vec{v}_i \in t^{(l)}.$$

Example 1: Function f_1(logical function NAND) is defined by

$$\begin{array}{c|cc} f_1 & 0 & 1 \\ \hline 0 & 1 & 1 \\ 1 & 1 & 0 \end{array}$$

For $\vec{v}_0 = \begin{pmatrix} 0 \\ 1 \\ 1 \end{pmatrix}$, $\vec{v}_1 = \begin{pmatrix} 1 \\ 1 \\ 0 \end{pmatrix}$ and $\vec{v}_2 = \begin{pmatrix} 1 \\ 0 \\ 1 \end{pmatrix}$, $f_1^{(3)}(\vec{v}_1, \vec{v}_2) = \begin{pmatrix} f_1(1,1) \\ f_1(1,0) \\ f_1(0,1) \end{pmatrix} = \begin{pmatrix} 0 \\ 1 \\ 1 \end{pmatrix} = \vec{v}_0$

Definition 2 (similar matrices)
Let $\vec{u}_i, \vec{v}_i \in t^{(l)} (i \in [1, k])$. Consider $(\vec{u}_1, \vec{u}_2, \cdots, \vec{u}_k)$ and $(\vec{v}_1, \vec{v}_2, \cdots, \vec{v}_k)$ as two $l \times k$ matrices. They are said to be similar, denoted by $(\vec{u}_1, \vec{u}_2, \cdots, \vec{u}_k) \sim (\vec{v}_1, \vec{v}_2, \cdots, \vec{v}_k)$, if and only if they can be transformed into each other by row exchanges. (It is easy to see that $\sim$ is an equivalence relation.)

For example, $\begin{pmatrix} 0 & 1 \\ 1 & 0 \\ 1 & 1 \end{pmatrix} \sim \begin{pmatrix} 0 & 1 \\ 1 & 1 \\ 1 & 0 \end{pmatrix} \sim \begin{pmatrix} 1 & 1 \\ 1 & 0 \\ 0 & 1 \end{pmatrix}$. For the arrangement of a uniform tree $T_b^{(n)}$, we are concerned about a predefined property which is expected to be satisfied for every b-cell in the tree. We use the *predicate* P_b to describe this property. The following is the formal definition of arrangement problem. An example following the definition gives a further explanation of it.

Definition 3 (arrangement, arrangement complexity)
Given a function $b : t^k \longrightarrow t$ *and a predefined property* P, *we define the predicate* P_b *as*

$$P_b(\vec{v}_0, \vec{v}_1, \cdots, \vec{v}_k) = \begin{cases} \text{true} & : \quad \begin{aligned} \vec{v}_0 &= b^{(l)}(\vec{v}_1, \cdots, \vec{v}_k) \quad \text{and} \\ (\vec{v}_0, \vec{v}_1, &\cdots, \vec{v}_k) \text{ has property } P \end{aligned} \\ \text{false} & : \quad \text{otherwise} \end{cases} \tag{1}$$

where l *is an arbitrary integer in* N, *and* $\vec{v}_i \in t^{(l)}$ *for* $i \in [0, k]$. *In addition, the predicate satisfies (2)*

$$(\vec{u}_0, \vec{u}_1, \cdots, \vec{u}_k) \sim (\vec{v}_0, \vec{v}_1, \cdots, \vec{v}_k) \Longrightarrow P_b(\vec{u}_0, \vec{u}_1, \cdots, \vec{u}_k) = P_b(\vec{v}_0, \vec{v}_1, \cdots, \vec{v}_k) \tag{2}$$

We call n *l-dimensional vectors of* $t^{(l)}$ *(l n-component patterns of* t^n*) a complete arrangement set for* $T_b^{(n)}$ *if by applying them to the* n *primary input lines of* $T_b^{(n)}$, $P_b(\vec{v}_0, \vec{v}_1, \cdots, \vec{v}_k)$ *is true for every* b-cell *in* $T_b^{(n)}$. *Here,* $\vec{v}_0$ *is the output vector and* $\vec{v}_1, ..., \vec{v}_k$ *are the input vectors of the cell.*

The arrangement complexity l *of* $T_b^{(n)}$ *is defined as the minimum of the dimensions of the complete arrangement sets for* $T_b^{(n)}$.

For example, if we define the predicate P_b as the following

$$P_b(\vec{v}_0, \vec{v}_1, \cdots, \vec{v}_k) = \begin{cases} \text{true} & : \quad \begin{aligned} \vec{v}_0 &= b^{(l)}(\vec{v}_1, \cdots, \vec{v}_k) \quad \text{and} \\ t^k &\subset \{(v_{i1}, \cdots, v_{ik}) | i = 1, 2, ..., l\} \end{aligned} \\ \text{false} & : \quad \text{otherwise} \end{cases}$$

where $\vec{v}_i \in t^{(l)}$, then the input set to every b-cell in the tree includes t^k, namely all possible input combinations, and the above arrangement problem becomes the assignment problem[Wu93].

It can be shown that the arrangement problem becomes a test problem when we give another interpretation to the function b and the predicate P_b[Wu92].

3 $\Theta(1)$ Arrangeable Trees

The arrangement complexity of $F \in \mathcal{A}$ depends on the property of $\phi_2(B)$, namely b. In the following, we show that one can construct a complete arrangement set of a constant size for every $F \in \mathcal{A}$ if the function b has a special property described later. In order to describe this property, we require a new symbol D_u^i which is defined for all $u \in T^*$ by

(1) $D_u^2 = D_u$,   (2) $D_u^{i+1} = (D_u^i \times L_u) \circ D_u$.

The logical structure of D_u^{i+1} is illustrated by Fig. 6

In the rest of the paper, we use σ to denote the type of $\underbrace{t \cdots t}_{k}$,

Definition 4 (b-stable set)
A set $S \subset t^k$ is b-stable if and only if there are bijective mappings $\pi_1, ..., \pi_k : S \to S$ such that $(b \circ \pi_1 \times \cdots \times b \circ \pi_k) \circ D_\sigma^k(S) = S$.

The following lemma states that if the set $S \in t^k$ is b-stable, we can construct an identity mapping for the set S, and the mapping includes the function b as its component.

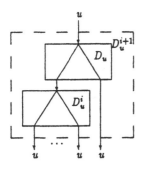

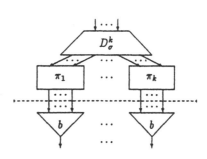

Fig. 6 D_u^{i+1} Fig. 7 f_b

Lemma 1 *If set $S \subset t^k$ is b-stable, there are k bijective mappings $\pi_1, ..., \pi_k : S \to S$ such that*

$$\underbrace{(b \times \cdots \times b)}_{k} \circ (\pi_1 \times \cdots \times \pi_k) \circ D_\sigma^k \tag{3}$$

is the identity on S.

Proof: Suppose $S \subset t^k$ is b-stable and $(b \circ \pi_1 \times \cdots \times b \circ \pi_k) \circ D_\sigma^k$ is a bijective mapping from S to S. Define a bijective mapping $\pi_0 : S \to S$ as the inverse mapping of $(b \circ \pi_1 \times \cdots \times b \circ \pi_k) \circ D_\sigma^k$. Hence,

$$(b \circ \pi_1 \times \cdots \times b \circ \pi_k) \circ D_\sigma^k \circ \pi_0|_S \;=\; id|_S,$$

where $id|_S$ is the identity on S. Because $D_\sigma^k \circ \pi_0 = \underbrace{(\pi_0 \times \cdots \times \pi_0)}_{k} \circ D_\sigma^k$, it holds

$$(b \circ \pi_1 \times \cdots \times b \circ \pi_k) \circ D_\sigma^k \circ \pi_0 \;=\; (b \circ \pi_1 \times \cdots \times b \circ \pi_k) \circ \underbrace{(\pi_0 \times \cdots \times \pi_0)}_{k} \circ D_\sigma^k$$

$$=\; (b \times \cdots \times b) \circ (\pi_1 \circ \pi_0 \times \cdots \times \pi_k \circ \pi_0) \circ D_\sigma^k.$$

By substituting $\pi_i \circ \pi_0$ with π_i, we obtain the lemma.

Q.E.D.

We use f_b to denote the mapping defined by (3). Fig. 7 illustrates the structure of f_b. It consists of two parts. The upper part $(\pi_1 \times \cdots \times \pi_k) \circ D_\sigma^k$ is a fanout mechanism, and it has one input line and k output lines of type σ (k input lines and k^2 output lines of type t) and implements a mapping from t^k to t^{k^2}. The lower part $\underbrace{(b \times \cdots \times b)}_{k}$ consists of k parallel b cells. A b-cell can be considered as a uniform tree with k input lines of type t (an input line of type σ) and an output line of type t. Then, $\underbrace{(b \times \cdots \times b)}_{k}$ can be considered as a building block made up of k uniform trees. It has k input lines and one output line of type σ and implements a mapping from t^{k^2} to t^k. The two parts together realize the indentity mapping on t^k according to Lemma 1. The idea

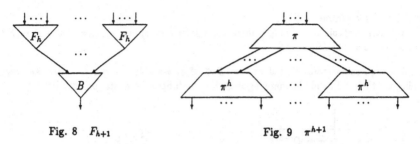

Fig. 8 F_{h+1} Fig. 9 π^{h+1}

here is to construct a building block which includes uniform trees and realizes the identity on a set S. By applying S to the building block, S is assigned to every uniform tree inside the building block. In the following we use this idea again to construct a family of identity mappings $F^h (h \in \mathbf{N})$. F^h includes h-level balanced uniform trees based on b.

We use π to denote $(\pi_1 \times \cdots \times \pi_k) \circ D_\sigma^k$. Thus, f_b represents $\underbrace{(b \times \cdots \times b)}_{k} \circ \pi$. At first, we give the recursive definitions of the balanced uniform trees F_h and the fanout mechanisms $\pi^h (h \in \mathbf{N})$.

The recursive definition for F_h is the following:

$$F_0 = L_t \tag{4}$$
$$F_{h+1} = B \circ \underbrace{(F_h \times \cdots \times F_h)}_{k}, \quad h \in \mathbf{N} \tag{5}$$

Fig. 8 shows F_{h+1}. It is easy to see that F_h $(h \in \mathbf{N})$ is a balanced uniform tree of level h. The π^h-family is defined as follows:

$$\pi^0 = L_t \tag{6}$$
$$\pi^{h+1} = \underbrace{(\pi^h \times \cdots \times \pi^h)}_{k} \circ \pi, \quad h = 1, 2, \dots \tag{7}$$

Fig. 9 shows π^{h+1}. Using F_h and π^h we can define the F^h-family by

$$F^h = \underbrace{(F_h \times \cdots \times F_h)}_{k} \circ \pi^h, \qquad h \in \mathbf{N} \tag{8}$$

To put it differently, it holds

$$F^h = \underbrace{(F_h \circ \pi^{h-1} \times \cdots \times F_h \circ \pi^{h-1})}_{k} \circ \pi \tag{9}$$

Fig. 10 shows F^h.

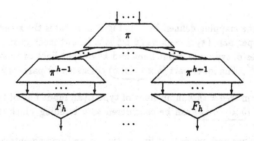

Fig. 10 F^h

According to the above definition, we have

$$\phi_2(F^1) = \phi_2(\underbrace{(B \times \cdots \times B)}_{k} \circ \pi) = f_b.$$

Let $f^h = \phi_2(F^h)$ for $h \in \mathbb{N}$. Then, f^h is a mapping from S to S and it is a generalization of f_b. The following lemma holds.

Lemma 2 $f^h|_S = id|_S$ holds for all $h \in \mathbb{N}$.

Proof: We prove this lemma by using induction on the parameter h. For $h = 1$, we have $f^1 = f_b$ and $f^1|_S = id|_S$. Suppose $f^{l-1}|_S = id|_S$ holds. According to the above definition

$$
\begin{aligned}
F_h \circ \pi^{h-1} &= B \circ \underbrace{(F_{h-1} \times \cdots \times F_{h-1})}_{k} \circ \pi^{h-1} \\
&= B \circ F^{h-1}, \qquad\qquad\qquad h \in \mathbb{N}.
\end{aligned}
$$

Hence

$$
\begin{aligned}
F^l &= \underbrace{(F_l \times \cdots \times F_l)}_{k} \circ \pi^l \\
&= \underbrace{(F_l \times \cdots \times F_l)}_{k} \circ \underbrace{(\pi^{l-1} \times \cdots \times \pi^{l-1})}_{k} \circ \pi \\
&= \underbrace{(F_l \circ \pi^{l-1} \times \cdots \times F_l \circ \pi^{l-1})}_{k} \circ \pi \\
&= \underbrace{(B \circ F^{l-1} \times \cdots \times B \circ F^{l-1})}_{k} \circ \pi \\
&= \underbrace{(B \times \cdots \times B)}_{k} \circ \underbrace{(F^{l-1} \times \cdots \times F^{l-1})}_{k} \circ \pi.
\end{aligned}
$$

Thus

$$
\begin{aligned}
f^l|_S &= \phi_2(F^l)|_S \\
&= \underbrace{(b \times \cdots \times b)}_{k} \circ \underbrace{(f^{l-1} \times \cdots \times f^{l-1})}_{k} \circ \pi|_S \\
&= \underbrace{(b \times \cdots \times b)}_{k} \circ \pi|_S \\
&= f^1|_S \\
&= id|_S.
\end{aligned}
$$

Thus, $f^h|_S = id|_S$ holds for all $h \in \mathbb{N}$.

Q.E.D.

Theorem 1 *If $S \subset t^k$ is b-stable and a minimal arrangement set for cell B, $\#S$ is an upper bound to the minimum of the cardinalities of the complete arrangement sets for each of the trees in $\mathcal{A}$.*

Proof: Given a tree $T' \in \mathcal{A}$, one can always find a balanced tree $T \in \mathcal{A}$ such that T' can be embedded into T. The arrangement complexity of T is an upper bound for that of T'. We can construct a complete arrangement set of a constant size for every tree in $\mathcal{A}$, if we can construct a complete arrangement set of a constant size for every balanced tree in $\mathcal{A}$. In other words, all trees in $\mathcal{A}$ are constant arrangeable if all balanced trees in $\mathcal{A}$ are constant arrangeable.

A balanced tree $F_{h+1} \in \mathcal{A}$ has the structure $B \circ (\underbrace{F_h \times \cdots \times F_h}_{k})$. Suppose $S \subset t^k$ is b-stable and an arrangement set for cell B. In the above, we showed that for every $h \in \mathbb{N}$, it holds

$$\phi_2(F^h) = \phi_2((\underbrace{F_h \times \cdots \times F_h}_{k}) \circ \pi^h|_S) = id|_S$$

and $(\underbrace{F_h \times \cdots \times F_h}_{k}) \circ \pi^h(S) = S$. This indicates that when $\pi^h(S)$ is applied to the primary input lines of F_{h+1}, the vectors applied to an arbitrary cell B inside F_{h+1} comprise an arrangement set. Thus $\pi^h(S)$ is just a complete arrangement set for F_{h+1} and $\#S$ is an upper bound to the minimum of the cardinalities of the complete arrangement sets for F_{h+1}.

$$\text{Q.E.D.}$$

Corollary 1 *If $S \subset t^k$ is b-stable and an optimal arrangement set for cell B, $\pi^h(S)$ is an optimal complete arrangement set for F_{h+1}.*

Theorem 2 *The arrangement complexity of $T_b^{(n)}$ is $\Theta(1)$, if there exist an $i \in \mathbb{N}$, a subset $S \subset t^{k^i}$ and k^i bijective mappings $\pi_1, ..., \pi_{k^i} : S \longrightarrow S$ such that S is a complete arrangement set for F_i and it holds*

$$(\underbrace{F_i \times \cdots \times F_i}_{k^i}) \circ (\underbrace{\pi_1 \times \cdots \times \pi_{k^i}}_{k^i}) \circ D_\sigma^{k^i}(S) = S.$$

Proof: Suppose there are an $i \in \mathbb{N}$, a subset $S \subset t^{k^i}$, and k^i bijective mappings $\pi_1, ..., \pi_{k^i} : S \longrightarrow S$ such that S is a complete arrangement set for F_i and

$$(\underbrace{F_i \times \cdots \times F_i}_{k^i}) \circ (\underbrace{\pi_1 \times \cdots \times \pi_{k^i}}_{k^i}) \circ D_\sigma^{k^i}(S) = S. \tag{10}$$

Let $\kappa = k^i$ and $g = \phi_2(F_i)$. Based on (10), S is g-stable. Let $l = \#S$. We define

$$\mathbf{P}_g(\vec{v}_0, \vec{v}_1, \cdots, \vec{v}_\kappa) = \begin{cases} \text{true} & : & \begin{aligned} &\vec{v}_0 = g^{(l)}(\vec{v}_1, \cdots, \vec{v}_\kappa) \quad \text{and} \\ &(\vec{v}_1, \cdots, \vec{v}_\kappa) \text{ is a complete arrangement for } F_i \end{aligned} \\ \\ \text{false} & : & \text{otherwise} \end{cases}$$

where $\vec{v}_i \in t^{(l)}$. As mentioned above, S is g-stable. Based on Theorem 1, we can state that $\#S$ is an upper bound to the minimum of the cardinalities of the arrangement sets for $T_g^{(n)}$ and that the arrangement complexity of $T_b^{(n)}$ is $\Theta(1)$.

$$\text{Q.E.D.}$$

The proofs of Theorem 1 and 2 are constructive. In fact, we can derive algorithms to construct a minimal complete arrangement set for the balanced uniform tree based on function b.

4 The Jump from $\Theta(1)$ to $\Omega((\lg n)^\gamma)$

In this section, we give another criteria of $\Theta(1)$ arrangeable uniform trees and show that the arrangement complexity of $T_b^{(n)}$ is either $\Theta(1)$ or $\Omega((\lg n)^\gamma)(\gamma > 0)$.

We assign every line and b-cell in $T_b^{(n)}$ a unique level. The levels will be arranged in ascending order from the primary output to the primary inputs of $T_b^{(n)}$. The primary output is assigned level 0. A b-cell and all its input lines are assigned level $k + 1$, if its output line is in level k. $T_b^{(n)}$ is said to be of k-level, if it has k levels.

According to the definition of the complete arrangement set, we can define a predicate $\mathbf{P}_b$ based on the given function $b : t^k \longrightarrow t$ and the predefined property P, such that n l-dimensional vectors of $t^{(l)}$ comprise a complete arrangement set for $T_b^{(n)}$ if and only if by applying them to the n primary inputs lines of $T_b^{(n)}$, $\mathbf{P}_b(\vec{v}_0, \vec{v}_1, \cdots, \vec{v}_k)$ is true for every b-cell inside $T_b^{(n)}$. Here, $\vec{v}_0$ is the output vector and $\vec{v}_1, \cdots, \vec{v}_k$ are input vectors of that b-cell.

Lemma 3 $T_b^{(n)}$ is $\Theta(1)$ arrangeable if there are an $l \in \mathbf{N}$ and a set $W \subset t^{(l)}$ such that for every $\vec{v}_0 \in W$, there are k vectors $\vec{v}_1, \vec{v}_2, \cdots, \vec{v}_k$ in W and $\mathbf{P}_b(\vec{v}_0, \vec{v}_1, \cdots, \vec{v}_k)$ is true. Put it formally:

$$\exists l \in \mathbf{N} \; \exists W \subset t^{(l)} \; \forall \vec{v}_0 \in W \; \exists \vec{v}_1, \cdots, \vec{v}_k \in W \; \{\mathbf{P}_b(\vec{v}_0, \vec{v}_1, \cdots, \vec{v}_k)\} \tag{11}$$

Proof: Suppose $\exists l \in \mathbf{N} \; \exists W \subset t^{(l)} \; \forall \vec{v}_0 \in W \; \exists \vec{v}_1, \cdots, \vec{v}_k \in W \; \{\mathbf{P}_b(\vec{v}_0, \vec{v}_1, \cdots, \vec{v}_k)\}$. We prove that for every N-level $T_b^{(n)} (n \leq k^N)$, there are n vectors $\vec{v}_1, \cdots, \vec{v}_k$ in W and they comprise a complete arrangement set for $T_b^{(n)}$. This can be done by induction on the number of the levels of $T_b^{(n)}$.

In the case $N = 1$, the tree has only one cell. We choose $\vec{v}_0 \in W$ arbitrarily, then determine k vectors $\vec{v}_1, \vec{v}_2, \cdots, \vec{v}_k \in W$ such that $\mathbf{P}_b(\vec{v}_0, \vec{v}_1, \cdots, \vec{v}_k)$ is true. It is clear that $(\vec{v}_1, \vec{v}_2, \cdots, \vec{v}_k)$ is an arrangement set for cell B, a tree having only one cell.

Assume that for $N = i$, the vectors $\vec{v}_{1,0}, \vec{v}_{2,0}, \cdots, \vec{v}_{k^i,0} \in W$ comprise a complete arrangement set for $T_b^{(k^i)}$. Suppose $T_b^{(k^{i+1})}$ is of $(i+1)$ levels and is constructed by connecting every primary input line in $T_b^{(k^i)}$ to the output line of a b-cell. According to the assumption,

$$\forall j \in [1, k^i] \; \exists \vec{v}_{j,0}, \vec{v}_{j,1}, \cdots, \vec{v}_{j,k} \in W \; \{\mathbf{P}_b(\vec{v}_{j,0}, \vec{v}_{j,1}, \cdots, \vec{v}_{j,k})\}.$$

Hence, $(\vec{v}_{j,0}, \vec{v}_{j,1}, \cdots, \vec{v}_{j,k})$ is an arrangement set for a b-cell. When $\vec{v}_{j,1}, \vec{v}_{j,2}, \cdots, \vec{v}_{j,k}$ are applied to the k input lines of the cell B directly linked to the jth input line in the level i, the vector offered to this input line is just $\vec{v}_{j,0}$. Thus, we can state that the k^{i+1} l-dimensional vectors $\vec{v}_{1,1}, \vec{v}_{1,2}, \cdots, \vec{v}_{1,k}, \vec{v}_{2,1}, \cdots, \vec{v}_{k^i,k}$ comprise a complete arrangement set for $T_b^{(k^{i+1})}$.

Q.E.D.

Corollary 2 $T_b^{(n)}$ is $\Theta(1)$ arrangeable if

$$\exists l \in \mathbf{N} \; \exists W' \subset t^{(l)} \; \forall \vec{u}_0 \in W' \; \exists \vec{v}_0, \vec{v}_1, \cdots, \vec{v}_k \in W' \; \{\mathbf{P}_b(\vec{v}_0, \vec{v}_1, \cdots, \vec{v}_k) \wedge \vec{u}_0 \sim \vec{v}_0\} \tag{12}$$

Proof: Given a set $W' \subset t^{(l)}(l \in \mathbf{N})$, we can always induce a set W such that

$$\forall \vec{v} \in t^{(l)} \; \{\exists \vec{u} \in W' \{\vec{u} \sim \vec{v}\} \Longrightarrow \vec{v} \in W\} \wedge \forall \vec{v} \in W \; \exists \vec{u} \in W' \{\vec{u} \sim \vec{v}\}.$$

The set W includes every vector which is *similar* to a vector in W'. It is obvious that such a W satisfies (11) if W' fulfills (12).

Q.E.D

Assume that $T_b^{(n)}$ consists of b-cells $C_{1,1}, C_{2,1}, C_{2,2}, ..., C_{k,m}, ...$, and cell $C_{i,j}$ is the jth cell in the ith level of $T_b^{(n)}$. Let A denote n vectors in $t^{(l)}$ and apply A to this tree. Let W denote the corresponding set including A and all other vectors delivered to other lines in every level of $T_b^{(n)}$. We use (A, i, j, m) to represent the corresponding vector applied to the mth input line of $C_{i,j}$, and $(A, i, j, 0)$ to represent the vector delivered to the output line of $C_{i,j}$.

Given a complete arrangement set A for an N-level $T_b^{(n)}$, we determine N sets in the following way:

$$W_s(A) := \left\{ (A, i, j, m) \mid i \in [1, s], j \in [1, k^{i-1}], m \in [0, k] \right\}, \quad s \in [1, N] \tag{13}$$

$W_s(A)$ includes all vectors delivered to a line in level i ($i \in [1, s]$) and the vector delivered to the primary output line. According to Definition 2, $\sim$ is an equivalence relation. $W_s(A)$ can be partitioned into equivalence classes according to the equivalence relation $\sim$ and we use $\#W_s(A)/\sim$ to denote the number of equivalence classes in $W_s(A)$. The following observation is obvious:

Observation 1 *Assume A to be a complete arrangement set for an N-level $T_b^{(n)}$. Then it holds*

1. $\forall s \in [2, N] \left\{ W_{s-1}(A) \subseteq W_s(A) \subseteq t^{(l)} \right\}$.

2. $\forall s \in [2, N] \{1 \leq \#W_{s-1}(A)/\sim \leq \#W_s(A)/\sim \}$.

Lemma 4 *Assume A to be a complete arrangement set for an N-level $T_b^{(n)}$. Then, $T_b^{(n)}$ is $\Theta(1)$ arrangeable if $\#W_s(A)/\sim = \#W_{s-1}(A)/\sim$ for an $s \in [2, N]$.*

Proof: Assume A to be a complete arrangement set for an N-level $T_b^{(n)}$. Suppose $\#W_s(A)/\sim = \#W_{s-1}(A)/\sim$ for an $s \in [2, N]$. Based on Observation 1, $W_{s-1}(A) \subseteq W_s(A)$ for all $s \in [2, N]$. According to the definition of $W_s(A)$, we can state that

$$\forall \vec{u}_0 \in W_s(A) \, \exists \vec{v}_0, \vec{v}_1, \cdots, \vec{v}_k \in W_s(A) \, \{ \mathbf{P}_b(\vec{v}_0, \vec{v}_1, \cdots, \vec{v}_k) \wedge \vec{u}_0 \sim \vec{v}_0 \}.$$

Based on Corollary 2, $T_b^{(n)}$ is $\Theta(1)$ arrangeable.

Q.E.D.

Lemma 5 *For every complete arrangement set A for an N-level $T_b^{(n)}$, it holds*

$$\forall s \in [1, N] \{ \#W_s(A)/\sim \geq s \} \tag{14}$$

if $T_b^{(n)}$ is not $\Theta(1)$ arrangeable.

Proof: Suppose $T_b^{(n)}$ is not $\Theta(1)$ arrangeable. According to Observation 1 and Lemma 4,

$$(\#W_1(A)/\sim \geq 1) \wedge (\forall s \in [2, N] \{ \#W_s(A)/\sim > \#W_{s-1}(A)/\sim \}).$$

Therefore, $\#W_s(A)/\sim \geq s$.

Q.E.D.

Given an arbitrary $l \in N$, we can partition $t^{(l)}$ into a number of equivalence classes according to the equivalence relation $\sim$. Let $\#t^{(l)}/\sim$ denote the number of equivalence classes of $t^{(l)}$.

Observation 2 *For every N-level $T_b^{(n)}$, its complete arrangement A consists of vectors in $t^{(l)}$ for an $l \in N$ and satisfies*

$$1 \leq \#W_N(A)/\sim \leq \#t^{(l)}/\sim \tag{15}$$

Theorem 3 *$T_b^{(n)}$ is $\Theta(1)$ arrangeable if and only if there are an $l \in N$ and a set $W \subset t^{(l)}$ such that*

$$\forall \vec{u}_0 \in W \, \exists \vec{v}_0, \vec{v}_1, \cdots, \vec{v}_k \in W \, \{ \mathbf{P}_b(\vec{v}_0, \vec{v}_1, \cdots, \vec{v}_k) \wedge \vec{u}_0 \sim \vec{v}_0 \} \tag{16}$$

Proof: The *if* part follows immediately from Corollary 2. Assume $T_b^{(n)}$ to be $\Theta(1)$ arrangeable. There is a constant $l \in N$, and one can determine a complete arrangement set A, which is made up of vectors in $t^{(l)}$, to an arbitrary $T_b^{(n)}$. Suppose $\lceil \lg n \rceil = N$ and $N > \#t^{(l)}/\sim$. Since

$$\forall s \in [1, N] \left\{ \#W_s(A)/\sim \leq \#t^{(l)}/\sim < N \right\},$$

there must be such an $s \in [2, N]$ that $\#W_s(A)/_\sim = \#W_{s-1}(A)/_\sim$ and

$$\forall \bar{u}_0 \in W_s(A) \; \exists \bar{v}_0, \bar{v}_1, \cdots, \bar{v}_k \in W_s(A) \; \{P_b(\bar{v}_0, \bar{v}_1, \cdots, \bar{v}_k) \; \wedge \; \bar{u}_0 \sim \bar{v}_0\}$$

Q.E.D

Now, we show that the arrangement complexity of $T_b^{(n)}$ is either $\Theta(1)$ or $\Omega((\lg n)^\gamma)(\gamma > 0)$. In other words, there is a jump from $\Theta(1)$ to $\Omega((\lg n)^\gamma)$.

Theorem 4 *The arrangement complexity of $T_b^{(n)}$ is either $\Theta(1)$ or $\Omega((\lg n)^\gamma)$.*

Proof: Suppose the arrangement complexity of $T_b^{(n)}$ is not $\Theta(1)$ and A is a complete arrangement set for $T_b^{(n)}$. Let $s = \lceil \lg n \rceil$. Based on Lemma 5, we have

$$\#t^{(l)}/_\sim \geq \#W_s(A)/_\sim \geq s \geq \lg n$$

It is not hard to see that $\#t^{(l)}/_\sim$ is equal to the number of ways of inserting $l - 1$ spaces into the sequence of $|t|$ 1's (see Lemma 5, in Wu93). We can show that

$$\#t^{(l)}/_\sim = \binom{l + |t| - 1}{|t| - 1}$$

$$l^{|t|} > \binom{l + |t| - 1}{|t| - 1}$$

for $l > 1$. This means that $l \geq s^{\frac{1}{|t|}} \geq (\lg n)^{\frac{1}{|t|}}$. Hence, we have the theorem.

Q.E.D

A function f is said to be commutative, if for every permutation $(q_1, q_2, ..., q_k)$ of $(1, 2, ..., k)$, it holds $P_b(\bar{v}_0, \bar{v}_1, \bar{v}_2, \cdots, \bar{v}_k) = P_b(\bar{v}_0, \bar{v}_{q_1}, \bar{v}_{q_2}, \cdots, \bar{v}_{q_k})$.

Theorem 5 *For a commutative function b, the arrangement complexity of $T_b^{(n)}$ is $\Theta(1)$ if and only if there exist an $i \in \mathbb{N}$, a subset $S \subset t^{k^i}$ and k^i bijective mappings $\pi_1, ..., \pi_{k^i} : S \to S$ such that S is a complete arrangement set for F_i and*

$$\underbrace{(F_i \times \cdots \times F_i)}_{k^i} \circ \underbrace{(\pi_1 \times \cdots \times \pi_{k^i})}_{k^i} \circ D_\sigma^{k^i}(S) = S$$

where σ denotes the type of S.

Proof: Suppose f is commutative. The *if* part immediately follows from Theorem 2. We only have to treat the *only if* part.

In the same way used to analyze the assignment complexity of balanced uniform trees based on commutative functions(see Theorem 6 in Wu93), we can show that the arrangement complexity of $T_b^{(n)}$ is $\Theta(1)$ only if

$$\exists l \in \mathbb{N} \; \exists \bar{v}_0, \bar{v}_1, \bar{v}_2, \cdots, \bar{v}_k \in t^{(l)} \; \{P_b(\bar{v}_0, \bar{v}_1, \bar{v}_2, \cdots, \bar{v}_k) \; \wedge \; \forall j \in [1, k]\{\bar{v}_j \sim \bar{v}_0\}\}. \qquad (17)$$

Let l be the minimum of all integers satisfying (17). Then, there are an $i \in \mathbb{N}$ and k^i vectors $\bar{v}_1, \bar{v}_2, \cdots, \bar{v}_{k^i}$ in $t^{(l)}$ such that they are similar to each other and comprise a complete arrangement set for an i-level balanced uniform tree F_i. If we consider $(\bar{v}_1, \bar{v}_2, \cdots, \bar{v}_{k^i})$ as an $l \times k^i$ matrix, it contains no duplicate rows.

Let $\kappa = k^i$ and $v_{m,j}$ denote the mth component of $\vec{v}_j$. Define

$$S = \{(v_{m,1}, v_{m,2}, \cdots, v_{m,\kappa}) \mid m \in [1,l]\}.$$

Suppose that the output vector is $\vec{v}_0$ when S is applied to F_i. According to the assumption, it holds

$$\forall j \in [1,\kappa]\{(\vec{v}_j \sim \vec{v}_0)\}.$$

To put it differently, $\vec{v}_0$ can be transformed to every vector $\vec{v}_j (j \in [1,\kappa])$ by exchanging its component positions. This means that there are κ bijective mappings $\pi_1, ..., \pi_\kappa : S \to S$ such that

$$\underbrace{(F_i \times \cdots \times F_i)}_{k^i} \circ \underbrace{(\pi_1 \times \cdots \times \pi_{k^i})}_{k^i} \circ D_\sigma^\kappa(S) = S$$

where σ denotes the type of S. S is a complete arrangement set for F_i and the arrangement complexity of F_h is $\Theta(1)(h = i \times j, j \in N)$.

For an arbitrarily given $T_b^{(n)}$, we can always find an F_h such that F_h covers $T_b^{(n)}$. Thus, the arrangement complexity of $T_b^{(n)}$ is $\Theta(1)$.

Q.E.D

Conclusions

In this paper, we studied the arrangement complexity of uniform trees which can be used as mathematical models for information systems in different fields. In these trees, the information is received from the leaves, then transformed and propagated to their root. The arrangement complexity of a given tree is a measure of the minimal quantum of information required to be input to the leaves such that the input and output information of each of the nodes of the tree satisfies a predefined property. This paper shows that the arrangement complexity of a balanced uniform tree is either $\Theta(1)$ or $\Omega((\lg n)^\gamma)(\gamma > 0)$.

Suppose that every node of a given tree implements a mapping from t to t^k, and the information is received from the root of the tree, then transformed and propagated to the leaves. In contrast to the trees studied in this paper, such a tree can be considered as *contravariant tree*. It is worthwhile to study the arrangement complexity of the contravariant trees and the structure of their arrangement complexity.

References

[BeHa90] B. Becker, and J. Hartmann. Optimal-Time Multipliers and C-Testability. *Proceedings of the 2nd Annual Symposium on Parallel Algorithms and Architectures*, pp.146-154, 1990.

[BeSp91] B. Becker, and U. Sparmann. Computations over Finite Monoids and their Test Complexity. *Theoretical Computer Science*, pp.225-250, 1991.

[FSTH90] R. Fritzemeier, J. Soden, R. K. Treece, and C. Hawkins. Increased CMOS IC stuck-at fault coverage with reduced I_{DDQ} test sets. *International Test Conference*, pp.427-435, 1990

350

[Haye71] J. P. Hayes. On Realizations of Boolean Functions Requiring a Minimal or Near-Minimal Number of Tests. *IEEE Trans. on Computers* Vol. C-20, No. 12, pp.1506-1513, 1971.

[Hotz65] G. Hotz. Eine Algebraisierung des Syntheseproblems von Schaltkreisen. *EIK* 1, 185-205, 209-231, 1965.

[Hotz74] G. Hotz. **Schaltkreistheorie**. Walter de Gruyter · Berlin · New York 1974.

[HoWu95] G. Hotz, H. Wu. "On the Arrangement Complexity of Uniform Trees", Technical Report, SFB 124-B1, 05/1995, FB-14, Informatik, Universität des Saarlandes, Germany.

[SeKo77] S. C. Seth, and K.L. Kodandapani. Diagnosis of Faults in Linear Tree Networks. *IEEE Trans. on Computers*, C-26(1), pp.29-33, 1977.

[Wu92] H. Wu. On Tests of Uniform Tree Circuits. *Proceeding of CONPAR VAPP V*, pp.527-538, 1992.

[WuSp92] H. Wu, U. Sparmann. On the Assignments Complexity of Tree VLSI Systems. *Proceeding of 7th International Symposium on Computer and Information Sciences*, pp.97-103, 1992.

[Wu93] H. Wu. On the Assignments Complexity of Uniform Trees. *Proceeding of International Symposium on Symbolic and Algebraic Computation, ISSAC' 93*, pp.95-104.

[Wu94] H. Wu. On the Test Complexity of VLSI Systems, Dissertation, University of Saarland, 1994

A Relational-Functional Integration for Declarative Programming

Harold Boley

DFKI
Box 2080, 67608 Kaiserslautern, Germany
boley@informatik.uni-kl.de

Abstract. A relational-functional kernel language is introduced that integrates essential declarative constructs: logic variables and non-determinism from the relational paradigm with nested and higher-order operations from the functional paradigm. Operator definitions use 'valued clauses', subsuming relational Horn clauses and functional (conditional or unconditional) directed equations. Their semantics complements the atoms in relational Herbrand models by 'molecules', which pair functions, applied to argument terms, with returned-value terms. All abstract notions are illustrated by concrete declarative programs.

1 Introduction

The idea of declarative programming is to achieve the largest possible decoupling between the *what* of user-oriented specification from the *how* of machine-oriented control. Then, through a mechanization of the *how* a focussing on the *what* can be enabled. Classical disadvantages of declarativeness have been the less efficient program translation and execution; compensating advantages have been the more efficient program development and maintenance/porting.

The two major declarative constructs of relations (facts and rules for queries) and functions (equations for applications) were often studied separately. In fact, separate declarative paradigms emerged, already before OOP, namely relational (logic) and functional (equational) programming. Relational languages have been developing from Prolog to Gödel and Mercury; functional languages, from Lisp to ML and Haskell.

While the declarative disadvantages have decreased with better compilers [8], their advantages are still disturbed by the relational-functional paradigm gap. Hence there are now stronger attempts to integrate these declarative paradigms [4], especially motivated by the avoidance of duplication in documentation/standardization, development/maintenance/porting, and teaching, as well as by the research of common design principles, semantics (1st/higher-order operators), and implementation (WAM/SECD compilers).

Integrations of the relation and function constructs can be *loose* and *tight*, *practically* and *theoretically* oriented. Under this perspective, the integration in the historical Loglisp [7] is loose/practical, in the standard proposal Curry [5] is loose/theoretical, in Gödel's successor Escher [6] is tight/theoretical, and in our Relfun [1] is tight/practical.

In order to distinguish real integration constructs from additional 'features', research on *minimally necessary integrative notions* is required. Therefore we have studied the adaptation of basically relational notions for functions, mainly (R1) logic variables and (R2) non-determinism, as well as the adaptation of basically functional notions for relations, mainly (F1) operation nestings and (F2) higher-order operations.

2 The Two Paradigms and Their Amalgamation: Quicksort Example

Valued Clauses: Relfun's definition construct for minimal integration is *value-returning clauses*; these comprise three syntactic forms, with the boxed cues, where the middle one subsumes the other two:

| `:- .` | Horn clauses, i.e. rules that can specialize to facts, which are implicitly true-valued (to define relations).

| `:- & .` | Directed, conditional equations rewritten as clauses with an additional value-returning premise (to define functions with "if-part").

| `:& .` | Directed, unconditional equations, which return the value of their only premise (to define functions without "if-part").

Relational Paradigm: The quicksort relation qsort is defined and invoked like in Prolog (generally, Relfun variables are capitalized), but uses prefix notation also for "<" etc.

Facts & Rules:

```
qsort([],[]).
qsort([X|Y], XY-sorted) :-
   partition(X,Y,Sm,Gr),
   qsort(Sm,Sm-sorted),
   qsort(Gr,Gr-sorted),
   apprel(Sm-sorted, [X|Gr-sorted], XY-sorted).

partition(X,[Y|Z],[Y|Sm],Gr) :- <(Y,X),  partition(X,Z,Sm,Gr).
partition(X,[Y|Z],Sm,[Y|Gr]) :- <(X,Y),  partition(X,Z,Sm,Gr).
partition(X,[X|Z],Sm,Gr) :- partition(X,Z,Sm,Gr).
partition(X,[],[],[]).

apprel([],L,L).
apprel([H|R],L,[H|RL]) :- apprel(R,L,RL).
```

Queries (non-intended mode yields error):

```
>>>>>> qsort([3,1,4,2,3],Sorted)
true
Sorted=[1,2,3,4]
>>>>>> qsort(Unsorted,[1,2,3,4])
error: free variable can't be arg to builtin
```

Functional Paradigm: Here, $Pattern_{VAR}$.= $Application$ & $Expression_{VAR}$ is a valued "&"-conjunction representing a pattern-matching functional let expression let(($Pattern_{VAR}$, $Application$), $Expression_{VAR}$) in variables VAR.

Directed, conditional equations:
```
qsort([]) :& [].
qsort([X|Y]) :-
   seq[Sm,Gr] .= partition(X,Y) &
   appfun(qsort(Sm),tup(X|qsort(Gr))).

partition(X,[Y|Z]) :-
   <(Y,X), seq[Sm,Gr] .= partition(X,Z) & seq[[Y|Sm],Gr].
partition(X,[Y|Z]) :-
   <(X,Y), seq[Sm,Gr] .= partition(X,Z) & seq[Sm,[Y|Gr]].
partition(X,[X|Z]) :& partition(X,Z).
partition(X,[]) :& seq[[],[]].

appfun([],L) :& L.
appfun([H|R],L) :& tup(H|appfun(R,L)).
```

Application:
```
>>>>>> qsort([3,1,4,2,3])
[1,2,3,4]
```

Paradigm Amalgamation: As a preparatory stage for integration we now allow programs with functional-relational call alternations. The central constructs amalgamate by using qsort as a function with the ".="- subfunction call seq[Sm,Gr] .= partition(X,Y) replaced by the subrelation call partition(X,Y,Sm,Gr), and using partition as the unmodified relation.

Directed, conditional equations (with subrelation call):
```
qsort([]) :& [].
qsort([X|Y]) :- partition(X,Y,Sm,Gr) & appfun(qsort(Sm),tup(X|qsort(Gr))).
```

Relational-Functional Comparison: qsort is logically not meaningfully invertible (permutations of a necessarily sorted list!), in the implementation not at all (free variables as arguments of numerical comparisons lead to errors!). partition has two results (lists of smaller and greater elements), which can be delivered simply via *two* logic variables Sm and Gr as arguments, or awkwardly via collection into *one* return value (here: structure seq[Sm,Gr]).

Relational
  ⊖ qsort as relation suggests non-intended computation direction
  ⊕ partition as relation simplifies the delivery of two results
Functional
  ⊕ qsort as function shows intended computation direction
  ⊖ partition as function requires collection of two results into one value
Amalgamated
  ⊕ qsort as function shows intended computation direction
  ⊕ partition as relation simplifies the delivery of two results

3 Four Kernel Notions for the Integration: Serialization Example

(R1) Logic Variables: Function calls can, like relation calls, use (free) logic variables as actual *arguments* and, additionally, return them as *values*. Likewise, non-ground terms, which contain logic variables, are permitted. The processing is based on unification. The following example takes the free R as an argument and returns the non-ground [. . ., [...,Yi],. . .] as its value:

```
pairlists([],[]) :& [].
pairlists([X|L],[Y|M]) :& tup([X,Y]|pairlists(L,M)).

>>>>>> pairlists([d,a,1,1,a,s],R)
[[d,Y1],[a,Y2],[1,Y3],[1,Y4],[a,Y5],[s,Y6]]
R=[Y1,Y2,Y3,Y4,Y5,Y6]
```

(R2) Non-Determinism: Function calls are allowed to *repeatedly return values*, just as relation calls can *repeatedly bind query variables*. Thus, uniform ("don't know") non-determinism for solution search is obtained (implemented as in Prolog via backtracking).

Pure, ground-deterministic functions can also be called non-ground non-deterministically (e.g. *restriction-free*, with distinct logic variables). The enumeration of *computed answers* delivers pairs consisting of argument bindings and a return value (their ground instantiations for restriction-free calls constitute the *success set*):

```
>>>>>> pairlists(Q,R)
```

[]	[[X1,Y1]]	[[X1,Y1],[X2,Y2]]	[[X1,Y1],[X2,Y2],[X3,Y3]]	
Q=[]	Q=[X1]	Q=[X1,X2]	Q=[X1,X2,X3]	...
R=[]	R=[Y1]	R=[Y1,Y2]	R=[Y1,Y2,Y3]	

(F1) Operation Nestings: Functions and relations return general values and truth values, respectively. *Call-by-value* nestings in any combination, embedded logic variables, and embedded non-determinism are allowed, as shown via examples:

Function-Function:	appfun(qsort(...),...)
Relation-Relation:	or(and(true,false),true)
Function-Relation:	tup(apprel(L,M,[a,b,c]))
Relation-Function:	numbered(...,+(...,...))

The last kind of nesting, consisting of a relation call over the value of a function call, is most urgently missed in logic programming:

```
numbered([],N).
numbered([[X,N]|R],N) :- numbered(R,+(N,1)).
```

```
>>>>>> numbered([[a,Y2],[d,Y1],[1,Y3],[s,Y6]],1)
true
Y2=1,    Y1=2,    Y3=3,    Y6=4
```

(F2) Higher-Order Operations: Functional and relational arguments as well as values are permitted. A *restriction* to *named* functions and relations (no λ-expressions) is used, as they are dominant in practice and more easily integrated (avoids λ/logic-variable distinction and higher-order unification). This is just syntax, apply-*reducible* to 1st order, as shown by David H. D. Warren; but still it permits, say, a generic qsort definition via a comparison-relation (Cr) parameter, to be applied in partition:

```
qsort[Cr]([]) :& [].
qsort[Cr]([X|Y]) :-
   partition[Cr](X,Y,Sm,Gr) &
   appfun(qsort[Cr](Sm),tup(X|qsort[Cr](Gr))).

partition[Cr](X,[Y|Z],[Y|Sm],Gr) :- Cr(Y,X),  partition[Cr](X,Z,Sm,Gr).
partition[Cr](X,[Y|Z],Sm,[Y|Gr]) :- Cr(X,Y),  partition[Cr](X,Z,Sm,Gr).
partition[Cr](X,[X|Z],Sm,Gr) :- partition[Cr](X,Z,Sm,Gr).
partition[Cr](X,[],[],[]).

before([X1,Y1],[X2,Y2]) :- string<(X1,X2).

>>>>>> qsort[<]([3,1,4,2,3])              % Cr bound to <
[1,2,3,4]

>>>>>> qsort[before]([[d,Y1],[a,Y2],[1,Y3],[1,Y4],[a,Y5],[s,Y6]])
[[a,Y2],[d,Y1],[1,Y3],[s,Y6]]
Y4=Y3                                     % Cr bound to before
Y5=Y2
```

The Relational-Functional Kernel: We provide the four notions in an essential language kernel with an integrated relational/functional *operator* construct:

- Relfun functions (returning general values) can use logic variables (R1) and can be non-deterministic (R2).
- Relfun relations (returning truth values) can use nestings (F1) and can be of higher order (F2).
- Classical functions and relations become extrema in the 4-dimensional construct space shown in the figure.

Then, our new fundamental basis can be extended as a whole by finite domains, sort hierarchies, determinism specifications, etc. [1].

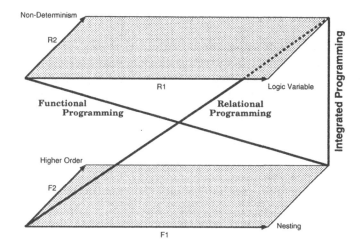

Serialization Program (R1,F1,F2): Suppose we are given the task to transform a list of symbols into the list of their lexicographic serial numbers. A sample transformation is `[d,a,l,l,a,s]` ⤳ `[2,1,3,3,1,4]`. The solution is obtained by combining previous examples of this section:

```
>>>>>> numbered(qsort[before](pairlists([d,a,l,l,a,s],R)),1)
       & R
[2,1,3,3,1,4]
R=[2,1,3,3,1,4]
```

Abstracting `[d,a,l,l,a,s]` to L gives us the `serialise` program:

```
serialise(L) :-
  numbered(qsort[before](pairlists(L,R)),1)
  & R.
```

This program incorporates the following novelties wrt the classical Prolog `serialise` of David H. D. Warren:

- The workhorse function `qsort` is separated out *reusably* (with `Cr = before`).
- Warren's purely relational program is changed into a *more concise integrated* one.
- The main function `serialise` specifies the *intended computation direction*, since it is not invertible (the builtin `string<` requires ground arguments).
- The subfunction `pairlists` binds the free 2nd argument to a list of logic variables, which become bound via their occurrences in the *returned* pair list.
- The subrelation `numbered` with an embedded "+" is used because of its "declarative binding side-effects". The parameterized subrelation `partition` is used to deliver multiple solutions.

Altogether, our `serialise` maps ground arguments deterministically to ground values, but for this essentially uses non-ground lists internally: Such a utilization of logic variables in functional programming leads to a higher (declarative) language level and (imperative) efficiency than obtained from an equivalent pure function without logic variables.

4 Generalized Herbrand Models: Component Example

Model-Theoretic Semantics: Herbrand model theory for kernel Relfun becomes possible via reduction of its restricted higher-order operations to 1st-order (valued Horn clauses). Generalized models of integrated programs, besides undirected elements for relations (ground atoms), also contain directed elements for functions (ground molecules). An *atom* applies a relation to argument terms. A *molecule* pairs a function, applied to argument terms, with a value term. The *ground atoms* in the model are exactly the *true ground queries* to the program. The *ground molecules* in the model are exactly the *ground pairs of application and value* of the program.

Thus, for relational programs we employ the usual Herbrand(-base) models; for functional programs we introduce Herbrand-*cross* models; for integrated programs we obtain the relational-functional union of Herbrand-*crossbase* models.

Material Components (R2,F1): The following table shows the reflexive-transitive closure over part relations and functions. Besides the individual models, the union of the first row has the second-row union as its crossbase model.

Relational program:	Functional program:
partr(W,W).	partf(W) :& W.
partr(W,P) :- mpartr(W,I), partr(I,P).	partf(W) :& partf(mpartf(W)).
partr(W,P) :- apartr(W,I), partr(I,P).	partf(W) :& partf(apartf(W)).
mpartr(feconcrete,concrete).	mpartf(feconcrete) :& concrete.
mpartr(feconcrete,steel).	mpartf(feconcrete) :& steel.
mpartr(steel,iron).	mpartf(steel) :& iron.
apartr(steel,carbon).	apartf(steel) :& carbon.
Least Herbrand-base model:	**Least Herbrand-cross model:**
{	{
partr(feconcrete, feconcrete),	*partf(feconcrete) :& feconcrete*,
...,	...,
partr(carbon, carbon),	*partf(carbon) :& carbon*,
partr(feconcrete, concrete),	*partf(feconcrete) :& concrete*,
partr(feconcrete, steel),	*partf(feconcrete) :& steel*,
partr(feconcrete, iron),	*partf(feconcrete) :& iron*,
partr(feconcrete, carbon),	*partf(feconcrete) :& carbon*,
partr(steel, iron),	*partf(steel) :& iron*,
partr(steel, carbon),	*partf(steel) :& carbon*,
mpartr(feconcrete, concrete),	*mpartf(feconcrete) :& concrete*,
mpartr(feconcrete, steel),	*mpartf(feconcrete) :& steel*,
mpartr(steel, iron),	*mpartf(steel) :& iron*,
apartr(steel, carbon)	*apartf(steel) :& carbon*
}	}

These models are equivalent to the relational-functional success sets of the Relfun interpreter, which basically realizes *"innermost, conditional narrowing"*. *Soundness* and *completeness* were shown generally [2].

5 Conclusions

The Relfun language is implemented by a combination of source-text transformers and compilers for Warren-Abstract-Machine (WAM) emulators [8] extended by value returning via the temporary WAM register X1 [1].

Contributions of this research to the state of the art may be summarized thus: (1) Kernel-notion integration by valued clauses (R1/R2/F1/F2 system). (2) Integrated extensions by finite domains, sort hierarchies, and determinism specifications. (3) Transfer of logic variables to the functional paradigm for computations with ground-I/O (encapsulated partial data structures). (4) Foundation of the semantics of functions on the same model-theoretic level as relations. (5) Development of relational-functional transformers, compilers, and abstract machines. (6) Application studies on declarative graph processing, materials selection, and NC-program generation [3].

Among the open questions let us mention search control (not only via determinism specifications but also via Relfun's sorts and modules), AND/OR-parallelism, more powerful higher-order operations, and denotational semantics for a full relational-functional language.

References

1. Harold Boley. Extended Logic-plus-Functional Programming. In Lars-Henrik Eriksson, Lars Hallnäs, and Peter Schroeder-Heister, editors, *Proceedings of the 2nd International Workshop on Extensions of Logic Programming, ELP '91, Stockholm 1991*, volume 596 of *LNAI*. Springer, 1992.
2. Harold Boley. A Direct Semantic Characterization of RELFUN. In E. Lamma and P. Mello, editors, *Proceedings of the 3rd International Workshop on Extensions of Logic Programming, ELP '92, Bologna 1992*, volume 660 of *LNAI*. Springer, 1993.
3. Harold Boley, Markus Perling, and Michael Sintek. Transforming Workpiece Geometries into Lathe-NC Programs by Qualitative Simulation. In *15th IMACS World Congress on Scientific Computation, Modelling and Applied Mathematics*. Wissenschaft und Technik Verlag, Berlin, August 1997.
4. Michael Hanus. The Integration of Functions into Logic Programming: From Theory to Practice. *Journal of Logic Programming*, 19,20:583–628, 1994.
5. Michael Hanus. A Unified Computation Model for Functional and Logic Programming. In *POPL'97*, Paris 1997.
6. John W. Lloyd. Combining Functional and Logic Programming Languages. In *1994 International Logic Programming Symposium*, ILPS'94.
7. J. A. Robinson and E. E. Sibert. LOGLISP: An Alternative to Prolog. *Machine Intelligence*, 10:399–419, 1982.
8. Peter Van Roy. 1983-1993: The Wonder Years of Sequential Prolog Implementation. *The Journal of Logic Programming*, 19,20:385–441, 1994.

Inside and Outside the Chinese Room

Siegfried Kanngießer

Universität Osnabrück

Abstract. In Searle's critique of what he calls strong Artificial Intelligence (AI) - a critique which consists essentially of the Chinese room gedankenexperiment - he argues „that strong AI must be false, since a human agent could instantiate the program and still not have the appropriate mental states." It is shown that Searle's gedankenexperiment - which rests last of all on an (incorrect) identification of knowledge in general with explicit knowledge and the (incorrect) assumption that a mental system must be transparent for itself - does not exemplify what it pretends to - namely the structure of a system of strong AI -, since the Chinese room must necessarily possess properties which are by no means properties which a computer system must have necessarily to be a language processing AI system. Therefore, the Chinese room doesn't instantiate such a system and, therefore, the gedankenexperiment doesn't tell anything about the possibility or impossibility of strong AI.

1 Turing's Test, AI, Searle's Room

„I distinguish between strong and weak AI. According to strong AI, appropriately programmed computers literally have cognitive states, and therefore the programs are psychological theories. I argue that strong AI must be false, since a human agent could instantiate the program and still not have the appropriate mental states" (Searle (1981), 282). - As is well known, Searle's argumentation against the possibility of strong Artificial Intelligence consists essentially of the famous Chinese room *gedankenexperiment* . The Chinese room scenario is well known, and there is no need to give a summary of it. But in order to discuss Searle's claim that strong AI must be false it seems usefully to repeat at least some of his basic assumptions.

Assumption A. The linguistic behavior of the Chinese room is indistinguishable from the linguistic behavior of a native Chinese speaker.

Assumption B. The man who is locked in the room - Tom Jones, to name the person - does not know any Chinese, and the other equipment of the room does not either. Therefore, one could say the Chinese room does not know any Chinese.

Assumption C. The Chinese room consisting of Tom Jones and the other equipment is an instance of the structure of a machine of strong AI.

Given these three assumptions one can conclude that strong AI must be false: an AI system behaves like a native speaker/listener but, nevertheless, it has not the knowledge of the language which must be ascribed to a native speaker of this language without any doubt. But are these assumptions as sound as they seem to be at the first glance?

Assumption A means that the Chinese room is able to pass the Turing test. There are reasons to contest such a far-reaching assumption (cf. Boden (1990), Harnad (1990a), Lenzen (1996), Rheinwald (1991a) for objections against assumption A.). But, contrary to some familiar but delusive biases, assumption A is not essential for Searle's attempt to give a refutation of the whole approach of strong AI since a refutation of assumption A would not imply a refutation of assumption B. To pass the Turing Test (TT) a system must be able to answer - among others - such questions as „What is the color of this flower?" or „What is the taste of this cake?". And to be able to answer such questions the system must be able to perceive its environment or, more generally, to make experiences. But within the scenario presented by Searle - and contrary to a genuine speaker/listener - the Chinese room is *not* able to perceive its environment and to have experiences. Therefore, it is not able to answer a question as „What is the color of this flower?", and this means that the Chinese room couldn't pass the TT. Nevertheless, the rejection of assumption A doesn't imply a rejection of assumption B. To pass the TT means that the system must *behave* in a certain manner. But as the discussion of the so called Other Mind Problem has shown, the behavior of a system tells nothing about its internal structure. The passed TT is incapable of guaranteeing the presence of mind (or of knowledge or of cognition), and not the failed TT is incapable of guaranteeing the absence of mind (or of knowledge and cognition). Therefore, it is not a critical question whether the Chinese room is able to pass the TT - the critical question is whether the Chinese room has the appropriate mental states. With respect to this, it seems to be admissible to neglect Assumption A within the further considerations.

Assumption B is commonly viewed as the kernel element of Searle's critique. It is discussed widely, intensively and controversially since Searle's thought experiment was published (cf. for instance the papers collected in Burkhardt (1990); cf. also Beckermann (1988), Boden (1990), Dennett (1980), Harnad (1989), Harnad (1990b), Rapaport (1988), Rheinwald (1991a), (1991b) and the literature cited there. Münch (1990) gives a summary of the discussion). The following considerations contribute only indirectly to this discussion: they are concerned primarily with assumption C.

Assumption C is an accepted assumption in the discussion of the Chinese room - it is accepted both by the opponents of Searle's critique and its proponents. Therefore, it doesn't play any rôle or even a prominent rôle in the discussion. It is generally taken for granted. *But assumption C is false.* It is the aim of the following considerations to show, why this is so. It should be obvious that its falseness bears consequences for the significance - and this means for the refuting power - of assumption B and, therefore, will also be taken into consideration.

2 Two Versions of the Chinese Room

As mentioned above, the Chinese room thought experiment has raised a lot of discussions. With respect to these discussions one could think of a dialogue between two people - Mr. Letter and Mr. Philo, to name these imaginary persons - which takes the following course:

Philo: One of the most prominent objections against Searle's thought experiment is the so called Systems Reply. Do you agree with the Systems Reply?

Letter: Excuse me, please - my erudition has its limits. What is the content of the Systems Reply?

Philo: It is quite simple. No part of the Chinese room does understand any Chinese. But the Chinese room as a whole understands Chinese. Therefore, Searle's critique collapses.

Letter: Tom Jones inside the room doesn't know any Chinese, and he knows that he doesn't know any Chinese. The other equipment of the room doesn't know any Chinese, and Tom Jones knows that the other equipment of the room doesn't know any. With respect to the knowledge of Chinese the Chinese room is completely empty. Without black magic it is not able to understand Chinese, even in part.

Philo: So you do agree with Searle's critique?

Letter: In this respect. His presentation of the Chinese room indeed excludes the possibility of any knowledge of Chinese inside the room. But I distrust his presentation. Especially, I distrust assumption C.

Philo: But why? If you are in agreement with assumption B you cannot argue against assumption C. Tom Jones inside the room doesn't know any Chinese, and Tom Jones is nothing else as an instance of a computer program. The Chinese room must be seen as a system of strong AI. You could not object to assumption C seriously.

Letter: Is Tom Jones really nothing else but an instance of a computer program? - Let me ask you a simple question: How is it possible for Searle to know that the Chinese room is - with respect to the knowledge of Chinese - cognitive empty?

Philo: This simple question requires a simple answer. Searle knows everything about the Chinese room Tom Jones knows about it, and the latter knows that the Chinese room is cognitive empty with respect to Chinese.

Letter: Of course. But this also means that Searle's conclusion that the Chinese room is cognitive empty is based on introspection. Namely, on Tom Jones' introspection. And, clearly, Tom Jones' introspection must be considered as an infallible one. - It should be obvious that there is no reason to assume a system of strong AI must be equipped necessarily with an infallible introspective access to its own internal structure. Moreover, it is not necessary to assume that a human agent is equipped with such an access to its own internal structure. On the contrary: it is well known that such an assumption would be a highly critical one.

Philo: I agree completely. But your claim is far away from a refutation of Searle's claim that strong AI must be false.

Letter: Though I don't think that it is of no importance to point out that Searle's critique presupposes the possibility of an exhaustive and infallible introspection, I also agree. And I hope you will also agree with me that Tom Jones is not a mere instance of a program but also something like a *cognitive probe* or a *cognitive detector* inside the room. And he can serve as a cognitive probe by means of his introspective power.

Philo: Obviously this is the case. But does it matter?

Letter: Do you think that it is necessary for a computer system to be a system of strong AI to have a cognitive probe or a cognitive detector inside? - No, you don't think so? - Then there is freedom to eliminate Tom Jones from the room and to substitute him by a symbol distribution device (SDD).

Philo: Clearly it is definitely possible to do so. But it wouldn't change the structure of the Chinese room essentially. Tom Jones does not know any Chinese, and the SDD - as a mere symbol distribution device - also does not know any Chinese. Therefore, the Chinese room does not know any Chinese.

Letter: We will discuss this later on. - But how do you *know* that the Chinese room in its SDD version doesn't know any Chinese? Let us reconsider Searle's argumentation. He argues „that strong AI must be false, since a human agent could instantiate the program and still not have the appropriate mental states." But this argument does not apply to the Chinese room in its SDD version, since no human agent instantiating a program is inside the room. And if the argument does not apply one cannot derive assumption B. Therefore, Searle's critique of the possibility of strong AI is empty.

Philo: I rather think your argumentation is misleading. If we can substitute Tom Jones by a SDD we can, conversely, also substitute the SDD by Tom Jones. Both substitutions don't change the situation: Tom Jones does not know Chinese, and the SDD does not either.

Letter: As we have seen before Tom Jones is something like a cognitive probe or a cognitive detector. By means of this probe we have insights in the internal structure of the Chinese room and its cognitive equipment. By means of the cognitive detector we are inside the room. Without it we are outside the room. And with the SDD inside the room we are outside the room, too. The two substitutions are *not* preserving information. Only if the cognitive probe is available one can make statements about the cognitive structure of the Chinese room. The SDD version of the Chinese room excludes this possibility. From outside, there is no insight in the internal structure of the Chinese room. We cannot decide whether the Chinese room is cognitive empty or not. All we can do is to observe its linguistic behavior and nothing else. And its linguistic behavior must be perfect, since assumption A holds.

Philo: But does this imply a refutation of Searle's critique? Do you really believe that the Chinese room in its SDD version is able to understand Chinese?

Letter: First, we have been in agreement with each other that it is not necessary for a computer system to be a system of strong AI to incorporate a cognitive probe. Therefore, it is admissible - and evidently possible - to transform every computer system and even every system of strong AI that contains a cognitive probe into a system without a cognitive probe inside. Secondly, we have seen that such a transformation implies an important reduction of the information available about the internal structure of the system. It brings us into a position outside the system. Thirdly, Searle presupposes presumably - at least implicitly - that every system of strong AI is or can be transformed into a system with a transparent internal structure in which the transformation does not change the original state of the system. But this presupposition does not hold. - The Chinese room in its Tom Jones version is an example of a system with an internal structure transparent from outside. But AI systems must not necessarily be transparent from outside. The Chinese room does not exemplify the general structure of a system of strong AI. Assumption C is wrong. - Without any doubts, the Chinese room in its version presented by Searle does not understand any Chinese. But since it is not an instance of a system of strong AI in this version it doesn't tell us anything about systems of strong AI or AI systems in general.

Philo: Nevertheless, I have to repeat my question: do you really believe that the Chinese room in its SDD version is able to understand Chinese? You cannot think so seriously. If the room with a human agent inside doesn't understand any Chinese, it must be the case *a fortiori* , that the room with a SDD instead of the human agent inside doesn't understand any Chinese.

Letter: Of course, your question is an important one. I believe strongly that the possibility of strong AI depends, *inter alia,* on the possibility of giving a positive answer to your question. But I will make no attempt to develop such an answer - it is of no interest presently. But the following seems to be obvious: only believing that the Chinese room in its SDD version is not able in principle to understand Chinese is not sufficient - in order to become arguments, beliefs must be substantiated. And I have tried to show that within Searle's argumentation there is no possibility to *demonstrate* the belief that the Chinese room in its SDD version is not able to understand Chinese. - Moreover, Searle is indeed well aware of this - he makes no attempt to apply his argumentation to entities of the type of the Chinese room in its SDD-Version. He asserts rather in general - and without arguments, as he concedes - that every attempt to ascribe mental states or cognitive qualities to such entities is annulling the demarcation between genuine mental systems and systems which are obviously pure physical systems and nothing else. He quotes McCarthy (1979): „Machines as simple as thermostats can be said to have beliefs [...]"(Searle (1981), 292). From Searle's point of view the implications of that remark are disastrous to the claim that AI is a cognitive inquiry: ascribing mental qualities to thermostats is to blur the distinction between persons and telephones.

Philo: But it is obvious that humans have beliefs and thermostats, telephones, and adding machines don't. - We want to know what distinguishes the mind from thermostats. And if McCarthy were right, strong AI hasn't a hope of telling us that.

Letter: It is not McCarthy's claim that thermostats have beliefs in the literal sense. McCarthy (1979) claimed that a description of thermostats is possible in terms of a mentalistic language within the framework of a default logic of counterfactuals. Of course, to adopt this possibility does not mean to blur the distinction between genuine mental systems and systems which are pure physical systems and nothing else.

Philo: So you are defending McCarthy's thesis?

Letter: It is not my concern whether McCarthy´s thesis is right. I am interested in Searle's critique only. I am interested to relieve that Searle's point of view is not a consequence of his Chinese room thought experiment. If Tom Jones is not inside the room, then there is no possibility to derive Searle's consequences from this thought experiment. And if Tom Jones is inside the room, then Searle's argumentation can not be applied to systems like the Chinese room in its SDD version or thermostats.

Philo: I have to admit that the numerous versions of the Chinese room scenario given by Searle are throughout versions with Tom Jones inside the room. The presence of a human agent acting inside the room seems to be necessary for Searle to establish his critique of the possibility of strong AI. But why is Searle committed to the presence of Tom Jones inside the room at all? Why is he compelled to this commitment?

The following considerations are an attempt to answer Mr. Philo's questions.

3 Explicit Knowledge and Implicit Knowledge

As mentioned above, Tom Jones inside the room serves as a cognitive probe. In order to serve as a cognitive probe Tom Jones has to fulfill certain conditions. Obviously, it is not sufficient that Tom Jones is able to communicate with Searle - Tom Jones has to communicate specific topics toSearle: he has to communicate to the states of the equipment of the Chinese room and, especially, his own mental states. In order to do so Tom Jones must have the exhaustive knowledge about his own mental states. It should be out of question that this requirement is necessary but by no means a trivial one - on the contrary: it is a highly critical one. But for the sake of argumentation it should be taken for granted that a cognitive probe is a system that has the complete knowledge about the system it is detecting. If Tom Jones wouldn't have knowledge about his own states, then Searle would be - so to say - outside Tom Jones as Mr. Philo, Mr. Letter and Searle are outside the Chinese room in its SDD version. - Now, in a reply to his critics, Searle makes a further claim: he claims that the bare existence of causal relations between a symbol and the referent is not sufficient for a system to understand a language. „To do that [the system] would have to have, for example, some *awareness* of the causal relation between the symbol and the referent" (Searle (1980), 454). That the system must be aware of the causal relation means that it has to know that it knows the causal relation - the referential knowledge of the system is only possible as explicit knowledge. With respect to this concept of knowledge it becomes clear what is meant, if Searle writes within his critique of the Systems Reply: „ The subsystem that understands English [...] knows that the stories are about restaurants and eating hamburgers, etc.; he knows that he is being asked questions about restaurants and that he is answering questions as best as he can by making various inferences from the content of the story, and so on. But the Chinese subsystem knows none of this; whereas the English subsystem knows that „hamburgers" refers to hamburgers, the Chinese subsystem [...]" (Searle (1981), 290). It should - with respect to the awareness-statement cited above - become obvious that „to know" is meant in this context as „to know explicitly". And with respect to this statement it should also become clear that Searle identifies „knowledge" with „explicit knowledge" in general. And this knowledge is not a second order knowledge - from Searle's point of view knowledge is generally *only* possible in form of explicit knowledge. And without doubt cognitive-intentional states are knowledge states. Therefore, Searle is obliged to the following assumption:

Assumption D. If I is an individual, and if Σ is a system of knowledge, then I is in the state of possessing Σ if and only if Σ is transparent for I. And if Σ is transparent for I, then I is in a cognitive intentional state.

Clearly, assumption D - the transparency assumption - means that the knowledge of an individual is possible only in form of explicit knowledge. And of course, the transparency assumption holds even for individuals which are AI machines: since AI machines are knowledge based systems, a system of knowledge must be incorporated in the machine. And if the Chinese room is an instance of an AI machine, a system of knowledge must be inside the Chinese room, and this system of knowledge must be transparent to itself. But where should such a system of knowledge be located inside the Chinese room? Obviously it is not reasonable to ascribe knowledge to three batches manipulated by Tom Jones. Therefore, the knowledge must be ascribed to Tom Jones himself: Tom Jones is the one and only element of the Chinese room that is without any doubt able to possess knowledge (in the sense of the transparency assumption). This shows that Tom Jones does *not* serve only as a cognitive probe inside the Chinese room - Tom Jones is also, at the same time, the knowledge base of the AI-system called „the Chinese room". And despite of the perfect linguistic behavior of the Chinese room its knowledge base is empty, since Tom Jones does not have explicit knowledge of Chinese. To put it in other words: Searle identifies the cognitive probe with the knowledge base of the system, and by means of this identification he is able to demonstrate that the Chinese room doesn't understand any Chinese. - Now it is easy to answer the questions raised by Mr. Philo.

Answer to Mr. Philo's questions. Tom Jones serves - by means of his introspective power - as a cognitive probe, and he serves as the empty knowledge base of the system. If there is no identification of the cognitive probe inside the Chinese room with the knowledge base of the system, the Chinese room thought experiment doesn't work, since then even the cognitive probe cannot tell *by means of its introspective power* anything about the cognitive state of the Chinese room. Therefore, Searle is committed to the presence of Tom Jones inside the Chinese room. Since Tom Jones is able - by means of the identification - to give exhaustive (and infallible) information about the state of the knowledge base of the system, Searle is able to draw his conclusions. If Tom Jones isn't inside the room, then there is no possibility for Searle to draw any conclusions.

Searle's thought experiment rests upon the transparency assumption. But is Assumption D correct? Is it indeed the case that knowledge is possible only as explicit knowledge? To put it in other words: Are cognitive-intentional states necessary states of consciousness? - By supposition, Tom Jones inside the room knows English, and he does have the appropriate mental states for understanding English. But even Tom Jones knowledge of English is *not* explicit knowledge, since Tom Jones can not *state* the rules and principles structuring his language. Nevertheless, Tom Jones is able *to execute* correctly these rules and principles - for instance, the principles of conjunctive coordination and word formation and the rules of predication -, and he is able to do so since he possesses *implicit* knowledge of these rules and principles. The linguistic knowledge of a native speaker/listener is in the normal case an implicit knowledge. (This is what Chomsky has claimed - cf. Chomsky (1980), for instance -, and it is what can be called Chomsky's hypothesis.) Tom Jones, as a native speaker/listener of English, *instantiates* a system of implicit linguistic knowledge. Being a native speaker/listener of a natural language it is not necessary to possess explicit knowledge of this language. Tom Jones does not have explicit knowledge of English, but he does have the appropriate mental states for understanding English. Therefore, with respect to Chomsky's hypothesis - a hypothesis which is uncontested for empirical reasons in linguistics, psychology and even in AI - Assumption D turns out to be false. (In defense of Assumption D Searle objects to Chomsky's hypothesis. Cf. Searle (1976) for the opening of the long-standing debate between Searle and Chomsky. For a conclusive refutation of Searle's assumption by Chomsky cf. Chomsky (1980), especially Chap. 3.)

A native speaker/listener does not possess explicit knowledge of his language. Therefore, for an AI system to be a language processing AI system it is not necessary to possess explicit knowledge of the language it is processing - and this means that the system does not have to be able to state the rules and principles it is executing in understanding a language. The system can be seen as an instantiation of a system of implicit linguistic knowledge in the very same sense in which Tom Jones, as a native speaker/listener of English, must be considered as an instantiation of a system of knowledge of English - a system of knowledge which is not transparent for Tom Jones himself. - To put it in other words: the linguistic knowledge of a genuine speaker/listener is not accessible for him by means of introspection. And, therefore, a language processing AI system must not possess explicit knowledge of the language it is processing. It must possess the relevant knowledge, but this knowledge must not be an explicit one. And this means, it must not be accessible to the system by means of introspection. Searle's critique includes the requirement that an AI system must obey the transparency assumption to be a system of knowledge that can have mental states in the proper sense. But the transparency assumption is misleading and, therefore, there is no need to fulfill Searle's requirement. Since there is no need to fulfill the requirement, Searle's critique collapses, and there is no reason to give up the idea of strong AI with respect to Searle's argumentation.

Nevertheless, it is possible in principle - though not necessary - to construct an AI system that possesses explicit knowledge - a system that knows what it is knowing, and that is able to state what its knowledge is. One can think of the SDD as the element of the system called „Chinese room" that is equipped with such a second order knowledge. It is notable that the SDD - as the system as a whole - must not at all be informed that the language the Chinese room is processing is called „Chinese". The knowledge available to the system must enable it to analyze certain linguistic inputs and to generate certain linguistic outputs and nothing else. One can think, furthermore, that the SDD is able to answer questions. Suppose that somebody wants to know what the system is doing while analyzing a certain input. The SDD wouldn't answer to his question, that the system is cognitive empty. The SDD would give an answer as, for instance, the following:

SDD: The system is applying grammar rule R 17 within a left corner parse with respect to the link relation.

Now, does this answer reflect knowledge of the language called „Chinese"? Does it reflect an appropriate mental state of the system? In the previous dialogue Mr. Philo raised the question whether the Chinese Room in its SDD version is able to

Rapaport, W. J. (1988), „To Think or not to Think - Critical Review of John Searle: „Minds, Brains, Programs"". In: *Noûs* 22, 585 - 609.

Rheinwald, R. (1991a), „Können Maschinen eine Sprache sprechen? Sind Computerprogramme syntaktisch oder semantisch"? In: *Kognitionswissenschaft* 2, 37 - 49.

Rheinwald, R. (1991b), „Menschen, Maschinen und Gödels Theorem". In: *Erkenntnis* 34, 1 - 21.

Searle, J. (1976), „The rules of the Language Game". In: *Times Literary Supplement,* September 10, 1976.

Searle, J. (1980), „Minds, Brains and Programs". In: *The Behavioral and Brain Sciences* 3, 417 - 424, 450 - 456.

Searle, J. (1981), „Minds, Brains and Programs". In: J. Haugeland (ed.), *Mind Design. Philosophy - Psychology - Artificial Intelligence.* Cambridge, Mass.: MIT Press. pp. 282 - 306.

Abstract Structures in Spatial Cognition[*]

Christopher Habel and Carola Eschenbach
University of Hamburg

Abstract. The importance of studying spatial cognition in cognitive science is enforced by the fact that the applicability of spatial concepts and spatial expressions is not limited to the spatial domain. We claim that common structures underlying both concrete, physical space and other domains are the basis for using spatial expressions, e.g., prepositions like *between*, with respect to space as well as time or other domains. This claim opposes the thesis that the common use is based upon an analogy between concrete space and other domains. The development of geometry from Euclid's *Elements* to more differentiated systems of diverse geometries and topologies can be perceived of as an example of the transfer from modeling concrete space towards describing abstract spatial structures.

1   The Current Interest in Spatial Cognition: Spatial Representations and Spatial Concepts

Human behavior is anchored in space and time. Spatial information, i.e., information about spatial properties of the entities in our environment, about spatial constellations in our surrounding, and about the spatial properties and relations of our bodies with respect to this surrounding, has a central position for human cognition. In the recognition of objects and events by different sensory channels, i.e., in visual, haptic or auditory perception, spatial information is involved. Motor behavior, i.e., locomotion and the movement of the body, is based on such information as well.

Beyond perception and motor action, some higher cognitive activities that interact indirectly with the spatial environment are coupled with spatial information, for instance, memory, problem solving and planning (cf. Eilan et al. 1993). The interaction of spatial cognition and other cognitive faculties is also exemplified by the ability to communicate information about spatial properties of the external world, especially about objects or constellations not directly perceivable (cf. Freksa & Habel 1990).

The cognitive science method of investigating and explaining cognition based on *computation* and *representation* has led to increasing research activities focusing on spatial representations and processes on such representations:

---

[*]   Parts of this paper are based on Habel & Eschenbach (1995). The research reported in this paper was carried out in connection to the project 'Axiomatik räumlicher Konzepte' (Ha 1237/7) supported by the Deutsche Forschungsgemeinschaft (DFG).
Thanks to an anonymous referee for comments and suggestions for improvements.
Address: FB Informatik (AB WSV) and Graduiertenkolleg *Kognitionswissenschaft*, Universität Hamburg, Vogt-Kölln-Str. 30, D-22527 Hamburg.
{habel, eschenbach}@informatik.uni-hamburg.de.

- In cognitive psychology spatial concepts are basic for thinking about objects and situations in physical space and therefore the necessary constituents for the integration of the central higher cognitive faculties with sensory, motor and linguistic faculties (cf. Miller 1978, Landau & Jackendoff 1993).[1]
- In linguistics spatial concepts are discussed as basic ingredients of the – mental – lexicon; the linguistic approach of *cognitive grammar* – with Lakoff, Langacker and Talmy as its most influential advocates – is committed to space as the foundation for semantics and for the general grammatical system.[2]
- In Artificial Intelligence spatial concepts are the basis for developing representational formalisms for processing spatial knowledge; for example, calculi of *Qualitative Spatial Reasoning* differ with respect to what their primitive terms are and which spatial expressions are definable on this basis (See, e.g., Freksa 1992, Hernández 1994, and Randell et al. 1992, Schlieder 1995a, b).

In the cognitive grammar approach as well as in most other discussions on spatial information the question what the basis of using the term *spatial* is seems to allow a simple answer: Space is identified with three-dimensional physical space. And by this, the concrete, physical space of our environment[3] is seen as the conceptual and semantic basis for a wide range of linguistic and non-linguistic cognition. Accordingly, *spatial concepts* concern size, shape or relative location of objects in three-dimensional physical space. This view is based on the judgment that direct interaction with concrete, physical space is the core of our experience and therefore of our knowledge.

Our spatial experience leads to groupings among spatial concepts depending on geometrical types of spatial characterizations. Examples of such groups, each of them corresponding to types of experience, are:

topological concepts
- based on relations between regions and their boundaries
- invariant with respect to elastic transformations

concepts of ordering
- based on relations between objects or regions with respect to the relative position in a spatial constellation.
- independent of the extensions and distances of the objects and regions in question

metric concepts
- include measures of distance and size of objects and regions.

---

[1] Following Miller (1978) we assume that the conceptual structure includes different types of concepts, e.g. concepts for objects, properties and relations. In this sense, spatial relations like touching or betweenness correspond to relational concepts, while shape properties like being round or angular correspond to predicative concepts.

[2] See, e.g., Lakoff (1987), Langacker (1986), Talmy (1983). Note that in the initial phase of this framework the term *space grammar* was used (Langacker 1982).

[3] Although it is often claimed that physical space is not concrete but an abstraction based on spatial properties and relations of material bodies, we will use the term *concrete space* to refer to physical space in contrast to *abstract spatial structures* referring to less restricted structures (such as topological, ordering or metric spaces) underlying physical space.

Aspects of this division are reflected by the contrast between qualitative and quantitative spatial reasoning. The means of qualitative spatial reasoning are in many cases restricted to topological terms (e.g., Randell et al. 1992) and terms of ordering (e.g., Schlieder 1995a, b).

An independent dimension of analysis concerns the distinction between concept types and types of spatial entities: On the one hand we deal with spatial relations between objects, their location or *relative position*. Characteristically these relations are independent of shape and extension, such that they can apply to points idealizing the place of the objects. On the other hand we are concerned with *shape properties* of extended objects or regions independent of their location. Shape properties are coined by the relative position of object parts among themselves. Concepts of *object orientation* combine both, shape of extended entities and spatial relations of their parts and other objects. These types of spatial concepts can be subdivided according to the dimension of geometrical type.

As a third dimension in classifying spatial concepts, we distinguish between *static* and *dynamic concepts*. Whereas the former concern properties and relations without consideration of time and change, the latter reflect the possibility of changes of spatial properties and relations over time. Since trajectories or paths of locomotion processes are extended spatial entities, spatial concepts are applicable to them as well as to material or geographical entities. (See Table 1 for an exemplification of some sections according to the three-dimensional classification scheme).

	static		dynamic	
	relation	shape	character of change	trajectory based
topological	interior, exterior, boundary, border, touch, contact, separation, ...	connection, hole, crack, fissure, ...	locomotion, separation, perforation, extension, ...	continuity, path, loop, ...
ordering	perspective, direction, horizontal, vertical, orthogonal, ...	cyclic, curve, convex, concave, corner, opening, indentation, ...	rotation, shift, deformation, bodily movement, ...	route, straight, turn, ...
metric	distance, angle, congruence, ...	length, volume, symmetry, proportions, curvature, ...	growth, shrinkage, approach, velocity, acceleration, ...	path length, ...

Table 1: Exemplification of some groups of spatial concepts

Generalizations from concrete experience in physical space lead to spatial concepts: Their spatial character corresponds to the spatial character of the corresponding properties and relations. Geometry and Topology are the most prominent representatives of formalizing spatial concepts and spatial structures. From one point of view, they can be seen as formal systems for modeling spatial circumstances. From another point of view, they can be seen as corresponding to guiding principles and constraints for representations of cognitive systems. We will exemplify both perspectives, i.e., the importance of abstract concepts for mathematics and spatial cognition, by the geometrical concept of ordering.

2 From Concrete Space to Abstract Spatial Structures: A Historical Journey

The development of mathematics is strongly connected to the development of geometry.[4] Euclid's *Elements* is one of the most influential books in the history of science, not only in mathematics (cf. Gray, 1989; Kline, 1972, chap. 4). This continual influence is based on the method as well as on the topic. The *Elements* are the origin of the axiomatic method. It is the first complete formal description of a part of mathematics, using definitions of the inventory of geometric and non-geometric notions, axioms to describe principles of general science and postulates to state the basic assumptions on the structure described by Geometry.

The topic of Euclid's *Elements* is the spatial surrounding of humans, i.e., concrete, three-dimensional physical space. The central philosophical assumption of Euclid – shared by Aristotle (cf. Kline 1972; p. 51) – is that the postulates of Geometry are a mathematically precise reflection of the facts of nature. In other words, the task of formulating the postulates of Geometry is the task of describing the essence of real space in an exact mathematical language. Therefore, Geometry produces a formal counterpart of reality, and thus, Euclid's axiomatization of Geometry is part of science, namely of physics. The term *Geometry* in this sense is a proper name, referring to the mathematics of concrete, physical space, and not a common noun, applicable to different theories of spatial structure.[5]

Under this perspective only one correct geometry is possible and desirable: This geometry is characterized by postulates which are committed to – and therefore describe – physical space. Taking this view led to the opinion – unquestioned for a long time – that non-Euclidean geometries are beyond the borderline of reasonable thinking. In Greek mathematics the main demand for the postulates of Geometry was their unquestionable evidence submitted by spatial experience.

In ancient mathematics plausibility of and evidence for Euclid's postulates was only queried with respect to the famous fifth postulate, the so-called *parallel postulate*. It was the formulation not the content of this postulate that was topic of debates (cf. Gray 1989, p. 32f.).[6] From Greek mathematics to modern times the debates about the fifth postulate focused mainly in attempting to prove the axiom of the parallels on the basis of other axioms and postulates, i.e., the attempt to demonstrate that it is only a consequence of other axioms and postulates and therefore

---

[4] Kline (1972) and Gray (1989) give detailed descriptions of the history of geometry in general and the "idea of space" in particular. The view we present in this section is influenced by both monographs.

[5] We continue to use capitalizing for signaling the proper name use, referring to Euclidean geometry, in contrast to the common noun use of *geometry*.

[6] What is seen as unintuitive and therefore as the core of the problem is the use of the idea that we can test whether any [finite] prolongations of two straight [finite] lines, meet. Note, that this test cannot in general be carried out 'in finite time' in the real world.

does not possess the status of an postulate of its own. A second branch of the debate was aimed at reformulating the postulate in a manner that corresponds to our intuitions about spatial experience.

The discussion about non-Euclidean geometries, i.e., geometries described by axiomatic systems that diverge from Euclid's with respect to the fifth postulate, did not start till the beginning of the 19th century: The development of non-Euclidean geometries by Bolyai and Lobatchevsky[7] created a new perspective on the relation between geometry and reality. Since then Euclidean geometry has been seen as one reasonable line of thought among others, and therefore the presupposition of Geometry as the unique mathematical discipline – without alternatives – describing the unique structure of physical space has been abandoned. Klein's (1872) "Vergleichende Betrachtungen über neuere geometrische Forschungen" ("A comparative review of recent researches in geometry") was the explicit formulation of the basic idea of a new program ("Erlanger Programm") for geometry (cf. Kline 1972, p. 917ff): The traditional mono-geometric view was replaced by a research program that led to a variety of geometries: Each geometry is basically characterized by a group of transformations (of space) and the task in the mathematical field of geometry is to investigate the invariances of these transformations and groups of transformations.

Beginning with the first investigations on non-Euclidean geometries the mathematics of space changed in the direction of increasing abstraction and focusing on general principles and structures. For instance, topology can be seen as the geometry of continuous transformations, i.e., a type of geometry that is concerned with homeomorphisms, often characterized informally as "rubber sheet geometry", concerned with "elastic deformations". The development from *geometria situs* to *topology* focuses on some mathematical notions, for example *interior, exterior, boundary, neighborhood* and *connection*, that were extraneous to Euclidean geometry. The topological perspective is also connected to separating aspects of measuring – with respect to distances and angles – and ordering from other aspects of spatiality and spatial extension, especially convergence. Topological spaces without a metric or even without the property of being metrizable are an independent topic or research.

Furthermore, the changed view about the relation between geometry and reality has had important consequences beyond mathematics. Non-Euclidean geometries have been successfully applied in the development of alternatives to Newtonian physics (cf. Gray 1989, part 3; Reichenbach 1958). Beginning with v. Helmholtz' classical studies in the second half of the 19th century, there has been some theoretical and empirical work on the geometry of visual perception. For example, Blank (1958) argues for hyperbolic geometry as basis of *visual space*.[8]

The development described above can be seen as a focus shift in mathematics: from the mathematics of space to spatial structures in mathematics. Notions as *dimension, distance, linearity* or *ordering*, which have their origin in spatial experience, have been generalized from Geometry to the structural inventory of

---

[7] See Kline (1972; chap. 36), Gray (1989; chap. 10).

[8] Cf. Roberts & Suppes (1967) and Indow (1991).

abstract spatial structures. Since other concrete domains – beyond physical space – are committed to the same principles and structural conditions, concepts successfully used with respect to physical space can be applied in these domains as well. Consequently the question "what is spatial" is not understood to be a mathematical question anymore.

3 Abstract Spatial Structures and Cognitive Representations

Some structures, which we observe in concrete, physical space, are also relevant in other domains. Starting from the assumption that language is a window to cognitive structures, the use of the same natural language expression in application to diverse domains produces evidence for the recognition of structural accordances between physical space and these domains. A similar view is held in *cognitive semantics* (cf. Gibbs & Colston, 1995).

The English preposition *between*, e.g., specifies spatial as well as temporal ordering: There are cities between Boston and New York and, usually, a lot happens between 10 o'clock and noon. On the other hand, there is a contrast between the spatial opposition pair *in front of / before – in back of / behind* and the temporal pair *before – after*.[9] That a term is used both spatially and temporally, permits several explanations. But a systematic explanation has to account for the fact that some terms are restricted to one domain. In the following we discuss two approaches, which are paradigmatic for the contrast of *space vs. spatial structure*.

The assumption that the concrete, three-dimensional physical space is cognitively dominant leads to the hypothesis that *between* is of primarily spatial character and that other uses of *between*, for example the temporal one, are derived from the spatial use (see Figure 1.a). From this perspective, the transfer from the spatial to the temporal domain is done by identifying time with one-dimensional space, i.e., by assuming processes of metaphorical transfer. The cognitive semantics approach is strongly committed to this idea of spatial metaphors in non-spatial domains (see, e.g., Lakoff 1987, Gibbs & Colston 1995). This explanation is able to motivate the agreement of spatial and temporal *between*, but an explanation gap arises with respect to the linguistic discrepancies of *before* and its opposites: If in the interpretation of *between* – and in some cases also of *before* – time is transformed to space, then the same mechanism should be applicable with respect to *in front of* or *behind*, i.e., a temporal use of these expressions would be expected. If temporal structure is understood as a sub-structure of space, why does not *after* have a spatial use or interpretation independent of time or movement?

As alternative explanation in the approach of abstract spatial structures we propose that different domains exhibit common structures (see Figure 1.b). Accordingly, linguistic expressions that are applicable in diverse domains specify restrictions regarding the structure of domains in which they are applicable without explicit

---

[9] This sketchy discussion of prepositions is not an attempt of a semantic analysis of the prepositions in question. It is only used here for exemplification of our approach. See, e.g., Habel (1990) on *between,* or Eschenbach et al. (1997) and Eschenbach and Kulik (1997) on *left–right, in front of–behind* and their German counterparts.

reference to these domains. Thus, their meaning is abstract in the following sense: meaning has not to be based on specific properties of individual domains but on more general properties which can be common for several domains.

The cognitively most relevant difference between space and time is the inherent direction of (cognitive) time.[11] The inherent orientation of time – often metaphorically described as the *arrow of time* – leads to fundamental asymmetries to be considered by a cognitive system. Straight lines in space are neutral with respect to direction. Therefore it is possible to augment straight lines in space by a direction; directions can be induced by the axes of the viewer's, speaker's or listener's body or by intrinsic direction of the environment (cf. Eschenbach & Kulik 1997). Therefore, locomotion on a straight line can be directed in two ways. In contrast, e.g., memory is bound to one direction of time and changes in time are understood to conform with this direction. This is inseparably connected to temporal ordering of cause-effect pairs.[12] Knowing the correspondence between causal relations and temporal direction can be seen as the core of a common sense theory of causality and physical time, which is part of our basic cognitive competence. Even pre-school children take the correspondence between temporal direction and causal relations into consideration (Bullock et al. 1982) and moreover there is empirical evidence that 6-month-old infants can perceive cause-effect relationship (Leslie & Keeble 1987).

To sum up, the domains of space and time have ordered geometry as a common structure, but they are fundamentally different with respect to the inherence of direction. The constraints for using prepositions as *between, before, in front of, behind* and *after* reflect the structural communities and differences of the domains. The common use of *between* in the spatial as well as in the temporal domain can be explained by assuming *between* to code a general, non-directed ordering relation (cf. Habel 1990). In contrast to this, the system of directional prepositions does not allow a canonical transfer from the spatial to the temporal domain: *in front of – behind* of the spatial case opposes temporal *before – after*. This difference can be related to whether the domain in question has an inherently distinguished direction.

The observation of cognitive grammar that a wide range of semantics is grounded on concrete space can – from the alternative perspective of abstract spatial structures – get another explanation: The recognition of common structures in different domains is the basis for the common use of linguistic expressions. This approach does not deny the central role of space and spatial cognition with respect to general cognition. Concrete space is a cognitively prominent domain that exhibits abstract spatial structures. Experience in concrete space can be the basis of abstraction in many ways.

The view of abstract structures underlying natural language terms presented here with reference to ordering extends to other domains than time and space. *Between* is applicable with respect to colors: Orange is between red and yellow, gray between black and white; with respect to organizational structures: departments are between

---

[11] See van Fraassen (1985, chap. III.3). Space possesses common properties for all directions and is therefore called *isotropic*. In contrast to this, in time are differences between the two directions, i.e., it is *anisotropic*.

[12] On the relation between causality and direction of time see: Reichenbach (1958, §21), van Fraassen (1985, chap. III.3, VI), Newton-Smith (1980, IX).

groups and corporations; and to any gradable property, i.e., properties that admit degrees[13] like age, speed, or even beauty.

4 Conclusion

The development of the mathematical discipline of geometry, from Geometry, i.e., from the geometry defined in Euclid's *Elements*, to a family of geometries, is an example for the transition from concrete space to abstract spatial structures. In cognitive science, a corresponding transition allows a systematic analysis of using spatial concepts in diverse domains. The relevance of concrete, three-dimensional physical space is not denied, but the focus of investigation and explanation is changed by the view presented in this paper: The analogy mapping between the spatial domain and other domains, which is central for cognitive grammar approaches, is replaced by mappings to common abstract structures, in which cognitive concepts are grounded.

References

Blank, A. (1958). Axiomatics of binocular vision: the foundations of metric geometry in relation to space perception. *Journal of the Optical Society of America, 48*, 328–333.

Bullock, M.; Gelman, R. & Baillargeon, R. (1982). The development of causal reasoning. In: W.J. Friedman (ed.), *The Developmental Psychology of Time* (pp. 209–254). New York: Academic Press.

Cresswell, M.J. (1976). The semantics of degree. In: B. Partee (ed.), *Montague Grammar* (pp. 261–292). New York: Academic Press.

Eilan, N.; McCarthy, R. & Brewer, B. (eds.) (1993). *Spatial Representations*. Oxford: Blackwell.

Eschenbach, C.; Habel, C. & Leßmöllmann, A. (1997). The interpretation of complex spatial relations by integrating frames of reference. Contribution to the Workshop "Language and Space", AAAI-97.

Eschenbach, C. & Kulik, L. (1997). An axiomatic approach to the spatial relations underlying *left–right* and *in front of–behind*. In: G. Brewka, C. Habel & B. Nebel (eds.), *KI-97 – Advances in Artificial Intelligence*. Berlin: Springer-Verlag.

Euclid. *Elements*. [transl. by T.L. Heath (1956)]. New York: Dover.

Freksa, C. (1992). Using orientation information for qualitative spatial reasoning. In: A. Frank, I. Campari & U. Formentini (eds), *Theories and Methods of Spatio-Temporal Reasoning in Geographic Space* (pp. 162–178). Berlin: Springer-Verlag.

Freksa, C. & Habel, C. (1990). Warum interessiert sich die Kognitionsforschung für die Darstellung räumlichen Wissens? In: C. Freksa & C. Habel (eds.), *Repräsentation und Verarbeitung räumlichen Wissens* (pp. 1–15). Berlin: Springer.

Gibbs, R.W. & Colston, H.L. (1995). The cognitive psychological reality of image schemata and their transformations. *Cognitive Linguistics, 6*, 347–378.

Gray, J. (1989; 2nd). *Ideas of Space*. Oxford: Clarendon Press.

Habel, C. (1990). Propositional and depictorial representations of spatial knowledge: The case of *path* concepts. In: R. Studer (ed.), *Natural Language and Logic* (pp. 94–117). Lecture Notes in Artificial Intelligence. Berlin: Springer.

---

[13] A huge class of adjectives specify such properties. The comparative form of natural language adjectives specify directed ordering relations, i.e., binary, transitive relations that need not be linear to justify this point (cf. Cresswell 1976, Pinkal 1990).

Habel, C. & Eschenbach, C. (1995). Abstrakte Räumlichkeit in der Kognition. *Kognitionswissenschaft, 4*, 171–176.

Hernández, D. (1994). *Qualitative Representation of Spatial Knowledge*. Berlin: Springer-Verlag.

Hilbert, D. (1956). *Grundlagen der Geometrie*. Stuttgart: Teubner.

Huntington, E.V. (1938). Inter-relations among the four principal types of order. *Transactions of the American Mathematical Society, 38*, 1–9.

Indow, T. (1991). A critical review of Luneberg's model with regard to global structure of visual space. *Psychological Review, 98*, 430–453.

Klein, F. (1872). Vergleichende Betrachtungen über neuere geometrische Forschungen. published 1893 in *Mathematische Annalen, 43*, 63–100.

Kline, M. (1972). *Mathematical Thought – From Ancient to Modern Times*. New York: Oxford University Press.

Lakoff, G. (1987). *Women, Fire, and Dangerous Things*. Chicago: University of Chicago Press.

Landau, B. & Jackendoff, R. (1993). "What" and "where" in spatial language and spatial cognition. *Behavioral and Brain Sciences, 16*, 217–238, 255–266.

Langacker, R.W. (1982). Space grammar, analysability, and the English passive. *Language, 58*, 22–80.

Langacker, R.W. (1986). An introduction to cognitive grammar. *Cognitive Science, 10*, 1–40.

Leslie, A.M. & Keeble, S. (1987). Do six-month-old infants perceive causality? *Cognition, 25*, 265–288.

Miller, G.A. (1978). Semantic relations among words. In: M. Halle, J. Bresnan & G. Miller (eds.), *Linguistic Theory and Psychological Reality* (pp. 60–117). Cambridge, MA: MIT-Press.

Newton-Smith, W.H. (1980). *The Structure of Time*. London: Routledge & Kegan Paul.

Pinkal, M. (1990). On the logical structure of comparatives. In: R. Studer (ed.), *Natural Language and Logic* (pp. 146–167). Lecture Notes in Artificial Intelligence. Berlin: Springer.

Randell, D.A.; Cui, Z. & Cohn, A.G. (1992). A spatial logic based on regions and connection. In: B. Nebel, C. Rich & W. Swartout (eds), *Principles of Knowledge Representation and Reasoning (KR'92)* (pp. 165–176). San Mateo, CA: Morgan Kaufmann.

Reichenbach, H. (1958). *The Philosophy of Space and Time*. New York: Dover.

Roberts, F.S. & Suppes, P. (1967). Some problems in the geometry of visual perception. *Synthese, 17*, 173–201.

Russell, B. (1903). *Principles of Mathematics*. Cambridge: Cambridge University Press.

Schlieder, C. (1995a). Reasoning about ordering. In: A.U. Frank & W. Kuhn (eds.), *Spatial Information Theory* (pp. 341–349). Berlin et al: Springer-Verlag.

Schlieder, C. (1995b). Qualitative shape representation. In: A. Frank (ed.), *Spatial Conceptual Models for Geographic Objects with Indeterminate Boundaries* (pp. 123–140). London: Taylor & Francis.

Talmy, L. (1983). How language structures space. In: H. Pick & L. Acredolo (eds.), *Spatial Orientation* (pp. 225–282). New York: Plenum.

Tarski, A. (1959). What is elementary geometry? In: L. Henkin, P. Suppes & A. Tarski (eds), *The Axiomatic Method, with Special Reference to Geometry and Physics* (pp. 16–29). Amsterdam: North-Holland Publ. (reprinted in: J. Hintikka (ed.) (1969), *The Philosophy of Mathematics* (pp. 164–175). Oxford: Oxford University Press.)

van Fraassen, B. (1985; 2nd.). *An Introduction to the Philosophy of Time and Space*. New York: Columbia University Press.

Spatial and Temporal Structures in Cognitive Processes[*]

Christian Freksa[#]

University of Hamburg

Abstract. The structures of space and time are identified as essential for the realization of cognitive systems. It is suggested that the omnipresence of space and time may have been responsible for neglecting these dimensions in knowledge processing in the past. The evolving interest in space and time in cognitive science and some of the current conceptions of space and time are briefly reviewed. It is argued that space and time not only structure cognitive representations and processes but also provide useful information for knowledge processing. Various ways of structuring space and time are discussed and the merits of different languages for describing space and time are addressed. In particular, qualitative and quantitative descriptions are related to local and global reference frames and crisp qualities are related to fuzzy quantities. The importance of selecting an appropriate level of interpretation for a given description is stressed. Examples of interpreting spatial and temporal object descriptions in various ways are presented.

The Ubiquity of Space and Time in Cognitive Systems

Space and time are everywhere – particularly in cognitive systems and around them. This situation – as trivial as it sounds – may be responsible for the fact that the relevance of space and time to cognition has been neglected in modeling cognitive representations and processes for a long time.

Perception, the origin of all cognition, takes place in spatially extended regions and requires time to be carried out; memory requires spatial extension and the processes of storage and retrieval require some time; processing perceived or recorded information takes place in space and requires time; actions carried out on the basis of computation require both space and time.

From an information processing perspective, something that is everywhere tends to be not very interesting: at first glance it appears unspecific and therefore not informative. Thus, it is not surprising that many knowledge representation approaches in artificial intelligence abstracted from time and space while truth and falsity were of central interest in these approaches[1]. Locations – in particular memory locations – were considered equivalent to one another and the times of occurrence of events were considered arbitrary – and therefore not relevant – in many models of the world.

---

[*] Support from the Deutsche Forschungsgemeinschaft is gratefully acknowledged.
[#] freksa@informatik.uni-hamburg.de FB 18, Vogt-Kölln-Str. 30, 22527 Hamburg, Germany.
[1] See also the debates on the role of logic in AI in *Computational Intelligence*, vol 3, no 3, August 1987 pp 149-237 and in *KI*, vol 6, no 3, September 1992.

But at second glance, the situation looks quite different: each location in space and each moment in time can be considered unique, and therefore very informative. However – unique entities are not interesting from an information processing point of view, as they are unpredictable; they are too specific to be useful for generalization.

Fortunately, at third glance we observe that space and time have rather regular structures. And structure means predictability. In other words, space and time bear the potential of being interpreted in very specific ways due to the specificity of their parts and of being interpreted in more general ways due to their regular structures; thus they behave in a predictable way and can be exploited by information processes in general and by cognitive processes in particular.

The structures of space and time serve as reference frames for our understanding of the world. Animals and people go to familiar places for security and sovereignty; they exploit the periodicity of events to predict new situations. We describe non-perceivable abstract dimensions in terms of the concrete dimensions space and time [cf. Freksa & Habel 1990];[2] in this way we can exploit our familiarity with those dimensions and convey dependencies in other domains.

During the last few years, the central roles of space and time for cognitive systems have been increasingly recognized. In artificial intelligence, a great interest has developed to understand and to model structures and uses of cognitive space and time. The work in this field is carried out in cooperation with other disciplines of cognitive science in an effort to jointly solve the puzzle of space, time, and their representation and use in cognitive systems.

Space and Time in Various Disciplines of Cognitive Science

Space and time have become of central interest to several branches of cognitive science. Psychologists study the cognition of perceived and imagined visual space, the cognition of large scale space, i.e. space which cannot be perceived from a single view point [cf. Lynch 1960], and the cognition of the duration of events. The relation between subjectively perceived duration and physically measured time in actual experience and in successive recollection hint at complex structures in the cognitive organization of time. Of particular interest in the cognition of space and time are questions of spatial and temporal reference frames, the relation between visual and haptic space, and the role of spatial scale for spatial cognition. Psychological experiments in spatial and temporal cognition are carried out by relating performance of human subjects in spatial and temporal tasks to models of spatial and temporal representation.

In the neurosciences, spatial and temporal cognition is investigated mainly by studying the effects of neurological deficits, for example deficits in the ability to correctly order sequences of events, deficits in the cognition of personal space, deficits in the cognition of locations, and deficits in the cognition of objects [cf. Andersen 1987]. Reference systems play a decisive role here too. The research in these areas is not restricted to the study of human spatial cognition, but extends to animals as well.

---

[2] See also: Habel & Eschenbach, Abstract structures in spatial cognition – this volume.

Linguistics studies adequate and inadequate use of language to describe space and time, for example the use of prepositions to describe and distinguish spatial and temporal arrangements of physical objects or events. Seemingly inconsistent usage of prepositions may be explained by identifying suitable reference systems [Retz-Schmidt 1988]. Philosophers have been asking questions about possible structures of space and time for more than 2500 years. An increasing number of interdisciplinary treatments is published like Landau and Jackendoff's [1993] much-discussed article "What and where in spatial language and spatial cognition", to mention one example.

Artificial intelligence has traditionally treated space and time mostly implicitly. Realizing that this may cause problems of restricted expressiveness and excessive complexity, AI researchers have been developing explicit representations of knowledge about space and time. Some of these representations may serve as operational models of spatial and temporal cognition and raise interesting questions both to empirical and to analytical approaches to cognitive science.

Abstract and Concrete Spaces

Two disciplines dealing extensively with space and time are mathematics and physics. One way of axiomatizing space in mathematics is as a structure made up of a set of points. Euclidean geometry builds a system of concepts on the basis of points, lines, and planes: distance, area, volume, and angle. In the context of spatial reasoning, Schlieder [1996] distinguishes between topological information (e.g. information about connectivity), orientation or ordering (e.g. information about convexity), and metric information (e.g. information about distances and angles).

Classical physics is concerned with concrete physical space. This space can be described in terms of orthogonal components to solve problems of classical mechanics. Physical space is positively extended, and movement can take place in any spatial direction. Unlike in classical physics, common sense notions of the world generally conceive time as directed (and therefore irreversible). Physical space and its elements are related to other physical quantities in many ways: movement relates time and (spatial) distance, atomic structures relate mass and spatial extension, gravity relates weight and mass, etc.

Cognitive systems appear to employ different conceptualizations of space. Central questions are: What are basic entities of the cognitive spatial structures? How are these entities related to one another? Which reference frames are employed? How are the entities and their relations cognitively processed? Which aspects of space are processed separate from others and which aspects are processed in an integrated manner? What is the role of spatial structures in generating and processing spatial metaphors?

Conceptions of Space and Time

When we speak about *space*, we refer to notions of location, orientation, shape, size (height, width, length and their combination), connection, distance, neighborhood, etc. When we speak about *time*, we refer to notions of duration, precedence, concurrency, simultaneity, consequence, etc. Some of the notions have well-defined meanings in disciplines like physics, topology, geometry, and theoretical computer science; but here we are concerned with the question how humans think and talk about them, how they represent such notions to get around in their spatio-temporal environment, how they reason successfully about the environment, and how they solve problems based upon this reasoning. In AI, these questions were first addressed in the framework of *naive physics* research [cf. Hayes 1978].

There is a multitude of ways in which space and time can be conceptualized, each of which rests on implicit assumptions or explicit knowledge about the physical structure of the world. We will start with a common sense picture, which could be something like: space is 'a collection of places which stand in unchanging relative position to one another and which may or may not have objects located at them'; time is 'an ever growing arrow along which changes take place'. Implicit in these pictures are the assumptions that the time arrow grows even when no other changes are taking place, that space is there even when there are no objects to fill it, and that spatial relations and changes can be observed and described. As these assumptions cannot be redeemed in practice, it is more reasonable to assume that objects and events *constitute* space or time, respectively.

Another distinction concerns the question whether space or time should be modeled by infinite sets of (extensionless) points or by finite intervals (or regions). If we talk about Rocquencourt being located South-West of Rostock, it is likely that we think of two geometric points (without spatial extension) on a map of Europe. If, in a different situation, we say that you have to follow a certain road through Rocquencourt to reach a particular destination, Rocquencourt will be considered to have a spatial extension.

Also, it is not clear from the outset whether a discrete, a dense, or a continuous representation of time and space may be more adequate for human cognition or for solving a given task [Habel 1994]: if we want to reason about arbitrarily small changes, a dense representation seems to be a good choice; if we want to express that two objects touch each other and we do not want anything to get in between them, a discrete representation seems preferable; if on one level of consideration a touching relation and on another level arbitrarily small changes seem appropriate, yet another structure may be required. Nevertheless, a continuous structure (e.g. R^2) is often assumed which provides a better correspondence with models from physics.

Description in Terms of Quantities and Qualities

Space and time can be described in terms of external reference values or by reference to domain-internal entities [e.g. Zimmermann 1995]. For external reference, usually standardized quantities with regular spacing (scales) are used; this is done particularly when precise and objective descriptions are desired; the described situations can be reconstructed accurately (within the tolerance of the granularity of the scale) in a different setting. In contrast, domain-internal entities usually do not provide regularly spaced reference values but only reference values which happen to be prominent in the given domain. The internal reference values define regions which correspond to sets of quantitatively neighboring external values. The system of internally defined regions is domain-specific.

Which of the two ways of representing knowledge about a physical environment is more useful for a cognitive system? In our modern world of ever-growing standardization we have learned that common reference systems and precise quantities are extremely useful for a global exchange of information. From an external perspective, the signals generated in receptor cells of (natural and artificial) perception systems also provide quantitative information to the successive processing stages. But already in the most primitive decision stages, for example in simple threshold units, rich quantitative information is reduced to comparatively coarse qualitative information, when we consider the threshold as an internal reference value.

We can learn from these considerations, that information reduction and abstraction may be worthwhile at any level of processing. As long as we stay within a given context, the transition from quantitative to qualitative descriptions does not imply a loss of precision; it merely means focusing on situation-relevant distinctions. By using relevant entities from within a given environment for reference, we obtain a customized system able to capture the distinctions relevant in the given domain. Customization as information processing strategy was to be considered expensive when information processing power was centralized; but with decentralized computing, as we find in biological and in advanced technical systems, locally customized information processing may simplify computation and decision-making considerably.

Local & Global Reference Systems and Conceptual Neighborhood

Significant decisions frequently are not only of local relevance; thus it must be possible to communicate them to other environments. How can we do this if we have opted for qualitative local descriptions? To answer this question, we must first decide which are the relevant aspects that have to be communicated. Do we have to communicate precise quantitative values as, for example, in international trade or do qualitative values like trends and comparisons suffice?

In cognitive systems, a qualitative description of a local decision frequently will suffice to 'get the picture' of the situation; the specific quantities taken into account may have no particular meaning in another local context. Qualitative descriptions can convey comparisons from one context to another, provided that the general structures of the two contexts agree. If the descriptions refer to the spatio-temporal structures of two different environments, this will be the case [cf. Freksa 1980].

Now consider qualitative spatio-temporal descriptions in a given environment. As they compare one entity to another entity with respect to a certain feature dimension, they form binary (or possibly higher-order) relations like *John is taller than the arch* or *Ed arrived after dinner was ready*. In concrete situations in which descriptions serve to solve certain tasks, it only makes sense to compare given entities to specific other entities. For example, comparing the size of a person to the height of an arch is meaningful, as persons do want to pass through arches and comparing the arrival time of a person to the completion time of a meal may be meaningful, as the meal may have been prepared for consumption by that person; on the other hand, it may not make sense to compare the height of a person to the size of a shoe, or the arrival time of a person at home with the manufacturing date of some tooth paste. For this reason, we frequently abbreviate binary spatial or temporal relations by unary relations (leaving the reference of the comparison implicit). Thus, to a person understanding the situation context, the absolute descriptions *John is tall* and *Ed arrived late* in effect may provide the same information as the previous statements in terms of explicit comparisons.

As long as it is clear from the situation context, that there is only one meaningful reference object and dimension for the implicit comparison, the descriptions can be considered crisp (as the description either is fully true or fully false in the reference world). However, in more realistic settings, situations are not completely specified and it is therefore not completely clear which should be considered the single relevant reference object. In fact, usually even the producer of a description himself or herself will not be able to precisely indicate which is the unique correct reference object. For example, when I assert *John is tall*, I am not able to uniquely specify with respect to which reference value I consider John to be tall. Why is the description still meaningful and why is it possible to understand the meaning of such a description?

In many cases, the reason that qualitative descriptions with indeterminate reference value work is that potential reference candidates provide a neighborhood of similar values, or – in terms of the terminology of qualitative reasoning – the values form a *conceptual neighborhood* [Freksa 1991]. Conceptual neighbors in spatial and temporal reasoning have the property that they change the result of a computation very little or not at all, in comparison to the original value. For example, in interpreting the description *John is tall* as an implicit comparison of the height of John with the height of other objects, it may not be critical whether I use as reference value the height of other people in the room, the average height of persons of the same category, or the median, provided that these values are in the same ballpark of values. On the other hand, if the context of the situation does not sufficiently specify which category of values provides an adequate reference for interpreting a given description, we may be in trouble. For example, if the description *John is tall* is generated in the context of talking about pre-school children, it may be inappropriate to interpret it with reference to the average height of the male population as a whole.

Crisp Qualities and Fuzzy Quantities

We have discussed descriptions like *John is tall* in terms of qualitative descriptions. The theory of fuzzy sets characterizes descriptions of this type in terms of fuzzy possibility distributions [Zadeh 1978]. What is the relation between the fuzzy set interpretation and the interpretation in terms of qualitative attributes?[3] The fuzzy set *tall* describes objects in terms of a range of (external objective) quantities. Having a range of quantities instead of a single quantity reflects the fact that the value is not precisely given with respect to the precision of the scale used. This is a simple granularity effect implicit also in crisp quantitative descriptions. For example,

---

[3] See also: Hernández, Qualitative vs. quantitative representations of spatial distance – this volume.

distance measures in full meters usually imply a range of 100 possible actual values in full centimeters or 1000 possible actual values in full millimeters, etc. The graded membership values associated with different actual values in addition account for the fact that in many descriptions not all actual values are possible to the same degree. Nevertheless, the description in terms of quantities with graded membership in a fuzzy set is a quantitative description.

The qualitative view directly accounts for the fact that the granulation of a scale in terms of meters, centimeters, or millimeters is somewhat arbitrary and does not directly reflect relevant differences in the domain described. Thus, the description *John is tall* can be viewed as a statement about the height category which John belongs to and whose distinction from other height categories is relevant in a certain context – for example when walking through an arch. In the qualitative view, the fact that the category *tall* can be instantiated by a whole range of actual height values is not of interest; the view abstracts from quantities. As fuzzy sets relate the qualitative linguistic terms to a quantitative interpretation, they provide an interface between the qualitative and the quantitative levels of description.

Levels of Interpretation

We have discussed a qualitative and a quantitative perspective on spatial and temporal representations and I have argued that the qualitative view uses meaningful reference values to establish the categories for the qualitative descriptions while the quantitative view relies on pre-established categories from a standard scale, whose categories are not specifically tuned to the application domain. In this comparison, the two approaches reflected by the two views are structurally not very different: both rely on reference values – the first from the domain, the second from an external scale. As a result of the adaptation to the specific domain, qualitative categories typically are coarser than their quantitative counterparts.

So what else is behind the qualitative / quantitative distinction? Let us consider again the qualitative / quantitative interface manifested in the fuzzy set formalism. A problem with the use of fuzzy sets for modeling natural language or other cognitive systems is that the interpretation of qualitative concepts is carried out through the quantitative level linked via the interface to the qualitative concept while cognitive systems seem to be able to abstract from the specific quantitative level [Freksa 1994]. For example, from *X is tall* and *Y is much taller than X* we can infer *Y is very tall*, independent of a specific quantitative interpretation of the category *tall*. How is this possible?

The answer is simple. The semantic correspondence between spatial and temporal categories should be established on the abstract qualitative level of interpretation rather than on a specific quantitative level. This requires that relations between spatial and temporal categories are established directly on the qualitative level, for example in terms of topological relations or neighborhood relations. In this way, the essence of descriptions can be transmitted and evaluated more easily.

An interesting aspect of transferring spatial and temporal operations from the quantitative level to the qualitative level is that fuzzy relations on the quantitative level may map into crisp relations on the qualitative level. For example, to compute the relation between the spatial categories *tall* and *medium-sized* on the quantitative level, fuzzy set operations have to be carried out. On the other hand, on the qualitative level, we may provide partial ordering, inclusion, exclusion, overlap information, etc. to characterize the categories and to infer appropriate candidate objects matching the description.

From a philosophical point of view, there is an important difference between the quantitative and the qualitative levels of interpretation. While quantitative interpretations – for example in terms of fuzzy sets – implicitly refer to a dense structure of target candidate values, qualitative interpretations directly refer to singular discrete objects which actually exist in the target domain. For this reason, certain issues relevant to fuzzy reasoning and decision making do not arise in qualitative reasoning. This concerns particularly the problem of setting appropriate threshold values for description matching.

Horizontal Competition – Vertical Subsumption

Creating and interpreting object descriptions with respect to a specific set of objects calls for the use of discriminating features rather than for a precise characterization in terms of a universally applicable reference system. This is particularly true when the description is needed for object identification where the reference context is available (as opposed to object reconstruction in the absence of a reference context).

When the reference context is available for generating and interpreting object descriptions, this context can be employed in two interesting ways. First of all, the context can provide the best discriminating features for distinguishing the target object from competing objects; second, the set of competing objects can provide the appropriate granulation for qualitatively describing the target object in relation to the competing objects. For example, when a description is needed to distinguish one person from one other person in a given situation, a single feature, say height, and a coarse granulation into qualitative categories, say *tall* and *short*, may suffice to unambiguously identify the target; if, on the other hand, in the interpretation of a description there are many competing objects, the description *tall* may be interpreted on a much finer granulation level distinguishing the categories *very tall, tall, medium-sized, short, very short*, which are subsumed by the coarser categories [Freksa & Barkowsky 1996].

Conclusion and Outlook

I have presented a view of cognitive representations of spatial and temporal structures and I have sketched a perspective for exploiting these structures in spatial and temporal reasoning. The discussion focused on the description and interpretation of actually existing concrete situations. The general arguments should carry over to non-spatial and non-temporal domains. However, difficulties can be expected in using the ideas for describing hypothetical worlds and impossible situations, as the approach relies heavily on the reference to spatially and/or temporally representable situations.

By carrying the principle of context-sensitive interpretation of the semantics of spatial and temporal categories a step further, we may get a rather different explanation of the meaning of semantic categories: whether a given category is applicable or not may not depend so much on their fulfilling certain absolute qualifying criteria as on the availability of potentially competing categories for description.

Acknowledgments

I thank Bettina Berendt, Reinhard Moratz, Thomas Barkowsky, and Ralf Röhrig for valuable comments and suggestions.

References

Andersen, R.A. 1987. Inferior parietal lobule function in spatial perception and visuomotor integration. In *Handbook of physiology, The nervous system* VI, Higher functions of the brain, part 2, ed. Plum, 483–518. Bethesda, Md.: American Physiological Society.

Freksa, C. 1980. Communication about visual patterns by means of fuzzy characterizations. *Proc. XXIInd Intern. Congress of Psychology*, Leipzig.

Freksa, C. 1991. Conceptual neighborhood and its role in temporal and spatial reasoning. In *Decision Support Systems and Qualitative Reasoning*, ed. Singh and Travé-Massuyès, 181–187. Amsterdam: North-Holland.

Freksa, C. 1994. Fuzzy systems in AI. In *Fuzzy systems in computer science*, ed. Kruse, Gebhardt, and Palm. Braunschweig/Wiesbaden: Vieweg.

Freksa, C., and Barkowsky, T., 1996. On the relation between spatial concepts and geographic objects. In *Geographic objects with indeterminate boundaries*, ed. Burrough and Frank, 109-121. London: Taylor and Francis.

Freksa, C., and Habel, C. 1990. Warum interessiert sich die Kognitionsforschung für die Darstellung räumlichen Wissens? In *Repräsentation und Verarbeitung räumlichen Wissens*, ed. Freksa and Habel, 1-15, Berlin: Springer-Verlag.

Habel, C. 1994. Discreteness, finiteness, and the structure of topological spaces. In *Topological foundations of cognitive science*, FISI-CS workshop Buffalo, NY, Report 37, ed. Eschenbach, Habel, and Smith, Hamburg: Graduiertenkolleg Kognitionswissenschaft.

Hayes, P. 1978. The naive physics manifesto. In *Expert systems in the microelectronic age*, ed. Michie. Edinburgh: Edinburgh University Press.

Landau, B. and Jackendoff, R. 1993. "What" and "where" in spatial language and spatial cognition, *Behavioral and Brain Sciences* 16: 217–265.

Lynch, K. 1960. *The image of the city*. Cambridge, Mass.: The MIT Press.

Retz-Schmidt, G. 1988. Various views on spatial prepositions. *AI Magazine*, 4/88: 95–105.

Schlieder, C. 1996. Räumliches Schließen. In *Wörterbuch der Kognitionswissenschaft*, ed. Strube, Becker, Freksa, Hahn, Opwis, and Palm, 608-609. Stuttgart: Klett-Cotta.

Zadeh, L.A. 1978. Fuzzy sets as a basis for a theory of possibility. *Fuzzy sets and systems* 1, 3–28.

Zimmermann, K. 1995. Measuring without measures: the delta-calculus. In *Spatial information theory. A theoretical basis for GIS*, ed. Frank and Kuhn, 59-67. Berlin: Springer.

Qualitative vs. Fuzzy Representations of Spatial Distance

Daniel Hernández

Fakultät für Informatik
Technische Universität München
80290 München

danher@informatik.tu-muenchen.de

Abstract Fuzzy set theory is a well-established modeling tool with applications in many domains, one of them being spatial reasoning. Qualitative approaches to the representation of spatial knowledge, by contrast, have become increasingly popular only in the last five years. In this paper, we compare fuzzy and qualitative approaches to the representation of the distance between two entities in physical space. We show commonalities and differences in the way the world is modeled, uncertainty handled, and inferences drawn in each framework, as well as possible combinations of both approaches. Furthermore, we discuss their relation to linguistic and cognitive issues, and how well each of them models human perception and expression of distance information.

1 Introduction

Distance is one of the very basic spatial concepts. At the same time, it is difficult to represent, as it is influenced by many factors, is context dependent, and often uncertain.

In what follows, we compare fuzzy and qualitative approaches to the representation of distance in space. We start by reviewing linguistic and psychological studies of cognitive distances to gain insights about their characteristic structure (section 2). We look then into the phenomenon of uncertainty uncovering various types and sources for it (section 3). This is followed by a brief description of fuzzy set (section 4) and qualitative (section 5) representations of distance knowledge leading to a comparison and discussion of both in section 6.

2 Spatial Distance

Cognitive distances are conceptualized first as a dichotomy between "proximity" (*near*) and "distality" (*far*). They express a relation between a reference object (RO) and a primary or localized object (PO) that is characterized by a relatively small region around the RO where a PO is considered to be close to the RO and a large or even infinite region where a PO is considered far away from the RO. The area around the RO, in which a particular relation is accepted as a valid description of the distance between two objects, is called "acceptance area". Contrary to the mathematical concept of distance, cognitive distances are often asymmetrical. For example, if a small village is considered to be close to a big city, the big city is likely to be considered far away from the small village as the perspective varies with the reference object. Furthermore, distances close to the reference objects are exaggerated whereas distances farther away tend to be underestimated.

Another interesting characteristic is that the extension of the objects involved, i.e., their size and shape, influence the size and shape of the acceptance areas for distance relations. The usual abstraction of the position of objects as points is valid only for objects *far away* from each other. In that case, the extension of the objects is small with respect to the distances between them and can be disregarded. Furthermore, the acceptance areas are likely to be concentric circles (assuming an isotropic space). If objects are in "close proximity" to each other, the distance is assessed with respect to the parts of the boundary of the two objects that are closest (Peuquet 1992). A primary object is said to be in "close proximity" of a reference object, if their extension cannot be disregarded with respect to their relative distances. In this case, the acceptance areas for distance relations strongly depend on the shape of the reference object. A circular object would maintain the same acceptance areas as in the case of point abstraction. In general, however, the acceptance areas are given by isometric lines that approximate the shape of the reference object as long as it is convex. If an object is not convex, then the relations of other objects lying inside its convex hull are difficult to express altogether. An acceptable simplification is to use encapsulating rectangles aligned with the frame of reference and let the acceptance areas be given by isometric lines that approximate a rectangle in close proximity of the object and tend to a circular shape moving toward the outside. Finally, in the case of connecting objects, the distance between their boundaries collapses to zero. Therefore, we can either describe the distances between two particular points of the objects, e.g., the two centroids or resort to topological relations.

The basic distance concepts are directly reflected in language. For example, Jackendoff and Landau (1992) show that in English there are basically only 3 degrees of distance distinctions: interior of reference object (*in, inside*), exterior but in contact (*on, against*), proximate (*near*), plus the corresponding "negatives": interior (*out of, outside*), contact (*off of*), proximate (*far from*). Furthermore, prepositions such as *among* and *between* also convey some distance information. A similar system with five distance distinctions is described by Pribbenow (1991): "inclusion" (acceptance area restricted to projection of reference object), "contact/adjacency" (immediate neighborhood of RO), "proximity" and "geo-distance" (surroundings of RO), and "remoteness" (defined as complement of the proximal region around the RO). Further linguistic studies of distance concepts are those by Bierwisch (1988) and Wunderlich and Herweg (1989) among many others.

As will be shown below, both "linguistic variables" in fuzzy sets and qualitative relations in the qualitative approach are heavily inspired by the way spatial information is expressed verbally. In particular, the relational nature of spatial expressions has a direct correspondence in the linguistic variables and qualitative relations. Also the semantics of such a label or relation is not seen in a direct relation between the objects involved, but rather, as in language, the reference object is used to define a region in which the primary object is located. However, the relation between the inventory of spatial constructs of a language and the possible combinations of basic spatial concepts is not a one-to-one mapping (Pribbenow 1991; Talmy 1983). For example, some prepositions might correspond to several different spatial relations depending on the context in which they are used (Herskovits 1986).

There have also been many psychophysical studies of the perception of distance and related cognitive issues. Downs and Stea (1973a) identify several characteristics of cognitive maps such as their incompleteness, the tendency to schematization and associated distortions and augmentations as well as significant intergroup and individual differences. Thus, the resulting representation resembles rather a collage of bits and pieces of spatial information rather than a map (Tversky 1993).

Cognitive distances in urban environments have been studied by Lee (1970), Briggs (1973), and Canter and Tagg (1975) among others. Studies of intercity distances (Stea 1969; Sadalla and Magel 1980) have suggested the influence of factors such as the attractiveness of and familiarity of the subjects with origin, goal, and interconnecting paths, as well as the kind and number or barriers along the way and the magnitude of the geographic distance.

In his extensive review of the psychological literature on the perception and cognition of environmental distances (i.e., those that cannot be perceived in entirety from a single point of view and thus require moving around for their apprehension) Montello (1995) identifies several processes as well as sources for distance knowledge. In general, knowledge of environmental distance depends on perception or awareness of body movement or change of position (based on vision, vestibular sensation, motor efference or auditory processes). Processes by which distance knowledge is acquired and used include working-memory, non-mediated, hybrid, and simple-retrieval processes. Knowledge about distances might be derived from many sources, including environmental features (turns, landmarks, barriers), travel time, and travel effort.

Given this complex interplay of information sources and processes determining cognitive distance concepts, it is not surprising that no exact models exist for them.

3 Uncertainty

Dealing with uncertainty is a common important motivation for the development of both fuzzy set and qualitative approaches to the representation of spatial knowledge. In this section, I want to comment on various types and sources of uncertainty and defer a discussion on how fuzzy and qualitative representations deal with it to the sections 4 and 5, respectively.

There is a great deal of disparity in the literature on concepts such as uncertainty, imprecision, vagueness, etc. Zimmermann (1992) distinguishes between stochastic uncertainty (lack of information about the future state of a system) and fuzziness (vagueness concerning the description of the semantic meaning of events), which can be either intrinsic (e.g., "tall men", since context dependent) or informational (e.g., "creditworthy customers", where domain too complex to be described completely). Dutta (1991) looks at inference procedures (presupposing a representation) and the environments or domains they deal with and lists the four cases: precise inference procedure in precise environment (e.g., Newtonian physics); imprecise inference procedure in precise environment (e.g., heuristics); precise inference procedure in imprecise environment (e.g., Dempster-Shafer, fuzzy logic); imprecise inference procedure in imprecise environment (e.g., heuristic prediction of stock markets). A different and more elaborated classification of knowledge types is described by Freksa (1994), who differentiates among others between certain and uncertain knowledge, complete and incomplete knowledge, and quantifiable and comparable uncertainty.

I want to propose here a simple classification scheme for various types and sources of uncertainty based on the classic representation paradigm of Palmer (1978). Within that framework, representation involves not only a mapping between a represented and a representing world but also the selection of objects, properties, and relations to be represented, i.e., the *modeling* of the domain, and the selection of corresponding elements in the representing medium, i.e., knowledge language design. There is, however, also a temporal component: We can usually represent the present (or past) state of the world, but only speculate about (or in benign cases: predict) the future state of a system.

These considerations allow us to distinguish between ontological and epistemological uncertainty about both present and future states of a world. *Ontological uncertainty* refers to inherent properties of the world itself, e.g., indeterminate boundaries of feature-defined regions such as polluted areas (present state) or the unpredictability of inherently random processes (future state). *Epistemological uncertainty* pertains to our imperfect knowledge about the world, e.g., contradictory information about the present state of a system of lack of information about an otherwise predictable future state.

The sources of uncertainty are varied and often interact in many ways making it difficult to keep them apart. Some of them are due to the impossibility of obtaining information, in particular in the case of ontological uncertainty: inherently random distributions and processes, and the unpredictability of the future are examples of this category. The lack of information is the primary source of epistemological uncertainty. Incomplete information might be due to the complexity of the domain, resource constraints, uncollaborative environments or measurement errors. Finally, the way we usually communicate being strongly context dependent might be the source of ambiguous or even contradictory information.

As far as distances are concerned, both types of uncertainty and all of their sources may be present. An example of ontological uncertainty appears when establishing distances between regions with indeterminate boundaries (Altman 1994). Examples of epistemological uncertainty are more common including measurement errors and the ambiguity in natural language statements about distances.

4 Fuzzy Set Representations

Many authors, among them Dutta (1991), Altman (1994), and Jorge and Vaida (1996) have suggested the use of linguistic variables (Zadeh 1973) to deal with the uncertainty of spatial knowledge. Linguistic variables are "variables whose values are not numbers but words or sentences in a natural or artificial language". Formally a linguistic variable is a quintuple $(x, T(x), U, G, M)$ (Zimmermann 1992), where x is the name of the variable (e.g., "proximity"), $T(x)$ is a set of names of linguistic values of x (e.g., {very close, close, ... }), with each value being a fuzzy variable over Universe U; G is a syntactic rule for generating the name, X, of values of x, while M is a semantic rule for associating with each X its meaning, which takes the form of a characteristic function (e.g., mapping small metric distances to a value near "1" and large metric distances to a value close to "0"). The motivation for the use of linguistic variables is that "linguistic characterizations are, in general, less specific than numerical ones" (Zadeh 1973, p. 3). This motivation is in the same spirit as the "making only as many distinctions as necessary" characterization of qualitative representations. There are, however, important differences, which we will discuss in section 6 after a more detailed review of some of the approaches just mentioned here and of qualitative presentations in the next section.

The work of Dutta (1991) aims at representing spatial constraints between a set of objects given imprecise, incomplete and possibly conflicting information about them. To do so, Dutta distinguishes between position and motion spatial constraints. Position constraints in turn can be "propositional" (i.e., qualitative), "metrical" (i.e., quantitative), a quantitatively specified range, or "visual" (i.e., only graphically depictable as a fuzzy area). The main idea is then to transform those constraints into an equivalent possibility distribution, in the two-dimensional case into distributions on the X and Y axes. These distributions can be generally approximated by triangular shapes and thus represented by fuzzy numbers of the form (mean value, left spread, right spread). Spatial reasoning is done in this framework by computing joint possibility distributions according to the compositional rule of inference (Zimmermann 1992).

Altman (1994) presents a treatment more specific to Geographic Information Systems (GIS) using fuzzy regions where the membership function is the concentration of some feature attribute at some point. He argues against converting imprecise data (e.g., *near*) to 'hard' data (e.g., *less than 5km*) at too early a stage in the analysis process, very much in the spirit of qualitative reasoning. Altman defines special distance and directional metrics on fuzzy regions as well as methods for their analysis and synthesis. The "distance" between two fuzzy regions is not a scalar as in other approaches but a new fuzzy set made out of the distances between elements in the Cartesian product of the two sets, and whose membership is the minimum membership of each element pair in the product. The type of uncertainty this deals with results from imprecision in the spatial delineation of the regions rather than from fuzziness in the position of point like objects as in Dutta's work.

Jorge and Vaida (1996) develop a fuzzy relational path algebra to reason about spatial relations involving distances and directions based on semirings. They aim at complementing qualitative distance and direction functions like those developed by Frank (1992) with degree of likelihood functions corresponding to membership functions of fuzzy predicates. Semirings are used as algebraic structures subsuming the formal properties of basic fuzzy set theory and the relational and path algebras of Smith and Park (1992) and Frank (1992) respectively.

Besides these approaches which deal specifically with distances in space, there is a considerable literature on fuzzy similarity relations (see, e.g., Dubois and Prade (1994) for an overview and further references), which are related to a more abstract concept of distance. Fuzzy similarity relations are a generalization of equivalence relations (with a special form of transitivity called max-* transitivity). Relations fulfilling only reflexivity and symmetry are called proximity relations and convey the closeness of an element to prototypical elements of a fuzzy set.

5 Qualitative Representations

Qualitative representations make only as many distinctions as necessary in a given context. They handle uncertainty by using coarse granularity levels, which avoid having to commit to specific values on a given dimension. With other words, the inherent "under-determination" of the representation absorbs the vagueness of our knowledge. Thus, in order to represent distances, qualitative approaches partition the space around a reference object in as many areas of acceptance as degrees of distance required in a given situation. As mentioned in section 2, these areas can be influenced by the shape and relative sizes of the objects involved (and maybe even other objects in the scene) and also by the uniformity or non-uniformity of the effort required to move from one position to another (isotropic and anisotropic spaces, respectively). Furthermore, the relative extension of the acceptance areas w.r.t. each other needs to be represented. Independently of this proportion among acceptance areas, *scale*, i.e., the proportion between represented and representing worlds needs to be taken into consideration. While in a strict sense this is only possible for analogical representations[1] and is often expressed quantitatively, there is also a qualitative

---

[1] Analogical representations have inherently the same structural characteristics as the represented aspects. A map, for example, is an analogical representation of planar positional information.

equivalent. For example, when using a city map, we are seldom aware of the numerical scale.

In (Hernández et al. 1995; Clementini et al. 1997) we have developed a qualitative representation of distances that formalizes many of the aspects mentioned above. We introduce the concept of *distance systems* made out of a totally ordered set of distance relations, an acceptance function mapping those relations to the corresponding geometric distance ranges in space, and an algebraic structure over intervals with comparative relations defining the structure of the distance system, i.e., how the distance relations relate to each other.

We capture much of the contextual information implied in distal expressions by explicitly stating their frame of reference. *Frames of reference* are attached to each distance relation and consist of the distance system the relation belongs to, the corresponding scale, and a *type*, which can be either intrinsic, extrinsic or deictic. These types are defined in analogy to the types of reference frames of projective or directional prepositions in natural language (Retz-Schmidt 1988): In the *intrinsic* case the distance is determined by some inherent property of the reference object (e.g., its size); if external factors such as costs or geographic conventions define the distance distinctions being made, we talk about an *extrinsic* frame of reference; finally, the point of view of a real or virtual observer might determine a *deictic* distance concept.

Given the relational nature of qualitative representations, the basic inference operation is the composition of relations. Spatial configurations described by a set of relations are usually stored as constraint networks, which are directed graphs, where nodes correspond to objects and arcs correspond to disjunctions of relations. Mechanisms such as constraint propagation and relaxation help to infer implied relations on demand and to maintain the consistency of the network whenever new relations are added (or old relations deleted).

Other qualitative approaches to the representation of distance, in particular in the context of geography, are those by Frank (1992) and Jong (1994). Zimmermann's Δ-calculus (Zimmermann 1995) deals with multiples and differences of symbolic quantities and could thus also be used to represent distances.

6 Comparison

Many of the commonalities and differences in the way fuzzy set and qualitative approaches deal with distances have become evident in the previous sections. In this section we summarize the most important aspects concerning modeling, uncertainty, structure, and inference.

The most important difference between fuzzy and qualitative approaches is obviously the way the domain, in this case "space", is modeled. Limiting our attention to the fuzzy approaches which make use of linguistic variables to denote distance concepts, we might be tempted to see a greater expressiveness in them as compared to qualitative approaches: Both make a number of distinctions labeled with symbolic names, but fuzzy numbers allow us to distinguish a gradual membership to each of them. On the other hand, it is not clear, where we could get those numbers from. Even more, we argued above, that in many situations making only as many distinctions as contextually relevant is the better way to model our cognitive distance concepts.

A further aspect is the representation of the domain structure. As compared to qualitative representations, fuzzy approaches are rather shallow representations that do not take the structure of the represented domain into consideration and consequently do not exploit the resulting neighborhood and symmetry constraints.

One of the sources of the uncertainty that both qualitative and fuzzy approaches intend to deal with is the need to express a certain relationship independently of the context in which it occurs.[2] In fuzzy approaches contextual information is encoded in a single number, the value of the membership function, which is not as expressive as the elaborated and explicit frame of reference concept of the qualitative representation introduced in section 5. Furthermore, a combination of named distances and comparatives, e.g., "far, but nearer than...", might be closer to our intuition than "0.6 far".

The quantitative characterization of the elasticity of constraints in fuzzy approaches contrasts with the more flexible concept of acceptance areas or distance ranges and their corresponding semantic interpretation in the qualitative model. This interpretation can assume strict (exact), overlapping or non-exhaustive intervals and even combine them heuristically allowing antecedent relations to denote non-exhaustive intervals, while consequent relations represent overlapping intervals to be shrunk in the next inference step (Mavrovouniotis and Stephanopoulos 1988).

Finally, the composition of fuzzy relations (done by min-max operations) yields a single membership value rather than a disjunction of possible relations as in the qualitative case. In order to verbalize the result of such reasoning a defuzzification process is required in the fuzzy model as opposed to a constraint selection in the qualitative model. While the discriminating power of single qualitative relations is kept intentionally low, the interaction of several relations can lead to arbitrarily fine distinctions. If each relation is considered to represent a set of possible values, the intersections of those sets correspond to elements that satisfy all constraints simultaneously.

In spite of the differences listed above, which result mainly from a purist and contrastive view of the approaches, they have the potential to enrich each other in various ways. For example, there is no reason why fuzzy representations could not be improved by the same type of domain structure resemblance and hierarchical granularity characteristic of qualitative representations. On the other hand, the varying information content of qualitative distinctions has already led to heuristics deferring the propagation of weak information. Fuzzy set operators and inference techniques offer well studied and much more powerful methods to improve those heuristics.

---

[2] This might be the case because the representation will be used later in a particular context, and thus, does not need to contain as much specific information itself.

Bibliography

Altman, D. (1994). Fuzzy set theoretic approaches for handling imprecision in spatial analysis. *International Journal of Geographical Information Systems, 8*(3), 271–289.

Bierwisch, M. (1988). On the grammar of local prepositions. In Bierwisch, Motsch, and Zimmermann, editors, *Syntax, Semantik und Lexikon*, Number 29 in Studia Grammatica, pages 1–65. Akademie-Verlag, Berlin.

Briggs, R. (1973). Urban cognitive distance. In Downs and Stea (1973b), pages 361–388.

Canter, D. and Tagg, S. K. (1975). Distance estimation in cities. *Environment and Behavior, 7*, 59–80.

Clementini, E., Di Felice, P., and Hernández, D. (1997). Qualitative representation of positional information. To appear in Artificial Intelligence.

Downs, R. M. and Stea, D. (1973a). Cognitive maps and spatial behavior: Process and products. In Downs and Stea (1973b), pages 8–26.

Downs, R. M. and Stea, D., editors (1973b). *Image and Environment: Cognitive Mapping and Spatial Behavior*. Aldine, Chicago.

Dubois, D. and Prade, H. (1994). Similarity-based approximate reasoning. In Zurada, J. M., editor, *Computational Intelligence: Imitating Life*, pages 69–80. IEEE Press, New York.

Dutta, S. (1991). Approximate spatial reasoning: Integrating qualitative and quantitative constraints. *International Journal of Approximate Reasoning, 5*, 307–331.

Frank, A. U. (1992). Qualitative spatial reasoning with cardinal directions. *Journal of Visual Languages and Computing, 3*, 343–371.

Frank, A. U. and Kuhn, W., editors (1995). *Spatial Information Theory. A Theoretical Basis for GIS. International Conference, COSIT'95*, Semmering, Austria, Volume 988 of *Lecture Notes in Computer Science*. Springer, Berlin.

Freksa, C. (1994). Fuzzy systems in AI: An overview. In Kruse, R., Gebhardt, J., and Palm, R., editors, *Fuzzy Systems in Computer Science*, pages 155–169. Vieweg, Wiesbaden.

Hernández, D., Clementini, E., and Di Felice, P. (1995). Qualitative distances. In Frank and Kuhn (1995), pages 45–57.

Herskovits, A. (1986). *Language and Spatial Cognition. An Interdisciplinary Study of the Prepositions in English*. Cambridge University Press, Cambridge, MA.

Jackendoff, R. and Landau, B. (1992). Spatial language and spatial cognition. In Jackendoff, R., editor, *Languages of the mind: Essays on mental representation*, chapter 6, pages 99–124. The MIT Press, Cambridge, MA.

Jong, J.-H. (1994). *Qualitative Reasoning about Distances and Directions in Geographic Space*. Ph.D. thesis, University of Maine.

Jorge, J. A. and Vaida, D. (1996). A fuzzy relational path algebra for distances and directions. In *Proceedings of the ECAI-96 Workshop on Representation and Processing of Spatial Expressions*, Budapest, Hungary.

Lee, T. R. (1970). Perceived distance as a function of direction in the city. *Environment and Behavior, 2*, 40–51.

Mavrovouniotis, M. L. and Stephanopoulos, G. (1988). Formal order-of-magnitude reasoning in process engineering. *Computer Chemical Engineering, 12*, 867–880.

Montello, D. R. (1995). The perception and cognition of environmental distance: processes and knowledge sources. Unpublished Manuscript, Department of Geography, University of California, Santa Barbara.

Palmer, S. E. (1978). Fundamental aspects of cognitive representation. In Rosch, E. and Lloyd, B. B., editors, *Cognition and Categorization*. Lawrence Erlbaum, Hillsdale, NJ.

Peuquet, D. (1992). An algorithm for calculating the minimum Euclidean distance between two geographic features. *Computers & Geosciences, 18*(8), 989–1001.

Pribbenow, S. (1991). *Zur Verarbeitung von Lokalisierungsausdrücken in einem hybriden System*. Ph.D. thesis, Universität Hamburg. Reprinted as IWBS Report 211, IBM Deutschland, 1992.

Retz-Schmidt, G. (1988). Various views on spatial prepositions. *AI Magazine, 9*(2), 95–105.

Sadalla, E. K. and Magel, S. G. (1980). The perception of traversed distance. *Environment and Behaviour, 12*, 65–79.

Smith, T. R. and Park, K. K. (1992). Algebraic approach to spatial reasoning. *International Journal of Geographical Information Systems, 6*(3), 177–192.

Stea, D. (1969). The measurement of mental maps: an experimental model for studying conceptual spaces. In Cox, K. R. and Golledge, R. G., editors, *Behavioral Problems in Geography: A Symposium*, pages 228–253. Northwestern University Press, Evanston, Ill.

Talmy, L. (1983). How language structures space. In Pick, H. L. and Acredolo, L. P., editors, *Spatial Orientation: Theory, Research and Application*. Plenum Press, New York.

Tversky, B. (1993). Cognitive maps, cognitive collages, and spatial mental models. In Frank, A. U. and Campari, I., editors, *Spatial Information Theory. A Theoretical Basis for GIS. European Conference, COSIT'93*, Marciana Marina, Italy, Volume 716 of *Lecture Notes in Computer Science*, pages 14–24. Springer, Berlin.

Wunderlich, D. and Herweg, M. (1989). Lokale und Direktionale. In von Stechow, A. and Wunderlich, D., editors, *Handbuch der Semantik*. Athenäum, Königstein.

Zadeh, L. A. (1973). The concept of a linguistic variable and its application to approximate reasoning. Memorandum ERL-M 411, University of California at Berkeley.

Zimmermann, H.-J. (1992). *Fuzzy set theory and its applications*. Kluwer, Dordrecht.

Zimmermann, K. (1995). Measuring without measures: The delta-calculus. In Frank and Kuhn (1995), pages 59–67.

What's a Part?
On Formalizing Part-Whole Relations

Simone Pribbenow*

University of Hamburg, Computer Science Department

Abstract. This paper deals with commonsense understanding of part-whole relations. A unifying definition for the different kinds of parts is proposed for one domain, that of rigid, man-made objects. First, the representation of objects via basic dimensions, reference systems and attributes is described. Then, different kinds of parts, based on the classification of Gerstl and Pribbenow (1996), are examined. Several problems with the seemingly uncomplicated notion of "part" are discussed. Modifying the representation of objects makes it possible to give one single definition of "a part P of an object O".

1 Introduction

The objective of this article is to investigate the following question: What are possible parts of objects of everyday use like cups, chairs or ball pens? The commonsense notion of part-whole relation(s) is an important aspect of knowledge representation, cognitive modeling as well as of the more technical area of knowledge engineering. The part-whole relation(s) are essential for different cognitive tasks, e.g., object recognition, reasoning about objects, and language understanding. The same hold for technical domains like model based configuration or diagnosis.

Part-whole relations are investigated from different perspectives.[1] Mereological approaches focus on calculi based on the "part-of" relation and their use in formal ontologies of different domains (e.g., Simons (1987), Smith (1982)). Linguistically oriented approaches examine the role of part-whole relations as semantic primitives and their relation to natural language expressions (e.g., Cruse (1979)). Psychological work concerns the role of parts in object recognition (e.g., Biederman (1987)) or in concept theory (e.g., Tversky (1990)). In cognitive science, classifications of part-whole relations are developed (e.g., Winston et al. (1987)) and in artificial intelligence, special formalisms for part knowledge are designed.

All approaches mentioned above concentrate on single topics. What is normally missing is a characterization of the notions of "part" and "whole" and the interaction between them. In order to achieve such a characterization, two questions must be answered:

---

* I wish to thank Emile van der Zee, Peter Gerstl, Eibo Thieme, and Bettina Berendt as well as two anonymous reviewers for their comments on the manuscript and for correcting my English. And it is also my dearest wish to thank Mr. and Mrs. Brauer for showing me that professional competence and warmth can go together very well.

[1] A more detailed overview over the current approaches to part-whole research can be found in Gerstl and Pribbenow (1995).

1.) What is a part? Is there any unique definition that formalizes the (commonsense) notion of a part?

2.) How can parts be combined to wholes? In which way do the features of the part contribute to the features of the whole object?

I will try to answer the first question in this paper for a restricted domain, the domain of man-made, rigid objects without taken temporal change into account. In this short paper, I will not try to answer the second question, but give a short outlook on the problems of the notion of a whole at the end of the paper.

2 The representation of objects

This paper considers only man-made, three-dimensional objects that do not have movable parts and that do not change their form in any other way. This means that liquids like (non-frozen) water are thus not considered. Artifacts are easier to examine than natural objects because their general structure and function is clearer to us as a result of their being designed by humans. Nevertheless, there is a good chance that the results can be extended to natural object. The objects should be rigid to allow for a simple spatial description of the whole. Additionally, the exclusion of time makes it impossible to describe the motion of parts and leads automatically into a domain of rigid objects. The timeless point of view also allows to ignore the problem of identity of one individual that undergoes any change in its parts, e.g., a chair of which one leg has fallen off and replaced by a new leg to get a complete, fully functioning chair again. Even though most objects in the domain form a spatially connected whole, self-connectedness is not a necessary condition. The object can have removable parts like the cap of a bottle or the parts can be disconnected in space like in a deck of cards.

The objects in the domain are described by basic dimensions and attributes. Before I start with the analysis of parts, a first approach to the representation of objects will be given. The result of the analysis of parts will reveal whether this approach is sufficient or should be modified.

Basic dimensions
As stated above, the basic dimensions of our domain are three spatial dimensions and each object is associated with its "spatial extent", that is the subspace occupied by the object. It is possible to infer the volume, the form, and gestalt aspects like squareness from the spatial extent of an object. The extent of an object remains the same under spatial translation (shift from one position in space to another) or rotation. One result of these invariances is that extent does not take into account the position of an object. The extent of an object is normally connected but it could be scattered as in the above mentioned case of the single cards of a deck.

To each object, an own reference system consisting of three axes is assigned that reflects the canonical alignment of the object (see Figure 1b).[2] The object´s reference system is augmented by labels to make it possible to differentiate between the

---

[2] For artifacts, the three axes of the object´s reference system almost always are straight and orthogonal. In the domain of natural objects, exceptions from straightness are, for example, streets or rivers with one curved axis and exceptions from orthogonality are, for example, crystals.

different sides of the object, e.g., its top and its bottom. If such canonical orientations do not exist at all as in the case of a perfect sphere or not for all axes as in the case of a pencil which lacks the top/bottom and the left/right orientation, the undetermined dimension axes are chosen arbitrarily. To distinguish object-determined from arbitrary axes, the two directions of the object-determined ones are labelled with the alignment they represent, e.g., top - bottom for the vertical axis, while the arbitrary ones do not get any labeling. An object´s reference system can be related to the basic dimensions if this relational information is needed for some task.

As shown in definition (Def 1), an object is described along the basic dimensions by its extent, its reference system, and the labels of its reference system.[3]

(Def 1): Basic representation of an object

Basic dimensions: $\mathbf{D} = D_1 \times D_2 \times D_3$ with Di and Dj orthogonal

Extent: ext: {objects} --> $\mathbf{P}(\mathbf{D})$ a function that assigns to each object O its extent

Ref. system: rs: {objects} --> $\{(R_1, R_2, R_3)\}$

Labels: label: {objects) --> $\{(R_i, (L1, L2))$ for each canonically aligned R_i of rs(O)}

Object O: $\mathbf{D} \supset$ ext(O)   the extent of an object, a subspace of $\mathbf{D}$

    rs (O)   the object´s reference system

    label (O)   the set of labels belonging to the object´s reference system

---

Attributes

All other knowledge about an object is given by attributes or features. As objects are concrete entities they have a unique unambiguous name or reference. They are instances of a concept from which they inherit what attributes are applicable together with the possible value range of these attributes. In the chosen domain, the most important attributes are the features "material", "color", or "function". Other possible (abstract) features are the monetary or subjective "worth", "beauty", or "dangerousness". For the characterization of an object the attribute slots inherited by the appropriate concept are filled with concrete values, e.g., the set of specific materials from which the object is built up. The basic representation of an object given in (Def 1) is now augmented by attributes as shown in (Def 2).

(Def 2): Complete representation of an object O

Basic representation: ext(O), rs (O), label (O)   extent, reference system, and labels of O

Attributes:

reference (O), concept (O)   unique name and concept of O

$\{(attr_i (O): values)\}$ concrete values for all attributes inherited by the concept (O)

Figure 1a shows a concrete object, my personal Biedermeier lady´s desk. Its extent and the object-determined reference system is shown in Figure 1b. My desk is an instance of the concept "desk" which is a subconcept of "table". The material is wood and leather (at the top), the colors are dark brown and dark green. Its function is to serve as a desk and to contain things in its drawers. A partial attribute description is given in Figure 1c.

---

[3] Similar theoretical considerations about object representation have been made by Landau and Jackendoff (1993) and van der Zee (1996).

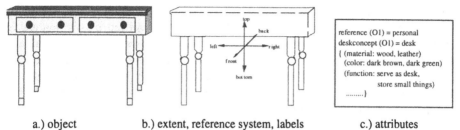

| a.) object | b.) extent, reference system, labels | c.) attributes |

Fig. 1. Representation of my personal Biedermeier lady´s desk

3 What can be a part?

Let´s go back to the main question of the paper about the nature of the parts of an object. Examples of different kinds of parts are given which constitute different kinds of relations between a part and the corresponding whole. In this article, only examples are given. A classification of part-whole relations, its comparison with other approaches, and examples for its use can be found in the papers of Gerstl and Pribbenow (1995, 1996).[4] Further information on how the different kinds of parts can be represented and/or constructed in a mental model approach can be found in Pribbenow (1996).

In the following, for each kind of part-whole relation the underlying definition of a part is given in terms of definition (Def 2).

Structure dependent parts

1a.) the top / a leg - my desk   a component of a complex object

1b.) one card - a deck   an element of a collection object

The pairs under 1a.) are examples for the most typical notion of "part". The top or a leg are so-called *components* of a desk or a table where the whole is conceptualized as a complex object. Complexes are wholes with an inherent part structure, where all parts play a special role with respect to spatial, temporal, functional, and other aspects. In example 1b.), the deck is composed of a number of cards which are uniform under the chosen perspective. In this case, the whole object is a collection of undistinguishable *elements*. Components and elements are called structure dependent parts because in both cases the dismantling of the respective whole in parts is given a priori by conceptual knowledge.

Each component or element has a three-dimensional extent and an object reference system that may be different from that of the whole. It has a unique reference, is an instance of a concept, and is described by the attributes inherited from its concept. The only difference between components and elements is that components are described by different concepts while all elements of a collection by definition belong to the same class.

Some of the attributes of components and elements are the same as those that hold for the whole object, e.g., "material", "color", "function", or "worth". The values of the attributes are in general different from those of the whole, except the values of the

---

[4] In the examples, the quantity - mass relation (see Gerstl & Pribbenow 1995, 1996) is omitted because mass objects like liquids do not belong to the domain under consideration.

substantial attributes like "material" which are a subset of those of the whole. To account for that difference, the definition (Def 2) is modified by distinguishing between substantial and abstract attributes. An attribute is called substantial if it is defined for all – material – pieces of the whole object and if the attribute´s values can be determined for all materially occupied subspaces of the object´s extent. Opposite to that, abstract attributes like "function" or "beauty" are restricted in their applicabi-lity and are only defined for the whole object and – at most – certain parts of it. For example, there may exist attributes for the whole that cannot be used for all of its parts like "maximum load" for "table" but not for "table top". Therefore, the differen-ce between substantial and abstract features is not the difference between physically concrete and abstract attributes but between overall defined and restricted attributes.

(Def 2'): Modified complete representation of an object O
Attributes:
substantial ones {(attr$_i$(O): values)}   attribute-value pairs defined for all pieces of O
abstract ones {(attr$_j$:(O) values)}   attribute-value pairs defined for O or some parts of O
The rest of the definition remains the same

At first glance, components and elements can be described in nearly the same way as whole objects and definition (Def 2') seems to be a correct and exhaustive way to represent the structure dependent parts. This is true for most cases although there are exceptions like 1c.) and 1d.).

1c.) the left drawer´s interior - my desk   a component of a complex object
1d.) the keyhole - a lock   a component of a complex object

The drawer and its interior are surely important parts of my desk because they allow me to store objects like pencils and papers. The dimensions of the interior and not that of the whole drawer determine what objects can be put into the drawer. In example 1d.), the keyhole is regarded as an essential part of a lock. The two examples show that it is necessary to consider non-material components.[5] They form dependent parts of an object because they could not exist independently of the whole like a drawer or a leg. In all other ways, dependent components equal "normal" components. In order to deal with those dependent but sometimes essential parts, definition (Def 1) must be extended. The whole object must include its non-material components like the interior of rooms, drawers or cups. Therefore, the extent of an object must be defined as the sum of the materially occupied spaces and the associated spaces of an object (see Def 1'). This definition corresponds to the extent shown in Figure 1b) that included the interior of the drawers.

(Def 1'): Modified basic representation of an object
Extent: ext: {objects} --> **D**   a function that assigns to each object O as extent its material occupied and associated spaces
The rest of the definition remains the same

Summary: Considering components and elements together with (Def 1'), a part can be defined as a subspace of the extent of the whole object but with a different reference system. A part can be described along the lines of definition (Def 2'). Each

---

[5] Landau and Jackendoff (1993) also consider this kind of parts. They call them "negative parts".

part has a unique reference, a concept, and is characterized by concrete values of the attributes inherited and restricted by its concept. The values of the substantial attributes are restricted by the values of the whole object.

Temporarily constructed parts

2a.) the wooden parts of my desk   a portion of an object
2b.) the upper half of my desk   a spatial segment of an object

In example 2a.), the wooden parts are that portion of the desk that are made out of a specific material. To compute *portions*, properties of the whole object are used to select those parts of the whole that have special values for certain attributes. To construct portions it is necessary to know the possible attributes of an object and their value distribution over the object. The upper half in example 2b.) is a *segment* of the spatial extent of the object, computed with the help of the object´s or an external (deictic) reference system and based on volume proportion.

In general, spatial segments like halves or corners are determined by the spatial properties of volume proportion and gestalt/form of whole and part while portions make use of attributes provided by the concept of the whole. Although the construction procedures are quite different, both kinds of parts can be defined as a subspace of the extent of the whole object, including non-material parts if necessary. As opposed to components and elements, segments and portions cannot be described using all features of definition (Def 2) because they are temporarily constructed by attributes or schemata and therefore are not necessarily instances of a concept.[6] In general, segments and portions can only be described by the substantial attributes of the whole object like "material" or "color", an exception is the description of a portion by the abstract attribute that was used to define it. As segments and portions are subspaces of the spatial extent it is possible to infer volume or form aspects (see section 2, "Basic dimensions").

As the considerations above show, a segment or portion can be described along the same basic dimensions as its whole and by the substantial attributes of the whole. A problem with this rather elegant and satisfying part definition arises if examples like 2c.) are considered:

2c.) the upper surface of my desk   a spatial segment of an object

A surface is normally defined as a two-dimensional entity that cannot exist - like an interior - independently of the whole. A surface is a rather problematic entity: It has no volume but a form/gestalt, the attribute "material" is not applicable but "texture" and "color" normally are. If such entities are accepted as parts, the general notion of a part cannot any longer be described by the same basic dimensions as its whole because it might not be three-dimensional. There are three ways out of this dilemma:

A. Allow only three-dimensional parts and interpret a surface as a three-dimensional part with minimal thickness analog to the view of wallpaper as surface of a wall.

---

[6] Especially for artifacts, portions tend to correspond to one or a small number of components because most components are designed for providing one function, being made of one material, and so on.

B. Allow only three-dimensional parts and interpret a surface as an abstract construction that is not a "real" part.

C. Change the definition of a part radically to the following: A part is a zero- to three-dimensional entity embedded in the extent of the whole. If it is more than zero-dimensional it has an appropriate reference system and the substantial attributes appropriate to the given dimensions.

All alternatives have advantages and disadvantages. Alternative A implies a satisfying definition of "part" and follows the philosophy that our world has a three-dimensional nature but it does not take into account the rather abstract mathematical notion of a surface.[7] Alternative B also implies a satisfying definition but at the cost that it restricts the possible parts. Alternative C gives a liberal definition of part by which, in consequence, a part can no longer be described as a subspace of the extent of its whole. The alternative to be chosen partially depends on the application. For tasks involving mathematical or formal thinking, the abstract notion in C might be appropriate. For purely commonsense tasks, the three-dimensional nature is important and therefore C is excluded. Alternative B is not a good alternative if the whole range of part phenomena should be considered. Therefore, alternative A is chosen for the definition given in this paper.

Summary: Considering segments and portions, a part can be defined as a subspace of the extent of the whole object. Normally it does not belong to a concept and has no reference system. In general, a part can be described by the substantial attributes of the whole object where the part´s values of these attributes are a subset of the values provided by the whole.

Arbitrary parts
3.) a splinter of the top of my desk   an arbitrary piece of an object

Arbitrary parts could be regarded as segments without a definite spatial characterization or as portions without a characterization via the values of some attributes. Therefore, these parts could be defined with the definition of segments and portions given above.

Given the considerations about structure dependent parts (components and elements), temporarily constructed parts (segments and portions), and arbitrary parts, the notion of a part can be determined as given in (Def 3) that is based on the definitions (Def 1') and (Def 2').

(Def 3): Definition of a part P of an object O
P is a part of O iff
(1)   P is described by the basic dimensions **D** with the additional condition
$ext(O) \supset ext(P)$
(2)   P is described with the same substantial attributes as the whole with the condition
$values_O \supset values_P$ for all substantial attributes

Following this definition, everything is a part that shares extent and certain attribute values. The definition does not say anything about which kind of part, e.g., a

---

[7] Although alternative A interprets a surface as three-dimensional, this does not prevent the surface from being conceptualized as a two-dimensional entity for some tasks.

component or an arbitrary part, a specific part belongs to. This simple definition is only possible because the extent of a whole was extented to associated, not materially occupied spaces and the possible attributes were distinguished in substantial and abstract ones.

4   Outlook

As stated in the introduction, the characterization of the commonsense notion of part-whole relations consists of two subquestions. In this paper, I have tackled the first question about the definition of the notion of "part". The second question to be discussed concerns the notion of "whole" and how a whole is constructed out of its parts. The answer to that question is a current research topic, of which only a brief outlook can be given at the moment. Following an old proverb, a whole is more than the sum of its parts. Therefore, the commmonsense notion of a (complex) whole assumed an additional structure between the different parts in order to build up the whole. This structure involves at least spatial and functional aspects of the part-structure. As a consequence, the notion and construction of a whole cannot be regarded as the mere inverse of the notion of a part.

References

Biederman, I. (1987): Recognition-by-Components. A Theory of Human Image Understanding. Psychological Review 94, 115–147

Cruse, D. A. (1979): On the Transitivity of the Part-Whole Relation. Journal of Linguistics 15, 29-38

Gerstl, P. / Pribbenow, S. (1995): Midwinters, End Games, and Bodyparts: A Classification of Part-Whole Relations. International Journal of Human-Computer Studies 43, special issue on "Formal Ontology in Conceptual Analysis and Knowledge Representation", 865-889

Gerstl, P. / Pribbenow, S. (1996): A Conceptual Theory of Part-Whole Relations and its Applications. Data and Knowledge Engineering 20 (3), special issue on "Part-Whole Relations", 305-322

Landau, B. / Jackendoff, R. (1993): "What" and "where" in spatial language and spatial cognition. Behavioral and Brain Sciences, 16, 217-238

Pribbenow, S. (1996): Parts and Holes and their Relations. to appear in: Ch. Habel / G. Rickheit (eds.): Mental Models in Discourse Processing and Problem Solving

Simons, P. (1987): Parts. A Study in Ontology. Clarendon Press: Oxford

Smith, B. (1982) (ed.): Parts and Moments. Studies in Logic and Formal Ontology. Philosophia: Munich

Tversky, B. (1990): Where Partonomies and Taxonomies Meet. In: S. L. Tsohatzidis (ed.): Meanings and Prototypes: Studies in Linguistic Categorization. Routledge: New York, 334-344

van der Zee, E. (1996): Spatial Knowledge and Spatial Language. Dissertation, ISOR/Utrecht University, Utrecht, The Netherlands

Winston, M. / Chaffin, R. / Herrmann, D. (1987): A Taxonomy of Part-Whole Relations. Cognitive Science 11, 417-444

SPOCK: A Feasibility Study on the Completeness of Parts Lists

Claus R. Rollinger

Universität Osnabrück
Institut für Semantische Informationsverarbeitung
D-49069 Osnabrück
Tel.: +49-541-969-2583
email: Claus.Rollinger@cl-ki.uni-osnabrueck.de
FAX: +49-541-969-2500

Abstract Parts lists in motor-industries are very complex and as well very dynamic entities. They are changed up to 600 times a year. New parts are constructed in the context of an already existing parts list. Verifying and certifying the completeness of such lists is an expensive and time-intensive job which requires several experts' work. In this paper we present the results of a feasibility study performed together with the Messrs. Wilhelm KARMANN GmbH. The goal was to verify the completeness of parts lists of the tailgates of the GOLF. To fulfil this task we developed the SPOCK system on the basis of the configuration tool PLAKON [Cunis et al. 1991]. At the end all missing and surplus parts of variants parts lists were identified, even those that were missed by the experts of Karmann.

1 Introduction

From our point of view the aim of SPOCK[1][Domcke et al. 1995], was to show if and how far knowledge-based configuration methods and tools are suitable to perform the task of verifying the completeness of parts lists as a decisive factor within the manufacturing process. The work of many departments, such as technical development, technical planning, technical series service in vehicle engineering, manufacturing control, quality supervision, purchasing, disposition and sales is directly and crucially depends on parts lists. Faultlessness of parts lists that is of great importance to all these departments is hard to be achieved since parts lists are subject to intensive dynamics due to constructional changes and improvements (approx. 600 modifications p.a.). Thus Karmann's main interest was to find out if knowledge-based methods provide a solution reducing the costs of the traditional (intellectual) way of controlling the completeness of parts lists.

The goal of the study was the development of a completeness test able to indicate all faults that may occur in variants parts lists (fault recording). A

---

[1] Planning, organisation and computer-based configuration of parts lists, a feasibility study, performed in co-operation with Messrs. Wilhelm Karmann GmbH)

parts list of some product is called complete if all and exactly those parts which actually are needed within the construction process for all variants are listet. We selected the tailgate of a vehicle (VW Golf) to be subject of the test since it represents a distinct and representative section of a parts list that is mainly assembled by Karmann. The SPOCK-system developed on the basis of the configuration tool PLAKON [Cunis et al. 1991] to perform the completeness test is able to identify all missing and surplus parts in variants parts lists of tailgates, even those missed by the experts of Karmann.

Although we succeeded in performing completeness tests for variants parts lists successfully, we realised that the application of our solution within the normal operational process was out of question. This is mainly caused by the fact that parts lists in motor-industries are highly dynamic entities. They are changed up to 600 times a year because certain parts of a car have to be substituted by new constructed ones to increase the product quality. These modifications often demand for revisions of the knowledge base and the underlying knowledge representation language. Nonmonotonic changes of the knowledge base and revisions of the knowledge representation language have to be carried out by a knowledge engineer and cannot be performed by the end user. Thus, modifications become very expensive. For that reason and because of the very many modifications in this application area Karmann decided against the integration of SPOCK within its normal operational process.

2 The principles of a parts list and occurring errors

A parts list specifies all parts belonging to a certain product. It results from a number of modification lists established by the technical development upon request of an engineer. These modification lists are integrated into an existing parts list or converted into a new one, respectively, by the department of technical development.

The dependencies within the parts lists are managed by means of PR numbers. PR numbers represent the key numbers for the primary characteristics. These numbers are required to select parts for a certain variant of a vehicle; e.g. the attachment a certain car shall have is defined by these numbers (for more details cf. [SPOCK 1994] and [Rollinger 95 a]. In practice more than one million variants of a car are possible, even if many of them are never built.

- The part number is a clear identification feature and gives the expert a rough indication about the part's location within the vehicle.
- Sequence indicates the parts list's structural order.
- The Y-structure is kind of a has-part-relation defining complex parts.
- The Description delivers a simple name for a specific part.
- The Quantity fixes the required number of parts.
- The PR-numbers represent the primary characteristics of the car

PR-numbers consist of 3 characters being combined with each other by + or / (logical and/or). The encoding method for primary characteristics provides for

Part no.	Sequence	Y-structure	Description	Quantity	PR-no.
1H0419100	847000	3Y	ZSB Steering system right	1	+LOR
1H0419101	847005	3Y	ZSB Steering system left	1	+LOL
1H0419223	847015	3	Steering wheel	1	
N 567984	847025	3	Hexagonal nut	4	
1H0419236	847100	4Y	ZSB steering column	1	+LOR
1H0419237	847110	4Y	ZSB steering column	1	+LOL
1H0419451	847120	4	Upper steering tie rod	1	
1H0419854	847130	4	Swivel joint right	1	+LOR
1H0419855	847140	4	Swivel joint left	1	+LOL
1H0419452	847150	4	Lower steering tie rod	1	

Figure1. A parts list with PR-numbers (LOL = left-hand drive, LOR = right-hand drive)

a unique family sign for the corresponding characteristics family. The selection of PR numbers from one of about 70 families is strictly restricted to one, since otherwise the model of this vehicle would either be overdefined (two gear boxes specified) or underdefined (no gear specified). Without a PR-number for a certain part, this part is installed in every model variant of the vehicle. If a PR-number is available, the part will not be installed but into only a certain variant of the car.

Upon receipt of an order (a list of PR-numbers) a variants list is generated from the parts list. This variants list indicates all parts required to assemble that very car. It is forwarded to the production department.

Example: The order of a car with a right-hand steering wheel contains the PR-number LOR. The sections of the parts list indicating those parts required for a right-hand steering wheel will show the PR-number LOR, which means that these parts will be installed in such cars only. These parts are copied into the variants list.

Part no.	Sequence	Y-str.	Description	Application	Nonapplic.
1H0805123	066110	2Y	ZSB front construction	020591	
1H0805558	066120	2	center storage console	020591	
1H0300412	610100	3Y	Automatic gear	020591	270493
1H0300412A	610105	3Y	Automatc gear	270493	250693
1H0300412B	610106	3Y	Automatic gear	250693	010194
1H0300412C	610107	3Y	Automatic gear	010194	999999
1H0300413	610108	3Y	Automatic gear	999999	

Figure2. Application and nonapplication dates of a parts list

The application date specified for each part in a parts list indicates from which day on a new part is installed in a vehicle. This date represents an intended date which in case of any delay may be postponed. The nonapplication date is directly related to the application date of a new part and therefore may be postponed as well. It specifies from which day on a certain part is no longer installed.

The continuous modification process within the parts list is due to the fact that parts recurrently become invalid and are replaced by new ones. Two parts, replaced one by the other, require an application date of the new part complying with the nonapplication date of the old one. It may otherwise lead to the existence of two similar parts being valid at the same time or to nonreplacement of a certain part by a new one.

The following errors occur within a parts list (fault classes):

- Faulty application or nonapplication date. The example of fig. 2 deals with the installation of a gear. The parts list indicates 3 automatic gears. The first gear is installed from 03-05-93 on and shall become invalid from 22-08-94. The second gear is applicable from 22-08-94 and becomes invalid from 05-04-94, which means that is not yet installed. The third gear is installed from 05-04-94. The mistake is that during the period of 05-04-94 to 22-08-94 two gears are valid, the first and the third one. Consequently, two gears at a time are installed in one car, which is of course unusual.
- Errors in the PR-number system (Vehicle with automatic gear and clutch pedal)
- Errors in the Y-structure (clutch pedal as part of the steering column assembly)
- Errors in part numbers
- Omitted parts to be constructed (e.g. trunk-grid)

3 Modelling generic parts lists

An essential task of the study was the development of a generic tailgate model serving as reference in completeness tests for variants parts lists. Furthermore, we investigated how to support the development of new parts lists by means of this reference tailgate. Because of its attractive knowledge representation capabilities ('is_a' - and 'has_parts'-relations, constraints and constraint-propagation, explicit control-knowledge) we decided to use the configuration system PLAKON as the base system. A pragmatic reason for choosing PLAKON instead of any other system was the availability of PLAKON and the support we got from the PLAKON developers.

Modelling the reference tailgate as a PLAKON knowledge base we first concentrated on the completeness test for an exemplary tailgate parts list. In a second phase we concerned with the question of how to generalise the reference tailgate to serve as test for further tailgate parts lists and the development of new parts lists in the context of constructing a new vehicle.

PLAKON offers two essential relations to model knowledge:

- The 'is_a'-relation to represent classificatory knowledge that does not play an important role within a parts list as explicit knowledge. It is obvious that within the completeness test classificatory knowledge is very important, because each single element of a variants parts list has to be classified correctly to decide whether it is needed or not.

- The relation 'has_parts' (and its inverse relation 'part_of') to represent the part-whole-relation can be used to represent the important treelike organisation of the elements within a parts list. Using this relation we define complex objects up to the tailgate itself.

The possible variants of a tailgate are clearly defined by the PR-number combinations. Each PR-number combination defines which optional part is installed and which special form a part to be installed is going to have (i.e. gas spring Hk1 or gas spring Hk3). Thus the PR-number system represents the disjunction in the parts list that can be seen as a special kind of an and-or-graph. A variants parts list is a pure and-tree, because one special alternative of those the parts list dispose was chosen.

The insights that the functions of the parts of a parts list represent the and-part of the and-or-graph and that the alternatives to realise these functions represent the or-part of the graph led to the development of a universal functional structure [Reinecke 1994]. This structure is recurrently established:

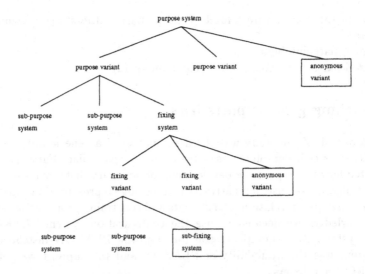

Figure3. Function driven modelling

In case a completely new variant has to be constructed instead of taking one of the known alternatives, anonymous variants offer new alternatives to the engineer. So-called PDM-sheets (product, detail manufacturing) were used along with the parts list to develop the above structure to receive further information about the function of each single tailgate part. Being more adaptive to the requirements and mentality of the engineer is the main advantage of such a domain dependent knowledge base structure which obeys the functional character of all functions of objects in the domain under consideration.

4 The architecture of SPOCK

The input to SPOCK is a variant parts list and the respective PR-number specification (the order). The PR-numbers are used as search arguments defining parts from the reference model of the tailgate as necessary parts. The result is a variant reference tailgate part of the reference model. Then the variant parts list and the variant reference tailgate are compared with each other. This is realised as the configuration of the variant taking the variant parts list as its specification. The deviations from the variant reference tailgate are faults within the variants parts list caused by faults of the parts list.

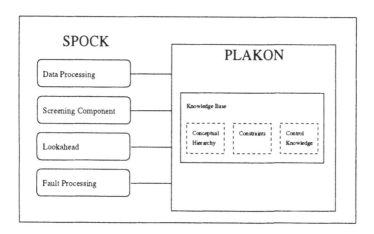

Figure4. The architecture of Spock

PLAKON as kernel of the system provides the essential part of the needed functionality and therefore takes of course a central position together with the components of the knowledge base (conceptional hierarchy, constraints and control knowledge) within the architecture of the system. Bound to its kernel PLAKON, the SPOCK system is implemented in Common LISP.

The components of SPOCK and the system's working cycle:

- *Data processing:* This component transforms variants parts list into Lisp-hashtables, which lateron are available for the screening and fault processing components.
- *Screening component:* Computes the variant reference tailgate using the PR-number specification (the order).
- *Lookahead component:* Controls the configuration process. During the process of definite specialisation of the individual parts the screening component

becomes active and looks for parts in the variants parts list which match according parts of the variant reference tailgate. The data achieved during this phase is finally used by the fault processing component to produce a detailed fault record.

- *Fault processing:* Classifies faults, searches for combinations of certain faults, interprets the detected faults, allowing for conclusions as to their causes. Together with the fault categories these interpretations are finally issued by the fault processing component.

The universality of this process is restricted by the application of PR-numbers, the specification system of the VW corporation. It is this special part of the system that has to be redeveloped in case of applying it on parts lists of another manufacturer. But in case of an error-free reference tailgate such system will be capable of detecting all missing and surplus parts of a variants list's.

5   Outcomes

SPOCK gives a positive answer to the question whether a knowledge-based configuration tool is capable of successfully performing a completeness test in parts lists. It is able to detect the various faults in tailgate variants lists together with the information on kind, scope, and possible causes of these faults. A fault report is given to the user to enable him to correct the parts list. Compared to this benefit, the efforts of modelling and maintenance were too extensive: The need for continuous modification of the knowlege base by some knowledge engineers because of the ongoing constructional modifications was the reason for not to follow up the SPOCK-approach.

The exchange of knowledge between Messrs. Wilhelm KARMANN GmbH and the University of Osnabrück in the field of knowledge-based configuration tools may be considered to be a further result. It supported KARMANN in gathering know-how and led the project staff to become deeply sensible of the problems a parts list in motor-industries may cause. This understanding led to the insight that to ensure the completeness of (variants) parts lists it is more reasonable to apply knowledge based technology at the beginning (the formation process of creating parts lists) instead of proving the completeness on variants parts lists at the end: The cause is to be fighted off instead of the effect. One might ask why it needed a project to come to this very obvious realisation. The reason is as well trivial: The user's understanding of the possibilities and function of knowledge-based technology was almost completely absent and vice versa the parts list problem was untouched ground to the project staff. It took almost half a year of intensive co-operation until the mutual understanding had grown far enough to realise this.

Because of this insight supporting the formation process of creating parts lists using the specifications of future products came as a second requirement. Various alternatives of representing the respective knowledge in PLAKON were evaluated until we succeeded with the universal functional structure as a solution capable of meeting these numerous requirements. It became obvious that to model the domain knowledge an upper structure of the underlying ontology and knowledge about the main functions of its objects are very helpful. This result stands in contrast to the problem solving methods oriented KADS approach [Wielinga 1992] that does neither consider the ontology of the domain in question nor its structure in a satisfactory way.

For the time being, adaptation of a knowledge base to environmental changes is still be done manually by knowledge engineers, who should work along with the engineer to achieve a modified knowledge base upon completion of a re-construction. This situation has to be changed in a way that the engineer may dispose of tools capable of supporting him in fulfilling a constructional task proposing the whole range of alternative solutions, and capable of jointly extending and modifying the systems knowledge base in the course of his construction task. Unfortunately, the very aspect of the dynamics of knowledge bases exceeding predictable extensions up to now did not play an important role in the field of knowledge-based methods. To us this experience proves the necessity of a problem-oriented technology transfer [Rollinger, Herzog 1994], which allows for a deeper understanding of relevant application problems.

As a last result we learned how difficult it is to develop systems capable of detecting, understanding, and correcting faults. It seems to be a substantial intellectual ability of humans to manage errors, contradictions, irregularities, and conflicts worth to be subject of further investigations.

6   Related Work

Configuration systems like R1 [McDermott 1982] were under the first successful applications of knowledge based technology. Still today configuration tools are developed and brought into action successfully [Wright et al. 1993] but most applications of knowledge-based (configuration) systems are successful in domains of relatively low dynamics e.g. [Bachmann 1993]. We find few applications in the field of construction e.g. [Descotte, Latombe 1985], where innovation requires complex changes of the knowledge base or (more complicated) changes of the knowledge representation language.

Nonmonotonic reasoning systems like ATMS [Reiter, de Kleer 1987] or the approach of Makinson [Makinson et al. 1985a, Makinson et al. 1985b] enable to compute the consequences of nonmonotonic changes of a knowledge base. There are several approaches to use ATMS in configuration systems [Paulokat 1992] but NMR neither supports the creation of some new part of the knowledge base nor does it provide any help in modifying the representation language to represent unforeseen relations and attributes.

To change this situation continuous and unforeseeable modifications of knowledge bases and their underlying representation languages have to play a key role in the future development of knowledge-based methods.

References

[Bachmann 1993] Bachmann, Reinhard: Gründe und Bedingungen des Erfolgs wissensbasierter Konfigurationssysteme, in: KI 1/93, pp. 48 - 50 (1993).

[Cunis et al. 1991] Cunis, R., A.Günter, H.Strecker (1991): Das PLAKON-Buch. Springer-Verlag, Informatik Fachberichte 266.

[Descotte, Latombe 1985] Descotte, Y., J. Latome: Making Compromises among Antagonist Constraints in a Planner, in: Artificial Intelligence Journal Vol. 27, pp. 183 - 217 (1985).

[Domcke et al. 1995] Domcke, J., Gieseke, W., Ksell, P., Lenschow, N.: "Studienprojekte am Beispiel SPOCK", in: KI 5/95.

[Makinson et al. 1985a] Makinson, Davis, Carlos Alchourron: On the Logic of Theory Change: Safe Contraction, in: Studia Logica 44, pp. 405 - 422 (1985).

[Makinson et al. 1985b] Makinson, Davis, Carlos Alchourron, Peter Gärdenfors: On the Logic of Theory Change: Partial Meet Functions for Contraction and Revision, in: Journal of Symbolic Logic 50, pp. 510 - 530 (1985).

[McDermott 1982] McDermott, J.: R1: A Rule-Based Configurer of Computer Systems, in: Artificial Intelligence Journal Vol. 19 (1), pp. 39 - 88 (1982).

[Paulokat 1992] Paulokat, H.-J. (ed.): (A)TMS in Expert Systems, SEKI-Report SR 92- 06. Univ. Kaiserslautern (1992).

[Reinecke 1994] Reincke, K. (1994): Prinzipienbasiertes Modellieren, Bericht des Instituts für Semantische Informationsverarbeitung der Universität Osnabrück.

[Reiter, de Kleer 1987] Reiter, Raymond, Johan de Kleer: Foundations of Assumption-Based Truth Maintenance Systems: Preliminary Report, in: Proceedings of the AAAI-87, pp. 183 - 188 (1987).

[Rollinger 95 a] Rollinger, C. R. (1995 a): Plausibilitätsaussagen über Stücklisten; Osnabrück 1994, Arbeitsmaterialien für den Kurs "Vollständigkeits- und Konsistenzüberprüfung von Stücklisten in der Automobilindustrie" der KIFS 95, 15 S.

[Rollinger, Herzog 1994] Rollinger, C. R., O. Herzog (1994): Grundzüge eines Konzepts zum problemorientierten Technologietransfer, in KI-Sonderheft zur KI-94, pp. 57 - 61.

[SPOCK 1994] SPOCK-Projekt Abschlußbericht (1994), Bericht des Instituts für Semantische Informationsverarbeitung, Universität Osnabrück.

[Wielinga 1992] Wielinga, B. J., A. Th. Schreiber u. J. A. Breuker (1992): KADS: a modelling approach to knowledge engineering; in: Knowledge Aqkuisition 4; pp. 5 - 53.

[Wright et al. 1993] Wright, Jon R., Elia S. Weixelbaum, Gregg T. Vesonder, Karen E. Brown, Stephen R. Palmer, Jay I. Berman, and Harry H. Moore: A Knowledge-Based Configurator That Supports Sales, Engineering, and Manufacturing at AT&T Network Systems, in: AI Magazine Vol. 14 (3), pp. 69 - 80 (1993).

Decision Support Systems with Adaptive Reasoning Strategies

Kerstin Schill

Institut für Medizinsche Psychologie,
Ludwig-Maximilians-Universität,
80336 München
kerstin@imp.med.uni-muenchen.de

Abstract. The ultimate goal in the development of decision support systems is to reach the competence and flexibility set by the human standard. We present an approach which is aimed at the efficient handling of situations with incomplete and partially inconsistent data. Its static structure is derived from a hierarchical implementation of the Dempster/Shafer Belief theory, which is extended towards a multi-layered representation by a set of hierarchies. The dynamic behavior is controlled by an *adaptive* strategy which can reduce the specific problems which may arise due to the predetermined strategies like "best hypotheses", "establish-refine-techniques", "hypothetic-deductive strategies". The suggested strategy is based on the principle of maximum information gain and is able to take the complete "activation pattern" of the representation into account. Acting together, both components can provide reasonable reactions even in ambiguous and ill-defined situations.

1 Introduction

The performance of a decision support system is crucially influenced by both its static structure and its dynamic behavior. The static properties are mainly determined by the method used for the representation of the domain knowledge, whereas the dynamic aspect is dependent on the problem solving strategy. The question of whether these two aspects can be considered independent of each other, and the analysis of suitable basic methods for them, has been the main research focus in the development of decision support systems [5]. However, despite of the availability of a wide range of methods and design tools, there are still some problems which require basic research. Important among them are the ability of a system to deal with inconsistent and unclear data configurations, and the systems potential for an adaptive, situation-specific behavior [2]. Furthermore, an ideal system design must not only optimize the static and dynamic aspects separately, but must take into account their interdependencies as well. The main challenge of decision support systems is thus not the most efficient handling of well defined situations, but rather the provision of an acceptable reaction in situations where the available data are incomplete, partially inconsistent, widely scattered across the knowledge base, and supportive of several contradictory hypotheses.

   In the following sections we provide some suggestions on how these problems may be approached. The main part of the paper will be devoted to the description of a novel kind of problem solving control strategy, which is based on the concept of maximum information gain and the Belief theory of Dempster and Shafer. The resulting strategy selects the most appropriate action at every step on the basis of the associated possible information gain, which is calculated as the difference between the actual and the potential belief distribution. This allows for a parallel consideration of all available data during the entire course of the consultation process.

How strongly the overall system behavior is influenced by interdependencies between the knowledge representation and the control strategy is illustrated in the third section, where we extend the knowledge representation towards a multi-layer knowledge base which organizes a set of elementary knowledge entities into multiple hierarchical structures. The maximum information gain strategy is then applied in parallel to all layers, and the "winner" determines the system's reaction. The interplay between this new data structure and the control strategy generates a new set of interesting "behaviors" not seen with the single-layer hierarchy.

2 Inference by Information Gain (IBIG)

2.1 The Management of Uncertainty in IBIG

To support the selection of a suitable method for the management of uncertainty in a given problem domain we have developed a theoretical framework by which most of the known uncertainty theories can be mapped and compared [13]. In the following proposed system the management of uncertain knowledge is based on Shafer's Belief Theory [10]. The theory enables the use of the subjective belief of experts which is advantageous in case no a priori probabilities are available. Shafer's theory modifies the additive axiom of Bayes theory to the axiom $Bel(A) + Bel(A^C) \leq 1$ which enables one to quantify belief in a certain proposition without determining the belief in its negation and vice versa. The axiom thus provides a distinction between lack of knowledge and the assignment of belief to the negation of a set. A central concept in this theory is the so called frame of discernment, denoted by θ, which is a set of propositions about the mutually exclusive and exhaustive possibilities in a domain.

The theory is based on a function m, called basic belief assignment [12] which obeys the following three axioms:

$$m: 2^{\theta} \longrightarrow [0,1] \tag{1}$$

$$m(\emptyset) = 0 \tag{2}$$

and

$$\sum_{A \subseteq \theta} m(A) = 1 \tag{3}$$

In terms of this basic belief assignment, the belief in a proposition $A \in 2^{\theta}$ can be expressed as:

$$Bel(A) = \sum_{B \subseteq A} m(B) \tag{4}$$

Pieces of evidence are combined by the application of Dempster's rule of combination [10] on the basic belief assignments. The combination of two basic belief masses is defined by:

$$m_{12}(A) = K* \sum_{i,j,\ A_i \cap B_j = A} m_1(A_i) * m_2(B_j) \tag{5}$$

with the normalization constant K:

$$K = (1 - \sum_{i,j,\ A_i \cap B_j = \varnothing} m_1(A_i) * m_2(B_j))^{-1} \tag{6}$$

A major drawback for practical implementation of the "Dempster-Shafer" theory of evidence has been its computational complexity. Barnett [1] reduces this complexity from exponential to linear by assuming that each piece of evidence either confirms or denies a single proposition rather than a disjunction. From that follows the definition of simple support functions (a subclass of Belief functions), with which the confirming and non-confirming belief of a set or proposition can be calculated as follows:

Given a collection of basic belief masses m_{ij}, induced by n pieces of evidence indexed by j (j=1,..n) in favour of a proposition $X_i \subset \theta$, one can calculate the confirming belief with:

$$m_{x_i}(X_i) = 1 - \prod_{j=1}^{n}(1-m_{ij}) \tag{7}$$

Likewise, the non-confirming belief, as resulting from a collection $m_{ij}{}^c$ of m pieces of evidence against X_i, is given by:

$$m_{x_i}{}^c(X_i{}^c) = 1 - \prod_{j=1}^{m}(1-m_{ij}{}^c) \tag{8}$$

Based on these definitions Gordon and Shortliffe [3] have developed an approximation of the Belief theory which is applicable to tree-like knowledge structures and allows the calculation of the belief $m_T(X_i)$ for each set X_i in the tree T.

This approach has been modified by us with respect to the calculation of the normalization constant [9].

The availability of methods for propagating evidence in networks like the one introduced by Gordon and Shortliffe or in related approaches based on Bayesian belief opened a wide range of applications (e.g. Pearl [6]). However, a still critical issue is the optimal usage of the belief distribution resulting from such network calculation schemes - in other words, how to reason on the basis of the propagated belief?

2.2 The Information Increment Strategy

Common reasoning strategies can be characterized by the principle of partitioning [8]. In rule-based systems a single hypothesis or an agenda with a small number of probable hypotheses are evaluated on the basis of some initial data. The selected hypothesis then determines the subsequent data collection process (e.g. MYCIN [11]). In tree-like knowledge bases a continuous partitioning process (establish-refine-technique) which starts at the root guides the selection process of the data (Fig.1).

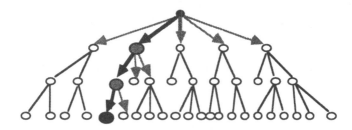

Fig. 1. Efficient successive partitioning in a clear and unambiguous case

The main problem of these partitioning principles arises in unclear consultation cases, as for example in cases where large lists of weakly supported hypotheses are given. In such cases, an incorrect selection may lead to a "dead end" with no solution, requiring an expensive back tracking (Fig.2).

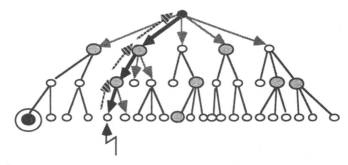

Fig. 2. Dead-end behavior in cases of unclear and ambiguous data situations

The development of our control strategy was guided by two main ideas. First, that the strategy should adapt itself to the activation pattern of the current data distribution instead of being predetermined like the established partitioning strategies. Second, it should not be based on heuristic considerations but should be closely related to fully axiomatised theoretical frameworks.

The basic principle of our strategy, as described in [9], is to determine those data which, when collected next, can yield the largest information gain with respect to the actual evidence distribution. The evidence distribution can be related to the activity pattern of units in a network-like structure and represents the support assigned to propositions, as modeled on a "cognitive" level [4]. The information gain is calculated by the difference between the current belief distribution in the hierarchy, induced by the pieces of evidence as yet available, and the "potential belief distribution" which can result from future input.

The belief distribution is calculated according to Gordon and Shortliffe's approach [3]. The potential belief of a set X_i in the hierarchy T is, roughly speaking, the belief that the hypothesis set could achieve in the subsequent consultation process. Each set X_j in T is associated with a number of data items whose collection can induce confirming or non-confirming belief for the set. The confirming belief a data item might induce for a set X_j is expressed by an a priori given confirming belief mass $\hat{m}_{jk}$. Analogously, the non-confirming belief is expressed by an a priori given non-confirming belief mass $\hat{m}^c_{jk}$.

Corresponding to (7) we can define the potential confirming belief of a set X_j by:

$$\hat{m}_{x_j}(X_j) = 1 - \prod_{k=1}^{n}(1-\hat{m}_{jk}) \tag{9}$$

where $\hat{m}_{jk}$ are the a priori given potential confirming belief masses.

Corresponding to (8) the potential non-confirming belief

$$\hat{m}_{x_j}^c(X_j^c) = 1 - \prod_{k=1}^{m}(1-\hat{m}_{jk}^c) \tag{10}$$

where $\hat{m}_{jk}^c$ are a priori given potential non-confirming belief masses.

The next step is to analyze how the two potential belief masses $\hat{m}_{x_j}(X_j)$ and $\hat{m}_{x_j}^c(X_j^c)$ of each node X_j influence the actual belief distribution. For this analysis, we examine elementary evidence situations in the hierarchy consisting of only one set X_i with belief. It is assumed that more complex belief situations can be approximated by the superposition of such elementary evidence situations. The effect of the potential belief mass of a node X_j on the actual belief $m_T(X_i)$ of a node X_i is determined by the relations between the two sets within the hierarchy, and is denoted by $\hat{m}_T(X_i)$. The information increment for X_i arising from X_j is defined by the difference between the current and the potential belief masses:

$$I(X_i) = |m_T(X_i) - \hat{m}_T(X_i)| \tag{11}$$

One has to take into account that X_j might influence the belief of X_i by both its potential confirming as well as its potential non-confirming belief. In addition, these influences depend on the relations between X_j and X_i in the tree (i.e. the intersections of these sets). Therefore, a number of different cases for the calculation of the information increment have to be derived.

We will exemplify the principle by considering one of these cases. Here the information increment is derived for a set X_i with $X_j \not\supseteq X_i$ and we investigate the influence of the potential confirming belief $\hat{m}_{x_j}(X_j)$ of X_j. Henceforth this type of relation is indicated as pattern p_1.

The corresponding belief m_T can be calculated by [9, 3]:

$$m_T (X_i, X_j, p_1) = m_T(X_i) * m_{x_j}(\theta) * K \tag{12}$$

i.e. that the set X_j influences $m_T (X_i)$ by its current belief on θ. This current belief on θ is calculated by:

$$m_{x_j}(\theta) = 1 - m_{x_j}(X_j) \tag{13}$$

Replacing this current belief mass in (12) by the potential belief mass

$$\hat{m}_{x_j}(\theta) = 1 - \hat{m}_{x_j}(X_j) \tag{14}$$

defines the potential belief

$$\hat{m}_T (X_i, X_j, p_1) = m_T(X_i) * \hat{m}_{x_j}(\theta) * \hat{K} \tag{15}$$

which the set X_i may reach due to the potential confirming belief of X_j .

The information increment for the set X_i as induced by the set X_j according to the pattern p_1, is then the difference between the current belief m_T and the potential belief $\hat{m}_T$ as:

$$I(X_i, X_j, p_1) = |1 - \hat{m}_{x_j}(\theta) * \hat{K}| * m_T(X_i) \tag{16}$$

where $$\hat{K} = (1 - \hat{m}_{x_j}(X_j)) * \sum_{\substack{X_k \cap X_j = \emptyset \\ X_k \in T}} m_T(X_k))^{-1} \tag{17}$$

To take into account all possible intersections between sets X_j and X_i in the tree-like network, as well as both types of potential beliefs, we have derived six different patterns p_k corresponding to the possible intersections [9]. If more than one pattern is applied to X_j, the information increment is superimposed:

$$I_{X_j} = \sum_{i,k} I(X_i, X_j, p_k) \tag{18}$$

To summarize so far: on every node X_i in the hierarchy the six patterns p_k are applied. The information-increments arising for a set X_i from a set X_j are superimposed and are allocated to X_j. The node X_j with the largest information gain is the one which determines the data-collection process in the next step. After the data collection the new potential belief masses and the actual belief masses are recalculated and the patterns are again applied.

The information increment has been applied in a decision support system for aphasia and has been tested successfully by a number of experts. However, the domain of aphasia requires no huge database and can only represent a subset of the variety of database configurations that may occur with different knowledge domains. To enable a more general analysis of the behavior of the strategy we have thus performed extended simulations with various artificially created databases. We have investigated both the scaling of runtime in dependence on the size of the database and the typical behaviors of the strategy resulting from different database configurations and activation patterns.

The computational complexity depends on the percentage of activated nodes. In cases where only a few sets m have received actual belief, it is close to linear, whereas for a fully activated hierarchy the upper limit of the complexity is $O(n^2)$. Runtime simulations have shown that with realistic sizes of artificially created knowledge bases (400 sets in the hierarchy) each consultation step (a complete max. information gain calculation) requires about 15 sec. For most of the simulations that we performed with respect to the behavior of the strategy we have assumed that the potential confirming and non-confirming beliefs of all sets in the tree are equal, and that the activated nodes are randomly distributed, whereas in most realistic applications only few nodes will have significant activation values. Our simulations thus tend more towards a worst-case situation concerning the complexity. The simulations performed with different configurations and activation states have shown that the information increment strategy can result in a variety of adaptive behaviors [7]:

If a set of the tree has received some confirming belief and if there is no evidence for "competing branches", then the subtree below the activated node is top-down partitioned as known from classical search strategies. In this case, the data collection process is determined by the "nodes" in the subtree which still have promising information gain due to their associated potential of confirming belief.

Another behavior can arise if a set on a more specific level, e.g. "near a leaf node", has received confirming belief, and if its father nodes still have potential non-confirming belief. The strategy then shows a bottom up verification behavior. Here the supersets of the concerned hypotheses set are determining which data should be collected next.

In cases in which a number of actual data are lying on one single path in the tree, top down and bottom up partitioning behavior can arise simultaneousley. This may happen if the father nodes still have potential non-confirming belief and the son nodes have potential confirming belief.

The observed behaviors may be summarized as follows: if the actual data situation is unambigous and consistent, the information increment strategy will show one of the classical search behaviors, i.e. it will yield a tree partitioning or a confirmation of the "best" hypothesis dependent on the type of activation state. However, if the situation comprises incoherent activations, a more complicated "mixed" behavior may result.

But is such a complicated behavior really the better solution? To answer this question we have compared the runtime of our strategy with that of a classical partitioning search for a number of prototypical ambiguous data situation [7]. In all cases, the proposed strategy required fewer steps, i.e. less data had to be collected until the solution was found.

The following figures illustrate the behavior of the strategy in ambiguous situations. Figure 3 shows the initial configuration used in these examples. Three sets of a tree (indicated by shaded circles respectively) have attained equal current belief $m_{X_i}(X_i) = 0.5$. With each set, two potential confirming and potential non-confirming beliefs should be associated, with a resulting $\hat{m}_{x_j}(X_j) = 0.88$ and $\hat{m}_{x_j^c}(X_j^c) = 0.88$.

Application of the information increment strategy yields the maximum information gain for the two son nodes of the root, and we assume that the left one is selected. We now consider three different cases, depending on which hypothesis is the correct solution.

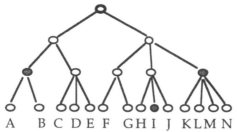

Fig. 3. The initial configuration with three sets on different branches with equal current belief

1. The solution is B: The resulting sequence of the data collection process is shown in Fig.4. First the set A will be examined. Since this will provide only non-confirming belief for A, the strategy tries to confirm the set AB by examining its remaining potential confirming belief. This confirms the supposition that the sought hypothesis is a subset of AB. The set B will be examined in the fourth step. After the data collection process it has a belief of 0.98.

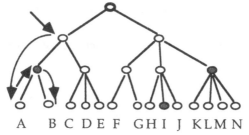

Fig. 4. Sequence of the Information Increment strategy in case the set B is the solution

2. The solution is I: The resulting sequence of the data collection process is illustrated in Fig.5. After 3 data collection steps the set I has attained a belief of 0.93.

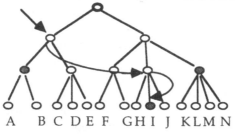

Fig. 5. Sequence of data collection by the Information Increment strategy as resulting for solution I.

3. The solution is L: The resulting sequence of data collection is shown in Fig.6. The strategy switches immediately into the other subtree. The solution is reached in three steps with a belief of 0.88.

A   B C D E F   G H I J K L M N

Fig. 6. Sequence of data collection by the Information Increment strategy as resulting for solution L

Since the strategy is acting in a parallel fashion on all actually available knowledge in the database it can work on more than one focus of belief at the same time. It can thus avoid the time-consuming back tracking procedure, required by systems which pursue a "best hypothesis". This is achieved by the continuous competition between the different foci as being established by all parallel branches in the tree for which evidence is given. The set promising the highest information gain among all those branches determines the next step in the data collection process. However, the strategy may easily jump between branches, while showing at the same time the classical top down and bottom up behaviors within the branches.

3   The Application to a Multi-Layered Hierarchical Knowledge Base

Even with such an adaptive strategy overly strong restrictions are imposed in many practical cases by the selection of one single structuring principle for the database. In general, there seems to be no best structuring principle which is equally well suited for the representation of all kinds of problems [8]. Optimally, all entities and a variety of possible relationships between them should be taken into account in order to account for the knowledge of human experts. Thus, a knowledge-base structure is required which allows the parallel representation of diverse relationships between the basic knowledge entities. On the other hand, the resulting knowledge base should not just represent a chaotic mixture, since this will prevent both the evaluation and the easy updating of the structure.

We have tried to meet these requirements by introducing a knowledge base which is modeled by the parallel representation of an arbitrary number of separate layers [9]. On each of the layers the knowledge entities can be linked with only one specific type of relationship, while across the layers different types of relationsships can be realized. In the actual version of our system we have restricted the knowledge base to a multi-hierarchical structure, i.e. a number of layers each representing one hierarchy. This has several advantages, among them a guaranteed consistent propagation of uncertainty on each layer.

Given such a knowledge base and some preliminary evidence on one or more hierarchies, the information increment strategy calculates in parallel the belief distribution for every separate hierarchy. Also, the information gains are computed separately for each layer. The hypothesis set with the maximal information gain with respect to all layers then determines the next consultation step. The unknown or as yet uncollected data of the respective node will be collected and, based on this new data, the belief situation is recalculated at all layers in the knowledge base. The control strategy applied to the multi-layered hierarchy structure can thus be seen as a simple extension of the original strategy for single hierarchies.

However, the interdependence between the strategy and the knowledge structure generates new types of behavior. Depending on the actual consultation, the control strategy might, for example, select one layer in the initial phase on which it then stays for the remainder of the decision process. Alternatively, it might continuously switch between layers. The former behavior appears whenever the structure of the problem-solving task fits well into the format of the initially selected hierarchical structure. The latter behavior results if there is no such fit between the data and the structure used for their representation. The data collected by the largest information increment at a suboptimal hierarchy will then allow the strategy to switch to another hierarchy, which might provide improved conditions for the subsequent decision process.

4 Conclusions

We have derived some suggestions for the design of decision support systems. Obviously, both the knowledge representation and the control strategy have to be improved in order to derive more powerful systems. Furthermore, however, the interdependence of both aspects has to be taken into account. The suggested adaptive control strategy is based on the concept of maximum information. This strategy can be applied to various types of hierarchical knowledge bases. In contrast to common strategies of knowledge based systems, no predetermined direction in the form of a certain type of partitioning is given. The information increment strategy acts in parallel on the represented knowledge, while it organizes itself depending on the evidence distribution as induced by the available data. The reasoning behavior is determined by the permanently changing relationship between the fixed knowledge structure and the growing corpus of actually available data. This relation is evaluated in terms of belief distributions, as introduced in the evidence theory of Dempster & Shafer. In each step it is used to determine the question/action which yields the data that can give rise to a maximal change of the "state of knowledge", i.e. can provide the maximal information gain. Theoretical and practical analysis of the proposed system reveals that the resulting behavior includes the classical principles.

The power of the strategy can be further improved when it is combined with a more sophisticated knowledge structure. In Section 3 we have shown, how the strategy can be combined with a multi-layer knowledge representation, thereby enabling an even more flexible adaptation to the actual situation. With such an architecture, the system reacts to impending dead ends in a manner which is reminiscent of the human behavior: "spontaneous restructuring".

References

1. J.A. Barnett, Computational Methods for a Mathematical Theory, *Proceedings of the Seventh International Joint Conference on Artificial Intelligence*, Vancouver, 1981, 868-875.

2. S. Goontalike, S. Khebbal, Intelligent Hybrid Systems: Issues, Classifications and Future Directions, in S. Goontalike, S. Khebbal (Eds.), *Intelligent Hybrid Systems*, John Wiley & Sons, Chichester, 1995.

3. J. Gordon, E. H. Shortliffe, A Method for Managing Evidential Reasoning in a Hierarchical Hypothesis Space, *Artificial Intelligence*, 26, 1985, 323-357.

4. S. Hruska, T. Whitfield, Expert Networks: Theory and Applications, in L. Medsker, *Hybrid Intelligent Systems*, Kluwer Academic Publishers, Boston, 1995.

5. P. Jackson, *Introduction to Expert Systems*, 2nd. ed. Addison-Wesley, Reading, 1990.

6. J. Pearl, *Probabilistic Reasoning in Intelligent Systems: Networks of Plausible Reasoning*, Morgan Kaufmann, San Mateo, 1988.

7. F. Röhrbein, *Weiterentwicklung und Analyse einer Informationsbasierten Inferenzstrategie*, Diplomarbeit am Institut für Informatik der TU München, 1995.

8. K. Schill, *Medizinische Expertensysteme, Band 1: Methoden und Techniken*, R. Oldenbourg Verlag, Munich, 1990.

9. K. Schill, Analysing Uncertain Data in Decision Support Systems, *Proceedings of the Third International Symposium on Uncertainty Modeling and Analysis & Annual Conference of the North American Fuzzy Information Processing Society*, IEEE Computer Society Press, College Park, Maryland, 1995, 437-442.

10. G. Shafer, *A Mathematical Theory of Evidence*, Princeton University Press, Princton, 1976.

11. H. Shortliffe, *Computer Based Medical Consultations: MYCIN*, Elsevier, New York, 1976.

12. P. Smets, Belief Functions, in P. Smets, E.H. Mamdani, D. Dubois, H. Prade (Eds.), *Non-Standard Logics for Automated Reasoning*, Academic Press, London, 1988, 253-286.

13. E. Umkehrer, K. Schill, A Classification System for Uncertainty Theories: How to Select an Appropriate Formalism?, in H.-H. Bock, W. Polasek (Eds.), *Data Analysis and Information Systems*, Springer, Heidelberg, 1996.

Knowledge Discovery in Databases – An Inductive Logic Programming Approach

Katharina Morik

Univ. Dortmund, Computer Science Department, LS VIII

Abstract. The need for learning from databases has increased along with their number and size. The new field of Knowledge Discovery in Databases (KDD) develops methods that discover relevant knowledge in very large databases. Machine learning, statistics, and database methodology contribute to this exciting field. In this paper, the discovery of knowledge in the form of Horn clauses is described. A case study of directly coupling an inductive logic programming (ILP) algorithm with a database system is presented.

1 Introduction

Databases are used in almost all branches of industry and commerce. The aim of KDD is to discover rules hidden in these collected data.

The task of KDD is challenging, for the following reasons:

- The amount of database tuples from which an algorithm learns exceeds the number of examples that are usually handled by a learning algorithm or a statistical procedure. Real-world KDD applications have to cope with a number of tuples on the order of several hundred thousand.
- The amount of database attributes (on the order of several hundred) exceeds the number of features that are usually handled by a learning algorithm.
- The task of finding all valid rules hidden in a database is more difficult than other learning tasks (see Section 2).

Several such learning algorithms for KDD exist: Bayesian and Neural Networks, induction of decision trees, minimal description length algorithms, learning of association rules – to name but the most common ones [1]. In order to reduce the number of attributes, these algorithms reduce the database in one or both of the following ways:

- Analysis is only done of one database attribute or of the equivalent set of attributes with binary values.
- Analysis is only done on one database table comprised of the most interesting attributes. Frequently, this table is created in a pre-processing step. [2]

---

[1] The KDD books give a comprehensive overview of the field [10] [4]. For fast neural learning see also [11]

[2] In principle, learning from just one database table is not a restriction – it could be the universal relation and cover what was originally stored in many tables. In practice, however, the universal relation of real-world databases is so large that it cannot be efficiently managed, nor can the learning algorithms handle it.

In addition to restricting the database, most algorithms restrict the discovered knowledge to an attribute-value representation (propositional logic), possibly with the extension of probabilistic annotations or certainty factors. This is a severe restriction, since it excludes relational or structural knowledge. Saso Dzeroski has given a nice example to illustrate this [3]: Figure 1 shows data in two tables of a database. If restricted to propositional knowledge, an algorithm could discover the following rules in the data:

$income(Person) \geq 100000 \rightarrow customer(Person) = yes$

$sex(Person) = f \& age(Person) \geq 32 \rightarrow customer(Person) = yes$

Rules like the following cannot be expressed (and therefore not be learned) by these algorithms:

(i) $married(Person, Spouse) \& customer\_yes(Person)$
    $\rightarrow customer\_yes(Spouse)$

(ii) $married(Person, Spouse) \& income(Person, \geq 100000) \rightarrow customer\_yes(Spouse)$

potential customer				married	
person	age	sex	income	customer	husband	wife
Ann Smith	32	f	10 000	yes	Jack Brown	Jane Brown
Joan Gray	53	f	1 000 000	yes	Bob Smith	Ann Smith
Mary Blythe	27	f	20 000	no		
Jane Brown	55	f	20 000	yes		
Bob Smith	30	m	100 000	yes		
Jack Brown	50	m	200 000	yes		

Fig. 1. Relational database with two tables

Other relations that cannot be expressed or characterized in propositional logic include spatial relations, time relations, or the connectivity of nodes in a graph. For such knowledge, a (restricted) first-order logic is necessary. Inductive Logic Programming (ILP) is the field within machine learning which investigates Learning hypotheses in a restricted first-order logic. In Section 3 we show how to overcome the common restrictions (learning propositional rules from one attribute or one database table) by an ILP algorithm without becoming inefficient.

2   The Learning Task in a Logical Setting

The task of knowledge discovery in a broad sense includes interaction with the knowledge users, the database managers and data analysts. Learning rules from data is then one important part of the overall task of KDD. The rule learning task has been stated formally by Nicolas Helft [5] using the logical notion of minimal models of a theory $\mathcal{M}^+(Th) \subseteq \mathcal{M}(Th)$.

Minimal model. An interpretation I is a model of a theory Th, $\mathcal{M}(Th)$, if it is true for every sentence in Th. An interpretation I is a *minimal model* of Th, written $\mathcal{M}^+(Th)$, if I is a model of Th and there does not exist an interpretation I' that is a model of Th and $I' \subset I$.

Rule learning

Given observations $\mathcal{E}$ in a representation language $\mathcal{L}_\mathcal{E}$ and background knowledge $\mathcal{B}$ in a representation language $\mathcal{L}_\mathcal{B}$,
find the set of hypotheses $\mathcal{H}$ in $\mathcal{L}_\mathcal{H}$, which is a (restricted) first-order logic, such that

(1) $\mathcal{M}^+(\mathcal{B} \cup \mathcal{E}) \subseteq \mathcal{M}(\mathcal{H})$ (validity of $\mathcal{H}$)
(2) for each $h \in \mathcal{H}$ there exists $e \in \mathcal{E}$ such that $\mathcal{B}, \mathcal{E} - \{e\} \not\models e$ and $\mathcal{B}, \mathcal{E} - \{e\}, h \models e$ (necessity of h)
(3) for each $h \in \mathcal{L}_\mathcal{H}$ satisfying (1) and (2), it is true that $\mathcal{H} \models h$ (completeness of $\mathcal{H}$)
(4) There is no proper subset $\mathcal{G}$ of $\mathcal{H}$ which is valid and complete (minimality of $\mathcal{H}$).

Since the hypotheses $\mathcal{H}$, i.e. sets of rules, are valid in all minimal models of background knowledge and examples, the first condition asks for a deductive step. It corresponds to the application of the closed-world assumption, i.e. all but the stated assertions are false. The second condition restricts the learning result to those rules that are related to given observations. There might be additional valid rules, for instance tautologies, but we are not interested in them. The most important condition is the third one which demands that *all* valid and necessary rules must be found. Condition (4) formalizes the non-redundancy requirement. This learning task has been taken up by several ILP researchers, e.g., [7], [2]. It is more difficult than the classical concept learning task described below:

Concept learning

Given positive and negative examples $\mathcal{E} = \mathcal{E}^+ \cup \mathcal{E}^-$ in a representation language $\mathcal{L}_\mathcal{E}$ and background knowledge $\mathcal{B}$ in a representation language $\mathcal{L}_\mathcal{B}$,
find a hypothesis $\mathcal{H}$ in a representation language $\mathcal{L}_\mathcal{H}$, which is a (restricted) first-order logic, such that

(1) $\mathcal{B}, \mathcal{H}, \mathcal{E}^+ \not\models \square$ (consistency)
(2) $\mathcal{B}, \mathcal{H} \models \mathcal{E}^+$ (completeness of $\mathcal{H}$)
(3) $\forall e^- \in \mathcal{E}^- : \mathcal{B}, \mathcal{H} \not\models e^-$ (accuracy of $\mathcal{H}$)

The difference between the two learning tasks can be illustrated by our small example database (Figure 1). For the sake of clarity, let us reduce the table *potential customer* to the attributes *customer* and *income* and replace the numerical values of *income* by *low, high* in the obvious way. We consider the observation $\mathcal{E}$ to be the attribute *customer* and the background knowledge $\mathcal{B}$ to be *income* and *married_to*. In addition to rules (i) and (ii) – where ≥ 100000 is replaced by *high* – rule learning will find

(iii) $income(Person, high) \rightarrow customer\_yes(Person)$

Let us now inspect two variants of our example in order to clarify the differences. Case 1: It is unknown whether *jane* is a customer. Case 2: Both, the income of *jack* and whether *jane* is a customer are unknown. In the first case, condition (1) of rule learning leads to the rejection of rules (i) and (ii), since *jane* is not a customer in all minimal models of $\mathcal{E}$ and $\mathcal{B}$. Only rule (iii) is valid regardless of whether or not *jane* is a customer. If we regard the attribute value *yes* of *customer* as the classification of positive examples and the value *no* as the classification of negative examples, then we can apply concept learning on *customer_yes*. Not knowing whether *jane* is a customer does not prevent concept learning from finding rules (i) and (ii). *customer_yes(jane)* will be predicted. Concept learning will deliver (i) and (iii), or (ii) and (iii), depending on its preference. The task of deriving the positive examples is accomplished with either of the two sets of rules. If negative examples are not explicitly stated but are derived using the closed-world assumption, however, concept learning rejects rules (i) and (ii) (accuracy condition of concept learning). Rule (iii) alone cannot derive that *ann* is a customer. Because of its completeness condition, concept learning fails when using the closed-world assumption.

In the second case, the rules (i) – (iii) cannot derive *customer_yes(jack)*. The completeness condition of concept learning leads to the rejection of rules (i) – (iii). Even without the closed-world assumption, concept learning does not deliver a result at all. Rule learning still finds rule (iii). In summary, rule learning finds rules in all cases, whereas concept learning fails to find any rule in case 2 and under the closed-world assumption in case 1. The rules found by rule learning are closer to the data (i.e. less predictive) than the rules found by concept learning. The rule learning task is more difficult than the concept learning task because there are learning problems that can be solved by rule learning, but not by concept learning (case 2), and there are no learning problems that can be solved by concept learning but not by rule learning [3]. The completeness condition of finding *all* valid and possibly interesting rules is the formalization of the learning task in KDD.

3 Discovery of Horn Clauses

The previous section states formally what it means to find *all* valid, necessary, and non-redundant rules. In addition, the user indicates the kind of hypotheses in which he or she is interested. The system then restricts $\mathcal{L}_{\mathcal{H}}$ to those hypotheses that fit the user-given declarative bias. This method offers two advantages: it allows users to tailor the learning procedure to their goals and, by restricting the space of all hypotheses, it makes rule learning feasible. Of course, there is a price to pay: the tailored learning procedure misses interesting rules that do not fit into the user-given hypothesis space. Our learning procedure, the Rule Discovery Tool

---

[3] Stephen Muggleton and Luc De Raedt have shown for languages $\mathcal{L}_{\mathcal{B}}$ and $\mathcal{L}_{\mathcal{H}}$ being restricted to definite clauses that rule learning covers concept learning [9]. Jörg-Uwe Kietz has generalized their finding and gives proofs of the difficulty of learning for various restrictions of first-order logic [6].

(RDT) and its adaptation in order to learn directly from databases (RDT/DB) has been described elsewhere [7], [8], [1]. Here, we shortly summarize its main algorithm and give an example of its declarative bias.

The user-given bias is a set of rule schemata. A rule schema has predicate variables that can be instantiated by predicates of the domain. An instantiated rule schema is a rule. Rule schemata are partially ordered according to their generality. For our small database, a user might specify the following rule schemata $m1$, $m2$, and $m3$ which restrict hypotheses to one or two conditions for the conclusion. An additional predicate in the premise makes a rule more specific.

m1(P, Q): $P(X) \rightarrow Q(X)$
m2(P1, P2): $P1(X)\&P2(X) \rightarrow Q(X)$
m3(P1, P2): $P1(X,Y)\&P2(Y) \rightarrow Q(X)$

RDT's learning procedure consists of two steps: hypothesis generation and testing. In a top-down, breadth-first manner, all possible instantiations of the rule schemata are generated and tested via SQL-queries to the database. The following rules instantiate $m1$ in our example:

$age\_young(X) \rightarrow customer\_yes(X)$
$age\_middle(X) \rightarrow customer\_yes(X)$
$age\_old(X) \rightarrow customer\_yes(X)$
$sex\_f(X) \rightarrow customer\_yes(X)$
$sex\_m(X) \rightarrow customer\_yes(X)$
$income\_high(X) \rightarrow customer\_yes(X)$
$income\_low(X) \rightarrow customer\_yes(X)$

Rules and rule schemata depend on a mapping from the database representation to predicates. Here, we have chosen a representation in propositional logic for the *customer* table. The discretized attribute values are used as predicates. The name of the person (i.e. the key of the table) is the only argument of these predicates. An alternative mapping is implicitly given by rule (iii) above. There, the attribute of the database becomes the predicate; the key and the attribute value become its arguments. Another alternative is to map the table name onto the predicate and have all attributes as arguments. This is the natural mapping for the *married* table as is implicit in rules (i) and (ii). The user can specify a mapping from the database to the rule representation.

Hypothesis testing uses the specified mapping when creating SQL queries. A user-given acceptance criterion is used to decide whether the result of the queries for supporting and non supporting tuples is sufficient for accepting the hypothesis. If a rule has enough support but too many non supporting tuples, it is considered too general. Later on, it becomes a partial instantiation of a more specific rule schema if this exists. If a rule does not have enough support, it is considered too specific. In this case, the rule need not be specialized further, since this cannot increase the number of supporting tuples. RDT safely prunes the search in this case. RDT learns all valid rules that fit the declarative bias. The important points of this learning procedure its declarative bias and its top-down, breadth-first refinement strategy which allows the pruning of large parts of the hypothesis space. This makes rule learning from very large databases tractable.

4 Experiments

We have run RDT/DB on various large data sets. An illustrative example is vehicle data from Daimler Benz AG. Here, we have solved two learning problems. First of all, we learned characteristics of warranty cases. This learning task is close to concept learning, since the learned rules characterize cars of one class or concept, namely the warranty cases. However, the task was not to find a set of rules that completely derives all warranty cases (the completeness condition of concept learning). Instead, the task was to find all relevant rules about warranty cases (the completeness condition of rule learning). That is, we wanted to find out what the data tell us about warranty cases.

RDT/DB accomplishes this learning task by instantiating the predicate variable of the conclusion in all rule schemata by the predicate $warranty(X)$. Following the advice of the Mercedes technicians, we separated the data into three subsets: gasoline engines and manual gearshift, gasoline engines and automatic gearshift, and diesel engine and automatic gearshift. In each of these subsets, the number of database tables is 23, and the largest number of tuples in a database table was 111,995. We selected up to 3 relevant attributes of each table so that one observation consists of 26 attributes which must be collected using 23 database tables. Using 3 rule schemata, RDT/DB learned rules like the following:

(iv) $rel\_niveaureg(X) \rightarrow warranty(X)$ stating that vehicles with the special equipment of *Niveauregulierung* are more likely to be warranty cases than all other cars, taking into account the distribution of cars with this equipment.

(v) $motor\_e\_type(X, Type)\&mobr\_cyl(Type, 6.0) \rightarrow warranty(X)$ stating that vehicles of an engine type that has 6 cylinders are more likely to be warranty cases than one would predict on the basis of the overall warranty rate and the proportion of cars with this characteristic.

The second learning task was to analyze warranty cases in which parts of a particular functional or spatial group (e.g., having to do with fuel injection) were claimed to be defective. We investigated 9 groups of car parts. Here, RDT/DB inserted – one after the other – 9 predicates as the conclusion of all rule schemata. We used 13 rule schemata. We specified an acceptance criterion inspired by Bayes:

$$\frac{pos}{pos+neg} \geq \frac{concl}{concl+negconcl}$$

where *pos* is the number of tuples for which the premise and the conclusion are true, *neg* is the number of tuples for which the premise is true but the conclusion is not true, *concl* is the number of tuples for which the conclusion is true, regardless of any premise, and *negconcl* is the number of tuples for which the conclusion is not true. The first expression corresponds to the conditional probability of the conclusion given the conditions described by the premise. The second expression corresponds to the a priori probability of the conclusion [4].

---

[4] Note that the data set is complete, i.e. all vehicles of a certain engine and gearshift are known to the system. This means that prior probabilities can be reduced to

we have adopted the approach of ILP, which can express rules in restricted FOL. We have shown that RDT/DB, an ILP algorithm which directly accesses ORACLE databases, is capable of solving the difficult task of rule learning. Using a declarative bias which narrows the hypothesis space allows RDT/DB to learn first-order logic rules from diverse tables, even when the number of tuples is large. However, directly using the database makes hypothesis testing inefficient. Each hypothesis is tested using two SQL queries, which count supporting and non supporting tuples. These tuples are not stored in the main memory under the control of the learning system. If a hypothesis is specialized later on, a subset of the already computed set of tuples must be selected. In our approach, however, the result of previous hypothesis testing is lost and the new SQL query computes the large set of tuples anew and then selects within it. Now that we have restricted hypothesis generation successfully, improvements to hypothesis testing are necessary.

References

1. Peter Brockhausen and Katharina Morik. A multistrategy approach to relational knowledge discovery in databases. *Machine Learning Journal*, to appear 1997.
2. L. DeRaedt and M. Bruynooghe. An overview of the interactive concept–learner and theory revisor CLINT. In Stephen Muggleton, editor, *Inductive Logic Programming.*, number 38 in The A.P.I.C. Series, chapter 8, pages 163–192. Academic Press, London [u.a.], 1992.
3. Saso Dzeroski. Inductive logic programming and knowledge discovery in databases. In Usama M. Fayyad et al., editors, see 4., pages 117–152.
4. Usama M. Fayyad, Gregory Piatetsky-Shapiro, Padhraic Smyth, and Ramasamy Uthurusamy, editors. *Advances in Knowledge Discovery and Data Mining.* AAAI Press Series in Computer Science. A Bradford Book, The MIT Press, Cambridge Massachusetts, London England, 1996.
5. Nicolas Helft. Inductive generalisation: A logical framework. In *Procs. of the 2nd European Working Session on Learning*, 1987.
6. Jörg Uwe Kietz. *Induktive Analyse relationaler Daten.* PhD thesis, Technische Universität Berlin, 1996.
7. Jörg-Uwe Kietz and Stefan Wrobel. Controlling the complexity of learning in logic through syntactic and task–oriented models. In Stephen Muggleton, editor, *Inductive Logic Programming*, chapter 16, pages 335–360. Academic Press, London, 1992.
8. Guido Lindner and Katharina Morik. Coupling a relational learning algorithm with a database system. In Kodratoff, Nakhaeizadek, and Taylor, editors, *Statistics, Machine Learning, and Knowledge Discovery in Databases*, MLnet Familiarization Workshops, pages 163 – 168. MLnet, April 1995.
9. S. Muggleton and Luc De Raedt. Inductive logic programming: Theory and methods. *Journal of Logic Programming*, 19/20:629–679, 1994.
10. Gregory Piatetsky-Shapiro and William J. Frawley, editors. *Knowledge Discovery in Databases.* The AAAI Press, Menlo Park, 1991.
11. J. Schmidhuber and D. Prelinger. Discovering predictable classifications. *Neural Computation*, 5(4):625 – 635, 1993.

The Composition Heuristic[*]

Kurt Ammon[**]

Hamburg

Abstract. An essential heuristic in the SHUNYATA program is the composition heuristic which produces predicates and formulas forming the central "ideas" of proofs. In the proof of a rather simple theorem in mathematical logic, it generates a predicate. In the proof of Gödel's incompleteness theorem, it generates an undecidable formula. The construction of the above predicate and the undecidable formula ordinarily requires the application of Cantor's famous diagonal method. The composition heuristic was originally developed as a learning procedure which generates theorem provers automatically.

1 Introduction

The SHUNYATA program focusses on the development of control procedures which is a basic problem in automated theorem proving. An essential procedure in SHUNYATA is the composition heuristic introduced in Section 2. Section 3 shows how the heuristic generates the central "idea" of a proof of a rather simple theorem in mathematical logic. Section 4 describes how it can produce an undecidable formula which is the central "idea" of the proof of Gödel's incompleteness theorem. Section 5 discusses why resolution provers cannot generate the predicates and formulas produced by the composition heuristic.

2 Composition Heuristic

The composition heuristic constructs formulas and predicates by applying rules for the formation of formulas and predicates to preceding proof steps. Roughly speaking, the rules give the domains and ranges of elementary functions which form the elementary building stones of the new formulas and predicates. The application of the rules yields compositions of the elementary functions. Some of these compositions are formulas or predicates.

In order to construct a predicate $P(x)$ on a given set S, the composition heuristic first introduces a variable $x \in S$. Then, it applies universal propositions

---

[**] Correspondence to Kurt Ammon, Hamburg, Germany, Fax: +49 40 8317876, Email: ammon@compuserve.com

1.	$T \subseteq S$	Preceding proof step
2.	*assume* $x \in S$	Composition
3.	$predicate(x \in T)$	Composition, Rule 1
4.	$predicate(\neg x \in T)$	Composition, Rule 2

Table 1. The construction of a predicate by the composition heuristic

in preceding proof steps to the proposition $x \in S$. Finally, the application of rules for the construction of predicates yields predicates $P(x)$ on S. The predicates $P(x)$ can be used to define subsets

$$\{x \in S : P(x)\}$$

of the set S.

Table 1 illustrates the construction of a predicate for the definition of a subset of a set S. Step 1 in Table 1 indicates that a preceding step contains a subset relation $T \subseteq S$, i.e., T is a subset of the set S. In order to construct a predicate for the definition of the new subset of S, the composition heuristic introduces a variable x for an element of the set S in step 2. Examples of rules for the formation of predicates are:

Rule 1. If T is a subset of a set S and x is an element of S, then $x \in T$ is a predicate. A formalization is:

$$\forall T, S, x(T \subseteq S \wedge x \in S \rightarrow predicate(x \in T))$$

Rule 2. If A is a predicate, then the negation $\neg A$ of A is also a predicate. A formalization is:

$$\forall A(predicate(A) \rightarrow predicate(\neg A))$$

The application of Rule 1 to the propositions $T \subseteq S$ and $x \in S$ in steps 1 and 2 yields the predicate $x \in T$ in step 3. The application of Rule 2 to the predicate $x \in T$ yields the predicate $\neg x \in T$ in step 4. This predicate defines a new subset

$$\{x \in S : \neg x \in T\}$$

of S which represents the complement of T in S.

3 Cantor's Diagonal Method

A rather simple theorem in mathematical logic, whose proof ordinarily requires the application of Cantor's famous diagonal method [9, pp. 6–8], is:

Theorem 3. The set of all sets of natural numbers is not enumerable, i.e., there is no function f on the set of natural numbers $\mathbf{N}$ into the subsets of $\mathbf{N}$ such that for all subsets $S \subseteq \mathbf{N}$, there is a natural number $n \in \mathbf{N}$ with $S = f(n)$. A formalization is:

$$\neg \exists f(function(f, \mathbf{N}) \wedge$$
$$\forall n(n \in \mathbf{N} \rightarrow f(n) \subseteq \mathbf{N}) \wedge$$
$$\forall S(S \subseteq \mathbf{N} \rightarrow \exists n(n \in \mathbf{N} \wedge S = f(n))))$$

1. assume $f(function(f, \mathbf{N}) \wedge$	Contradiction
$\forall n(n \in \mathbf{N} \to f(n) \subseteq \mathbf{N}) \wedge$	
$\forall S(S \subseteq \mathbf{N} \to \exists n(n \in \mathbf{N} \wedge S = f(n))))$	
2. assume $n \in \mathbf{N}$	Composition
3. $f(n) \subseteq \mathbf{N}$	Composition, steps 1, 2
4. $predicate(n \in f(n))$	Composition, Rule 1, steps 2, 3
5. $predicate(\neg n \in f(n))$	Composition, Rule 2, step 4

Table 2. The construction of a predicate on $\mathbf{N}$ by the composition heuristic

In the ordinary proof, the diagonal method produces a predicate

$$\neg n \in f(n) \tag{1}$$

defining a set

$$S = \{n \in \mathbf{N} : \neg n \in f(n)\} \tag{2}$$

of natural numbers. In SHUNYATA's proof of Theorem 3, the predicate (1) defining the set (2) is produced by the composition heuristic [4, pp. 682–683].

SHUNYATA generates the proof as follows: Because Theorem 3 is the negation of a proposition, the contradiction heuristic introduces the assumption in step 1 in Table 2 that the proposition holds [4, p. 682]. In order to apply the proposition

$$\forall S(S \subseteq \mathbf{N} \to \exists n(n \in \mathbf{N} \wedge S = f(n))) \tag{3}$$

in step 1 in Table 2, whose antecedent contains a subset $S \subseteq \mathbf{N}$, SHUNYATA calls the composition heuristic to construct a predicate on the set of natural numbers $\mathbf{N}$ defining a subset $S \subseteq \mathbf{N}$. The composition heuristic first introduces a variable $n \in \mathbf{N}$ in step 2 in Table 2. Then, it applies universal propositions in preceding proof steps to the assumption in step 2 which yields step 3. Finally, the application of Rules 1 and 2 yields the predicates in steps 4 and 5. The predicate in step 5 corresponds to the predicate (1) defining the set S in (2). The predicate (1) forms the central "idea" of the proof because, according to (3), there is a natural number $n \in \mathbf{N}$ with $S = f(n)$, which immediately produces contradictions for the assumptions $n \in S$ and $\neg n \in S$ [4, pp. 682-683].

Rules 1 and 2 are elementary, general, and well-known. Rule 1 is the formation rule for the most elementary predicate in Theorem 3, i.e., the element predicate, and Rule 2 the formation rule for the most elementary propositional connective, the negation $\neg$, which is also occurs in the theorem to be proved (see [12, p. 12]). The composition heuristic first applies rules containing elementary concepts or concepts occurring in the theorem to be proved (see [5, p. 303]). Therefore, Rules 1 and 2 can easily be selected from a knowledge base containing many rules (see [3, pp. 15–16]). Because the construction of the predicate (1) defining set (2) ordinarily requires Cantor's diagonal method, the composition heuristic does not contain the diagonal method, and Rules 1 and 2 are elementary, general, and can easily be selected from a knowledge base, it seems justified to say that the composition heuristic can implicitly rediscover the diagonal method in the proof of Theorem 3.

4 An Undecidable Formula

Gödel's incompleteness theorem says that every formal number theory contains an undecidable formula, i.e., neither the formula nor its negation are provable in the theory. The composition heuristic can construct an undecidable formula on the basis of elementary rules for the formation of formulas [5]. Ordinarily, the construction of an undecidable formula is achieved by Cantor's diagonal method [9, p. 207].

The composition heuristic can construct an undecidable formula on the basis of the following rules [5, p. 295]:

Rule 4. A formal number theory contains a variable x. A formalization is:

$$all\ T(fnt(T) \rightarrow variable(\mathrm{x}, T))$$

Rule 5. A formal number theory contains a variable y. A formalization is:

$$all\ T(fnt(T) \rightarrow variable(\mathrm{y}, T))$$

Rule 6. A formal number theory contains a formula A(x, y) (see Lemma 1 in [5, p. 298]). A formalization is:

$$all\ T(fnt(T) \rightarrow formula(\mathrm{A(x, y)}, T))$$

Rule 7. If F is a formula of a formal number theory, then $\neg F$ is also a formula. A formalization is:

$$all\ T, F(fnt(T) \wedge formula(F, T) \rightarrow formula(\neg F, T))$$

Rule 8. If F is a formula and x a variable, then $\forall x F$ is a formula. A formalization is:

$$all\ T, x, F(fnt(T) \wedge variable(x, T) \wedge formula(F, T) \rightarrow formula(\forall x F, T))$$

Rule 9. The Gödel number of a formula is a natural number. A formalization is:

$$all\ T, F(fnt(T) \wedge formula(F, T) \rightarrow natural\text{-}number(gn(F)))$$

Rule 10. If $F(x)$ is a formula with a variable x and n a natural number, then the formula $F(n)$ resulting from substituting the numeral n for the variable x in $F(x)$ is a formula. A formalization is:

$$all\ T, F, n(fnt(T) \wedge formula(F, T) \wedge variable(x, T) \wedge natural\text{-}number(n) \rightarrow$$
$$formula(sub(F, x, num(n)), T))$$

1. *assume T* $(fnt(T))$	Universal
2. *variable*(x, T)	Composition, Rule 4, step 1
3. *variable*(y, T)	Composition, Rule 5, step 1
4. *formula*$(A(x, y), T)$	Composition, Rule 6, step 1
5. *formula*$(\neg A(x, y), T)$	Composition, Rule 7, steps 1, 4
6. *formula*$(\forall y \neg A(x, y), T)$	Composition, Rule 8, steps 1, 3, 5
7. *natural-number*$(gn(\forall y \neg A(x, y)))$	Composition, Rule 9, steps 1, 6
8. *formula*$(sub(\forall y \neg A(x, y), x,$	Composition, Rule 10, steps 1, 2, 6, 7
$\quad num(gn(\forall y \neg A(x, y)))), T)$	

Table 3. The construction of an undecidable formula in formal number theory

In order to prove Gödel's theorem, the universal heuristic first introduces the assumption in step 1 in Table 3 which says that the antecedent of the theorem holds (see [5]). Then, the composition heuristic constructs formulas by applying the above rules. Steps 2–8 in Table 3 show the construction of the undecidable formula. Steps 2, 3, and 4 result from an application of Rules 4, 5, and 6 to the first step in Table 3. Then, the application of Rules 7, 8, 9, and 10 produces the undecidable formula in step 8. The ordinary representation of the formula is

$$\forall y \neg A(\mathbf{k}, y), \tag{4}$$

where $\mathbf{k}$ denotes the numeral of Gödel number of the formula

$$\forall y \neg A(x, y) \tag{5}$$

in step 7 (see [5, pp. 300–301]). The substitution of the numeral $\mathbf{k}$ for the variable x in the formula (5) itself ordinarily involves the application of Cantor's diagonal method [9, p. 207].

The composition heuristic can also be used to construct the predicate $A(k, n)$ in Definition 3 in [5, pp. 297–298]. The construction requires three additional rules.[3] The first two rules initialize the construction by introducing the variables F and n which occur in the formalization of Definition 3.

Rule 11. The variable F represents a formula in the formal number theory T. A formalization is:

$$formula(F, T)$$

Rule 12. The variable n represents a natural number. A formalization is:

$$natural\text{-}number(n)$$

The third rule refers to a predicate $gnp(n, F)$ which says that the natural number n is the Gödel number of a proof of the formula F:

---

[3] The construction of the predicate $A(k, n)$ is not yet implemented in SHUNYATA.

1. *assume T (fnt(T))*	Universal
2. *formula(F, T)*	Composition, Rule 11
3. *natural-number(n)*	Composition, Rule 12
4. *variable*(x, *T*)	Composition, Rule 4, step 1
5. *natural-number(gn(F))*	Composition, Rule 9, step 2
6. *formula(sub(F,* x, *num(gn(F))), T)*	Composition, Rule 10, steps 1, 4, 5
7. *predicate(gnp(n, sub(F,* x, *num(gn(F))))))*	Composition, Rule 13, steps 1, 3, 6

Table 4. The construction of the predicate $A(gn(F), n)$ in Definition 3

Rule 13. If n is a natural number and F is a formula, then $gnp(n, F)$ is a predicate. A formalization is:

all T, F, n(fnt(T) $\wedge$ formula(F, T) $\wedge$ natural-number(n) $\rightarrow$ predicate(gnp(n, F)))

Table 4 shows the construction of the predicate $A(gn(F), n)$ in the formalization of Definition 3 in [5, pp. 297–298]. In steps 2 and 3, Rules 11 and 12 introduce the variables F and n in the formalization of Definition 3. The application of Rules 4, 9, 10, and 13 then yields the predicate

$$gnp(n, sub(F, x, num(gn(F))), T) \tag{6}$$

in step 7 which defines the predicate $A(gn(F), n)$ in Definition 3.

Rule 6 states that the formula A(x, y) in Lemma 1 is a formula [5, p. 298]. The lemma says that A(x, y) expresses the predicate (6) in Definition 3 which can be constructed by the composition heuristic (see Table 4). Gödel [8, p. 186] contents to "indicate the outline of the proof" of his Theorem V, which corresponds to Lemma 1, "since it offers no fundamental difficulties ...". Rule 9 says that the Gödel number of a formula is a natural number. Rule 13 refers to the predicate $gnp(n, F)$ which says that the natural number n is the Gödel number of a proof of the formula F. The concept of Gödel numbers is rather simple. Roughly speaking, a Gödel numbering is just an encoding of the expressions of a formal theory into natural numbers [12, p. 136]. For example, the binary numbers representing characters and strings in a computer can be regarded as their Gödel numbers. The concept of formal proofs used in Rule 13 is already contained in the Principia Mathematica [8, p. 5].

The remaining rules used for the construction of the undecidable formula (4) and the predicate (6) are elementary, general and were well-known when Gödel discovered his proof. Obviously, this applies to Rules 4, 5, 11, and 12 which state that x and y are variables, F is a formula, and n is a natural number. It also applies to Rules 2 and 8 which state that $\neg F$ and $\forall x F$ are formulas for any formula F and any variable x. These rules are ordinarily used to define well-formed formulas in first-order logic. It is worth mentioning that any well-formed formula can be constructed by means of these two rules and the rule that $A \rightarrow B$ is a formula for any formulas A and B [12, pp. 46–47]. Rule 10 is also elementary and general because it resembles the fundamental operation of substitution in formal number theory [12, p. 48].

Lemmas 2–5 in [5, p. 298] are so trivial that many presentations of Gödel's proof contain no proofs of most lemmas. Rather, it is assumed that the readers know or can easily prove them. For example, Gödel [8, p. 188] writes that "every ω-consistent system is obviously also consistent" which corresponds to Lemma 3.

Because the construction of the undecidable formula (4) ordinarily requires Cantor's diagonal method, the composition heuristic does not contain the diagonal method, and, for the reasons given above, the rules used for the construction of the formula are elementary and general or refer to the rather simple concept of Gödel numbers, it is justified to say that the composition heuristic can implicitly rediscover Cantor's diagonal method while it is constructing an undecidable formula. The formula can be regarded as the central "idea" of Gödel's proof. It is worth mentioning that the diagonal method was discovered over five decades before Gödel published his theorem [9, p. 7].

5 Discussion

The power of SHUNYATA is due to its heuristics, which guide the search for a proof, and the language CL, which models the representation of proofs in textbooks [5, p. 303–304]. Loveland [11, p. 4] writes that the "design of strong guidance systems is very difficult, indeed beyond our present capabilities except for very small, highly structured domains." Referring to theorem provers using resolution or his connection method, Bibel [6, p. 265] assumes that a manual analysis and encoding of control strategies for many different fields of mathematics is not realistic. SHUNYATA contains surprisingly simple and general heuristics producing substitutions and terms which form the central "ideas" of proofs. For example, it uses subterms of the theorem to be proved as substituents and then simplifies the resulting terms [4, pp. 683–685]. By means of this simple heuristic, proofs of a number of theorems in group theory and of SAM's lemma are rather trivial.[4] The substituents taken from the theorems form the central "ideas" of the proofs. Because substitutions in resolution provers are computed by unification, it is rather difficult to use subterms of the theorem to be proved as substituents in these provers. Another example is the composition heuristic which also produces the central "ideas" of proofs such as an undecidable formula in the proof of Gödel's theorem. Theorem provers based on the resolution method or variants of it such as Bibel's connection method cannot generate the undecidable formula [7].[5] The composition heuristic was originally developed as

---

[4] A pupil at a secondary school used the heuristic to generate proofs of simple theorems in number and group theory, for example, a proof of the theorem that linear equation solvability implies the existence of an identity in a group [1, p. 244]. Letz et al. [10, p. 203] regard such theorems as "interesting" problems for their high-performance prover SETHEO which uses Bibel's connection method.

[5] In their experiment [7], Brüning et al. furthermore used definitions and lemmas different from those in [5]. Rather, the input of SETHEO implicitly contained the proof it produced. For example, the definitions and lemmas additionally included specialized equality relations containing particular formulas, Gödel numbers, and constants

a learning procedure which generates theorem provers automatically [2]. This also illustrates its generality.

6 Conclusion

The composition heuristic constructs formulas and predicates by applying rules for the formation of formulas and predicates to preceding proof steps. Roughly speaking, the rules give the domains and ranges of elementary functions which form the elementary building stones of the new formulas and predicates. In the proof of the theorem that the set of sets of natural numbers is not enumerable, the heuristic produces a predicate on the set of natural numbers. In the proof of Gödel's incompleteness theorem, it produces an undecidable formula. In the proof of each of the two theorems, the heuristic implicitly rediscovers Cantor's famous diagonal method. Because substitutions in resolution provers are computed by unification, these provers have great difficulty in generating the expressions produced by the composition heuristic and other heuristics in SHUNYATA. This explains problems in developing control strategies for resolution provers.

Acknowledgements. I wish to thank reviewers for valuable suggestions which improved my appreciation of my own work. I also thank Sebastian Stier for useful information and helpful comments on an earlier draft of this paper.

References

1. Ammon, K., *The Automatic Development of Concepts and Methods.* Doctoral dissertation, Department of Computer Science, University of Hamburg, 1988.
2. Ammon, K., The automatic acquisition of proof methods, *Seventh National Conference on Artificial Intelligence*, Saint Paul, Minnesota, 1988.
3. Ammon, K., Automatic proofs in mathematical logic and analysis. *11th International Conference on Automated Deduction*, Saratoga Springs, NY, 1992.
4. Ammon, K., The SHUNYATA system. *11th International Conference on Automated Deduction*, Saratoga Springs, NY, 1992.
5. Ammon, K., An automatic proof of Gödel's incompleteness theorem. *Artificial Intelligence* 61, 1993, pp. 291–306.
6. Bibel, W., *Automated Theorem Proving.* Vieweg, Braunschweig, 1982.
7. Brüning, S., Thielscher, M., and Bibel, W., Letter to the Editor, *Artificial Intelligence* 64, 1993, pp. 353–354.
8. Gödel, K., Über formal unentscheidbare Sätze der Principia Mathematica und verwandter Systeme I. Monatshefte für Mathematik und Physik, Vol. 38, pp. 173–198.
9. Kleene, S. C., *Introduction to Metamathematics.* North-Holland, Amsterdam, 1952.
10. Letz, R., Schuhmann, J., Bayerl, S., and Bibel, W., SETHEO: A high-performance prover. *Journal of Automated Reasoning* 8, 1992, pp. 182–212.
11. Loveland, D. W., *Automated Theorem Proving: A Logical Basis.* North-Holland, Amsterdam, 1978.
12. Mendelson, E., *Introduction to Mathematical Logic.* Van Nostrand Reinhold, New York, 1964.

---

customized to Gödel's proof. Therefore, it cannot at all be said that SETHEO produced a proof from the same information.

The Job Assignment Problem: A Study in Parallel and Distributed Machine Learning

Gerhard Weiß

Institut für Informatik, Technische Universität München D-80290 München, Germany
weissg@informatik.tu-muenchen.de

Abstract. This article describes a parallel and distributed machine learning approach to a basic variant of the job assignment problem. The approach is in the line of the multiagent learning paradigm as investigated in distributed artificial intelligence. The job assignment problem requires to solve the task of assigning a given set of jobs to a given set of executing nodes in such a way that the overall execution time is reduced, where the individual jobs may depend on each other and the individual nodes may differ from each other in their execution abilities. Experimental results are presented that illustrate this approach.

1 Introduction

The past years have witnessed a steadily growing interest in parallel and distributed information processing systems in artificial intelligence and computer science. This interest has led to new research and application activities in areas like parallel and distributed algorithms, concurrent programming, distributed database systems, and parallel and distributed hardware architectures. Three basic, interrelated reasons for this interest can be identified. First, the willingness and tendency in artificial intelligence and computer science to attack increasingly difficult problems and application domains which often require, for instance, to process very large amounts of data or data arising at different geographcial locations, and which are therefore often to difficult to be handled by more traditional, sequential and centralized systems. Second, the fact that these systems have the capacity to offer several useful properties like robustness, fault tolerance, scalability, and speed-up. Third, the fact that today the computer and network technology required for building such systems is available. A difficulty with parallel and distributed information processing systems is that they typically are rather complex and hard to specify in their dynamics and behavior. It is therefore broadly agreed that these systems should be able, at least to some extent, to self-improve their future performance, that is, to learn. Not surprisingly, today a broad range of work on learning in parallel and distributed information processing systems, or parallel and distributed machine learning for short, is available. Much of this work is centered around large-scale inductive learning (e.g., [1, 3, 7, 9]) and multiagent learning (e.g., [8, 10, 11]). What should be also mentioned here is the theory of team learning, which might be considered as an important contribution on the way toward a general theory of parallel and distributed machine learning (e.g., [2, 5, 6]). The major property of this kind of learning is that the learning process itself is logically or geographically distributed over several components of the overall system and that these components conduct their learning activities in parallel. The field of parallel and distributed machine learning is of considerable importance, but also is rather young and still searching for its defining boundaries and shape. The work described in this article may be considered as an attempt to contribute to this search.

A problem being well suited for studying parallel and distributed learning is the job assignment problem (JAP). The basic variant of the JAP studied here requires to assign jobs to executing nodes such that the overall completion time is reduced, where there may be dependencies among the individual jobs and differencies in the execution abilities of the individual nodes. Obviously, the JAP inherently allows for parallelism and distributedness, simply because the jobs to be executed can be distributed over several nodes and because the nodes can execute different jobs in parallel. In addition to that, there are two further reasons why the JAP is an interesting and challenging subject of research not only from the point of view of machine learning. One reason is the complexity of this problem. The JAP is non-trivial and known to be a member of the class of NP-hard problems [4], and therefore in many cases it is even very difficult "to find a reasonable solution in a reasonable time". The other reason is that this problem is omnipresent in and highly relevant to many industrial application domains like product manufacturing and workflow organization. This is because the JAP constitutes the core of most scheduling tasks, and the effectiveness and efficiency of whole companies and organizations is therefore often considerably affected by the way in which they solve this problem in its concrete appearance.

The parallel and distributed learning approach to the JAP as it is introduced in this article follows the multiagent learning paradigm known from the field of distributed artificial intelligence. According to this approach, the nodes are considered as active entities or "agents" that in some sense can be said to be autonomous and intelligent, and the jobs are considered as passive entities or "resources" that in some way are used or handled by the agents. The individual agents are restricted in their abilities and, hence, have to interact somehow in order to improve their use and handling of the resources with respect to some predefined criteria. Learning in such a scenario can be interpreted as a search through the space of possible interaction schemes. Starting out from the concept of the estimates of the jobs' influence on the overall time required for completing all jobs, the described approach aims at appropriately adjusting these estimates by a parallel and distributed reinforcement learning scheme that only requires low-level communication and coordination among the individual nodes. This low-level characteristic makes this approach different from most other available multiagent learning approaches.

The article is structured as follows. The job assignment problem and three concrete instantiations of it are described in section 2. The learning approach is presented in detail in section 3. Experimental learning results for the three

TABLE 1:

job	<	time		
		N_1	N_2	N_3
1	2	40	80	100
2	8, 9	30	110	120
3	9	60	20	70
4	9	100	30	100
5	6	10	10	50
6	9	20	20	20
7	9, 10	70	50	20
8	–	40	20	80
9	–	30	90	80
10	–	60	50	20

TABLE 2:

job	<	time		
		N_1	N_2	N_3
1	2	10	50	50
2	3	10	40	70
3	4	10	100	50
4	5	10	60	90
5	6	10	100	50
6	–	10	50	80
7	–	40	80	80
8	–	100	120	60
9	–	60	30	70
10	–	20	90	80
11	–	100	100	30
12	–	60	20	50
13	–	10	40	70

TABLE 3:

job	<	time			
		N_1	N_2	N_3	N_4
1	–	70	10	10	10
2	–	60	10	10	10
3	5, 6	100	120	20	120
4	5, 6	110	120	80	20
5	7	60	90	10	100
6	8	50	140	100	10
7	–	100	150	20	70
8	–	90	100	140	10
9	–	10	10	10	60
10	–	140	100	20	120
11	–	70	10	80	90

instantiations of the JAP are shown in section 4. A brief summary and an outlook on future work is offered in section 5.

2 The Job-Assignment Problem (JAP)

The JAP as it is considered within the frame of the work described here can be formally described as follows. Let $J = \{J_1, \ldots, J_n\}$ be a set of jobs and $N = \{N_1, \ldots, N_m\}$ be a set of nodes, where each job can be executed by at least one of the nodes ($n, m \in \mathcal{N}$). The individual jobs may be ordered by a dependency relation, $<$, where $J_k < J_l$ means that J_k has to be completed before the execution of J_l can be started. J_k is called a predecessor of J_l, and J_l is called a successor of J_k. The nodes may differ from each other in as far as the time required for completing a job may be different for different nodes. The problem to be solved is to find an assignment of the jobs to the nodes such that the overall time required for completing all jobs contained in J is minimal. Because this problem is NP-hard, usually it is reformulated such that it is just required to find an almost optimal solution in polynomial time. The learning approach described in this article follows this reformulation, and aims at producing satisfying (and not necessarily optimal) solutions in reasonable time.

The tables 1 to 3 show three instantiations of the JAP, subsequently referred to as $I1$, $I2$, and $I3$, respectively. Consider the table 1 (the others are to be read analogously). There are 10 jobs and 3 nodes, and there are dependencies among some of the jobs. For instance, job J_1 has to be completed before job J_2 can be started, and the execution of job J_9 requires the completion of the jobs J_2, J_3, J_4, J_6, and J_7. Each job can be executed by each node, but there are differences in the time required by the nodes for executing the jobs. For instance, the nodes N_1, N_2, and N_3 need 40, 80, and 100 units of time, respectively, for completing the job J_1. As this table also shows, a node may require different time intervals for completing different jobs. For instance, the node N_1 needs 40, 30, and 60 units of time for completing the jobs J_1, J_2, and J_3, respectively.

3   The Learning Approach

The basic idea underlying the multiagent learning approach described here is that each job is associated with an estimate of the job's influence on the overall completion time, and that these estimates are improved in the course of learning. As it is described in more detail below, this improvement as well as the execution of the jobs is done by the involved nodes in a parallel and distributed way. A high estimate indicates a significant impact on the overall completion time, and a job being associated with a high estimate therefore is identified as "critical" and should be completed as soon as possible. Learning proceeds in episodes, where an episode consists of the time intervall required for completing all jobs. The basic working steps realized during an episode can be conceptually described as follows:

> until all jobs are completed do
> (1) The idle nodes choose among the executable jobs, and this choice is done dependent on the nodes' execution times and the job estimates.
> (2) The nodes execute their chosen jobs.
> (3) If a node completes a job, then it adjusts the estimate of this job.

When an episode t is finished, the next episode $t+1$ starts and learning continues on the basis of the adjusted job estimates that are available at the end of episode t. This is iterated for a predefined, maximum number of episodes. The best solution found during these episodes is offered as the solution of the overall learning process. (A solution found in an episode need not necessarily be as good as the solution found in the preceding episode. Due to its statistical nature this approach does not guarantee a monotonic improvement of the solutions found in the course of learning.) The approach is parallel and distributed in as far as both job execution (2) and estimate adjustment (3) is done by different agents. A synchronization of the agents' activities occurs in step (1). This also shows the potential advantages of this kind of learning over centralized learning approaches: it is more robust (e.g., failure of an individual node does not damage the overall learning process); it is more flexible (e.g., new nodes can be easily integrated in an ongoing learning process); and it is faster (because of inherent task and result sharing).

Many concrete forms of this conceptual description are possible. It was not the goal of the described work to exhaustively investigate all these forms. Instead, the work aimed at an improved understanding of the potential benefits and limitations of parallel and distributed machine learning in general, and therefore a concretization has been chosen that realizes this type of learning in an intuitive and relatively simple way and at the same time enables a conclusive and efficient experimental investigation. In the actual implementation, step (1) realizes a rank-based assignment of the executable jobs. This means that the job being associated with the highest estimate is assigned first, the job having the second highest estimate is assigned next, and so forth. Moreover, if the assignment of a job is ambitious in the sense that there are several idle nodes capable of executing this job, then the node offering the shortest (job-specific) execution time is selected with highest probability. Formally, if $N[J_k]$ denotes the set of all idle nodes capable of executing a job J_k (at some time during an episode) and $T[i, k]$ denotes the time required by $N_i \in N[J_k]$ for completing J_k, then the probability that N_i executes J_k can be described by

$$\frac{T[i, k]}{\sum_{N_j \in N[J_k]} T[j, k]} \quad . \tag{1}$$

The actual implementation of step *(3)* offers two slightly different schemes, subsequently referred to as $A1$ and $A2$, for the adjustment of the job estimates. In the following, let E_k^t denote the estimate of job J_k at the beginning of episode t, let C_k^t denote the completion time of J_k in episode t, and let $\overline{C_k^t} = \frac{1}{t} \sum_{\tau=1}^{t} C_k^\tau$ denote the average completion time of J_k in the episodes 1 to t. According to the adjustment scheme $A1$, the estimates are updated immediately after job completion. Whenever a node finished a job J_k during an episode t, it modifies E_k^t according to

$$E_k^{t+1} = E_k^t + \alpha(C_k^t - \overline{C_k^t}) \quad , \tag{2}$$

where α is a factor called learning rate. The resulting estimate E_k^{t+1} is used for ranking in step *(1)* of episode $t + 1$. The later (earlier) a job is completed, the higher (lower) is its estimate at the beginning of the next episode and, hence, the higher (lower) is the probability of an earlier execution of this job. According to the adjustment scheme $A2$, the job estimates are updated at the end of each epiode. In contrast to $A1$, this scheme explicitly takes into consideration that there may be dependencies among the jobs. Consider the situation at the end of episode t. Let $Pred(J_l)$ denote the set of all predecessors of J_l, let $Succ(J_l)$ denote the set of all successors of J_l, and let C^t denote the overall completion time in the episode t. For each $J_k \in Pred(J_l)$, the node which executed J_l pays a certain amount P_{lk}^t to the node which executed J_k during this episode. This amount is given by

$$P_{lk}^t = \begin{cases} (C_l^t - C_l^{t-1})(C^t - C^{t-1}) + P_l^t & \text{if } Succ(J_l) \neq \emptyset \\ (C_l^t - C_l^{t-1})(C^t - C^{t-1}) & \text{otherwise} \end{cases} , \tag{3}$$

where P_l^t is the sum of all payments that the node which executed J_l received from the nodes which executed the successors of J_l at the end of the episode t, this is,

$$P_l^t = \sum_{J_i \in Succ(J_l)} P_{il}^t \quad . \tag{4}$$

After the node which executed a job J_k received all payments for this job from the nodes which executed this job's successors, it adjusts the estimate of J_k according to

$$E_k^{t+1} = E_k^t + \alpha(C_k^t - C_k^{t-1})(C^t - C^{t-1}) + \beta P_k^t \quad , \tag{5}$$

where α and β are factors called learning rates. The mechanism underlying this update scheme is illustrated in table 4. For instance, as this table shows, if a job J_k is finished later in episode t than in episode $t-1$ (i.e., $C_k^t - C_k^{t-1} > 0$) and the overall completion time increased (i.e., $C^t - C^{t-1} > 0$), then the estimate of J_k tends to increase (because the product $(C_k^t - C_k^{t-1})(C^t - C^{t-1})$ is positive, as expressed by the $+$). As a result, in this case it is likely that the job J_k will be executed earlier and, provided that there is a causal relationship between the completion time of J_k and the overall completion time, that an improved assignment will be generated in the next episode $t+1$. The effect of the

TABLE 4:

influence on E_k^t		$C^t - C^{t-1}$	
		> 0	< 0
$C_k^t - C_k^{t-1}$	> 0	$+$	$-$
	< 0	$-$	$+$

payments is that potential causal relationships between the completion time of the jobs and the overall completion time are propagated backwards through the job dependency network. All together, this adjustment scheme takes particularly care of "critical" dependency paths, that is, paths resulting in a late overall completion.

Learning according to this approach occurs in a parallel and distributed way. In particular, the estimates of different jobs may be adjusted concurrently, and all processors involved in job execution are also involved in the adjustment of the estimates. There are two major characteristics of this approach. First, it realizes a basic form of reinforcement learning. The only available learning feedback is the completion time of the individual jobs. This also means that there is no explict information available about how to gain an improved job assigment. Second, learning is just based on a low-level communication and coordination among the individual nodes. This also means that there is no time- or cost-consuming need for exchanging complex information or conducting complex negotiations in order to realize learning.

4 Experimental Results

The figures 1, 2, and 3 show for the JAP instantiations $I1$, $I2$, and $I3$, respectively, the best solutions learnt after 20 episodes by the adjustment schemes $A1$ and $A2$. In all experiments described here the learning rates α and β were set to one, and the parameters E_i^0, C_i^0, and C^0 where all initialized with zero. As figure 1 shows, the shortest overall completion times for $I1$ generated by $A1$ and $A2$ were 140 and 110, respectively; as figure 2 shows, the shortest overall completion times for $I2$ generated by $A1$ and $A2$ were 150 and 130, respectively; and as figure 3 shows, the shortest overall completion times for $I3$ generated by $A1$ and $A2$ were 130 and 160, respectively. As these figures also show, the scheme $A2$ produced slightly better results than the scheme $A1$ for the instantiations $I1$

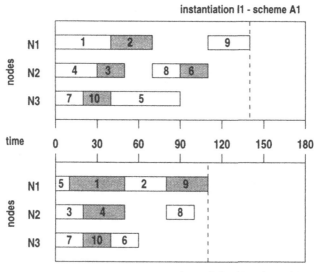

FIGURE 1:

instantiation I1 - scheme A1

instantiation I1 - scheme A2

and *I*3. This observation has been also made in a number of other experiments not described here, and indicates that in general it is worth to explicitly take the dependencies among the jobs into consideration. This is not very surprising. The interesting point here is that good results could be also achieved if the dependencies are not explicitly taken into consideration - as the results for scheme *A*1 illustrate. This shows that the described learning approach is also of interest for domains in which the dependencies are unknown. In order to be able to evaluate these learning results, 20 random solutions for each of the three instantiations have been generated. The best random solutions found for *I*1, *I*2, and *I*3 had overall completion times of 230, 200, and 210, respectively. Obviously, both adjustment schemes clearly outperformed random search. Another measure of evaluation is given by the optimal overall completion times, which are 100 for *I*1, 130 for *I*2, and 100 for *I*3. It should be noted that the three instantiations under consideration were designed as test cases whose optimal solution are known – as mentioned above, the JAP is too complex to be optimally solved in general. A comparison with the optimal solutions shows that the optimum was found for *I*2 and was closely approached for *I*1 and *I*3. This qualitatively coincides with the comparative results gained in several other experiments. For reasons of completeness is should be mentioned that the optimal solution for *I*1 was found after 62 episodes (by *A*1) and for *I*3 after 41 episodes (by *A*2). It has to be stated, however, that the schemes *A*1 and *A*2 are not proven to always converge to the optimal solution, and therefore leave room for improvement.

Figure 2:

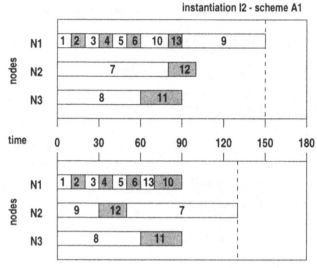

Figure 3:

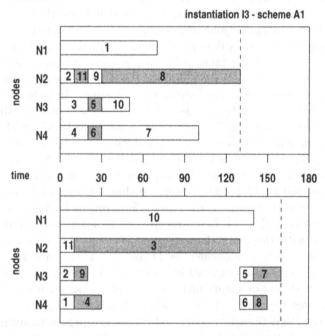

5 Conclusion

The work described in this article applies parallel and distributed machine learning to a basic variant of the job-assignment problem. The learning approach bases on the multiagent learning paradigm known from distributed artificial intelligence, and ascribes the jobs the passive role of resources and the nodes the active role of agents. The concept of the estimates of the jobs' influence on the overall completion time is introduced, and the job estimates are adjusted in a reinforcement learning style and without requiring intensive communication and

4. Garey, M.JR., & Johnson, D. (1979). *Computers and intractability*. New York: Freeman.
5. Jain, S., & Sharma, A. (1995). On aggregating teams of learning machines. *Theoretical Computer Science A*, 137(1), 85–108.
6. Pitt, L., & Smith, C. (1988). Probability and plurality for aggregations of learning machines. *Information and Computation*, 77, 77-92.
7. Provost, F.J., & Hennessy, D.N. (1995). Distributed machine learning: Scaling up with coarse grained parallelism. In *Proceedings of the Second International Conference on Intelligent Systems for Molecular Biology* (pp. 340–348).
8. Sen, S. (Ed.) (1996). *Adaptation, coevolution and learning in multiagent systems. Papers from the 1996 AAAI Symposium*. Technical Report SS-96-01. AAAI Press.
9. Sikora, R., & Shaw, M.J. (1991). *A distributed problem-solving approach to inductive learning*. Faculty Working Paper 91-0109. Department of Business Administration, University of Illinois at Urbana-Champaign.
10. Weiß, G. (Ed.) (1997). *Distributed artificial intelligence meets machine learning*. Lecture Notes in Artificial Intelligence, Vol. 1221. Springer-Verlag.
11. Weiß, G., & Sen, S. (Eds.) (1996). *Adaption and learning in multi-agent systems*. Lecture Notes in Artificial Intelligence, Vol. 1042. Springer-Verlag.

Self-Improving Behavior Arbitration

2 Control Architecture

To deal with goal-orientation, reactivity, and flexibility and consequently with autonomy in the control system of a mobile robot we investigate a methodology using concurrent processes (behavior modules) and a priority-based arbitration scheme. Two levels of arbitration are needed, a local level which accounts for interactions among behaviors and interactions between behaviors and the environment at a given situation, and a global level which ensures that the robot's reactions are consistent with the required goal. Each behavior has therefore at each time-step a local and a global priority. The local priority reflects how good is the behavior to survive in the current world situation. The global priority reflects how good is the behavior for reaching the goal (fulfilling the required task) from the current world situation. These priorities are then combined and used to determine the behavior that will get control in the next cycle. The architecture allows also the integration of learning capabilities. In the following sections emphasis is put on the local arbitration level.

3 Local Priorities

An agent is viewed as having a set of behaviors it can engage in. The local priority for a given behavior at a given time consists of an activity value and a connection value. The activity value reflects the impact of the stimuli on the behavior. The connection value allows to integrate some other considerations such as the relative importance of behaviors or the interaction between them (e.g. expected sequence of behaviors).

Activity value. The activity value AV of a behavior B_i at a given time t is computed as follows:

$$AV(B_i, t) = \frac{1}{2}\left[1 + \frac{1}{n}\sum_{j=1}^{n} f_{i,j}(s_j(t))\right] \tag{1}$$

$f_{i,j}(s_j(t))$ denotes the effect of perceptual value s_j on behavior B_i at time t and n is the number of perceptual values. The result is a value in $[0, 1]$. The function $f_{i,j}$ describes the effect of each possible value delivered by the sensor on the activity of the behavior. To deal with more complex sensors such as a CCD camera, a preprocessing step that divides the sensor space is necessary. Preprocessing the raw sensor data first yields quantities that influence the activity of the behavior independently (e.g., distance and angle information extracted from an image). These quantities can be thought as being delivered by different sensors. The second step in the preprocessing consists in segmenting the domain of nonlinear quantities by clustering their possible values. Similar ideas of segmenting the sensor space for a vision-based mobile robot that tries to shoot a ball into a goal can be found in [2]. There, the domain of the ball image, for example, is divided into 9 clusters, combinations of three positions (left, center, and right) and three sizes (large (near), medium, and small (far)).

Connection Value. The interactions among behaviors are modeled using a network. The nodes of the network represent the different behaviors. The links represent relations among them. The links are given weights. The weight for of the first part. Figure 1 shows the integration of the association network in the existing model for computing activity values. Two types of learning are being simultaneously applied: unsupervised learning concerned with building the self-organizing map and supervised learning in each behavior concerned with integrating the knowledge of the designer (the AV-component) into the system by associating each region of the map (each neural unit) with an activity value.

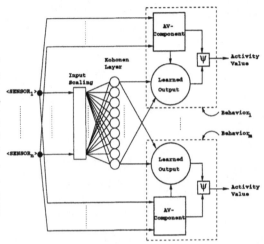

Fig. 1. *Addition of an association network to the existing model for computing activity values. Input values are routed both to the network and to the AV–component of each behavior. The output of the AV–component is used to update the output of the Kohonen layer and influences the resulting activity value depending on the weighting factor ψ, which grows from 0 at start-up to a value of 1 at the end of the learning phase.*

During the interaction with the environment the method presented generates a table for the mapping between raw sensor data and activity values that is capable of generalization. This table can also be kept dynamic even after a long learning phase by allowing the network to adjust its weights in small increments. This provides a continuous adaptation to changes in the environment-agent relationship. Another advantage of the learning algorithm is the possibility of parallel computations (each behavior computes its own mapping).

The critical aspects when computing the activity value are: (i) which inputs (perceptual values) are relevant and should be included and (ii) how are these inputs evaluated to generate the activity value of a behavior. These problems have only been partially addressed by the associative mechanisms presented above. The associative net is only able to learn mapping from inputs to the predefined (by the designer) output. However, since the problem of generalization over states was solved by the table generated by the associative net, these problems can be worked around by combining the described method with reinforcement learning [14]. Although, many studies (e.g., Chapman and Kaelbling [4]) have found that reinforcement learning algorithms often converge slowly, some real robot applications (e.g., Asada et al [2]) exist that show how these algorithms can be used in realizing autonomous agents. In addition the proposed combination has the advantage that the agent has a minimum level of ability while the learning and adaptive mechanisms are initialized and consequently does not need to wait until learning converges in order to act in a somewhat reliable manner. Reinforcement learning is integrated as follows: each time a behavior is selected, the output of the corresponding neural unit (situation) is updated using a reinforcement signal which depends on the success of the behavior in permitting the agent to survive. As a result, the designer of the agent has only to specify an initial control structure which does not need to be optimal. This structure will be automatically improved as the agent gains experience in its environment.

Learning Connection Values. The learning task is to incrementally change the weights of links among behaviors so that gradually only transitions between "appropriate" behaviors are made (a behavior is "appropriate" within a certain environmental situation if its local priority surpasses a threshold θ_{above} and it is "not appropriate" if its local priority drops under a threshold θ_{below}). Behaviors that were "appropriate" at time $(t-1)$ increase therefore the weights of their links to behaviors that are "appropriate" at time t and decrease the weights of their links to behaviors that are "not appropriate". The weight of a link from a behavior B_i that was "appropriate" at the previous time-step to a behavior B_j is updated as follows:

$$w_{i,j}(t) = \begin{cases} w_{i,j}(t-1) + \Delta(\eta_i) & : & app(B_j, t) \\ w_{i,j}(t-1) - \Delta(\eta_i) & : & notapp(B_j, t) \\ w_{i,j}(t-1) & : & otherwise \end{cases} \quad (3)$$

η_i is the number of times behavior B_i was "appropriate" in the past and $\Delta(\eta_i) = \begin{cases} h(\eta_i) - h(\eta_i - 1) & : & \eta_i \geq 1 \\ 0 & : & \eta_i = 0 \end{cases}$ where h is a monotonic increasing function having values ranging from -1 to 1 (e.g. $h(x) = tanh(\frac{x}{k})$). h determines how the weights are updated and k can be used to change the shape of the function and thus provides the possibility to influence the learning process.

Again, the algorithm is completely distributed (each behavior learns the weights of its links to other behaviors) and a range of different learning styles can be implemented by initializing and tuning the different parameters.

5 Experiments

In order to test the ideas outlined so far, a simulated dynamic environment similar to the one developed in [10] was used as a testbed. The dynamic environment is a 25×25 cell world. A sample environment is shown in figure 2. There are four kinds of objects in the environment: the agent ("R"), food ("$"), enemies ("E"), and obstacles ("O"). The perimeter of the world is considered to be occupied by obstacles. At the start, the agent and four enemies are placed in their initial positions as shown in figure 2, and fifteen pieces of food are randomly placed on unoccupied cells. At each timestep the agent has four behaviors to choose from: "move forward", "move backward", "move left", and "move right". Each of these behaviors allows the agent to walk to one of the four adjacent cells.

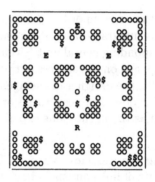

Fig. 2. *A dynamic environment involving an agent (R), enemies (E), food ($), and obstacles (O).*

After the agent moves, each of the enemies is allowed to stay or move to an adjacent cell that is not occupied by obstacles or food. To allow the agent to escape from chasing enemies, the enemy speed is limited to 80 % of the full speed of the agent. The enemies move randomly, but tend to move towards the agent; the tendency becomes stronger as the agent gets closer.

A play ends when the agent dies. The agent dies when it collides with an enemy or an obstacle. At the start of a new play, the agent is given a fixed amount of energy. Each piece of food provides the agent with 15 units of additional energy, and each move costs the agent 1 unit. When the agent runs out of energy it remains at the same position until it is caught by an enemy.

The agent is allowed to see only the area surrounding it. It has 8 sensors:S_F, S_B, S_L, S_R, S_{FL}, S_{FR}, S_{BL}, and S_{BR}. These are used to sense objects respectively in the directions Forward, Backward, Left, Right, Forward-Left, Forward-Right, Backward-Left, and Backward-Right. Each of the sensors delivers a real perceptual value $\in [-1, 1]$ (this can be thought as being a repulsive force acting on the agent) which depends on the kind of the detected object and its distance from the agent. The delivered value is given by s for the sensors $\{S_F, S_B, S_L, S_R\}$ and by s' for the sensors $\{S_{FL}, S_{FR}, S_{BL}, S_{BR}\}$:

$$s = \begin{cases} 0.75/distance^3 & : \quad if\ object = \text{``}O\text{''} \\ -1.0/distance & : \quad if\ object = \text{``}\$\text{''} \\ 1.0/distance & : \quad if\ object = \text{``}E\text{''} \end{cases} \quad s' = \begin{cases} 0 & : \quad if\ object = \text{``}O\text{''} \\ -0.5/distance & : \quad if\ object = \text{``}\$\text{''} \\ 0.5/distance & : \quad if\ object = \text{``}E\text{''} \end{cases}$$

From the agent's point of view, the world is nondeterministic, not only because the enemies behave randomly, but also because the world is only partially observable. The task of the agent is to survive in this environment. This means it must always try to get food (in order to get energy and consequently be able to move), avoid obstacles and escape from chasing enemies. To evaluate the performance of the different frameworks and algorithms the probability distribution of the length of a play, i.e., for each time-step the probability that the agent dies at this time-step, is used as performance measure.

Activity values. We started first with using only activity values to control the agent. The effects of perceptual values on behaviors were chosen as shown in figure 3.

Sensors / Behaviors	S_F	S_B	S_L	S_R	S_{FL}	S_{FR}	S_{BL}	S_{BR}
move forward	f_2	f_1	f_1	f_1	f_2	f_2	f_1	f_1
move backward	f_1	f_2	f_1	f_1	f_1	f_1	f_2	f_2
move left	f_1	f_1	f_2	f_1	f_2	f_1	f_2	f_1
move right	f_1	f_1	f_1	f_2	f_1	f_2	f_1	f_2

Fig. 3. *Dependency of behaviors on sensors described using the functions* $f_0(x) = 0$, $f_1(x) = x$, *and* $f_2(x) = -x$.

Figure 4(A) shows the performance of the agent and especially how this performance becomes better with more input information. In the first case (curve $c1$) the agent has not used any sensor inputs. At each time-step it selected a behavior randomly. In the second case (curve $c2$) only input from the sensors S_F, S_B, S_L, and S_R was considered. In the third case (curve $c3$) all the eight sensors were used.

Map-building and learning activity values. In a second study we were concerned with building the self-organizing map and learning activity values. Figure 4(B) shows the performance of the agent after a learning period of 100000 time-steps (curve $c2$). This performance is almost the same as that of the teacher (curve $c1$) which means that a sufficiently consistent self-organizing map was built. During the learning phase the robot was controlled only by activity values computed from the sensors S_F, S_B, S_L, and S_R. The self-organizing network was a two-dimensional network with 50×50 cells. The parameter ψ was set during learning to 0 and after learning to 1 which means that after learning the agent is controlled using only the learned activity values.

One of the main reasons for using the neural network was its ability to deal with noisy or incomplete input. It is therefore expected that the robustness of the agent becomes better after learning. The results shown in figure 4(C) highlight this very clearly. In this experiment the sensor S_F was supposed to be defective and delivers always the value 0. Curve $c1n$ shows the bad performance without learning. Curve $c2n$ shows that there is only a small performance deviation when the agent uses the already learned map and activity values. Curves $c1$ and $c2$ are those of figure 4(B).

Improving activity values. In this study we were concerned with improving an initial control structure using reinforcement learning. The designer of the agent is supposed to know only the dependency of the behaviors on the sensors S_F, S_B, S_L, and S_R. The effects of the sensors S_{FL}, S_{FR}, S_{BL}, and S_{BR} were unknown and therefore modeled with the function $f_0(s) = 0$. The agent was allowed first to build a self-organizing map and learn the activity values using

462

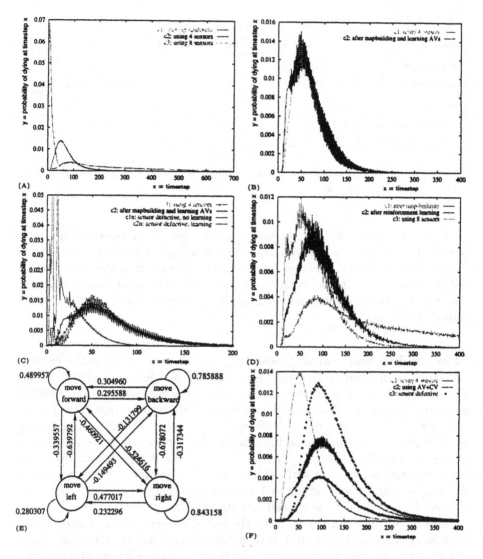

Fig. 4. *(A) Performance of the agent when using only activity values. (B) Performance of the agent after map-building and learning activity values. (C) Performance of the agent when sensor S_F is defective. (D) Improving an initial control structure using reinforcement learning. (E) Network modeling the relations among behaviors obtained after 10000 time-steps of experience. (F) Performance of the agent when connection values are considered.*

the initial control structure. This happened in the same way as in the previous study except that in this case all eight sensors were used when building the self-organizing map. The performance of the agent after map-building is shown in figure 4(D) (curve $c1$). After that the obtained activity values were changed using reinforcement learning. We used a simple version of the Q-learning algorithm as described in [2]. The reinforcement signals were choosen as follows: -0.8 if the agent dies, 0.4 if the agent gets food, and 0.0 otherwise. Curve $c2$ (figure 4(D)) shows the performance of the resulting control structure.

The performance became clearly better after using reinforcement learning, however, the agent failed to reach the performance shown by curve $c3$ (performance reached when all eight sensors were used to compute the activity values). The reason for this may be that the local information used by the agent was insufficient, i.e., the self-organizing map was not good enough, or that more parameter tuning must be done.

Connection values. In this study we were interested in the effects of using and learning connection values. As at the beginning the interconnections between behaviors were not known, the agent was first allowed to learn them using an initial control structure which was supposed to be sufficiently good. The initial control structure used only activity values which were computed using only the four sensors S_F, S_B, S_L, and S_R. The obtained network is shown in figure 4(E). The parameter settings used to generate these weights were as follows: the initial weights and values for η were set to 0, θ_{above} was chosen to be always the highest local priority at the given time-step, θ_{below} was chosen to be always the smallest local priority at the given time-step, $h(x) = tanh(\frac{x}{k})$, $k = 100$, and the learning period was 10000 time-steps.

This network was then used to compute the connection values which were combined with activity values to build the local priority. The resulting performance was surprisingly better than that of the initial control structure (curve 2 in figure 4(F)) . To test the robustness of the system the sensor S_F was supposed again to be defective and delivered always the value 0. As expected, the robustness became better. This can be seen by comparing curve 3 in figure 4(F) (connection values were also considered) with curve $c1n$ in figure 4(C) (only activity values were considered). In this experiment the parameter α was set to the value 0.7 which gave roughly the best performance in this case.

6 Conclusions

This paper has introduced a new scheme for integrating behaviors in a behavior-based architecture using priorities and learning techniques. Despite the simplicity of the test-bed, the results are encouraging and suggest that this architecture is a promising approach to building autonomous learning systems. Ongoing work is focused on testing the model in a more realistic computer simulation that reflects the real world as good as possible. The merit of such a computer simulation will not only be to check the validity of the algorithms, but also to save the runnnig cost of the real robot during the learning process. The design process therefore consists of two parts: first, learning the optimal control structure through the computer simulation and then, applying the learned structure to a real situation. Because the computer simulation cannot completely simulate the real world, learning should continue in the real world situation in order to provide a continuous adaptation. This is certainly possible when using the algorithms presented in this paper.

Our work is also concentrated on improving this model and on extending it by integrating global priorities and global learning.

References

1. R.C. Arkin. Integrating behavioral, perceptual, and world knowledge in reactive navigation. *Robotics and Autonomous Systems*, 6:105–122, 1990.
2. M. Asada, S. Noda, S. Tawaratsumida, and K. Hosoda. Vision-based behavior acquisition for a shooting robot by using a reinforcement learning. In *Proceedings of The IAPR/IEEE Workshop on Visual Behaviors-1994*, pages 112–118, 1994.
3. R. A. Brooks. A robust layered control system for a mobile robot. *IEEE Journal of Robotics and Automation*, RA-2(1), April 1986.
4. D. Chapman and L.P. Kaelbling. Input generalization in delayed reinforcement learning: An algorithm and performance comparisons. In *Proceedings of The International Joint Conference on Artificial Intelligence, IJCAI-91*, 1991.
5. R.J. Firby. Adaptive execution in complex dynamic worlds. Ph.D. Dissertation YALEU/CSD/RR#672, Yale University, Jan. 1989.
6. E. Gat. Integrating planning and reacting in a heterogeneous asynchronous architecture for controlling real-world mobile robots. In *Proceedings of AAAI-92*, pages 809–815, San Jose, CA, July 1992.
7. M. S. Hamdi. A goal-oriented behavior-based control architecture for autonomous mobile robots allowing learning. In M. Kaiser, editor, *Proceedings of the Fourth European Workshop on Learning Robots*, Karlsruhe, Germany, December 1995.
8. M. S. Hamdi and K. Kaiser. Adaptable local level arbitration of behaviors. In *Proceedings of The First International Conference on Autonomous Agents, Agents'97*, Marina del Rey, CA, USA, February 1997.
9. T. Kohonen. *Self-Organization and Associative Memory*. Springer Series in Information Sciences 8, Heidelberg. Springer Verlag, 1984.
10. L.-J. Lin. Self-improving reactive agents based on reinforcement learning, planning and teaching. *Machine Learning*, 8(3/4):293–321, 1992.
11. S. Mahadevan and J. Connell. Automatic programming of behavior-based robots using reinforcement learning. *Artificial Intelligence*, 55(2):311–365, 1992.
12. J.d.R. Millàn and C. Torras. Efficient reinforcement learning of navigation strategies in an autonomous robot. In *Proceedings of The International Conference on Intelligent Robots and Systems, IROS'94*, 1994.
13. N. Nilsson. Shakey the robot. Technical Note 323, SRI AI center, 1984.
14. Richard S. Sutton. Reinforcement learning architectures for animats. In Jean-Arcady Meyer and Stewart W. Wilson, editors, *Proceedings of the First International Conference on Simulation of Adaptive Behavior*. MIT Press, Cambridge, Massachusetts, 1990.

Neural Networks for Manipulator Path Planning

Margit Sturm*

Siemens AG, Corporate Technology, Department Information and Communication,
D-81730 Munich

Abstract In order to manipulate objects, robot arms need to approach

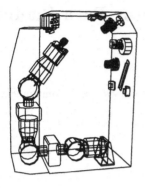 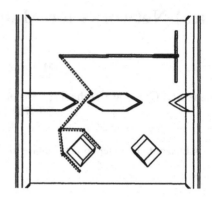

Figure1. Left: ROTEX: The 6-DOF manipulator used in the D2 space mission; Right: a 10-DOF gripper used for simulation purposes.

be transformed to polynomial surfaces in configuration space. This is due to transcentendal angle equations. However, path planning based on a polynomial surface representation is extremely difficult. A representation of free configuration space which simplifies path planning is thus a crutial point. Figure 2 gives an example of a toy manipulator and the surrounding objects at left and the corresponding configuration space at right.

Section 2 reviews the essential classes of path planning algorithms briefly. Section 3 presents the combination of an adaptive neural network representation of free space with graph-based path planning methods. Results and conclusion follow in sections 4 and 5. For a detailed description see [5].

2 Path Planning Algorithms

In order to learn about the free configuration space, i.e. to build a model of the configuration space, collision checks can be performed. The collision check of a certain configuration is a basic operation of any path planning algorithm. Concerning computational costs, it is a very expensive one: A collision check requires an analytical computation of whether any of the manipulator links intersect with any of the obstacles. Two main streams for configuration space modeling based on collision checks have emerged: Cell decomposition methods and the construction of a graph. [7] gives a thorough overview of manipulator path planning methods.

2.1 Cell Decomposition Methods

Cell decomposition means that the configuration space is decomposed regularly into hyper-cubic cells, which will be marked off-line as free cells or as obstacle cells. A cell ist generally defined as obstacle cell if the manipulator collides at

Figure2. Left: A two-jointed toy manipulator (joint angles Θ_1 and Θ_2) with rectangular joints. The robot is shown both in a start position S (solid rectangles) and in a goal position Z (dotted rectangles). $\Theta_1 = 0$ when the first joint heads downwards. $\Theta_2 = 0$ when the second joint is stretched out. One possible end effector movement from S to Z is along the bold, curved line. Right: The corresponding configuration space with configuration obstacles drawn in black. The black regions at the left and right border e.g. result from the quader below the base of the robot.

the configuration in the center of the cell. Otherwise, a cell is in free space per definition.

Path planning to a certain goal cell is mostly realized as a diffusion process on the grid of cells: Analog to a wave front expanding from the goal cell, the manhattan distance in the grid from each cell to the goal cell is calculated. As soon as the start cell will be reached, a path can be found by searching for the negative gradient of the stored distances.

Clearly, cell decomposition only *approximates* the configuration space. It has to be a fairly coarse approximation, since the number of cells is exponential in die number of DOFs. Ongoing research aims at breaking down the curse of dimensions. PartiGame [8] for example generates higher resolutions of the grid dynamically in critical regions of the configuration space. Whenever a goal cannot be reached on the current grid, a smart exploration strategy starts and refines the grid. However, due to the exploration, an immense number of collision checks are necessary on-line. This restricts the use of PartiGame to simply modeled manipulators and obstacles.

2.2 Graph Construction Methods

An interesting alternative is the representation of free space in a graph. Its vertices are configurations, its edges collision-free straight paths between the two configurations. Once a graph has been constructed, path planning can be reduced to finding a collision-free connection from start and goal to vertices the graph, followed by a graph search from the start vertex to the goal vertex.

The advantage of graphs compared to cell decompositions is that the number of their nodes is not necessarily exponential in the dimension of the space. Furthermore, the graph construction algorithm can e.g. easily enforce that the number of nodes in a region reflects the local clutter of the configuration space [4].

The major drawback of graph-based planning are the immense computational costs for collision checks along potential edges of the graph. [4] state that their graph construction is only feasible for links of manipulators being modeled as lines instead of cuboids, and objects being modeled very roughly by a very few facets.

3   The Ellipsoidal Map: Combining Neural Networks and Graph-Based Techniques

Since the crucial point with graph construction methods is the number of edges to be checked for collision, the following concept seems promising: Store any path which is known to be collision-free, wherever this knowledge comes from, and however the path is like, in a way that a maximum of information about free space is extracted from this path while memory is used very sparingly, and thereby build a graph of free space. In other words: Generalize from any path to assumed free space. This generalization has been achieved by developing the *Ellipsoidal Map*, a graph of connected ellipsoids. The ellipsoids model the assumed free space along paths. The edges in this graph are labelled with "transition" configuration being a good subgoal when going from inside one ellipsoid into a neighbor's. The choice of ellipsoids has several reasons: Ellipsoids can on the one hand model paths fairly good (see figure 3, left), and are on the other hand flexible in orientation and can therefore model larger regions in free space appropriately. Their shape, position and orientation can easily be modeled by a matrix.

Figure3. The Ellipsoidal Map after the first (left), the third (middle) and the 50th (right) path stored. The basic assuption is that there is some free space along paths. The free space is modelled by adaptive ellipoids growing along the path.

Since generalizing from example data is the core of neural networks, we implemented an ellipsoid as the receptive field of a neuron. We use the classical hyper-RBF neuron [9] known from function approximation. Its activation function is defined as

$$d_i : x \in \mathbf{R}^n \mapsto \|M_i(x - x_i)\|_2 \in \mathbf{R}, \tag{1}$$

where $\|.\|_2$ denotes the usual Euclidian norm $\|x\|_2 = \sqrt{x^T x}$, M_i is a positive definite matrix $M_i \in \mathbf{R}^{n \times n}$ and x_i denotes the receptive field's center $x_i \in \mathbf{R}^n$.

3.1 Adapting the Ellipsoidal Map to Example Paths

First the path is discretized into small path "steps". Next, the map is sequentially adapted to the single path steps. This is done by finding the neuron which can be adapted best[4]. If none can be adapted reasonably to match, a new neuron is created. The adaptation of a neuron to a path step is reduced to adapting it to both the first and the last configuration of the step. If these two points are properly represented by the neuron, so is the whole path step—due to the convexity of the ellipsoidal shape.

Adapting an existing ellipsoid If a point is already inside the ellipsoid, nothing is done. Otherwise, the idea is to move the ellipsoid's center towards the point and then "stretch" the ellipsoid along the movement direction such that the old border point in the opposite direction remains a border point.

To be more explicit, let p be the point to adapt to, M_i be the old transformation matrix and x_i be the old center. Then the new center is $x'_i := x_i + \beta(p - x_i)$, where β determines how far the motion goes. The new transformation matrix is given as $M'_i := (E_n + (\alpha - 1)aa^T)M_i$, with $a := \frac{M_i(p - x_i)}{\|M_i(p - x_i)\|_2}$. It follows that $\alpha := 1/(1 + \|\beta M_i(p - x_i)\|_2)$. Note that enlarging the ellipsoid means that its transformation matrix makes the vectors shorter, therefore $\alpha < 1$.

What has been left out is the determination of β, i.e. how far to move the ellipsoid. Here the following simple idea, borrowed from physics, is used: With each point, a unit mass is associated. The center of the ellipsoid is chosen such that it is the center of mass of all points the ellipsoid was adapted to. For this purpose, a mass m_i is given to each neuron. We get $\beta := 1/(m_i + 1)$ and the new mass is $m'_i := m_i + 1$. Also, the adaptability of a neuron may be reduced or increased by changing its mass. This adaptation algorithm realizes the generalization from paths to assumed free space, which is heuristic in nature. Thus, collisions on a generated path might occur. They lead to a retraction of the corresponding ellipsoid from the collision point, which is realized exactly inverse to the enlargement of ellipsoids.

---

[4] In other existing unsupervised learning architectures (e.g. [6]), the best-matching unit is also the "best-adaptable" one. This is not true for ellipsoids. See [1] for the exact definition of our attribute "best-adaptable".

Creating a new ellipsoid The initial ellipsoidal receptive field will simply have a principal axis along the path step, such that both end-points of the step lie on the border. The remaining perpendicular axes are initialized with a user-specified width ρ_0. The mass is initialized as $m_i := 2$, taking into account the two points represented.

Updating the neighborhood structure As mentioned, the neurons are connected according to their neighborhood structure. By observing when the best-matching neuron changes, the information is gained which neurons have "neighboring" receptive fields. Such neighboring neurons will be connected and a configuration will be associated with the connection. This configuration is averaged from all corresponding transition configurations (where the best-matching neuron changes) observed in the example paths.

3.2 Path Planning

To generate a path for a given task, the graph is used by finding the best-matching neurons for the start and goal configurations and generating a path via the transition points according to the connectivity structure of these neurons. If a generated path leads to a collision, the ellipsoidal graph gets adapted by shrinking the responsible neurons' receptive fields and possibly deleting connections between neurons.

When confronted with a new path planning task, the graph of ellipsoids can first be seen as a background process which collects information contained in collision-free paths. Very soon, it gets able to plan paths for more and more tasks, while paths can still be stored and collision information can be used to correct the graph.

An exploration component [11] was realized in order to also reach goals for which paths cannot yet be found in the *Ellipsoidal Map*. It aims at connecting unconnected components of the graph by as short paths as possible, which then have to be checked for collisions. [1] describes the *Ellipsoidal Map* in more detail.

Another recent combination of neural network techniques and graphs can be found in [3].

4 Simulation Results

We will briefly report on planning results concerning the ROTEX manipulator. For an indeep study of different scenario, and a thorough comparison to other research, we refer to [5]. A brief comparison is not possible, since the different approaches are all specialized to different scenarios, such as line or cuboid manipulator links, simple or complex objects, static or dynamic environments, the number of links.

Path planning for the ROTEX manipulator was started from scratch with the empty *Ellipsoidal Map*. Several epochs of 100 planning tasks to random goals each were performed. For each epoch, the average rate of successfully planned paths was measured. It is denoted as "success per epoch" in figure 4. Furthermore, the "exploration rate" tells us how often exploration had to be initiated in order to find a path to the goal. On top, the "total success rate" monitors the average success rate of all planning attempts.

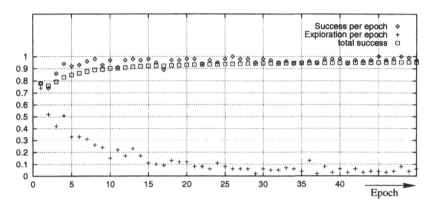

Figure4. Evolution of the Ellipsoidal Map for the ROTEX manipulator

A success rate of 85% was already reached in the third epoch, which is far more than the 20% start/goal-pairs which can be trivially connected by a straight line. However, 100% can never be guaranteed, since the configuration model is an approximative one, and planning is heuristic. The computation time is only 2.5 seconds[5] even for the first epoch, which is highly satisfactoy compared to other approaches.

5 Conclusion

The combination of neural networks to represent free space efficiently and graph theoretic methods to capture the connectivity of regions in free space has some considerable properties:

The curse of dimensions, onhand at cell decomposition methods, gets dissolved by modeling free space—and only free space—adaptively by ellipsoids. The connectivity of ellipsoidal regions is captured in a graph, opening the possibility to use efficient graph search methods to plan paths.

The adaptive representation of free space is achieved by storing collision-free paths in a generalizing fashion in the so-called *Ellipsoidal Map*. Either existing ellipsoids grow along each stored path, or, whenever a path is too far from ellipsoidal regions, new ellipsoids get inserted. Technically, the adaptive of ellipsoids are realized as generalized radial basis functions (RBF) [10], well known in the area of artificial neural networks. Ellipsoids along the same path get connected by edges in a graph. Path planning maps start and goal configuration to nodes

---

[5] on a Sun SPARCstation 20 (80.1 SPECfloat92; 76.9 SPECint92)

in the graph, which is realized by the neural activation of the nodes. Afterwards, an A^* graph search [2] results a path to the goal.

6 Acknowledgement

This research was conducted at Professor Dr. Dr. h.c. W. Brauer's lab at the Technical University Munich. The author wishes to thank Dr. Brauer for the fruitful and valuable discussions as well as for the highly motivating atmosphere at his lab.

References

[1] Brychcy, T. , Kinder, M.: A neural network inspired architecture for robot motion planning. In Bulsari, A. , Kallio, S. (Hrsg.), *Engineering Applications of Artificial Neural Networks: Proceedings of the International Conference EANN '95, 21-23 August 1995, Otaniemi/Helsinki, Finland.* Finnish Artificial Intelligence Society, 1995, S. 103-110.

[2] Dijkstra, E.: A note on two problems in connection with graphs. *Numerische Mathematik, Bd. 1* [1959], S. 269-271.

[3] Eldracher, M.: *Planung kinematischer Trajektorien für Manipulatoren mit Hilfe von Subzielen und neuronalen Netzen.* Dissertation, Technische Universität München, München 1995.

[4] Kavraki, L. , Latombe, J.-C.: Randomized preprocessing of configuration space for fast path planning. In *1994 IEEE International Conference on Robotics and Automation, San Diego,* 1994, S. 2138-2145.

[5] Kinder, M.: *Pfadplanung für Manipulatoren in komplexen Umgebungen mittels generalisierender Pfadspeicherung in Ellipsoidkarten.* Reihe 8: Meß-, Steuerungs- und Regelungstechnik, Nr. 580, VDI Verlag, Düsseldorf 1996. in German.

[6] Kohonen, T.: *Self-Organization and Associative Memory.* 2. Auflage. Springer, Berlin, Heidelberg, New York, London, Paris, Tokyo 1988.

[7] Latombe, J.-C.: *Robot Motion Planning.* 3. Auflage. Kluwer Academic Press, Boston 1991.

[8] Moore, A. W.: The partigame algorithm for variable resolution reinforcement learning in multidimensional statespaces. In *Neural Information Processing Systems 6.* Morgan Kaufmann, 1994, S. 711-718.

[9] Poggio, T. , Girosi, F.: Networks for Approximation and Learning. In *Proceedings of the IEEE*, Bd. 78, 1990, S. 1481-1497.

[10] Powell, M.: Radial basis functions for multivariable interpolation: A review. In *IMA conference on "Algorithms for the Approximation of Functions and Data".* RMCS Shrivenham, 1985.

[11] Stutz, C.: Pfadplanung für Manipulatoren durch Aufbau eines Graphen aus Ellipsoiden mit Hilfe von Explorationsmethoden. Diplomarbeit, Institut für Informatik, Technische Universität München 1995.

Path Planning Using a Subgoal Graph

Martin Eldracher and Thomas Pic

Fakultät für Informatik, Technische Universität München, 80290 München, Germany

Abstract This article is concerned with generation of kinematic trajectories for manipulators. For quick planning we use a graph-based
algorithm that already allows to plan at least some motions from the
beginning of the graph construction process, and hence omits long preprocessing phases. Unless specific tasks are given, we use random configurations for incremental graph construction. The graph is constructed
in configuration-space of manipulators. Its nodes serve as subgoals and
its edges as collision free sub-trajectories for planning new, unknown trajectories. We show the high performance of this approach with respect to
preprocessing and trajectory generation time, as well as planning success
in a realistic simulation of a real world manipulator task.

1 Introduction

Our task is to plan collision-free paths (trajectories) connecting arbitrary start-
and end-positions of an industrial robot (manipulator) in an previously unknown
environment (see e.g. [6, 3]). Since optimization can be performed independently
[2, 11], we aim at quick planning of any collision-free trajectory, but not on
optimal paths with respect to smoothness or length of the path. Usually in
robotics tasks are not given in (work-space) positions but in configurations in
the manipulator's configuration-space. The calculation of a configuration that
brings the manipulator (or better its tool-center-point) on a certain position
can be calculated using the inverse kinematics[1]. Given work-space obstacles, the
computation of the configuration-space obstacles is exponential in the dimension
of configuration-space and polynomial in both the degree of the polynomials
describing the obstacles in work-space and the number of these polynomials
[8]. Hence it is computationally not feasible to compute in advance a complete
model with reasonable accuracy. In dynamically changing environments this is
even theoretically impossible. Therefore information for any planning must be
produced by sensors during operation. The only available, reasonably priced
sensor is a force-torque-sensor to be integrated into each joint of the manipulator.
The force-torque-sensor indicates whether the manipulator hits an obstacle, i.e.
whether the current configuration is collision free. Using only this information,
calculated in the manipulator simulation, we present an approach that constructs
a subgoal-graph in configuration-space $\mathcal{C}$ using random configurations. To plan a
trajectory for arbitrary start and goal configurations, only sub-trajectories from

---

[1] In general there is no algebraic solution for the inverse kinematics of arbitrary manipulators, however, closed formulas exist for nowadays industrially used manipulators.

start and goal to one of the subgoals must be found. The rest of the trajectory is generated using graph search methods as A^*, without further sensor-information required. In that way we achieve quick trajectory generation with only using our graph and inspecting one-dimensional sub-spaces by simulation of straight line connections between configurations, but without computing a complete model.

2 Subgoal-Graph Construction

Before describing the construction of the subgoal-graph, we need two prerequisites. First a definition to distinguish whether we already know how to move from one to another specific configuration, what we call *connected*. Second a strategy how to extend our graph using knowledge about already connected configurations.

First, if a configuration $c_2 \in C$ can be reached collision-free from a configuration $c_1 \in C$ using a straight line in configuration-space, we say c_1 is *connected* to c_2, and vice versa. We search a set $\mathcal{SG}$ of *subgoals* sg in free(-configuration)-space C_{free} that is as small as possible with properties:

1. Any configuration $c \in C_{free}$ is connected to at least one subgoal $sg \in \mathcal{SG}$, a node in the subgoal-graph.
2. Each $sg_1 \in \mathcal{SG}$ is connected to some other $sg_2 \in \mathcal{SG}$, what is denoted with an edge between sg_1 and sg_2 in the subgoal-graph.

Second, during construction of the subgoal-graph, each subgoal $sg_i \in \mathcal{SG}$ is provided with a set $\mathcal{K}_i$ of *candidates* $k \in C_{free}$ that are connected to their subgoal. Candidates serve to extend the subgoal-graph. Graph construction basically is governed by three parameters: the number anz_{it} of random configurations to use for the initial graph construction[2], the number anz_{cand} of candidates for each subgoal, and the strategy to decide whether a new configuration will be included in the candidate set $\mathcal{K}_i$ for the Euclidean nearest subgoal sg_i. Two strategies will be evaluated to decide whether a new configuration replaces an old candidate:

- "distance (d)":
  Candidates for sg_i have the largest Euclidean distance to sg_i.
- "angle sum times distance (a*d)":
  Candidates for sg_i have the largest product of Euclidean distance to sg_i and angle[3] sums to all other candidates within $\mathcal{K}_i$.

If a candidate is inserted into the subgoal-graph, both strategies maximally extend the graph into areas that are not-modeled up to now. Furthermore, strategy "(a*d)" tries to maximally distribute the candidates in C_{free}.

For graph construction first a random configuration is defined to be the subgoal-graph. Then further random configurations are either used to start a

---

[2] Since we use an incremental algorithm, we use this parameter for speed-up, but can continue the construction of the graph whenever necessary.

[3] Angles between candidates $k \in \mathcal{K}_i$ are computed with respect to the subgoal sg_i.

new component of the subgoal-graph, if they are not connected to the current graph[4], or they are possibly inserted as candidates to a subgoal of the current subgoal-graph following the chosen strategy. Finally we merge all components, if this is possible with our current knowledge, at all.

The graph construction follows the heuristics described below:

Subgoal Graph Construction Algorithm

1. Define random configuration sg $\in \mathcal{C}_{free}$ as set of subgoals: $\mathcal{SG} := \{\text{sg}\}$
2. While |generated random configurations| $< anz_{it}$ do:
   (a) Choose random configuration $c \in \mathcal{C}_{free}$.
   (b) Test if c is connected to any subgoal sg $\in \mathcal{SG}$
   (c) Case 1: c is connected to at least one subgoal sg $\in \mathcal{SG}$.
       - Find subgoal sg_i with smallest Euclidean distance.
       - Eventually store c as candidate in $\mathcal{K}_i$ according chosen strategy.
   (d) Case 2: c is not connected to any subgoal sg $\in \mathcal{SG}$.
       - Test if c connected to any candidate $k \in \mathcal{K} := \bigcup \mathcal{K}_i$
       - If yes: Insert candidate in subgoal-set, $\mathcal{SG} := \mathcal{SG} \cup \{k\}$. Store c as candidate for $k \in \mathcal{SG}$. Delete k from $\mathcal{K}$.
       - If no: Start a new component in the set $\mathcal{SG}$ with c.
3. Try to merge components in $\mathcal{SG}$ (take all candidates and subgoals instead of random configurations and perform the upper loop for each of them)[5].

3   Results

The *task* is to generate collision free trajectories for arbitrary start-goal-combinations. We use two example environments. A 2-dof[6] environment (Fig. 1) to illustrate some basic concepts, and a 6-dof environment (Fig. 2), with manipulator ROTEX in its original work-cell of the german D2 space mission, which is extremely narrow, making trajectory generation very difficult.

Figure 3 shows results in configuration-space of Figure 1 with both strategies for candidate insertion (see Section 2) after graph construction with 1000 random configurations. Squares denote subgoals, and circles denote candidates. Candidates are connected to their subgoals. Despite the different candidate distribution, the constructed graphs are nearly equal.

Table 1 shows results for graph construction in ROTEX environment with different parameters. Columns "anz_{it}", "anz_{cand}", and "strat" give the number of random configurations, candidates, and the strategy, respectively. Column "#components" shows the number of subgoal-graph components after (before) merging the graph components. Column "#sg" gives the number of subgoals

---

[4] Introducing several components into the subgoal-graph is more efficient than disregarding this random configuration. Using a real manipulator instead of simulation, we would have to disregard this configuration as in Eldracher [4]. However, apart from loosing some efficiency the basic algorithm stays the same.

[5] Should this not work completely, only the biggest component will be retained.

[6] "dof" denotes "degrees of freedom". In our examples dof is always equal to the number of joints, or the dimension of configuration-space, respectively.

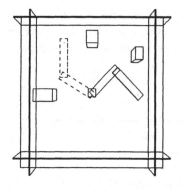

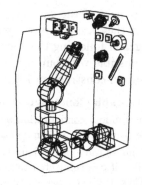

Figure1. *2-dof example environment.*   **Figure2.** *6-dof ROTEX environment.*

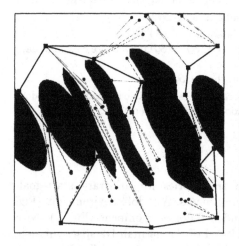 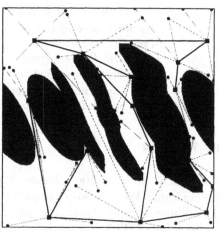

Figure3. *Results with strategy "d" (left) and "a∗d" (right) for graph construction with 1000 random configurations and four candidates.*

after (before) merging. Column "success" gives first the number of random test start-goal-combinations connected to one component of the subgoal-graph only using subgoals, that is the number of solved tasks[7]. The second number shows the number of additionally solved tasks also using the candidates. The last number gives not solved tasks. Column "time" gives the time for graph construction/merging in seconds on a HP Series 9000 Model 720 in multi-user operation.

Less candidates generate more components of the subgoal-graph before merging, because there are less candidates that can connect a random configuration to an existing component. After merging no significant differences remain. Especially with fewer candidates, the simpler strategy "d" needs more subgoals to model the whole configuration-space. This is mainly a result of the many subgoal-graph components that have to be merged using many additional subgoals. After

---

[7] A collision free trajectory is found for an arbitrary start-goal-combination.

5000	2	a∗d	2 (20)	58 (50)	993/4/3	1953s/127s
5000	4	a∗d	1 (17)	55 (50)	995/4/1	2043s/123s
5000	6	a∗d	1 (15)	55 (50)	996/4/0	1857s/ 90s
5000	8	a∗d	1 (14)	53 (47)	994/6/0	1905s/ 19s
5000	10	a∗d	1 (14)	53 (47)	992/8/0	1911s/100s

Table1. *Results of the graph construction in ROTEX environment for different numbers of candidates and both candidate insertion strategies.*

subgoal-graph construction with more than two candidates, always more than 99% of the test tasks are solved. Also using the already produced candidates this ratio rises to the optimum of 100%. Strategy "a∗d" seems to be a little bit better with respect to less components of the subgoal-graph, less subgoals, and higher success ratios. However, the differences are not significant. There is only one significant difference using two candidates and strategy "d". But additional experiments with different random configurations show that results of the same quality as with more candidates can be reached. Thus the only conclusion that must be drawn is that two candidates are too few in order to guarantee a good subgoal-graph. If more than two candidates are allowed, the algorithm is insensitive to changes in the parameters. Given the graph, the generation of a trajectory only takes some tenths of a second.

4 Speedup Using Neural Preprocessing

The graph construction process (Section 2) should be speeded up, but in no case any inexactness from the neural preprocessing may be introduced to trajectory generation. The above algorithm tests possible connections to all subgoals for each new random configuration. For the Euclidean nearest connected subgoal the current random configuration may be inserted as a candidate[8]. If some perfect storage correctly told us which subgoal is the nearest connected, we would not need any further slow, simulation intensive search for a connected subgoal[9].

---

[8] This is the average case (Case (1) in algorithm below) after some ten configurations are already used to construct the graph. In the worst case also all candidates have to be tested.

[9] In order to get speed up not only during graph construction but also when using the graph for trajectory planning, we need storage that can be trained online and incrementally.

As storage we use a slightly modified CMAC [1, 10], which is a general, locally generalizing function approximator. CMAC learns to map each configuration $c \in C_{free}$ on to a connected subgoal sg $\in SG$ with small Euclidean distance. Since CMAC is not perfect, we have to verify its information. If CMAC's information is correct, we can stop the expensive simulations. If CMAC is wrong, in comparison to our first algorithm only the order of testing the subgoals is changed but not the number of subgoals to test.

Basically only two things must be changed in the graph construction algorithm. First, we have to incorporate CMAC training. Second, the first subgoal that is tested for each random configuration is determined by CMAC. The modified algorithm therefore is:

Subgoal Graph Construction with Neural Preprocessing

1. Define random configuration sg $\in C_{free}$ as set of subgoals: $SG := \{sg\}$
2. While |generated random configurations| $< anz_{it}$ do:
   (a) Choose random configuration $c \in C_{free}$.
      Let sg_{CMAC} be the output of CMAC for input c.
      Let $sg_i \in SG$ be the subgoal with smallest Euclidean distance to sg_{CMAC}.
   (b) Case 1: c is connected to sg_i.
      − Verify that c is connected to subgoal sg_i
      − Eventually store c as candidate in K_i according chosen strategy.
      − Train CMAC with example $c \mapsto sg_i$.
   (c) Case 2: c not connected to sg_i but to some other subgoal sg $\in SG \setminus \{sg_i\}$.
      − Test if c is connected to any subgoal $sg_i \in SG$
      − Find connected subgoal sg_j with smallest Euclidean distance to c.
      − Eventually store c as candidate in K_j according chosen strategy.
      − Train CMAC with example $c \mapsto sg_j$.
   (d) Case 3: c is not connected to any subgoal sg $\in SG$.
      − Test if c connected to any candidate $k \in K := \bigcup K_i$
      − If yes: Insert candidate in subgoal-set, $SG := SG \cup \{k\}$. Store c as candidate for $k \in SG$. Delete k from K. Train CMAC with $c \mapsto k$.
      − If no: Start a new component in the set SG with c. Train CMAC with $c \mapsto c$.
3. Try to merge components in SG.

The speed up is determined by the quality of CMAC mapping and the number of subgoals in the graph. Neural preprocessing accelerated the algorithm by a factor of ten in the 2-dof environment. A factor of four was reached for ROTEX, which is harder to train with CMAC[10]. After a better implementation of the graph construction algorithm the versions with and without neural preprocessing are now nearly equally fast for ROTEX. But for more complex environments (e.g. a 10-dof gripper [7]) still a speed up of nearly 30% is obtained [9]. That is, the higher dimensional and the more cluttered an environment is, the more advantage can be drawn from neural preprocessing.

---

[10] Hence a smaller generalization must be used. Besides more subgoals are inserted, therefore CMAC must change its mapping more often. That is, during training the mapping more often is wrong, no speed up is obtained for this step.

5 Discussion

Usually classical graph based algorithms are based on geometrical preconditions that do not hold for higher dimensional spaces or are difficult to calculate. Our randomized approach does not use any preconditions. Our approach even does not need to take into account any informations about the manipulator domain, and can be applied to arbitrary process spaces as well.

In dynamic environments most classical algorithms require a complete recomputation of all configuration-space obstacles even for small changes in configuration-space, unless additional knowledge, e.g. the exact movement of all obstacles, is used. In comparison, our graph can be changed online while collecting sensor information during operation of the planner; only parts of the configuration-space must be reconstructed. Which parts can be decided via direct sensor information, whenever the manipulator tries to use a trajectory that is erroneously thought to be collision free. The most simple form of adaption is to delete edges with collisions and keep the graph working using the construction process also during the trajectory planning phase.

In our approach only some thousand random configurations (and one dimensional sub-spaces between them) must be tested, in order to solve arbitrary tasks, while most of the configuration-space must not be regarded at all. This is a substantial difference to classical approaches, which assume to know exactly the work-space geometry in order to compute configuration-space. We base our exploration purely on local sensor information from force-torque-sensors that are technically available. This yields further difficulties, but seems to be more realistic. Nevertheless, we solve realistic 6-dof environments, while classical approaches as e.g. cell decomposition methods can only be used up to 4-dof environments [8].

We need approximately half an hour to completely construct a graph for ROTEX[11]. But most of the time in our algorithm is used for collision checking. Kavraki and Latombe [7] only need some hundred seconds to build up a graph with some 10,000 nodes for trajectory generation for a 10-dof manipulator in a two-dimensional work-space. This can be achieved for two-dimensional work-spaces via computing in advance all possible collisions, but inherently forbids applications in dynamic environments. Admitting complexity problems for three dimensional work-spaces, furthermore each joint angle is discretized in only 128 steps and the manipulator has no spatial extension, which both speed up collision checking significantly. To guarantee collision free continuous trajectories we perform simulations with spatially extended manipulators. Horsch et. al. [5] also simulate continuous trajectories with spatially extended obstacles. They give times around six hours for graph construction for a manipulator similar to ROTEX. That is, to reach a 100% solving ratio, our approach uses either much less random configurations, or is quicker compared to similar approaches. However, there is a main difference between our approach and Kavraki and Latombe's [7],

---

[11] Generally only 1500 instead of 5000 random configurations suffice to construct the graph, yielding construction times of approximately 15 minutes.

which first generates some thousand random configurations and construct the graph afterwards: Our approach is incremental, we extend the graph with each new random configuration. So we can plan some trajectories from the first random configuration on, and intermit planning and graph construction. This is not only interesting for improving the graph during operation in static environments, but also a prerequisite for adaptive modeling in dynamic environments.

References

1. J.S. Albus, editor. *Brains, Behaviour, and Robotics*. Byte Books, 1981.
2. S. Berchtold and B. Glavina. A scalable optimizer for automatically generated manipulator motions. In *Proc. of IEEE/RSJ/GI Int. Conf. on Intelligent Robots and Systems IROS-94*, pages 1796–1802, Munich, Germany, September 1994.
3. A.P. del Pobil and M.A. Serna. *Spatial Representation and Motion Planning*, volume 1014 of *Lecture Notes in Computer Sciences*. Springer, Berlin, 1995.
4. M. Eldracher. Neural subgoal generation with subgoal graph: An approach. In *World Congress on Neural Networks WCNN-94, San Diego*, pages II-142 – II-146. Lawrence Erlbaum Associates, Inc., Publishers, Hillsdale, June 1994.
5. Th. Horsch, F. Schwarz, and H. Tolle. Motion planning with many degrees of freedom – random reflections at c-space obstacles. In *1994 IEEE International Conference on Robotics and Automation, San Diego*, pages 3318–3323, 1994.
6. Y.K. Hwang and N. Ahuja. Gross motion planning. a survey. *ACM Computing Surveys*, 3(24):219–291, 1992.
7. L. Kavraki and J.C. Latombe. Randomized preprocessing of configuration space for fast path planning. In *1994 IEEE International Conference on Robotics and Automation, San Diego*, pages 2138–2145, 1994.
8. J.C. Latombe. *Robot Motion Planning*. Kluwer Academic Press, Boston, 1991.
9. Th. Pic. Versuche zur neuronalen Subzielgenerierung. Fortgeschrittenenpraktikum, Prof. Dr. Brauer, October 1994. Technische Universität München.
10. H. Tolle and E. Ersü. *Neurocontrol. Learning Control Systems Inspired by Neuronal Architectures and Human Problem Solving Strategies*, volume 172 of *Lecture Notes in Control and Information Sciences*. Springer, Berlin, 1992.
11. O. v. Stryk. *Numerische Lösung optimaler Steuerungsprobleme: Diskretisierung, Parameteroptimierung und Berechnung der adjungierten Variablen*. PhD thesis, Mathematisches Institut, Technische Universität München, 1994.

A Nonlinear Markovian Characterization of Time Series Using Neural Networks

Christian Schittenkopf[1,2] and Gustavo Deco[1]

[1] Siemens AG, Corporate Technology, Dept. ZT IK 4
Otto-Hahn-Ring 6, 81730 Munich, Germany
[2] Technische Universität München
Arcisstraße 21, 80290 Munich, Germany

Abstract. The goal of our approach is the determination of the order of the Markov process which explains the statistical dependencies of an observed time series. Our method measures the information flow of the time series indirectly via higher order cumulants considering linear and nonlinear correlations. The main point of our method, which is an extension of the method of surrogate data, is that the time series is tested against a hierarchy of nonlinear Markov processes, whose probability densities are estimated by neural networks.

1 Introduction

The application of concepts from information theory has been a very fruitful approach to the analysis of time series for nearly two decades. The recently introduced concept of information flow [3] measures the decay of linear and nonlinear statistical dependencies between the entire past and the future of a time series. The information flow is characterized by the conditional entropy which generalizes the Kolmogorov-Sinai entropy to the case of observing the uncertainty for more than one step into the future. Due to the problems in the empirical estimation of the involved entropies, a cumulant-based measure of the loss of statistical correlations, which is easy to calculate, will be used as the discriminating statistic in the framework of the method of surrogate data [9]. This quantization of statistical dependencies by higher order cumulants [2] is also preferable from the point of view that experimental time series are usually short and noisy.

In this paper we extend the method of surrogate data to study the information flow of a time series. The extension is twofold: First, a *hierarchy* of null hypotheses corresponding to nonlinear Markov processes of increasing order is tested. Therefore our surrogate data sets approximate the linear and nonlinear correlations of the time series with increasing accuracy. The probability density functions of the nonlinear Markov processes are estimated by neural networks. Secondly, the discriminating statistic, which measures the statistical dependencies between the past and the future of a time series in Fourier space, is not a single number but a function, namely the *cumulant-based information flow*. Our method is iterative in the following sense: Whenever a null hypothesis is rejected, a new Markov process (of higher order), which approximates the information flow of the time series in a better way, can be generated and tested.

In section 2 we define cumulant-based measures of statistical dependence which measure the information flow indirectly. The iterative procedure for testing nonlinear Markov processes is explained in section 3. Section 4 describes our experimental results. We conclude in section 5.

2 Measures of Statistical Dependence

Given a time series $\{x_t\}, t = 1, 2, \ldots, N$ a meaningful measure of the statistical dependencies (linear and nonlinear) between n subsequent observations of the time series and the point which is r time steps into the future (look-ahead r), can be formulated in Fourier space [2, 8] as

$$m(r) = \sum_{i_1=1}^{n} \mathcal{K}_{i_1 n+r}^2 + \sum_{i_1=1}^{n} \sum_{i_2=i_1}^{n+r} \mathcal{K}_{i_1 i_2 n+r}^2 + \sum_{i_1=1}^{n} \sum_{i_2=i_1}^{n+r} \sum_{i_3=i_2}^{n+r} \mathcal{K}_{i_1 i_2 i_3 n+r}^2 \quad (1)$$

where $\mathcal{K}_{i_1 \ldots i_j}$ denotes a cumulant of order j [5]. Calculating $m(r), r = 1, 2, \ldots$ we obtain a cumulant-based characterization of the information flow of the time series because we measure the decay of all kinds of correlations as a function of the look-ahead r. The minimal value of $m(r)$, i. e. $m(r) = 0$, indicates statistical independence and increasing positive values of $m(r)$ express increasing dependencies in the time series. For practical purposes n must be limited to a finite value. In principle, one would have to consider the whole past of the time series $(n \to \infty)$. If the time series is shifted so that it has a mean value of zero, the cumulants in Eq. (1) are given by

$$\mathcal{K}_{i_1 i_2} = C_{i_1 i_2}, \mathcal{K}_{i_1 i_2 i_3} = C_{i_1 i_2 i_3}, \quad (2)$$

$$\mathcal{K}_{i_1 i_2 i_3 i_4} = C_{i_1 i_2 i_3 i_4} - C_{i_1 i_2} C_{i_3 i_4} - C_{i_1 i_3} C_{i_2 i_4} - C_{i_1 i_4} C_{i_2 i_3} \quad (3)$$

where the moments $C_{i_1 \ldots i_j}$ of order j can be estimated empirically by

$$C_{i_1 \ldots i_j} = \frac{1}{N - n - r + 1} \sum_{t=0}^{N-n-r} x_{t+i_1} \ldots x_{t+i_j}. \quad (4)$$

Note that the cumulants of order three and four take also nonlinear dependencies of the time series into account. More details concerning computational aspects will be given in section 4.

3 Markovian Characterization

3.1 The Method of Surrogate Data

Since the publication of the paper of Theiler et al. [9] statistical hypothesis testing has become one of the most frequently used techniques in the analysis of time series. The first step is to make an assumption about the time series, for example, that it is white noise or that all statistical dependencies are linear or any potential property of the time series which we are interested in. This assumption is called *null hypothesis* and our goal is to test it. The second step is to generate several new "versions" of the time series (the *surrogate data sets*) which have the hypothesized property. For example, if we test for white noise the surrogate data sets are generated by shuffling the time series the temporal order of which is destroyed. If we test for linearity the surrogate data sets are constructed to have the same Fourier spectrum as the time series. The final step is to calculate a so-called *discriminating statistic* for the original time series and for the surrogate data sets and to accept or reject the null hypothesis according to the *two-sample Student t test*: Let D_O and D_{S_i} denote the statistic computed for the time series and for the i-th surrogate data set, respectively. Estimating the mean value and the standard deviation by

$$\mu_S = \frac{1}{M}\sum_{i=1}^{M} D_{S_i} \text{ and } \sigma_S = \sqrt{\frac{1}{M-1}\sum_{i=1}^{M}(D_{S_i} - \mu_S)^2} \tag{5}$$

where M denotes the number of surrogate data sets, the random variable

$$t = \sqrt{\frac{M}{M+1}}\frac{\mu_S - D_O}{\sigma_S} \tag{6}$$

is t-distributed with $M-1$ degrees of freedom [1]. The result of the test (accepting or rejecting the null hypothesis) is correct with probability $1 - p$ only since M is finite. The probability p of an incorrect result is also called p-value and it is fixed (usually at 1, 5 or 10 %) before the test is made. The null hypothesis is rejected if the absolute value $|t|$ is larger than $\hat{t}$. The value of $\hat{t}$ depends on p and M and can be found in tables of t-distributions (cf. [1] for example). If the null hypothesis is rejected our assumption about the original time series was inadequate. More precisely, if the hypothesis is true, the probability of rejection is smaller than p. The following subsection tries to explain in detail our method including the new null hypothesis that the time series can be explained by a *nonlinear* Markov process.

3.2   A Hierarchy of Nonlinear Markov Processes

A schematic illustration of our method is depicted in Fig. 1. The first step is a preprocessing of the time series $\{x_t\}, t = 1, 2, \ldots, N$ to obtain a Gaussian marginal probability distribution [9]. For this purpose Gaussian random numbers $\{y_t\}, t = 1, 2, \ldots, N$ are computed and re-ordered so that the ranks of both time series agree. As a result, we get a new time series with a Gaussian distribution and with the same "temporal behavior" as the original time series. The next step is to determine the order m of the nonlinear Markov process which is supposed to approximate the information flow of the transformed time series $\{y_t\}$. If we do not have detailed knowledge about the original time series we will usually start with $m = 1$. We neglect the case $m = 0$ (white noise) in this paper since an appropriate test (with shuffled time series) was already described in [9]. In order to obtain the corresponding Markov process of order m two-layered feed-forward neural networks are trained to perform an estimation of the conditional density $\rho(y_t|y_{t-1}, \ldots, y_{t-m})$. In principle, any estimator for conditional densities can be used. However, it has been shown that nonlinear neural networks are very suitable for this purpose [6], and therefore, in this paper all density functions are approximated by

$$\rho(y_t|y_{t-1}, \ldots, y_{t-m}) = \sum_{h=1}^{k} \frac{u_h}{\sqrt{2\pi\sigma_h^2}} \exp\left(-\frac{(y_t - \mu_h)^2}{2\sigma_h^2}\right), \tag{7}$$

$$u_h = v_{h0} + \sum_{i=1}^{l} v_{hi} \tanh\left(w_{hi0} + \sum_{j=1}^{m} w_{hij} y_{t-j}\right), \tag{8}$$

$$\mu_h = \tilde{v}_{h0} + \sum_{i=1}^{l} \tilde{v}_{hi} \tanh\left(\tilde{w}_{hi0} + \sum_{j=1}^{m} \tilde{w}_{hij} y_{t-j}\right), \tag{9}$$

$$\sigma_h^2 = \hat{v}_{h0} + \sum_{i=1}^{l} \hat{v}_{hi} \tanh\left(\hat{w}_{hi0} + \sum_{j=1}^{m} \hat{w}_{hij} y_{t-j}\right) \tag{10}$$

where k denotes the number of Gaussians, l is the number of hidden neurons and $v_{hi}, w_{hij}, \tilde{v}_{hi}, \tilde{w}_{hij}, \hat{v}_{hi}$, and $\hat{w}_{hij}$ are the parameters of the networks. Additionally, the constraint $\sum_{h=1}^{k} u_h = 1$ holds to ensure that the sum (7) is really a density function. In other words, the conditional probability density is represented by a weighted sum of normal distributions whose weights, means, and variances are the output of different neural networks (multi-layer perceptrons, Eqs. (8) – (10)) to the m-dimensional input $(y_{t-m}, \ldots, y_{t-1})$. The training is performed following the maximum likelihood principle [7] in the sense that the parameters of the networks, i. e. $v_{hi}, w_{hij}, \tilde{v}_{hi}, \tilde{w}_{hij}, \hat{v}_{hi}, \hat{w}_{hij}, 1 \leq h \leq k, 1 \leq i \leq l, 1 \leq j \leq m$, are updated according to gradient descent on the log-likelihood function

$$-\sum_{t=m+1}^{N} \log \rho(y_t; u_1, \mu_1, \sigma_1^2, \ldots, u_k, \mu_k, \sigma_k^2). \tag{11}$$

We emphasize that the parameters are *nonlinear* functions of the input components, i. e. $u_1 = u_1(y_{t-m}, \ldots, y_{t-1}), \ldots$. It is also worth mentioning that the training procedure can be accelerated by second order methods and a line search routine since the calculated gradients are quite small.

After the training period the surrogate data sets $S_1, \ldots, S_M$ are generated in the following way: The first m values $(y_1, \ldots, y_m)$ of the time series are fed into the networks which predict the parameters of the probability density of the next value. The next value z_1 is drawn according to the corresponding probability distribution. Then the input vector $(y_2, \ldots, y_m, z_1)$ is fed into the networks

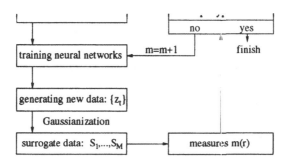

Fig. 1. A schematic illustration of the iterative procedure to detect the Markov order of a time series. See text for detailed explanation.

and the value z_2 is drawn. The iteration of this procedure yields a time series $\{z_t\}, t = 1, 2, \ldots, N$ which is Gaussianized and forms the first surrogate data set S_1. Consequently, S_1 is a Markovian approximation of the time series $\{y_t\}, t = 1, 2, \ldots, N$. An arbitrary number M of surrogate data sets can be generated by repeating this procedure. The surrogate data sets $S_1, \ldots, S_M$ are, of course, different because the values z_t are generated by a *stochastic* process, which is defined by the conditional probability densities, respectively. The next step of our method is to calculate the measures $m(r)$ for $\{y_t\}, S_1, \ldots, S_M$. If the hypothesis, that the nonlinear Markov process of order m is appropriate for modelling the time series, is rejected, the order is increased to $m + 1$ and the procedure is repeated (starting with the training of the neural networks).

4 Experimental Results

The described experiments are only a small subset of our numerical investigations. In this paper we present results for linear (autoregressive) and nonlinear (noisy chaotic) computer-generated and real-world time series (for more results cf. [8]). The measures of statistical dependence $m(r)$ (see Eq. (1)) were calculated using the parameter values $n = 10$ and $1 \leq r \leq 10$. In all experiments $M = 10$ surrogate data sets were generated and we thus get $\hat{t} = 1.833$ for $p = 0.1$ (rejection criterion). In all figures, $m(r)$ of the original time series and the mean value $\mu_S = \mu_S(r)$ of the surrogate data sets are plotted versus the look-ahead r. In parentheses the mean value of $|t| = |t(r)|$ over r (see Eq. (6)) is given for the corresponding Markov process. The curves in the figures are normalized so that $m(1) = 1$ holds for the original time series. In all experiments two or three Gaussians ($k = 2, 3$) and three hidden neurons ($l = 3$) were used (see Eqs. (7) – (10)). The given parameter values for n, r, M, p, k, and l are by no means restricted to these values. They just represent a good choice for time series of moderate length ($N \simeq 10000$).

A special class of linear Markov processes is given by the autoregressive processes of order q (AR(q)) defined by $x_{t+1} = \sum_{i=0}^{q-1} a_i x_{t-i} + \sigma e_t$ where e_t denotes zero mean Gaussian noise of variance one and where $a_i, 0 \leq i \leq q - 1$ and σ can be chosen to simulate a time series in terms of the autocorrelation function for lags not larger than q. Fig. 2 shows our experimental results for the AR(5) process with $a_i = 0.1, 0 \leq i \leq 4$, and $\sigma = 0.1$. The hypotheses corresponding to Markov processes of order one, two, three, and four are clearly rejected. Only the correct, fifth order process is accepted. Therefore the true order of the time series is detected.

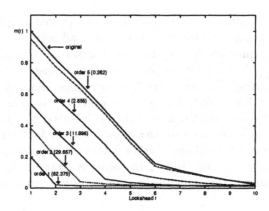

Fig. 2. An AR(5) process and Markovian approximations of first to fifth order.

Chaotic dynamical systems are known to have infinite memory which means that for arbitrary fine partitions of phase space the whole past influences the future behavior (for an excellent overview cf. [4] for example). However, for practical purposes the case of a chaotic time series distorted by white noise is more important because any measuring device induces random fluctuations which do not result from the underlying dynamics. The presence of noise means a restriction of the memory to a finite number of steps and therefore Markov processes are appropriate models. Clearly, the larger the noise level the smaller the order of the Markov process.

For demonstration purposes, we studied the logistic map $x_{t+1} = 3.9x_t(1 - x_t)$ with additive, zero mean Gaussian noise of variances 0.1 and 0.5, respectively. The numerical results are depicted in Fig. 4. In the first case the simplest process which is not rejected, is of order eight (left-hand side). Note that the seventh order process is far from being accepted. If the noise level is increased, the order decreases to five (right-hand side). In a control experiment we also calculated the cumulant-based information flow of the sixth order approximation but this did not give any substantial improvement.

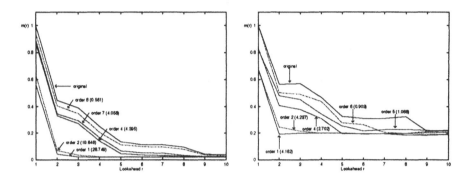

Fig. 3. (Left) A logistic map with additive noise resembles a higher order Markov process concerning the information flow. (Right) The same process with increased noise level.

The time series of yearly sunspot numbers has been extensively studied in the literature. We chose the monthly time series[3] because of the larger number of data points ($N = 2809$). The results of our numerical experiments on this real-world time series are depicted in Fig. 4. We found out that the order of an acceptable process is quite low ($3 - 4$). In order to test the influence of nonlinearities an AR(4) process was fitted to the Gaussianized time series, ten surrogate data sets were generated and Gaussianized and the measures $\mu_S(r)$ were calculated. The mean value of $|t| = |t(r)|$ was 1.105. Therefore the linear process is still good enough to be accepted ($\hat{t} = 1.833$), although the nonlinear approximation gives a better explanation of the information flow. Consequently, the time series of monthly sunspot numbers can be modelled by a low order Markov process and good results can already be achieved by a linear ansatz.

5 Conclusion

Our method characterizes the statistical dependencies of a time series by determining the order of the Markov process which has the same cumulant-based information flow as the time series. The probability densities of the tested Markov processes are estimated by neural networks. Experimental results for artificial data sets and one real-world time series demonstrate the applicability of our method.

---

[3] The authors want to thank the Sunspot Index Data Centre, Brussels, Belgium for making the monthly sunspot time series available to them.

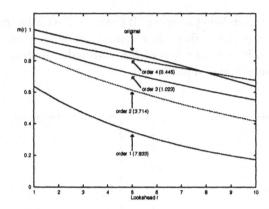

Fig. 4. The monthly sunspot time series and several Markovian approximations.

References

1. Breiman, L.: Statistics: With a View Toward Applications (Houghton Mifflin, Boston, 1973)
2. Deco, G., Obradovic, D.: An Information Theoretic Approach to Neural Computing (Springer, New York, 1996)
3. Deco, G., Schittenkopf, C., Schürmann, B.: Determining the Information Flow of Dynamical Systems from Continuous Probability Distributions. Phys. Rev. Lett. **78** (1997) 2345–2348
4. Eckmann, J.-P., Ruelle, D.: Ergodic Theory of Chaos and Strange Attractors. Rev. Mod. Phys. **57** (1985) 617–656
5. Gardiner, C.W.: Handbook of Stochastic Methods (Springer, Berlin, 1990)
6. Neuneier, R., Finnoff, W., Hergert, F., Ormoneit, D.: Estimation of Conditional Densities: A Comparison of Neural Network Approaches, p. 689 in Intern. Conf. on Artificial Neural Networks, ICANN (Springer, 1994)
7. Papoulis, A.: Probability, Random Variables, and Stochastic Processes (McGraw-Hill, Singapore, 1991)
8. Schittenkopf, C., Deco, G.: Testing Nonlinear Markovian Hypotheses in Dynamical Systems. Physica D **104** (1997) 61–74
9. Theiler, J., Eubank, S., Longtin, A., Galdrikian, B., Farmer, J.D.: Testing for Nonlinearity in Time Series: The Method of Surrogate Data. Physica D **58** (1992) 77–94

Feature-Based Perception of Semantic Concepts

Gabriele Scheler

Institut für Informatik
TU München
D 80290 München
scheler@informatik.tu-muenchen.de

Abstract. In this paper we shall point to some principles of neural computation as they have been derived from experimental and theoretical studies primarily on vision. We argue that these principles are well suited to explain some characteristics of the linguistic function of semantic concept recognition. Computational models built on these principles have been applied to morphological-grammatical categories (aspect), function words (determiners) and discourse particles in spoken language. We suggest a few ways in which these studies may be extended to include more detail on neural functions into the computational model.

1 Introduction

When we attempt to model the human capacity for processing language in the context of recent advances in the computational and cognitive neurosciences, we may adopt the biological-genetic view of looking at primary, simple capacities within the complex linguistic behavior. A candidate for such a simple capacity is the construction and recognition of linguistic categories, i.e. phonemes, morphemes or lexemes.

The first linguistic ability present in young children (one-word phase) relates to categorization of objects and situations according to their perceived similarity (cf. [6],[20]). Arguably the use of words as full utterances, which is based on the ability to categorize objects and actions and uses the principle of categorical perception, is a phylogenetic precursor of a full linguistic system as well ([12]).

Models of neural computation, which are historically closely linked to experimental research on visual perception, have focused on processes of categorization, pattern recognition and learning/generalization on the basis of similarity.

Recently a number of attempts have been made to fit the study of linguistic meaning - semantics and pragmatics - into a neurocomputational (connectionist) framework ([27, 7, 24, 32, 30]). However, a number of different approaches may be taken, and in this paper we want to describe a computational model that shows a close correspondence to models of visual and auditory perception.

An experimentally established concept of auditory perception is the notion of categorical perception, which refers to a discretization of continuous physical dimensions, i.e. a categorization of auditory stimuli. Both prototype effects and boundary effects have been observed. It has been shown to exist both in animal and human perception of speech sounds and provides an empirical background for (independently established) segmental phonological theory ([17], [8], [11]).

Linguistic semantic theory derives its strongest influences from logical semantics and cognitive linguistics, but feature-based, configurational accounts of meaning ([10],[21, 22]) have made a strong appeal in bridging the gap between empirical and theoretical analyis.

Logical semantics ([25], [1], [13]) with its core concept of truth values provides a mathematical framework to elucidate and formalize a great range of intuitive meanings. According to its philosophical interest this has been mostly applied to the abstract meanings of grammatical morphemes, but also to some degree to lexematic meanings (cf. [14]). However, there is no direct relationship between this mathematical framework (model theory and higher-order logic) and the processes of neural computation as they have emerged in the last few decades.

Cognitive linguistics ([3], [19], [9], [18]), on the other hand, provides an informal, empirical approach to semantics, and has influenced and informed connectionist semantic theories, e.g. with respect to the study of verbal frames, deixis and spatial expressions.

Semantic feature theory may be made compatible with logical semantics by redefining semantic features as atomic operators with a corresponding axiomatization (cf. e.g. [33] for such an account). In this way it is possible to define non-arbitrary, linguistically established semantic features and draw on the range of established meaning correspondences to logical models.

In the following we shall outline some basic principles of neural categorization as they are put forward in the context of visual perception. We shall then explain an existing computational model of semantic processing, called NEUROSEM, and point out the new focus on feature discovery and feature extraction that is implied with this and related models.

Furthermore we attempt to relate the computational model to more detailed accounts of neural functions and suggest a number of ways for improvement of the model. We shall focus on lateral inhibition as a principle of self-organization and phase locking as a mechanism for feature binding. We conclude with an outlook where we place the theory of feature-based perception into the context of the language processing capability and suggest that neural circuits derived from other evolutionary sources may be critically implicated for the complex faculty.

2 Some Principles of Visual Perception

In visual perception, certain features are extracted from the retinal (preprocessed) image, and relayed through several centers. In the early stages of visual processing, afferent and lateral connections form self-organizing maps by adjusting synaptic efficacies on coincident pre– and postsynaptic activity (Hebbian learning). Lateral connections which may be enabling or inhibitory (forming cooperative or competitive feature assemblies) are formed according to the statistical properties of the input, and store patterns of correlation of the input.

Since they may be regarded as a form of implicit memory, influencing the perception of further signals, they are a part of recent theories of "active vision" ([5]) regarding the role of stored memory in viewing and recognizing objects ("top-down processing").

Neuroanatomically, several distinctive pathways for types of information in the visual system can be differentiated. These pathways (vertical columns) selectively process information from one eye (ocular dominance columns), line orientation, color information, movement-related information etc. Within a pathway, there exist several 'relay centers' ("nodes"), which have some basic sequential arrangement, as well as afferent, lateral and feedback connections (cf. [43]). This means that in later (more central) stages features that are being extracted are increasingly complex and useful for the organism, remote from the perceptual input, and close to other modalities.

A problem for visual perception research concerns the hierarchical organisation of individual features into distinctive objects or perceptual gestalts. There are different ways of realizing such a feature-binding process within a neural network, such as making use of a sequence of afferent connections to higher-order features or using the temporal properties of neuronal output signals (spikes) to perform a discrimination of a large set of features to cluster features into objects ([45], [41]). The problem with cells responding to higher-order features only ("combination coding" [42]) lies in the inordinate amount of features that would have to be recruited for object recognition to function, and the lack of flexibility and rapidity in establishing a feature binding. Feature-binding by synchronization of neuronal spikes however allows transient feature binding which may be rapidly established and signals out the features defining an object from a larger amount of active neurons. There are a number of experimental studies suggesting that synchronization of neuronal firing may play a significant role in relating features into structures by temporal contiguity ([38], [37]).

3   A Computational Model of Semantic Processing

We start from the assumption that understanding simple words and morphemes in the adult and mature child is basically a two-stage process: The first stage aims at auditory recognition of word percepts (sound shapes) while the second stage aims at recognition of word concepts, i.e. lexematic or conceptual-grammatic units.

Auditory word recognition employs discretization of the acoustic signal into phonetic features and phoneme recognition together with other procedures for suprasegmental and syllabic recognition. (Since the latter are procedures that induce a hierarchical structure of the perceptual signal, they may also be regarded as feature-binding phenomena.)

The neural circuits that have evolved for primary perception may well be considered to be employed in the recognition of semantic concepts as well. Since the basic principles of cortical network organisation (rather than informational content) are not restricted to a particular species, dedicating a part of these neural circuits to concept recognition may have been a parsimonious way of evolving internal representations of abstract concepts ('reappropriation hypothesis', cf. [46] for a different interpretation of this notion.)

In order to investigate the practical feasibility of this basic intuition, we have performed interpretation and generation experiments using neural networks with different morphological units. The goal of these experiments was to assign the correct set of semantic features to a morpheme in a naturally occurring context, and to generate a morpheme (e.g., in another language) given this semantic representation. Obviously for the success of these experiments it is crucial to encode a sufficient amount of contextual information and to select a set of semantic features which capture the differences and the variablity in the meaning expressed. In particular, we have conducted this analysis on aspectual-temporal verb markers, on function words such as determiners and on discourse markers, i.e. discourse particles.

Based on a methodology of minimal contrasts, a number of semantic features defining oppositions in meaning may be established. Linking these features to a logical analysis allows to explore the logical relations between these features. These logical relations may be expressed as incompatibility (mutual exclusiveness), inferential relations, or conjunction of features. It is a simple logical operation to restructure the feature set according to a single type of logical relation. Using mutual exclusiveness we may structure the set of semantic features (typically less than 100) into separate "dimensions", where each percept (occurrence of a morpheme in a context) may activate an arbitrary number of dimensions but not more than a single feature within a dimension.

Given a full feature analysis for the semantic effect of morphological units, we may now use supervised classification methods for the interpretation of naturally occuring morphemes. Specifically, we trained fully connected back-propagation networks to assign meanings to grammatical morphemes or function words. The following interpretation effects occur within the computational model:

- for each form present in a real occurrence, we can assign a semantic feature representation given the morphological form and a set of contextual clues.
- morphological forms presented in isolation will yield a characteristic spectrum of semantic features, akin to a prototypical meaning for a specific form.
- especially when the contextual clues are significantly reduced, we can observe a prototypical filling-in effect, i.e. a pattern completion effect that results from the learned interaction between features.

Additionally, we may assume that semantic features that are critically implicated in the conceptualization of an event in one language, but less so in another language, may receive more attention in speakers of that language. Similar effects have been noted in the categorical perception of speech sounds and their mapping to phonemes ([16], [28]).

In any case, feature vectors as representations of semantic meaning can serve as target structures for other processes of neural computation such as unsupervised clustering, feature binding and feature discovery.

4 Extensions to the Model

In the following, we want to point to some characteristics of semantic processing that may merit further attention in biologically inspired theoretical models of language.

4.1 Lateral connections

Lateral connections, and more specifically, lateral inhibition in neurobiology is known to be a specific neuronal mechanism which serves to enhance recognition by reducing the signal/noise ratio ([36]).

Similarly, in our model, we may enhance recognition, when we use inhibitory links among competing values of a particular feature dimension. This shows the basic structure of a competitive clustering, i.e. a winner-take-all network linked by lateral inhibition. Furthermore we can enhance "top-down" effects of semantic pattern completion and overriding of weak contextual information on the basis of the stored conceptual information. Basically we may translate exclusive logical relations between features into inhibitory connections and arrive at a set of clusters of competitive interaction.

Relations between features do not have to be coded into the model. Both cooperative and competitive interactions within the cortex may be mediated by lateral connections. The pattern of these lateral connections can be altered by changing the input to the developing cortex. I.e., lateral connections may be derived on the basis of statistical correlations within the input patterns. In that case the hard constraints of the logical model are replaced by soft constraints of probabilistic enabling and inhibitory links. An interesting suggestion for training lateral connections between features and an application to both visual and lexical processing has been developed by Miikkulainen (FGREP and RF-LISSOM, [24], [23]).

The training of lateral connections involves long-term memory as it operates on a time-scale beyond immediate reaction times. However, once these constraints are established they may play a role in selective attention and suppressing feature activation for uncorrelated, asynchronous neuronal firing.

4.2 Feature binding

Feature binding processes studied in visual object recognition may also be implicated in semantic disambiguation (cf.[2] for a passing reference to that relation).

In a slightly simplified account of lexematic meaning assignment, a lexeme activates a set of features using contextual cues and constraints of lexical meaning[1] i.e. afferent signals and lateral interactions of stored feature relations. Features belonging to a single word may be perceived as a single entity by synchronization

---

[1] For lexematic meaning, i.e. the meaning of lexemes or content words, a distinction may be made between "lexical meaning", i.e. the stored meaning in an internal lexicon and "actual meaning", or the contextually appropriate meaning [29].

of neuronal firing. It takes about 400 ms to firmly establish a single, contextually appropriate meaning (cf.[44], [39], [40]). Before that a number of semantic meanings are activated (as shown in semantic priming effects) independent of their contextual appropriateness. The time-course of lexical interpretation is therefore compatible with the view that it is a process similar to object recognition in vision. Furthermore, just like objects in the visual world, the range of contextually appropriate meanings is not limited and meanings can not be fully retrieved from memory. This corresponds to the view that disambiguation (i.e. actual meaning assignment) is a contextual selection process and lexical meanings are created by other processes on a different time-scale [31].

However, the number of distinct firing rates limits the number of perceived objects in attention. On a phenomenological level illusionary perceptions, which occur as a result of accidental synchronies under attentional overload may be compared to increased mishearings of words and semantically-based errors in understanding under the same conditions.

Disambiguation processes in language occur at the syllabic, morphological, lexematic and syntactic levels. Thus we may have feature-binding processes on different levels of organization of the features that are being processed.

4.3 Feature discovery

A pressing issue from a practical point of view is the replacement of manually encoded feature sets for semantic representation by automatically constructed feature sets. At the same time, psychologists have pointed to the inadequacy of pattern recognition and learning methods on the basis of fixed feature sets (cf. [35],[26],[15]). In particular, discrimination shift tasks in concept learning show that human subjects create novel feature representations of visually presented stimuli which guide them in decision-making and influence their reaction times.

Feature sets may be induced from primary observations of statistical correlations in the input. Specifically, textual co-occurrences of lexemes can be used to infer a feature representation of their distributional properties. Feature detection, however, does not have to be limited to frequent co-occurence patterns. Novelty and relevance may also give rise to a primary observation entered into the feature detection process. This process may be modeled by minimum description length methods which can be used to account both for the construction and re-construction of features in on-line learning tasks and the long-term process of building a store of lexical word concepts.

It has been shown that the task of automatic lexical acquisition is well within the range of state-of-the art technology ([34], [4]). In the future the model that we are currently building by processes of statistical induction may be related to known processes of neural computation.

5   Conclusion: Language, Perception and Motoric Action

Semantic processing of morphemes and lexemes may be seen as a specific adjustment of general perceptual processes in humans - employing the same basic mechanisms that have been experimentally validated in the case of visual processing, and that can be formulated in the abstract language of neural computation.

For the syntax of language, which consists of phrase structure (chunking), hierarchical structures, and characteristics of linearization such as word order, congruence, ellipsis, long-distance dependencies and anaphora, a computational structure may have strong analogies to motoric action instead of perceptual image forming. The questions of code forming which result from the interaction of sensory and motoric processes could be investigated in a very precise way in the case of language: In particular, the phonological code is a well-established case of an internal representation which has arisen from an interaction of auditory percepts and articulatory action.

In general, we should not automatically assume that language is a 'higher-level' cognitive process, which builds on symbols and requires 'cognitive' rather than perceptual or motoric processes. Rather we may find that linguistic structures fit in with certain theories of basic neuronal mechanisms and that the study of linguistic functions may contribute towards an understanding of how specifically a human brain processes information.

Acknowledgments

The work reported in this paper was supported by a grant from the Deutsche Forschungsgemeinschaft (Br 609/7-1).

References

1. J. Barwise and J. Perry. *Situations and Attitudes.* MIT Press, 1983.
2. E. Bienenstock. In R. Eckmiller and C. v.d. Malsburg, editors, *Neural computers.* Springer, 1988.
3. M. Bierwisch. *Essays in the psychology of language.* Zentralinstitut für Sprachwissenschaft, 1983.
4. B. Boguraev and J. Pustejovsky, editors. *Corpus Processing for Lexical Acquisition.* MIT, 1996.
5. P. Churchland, V. Ramachandran, and T. Sejnowski. A critique of pure vision. In C. Koch and J. Davis, editors, *Large-Scale Neuronal Theories of the Brain.* MIT, 1994.
6. E. Clark. *The lexicon in acquisition.* Cambridge University Press, 1993.
7. G. Cottrell. *A Connectionist Approach to Word Sense Disambiguation.* Pitman, London, 1989.
8. G. Ehret. Categorical perception of sound signals: Facts and hypotheses from animal studies. In S. Harnad, editor, *Categorical perception*, pages 301–331. Cambridge University Press, 1987.
9. T. Givón. *Functionalism and grammar.* John Benjamins, 1995.
10. A.J. Greimas. *Structural Semantics.* University of Nebraska Press, 1983. (Translated from Semantique structurale, Gallimard, 1966.)
11. S. Harnad, editor. *Categorical Perception: The groundwork of Cognition.* Cambridge University Press, 1987.
12. M. Hauser. *The evolution of communication.* MIT Press, 1996.

13. H. Kamp and U. Reyle. *From Discourse to Logic: Introduction to Modeltheoretic Semantics of Natural Language, Formal Logic and Discourse Representation.* Studies in Linguistics and Philosophy. Kluwer, 1993.

14. H. Kamp and A. Rossdeutscher. Remarks on lexical structure and drs construction. *Theoretical Linguistics*, 20(2/3):97–164, 1994.

15. J. K. Kruschke and M. A. Erickson. Five principles for models of category learning. In Z. Dienes, editor, *Connectionism and Human Learning.* Oxford University, 1995.

16. P. Kuhl, K.A. Williams, F. Lacerda, K.N. Stevens, and B.Lindblom. Linguistic experience alters phonetic perception in infants by 6 months of age. *Science*, 255:606–608, 1992.

17. P.K. Kuhl and A.N. Meltzoff. Speech as an intermodal object of perception. In A. Yonas, editor, *Perceptual development in infancy*, pages 235–256. Lawrence Erlbaum, 1988.

18. G. Lakoff. *Women, Fire and Dangerous Things.* Chicago University Press, 1987.

19. R. Langacker. *Foundations of Cognitive Grammar.* Stanford University Press, 1987.

20. E. Markmann. Constraints children place on word meanings. *Cognitive Science*, 14:57–77, 1990.

21. I.A. Mel'cuk and A. Polguère. A formal lexicon in the meaning-text theory. *Computational Linguistics*, 13(3-4), 1987.

22. I. A. Mel'cuk. Semantic descriptions of lexical units in an explanatory combinatorial dictionary: Basic principles and heuristic criteria. *International Journal of Lexicography 1*, pages 165–188, 1988.

23. R. Miikkulainen, J. Bednar, Y. Choe, and J. Sirosh. Self-organization, plasiticity, and low-level visual phenomena in a laterally connected map model of the primary visual cortex. *Psychology of Learning and Motivation*, 1997.

24. R. Miikkulainen. *Subsymbolic Natural Language Processing: An Integrated Model of Scripts, Lexicon, and Memory.* Neural Network Modeling and Connectionism Series. MIT Press, 1993.

25. R. Montague. *Formal Philosophy.* Yale University Press, 1976.

26. M. Raijmakers. *Epigenesis of neural network models of cognitive development.* PhD thesis, University of Amsterdam, 1997.

27. T. Regier. *The Human Semantic Potential.* MIT, 1996.

28. J. Saffran, R. N. Aslin and E. L. Newport. Statistical learning by 8-months-old infants. *Science*, 274:1926, 1996.

29. G. Scheler. Three approaches to word meaning. Technical report, Computerlinguistik, Universität Heidelberg, November 1988.

30. G. Scheler. Generating English plural determiners from semantic representations. In S. Wermter, E. Riloff, and G. Scheler, editors, *Learning for natural language processing: Statistical, connectionist and symbolic approaches*, pages 61–74. Springer, 1996.

31. G. Scheler. Lexematische Äquivalenz in der maschinellen Übersetzung. Technical Report FKI-210, Institut für Informatik, TU München, 1996.

32. G. Scheler. Learning the semantics of aspect. In H. Somers, editor, *New Methods in Language Processing.* University College London Press, 1997.

33. G. Scheler and J. Schumann. A hybrid model of semantic inference. In Alex Monaghan, editor, *Proceedings of the 4th International Conference on Cognitive Science in Natural Language Processing (CSNLP 95)*, pages 183–193, 1995.

34. H. Schuetze. *Ambiguity Resolution in Language Learning*, volume 71 of *CSLI Publications.* Chicago University Press, 1997.

35. P. G. Schyns, R. L. Goldstone, and J. Thibaut. The development of features in object concepts. *Behavioral and Brain Sciences*, 21, 1997 (to appear).
36. G. Shepherd. *Neurobiology*. Oxford University Press, 3rd edition, 1994.
37. W. Singer. Synchronization of cortical activity and its putative role in information processing and learning. *Annual Reviews of Physiology*, 55:349–374, 1993.
38. W. Singer and C.M. Gray. Visual feature integration and the temporal correlation hypothesis. *Annual Reviews of Neuroscience*, 18:555–586, 1995.
39. D. Swinney. Lexical access during sentence comprehension: (re) consideration of context effects. *Journal of verbal learning and verbal behavior*, 6:645–659, 1979.
40. P. Tabossi. Sentential context and lexical acess. In S. Small, G. Cottrell, and M.Tanenhaus, editors, *Lexical Ambiguity Resolution*. Morgan Kaufman, 1988.
41. A. Treisman. The binding problem. *Current Opinion in Neurobiology*, 6:171–178, 1996.
42. J. Triesch and C. v.d.Malsburg. Binding - a proposed experiment and a model. In *Proceedings of ICANN*. Springer, 1996.
43. D. C. Van Essen and E. A. Deyoe. Concurrent processing in the primate visual cortex. In M. Gazzaniga, editor, *The Cognitive Neurosciences*. MIT Press, 1995.
44. C. Van Petten and M. Kutas. Ambiguous words in context: An event-related potential analysis of the time course of meaning activation. *Journal of Memory and Language*, 26:188–208, 1987.
45. C. von der Malsburg. The correlation theory of brain function. In K. Schulten and L van Hemmen, editors, *Models of Neural Networks 2*. Springer, 1994.
46. J. Wilkins and J. Wakefield. Brain evolution and neurolinguistic preconditions. *Behavioral and Brain Sciences*, 18:161–226, 1995.

Automatic Detection of Thesaurus Relations for Information Retrieval Applications

Gerda Ruge

Computer Science, Technical University of Munich

Abstract. Is it possible to discover semantic term relations useful for thesauri without any semantic information? Yes, it is. A recent approach for automatic thesaurus construction is based on explicit linguistic knowledge, i.e. a domain independent parser without any semantic component, and implicit linguistic knowledge contained in large amounts of real world texts. Such texts include implicitly the linguistic, especially semantic, knowledge that the authors needed for formulating their texts. This article explains how implicit semantic knowledge can be transformed to an explicit one. Evaluations of quality and performance of the approach are very encouraging.

1 Introduction

In most cases, when the expression *information retrieval* is used text retrieval is meant. Information retrieval systems manage large amounts of documents. A database containing 1,000,000 documents is a normal case in practice. Some database providers e.g. NEXUS have to deal with millions of documents a week. The special purpose that retrieval systems are designed for, is the search for relevant items with respect to an information need of a user. This would ideally be realized by a system that understands the question of the user as well as the content of the documents in the database – but this is far from the state of the art.

The requirements of information retrieval systems – domain independence, efficiency, robustness – force them to work very superficially in the case of large databases. The search is usually based on so-called terms. The *terms* are the searchable items of the system. The process of mapping documents to term representations is called *indexing*. In most retrieval systems, the index terms are all words in the documents with the exception of *stopwords* like determiners, prepositions or conjunctions. A *query*, i.e. the search request, then consists of terms; and the documents in the result set of the retrieval process are those that contain these query terms. Most of the work in retrieval research in the last decades have been concentrated on refining this term based search method. One of these refinements is to use a thesaurus.

A *thesaurus* in the field of Information and Documentation is an ordered compilation of terms which serves for indexing and retrieval in one documentation domain. A central point is not only to define terms but also relations between terms[2]. Such relations are synonymy ("container" – "receptacle"), broader terms or hyperonyms ("container" – "tank"), narrower terms or hyponyms ("tank" – "container"), the part-of-relation or meronymy ("car" – "tank") and antonymy ("acceleration" – "deceleration"). The concept *semantically similar* subsumes all these thesaurus relations.

It is difficult for retrieval system users to bring to mind the large number of terms that are semantically similar to their initial query terms. Especially untrained users formulate short queries. For the original query {WORD, CLUSTERING, TERM, ASSOCIATION} the following terms could be found in the titles of relevant documents like "Experiments on the Determination of the Relationships between Terms" or "A Taxonomy of English Nouns and Verbs":

Example 1.

TERM, KEYWORD, DESCRIPTOR, WORD, NOUN, ADJECTIVE, VERB, STEM, CONCEPT, MEANING, SENSE, VARIANT, SEMANTIC, STATISTIC, RELATED, NARROWER, BROADER, DEPENDENT, CO-OCCURRENCE, INTERCHANGABLE, FIRST ORDER, SECOND ORDER, CLUSTER, GROUP, EXPANSION, CLASS, SIMILARITY, SYNONYMY, ANTONYMY, HYPONYMY, HYPERONYMY, ASSOCIATION, RELATION, RELATIONSHIP, TAXONOMY, HIERARCHY, NETWORK, LEXICON, DICTIONARY, THESAURUS, GENERATION, CONSTRUCTION, CLASSIFICATION, DETERMINATION

Such additional terms would support the users in formulating their queries. Therefore one important direction of research in automatic thesaurus construction is the detection of semantically similar terms as candidates for thesaurus relations.

2 Various Approaches for the Automatic Detection of Semantic Similarity

There is a large variety of approaches for automatic detection of thesaurus relations, mainly suggested by retrieval researchers and also by linguists. In the following, a selection of basic approaches are listed with brief characterizations.

In statistical term association, co-occurrence data of terms are analysed. The main idea of this approach relies in the assumption that terms occurring in similar contexts are synonyms. The contexts of an initial term are represented by terms frequently occurring in the same document or paragraph as the intitial term. In theory, terms with a high degree of context term overlap should be synonyms, but in practice no synonyms could be found by this method [8].

Co-occurrence statistics can be refined by using singular value decomposition. In this case the relations are generated on the basis of the comparision of the main factors extracted from co-occurrence data [12]. Even though this approach does not find semantically similar terms, the use of such term associations can improve retrieval results. Unfortunately, singular value decomposition is so costly, that it can only be applied to a small selection of the database terms.

Salton [14] gives a summary of work on pseudo-classification. For this approach, relevance judgements are required: Each document must be judged with respect to relevance to each of a set of queries. Then an optimization algorithm can be run: It assigns relation weights to all term pairs, such that expanding the query by terms related with high weights leads to retrieval results as correct as possible. This is the training phase of the approach. After the training, term pairs with high weights represent thesaurus relations. A disadvantage of this approach lies in its high effort for the manual determination of the relevance judgements as well as for the automatic optimization. The manual effort is even comparable to manual thesaurus construction.

Hyponyms were extracted from large text corpora by Hearst [5]. She searched for relations directly mentioned in the texts and discovered text patterns that relate hyponyms, e.g. "such that". Frequently this method leads to term pairs that – out of context – are not directly related in the hyponymy hierarchy like "species" and "steatornis oilbird" or "target" and "airplane".

Hyperonyms can also be detected by analysing definitions in monolingual lexica. A hyperonym of the defined term is the so-called *genus term*, the one that gives the main characterization of the defined term [1]. Genus terms can be recognized by means of syntactic analysis. A further approach is based on the idea that semantically similar terms have similar definitions in a lexicon. Terms that have many defining terms in common are supposed to be semantically similar or synonyms [13]. These lexicon based approaches seem very plausible, however they have not been evaluated. One problem of these approaches is their coverage. Only terms that are filed in a lexicon can be dealt with, thus many relations between technical terms will stay undiscovered.

Güntzer et al. [4] suggested an expert system that draws hypotheses about term relations on the basis of user observations. For example, if a retrieval system user combines two terms by OR in his/her query (and further requirements hold) these terms are probably synonyms. The system worked well, but unfortunately the users capability of bringing to mind synonyms is very poor. Therefore the majority of the term pairs found were either morphologically similar like "net" and "network" or translations of each other like "user interface" and "Benutzer-oberfläche". Other synonyms were hardly found.

These examples of approaches for the detection of semantically similar terms show clearly that the main ideas can be very plausible but nevertheless do not work in practice. In the following, a recent approach is explained that has been confirmed by different research groups.

3 Detection of Term Similarities on the Basis of Dependency Analysis

In this section we describe a method that extracts term relations fully automatically from large corpora. Therefore, domain dependent thesaurus relations can be produced for each text database. The approach is based on linguistic as well as statistic analysis. The linguistic background of this approach is dependency theory.

3.1 Dependency Theory

The theory of dependency analysis has a long tradition in linguistics. Its central concept, the dependency relation, is the relation between heads and modifiers. *Modifiers* are terms that specify another term, the *head*, in a sentence or phrase. Examples 2, 3 and 4 below include the head modifier relation between "thesaurus" and "construction".

Example 2. thesaurus construction

Example 3. construction of a complete domain dependent monolingual thesaurus

Example 4. automatic thesaurus generation or construction

In example 3, the head "thesaurus" has three modifiers: "complete", "dependent", and "monolingual". A modifier might have more than one head in case of conjunctions. In example 4, the modifiers "automatic" and "thesaurus" specify both heads, "generation" and "construction".

In dependency trees, the heads are always drawn above their modifiers. A line stands for the head modifier relation. For the purpose of information retrieval, stopwords like determiners, prepositions and conjunctions are usually neglected, such that the tree only contains relations between index terms. Such dependency trees differ from syntax trees of Chomsky grammars in representing not the sentence structure but the specification relations between words in the sentence; e.g. example 5 has the same dependency tree as example 6 but different syntax trees (not shown).

Example 5. Peter drinks a sweet hot coffee.

Example 6. Peter drinks a coffee which is sweet and hot.

3.2 Head and Modifier Extraction from Corpora

Some implementations of dependency analysis are practically applicable to large amounts of text because they realize a very quick and robust syntactic analysis. Hindle [6] reports of a free text analysis with subsequent head modifier extraction which deals with one million words over night. Strzalkowski [15] reports of a rate of one million words in 8 hours. The last version of our own parser described in [11] is much faster: 3 MB per minute real time on a SUN SPARC station; that is approximately 15 minutes for one million words. Such a parser works robustly and domain independently but results only in partial analysis trees. Our dependency analysis of noun phrases has been evaluated with respect to error rates. 85% of the head modifier token were determined correctly and 14%

were introduced wrongly. These error rates are acceptable because the further processing is very robust as shown by the results below. Table 1 shows the most frequent heads and modifiers of the term "pump" in three annual editions of abstracts of the American Patent and Trademark Office.

pump			
Modifiers	Frequency	Heads	Frequency
heat	444	chamber	294
injection	441	housing	276
hydraulic	306	assembly	177
vacuum	238	system	160
driven	207	connected	141
displacement	183	pressure	124
fuel	181	piston	120
pressure	142	unit	119
oil	140	body	115

Table 1. Most frequent heads and modifiers of "pump" in 120 MB of patent abstracts

3.3 Semantics of the Head Modifier Relation

Head modifier relations bridge the gap between syntax and semantics: On the one hand they can be extracted on the basis of pure syntactic analysis. On the other hand the modifier specifies the head, and this is a semantic relation. How can the semantic information contained in head modifier relations give hints about semantic similarity? Different semantic theories suggest that terms having many heads and modifiers in common are semantically similar. These connections are now drafted very briefly.

Katz and Fordor [7] introduced a feature based semantic theory. They claimed that the meaning of a word can be represented by a set of semantic features, for example {+human, +male, -married} is the famous feature representation of "bachelor". These features also explain which words are compatible, e.g. "bachelor" is compatible with "young", but not with "fly". The selection of all possible heads and modifiers of a term therefore means the selection of all compatible words. If the corpus has a large coverage and all heads and modifiers of two terms are the same, they should also have the same feature representation, i.e. the same meaning.

Wittgenstein's view of the relation of meaning and use was mirrored in the co-occurrence approach in Sect. 2. Terms appearing in similar contexts were supposed to be synonyms. Probably, this idea is correct if the contexts are very small. Heads and modifiers are contexts and these contexts are as small as possible – only one term long. Thus, head and modifier comparison implements smallest contexts comparison.

In model theoretic semantics the so-called extensional meaning of many words is denoted by a set of objects, e.g. the set of all dogs in the world represents the meaning of the word "dog". If two terms occur as heads and modifiers in a real world corpus, in most cases it holds that the intersection of their representations in not empty. Thus the head modifier relation between two terms means that each term is a possible property of the objects of the other term. Head modifier comparison therefore is the comparison of possible properties.

Head modifier relations can also be found in human memory structure. A variety of experiments with human associations suggest that in many cases heads or modifiers are responses to stimulus words, e.g. stimulus "rose" and response "red". As stimulus words, terms with common heads and modifiers therefore can effect the same associations.

3.4 Experiments on Head-Modifier-Based Term Similarity

According to the theories in Sect. 3.3, terms are semantically similar if they correspond in their heads and modifiers. Section 3.2 shows that masses of head modifier relations can be extracted automatically from large amounts of text. Thus semantically similar terms can be generated fully automatically by means of head modifier comparision. Implementations of this method are described by Ruge [9], Grefenstette [3] and Strzalkowski [16]. Table 2 gives some examples of initial terms together with their most similar terms (with respect to head and modifier overlap). The examples contain different types of thesaurus relations: synonyms ("quantity" – "amount"), hyperonyms ("president" – "head"), hyponyms ("government"– "regime") and part-of-relations ("government"– "minister").

quantity	government	president
amount	leader	director
volume	party	chairman
rate	regime	office
concentration	year	manage
ratio	week	executive
value	man	official
content	minister	head
level	president	lead

Table 2. Most similar terms of "quantity" [9], "government" [3] and "president" [16]

The comparison of heads and modifiers is expressed by a value between 0 (no overlap) and 1 (identical heads and modifiers). This value is determined by a similarity measure. I found that the cosine measure with a logarithmic weighting function (1) works best ([9], [10]).

$$sim(t_i, t_j) = \frac{1}{2} \cdot \frac{h_i^{ln} \cdot h_j^{ln}}{\left\| h_i^{ln} \cdot h_j^{ln} \right\|} + \frac{1}{2} \cdot \frac{m_i^{ln} \cdot m_j^{ln}}{\left\| m_i^{ln} \cdot m_j^{ln} \right\|} \tag{1}$$

In Eq. (1), $h_i^{ln} = (ln_0(h_{i1}), \ldots, ln_0(h_{in}))$. h_{ik} stands for the number of occurrences of term t_i as head of term t_j in the corpus. $ln_0(r) = ln(r)$ if $r > 1$ and 0 otherwise. m_i^{ln} is defined analogously for modifiers. The cosine measure in principle gives the cosine of the angle between the two terms represented in a space spanned by the heads or spanned by the modifiers. In *sim*, the weights of the heads and modifiers were smoothed logarithmically. *sim* gives the mean of the head space cosine and the modifier space cosine of the two terms.

The head modifier approach has been examined on different levels of evaluation. First, the rate of semantically similar terms among the 10 terms with highest *sim*-values for 159 different initial terms has been evaluated ([9], [10]). About 70% of the terms found were semantically similar in the sense that they could be used as additional terms for information retrieval. Grefenstette [3] and Strzalkowski [16] clustered those terms that had a high similarity value. Then they expanded queries by replacing all query terms by their clusters. The expanded queries performed better than the original queries. Strzalkowski found an improvement in the retrieval results of 20%. This is a very good value in the retrieval context. Unfortunately, the effect of query expansion alone is not known, because Strzalkowski used further linguistic techniques in his retrieval system.

4 Conclusions

A disadvantage of most information retrieval systems is that the search is based on document terms. These term based systems can be improved by incorporating thesaurus relations. The expensive task of manual thesaurus construction should be supported or replaced by automatic tools. After a long period of disappointing results in this field linguistically based systems have shown some encouraging results. These systems are based on the extraction and comparison of head modifier relations in large corpora. They are applicable in practice, because they use robust and fast parsers.

References

1. Das-Gupta, P.: Boolean Interpretation of Conjunctions for Document Retrieval. JASIS 38(1987) 245-254
2. DIN 1463: Erstellung und Weiterentwicklung von Thesauri. Deutsches Institut für Normung (1987), related standard published in English: ISO 2788:1986
3. Grefenstette, G.: Explorations in Automatic Thesaurus Discovery. Kluwer Academic Publishers, Boston, Dordrecht, London (1994)
4. Güntzer, U., Jüttner, G., Seegmüller, G., Sarre, F.: Automatic Thesaurus Construction by Machine Learning from Retrieval Sessions. Inf. Proc. & Management 25(1989) 265-273
5. Hearst, M.: Automatic Acquisition of Hyponyms from Large Text Corpora. Proceedings of COLING 92, Nantes, Vol.2(1992) 539-545
6. Hindle, D.: A Parser for Text Corpora. Technical Memorandum, AT&T Bell Laboratories (1990), also published in Atkins, A., Zampolli, A.: Computational Approaches to the Lexicon. Oxford University Press (1993)

7. Katz, J., Fordor, J.: The Structure of Semantic Theory. In Fordor, J., Katz, J.: The Structure of Language: Readings in the Philosophy of Language. Englewood Cliffs, NJ, Prentice Hall (1964) 479-518

8. Lesk, M.: Word-Word Associations in Document Retrieval Systems. American Documentation (1969) 27-38

9. Ruge, G.: Experiments on Linguistically Based Term Associations. Inf. Proc. & Mangement 28(1992) 317-332

10. Ruge, G.: Wortbedeutung und Termassoziation. Reihe Sprache und Computer 14, Georg Olms Verlag, Hildesheim, Zürich, New York (1995)

11. Ruge, G., Schwarz, C., Warner, A.: Effectiveness and Efficiency in Natural Language Processing for Large Amounts of Text. JASIS 42(1991) 450-456

12. Schütze, H., Pederssn, J.: A Cooccurrence-Based Thesaurus and Two Applications to Information Retrieval. Proceedings of RIAO94, New York (1994) 266-274

13. Shaikevich, A.: Automatic Construction of a Thesaurus from Explanatory Dictionaries. Automatic Documentation and Mathematical Linguistics 19(1985) 76-89

14. Salton, G.: Automatic Term Class Construction Using Relevance – A Summary of Work in Automatic Pseudoclassification. Inf. Proc. & Management 16(1980) 1-15

15. Strzalkowski, T.: TTP: A Fast and Robust Parser for Natural Language. Proceedings of COLING 92, Nantes, Vol.1(1992) 198-204

16. Strzalkowski, T.: Natural Language Information Retrieval. Inf. Proc. & Management 31(1995) 397-417

InfoSphere™-V: A New Approach to 3D-Visualization of Information

Leo Pfefferer and Dieter Schütt

Siemens AG, ZT IK 1
Otto-Hahn-Ring 6
81730 München

Abstract. Information highways are installed around the world and the impact on the business of companies like Siemens is tremendous. New techniques for information access, visualization and retrieval are required. Our approach at the Corporate Technology Department of Siemens is to provide better orientation in information bases by visualizing semantic content by information or contextual similarity. Integrating features for navigation instead of static representation enables the user to find the relevant information by browsing through the information space.

1 Introduction

Toward the end of the century, we are experiencing the fusion of telecommunications, electronics, entertainment, and service sectors to form the digital highway of the 'global village'. This technology enables us in new ways to meet people, provides entertainment, info, games and jobs opportunities.

But how can we manage the burst of news, messages and impressions that float back and forth? What is missing is an engineering-like approach that allows people to handle and process information in a systematic way over its entire life cycle. Information Engineering has a good chance of becoming one of the most suitable approaches [S-B 95].

With the InfoSphere™ project, we integrate various aspects of information processing. In addition to modeling and filtering of information, visualization techniques will improve methods to obtain information fast and at reasonable cost [G-S 96]. Within the InfoSphere™ project, InfoSphere™-V is geared toward visualization techniques.

2 Spatial Cognitivity and Context Analyzer (KOAN)

Every six years the knowledge of the world doubles. Thus, the major problem is to make adequate information available to the user. To fulfill this requirement new approaches and techniques are necessary. Visualization techniques have proven to be capable of handling such complexities.

The Context Analyzer (KOAN = 'Kontextanalysator' in German) is a tool, wich is oriented at the human capacity of association in a spatial environment [FJM 94, Pfe 96a, Pfe 96b, PFP 96].

In accordance with the principle that "content similarity corresponds to spatial proximity", information objects combined with their attributes are graphically presented in a spatial relationship in a so called 3D-information space.

3D-space corresponds to the familiar environment and to the interpretation procedures of human beings and allows the user to intuitively process and memorize large quantities of information and their correlation. The information objects and their attributes are visually identified by their specific shape and color, dependent on their meaning.

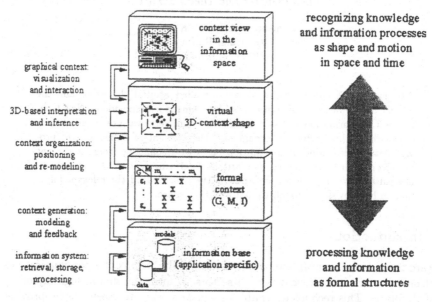

Fig. 1. The KOAN system architecture is composed of four stages for generating a visualization of an information base.

Figure 1 illustrates the system architecture of the KOAN system.

In most cases of data analysis the data records (obtained by measurements, interviews, collections) can be described by an application specific conceptual language. Data records will be represented by objects and their observed attributes by a so called "formal context", which is defined in the formal concept analysis.

A (single valued) formal context $K = (G, M, I)$ consists of the following information units [Wil 84]:

1. a set G of objects,
2. a set M of attributes and
3. a binary relation (incidence relation) $I \subseteq G \times M$
   between objects and attributes.

The relation gIm between an object g and an attribute m is interpreted as "the object g has the attribute m" or "m belongs to g". Such single valued formal contexts exist for example in literature data bases: The attribute set consists of relevant descriptors and of assignments of descriptors to supply the incidence relation. A picture of a formal context is shown in figure 2.

The data records which are to be evaluated, often exist in the form of a table whose rows are seen as objects and whose columns are qualified or quantified attributes. This situation is described by a multivalued context $K = (G, M, W, I)$, where W is called the attribute expression. $I \subseteq G \times M \times W$ is a ternary relation, so $(g, m, w) \in I$ is to be read as "the object g has attribute m with value w".

Such multivalued contexts can be transformed into single valued contexts by conceptual scaling. The loss of information is controlled by the conceptual language of scales [Pre 97].

Objects, attributes, and incidences generally span a multi-dimensional information space. However, applying the idea of representing content similarities by spatial proximity allows us to map information objects and their attributes as clusters into 3D-space.

attribute set

$$M = \{m_1, \ldots, m_k\}$$

M \ G	m_1	$\cdots$		m_k
g_1	X X		X	
.		X		
.		X X		X
g_n	X			X

object set

$$G = \{g_1, \ldots, g_m\}$$

Fig. 2. Description of a Formal Context. An "X" implies the relation glm: attribute m_j belongs to object g_i

The approximate embedding has to consider three spatial constraints for the object-object-, attribute-attribute-, and object-attribute-pairs, and is achieved by an iterative non-linear optimization method [FJM 94]:

1. The distance of two objects has to correspond to their similarity measure.
2. The distance of two attributes has to correspond to their equivalency measure.
3. The distance of an object and an attribute has to be smaller than the incidence distance boundary, if the attribute belongs to the object; otherwise the distance has to exceed the non-incidence boundary.

We apply similarity and equivalency measures from the theorie of cluster analysis (f.ex. Jaccard and Kulczynski metrics). The procedure of optimization is illustrated in figure 3.

After computing an optimized 3D-representation of the data, we project and display the information objects and attributes as color coded geometrical symbols on the computer monitor.

We have also implemented an interactive, 3D-graphical user interface. The screen representation can be moved, rotated and zoomed in order to optimally display the hidden structures within the information. By searching and browsing through the three-dimensional information galaxy, the user can satisfy his information requirement.

The method of context visualization in a 3D-space allows the user to rapidly scan large volumes of data and memorize its correlation.

3 Examples for KOAN-Applications

The range of application for contextual information processing extends from archiving and information retrieval through the operation of control rooms to the reengineering of software and planning such as in the scenario technique.

3.1 Alarm Surge Visual Analysis Using KOAN

Fault analysis in large high-tech plants requires the operator to identify the actual fault cause among the multitude of logged events. Because of the costs of developing plant specific knowledge bases, the use of expert systems is not economically efficient. Significant improvement can be obtained by a visualization of the event chain based on correlation of the events (provided by function diagrams) [FPP 96].

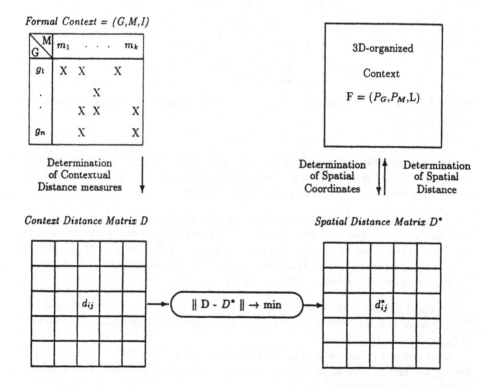

Fig. 3. Optimization process, computing a 3D-organized Context from a Formal Context.

For the Power Generation Group (KWU) of Siemens, we have developed a specialized version of KOAN, which converts the alarm surge text message and its hidden internal relations to function diagrams of the system into clearly arranged informative 3D-graphics.

The generated three-dimensional shape of KOAN assists the operator in finding the fault and locating its cause.

For this application, KOAN is based on alarm logs and function diagrams. It searches the specifically identified messages from the alarm logs, and puts these alarms into a process-engineering, logical or chronological correlation to other alarms. In the same way, the signals and logic operations from the function diagrams are put into correlation.

Knowing the process-engineering reasons and correlations that caused the alarm surge and being able to trace the faults back to their origin can greatly reduce the time required to find the actual fault cause. KOAN helps to reduce fault-related downtimes of a plant, and hence improves the cost-effectiveness of plant operation.

3.2   3D-Structure of Neural Nets with KOAN

In a new field we apply KOAN to visualize neural nets. When visualizing the learning process of a neural net, the user can influence the system early on and modify the structure of a particular neural net. Connections which have a low weight extending over a great distance in the 3D-representation space can be eliminated and the net structure can be simplified.

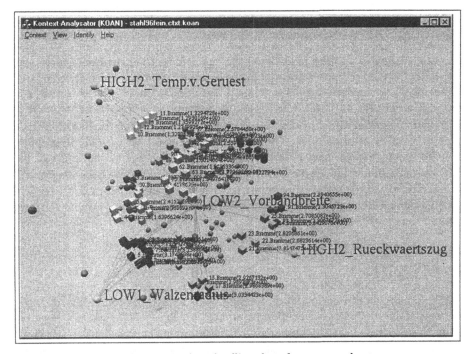

Fig. 4. 3D-context of steel rolling data from a neural net.

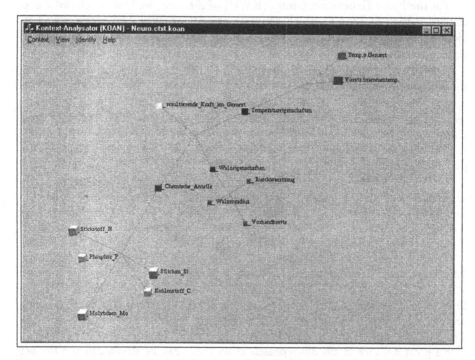

Fig. 5. 3D-structure of a neural net for steel rolling. In this simple example the input units are shown as three clusters, which generate a tree structure with a single output node as its root.

In the display cubes represent objects and spheres represent attributes. The line between a cube and a sphere indicates that the attribute belongs to this object. All attributes of an object have to be within the so called incidence distance boundary. The principle "contextual correlation ≅ spatial proximity" means that objects which are correlated in any way, i.e. they have common attributes, are in a closer proximity.

Beside the visualization of the procedure of learning, KOAN could also be applied to visualize net structures. The structure of a neural net with its three types of units (input, hidden, output) and the weights of each connection unit can be easily visualized in a 3D-representation using KOAN. The value of the weight can be interpreted as the measure of similarity.

An example for a 3D-structure of a neural net is shown in figure 5. Further research is required in this area.

4 Summary

The key challenge of information processing is to reduce the complexity of large amounts of data by new visualization paradigms.

In this paper we have introduced a novel data mining approach, using the visualization tool KOAN. This method of visualization supports associative and spatial perception of the human observer and provides rapid assessment of large volumes of data as well as detailed selective analysis of individual information.

It enables the user to access, structure. visualize and interactively retrieve information from a data base and helps the user to discover hidden relationships within the data.

Acknowledgements

We want to give our best thanks to Th. Führing, B. Kolpatzik, K. Jacoby, R. Michelis, J. Panyr, Th. Poppe, U. Preiser and M. Schlang.

References

[FJM 94] Führing, T. ; Jacoby, K. ; Michelis, R. ; Panyr, J.: Kontextgestaltgebung: Eine Metapher zur Visualisierung von und Interaktion mit komplexen Wissensbeständen. Nachtrag Schriften zur Informationswissenschaft Bd. 16; Rauch, W. ; Strohmeier, F. ; Hiller, H. ; Schlögl, C. (Hrsg.): Mehrwert von Information : Professionalisierung der Informationsarbeit (Proceedings des 4. Internationalen Symposiums für Informationswissenschaften (ISI 94) in Graz, Austria, 2.-4. November 1994). Konstanz : Universitätsverlag Konstanz (UVK), 1994

[FPP 96] Führing, T. ; Panyr, J.; Preiser, U.: 3D-Visualisierung von Prozeßinformation: Ein Ansatz zur Unterstützung der Störungsaufklärung in Kraftwerken. In: Krause, J. ; Herfurth, M. ; Marx, J. (Hrsg.): Herausforderungen an die Informationsvisualisierung und Datenvisualisierung (Tagungsband des 5. Internationalen Symposiums für Informationswirtschaft). Konstanz : Universitätsverlag Konstanz (UVK), 1996

[G-S 96] Gehmeyr, A. ; Schappert, A.: Relevance-based Information Exploration. submitted for the WWW97 Conference in Santa Clara, 1996

[Pfe 96a] Pfefferer, L.: Objektzentrierte Visualisierung mehrdimensionaler Daten als Erweiterung konventioneller Datenbankmodelle. München : Herbert Utz Verlag Wissenschaft, 1996

[Pfe 96b] Pfefferer, L.: Kontextvisualisierung mehrdimensionaler Daten. In: Conrad, S. ; Saake, G. ; Schmitt, I. ; Türker, C. (Hrsg.): Grundlagen von Datenbanken (Proceedings des 8. Workshop 'Grundlagen von Datenbanken' in Friedrichsbrunn/Harz, 28.-31. Mai 1996, veranstaltet vom Arbeitskreis 'Grundlagen von Informationssystemen' der GI-Fachgruppe 2.5) Magdeburg : Universitätsverlag, 1996, S. 66-71

[PFP 96] Panyr, J. ; Führing, T. ; Preiser, U.: Kontextuelle Visualisierung von Informationen. Proceedings des 19. Oberhofer Kolloquiums über Information und Dokumentation, Oberhof, 18.-20. April 1996, S. 217-228

[Pre 97] Preiser, U.: Structured Visualization of Search Result List. Proceedings der 21. Jahrestagung der Gesellschaft fr Klassifikation e.V. vom 12.-14. März 1997. To appear at Springer Publications, Heidelberg, 1997

514

[S–B 95]   Schütt, D. ; Bocionek, S.: InfoSphere: The Global Challenge for Siemens.
            Proceedings of APPT'95, Int. Workshop, Beijing, China,
            ISBN 7-5053-3304-6
[Wil 84]   Wille, R.: Liniendiagramme hierarchischer Begriffssysteme. In: Bock, H.H.:
            Anwendungen der Klassifikation: Datenanalyse und numerische Klassifika-
            tion. Frankfurt : INDEKS-Verlag, 1984, S. 32-51

Author Index

Springer
and the
environment

At Springer we firmly believe that an
international science publisher has a
special obligation to the environment,
and our corporate policies consistently
reflect this conviction.
We also expect our business partners –
paper mills, printers, packaging
manufacturers, etc. – to commit
themselves to using materials and
production processes that do not harm
the environment. The paper in this
book is made from low- or no-chlorine
pulp and is acid free, in conformance
with international standards for paper
permanency.

Lecture Notes in Computer Science

For information about Vols. 1–1265

please contact your bookseller or Springer-Verlag

Vol. 1302: P. Van Hentenryck (Ed.), Static Analysis. Proceedings, 1997. X, 413 pages. 1997.

Vol. 1303: G. Brewka, C. Habel, B. Nebel (Eds.), KI-97: Advances in Artificial Intelligence. Proceedings, 1997. XI, 413 pages. 1997. (Subseries LNAI).

Vol. 1304: W. Luk, P.Y.K. Cheung, M. Glesner (Eds.), Field-Programmable Logic and Applications. Proceedings, 1997. XI, 503 pages. 1997.

Vol. 1305: D. Corne, J.L. Shapiro (Eds.), Evolutionary Computing. Proceedings, 1997. X, 307 pages. 1997.

Vol. 1306: C. Leung (Ed.), Visual Information Systems. X, 274 pages. 1997.

Vol. 1307: R. Kompe, Prosody in Speech Understanding Systems. XIX, 357 pages. 1997. (Subseries LNAI).

Vol. 1308: A. Hameurlain, A M. Tjoa (Eds.), Database and Expert Systems Applications. Proceedings, 1997. XVII, 688 pages. 1997.

Vol. 1309: R. Steinmetz, L.C. Wolf (Eds.), Interactive Distributed Multimedia Systems and Telecommunication Services. Proceedings, 1997. XIII, 466 pages. 1997.

Vol. 1310: A. Del Bimbo (Ed.), Image Analysis and Processing. Proceedings, 1997. Volume I. XXII, 722 pages. 1997.

Vol. 1311: A. Del Bimbo (Ed.), Image Analysis and Processing. Proceedings, 1997. Volume II. XXII, 794 pages. 1997.

Vol. 1312: A. Geppert, M. Berndtsson (Eds.), Rules in Database Systems. Proceedings, 1997. VII, 214 pages. 1997.

Vol. 1313: J. Fitzgerald, C.B. Jones, P. Lucas (Eds.), FME '97: Industrial Applications and Strengthened Foundations of Formal Methods. Proceedings, 1997. XIII, 685 pages. 1997.

Vol. 1314: S. Muggleton (Ed.), Inductive Logic Programming. Proceedings, 1996. VIII, 397 pages. 1997. (Subseries LNAI).

Vol. 1315: G. Sommer, J.J. Koenderink (Eds.), Algebraic Frames for the Perception-Action Cycle. Proceedings, 1997. VIII, 395 pages. 1997.

Vol. 1316: M. Li, A. Maruoka (Eds.), Algorithmic Learning Theory. Proceedings, 1997. XI, 461 pages. 1997. (Subseries LNAI).

Vol. 1317: M. Leman (Ed.), Music, Gestalt, and Computing. IX, 524 pages. 1997. (Subseries LNAI).

Vol. 1318: R. Hirschfeld (Ed.), Financial Cryptography. Proceedings, 1997. XI, 409 pages. 1997.

Vol. 1319: E. Plaza, R. Benjamins (Eds.), Knowledge Acquisition, Modeling and Management. Proceedings, 1997. XI, 389 pages. 1997. (Subseries LNAI).

Vol. 1320: M. Mavronicolas, P. Tsigas (Eds.), Distributed Algorithms. Proceedings, 1997. X, 333 pages. 1997.

Vol. 1321: M. Lenzerini (Ed.), AI*IA 97: Advances in Artificial Intelligence. Proceedings, 1997. XII, 459 pages. 1997. (Subseries LNAI).

Vol. 1322: H. Hußmann, Formal Foundations for Software Engineering Methods. X, 286 pages. 1997.

Vol. 1323: E. Costa, A. Cardoso (Eds.), Progress in Artificial Intelligence. Proceedings, 1997. XIV, 393 pages. 1997. (Subseries LNAI).

Vol. 1324: C. Peters, C. Thanos (Eds.), Research and Advanced Technology for Digital Libraries. Proceedings, 1997. X, 423 pages. 1997.

Vol. 1325: Z.W. Raś, A. Skowron (Eds.), Foundations of Intelligent Systems. Proceedings, 1997. XI, 630 pages. 1997. (Subseries LNAI).

Vol. 1326: C. Nicholas, J. Mayfield (Eds.), Intelligent Hypertext. XIV, 182 pages. 1997.

Vol. 1327: W. Gerstner, A. Germond, M. Hasler, J.-D. Nicoud (Eds.), Artificial Neural Networks – ICANN '97. Proceedings, 1997. XIX, 1274 pages. 1997.

Vol. 1328: C. Retoré (Ed.), Logical Aspects of Computational Linguistics. Proceedings, 1996. VIII, 435 pages. 1997. (Subseries LNAI).

Vol. 1329: S.C. Hirtle, A.U. Frank (Eds.), Spatial Information Theory. Proceedings, 1997. XIV, 511 pages. 1997.

Vol. 1330: G. Smolka (Ed.), Principles and Practice of Constraint Programming – CP 97. Proceedings, 1997. XII, 563 pages. 1997.

Vol. 1331: D. W. Embley, R. C. Goldstein (Eds.), Conceptual Modeling – ER '97. Proceedings, 1997. XV, 479 pages. 1997.

Vol. 1332: M. Bubak, J. Dongarra, J. Waśniewski (Eds.), Recent Advances in Parallel Virtual Machine and Message Passing Interface. Proceedings, 1997. XV, 518 pages. 1997.

Vol. 1333: F. Pichler. R.M. Díaz (Eds.), Computer Aided Systems Theory – EUROCAST'97. Proceedings, 1997. XI, 626 pages. 1997.

Vol. 1334: Y. Han, T. Okamoto, S. Qing (Eds.), Information and Communications Security. Proceedings, 1997. X, 484 pages. 1997.

Vol. 1335: R.H. Möhring (Ed.), Graph-Theoretic Concepts in Computer Science. Proceedings, 1997. X, 376 pages. 1997.

Vol. 1336: C. Polychronopoulos, K. Joe, K. Araki, M. Amamiya (Eds.), High Performance Computing. Proceedings, 1997. XII, 416 pages. 1997.

Vol. 1337: C. Freksa, M. Jantzen, R. Valk (Eds.), Foundations of Computer Science. XII, 515 pages. 1997.

Vol. 1338: F. Plášil, K.G. Jeffery (Eds.), SOFSEM'97: Theory and Practice of Informatics. Proceedings, 1997. XIV, 571 pages. 1997.

Vol. 1339: N.A. Murshed, F. Bortolozzi (Eds.), Advances in Document Image Analysis. Proceedings, 1997. IX, 345 pages. 1997.

Vol. 1340: M. van Kreveld, J. Nievergelt, T. Roos, P. Widmayer (Eds.), Algorithmic Foundations of Geographic Information Systems. XIV, 287 pages. 1997. ·

Vol. 1341: F. Bry, R. Ramakrishnan, K. Ramamohanarao (Eds.), Deductive and Object-Oriented Databases. Proceedings, 1997. XIV, 430 pages. 1997.

Vol. 1342: A. Sattar (Ed.), Advanced Topics in Artificial Intelligence. Proceedings, 1997. XVIII, 516 pages. 1997.

Vol. 1344: C. Ausnit-Hood, K.A. Johnson, R.G. Pettit, IV, S.B. Opdahl (Eds.), Ada 95 – Quality and Style. XV, 292 pages. 1997.